At the
Right Time

Dating the Events of the New Testament

At the
Right Time

•

Dating the Events of the New Testament

Jerome R. Johnson

**For while we were still helpless,
at the right time
Christ died for the ungodly. — Romans 5:6**

Bathkol Books
Box 999
Havre de Grace, Maryland
www.atrt.com

Bathkol Books
Box 999
Havre de Grace, Maryland 21078

Scripture taken from The New American Standard Bible
Copyright © The Lockman Foundation 1960, 1962, 1963, 1968, 1971, 1972, 1973, 1975, 1977, 1988, 1995
Used by Permission.

Star charts and moon phase graphics generated using The Sky: Astronomy Software Version 4
Copyright © Software Bisque 1992-6
Used by Permission

Maps generated using PC Bible Atlas for Windows
Copyright © Parsons Technology 1993-4
Used by permission

LIBRARY OF CONGRESS CATALOGING – IN – PUBLICATION DATA

Jerome R. Johnson
At the Right Time: Dating the Events of the New Testament/ Jerome R. Johnson

Includes bibliographical references and indexes.

ISBN 0-9665749-0-7

1. Chronology — New Testament. 2. Jewish Calendars — 10 B.C. – A.D. 70.
3. Synopsis — Gospels. 4. Calendars — Jewish, Julian & Gregorian.

Printed in the United States of America
        by Kogan Hickory Printing, Baltimore, Maryland

For my mother
Sylvia

She gave me life
She gave me love,
And pointed my soul
To heaven above.

Acknowledgment

Although assistance in this study has been received from many people, the contribution of Ron and Pam Tabor must be especially noted. Pam Tabor designed the entire volume, and any attractiveness and readability it possesses is due primarily to her efforts. Ron and Pam Tabor have proofread the book and have made many helpful suggestions and corrections. In fact, without the efforts of the Tabors, this volume would have probably never reached the printers. Cindy Benedict also proofread the entire volume. However, in spite of the best efforts of these talented people, it seems unlikely that they have succeeded in eliminating all the mistakes of the author, who would appreciate comments from readers that might improve future editions of this book. Comments should be sent to: Jerome R. Johnson, Bathkol Books, Box 999, Havre de Grace, Maryland 21078.

I would like to thank the following organizations for graciously granted the author permission to use their products in the production of this book: the Lockman Foundation, which granted permission to quote Scriptures from the New American Standard Bible, Parsons Technology, which granted permission to use maps generated with their computer program PC Bible Atlas, and Software Bisque, which granted permission to use graphics generated with their astronomy program The Sky.

I would also like to thank Steve Sheppard and Gary Snyder, of Kogan Hickory Printing, who patiently turned my computer files into this printed volume.

**About
the
Author**

Jerome (Jerry) Johnson is a mathematician and physical scientist. He received a B.S. degree in Mechanical Engineering and a M.S. degree in Mathematics from Purdue University and a Ph D. degree in Applied Science from the University of Delaware. He has specialized in safety and reliability studies and he has worked as an engineer, mathematician and supervisory physical scientist at both the U.S. Army Ballistics Research Laboratory and the U.S. Army System Analysis Activity. He has also taught probability and statistics courses for the University of Delaware. Dr. Johnson has studied and traveled extensively in the Holy Land, and he has been a student of the Bible and a member of the Christian Church since his youth. He was born in Indiana, but currently lives in Maryland on the upper reaches of the beautiful Chesapeake Bay.

Contents

Preface

Interest in dating the events of the New Testament can be traced to the very beginning of Christianity. In fact, one of the purposes of the writers of the New Testament was to address this interest. John, in his gospel, mentioned many Jewish feast days in connection with the events he wrote about; and since these feast days occurred on fixed dates of the Jewish calendar, he was giving the dates of occurrence of these events. The other gospel writers also supplied chronological information. Paul, in some of his letters such as the letter to the Galatians, gave detailed chronological information. Although this chronological information would have been clear to the first century A.D. reader of the New Testament, especially the Jewish readers, this is often not the case for today's reader. Through the centuries, much of the chronological information of the New Testament has been lost or at least obscured. In this book I shall undertake the exciting task of attempting to clear away the dust and debris that obscure the dates of occurrence of the most significant events in human history.

Through the centuries much has been written concerning our subject, but this work will not be a review of past studies. For such information, the reader is referred to Jack Finegan's excellent book, *Handbook of Biblical Chronology*. In this volume, we shall be primarily concerned with a new assessment of the data that is available from ancient sources and shall make use of results from archaeology, astronomy, numismatics, geography and the power of the modern computer to make this assessment. I have undertaken a new assessment, not to minimize the importance of past studies, but to permit us to focus on the primary sources of information and to make as clear as possible the methods used in making inference from these primary sources. A list of references used is given at the end of the book. Many of these references have been very helpful in suggesting approaches that were used in this study; however, each approach has been reassessed, and the conclusions reached in this study may not agree with those of the reference that suggested the approach.

I first became interested in New Testament chronology after reading Ernest L. Martin's book, *The Birth of Christ Recalculated*. In investigating the chronology of the New Testament, I soon realized that I needed the Jewish calendars for New Testament times in order to convert the chronological information of the New Testament into dates on our calendar. I found several published collections of calendars that appeared to supply the required Jewish calendars, but in each case it turned out that these calendars were projections of the present Jewish calendar back to the first century A.D. rather than the observational Jewish calendar used in New Testament times. It was therefore necessary to construct a set of Jewish calendars for the time of the New Testament using computer-generated astronomical data. These calendars appear in Appendix D and permit the translation of dates on the Jewish calendar used during New Testament times into dates on the Gregorian calendar that we use today. A detailed study of the chronology of the New Testament was then carried out using the calendars of Appendix D. Each verse of the four Gospels and the book of Acts was then dated. Finally, using the internal information of the New Testament and the testimony of the church fathers, a determination was made of the year when the writing was completed for each book of the New Testament.

It is very fortunate that the reckoning of time in the New Testament was based on observations of the sun and the moon rather than some manmade approximation, since computer programs permit us to reproduce these observations today. In the same way the New Testament provides God's direct revelation of Himself and His will. If we want to know about God, we should go directly to the Word of God. Unfortunately, as was the case with the calendar, man has tried to improve on the Word of God. Jesus, in Matthew 15:9, rebukes the Pharisees and scribes by quoting Isaiah "'BUT IN VAIN DO THEY WORSHIP ME, TEACHING AS DOCTRINES THE PRECEPTS OF MEN.'" All the doctrines that divide Christendom are just the precepts of men and Christians need to return to the Light, the Word of God. Then the Church can be one, which was the fervent prayer of Jesus (John 17:21).

Since the basis of this study of the chronology of the New Testament is the Bible, an accurate translation of the Bible will be of great importance. Of the available English translations, the author believes that the New American Standard Bible best meets this requirement, and the Lockman Foundation has graciously granted permission for its use. Other translations, in a laudable effort to make the meaning of the Scriptures clearer, have sometimes changed the Scriptures to say what the translators thought was intended rather than just translating what the Scripture writers actually said. In contrast, the New American Standard Bible translators have been content simply to give a literal translation of the Hebrew and Greek texts which provides the accurate details needed for this study.

Introduction

Is the Bible true? To the vast majority of the more than 1.5 billion Christian adherents in the world (Barrett, *World Christian Encyclopedia*, page 4), there is no question that the Bible is true and they may be offended that the question is even asked. However, to many in the scholarly community, the truth of the Bible is open to question. In this book we shall be primarily concerned with the New Testament; however, the validity of the entire Bible will be important to our study.

Authors of the Gospels

Practically all of our chronological information concerning the earthly ministry of Jesus will depend on the information given in the four Gospels: Matthew, Mark, Luke and John. But do these Gospels provide historically accurate information concerning the earthly ministry of Jesus? How we answer this question will, to a large extent, depend on when and by whom the Gospels were written. If the Gospels reflect the eyewitness testimony of the Apostles, speaking under the guidance of the Holy Spirit, then these Gospels should be historically accurate and reliable. However, in recent years, critical scholarship has challenged the idea that the Gospels directly reflect the eyewitness testimony of the Apostles. Rather, these critical scholars have asserted that the Gospels are the product of unknown authors. These unknown authors supposedly based their Gospel on oral tradition and written sources, such as the Document Q, which were subsequently lost and were not mentioned by any of the early church writers. Supposedly, these unknown authors produced their Gospels by editing these oral and written sources to accomplish their own theological purposes and to support the teachings and practices of the church of their day. If these assumptions are correct, then the historical accuracy of the Gospels can be questioned.

In order to answer these questions concerning the authorship of the Gospels, we shall first consider the testimony of the early church fathers. This testimony of the early leaders and writers of Christ's Church can be summarized by a statement of Irenaeus (A.D. *c*. 130 — 200). This statement is from Book III of "Refutation and Overthrow of False So-Called Knowledge*"The Ante-Nicene Fathers, Volume 1*, page 414. Irenaeus was born in Asia Minor and was a pupil of Polycarp who was a disciple of the Apostle John (*Chambers Biographical Dictionary*, page 760).In this work, Irenaeus says:

> Matthew published a written gospel for the Hebrews in their own tongue, while Peter and Paul were preaching the gospel in Rome and founding the church there. After their passing, Mark also, the disciple and interpreter of Peter, transmitted to us in writing, the things preached by Peter. Luke, the follower of Paul, set down in a book the gospel preached by him. Lastly John, the disciple of the Lord who had leant back on His breast, once more set forth the gospel, while residing in Ephesus in Asia.

Thus the testimony of Irenaeus was that the four Gospels were written by the persons to whom they are ascribed in our Bible and that these Gospels were written in the order that they appear in our Bible. Although the designations of the author were probably not part of the original gospel manuscripts, we have early and consistent testimony that these people were in fact the authors of the Gospels.

Thus we shall find that the testimony of all the church fathers was that: Matthew was written by the Apostle Matthew, Mark was written by Mark the companion of the Apostle Peter, Luke was written by Luke the companion of the Apostle Paul and finally John was written by the Apostle John. The relationship between the four gospels is illustrated by the *Diagram 1* below. This was the testimony of the church fathers and was accepted by the Church for 1800 years.

However, toward the close of the nineteenth century, a school of critical scholarship developed that began to question the testimony of the church fathers based on analysis of the text of the Gospels. Today many critical scholars would question that any of the Gospels reflect the eyewitness testimony of the Apostles. Although many conservative scholars do not fully accept the conclusions of critical scholarship, most of them have been greatly influenced by this work. Thus today very few New Testament scholars accept the Apostle Matthew as the author of the first Gospel. It is generally accepted that the Gospel of Mark was the first of the Gospels to be written, and some unknown author wrote the Gospel of Matthew using Mark as one of his sources.

The priority of the Gospel of Mark is considered to be one of the most firmly established conclusions of critical scholarship (the assured result); however, the arguments advanced by critical scholarship for this assertion are unconvincing to the author of this book. In its arguments to establish the priority of Mark, critical scholarship does not address the testimony of the church fathers, but rather postulates that either Mark was a condensed version of Matthew or Matthew was based on Mark and some unknown Q Document and possibly other unknown sources. However, no such simple dichotomy is suggested by the church fathers. According to the church fathers, Mark was transmitting the preaching of Peter, not just condensing the Gospel of Matthew. Therefore, the fact that Mark could clarify and amplify Matthew's Gospel does not indicate

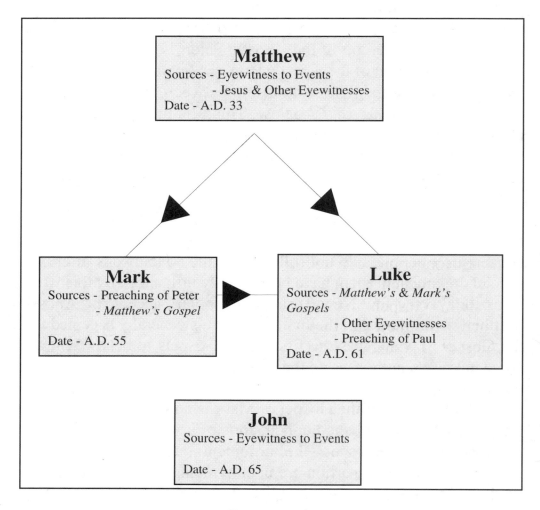

Diagram 1

that Mark's Gospel was written first or that Matthew used Mark's Gospel as a source of material for his Gospel. Rather, it indicates that Mark, using information he gained from the preaching of Peter, had information not contained in Matthew's Gospel, especially concerning the period of Jesus's ministry prior to Matthew's call to discipleship and for events to which Matthew was not an eyewitness.

The greater freshness of Mark's Gospel, as compared to the greater formality of Matthew's Gospel reflects the difference in the author's style and purpose rather than any indication of priority. Mark emphasized what Jesus did while Matthew was more concerned with what Jesus said. Also, the fact that Luke frequently agrees with Mark's Gospel against Matthew's Gospel only indicates that Mark, through the preaching of Peter, had properly clarified Matthew's Gospel.

None of the arguments advanced by critical scholarship offers any evidence that the Gospel of Mark was written first and then was used as a source for the Gospel of Matthew. The fact that, for those narratives that are common to Matthew and Mark, Mark's narratives are usually longer probably indicates that Mark tended to select those incidents for which he had additional information from Peter to include in his Gospel. Finally, the fact that practically all of Mark is contained in Matthew and Luke does not show that Mark was written first. Rather, it is evidence that Luke drew upon both Matthew and Mark, and this is consistent with Luke 1:1 which indicates that many gospel accounts preceded Luke's.

In Matthew 24:35 Jesus says: "Heaven and earth will pass away, but my words shall not pass away." If Jesus' words were to be preserved, would God have had the Christian community wait fifty to a hundred years to write them down? We are not told much about Matthew other than that he was a tax collector. However, Jesus must have selected each of the apostles carefully with a definite purpose in mind. Matthew, as a tax collector, was probably literate because it would be necessary to prepare reports concerning his collections for the authorities. Of the twelve original apostles, Matthew seems most likely to have been an educated man, other than Judas Iscariot, since most of the other apostles seemed to have been fishermen.

Acts 4:13 says:

> Now as they observed the confidence of Peter and John,
> and understood that they were uneducated and untrained
> men, they were marveling, and began to recognize them
> as having been with Jesus.

Thus Matthew seems to be the most likely candidate of the twelve to serve as a scribe to Jesus.

Shortly before recording his call as a disciple in Matthew 9:9, Matthew records in Chapters 5,6 and 7 Jesus' Sermon on the Mount. This is the most detailed record of any of Jesus' sermons, and it is possible that Matthew actually took notes during the sermon and then wrote down this sermon immediately afterwards. He would have naturally recorded the sermon in Aramaic which would be consistent with Irenaeus' statement concerning Matthew writing a gospel for the Hebrews in their own tongue. However, later Matthew could have prepared a Greek version of his Gospel replacing most of the Hebrew Scriptures with quotations from the Septuagint. The Apostle Paul was multilingual and if Matthew was to be Christ's primary scribe, there is no reason Matthew could not have been also. Seeing Matthew recording His words during the Sermon on the Mount may have prompted Jesus to call Matthew to discipleship shortly after this sermon. It is unimaginable that the Sermon on the Mount could be the product of some unknown church writer. It seems much more reasonable that these were the actual words of the Son of God recorded by the eyewitness Matthew. If, as Jesus claimed, He was the only begotten Son of God, speaking the very words of God, would it be reasonable that God would not have had these words preserved by an eyewitness to Jesus' ministry?

In the tenth chapter of Matthew, all twelve of the apostles are listed; however, only two of the twelve are singled out for special comment: Matthew, "the tax collector" and Judas Iscariot, "the one who betrayed Him." Both of these comments are unfavorable, and if the Apostle Matthew was the author of this Gospel, this would be in keeping with the modesty displayed by the other apostolic writers. Paul, in 1 Corinthians 15:9, says: "For I am the least of the apostles, who am not fit to be called an apostle, because I persecuted the church of God." Similarly, the Apostle John does not ever mention himself by name in his Gospel.

In addition to the testimony of Irenaeus concerning Matthew's writing of the first of the Gospels, Eusebius, in his *History of the Church* (page 152) records the testimony of Papias, Bishop of Hieropolis. Papias (c. A.D. 70—155) says: "So then, Matthew compiled the *Logia* in the Hebrew (Aramaic) language, but everyone interpreted them as he was able." Here Papias confirms that Matthew first wrote in the Hebrew (Aramaic) language, and the statement that everyone interpreted them as he was able suggests that Matthew was used by others (the other synoptic gospel writers).

Origen (c. A.D. 185-254) in his *Commentary on Matthew,* again preserved by Eusebius in the *History of the Church, Book VI, 25,* Page 265 says:

> I accept the traditional view of the four gospels which alone are undeniably authentic in the Church of God on earth. First to be written was that of the one-time exciseman who became an apostle of Jesus - Matthew; it was published for believers of Jewish origin and was composed in Aramaic. Next came that of Mark, who followed Peter's instructions in writing it, and who in Peter's general epistle was acknowledged as his son: "Greetings to you from the church in Babylon, chosen like yourselves, and from my son Mark." Next came

that of Luke, who wrote for Gentile converts the gospel praised by Paul. Last of all came John's.

Finally we have the testimony of Eusebius (c. A.D. 264-340), who was the father of church history. In his *History of the Church, Book III*, 24.5, Page 132, he said:

> Matthew had begun by preaching to Hebrews; and when he made up his mind to go to others too, he committed his own gospel to writing in his native tongue, so that for those with whom he was no longer present the gap left by his departure was filled by what he wrote. And when Mark and Luke had now published their gospels, John we are told, who hitherto had relied entirely on the spoken word, finally took to writing for the following reason. The three gospels already written were in general circulation and copies had come into John's hands. He welcomed them, we are told, and confirmed their accuracy, but remarked that the narrative only lacked the story of what Christ had done first of all at the beginning of His ministry.

Thus all of the church fathers accepted the Apostle Matthew as the author of the first Gospel. There is no record of any controversy concerning the acceptance of the Gospel of Matthew which again would support apostolic authorship. During the first two hundred years of the church, the Gospel of Matthew was the most often quoted and commanded the greatest respect of all the Gospels. Thus those who were in the best position to know about the authorship of the first Gospel accepted the Apostle Matthew as its author.

Not only did the church fathers support the Apostle Matthew as the author of the first Gospel, but there are many early quotations from Matthew which would support an early date for the writing of this Gospel which in turn would support the Apostle Matthew as the author of this Gospel. While the Apostle Matthew was still living, it is very unlikely that someone other than the apostle could gain acceptance of a work written in the name of the apostle. Ignatius of Antioch (c. A.D. 35-107) in his *Epistle to the Smyrneans*, Chapter 1:2 quotes Matthew 3:15 (D.A. Carson, *The Expositor's Bible Commentary, Matthew Vol. 8*, page 19). There are also numerous quotations from *Matthew* in the *Didache* which is widely recognized as dating from the first century A.D. (*Oxford Encyclopedia of the Early Church, Vol. I*, Page 235.) John Robinson (*Redating the New Testament*, page 535) dates the *Didache* from A.D. 40-60). All of these early quotations from Matthew suggest a very early date for the writing of Matthew.

Even within the New Testament itself, there is a strong indication that the Gospel of Matthew was written and accepted as Scripture at a very early date. In 1 Corinthians 15:3,4, Paul writes:

> For I delivered to you as of first importance what I also received, that Christ died for our sins according to the Scriptures, and that He was buried, and that He was raised on the third day according to the Scripture.

In Isaiah 53:8, it says:

> By oppression and judgement He was taken away; and as for His generation, who considered that He was cut off out of the land of the living, for the transgression of my people to whom the stroke was due?

Thus with reference to this Old Testament Scripture, Paul could say, that Christ died for our sins according to the Scripture. However, no Old Testament Scripture says that the Messiah was to be raised on the third day. Some commentators have pointed to Jonah 1:17, which relates that Jonah spent three days and three nights in the stomach of the fish as a source for Paul's comments in 1 Corinthians 15:4; however, it was not until Jesus himself, in Matthew 12:40, made the connection between Jonah's experience and His own coming experience that any connection existed. Thus, the Scripture to which Paul was referring was not an Old Testament Scripture. However, Matthew 16:21 says:

> From that time Jesus Christ began to show His disciples that He must go to Jerusalem, and suffer many things from the elders and chief priests and scribes and be killed, and be raised up on the third day.

This verse clearly states the prophecy by Jesus Himself that He would be raised on the third day. Thus the Scripture to which Paul appears to be referring is found in the Gospel of Matthew and thus Matthew appears to have been written and recognized as Scripture at the time of Paul's letter. Since Paul's first letter to the Corinthians can be dated to the spring of A.D. 55 (see Chapter 8), Matthew must have been written very early and therefore must have been written by the Apostle Matthew. Thus the assured conclusion of critical scholarship of the priority of Mark is actually highly questionable!

With such strong testimony that each of the four Gospels was either written by an apostle or directly reflect the teaching of an apostle, why would critical scholars be motivated to postulate that the Gospels were written by some unknown writers? It is difficult to determine motivation; however, the writings of most of the early critical scholars indicate that they generally reject the miracles recorded in the New Testament. If the Gospels actually reflect the eyewitness testimony of the apostles, why would they say that the miracles happened if they didn't, especially since most if not all of the apostles were martyred because of their teachings? On the other hand, if the Gospels were the product of later church writers trying to justify their own teachings and church practices, then it would become easier to reject part of their testimony. Thus the reader could become the judge of what was the word of God and what was something that was added later. Therefore, the desire of the early critical scholars to justify their rejection of the miracles of the New Testament may have played a part in their looking for alternate authors for the Gospels other than those supported by the testimony of the church fathers.

Use of the Gospels

How shall we use the four Gospels in determining the chronology of Jesus' earthly ministry? All of the four Gospels are trustworthy and accurate; however, the purpose of their authors differed. Matthew seemed to be primarily concerned with preserving the teachings of Jesus, but may not have always reported events in chronological order, particularly events in Jesus' ministry which he did not witness. Based on the preaching of Peter, Mark was able to supplement the information reported by Matthew, particularly with respect to the chronological order of events. Luke supplemented the information reported in Matthew and Mark, probably obtaining his information from the apostles and other eyewitnesses during his visits to Judea and elsewhere as a companion of Paul. Finally, after the first three Gospels were in circulation, Eusebius and the other church fathers indicate that John wrote his Gospel. Apparently, after seeing the other three Gospels, one of John's purposes was to report on those portions of Jesus' ministry that were not covered by the other Gospels. In fact, generally, the only common elements of the Gospel of John and the other Gospels are found in the events surrounding the feeding of the five thousand and the events of the final days of Jesus' ministry. The Gospel of John gives the most chronological information of any of the four Gospels. By mentioning a number of Jewish festivals, John gives the exact dates, in terms of the Jewish calendar, of a number of the events recorded in his Gospel.

The church father Papias (Eusebius, *The History of the Church*, page 152) disagrees with the conclusions that Mark, through the preaching of Peter, was able to correct the chronology of Matthew. Papias says:

> This, too, the presbyter used to say, "Mark who had been Peter's interpreter, wrote down carefully, but not in order, all that he remembered of the Lord's sayings and doings. For he had not heard the Lord or been one of His followers, but later, as I said, one of Peter's. Peter used to adapt his teaching to the occasion, without making a systematic arrangement of the Lord's sayings, so that Mark was quite justified in writing down some things just as he remembered them. For he had one purpose only—to leave out nothing that he had heard, and to make no misstatement about it."

However, Papias' statement probably reflects the higher regard he had for Matthew than for Mark rather than any apostolic teaching, since Papias knew that Matthew was the work of an apostle while *Mark* was the work of a non apostle, he assumed that whenever these Gospels differed, Matthew should always be followed. However, Luke, who lived during the lifetime of the apostles and "having investigated everything carefully from the beginning" (Luke 1:3), generally in chronological matters agreed with Mark against Matthew. Therefore, it appears that presenting the events in the exact chronological order was not one of the primary purposes of Matthew. We shall also find that Matthew did not become a disciple of Jesus until the second half of the first year of Jesus' ministry while Peter was one of Jesus' first disciples. Therefore, Mark, based on Peter's preaching had eyewitness chronological information possibly not available to Matthew.

The Gospel of John shall provide a framework of exactly dateable events during the ministry of Jesus. To this framework we shall add all the other events reported in John as well as in the other three Gospels. The date of occurrence of these events will be obtained by interpolating between the dates of the events for which exact dates are known. This interpolation will involve the use of the chronological information given in the text as well as estimated travel time between the locations of different events. Among the synoptic Gospels, precedence will be given to Mark's Gospel, not because it was written first, which it wasn't, but because Mark's Gospel is more event-oriented and reflects the preaching of Peter who was an eyewitness to almost all of Jesus' ministry. However, all the chronological information from each Gospel will be used and an effort will be made to place each verse of the four Gospels in their correct chronological order.

In the book of Acts the problem of precedence does not exist since there is only one book. Also, although the author, Luke, was probably not an eyewitness to any of the events of the Gospels, he was intimately involved and was an eyewitness to many of the events of Acts. Also, as a companion of Paul, he would have good access to information concerning those parts of Paul's ministry that Luke did not witness. Luke's detailed accounts of the events of the early church in Judea indicated he also had good access to the other apostles, particularly Peter. Thus we have in the four Gospels and the

Acts preserved the eyewitness testimony of the apostles and others that were present during Jesus' earthly ministry and during the first years of Christ's Church. The other books of the New Testament will be used when they can contribute chronological information for the events of this period; however, most of our chronological information will come from the first five books of the New Testament.

In this book we shall ask the question, "If the New Testament is true, what can we learn from it?" Thus, the truth and reliability of the New Testament will be accepted as given since after more than one hundred years, critical scholarship has been unable to disprove this assumption. If the New Testament is true, does this mean that any interpretation of the New Testament that we might make would automatically be true? Not at all, for 2 Peter 1:20-21 says:

> But know this first of all that no prophecy of Scripture
> is a matter of one's own interpretation, for no prophecy
> was ever made by an act of human will, but men moved
> by the Holy Spirit spoke of God.

The New Testament is true, but we must study to discover its truth. We must understand the language and customs of the people that wrote the New Testament so that we can understand what it meant to them. We should always question the truth of our interpretation of Scripture, but we should never question the inherent truth of the Scriptures themselves. If the Bible is not reliable, from where shall we gain our knowledge of God?

1

The Jewish Calendar

The idea of actually being able to date the events of the New Testament may seem incredible because of the time that has elapsed since the occurrence of these events and because they do not seem to be dated in the New Testament itself. However, probably due to the providence of God, the children of Israel used a calendar based on the observation of the phases of the moon, so that it will be possible to accurately date many of these events. This can be done today because of the computational power of the modern computer and our astronomical knowledge which makes possible the determination of the exact time of the occurrence of the various phases of the moon for New Testament times.

However, before we can begin dating the events of the New Testament, we must first become familiar with the method of reckoning time used in Judea at that time. Our goal will be to construct the Jewish calendar used during this period and relate it to the calendar that we use today. It will also probably be necessary to review some of the details of our own calendar which is called the Gregorian calendar after Pope Gregory XIII (1572-1585) under whom this calendar was first used. The Jewish calendar used in the New Testament times differs from the calendar currently used by the Jewish community, which was introduced under the rabbinical patriarch Hillel II in A.D. 358/9 (Meyers, page 78). Today's Jewish calendar is based on fixed lunar cycles and only approximates the observational calendar used in New Testament times. Therefore to obtain the calendar of the New Testament, we must turn to ancient sources to find out exactly how the Jewish calendar of that day was determined.

Sources of Information

Although the Bible itself gives us a considerable amount of information concerning the Jewish calendar, it will be necessary to supplement this Biblical information with information from other ancient sources. Among these extra-Biblical sources three are particularly important: the *Mishnah*, the *Talmud* and the writings of the Jewish historian Josephus. The *Mishnah* is a compilation and commentary on the Jewish oral law. Rabbi Akiba (c. A.D. 110-135) or possibly an earlier scholar made a comprehensive collection of the traditional oral law and then Judah Prince of Galilee in c.A.D. 200 produced the final written form of the *Mishnah*. After the completion of the *Mishnah*, two major schools of rabbinical studies developed, one in Palestine and one in Babylon. Each of these schools produced a *Talmud* and these *Talmuds* were called the *Palestinian Talmud* and the *Babylonian Talmud*. The *Talmud* contains the *Mishnah,* the oral law, and the *Gemara*, comments of Jewish rabbis on the *Mishnah*. References in this book to the *Talmud* will be to the *Babylonian Talmud* which is more complete and is generally considered to be more authoritative. Finally, Josephus was a Jewish historian, priest and general who wrote during the second half of the first century A.D. Although extra-Biblical sources will be used in this book, if there are any conflicts between the Bible and the extra Biblical sources, precedence will always be given to the Bible.

The Hour

The Jewish community of the first century A.D. measured time in terms of hours, days, weeks, months and years. Of course they did not use the English names for these periods of time, and they did not necessarily define these periods of time in the same way that we do today. In *John 11:9* Jesus, speaking to his disciples, said: "Are there not twelve hours of daylight?" The Jewish hours of daylight were measured from the time of sunrise. The correspondence between our time and the Jewish daylight hours for a day when the sun rises at 6:00 A.M. and sets at 6:00 P.M. is shown in *Table 1.1*.

This correspondence between our hour and the New Testament hour is demonstrated in *Matthew 20:1-16*. The landowner went out to hire laborers early in the morning, about the third hour, then again about the sixth hour and the ninth hour and finally about the eleventh hour and they laborer until evening. The first men that were hired grumbled that the last men that were hired worked only one hour and received the same wages as they received. The men stopped working at sunset so that the twelfth daylight hour would be the last hour before sunset and the eleventh hour would be the hour before that. The first hour would correspond to the time from sunrise until about 7:00 A.M.

Some commentators equate the New Testament hour to a specific time; for example, the sixth hour is equated to 12:00 noon. This is approximately correct, but actually the New Testament daylight hour was a period of time as indicated in *Table 1.1* rather than a specific time. The Jewish daytime hour represented a period

Table 1.1	
Jewish Daylight Hours (Measured from Sunrise)	**Our Corresponding Time*** (Measured from Midnight)
1st Hour	Sunrise — 7:00 A.M.
2nd Hour	7:00 — 8:00 A.M.
3rd Hour	8:00 — 9:00 A.M.
4th Hour	9:00 — 10:00 A.M.
5th Hour	10:00 — 11:00 A.M.
6th Hour	11:00 A.M. — 12:00 Noon
7th Hour	12:00 Noon — 1:00 P.M.
8th Hour	1:00 — 2:00 P.M.
9th Hour	2:00 — 3:00 P.M.
10th Hour	3:00 — 4:00 P.M.
11th Hour	4:00 — 5:00 P.M.
12th Hour	5:00 P. M. — Sunset

* For a day with Sunrise at 6:00 A.M. and Sunset at 6:00 P.M.

of time equal to one twelfth of the total time of daylight. Thus the length of the New Testament daylight hours varied with the season, being shorter in the winter and longer in the summer. The fact that the Jewish hour was a period of time rather than a specific time is indicated in the *Mishnah, Tractate Pesahim* (Feast of Passover), Danby, page 137. In this passage Rabbi Meir (c.A.D. 140-165) is discussing the burning of leaven on Nisan 14 and says: "They may eat through the fifth, but at the beginning of the sixth hour they must burn it." Clearly Rabbi Meir considers the fifth and sixth hours periods of time.

Without a clock, how would the New Testament observer determine the hour? This was probably done by noting the position of the sun. The sun moves across the sky at a rate of 15 degrees per hour (360 degrees in 24 hours) due to the rotation of the earth on its axis. Thus at the end of the third hour (approximately 9:00 A.M.) the sun would have moved 45 degrees along its path through the sky or to a position approximately halfway between its position at sunrise and its position at noon.

Sometimes in the New Testament, Roman time seems to be used where the hours are measured from midnight, as we do today, rather than from sunrise. Thus John 19:14 in describing the trial of Jesus before Pilate says: "Now it was the day of preparation for the Passover, it was about the sixth hour." If John was using Jewish time, this would indicate that the trial took place from about 11:00 A.M. to 12 noon. However, Mark 15:25 indicates that Jesus was crucified during the third hour and Matthew 27:45, Mark 15:52 and Luke 23:44 all indicate that darkness fell over the whole land during Jesus' crucifixion from the sixth until ninth hour. Thus John must have been using Roman time in his Gospel while Matthew, Mark and Luke were using Jewish time. Thus the sixth hour in John 19:14 would be the sixth hour from midnight so that Jesus' trial before Pilate took place from 5:00 - 6:00 A.M. which would be consistent with the times given in the other Gospels. The fact that John was using Roman time in his Gospel is also indicated in John 1:37-39 which says:

> And the two disciples heard him speak, and they followed Jesus. And Jesus turned and beheld them following and said to them, "What do you seek?" And they said to Him, "Rabbi (which translated means

> Teacher), where are you staying?" He said to them, "Come and you will see." They came therefore and saw where He was staying; and they stayed with Him that day, for it was about the tenth hour.

If John was using Jewish time, the tenth hour would be from about 3:00 to 4:00 P.M. and the day would be almost over. However, if John was using Roman time, then the tenth hour would be from 9:00 to 10:00 A.M. so that they could be said to have stayed the day with Jesus. Thus John seems to be using Roman time in his Gospel.

The Jewish nighttime was also divided into twelve hours with the hours measured from sunset. Table 1.2 indicates the correspondence between our time and the Jewish nighttime hours, again for a day with sunrise at 6:00 A.M. and sunset at 6:00 P.M. Thus Claudius Lysias, who is sending Paul to Caesarea to escape an ambush, in Acts 23:23b says "Get two hundred soldiers ready by the third hour of the night to proceed to Caesarea, with seventy horsemen and two hundred spearmen.." How would they know when the third hour had arrived without a clock? Again, the stars advance 15 degrees per hour due to the rotation of the earth on its axis. Thus, at sunset they could pick a prominent star near the eastern horizon and by the third hour of the night that star would have advanced 45 degrees or about halfway between its position at sunset and its zenith position at midnight. They might also have used the moon for this determination of the night time hour.

Table 1.2	
Jewish Nighttime Hours (Measured from Sunset)	**Our Corresponding Time*** (Measured from Midnight)
1st Hour	Sunset — 7:00 P.M.
2nd Hour	7:00 — 8:00 P.M.
3rd Hour	8:00 — 9:00 P.M.
4th Hour	9:00 — 10:00 P.M.
5th Hour	10:00 — 11:00 P.M.
6th Hour	11:00 P.M. — 12:00 Midnight
7th Hour	12:00 Midnight — 1 A.M.
8th Hour	1:00 — 2:00 A.M.
9th Hour	2:00 — 3:00 A.M.
10th Hour	3:00 — 4:00 A.M.
11th Hour	4:00 — 5:00 A.M.
12th Hour	5:00 A. M. — Sunrise

*For a day with Sunrise at 6:00 A.M. and Sunset at 6:00 P.M.

The Day

The New Testament day, as our day, corresponds to the time required for the earth to make one complete rotation on its axis. However, there was a significant difference between the Jewish day and our day because the Jewish day began at sunset while our day, following ancient Roman usage, begins at midnight. Thus the Jewish day consisted of twelve hours of darkness followed by twelve hours of daylight and would have begun approximately six hours earlier than our day. Thus *Genesis 1:5* says: "And there was evening and there was morning, one day."

We see the same usage in the New Testament. After Jesus had been teaching in the synagogue on the Sabbath, Mark 1:32-34 says:

> And when evening had come, after the sun had set, they began bringing to Him all who were ill and those who were demon-possessed. And the whole city had gathered at the door. And He healed many who were ill with various diseases, and cast out many demons; and He was not permitting the demons to speak, because they knew who he was.

After the sun had set, it was no longer the Sabbath, but the first day of the week, so the Jews of Capernaum were no longer under the Sabbath restrictions so that they felt free to bring the sick to see Jesus to be healed. Thus, this Scripture again indicates that the Jewish day began at sunset.

The Week

The Jews of the New Testament times had a seven-day week just as we do today. The Jewish days of the week were identified by number (see Genesis 1:1-2:3) except that the seventh day was also called the Sabbath (Shabbath) which means in Hebrew "to cease" and the sixth day was also called the Day of Preparation (preparation for the Sabbath). The seven-day week does not correspond to any known astronomical event like the 24- hour day. Rather, Genesis 1:1-23 says that God created the heavens and the earth in six days and God rested on the seventh day.

Table 1.3 lists the days of the week with their Jewish and Roman names. This table also indicates the meaning of the English and Roman names. The Roman names listed in Table 1.3 were taken from an inscription found in the city of Pompeii (Finegan, page 15) which was buried by an eruption of Mount Vesuvius in A.D. 79. The Roman names for the days come from the sun, the moon and the Roman gods associated with the five planets known to the ancient world. Our English names for the days follow the Roman names with a substitution of northern European gods for the Roman gods. Thus Tuesday came from Tiw's day where Tiw was the Old English god of war which corresponded to the Roman god Mars. Earlier the Romans had an eight-day week and only gradually adopted the seven-day week from the East.

Dio Cassius, who died c. A.D. 235, said,in his *Roman History (XXXVII, XVII-XIX)*, that the custom of referring the days of the week to the planets began in Egypt and in his day was found among all mankind. Dio Cassius, in the same reference, also said that the Jews dedicated to their God "the day called the day of Saturn." This is important because it indicates that the Jews numbered their days of the week the same as did the Romans. Thus Saturday (Saturn's Day) was the same day as the Jewish Seventh Day (the Sabbath). This is confirmed in Scripture by the fact that Luke, writing to the Roman, Theophilus, in Luke 20:1, for example, speaks of the "first day of the week" in connection with Jesus' resurrection without further qualification since the first day of the Jewish week was also the first day of the Roman week just as it is today. The fact that every Sabbath was a holy day served to maintain the cycle of the seven- day week

Table 1.3 Days of the Week		
English Designation of the Day (With Meaning)	**Jewish Designation of the Day**	**Roman Designation of the Day** (With Meaning)
Sunday (Sun Day)	First Day	Solis (Day of the Sun)
Monday (Moon Day)	Second Day	Lunae (Day of the Moon)
Tuesday (Tiw's Day)[1]	Third Day	Martis (Day of Mars)
Wednesday (Wooden's Day)[2]	Fourth Day	Mercurii (Day of Mercury)
Thursday (Thor's Day)[3]	Fifth Day	Jovis (Day of Jupiter)
Friday (Fria's Day)[4]	Sixth Day (Day of Preparation)	Veneris (Day of Venus)
Saturday (Saturn's Day)	Seventh Day (Sabbath)	Saturni (Day of Saturn)

1 Tiw was an Old English god of war identified with the Roman god Mars (From *Webster's Third International Dictionary*, Merriam Company: Springfield, MA, 1961).

2   Wooden was Old English for the Chief German god identified with the Roman god Mercury (ibid).

3 Thor was the Nordic god of thunder identified with the Roman god Jupiter (ibid).

4 Fria was the German goddess of love identified with the Roman god Venus (ibid)

back through the time of the exodus from Egypt, just as the Christian observance of Sunday has maintained the seven- day cycle unchanged since New Testament times. In 1582 when the Gregorian Calendar was first introduced, the date following October 4 (Julian) was called October 15, but October 4 (Julian) was Thursday and October 15 (Gregorian) was still Friday so that the weekly cycle of days remained unchanged.

It was necessary to drop ten days from the calendar because the year under the Julian calendar was too long so that approximately every 128 years the Julian calendar fell one more day behind. By 1582 the Julian calendar was ten days behind its correct date according to the earth's orbital position relative to the sun. Appendix A gives more information concerning these calendars.

The Month

The usual Hebrew word in the Old Testament for month was *chodesh* which is also the Hebrew word for new moon. This was the case because the Jewish month began on the night when the thin crescent of the new moon was first visible. Figure 1.1 shows a diagram of the illumination of the moon for various positions of the moon in its orbit around the earth. The view in the diagram is from a point above the north pole of the earth.

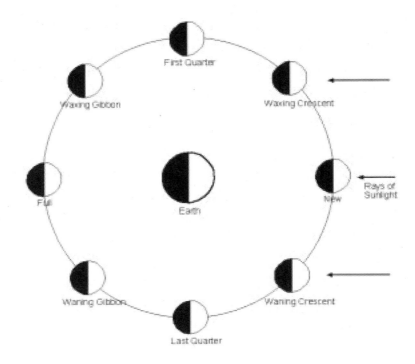

Figure 1.1
Phases of the Moon

Note that the side of the moon facing the sun is illuminated while the side of the moon away from the sun is dark. At the time of the new moon, the moon and the sun have the same celestial longitude (are in line as viewed from the earth) so that the side of the moon facing the earth is completely dark. However, generally by the evening of the day following the new moon, the moon will have advanced sufficiently along its orbit so that the thin crescent of the new moon will be visible just after sunset. This first visible crescent of the new moon marked the beginning of the Jewish month. As the earth rotated on its axis, this thin crescent moon will set about thirty minutes after the sun has set. The next evening a slightly thicker crescent of the moon will be visible and this crescent moon will set about 50 minutes after sunset. This process continues and by the seventh day about one-half of the moon will be illuminated with sunlight as seen from earth. This moon is called a first quarter moon because the moon has completed one quarter of its 29.5 day lunar cycle. The first quarter moon will set about midnight. As the lunar month progresses more than half of the moon's surface as viewed from earth will be illuminated and this moon is called a gibbon moon. As the illuminated area of the moon as seen from earth continues to increase in size on successive evenings, it is called a waxing moon. On about the fifteenth of the month (14¾ days into the lunar cycle), the entire surface of the moon facing the earth will be illuminated by sunlight, and we have a full moon. The full moon rises at sunset and doesn't set until sunrise.

As the moon proceeds along its orbit, about the 22nd day of the lunar cycle, the moon reaches its last quarter position, and again, one half of the moon's surface will be illuminated by the sun as seen from earth. Also, now the moon precedes the sun, thus rising before the sun rises and setting before the sun sets. The lunar cycle continues until the final thin crescent moon is seen just before sunrise, and then the next day will be the time of the new moon when again the celestial longitude of the sun and moon are equal and the side of the moon facing the earth is completely dark. Of course we can see the same lunar cycles in our night sky today. Since the whole lunar cycle takes about 29.5 days, the Jewish lunar months varied in length between 29 and 30 days. Figure 1.2 shows the approximate appearance of the moon on each day of April A.D. 33. For waning moons, the appearance of the moons are shown just after rising and for waxing moons the appearance is shown just before setting.

April
A.D. 33 (Gregorian)

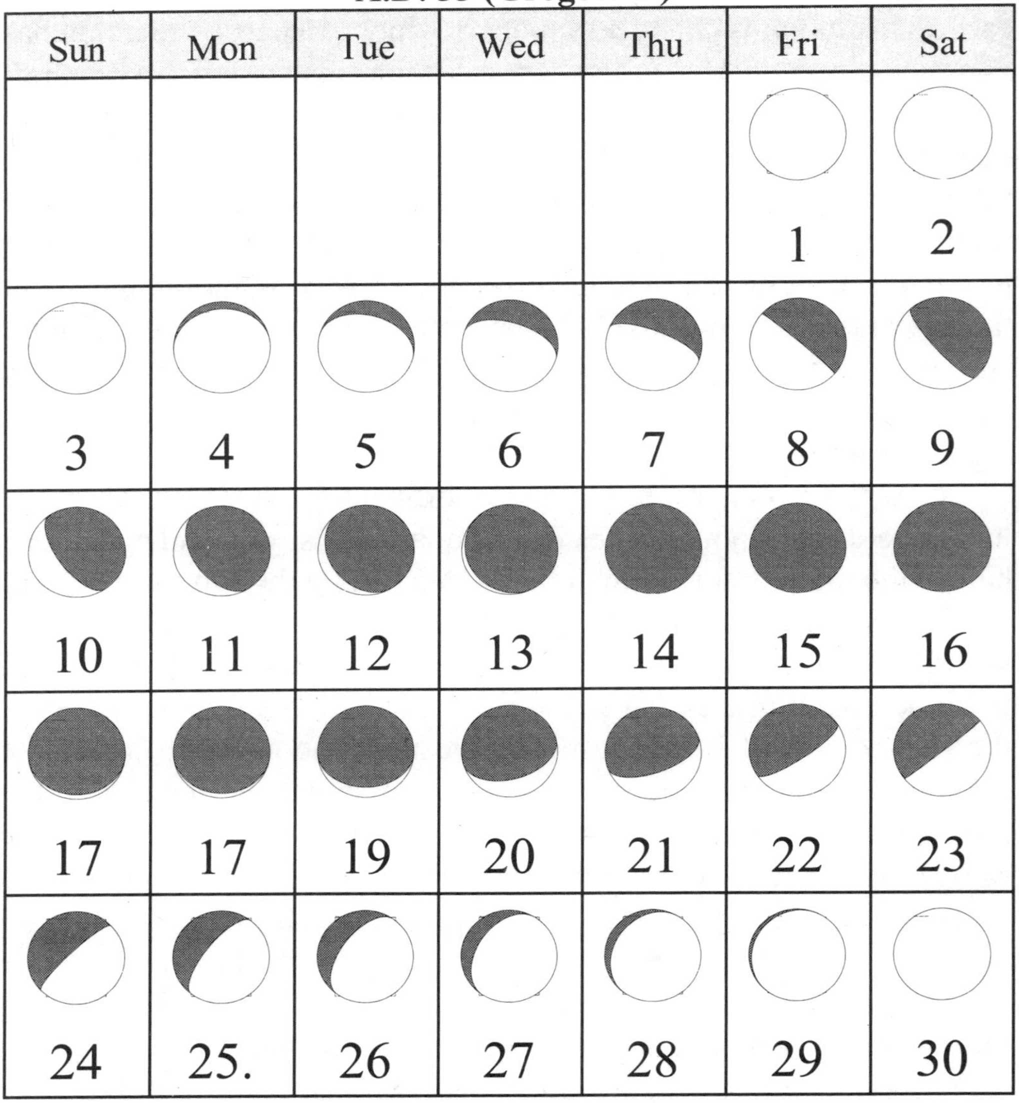

Sun	Mon	Tue	Wed	Thu	Fri	Sat
					1	2
3	4	5	6	7	8	9
10	11	12	13	14	15	16
17	17	19	20	21	22	23
24	25.	26	27	28	29	30

Daily Appearance of the Moon
Figure 1.2

Establishment of the New Moon

There are numerous references to the new moon in the Bible, for example: *Numbers 29:1-6, 1 Chronicles 23:31, 2 Chronicles 31:3, Nehemiah 10:33, Psalms 81:3* and *Colossians 2:16. Numbers 29:1-6* says:

> Now in the seventh month, on the first day of the month, you shall also have a holy convocation; you shall do no laborious work. It will be to you a day for blowing trumpets. You shall offer a burnt offering as a soothing aroma to the LORD: one bull, one ram, and seven male lambs one year old without defect; also their grain offering, fine flour mixed with oil: three-tenths of an ephah for the bull, two-tenths for the ram, and one-tenth for each of the seven lambs. Offer one male goat for a sin offering, to make atonement for you, besides the burnt offering of the new moon and its grain offering, and the continual burnt offering and its grain offering, and their drink offerings, according to their ordinance, for a soothing aroma, an offering by fire to the LORD.

Verse 1 of the above Scripture indicates that the offerings described are the offerings for the first day of the seventh month, and verse 6 indicates on that day they were to also offer the offering for the new moon. This is a direct indication in Scripture that the first day of the Jewish month was the day of the new moon. However, the Bible does not give a detailed description of exactly how the beginning of the Jewish month was determined because the authors of the Bible assumed that the Jewish calendar of their time was well known to their readers. Fortunately the Mishnah and the Talmud do give us considerably more details concerning the determination of the Jewish calendar while the Temple still stood (prior to A.D. 70).

In the *Mishnah, Tractate* (Portion) *Rosh ha–Shanah* (Feast of the New Year), considerable details are given as to how the witnesses were examined to establish the beginning of the Jewish month. There was a large courtyard in Jerusalem called Beth Yaazek where the prospective witnesses were assembled. These witnesses were examined by a court composed of three members of the Sanhedrin (according to *Tractate Sanhedrin)*. A large meal was prepared for the witnesses to encourage them to come. While the Temple still stood, a witness could violate the law which limited a Sabbath day's journey to 2000 cubits (about six tenths of a mile) in order to travel to Jerusalem and report seeing the first crescent of the new moon.

The witnesses were examined as follows: The witnesses were considered in pairs because to establish anything legally required the testimony of at least two credible witnesses (Deuteronomy 19:15). The pair of witnesses that arrived first was examined first. The elder of the two witnesses would be brought before the court first. He would be asked, "Where did you see the moon, before the sun or after the sun?" If he answered before the sun, his testimony would be rejected because the thin crescent of the moon that appears before the sun rises in the morning would be the final phase of the old moon and not the first crescent of the new moon that marks the beginning of the new month and appears just after sunset and would thus appear after the sun.

The court would also ask the witness if the moon was north or south of the sun? How high was it in the sky? To which side was it

Figure 1.3
Thin Crescent of the Setting Summer New Moon

leaning? And how broad was it? The moon always set in the west while the sun sets in the northwest in the summer and the southwest in the winter. Therefore, in the summer the moon would set south of the sun and in the winter the moon should set north of the sun. The illuminated portion of the moon always faces the sun so the tilt of the moon would depend on the position of the sun which would vary from season to season. *Figure 1.3* shows a summer crescent moon on the western horizon. At the spring equinox (about March 21) and at the autumn equinox (about September 23), the sun also sets due west so that the moon sets nearly parallel to the horizon as shown in *Figure 1.4*. At the summer and winter solstices, about June 22 and December 22 respectively, the crescent of the moon is most nearly vertical. These dates vary slightly because of leap year. Since the

Setting Crescent New Moon
At Spring and Autumn Equinoxes
Figure 1.4

horns or cusps of the crescent moon always point away from the sun, the horns of the new winter crescent moon would point north, while in the summer, the horns of the new moon would point south.

After examining the first witness, the court of the Sanhedrin would bring in the second witness and if his testimony agreed with the first witness and was acceptable to the court, there was sufficient evidence to establish the beginning of the new month. The other witnesses that had come were briefly examined so that they would be encouraged to come for future sightings when they might be the only witnesses. Members of the court also watched for the first crescent of the new moon and could serve as witnesses if needed.

When the sighting of the first crescent of the new moon had been established by the court, the chief of the court would say, "It is hallowed!" and all the people would answer, "It is hallowed! It is hallowed!" At that time a trumpet was sounded in accordance with Psalm 81:3,4 which says: "Blow the trumpet at the new moon, at the full moon, on our feast day, for it is a statute for Israel, an ordinance for the God of Jacob." To announce that a new month had begun, messengers were sent to surrounding areas with a Jewish population. These messengers were also exempted from the travel restriction on the Sabbath in order that the proper time for the set feasts and offerings would be known.

In general, the first crescent of the new moon will be visible just after sunset on the day following the new moon. The Jewish court that controlled the calendar in the first century A.D. knew that their month should have either 29 or 30 days because the lunar cycle is 29.5 days long. They would watch on the evening of the 30th day of the month and if the thin crescent of the new moon was seen by two credible witnesses, that day would be proclaimed the first day of the new month. Since, in the Jewish reckoning of time, the twelve hours of night preceded the twelve hours of daylight, the thin crescent of the new moon would be visible near the beginning of the Jewish day. Thus there would be almost twenty-four hours available for the witnesses to travel to Jerusalem and bear witness to the new moon before the end of that day. If the crescent of the new moon was not seen on the evening of the 30th day, then that day would be considered the 30th day of the previous month and the new month would begin with the next day. Even if the thin crescent of the new moon was seen by two credible witnesses, the *Mishnah* indicates that if the day was not hallowed (proclaimed) before sunset, that day would still be considered the 30th day of the preceding month. However, even if bad weather or other conditions prevented two witnesses from seeing the first crescent of the new moon, the calendar for that month would only be started at most a day late and the beginning of the next month would be based on new observations and would probably return to the exact lunar cycle. Although generally the months alternated between months of 29 and 30 days, it was possible to have two 29-day months or two 30-day months occurring consecutively due to the complexity of the lunar cycle.

Thus the Jewish calendar in New Testament times depended upon observing of the phases of the moon and the number of days in the month could not be determined until the end of the month. Also the new moon could occur on any day of the week. Therefore, the day of the week of feast days would vary from year to year just as the day of week of Christmas (December 25th) varies from year to year with our calendar. This situation was changed when Hillel II introduced the present calculated Jewish calendar during the fourth century of the Christian Era. Under the current Jewish calendar, certain feast days can only occur on certain days of the week (Parise, page 12).

Celestial Sphere

The celestial sphere is a conventional representation of the sky as a spherical shell on which the celestial bodies appear projected. The ecliptic is the sun's apparent annual path on the celestial sphere. The projection of the earth's equator on the celestial sphere is the celestial equator. These three dimensional circles are shown in *Figure 1.5*. The two intersections of the ecliptic with the celestial equator are called the spring (vernal) equinox and the autumn (autumnal) equinox. The two points on the ecliptic where the sun is furthest away from the celestial equator are called the summer and winter solstices.

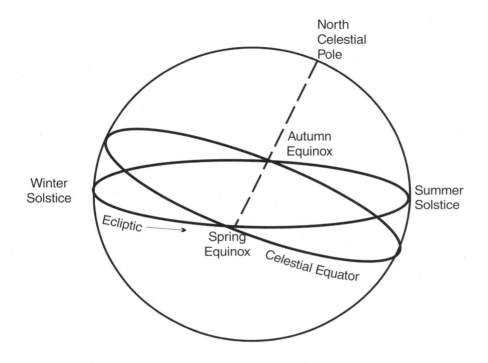

Celestial Sphere
Figure 1.5

Jewish Months

Table 1.4 gives a list of the numbers and names of the months of the Jewish calendars together with Scripture references to each month. In the Old Testament different names were used for the months prior to the Babylonian captivity. Only four of these early names appear in the Bible: Abib, the first month (Exodus 34:18, Deut. 16:1), Ziv, the second month (1 Kings 6:1, 1 Kings 6:37), Ethanim, the seventh month, (1 Kings 8:2) and Bul, the eighth month

Table 1.4 *Months of the Jewish Calendar During New Testament Times*		
Number of the Month	*Name of the Month*	*Scripture Reference*
1	*Nisan*	*Ex 12:2, Neh 2:1, Es 3:7*
2	*Iyyar*	*Gn 7:11*
3	*Sivan*	*Ex 19:1 Es 8:9*
4	*Tammuz*	*2 Ki 25:3*
5	*Ab*	*Nu 33:38*
6	*Elul*	*1 Ch 27:9 Ne 6:15*
7	*Tishri*	*Gn 8:4*
8	*Marheshvan*	*Zch 1:1*
9	*Kislev*	*Ezr 10:9 Ne 1:1 Zch 7:1*
10	*Tebeth*	*Gn 8:5 Es 2:16*
11	*Shebat*	*Dt 1:3 Zch 1:7*
12	*Adar*	*Es 3:7 Es 9:1 Ezr 6:15*

(1 Kings 6:38). The names of the months used after the Babylonian captivity and during the New Testament times appear in the Bible only in Ezra, Nehemiah, Esther and Zechariah, all of which were written after the Babylonian captivity, These names are similar to the names used in the Babylonian lunar calendar. All of the names listed in Table 1.4 are found in *Megillat Ta'anit* (*The Scroll of Fasting*, Finegan, page 39) probably written just after the beginning of the first century A.D. which indicates that these names were in use during New Testament times. Josephus, the first century Jewish historian, also uses many of these names for the Jewish months in his writings.

Thirteenth Month

There is still one aspect concerning the Jewish calendar of New Testament times that must be discussed. With the lunar cycle equal to 29.5 days, a Jewish year of twelve months would only have 354 days (12 times 29.5) and thus would be 11¼ days short of the 365¼ days of a solar year. Thus, in only three years, the spring feast of Passover would come more than a month early, and, in ten years, the Passover would be celebrated in the middle of winter rather than in spring. This problem was overcome by a systematic procedure for periodically inserting (intercalating) a thirteenth month into the Jewish year following the twelfth Jewish month of Adar. This thirteenth month was called Second Adar.

In *Antiquities of the Jews* (3.10.5, page 96), Josephus, the first century A.D. Jewish historian, wrote:

> In the month of Xanthicus, which is by us called Nisan, and is the beginning of our year, on the fourteenth day of the lunar month, when the sun

> is in Aries (for in this month it was that we were delivered from bondage under the Egyptians), and law ordains that we should every year slay that sacrifice which I before told you we slew when we came out of Egypt, and which is called Passover; and so we do celebrate this Passover in companies, leaving nothing of what we sacrificed till the day following.

Josephus' comment concerning the beginning of the Jewish year is significant because he was a Jewish priest during the first century A.D. and therefore would be familiar with how the Jewish calendar was determined in New Testament times. Josephus indicates that the sun must be in Aries, a constellation of stars located along the ecliptic when the new year begins and the Passover Feast is celebrated. Aries is one of the twelve Zodiac constellations of stars that are located along the apparent path of the sun through the sky. During the year the position of the sun among the stars changes from day to day and from month to month. This change in the apparent position of the sun among the stars as viewed from earth is of course caused by the earth revolving around the sun. During the $365\frac{1}{4}$ days of the year, the sun travels through all twelve of the zodiac regions. This annual journey of the sun through the twelve zodiac regions is shown for A.D. 33-34 in Table 1.5. An observer of course could not see the stars around the sun during the daytime, but by observing the constellation on the western horizon just after sunset and the constellation on the eastern horizon just before sunrise, it was possible to determine which of the zodiac regions contained the sun. From ancient times the ecliptic, the path of the sun through the stars, has been divided into twelve equal parts and each of these parts was named for the major constellation it contained.

Table 1.5 Sun's Journey Through the Zodiac Constellations A.D. 33-34	
Zodiac Region*	**Date Sun Entered Region**
Aries	March 20, A.D. 33
Taurus	April 21, A.D. 33
Gemini	May 22, A.D. 33
Cancer	June 23, A.D. 33
Leo	July 24, A.D. 33
Virgo	August 24, A.D. 33
Libra	September 23, A.D. 33
Scorpius	October 23, A.D. 33
Sagittarius	November 21, A.D. 33
Capricornus	December 21, A.D. 33
Aquarius	January 19, A.D. 34
Pisces	February 18, A.D. 34

* The Zodiac Regions are twelve equal regions, each of 30 degrees, marked off along the ecliptic and measured eastward from the position of the sun at the time of the spring equinox. These regions generally contain the position of the sun, moon and the five bright planets.

The following method seemed to have been used in determining whether or not a thirteenth month should be added to a given Jewish year. During the year the position of the sun among the zodiac constellations was followed. Josephus indicates that, at the time the Passover lamb was sacrificed at the close of the fourteenth day of the first Jewish month, the sun must be in the constellation Aries. If at the close of twelve lunar months, it was determined that the sun would be in Aries by the fourteenth of the next lunar month, then the next month was called Nisan and it would begin a new Jewish year. However, if it was determined that the sun would not reach the constellation Aries by the close of the fourteenth day of the next month, then a thirteenth month would be added to that Jewish year before the start of the new year.

A group of stars called the Pleiades, which is part of the zodiac constellation Taurus, probably played an important role in determining whether or not a thirteenth month was needed. The Pleiades are located on the western edge of Taurus right next to the constellation Aries. Thus, by observing how high the Pleiades were above the western horizon just after sunset at the end of the twelfth month, the Sanhedrin could determine the location of the sun on its yearly trek through the zodiac regions. If the Pleiades was near the western horizon just after sunset , then the sun was already in Aries and the next month would be Nisan the beginning of a new year. However, if the Pleiades was seen high above the horizon, the sun would not reach Aries by the fourteenth day of the next month and therefore a thirteenth month would be needed.

There are several references to the Pleiades in the Old Testament: Job 9:9, Job 38:31 and Amos 3:8. In Job 38:31-32, the Lord answered Job out of the whirlwind and said:

Can you bind the chains of the Pleiades,
or loose the cords of Orion?

Can you lead forth a constellation in its season
and guide the Bear with her satellites.

These verses not only indicate that the Jewish community was familiar with the Pleiades hundreds of years before New Testament times, but was also familiar with the idea that the position of the constellations in the sky were associated with the changing seasons. In Job 38:31, the Lord pointed out that Job could not supply the force to hold the stars of the Pleiades together or reach up and loosen the belt of Orion, another constellation of stars. Only God could do that!

Thus, by waiting to start the new year until the sun had entered the constellation Aries, the Jewish calendar was kept in step with the seasons. The court of the Sanhedrin, which controlled the calendar, would be watching the position of the sun during the entire twelfth month, and in most cases, could probably predict whether or not a thirteenth month would be needed before the end of the month. The significance of the sun being in the constellation Aries is that if the sun has reached Aries it has passed the spring equinox. The spring equinox is the position of the sun on the ecliptic where the ecliptic intersects the celestial equator with the sun going north (see Figure 1.5, page 39). When the zodiac constellations were established, several hundred years before the birth of Christ, the sun reached the spring equinox in the constellation Aries. However, due to the precession of the equinoxes, by the first century A.D. the spring equinox was now located in the eastern end of the zodiac constellation Pisces. This precession of the equinoxes is caused by a slow wobble in the earth's axis just as a slowly spinning top will wobble.

The above procedure for determining the start of the new Jewish year is also reflected in our date for the celebration of Easter. In the beginning of Christ's Church, Easter was celebrated in accordance with the Jewish calendar since all of its members were

Jews.   Jesus' crucifixion was celebrated on Nisan 14 and His resurrection was celebrated on Nisan 16 and this practice continued with the Asiatic churches for several centuries.   However, the Church at Rome began always to celebrate Easter on a Sunday and therefore a controversy arose concerning the proper time to celebrate Easter.   In A.D. 325, at the Council of Nicaea, it was ordained that Easter would always be celebrated on the first Sunday after the first full moon subsequent to the date of the spring equinox (Schaff page 218) and this is the date that we celebrate Easter today.

It may be surprising that the Zodiac, which is associated with astrology, could have played a role in the calendar used in the Bible. However, in Genesis 1:14 God said: "Let there be lights in the expanse of the heavens to separate the day from the night, and let them be for signs, and for seasons and for days and for years." Thus, the use of the Zodiac constellations to determine the calendar was one of their intended uses while their use for astrology is a misuse. A fourth century A.D. mosaic of the Zodiac signs and their Hebrew names was found in the floor of a Jewish synagogue at Hammat Tiberias on the Sea of Galilee. A sixth century A.D. synagogue at Bet Alpha, located about 20 miles southwest of the Sea of Galilee, also has a mosaic floor picturing the signs of the Zodiac with their Hebrew names. This further indicates that the signs of the Zodiac were known and used by the Jewish community in ancient times. *Table 1.6* gives the Latin (Roman) name and meaning of each of the twelve signs of the Zodiac together with their corresponding Jewish names. In general, the meaning of the Jewish (Hebrew) names are the same as that of the Roman names with one significant exception. The Jewish name of the first sign of the Zodiac, Taleh, means lamb rather than ram. The Passover Feast was celebrated when the sun was in the Zodiac constellation the Jews called Taleh (the lamb) and the lamb, of course, played an important part in this feast.

	Table 1.6 Signs of the Zodiac*	
	Latin Name (Meaning)	Jewish Name
1	Aries (the Ram)	Taleh
2	Taurus (the Bull)	Shor
3	Gemini (the Twins)	Teomin
4	Cancer (the Crab)	Sartan
5	Leo (the Lion)	Aryeh
6	Virgo (the Virgin)	Betulah
7	Libra (the Balance)	Moznayim
8	Scorpio (the Scorpion)	Aqrab
9	Sagittarius (the Archer)	Qeshet
10	Capricornus (the Goat)	Gedi
11	Aquarius (the Water Carrier)	Deli
12	Pisces (the Fishes)	Dagim

*Finegan, *Handbook of Biblical Chronology*, page 20.

Goldstine's Tables

Thus we know how the Jewish Sanhedrin of the New Testament Times determined the first day of their lunar month, but how can we reproduce their observations after almost 2000 years and relate these observations to our own calendar? In 1973 Herman H.

Goldstine, a member of the Institute for Advanced Study at Princeton University and Fellow of the International Business Machine Corporation published *New and Full Moons 1001 B.C. to A.D. 1651* which provided the answer to this question. Using an IBM 360 electronic computer, Dr. Goldstine computed, to the nearest minute, the exact instants when the celestial longitude of the sun and the moon were equal which is the exact time of the new moon. In these tables, he also gives the exact time when the celestial longitudes of the sun and the moon differ by 180° which is the instant of a complete full moon.

Goldstine's Tables give the time of the new moon in terms of the local time for an observer at ancient Babylon; however, by applying a constant correction of minus 39 minutes to the tabulated values to adjust for the difference in longitude between Jerusalem and ancient Babylon, the local Jerusalem time of the occurrence of each new moon that occurred during New Testament times can be determined. Prior to the publication of these tables, the time of the new moons during New Testament times could be computed, but it was a laborious calculation. Since the publication of these tables a number of programs for the personal computer have become available that permit the calculation of these times; however, Goldstine's Tables still provide a convenient source of the new moons for the time of the New Testament and much of the Old Testament as well.

Summary

Thus in the New Testament times each Jewish month began when the thin crescent of the new moon was first visible, and this was generally on the day following the occurrence of the exact instant of the new moon when the celestial longitude of the sun and the moon were equal. The Jewish year began with the month when the sun was in the constellation Aries. Since Goldstine's Tables give the exact time of each new moon that occurred during New Testament times, it is possible to construct the Jewish calendars for the years of the New Testament and to relate these first century A.D. Jewish calendars to our calendar. In *Appendix D* these Jewish calendars are given together with the corresponding Gregorian calendars (the calendar we are currently using) for the years 10 B.C. through A.D. 70. *Appendix D* also contains more details concerning exactly how these calendars were constructed.

Jewish Festivals

Since the Jewish months are not mentioned in the New Testament, how will the Jewish calendars of *Appendix D* be useful in dating the events of the New Testament? Although those Jewish months are not mentioned, a number of the Jewish festivals are mentioned in the New Testament and these festivals occur on fixed days of the Jewish calendar. *Table 1.7* lists the Jewish festivals mention in the New Testament together with their date on the Jewish calendar and Scriptural references concerning their observance. Many of the events of the New Testament are associated with these feast and fast days and thus it will be possible to date these events exactly in terms of the Jewish calendar. A more detailed discussion of the Jewish festivals is given in *Appendix C.*

Why are these New Testament Jewish calendars related in the Gregorian calendar instead of the Julian calendar, which was the Roman calendar of the first century A.D. and is the calendar used in most historical works for this period? The reason the Gregorian calendar is used in *Appendix D* is to permit us to know New Testament dates in terms of our current calendar. This is in accordance with our usual calendar practices. We, for example,

Table 1.7 Jewish Festivals		
Name	**Date**	**Scripture Reference**
Passover	Nisan 14	Ex 12:18, Lv 23:5
Feast of Unleavened Bread	Nisan 15-21	Lv 23:6
First Fruit's Offering	1st Sun. after Nisan 15	Lv 23:10ff
Pentecost	8th Sun. after Nisan 15	Lv 23:15ff
Day of Trumpets	Tishri 1	Nu 29:1, Lv 23:24
Day of Atonement	Tishri 10	Lv 16:29ff, Lv 23:27ff
Feast of Booths	Tishri 15-22	Lv 23:34ff
Dedication	Kislev 25 for 8 days	Jn 10:22

celebrate George Washington's birthday on February 22, according to our Gregorian calendar; however, a form of the Julian calendar was actually in use in England and the American colonies when Washington was born , and according to that calendar, Washington was born on February 11. Thus, we use the Gregorian calendar, which wasn't adopted by England and its colonies until 1752, to date Washington's birthday so that we will know the date of this event had our current calendar been in use at the time of his birth. In the same way, in *Appendix D*, we have extended the Gregorian calendar back to New Testament times so that we can date the events of the New Testament according to our current calendar. For further discussion of the Julian and Gregorian calendars, see *Appendix A*.

2

Jesus' Final Days

With the Jewish calendar for the years 10 B.C. to A.D. 70 of *Appendix D*, we have a powerful tool for establishing the dates of the events of the New Testament. However, in order to be able to relate the dates on the Jewish calendar of the New Testament times to our present Gregorian calendar, we need a point of reference. The situation is somewhat like having an old diary in which daily events are recorded together with the month and the day of the month, but not the year. We know the relative time of occurrence of all the events recorded, but we would not know the absolute time of occurrence of any of the events. However, as soon as we can determine the year of occurrence of any one event, then we can determine the exact date of occurrence of all the other events. The determination of New Testament chronology will not be quite that simple because we do not have a daily record of events; however, we do have a series of events, generally presented in chronological order with many of these events identified as to the month and the day of the month by indicating the time of their occurrence relative to the time of the Jewish festival days which occurred at known dates on the Jewish calendar.

The period of the New Testament for which we have the most detailed information is the final days of Jesus' earthly ministry. Thirty-six percent of the verses of *Matthew's Gospel* concern these final days. Thirty-seven percent of the verses of *Mark's Gospel*, twenty-five percent of the verses of *Luke's Gospel* and thirty-nine percent of the verses of *John's Gospel* also concern these final days. Thus, we shall begin our study by carefully reviewing the information contained in the four Gospels concerning the final days of Jesus' ministry, hoping to be able to date exactly one or more of the events during this period. If we can exactly date one event, this will provide the key to unlocking the chronology of the remainder of the New Testament.

Crucifixion

In describing Jesus' trial before Pilate in *John 18:28*, the Apostle John says:

> Then they led Jesus from Caiaphas into the Praetorium, and it was early; and they themselves did not enter into the Praetorium in order that they might not be defiled, but might eat the Passover.

This verse indicates that Jesus' trial before Pilate and Jesus' crucifixion took place before the Passover Feast or before Nisan 15 on the Jewish calendar. In *John 19:14*, when Pilate was passing judgment on Jesus, John says: "Now it was the day of preparation for the Passover, it was about the sixth hour and he said to the Jews, 'Behold your King.'" This verse indicates that the day of Jesus' Crucifixion occurred on the day of preparation for the Passover or on Nisan 14 of the Jewish calendar. In this verse in the New International Version of the Bible, the word "Passover" is replaced by "Passover

Week"; however, the word "week" does not appear in the Greek text. Finally, in *John 19:31*, John says:

> The Jews therefore, because it was the day of preparation, so that the bodies should not remain on the cross on the Sabbath (for that Sabbath was a high day), asked Pilate that their legs might be broken and that they might be taken away.

Thus, the day of Jesus' Crucifixion was not only the day of preparation for the Passover Feast, Nisan 14, but it was also the day of preparation for the Sabbath or the sixth day of the week, our Friday. " For that Sabbath was a high day"(literally for the day of that Sabbath was great) because it was the day of the Passover Feast.

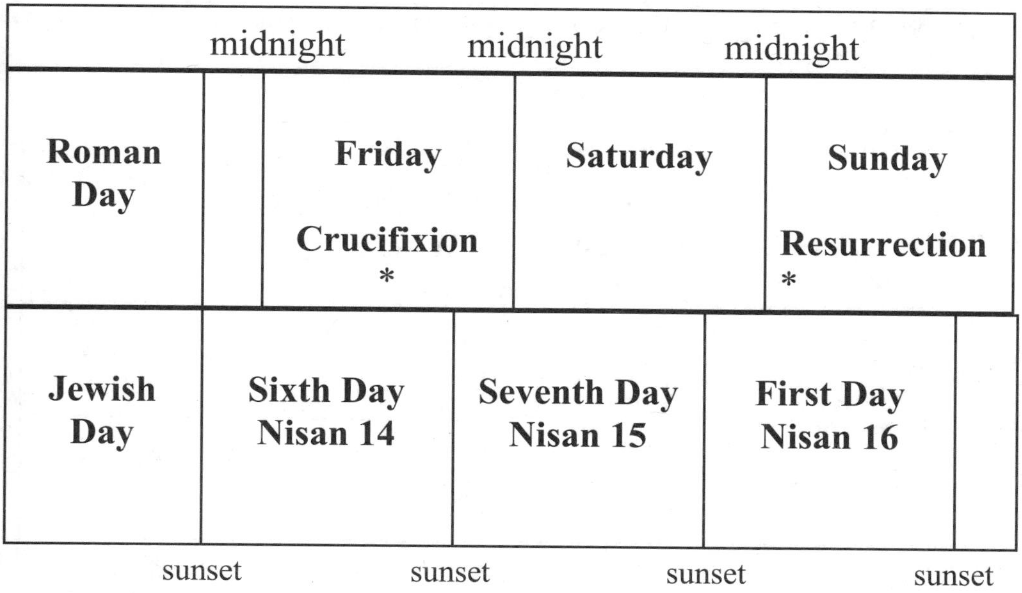

	midnight		midnight		midnight	
Roman Day		**Friday** **Crucifixion** *		**Saturday**	**Sunday** **Resurrection** *	
Jewish Day	**Sixth Day** **Nisan 14**		**Seventh Day** **Nisan 15**		**First Day** **Nisan 16**	
	sunset	sunset		sunset		sunset

Figure 2.1
Day of the Crucifixion

Figure 2.1 indicates the day of the Crucifixion both in terms of the Roman day, which is the same as our day, and the Jewish day. The fourth century Christian historian Eusebius, in *The History of the Church* (page 231), preserves a portion of a second century A.D. letter from Polycrates, an Asian bishop, to Victor, the bishop of Rome, that traces the Asian Church's observance of Nisan 14 as the day of Jesus' Crucifixion back to Philip, the evangelist and the Apostle John. Also, the *Babylonian Talmud, Tractate Sanhedrin*, page 281, indicates that *Yeshu* (Jesus) was executed on the eve of Passover. Thus, Jesus was crucified on Nisan 14 in a year in which that day ended on our Friday.

Since the calendars of *Appendix D* indicate the Gregorian date when the Jewish day begins, we shall be looking for a year in which Nisan 15 began on a Friday or equivalently, when Nisan 14 began on a Thursday. *Table 2.1* lists all the years during New Testament times when Nisan 15 began on a Friday. But during which of these years was Christ Crucified?

Table 2.1 **Gregorian Date of Nisan 15 For All Years Where Nisan 15 Began on a Friday (10 B.C. to A.D. 70)**			
Year	**Date**	**Year**	**Date**
A.D. 6	March 31	A.D. 40	April 13
A.D. 10	April 16	A.D. 54	April 10
A.D. 13	April 12	A.D. 60	April 2
A.D. 33	April 1	A.D. 64	April 18
A.D. 37	April 17	A.D. 67	April 15

Now in the fifteenth year of the reign of Tiberius Caesar, when Pontius Pilate was governor of Judea, and Herod was tetrarch of Galilee, and his brother Philip was tetrarch of the region of Ituraea and Trachonitis, and Lysanias was tetrarch of Abilene, in the high priesthood of Annas and Caiaphas, the word of God came to John, the son of Zacharias, in the wilderness (Luke 3:1-2).

In these verses Luke indicates that John the Baptist received his call from God to begin his ministry in the fifteenth year of the reign of the Roman Emperor Tiberius Caesar. Augustus Caesar died on August 19, A.D. 14 (Julian) and Tiberius effectively assumed control of the empire on Augustus' death. However, Tacitus, a first century A.D. Roman historian, in his *Annals of Imperial Rome*, (page 157) says: "In the consulships of Gaius Asinius Pollio (II) and Gaius Antistius Vetus (I), Tiberius now began his ninth year of national stability and domestic prosperity (the later, he felt, augmented by Germanicus' death)." *Table 2.2* lists the Roman consuls from 44 B.C. to A.D. 36.

From *Table 2.2* we can see that the consulship of Pollio and Vetus (Latin Pollione et Vetere) corresponded to the Julian calendar year A.D. 23. If the ninth year of the reign of Tiberius corresponded to A.D. 23, then *Table 2.3* shows that the first year of the reign of Tiberius was A.D. 15. It is significant that Tacitus says Tiberius began his ninth year in the consulship of Pollio and Vetus rather than that he served his ninth year under these consuls. Since the consuls take office on January 1 (Julian), then according to Tacitus, Tiberius couldn't have begun his ninth year before January 1, A.D. 23. Thus, although Tiberius assumed control of the empire on the death of Augustus on August 19, A.D. 14 (Julian), he did not count his years of reign as beginning until January 1, A.D. 15 according to Tacitus.

Table 2.2 Roman Consuls *			
Year	Consuls	Year	Consuls
44 BC	Caesare V et Antonino	24 BC	Augusto X et Flacco
43 BC	Pansa et Hirstio	23 BC	Augusto XI et Pisone
42 BC	Lepido et Planco	22 BC	Marcello et Arrutio
41 BC	Petate et Isaurico	21 BC	Lollio et Lepido
40 BC	Calvino et Pollione	20 BC	Apuleio et Nerva
39 BC	Censorino et Sabino	19 BC	Saturnino et Lucretio
38 BC	Pulchro et Flacco	18 BC	Lentulo et Lentulo
37 BC	Agrippa et Galio	17 BC	Turnio et Silato
36 BC	Publicula et Nerva	16 BC	Henobarbo et Scipione
35 BC	Cornificio et Pompeio	15 BC	Libone et Pisone
34 BC	Libone et Atratino	14 BC	Grasso et Augure
33 BC	Augusto II et Tullo	13 BC	Nerone et Varo
32 BC	Henobulbo et Sossio	12 BC	Messala et Quirino
31 BC	Augusto III et Messala	11 BC	Tuberone et Maximo
30 BC	Augusto IIII et Grasso	10 BC	Africano et Maximo
29 BC	Augusto V et Apuleio	9 BC	Druso et Crispino
28 BC	Augusto VI et Agrippa II	8 BC	Censorino et Gallo
27 BC	Augusto VII et Agrippa III	7 BC	Nerone et Pisone
26 BC	Augusto VIII et Tauro	6 BC	Balbo et Vetere
25 BC	Augusto VIIII et Silano	5 BC	Augusto XII et Sulla

*Based on the list given by the *Chronographer of Year 354* (see Finegan page 96).

Year	Consuls	Year	Consuls
4 BC	Sabino et Rufo	AD 17	Flacco et Rufo
3 BC	Lentulo et Messalino	AD 18	Tito III et Germanico II Caesare
2 BC	Augusto XIII et Silvano	AD 19	Silano et Balbo
1 BC	Lentulo et Pisone	AD 20	Messala et Cotta
AD 1	Caesare et Paulo	AD 21	Tito IIII et Druso II Caesare
AD 2	Vinicio et Varo	AD 22	Agrippa et Galba
AD 3	Lamia et Servilio	AD 23	Pollione et Vetere
AD 4	Catulo et Saturnino	AD 24	Caethego et Varro
AD 5	Voleso et Magno	AD 25	Agrippa et Lentulo
AD 6	Lepido et Arruntio	AD 26	Getulico et Sabino
AD 7	Cretico et Nerva	AD 27	Grasso et Pisone
AD 8	Camello et Quintiliano	AD 28	Silano et Nerva
AD 9	Camerino et Sabino	AD 29	Gemino et Gemino
AD 10	Dolabella et Silano	AD 30	Vinicio et Longino
AD 11	Lepido et Tauro	AD 31	Tiberio Caesare V solo
AD 12	Caesare et Capitone	AD 32	Arruntio et Ahenobarbo
AD 13	Planco et Silano	AD 33	Galba et Sulla
AD 14	duobus Sextis	AD 34	Vitello et Persico
AD 15	Druso Caesare et Flacco	AD 35	Camerino et Noniano
AD 16	Tauro et Libone	AD 36	Allieno et Plautino

Table 2.2
Roman Consuls*
(Continues)

*Based on the list given by the *Chronographer of Year 354* (see Finegan page 96).

Table 2.3 Years of Reign of Tiberius Caesar Based on Year 9 Corresponding to A.D. 23 (Tacitus)	
Year of Reign	Calendar Year (Julian)
1	A.D. 15
2	A.D. 16
3	A.D. 17
4	A.D. 18
5	A.D. 19
6	A.D. 20
7	A.D. 21
8	A.D. 22
9	A.D. 23
10	A.D. 24
11	A.D. 25
12	A.D. 26
13	A.D. 27
14	A.D. 28
15	A.D. 29

Therefore, the fifteenth year of Tiberius of *Luke 3:1* would correspond to the Julian calendar year of A.D. 29.

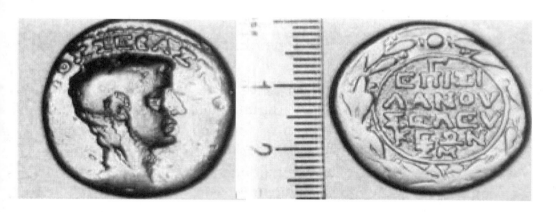

Obverse   Reverse

A Coin of Seleucia
Minted during the Reign of Tiberius Caesar
Figure 2.2

This dating of the years of reign of Tiberius is consistent with the dating of coins of the Roman empire minted during the reign of Tiberius. *Figure 2.2* shows photographs of an ancient coin minted in Seleucia which was the seaport of Antioch of Syria from which Paul began his first missionary journey (Acts 13:4). The obverse of this coin bears a portrait of Tiberius Caesar with the inscription "SEBASTOS SEBASTOU KAISAR." SEBASTOS is a Greek word for revered and is a translation of the Latin title Augustus given to Octavianus in 27 B.C. and to succeeding Roman emperors. Thus the inscription can be translated Augustus of Augustus Caesar. In the example of the coin pictured in Figure 2.2 only the middle of this inscription is clear, but other examples have the full inscription (see Greek Imperial Coins by David Sears, coin number 292.)

The Greek inscription in four lines on the field of the reverse of this coin is "EPI SILANOU SELEUKEON", which can be translated "Under Silanus, Seleucia." Silanus was the Legate of Syria from A.D. 11-17. The gamma above the field corresponds to year 3 of the reign of Tiberius. The ZM below the field corresponds to year 47 of the Actian Era. Year 1 of the Actian Era begins on September 2, 31 B.C. (Julian) which was the date of a great sea victory of Augustus Caesar (Octavianus) over the forces of Mark Anthony and Cleopatra that took place near the city of Actiun. Thus, year 47 of the Actian Era would indicate that this coin was minted between September 2, A.D. 16 and September 1, A.D. 17. *Table 2.3* indicates that the third year of the reign of Tiberius corresponded to the calendar year A.D. 17. Thus, the dating of this first century A.D. coin is consistent with the years of reign of Tiberius of *Table 2.3* which was based on the literary testimony of Tacitus. The two dates on this coin would indicate the coin was minted in the year A.D. 17 prior to September 2nd. Similar dating of the years of reign of Tiberius is found on coin number 290 (ibid.) issued by the city of Antioch of Syria which, according to the *Anti-Marcionite Prologue to the Gospel of Luke* (4th Century A.D.) was the hometown of the Gospel writer Luke (Tyndale's, *The Illustrated Bible Dictionary Volume 2*, page 919). Thus, there is strong evidence that the fifteenth year of Tiberius corresponded to the calendar year A.D. 29 and none of the ancient writers support the beginning of the years of reign of Tiberius before the death of Augustus on August 19, A.D. 14 (Julian).

We have somewhat belabored the establishment of the fifteenth year of the reign of Tiberius Caesar because this fixes the year that John the Baptist began his ministry and thus puts a lower limit on the beginning of Jesus' ministry. Let us return to *Table 2.2* and the question of in which year did the Crucifixion of Jesus take place? It is now obvious that any year prior to A.D. 29 must be eliminated because Jesus began His ministry after John the Baptist who was

Jesus' forerunner. In fact, Jesus began His ministry with His baptism by John the Baptist near the end of John's ministry. Thus we can eliminate the years A.D. 6, A.D. 10 and A.D. 13 from *Table 2.2*, as possible dates for the year of the Crucifixion and Resurrection of Jesus.

The *Gospel of John* mentions three different Passover Feasts during Jesus' earthly ministry: *John 2:13*, *John 6:4* and *John 11:55*. If A.D. 33 was the year of Jesus' crucifixion, then the calendars of Appendix D indicate that the third Passover Feast of *John 11:55* would have occurred on Friday, April 1, A.D. 33 (Gregorian), and the second Passover Feast of *John 6:4* would have occurred on Sunday, April 11, A.D. 32 and the first Passover Feast mentioned in John 2:13 would have occurred on Tuesday, March 25, A.D. 31. These dates for the ministry of Jesus fit well with John the Baptist's beginning his ministry in the fifteenth year of Tiberius or calendar year A.D. 29. The year A.D. 37 of *Table 2.1* for the Crucifixion or any later date would require a much longer ministry of Jesus than that indicated by the Gospel writers. We shall also find that events in the life of Paul, which can be independently dated and which are discussed in Chapter 7, would also preclude any date in Table 2.2 later than A.D. 33. Thus the year A.D. 33 must be the year of Jesus' crucifixion and resurrection.

Since in A.D. 33, Nisan 15 began at sunset on Friday, April 1, Jesus would have been crucified that day before sunset. *Mark 15:25* says: "It was the third hour when they crucified Him." Since the Passover Feast took place near the time of the spring equinox when the length of the day and the night are about equal, the sun would have risen about 6:00 A.M. and would have set about 6:00 P.M. Thus, Jesus would have been put on the cross between 8:00 and 9:00 A.M. (see Table 1.1, page 25). Then *Mark 15:33-37* says:

> When the sixth hour came, darkness fell over the whole
> land until the ninth hour. At the ninth hour Jesus cried

out with a loud voice, "ELOI, ELOI, LAMA SABACHTHANI?" which is translated, "MY GOD, MY GOD, WHY HAVE YOU FORSAKEN ME?" When some of the bystanders heard it, they began saying, "Behold, He is calling for Elijah." Someone ran and filled a sponge with sour wine, put it on a reed, and gave Him a drink, saying, "Let us see whether Elijah will come to take Him down." And Jesus uttered a loud cry, and breathed His last.

Thus, there would have been darkness over the whole land starting between 11:00 A.M. and 12:00 noon and continuing until between 2:00 and 3:00 P.M. Then between 2:00 and 3:00 P.M. Jesus died, during the ninth hour after sunrise.

Using astronomical data, C.J. Humpheys and W.G. Waddington in a December 1983 article entitled *"Dating the Crucifixion"* in the magazine *Nature*, conclude that the crucifixion of Jesus occurred on April 3, A.D. 33 (Julian) which is equivalent to April 1 (Gregorian).

Resurrection

Having established the exact date and time for the Crucifixion of Jesus, we almost immediately have the exact date of the Resurrection. However, there is a problem because the hour of the Resurrection is not clearly stated. We know from the Gospels that Jesus arose on the first day of the Jewish week, but because the Jewish first day of the week began at sunset on our Saturday, if the Resurrection occurred before midnight, then it would have occurred on our Saturday, April 2. However, if the Resurrection occurred at or after midnight, it would have occurred on Sunday, April 3. Thus, we need to examine the Gospels carefully for a clue as to the hour of the Resurrection. *Matthew 28: 1-11* says:

> Now after the Sabbath, as it began to dawn toward the first day of the week, Mary Magdalene and the other Mary came to look at the grave. And behold a severe earthquake had occurred, for an angel of the Lord descended from heaven and came and rolled away the stone and sat on it. And his appearance was like lightening, and his garment as white as snow; and the guards shook for fear of him, and became like dead men. And the angel answered and said to the woman, "Do not be afraid; for I know that you are looking for Jesus who has been crucified. He is not here, for He has risen, just as He said, Come, see the place where He was lying. And go quickly and tell His disciples that He has risen from the dead; and behold, He is going before you into Galilee, there you will see Him; behold I have told you.
>
> And they departed quickly from the tomb with fear and great joy and ran to report it to His disciples. And behold Jesus met them and greeted them. And they came up and took hold of His feet and worshiped Him. Then Jesus said to them, "Do not be afraid; go and take word to My brethren to leave for Galilee and there they shall see Me." Now while they were on their way, behold some of the guards came into the city and reported to the chief priests all that has happened.

The women came to the tomb, early in the morning on the First Day of the week. Since the angel was still at the tomb when the women arrived and the guards were just arriving in the city to report to the chief priests, it appears that the resurrection had only occurred shortly before the women arrived at the tomb. Therefore the resurrection must have occurred after midnight and on our Sunday, April 3, A.D. 33. An even stronger argument for the occurrence of the resurrection at or after midnight is the fact that while the apostles were still alive, the Gentile Christian Church, using the Roman method of reckoning time, made their day of worship the first day of the week instead of the seventh day because that was the day of Christ's Resurrection (*1 Corinthians 16:2, Acts 20:7*). If the Resurrection had taken place before midnight, the apostles would have known it and would not have sanctioned the Sunday celebration of the Resurrection. Thus, the fact that the early Gentile church, with the guidance of the apostles, considered Sunday as the day of Jesus' Resurrection is strong evidence that the Resurrection occurred at or after midnight and thus on April 3, A.D. 33.

Arrival at Bethany

Having established the date of the Crucifixion and the Resurrection, we shall now turn to the dates of the other events during the final days of Jesus' earthly ministry. *John 12:1-3* says:

> Jesus, therefore, six days before the Passover, came to Bethany where Lazarus was, whom Jesus had raised from the dead. So they made Him a supper there, and Martha was serving, but Lazarus was one of those reclining at the table with Him. Mary therefore took a pound of very costly perfume of pure nard, and anointed the feet of Jesus, and wiped His feet with her hair, and the house was filled with the fragrance of the perfume.

Although *Leviticus 23:5* uses the word "Passover" to refer to Nisan 14 when the lamb was killed, John seems to be using the word "Passover" to refer to the "Passover Feast" on Nisan 15. This would be consistent with *John 18:28*, previously quoted, in which John states that the Jewish officials did not enter into the Praetorium so that they could eat the Passover. Thus, counting the six days inclusively, Nisan 15 would be the first day, Nisan 14 would be the second day Nisan 13, the third day, Nisan 12, the fourth day and Nisan 11 the fifth day and Nisan 10 the sixth day before the Passover.

Using the calendar from *Appendix D*, we see that in A.D. 33, Nisan 10 began at sunset on our Sunday, March 27 which would be the Second Jewish Day of the week. Thus, Jesus would have probably arrived at Bethany about noon on Monday since the synoptic Gospels indicate that Jesus was coming from Jericho, a distance of only about twelve miles. In *John 12:2* we learn that they prepared Jesus a supper (the Greek word deipnon) which would have been the main meal served toward evening and probably a banquet. If the meal was served

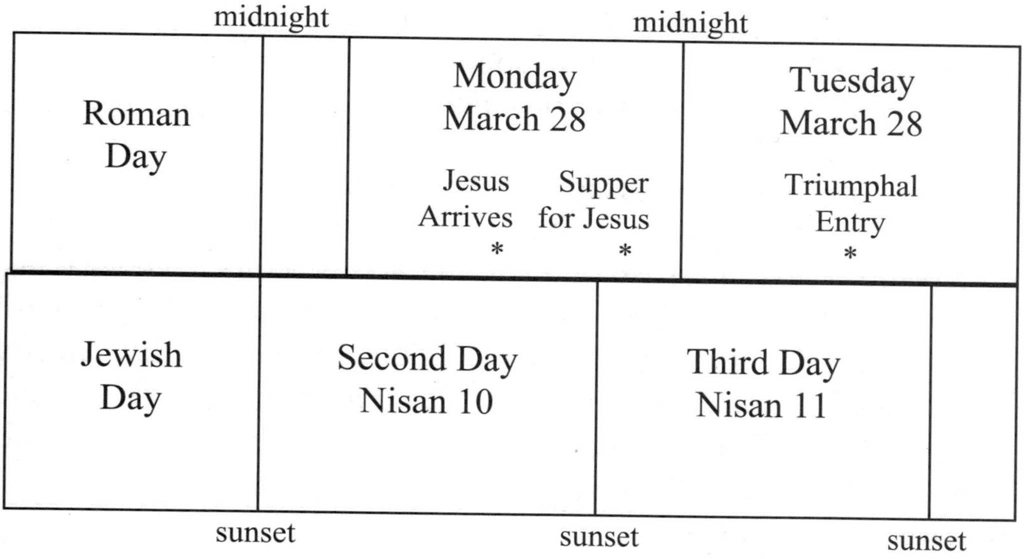

	midnight		midnight	
Roman Day		Monday March 28 Jesus Supper Arrives for Jesus * *	Tuesday March 28 Triumphal Entry *	
Jewish Day	Second Day Nisan 10		Third Day Nisan 11	
	sunset		sunset	sunset

Second and Third Day of Passover Week
A.D. 33
Figure 2.3

after sunset, it would be Nisan 11, but still Monday, March 28 according to our calendar. *Figure 2.3* gives time lines for the arrival of Jesus at Bethany both in terms of Roman time (our time) and Jewish time.

Triumphal Entry

Continuing in the *Gospel of John,* the next event recorded is Jesus' Triumphal Entry into Jerusalem. *John 12:12-13* says:

> On the next day the great multitude who had come to the feast, when they heard that Jesus was coming to Jerusalem, took the branches of palm trees, and went out to meet Him, and began to cry out "Hosanna! Blessed is He who comes in the name of the Lord, even the King of Israel." And Jesus finding a young donkey, sat on it; as it is written, "Fear not, daughter of Zion; behold, your King is coming, seated on a donkey's colt."

The next day would be Nisan 11 with the daylight hours coming on Tuesday, March 29 which would be the date of Jesus' Triumphal Entry into Jerusalem. Also on that same day certain Greeks that had come up to worship at the feast came to Philip and said, "Sir, we wish to see Jesus" (*John 12:20-21*). This day Jesus said, "Father, glorify Thy name." A voice out of heaven said, "I have both glorified it and will glorify it again" (*John 12:28*). Then Jesus departed and hid Himself from them (*John 12:36b*) and finally Jesus discussed His mission (*John 12:44-50*).

Cursing of the Fig Tree

The next chronological statement given by John in his Gospel is found in *John 13:1* and refers to the Last Supper that took place on Thursday evening; however, other details of Jesus' final days that occurred before the Last Supper are given in the synoptic Gospels: *Matthew*, *Mark* and *Luke*. In *Mark 11:1-11* is recorded the Triumphal Entry (Tuesday, March 29) and then *Mark 11:12-14* says:

> And on the next day, when they had departed Bethany, He became hungry. And seeing at a distance a fig tree in leaf, He went to see if perhaps He would find anything on it; and when He came to it, He found nothing but leaves, for it was not the season for figs. And He answered and said to it, "May no one ever eat fruit from you again!" And His disciples were listening.

The cursing of the fig tree occurred on Wednesday, March 30 (see *Figure 2.4*). Why did Jesus curse the fig tree for not having figs if it was not the season for figs? Generally fig trees lose their leaves during the winter and new leaves and small green figs appear together in the spring. However, these green figs do not ripen, in the Jerusalem area, until June, thus Marks says it was not the season for figs. If it was not the season for figs, why did Jesus expect to find figs on this tree? The answer is probably that this fig tree was in a sheltered location and possibly it had been a mild winter so that this fig tree had not lost its leaves during the winter. If this tree had mature leaves that had survived the winter, then it could have mature fruit. However, Jesus found only leaves on the tree. Thus the fig tree gave the promise of bearing fruit, but was barren which is why Jesus cursed it. During this period of His ministry, Jesus was dealing with the Jewish religious leaders who gave the appearance of being very pious, but were also barren of godly fruit. Thus the cursing of the fig tree is probably an acted parable concerning the danger of false piety.

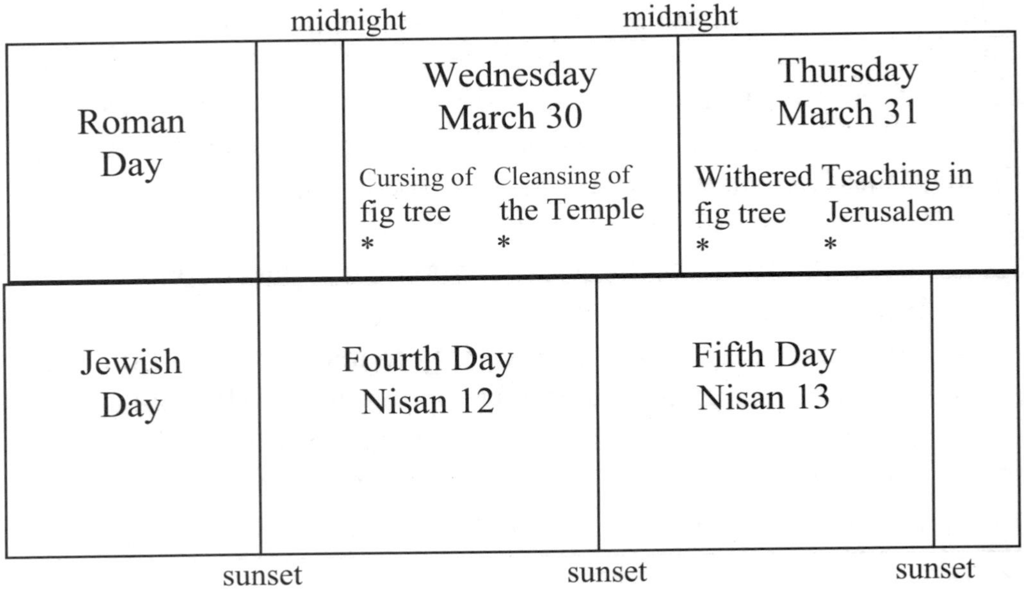

		midnight		midnight	
Roman Day		Wednesday March 30 Cursing of fig tree *	Cleansing of the Temple *	Thursday March 31 Withered fig tree *	Teaching in Jerusalem *
Jewish Day		Fourth Day Nisan 12		Fifth Day Nisan 13	
	sunset		sunset		sunset

Figure 2.4
Fourth and Fifth Day of Passover Week
A.D. 33

Cleansing of the Temple

Later on Wednesday, Jesus cleanses the Temple. *Mark 11:15-17* says:

> And they came to Jerusalem. And He entered the temple and began to cast out those who were buying and selling in the temple, and overturned the tables of the moneychangers and the seats of those who were selling doves; and He would not permit anyone to carry goods through the temple. And He began to teach and say to

them, "Is it not written, 'My house shall be called a
house of prayer for all the Nations'? But you have made
it a robbers' den."

Continuing on in Mark's 11th chapter, *Mark 11:20* says: "And as they
were passing by in the morning, they saw the fig tree withered from
the roots up." This would now be on Thursday, March 31 (see *Figure
2.4*). When Peter pointed out that the fig tree had withered, Jesus
taught His disciples about the power of prayer.

Teaching in Jerusalem

Mark 11:27 indicates that Jesus and His disciples then came
again to Jerusalem. While in Jerusalem on Thursday, March 31, A.D.
33, the four Gospels indicate that Jesus did a great deal of teaching
which is listed in *Table 2.4* which summarizes all of the events during
the final days of Jesus' earthly ministry together with their dates of
occurrence.

One of the important lessons Jesus taught on that day
concerned the paying of tribute to Caesar. Matthew 22:15-22 says:

Then the Pharisees went and counseled together how
they might trap Him in what He said. And they sent
their disciples to Him, along with the Herodians, saying,
"Teacher, we know that You are truthful and teach the
way of God in truth, and defer to no one; for You are not
partial to any. Tell us therefore, what do You think? Is
it lawful to give a poll-tax to Caesar, or not?" But Jesus
perceived their malice, and said, "Why are you testing
Me, you hypocrites? Show Me the coin used for the
poll-tax."And they brought Him a denarius. And He
said to them, "Whose likeness and inscription is this?"

They said to Him, "Caesar's." Then He said to them, "Then render to Caesar the things that are Caesar's; and to God the things that are God's." And hearing this, they marveled, and leaving Him, they went away.

Figure 2.5 is a picture of the most common Roman denarius circulating throughout the Roman empire at that time and this denarius is probably like the one brought to Jesus. This coin is

Obverse   Reverse

Figure 2.5
Denarius of Tiberius

actually only about the size of a current U.S. dime. The obverse side of the coin bears the likeness of Tiberius Caesar and an inscription which says, beginning at 5:00 o'clock and reading counterclockwise, "TI CAESAR DIVI AVG F AVGVSTVS" or "Tiberius Caesar, son of the divine Augustus, Augustus." The reverse side of the coin pictures a female figure, possibly Livia, Tiberius' mother, with the inscription, "PONTIF MAXIM" which is an abbreviation for the title Pontiflex Maximus. This coin was proclaiming the Roman emperor, Tiberius, to be the son of a god (son of the divine Augustus) and the supreme authority in religious matters (Pontiflex Maximus). Thus when Jesus said, "Then render to Caesar the things that are Caesar's and to God the thing's that are God's," He was rebuking not only the Pharisees, who didn't want to pay their taxes, but also the Romans who were claiming authority and a title that rightfully belonged to God and His only begotten Son, Jesus!

Following the description of Jesus' teaching on Thursday, *Mark 14:1-2* says:

> Now the Passover and Unleavened Bread were two days away; and the chief priests and the scribes were seeking how to seize Him by stealth and kill Him; for they were saying, "Not during the festival, otherwise there might be a riot of the people."

When *Mark* mentions in this passage that the Passover and Unleavened Bread was two days off, he is speaking of the week of the Passover Feast which begins with Nisan 14. Using inclusive counting, which was the practice in New Testament times, the present day, Thursday, Nisan 13, would be counted as day 1 and the next day, Friday, Nisan 14, would be day 2. This again would confirm that the current day was Thursday, Nisan 13.

At this point in *Mark's Gospel*, he recounted the anointing of Jesus with pure nard and gives the additional details that the event took place at the home of Simon the leper, that the nard was in an alabaster vial and that Mary also anointed Jesus' head. From the position of this account in *Mark's* and *Matthew's Gospels*, we might think that the events took place on Thursday, March 31; however, both *Matthew* and *Mark* only say that this event took place when Jesus was in Bethany (*Matthew 26:6, Mark 14:3*) while *John 12:1* gives an exact date for this event (six days before the Passover). Therefore we shall rely on *John's Gospel* to date this event.

Matthew 26:14-16 and *Mark 14:10-11* tell of Judas' bargain with the chief priests to betray Jesus. Since earlier on Thursday the chief priests and scribes were still seeking how to kill Jesus (*Mark 14:1-2*), Judas must have made his bargain with the chief priests sometime later Thursday, but before the Last Supper which is the next chronological event recorded in the Gospels.

The Last Supper

> And on the first day of Unleavened Bread, when the Passover lamb was being sacrificed, His disciples said to Him, "Where do You want us to go and prepare for You to eat the Passover?"(Mark 14:12)

Clearly the reference here is to Nisan 14 since *Mark* says, "when the Passover lamb was being sacrificed," but *John 19:14* indicated that Jesus was tried and crucified on the day of preparation for the Passover or on Nisan 14. How can these two Scriptures be reconciled?

Since Jesus' disciples were concerned about where they would celebrate the Passover Feast, they would have reasonably come to Jesus at the beginning of the day of Preparation for the Passover, not at the end of that day. Therefore, they would have come to Jesus on Thursday, just after sunset. They would have probably expected to celebrate the Passover Feast at the regular time on Nisan 15; however, from all four Gospel accounts, it is clear that the Last Supper took place on Thursday evening. Thus, when the disciples came to Jesus, they would have learned that Jesus had already made arrangements to eat the Passover Feast Thursday evening. But how would this be possible since the Passover lambs were not to be sacrificed until Friday afternoon between the ninth and eleventh hours or from 2:00 - 5:00 P.M. (*Josephus, Wars 6.9.3*, page 749)?

A possible explanation is found in the fact that the Essenes, one of the three major Jewish religious groups during New Testament times, seemed to have followed the calendar of the *Book of Jubilee* (*Finegan*, page 56). The calendar of the *Book of Jubilee* began each Jewish year on the fourth day of the week (Wednesday) so that Nisan 1 and therefore Nisan 15 would always fall on the fourth day of their week. Thus in A.D. 33 the Essenes would have celebrated the Passover before the rest of the Jewish community, and therefore it is possible that they could have supplied Jesus and His disciples with a lamb for the Passover feast on Thursday. Actually, there is no mention of a lamb being part of the Last Supper, and today the Jewish community celebrates the Passover Feast each year without a lamb. There may be some indication in both *Mark's* and *Luke's Gospel* that Jesus and His disciples celebrated the Passover Feast with the Essenes community. *Mark 14:13-17* says:

> And He sent two of His disciples, and said to them, "Go into the city, and a man will meet you carrying a pitcher of water; follow him; and wherever he enters, say to the owner of the house, 'The Teacher says, "Where is My guest room in which I may eat the Passover with My disciples?"' And he himself will show you a large upper room furnished and ready; and prepare for us there." And the disciples went out, and came to the city, and found it just as He had told them, and they prepared the Passover. And when it was evening He came with the twelve.

To see a man carrying a water jar in Jerusalem in New Testament times would have been an unusual sight because carrying water was considered to be a woman's work. However, *Josephus* says that the Essenes disdained marriage and therefore would not have had women to carry their water. Therefore, the man with the water jar that the disciples (Peter and John - *Luke 22:80*) followed quite possibly was an Essene, and the house to which he led them then would have been a house in the Essene community of Jerusalem. Interestingly, very near the traditional site of the Last Supper on Mount Zion is an ancient gate in the wall which *Josephus* says was called the Gate of the Essenes. This probably indicates that there was an Essene community residing in this area during New Testament times. Thus, Peter and John went to this upper room, which was already finished and ready, early Thursday evening, March 31st and then later Thursday evening, Jesus and the other disciples came to celebrate the Passover Feast (see *Figure 2.6*).

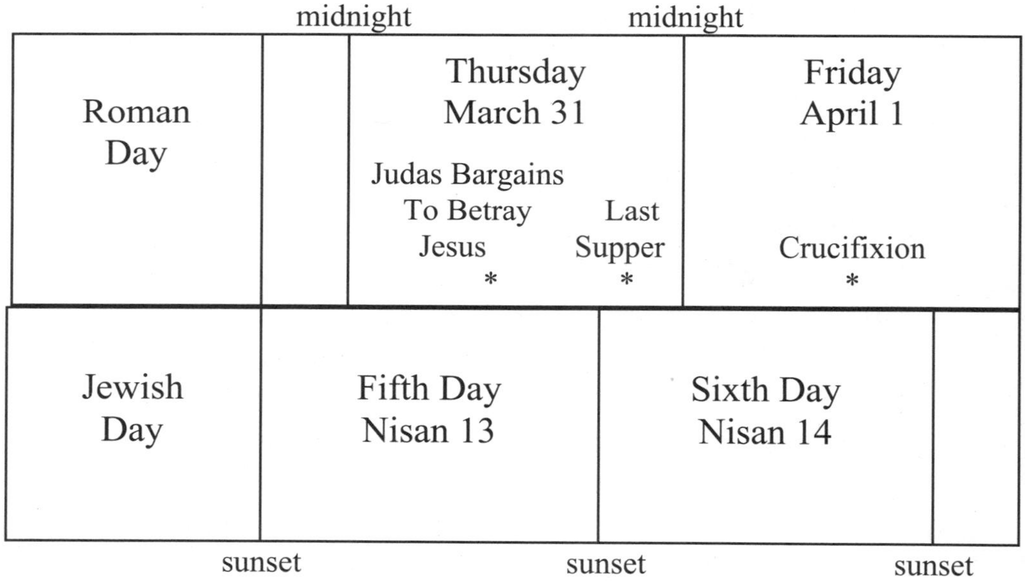

	midnight		midnight
Roman Day		Thursday March 31 Judas Bargains To Betray Jesus *	Last Supper *	Friday April 1 Crucifixion *
Jewish Day	Fifth Day Nisan 13	Sixth Day Nisan 14	
	sunset	sunset	sunset

Fifth and Sixth Day of Passover Week
A.D. 33
Figure 2.6

In *Luke 22:15* Jesus says: "I have earnestly desired to eat the Passover with you before I suffer." Thus, the Last Supper was clearly an observance of the Passover Feast. However, the Last Supper was more than just an observance of the Passover Feast, because during that evening Jesus instituted the Lord's Supper which was one of the primary observances of the Apostolic Church. It was also Jesus' final discourse with the eleven apostles. John considered these aspects of the Last Supper so important that he does not even mention the Passover Feast in his description of the events of that evening apparently relying on the synoptic Gospels to supply that information. That same Jewish day, Nisan 14, Jesus would be sacrificed at the proper hour as the perfect "Lamb of God who takes away the sins of the world" (*John 1:29*)! In *1 Corinthians 5:7b*, Paul says: "For Christ our Passover also has been sacrificed." Thus, the Passover Feast which commemorated God's deliverance of the Children of Israel from slavery in Egypt, foreshadowed our deliverance from slavery to sin by Christ's atoning death on the cross. Christ's death on the cross was now to be commemorated by the Lord's Supper. Thus, there are really no inconsistences among the accounts of the Last Supper in the four Gospels.

After the Last Supper, but still on Thursday night, March 31, Jesus and the eleven apostles sang a hymn and then went out to the Mount of Olives (*Matthew 26:30*). Then Jesus said, "You will all fall away because of Me this night, for it is written, 'I will strike down the Shepherd, and the sheep of the flock shall be scattered'" (*Matthew 26:31*). Then Jesus and the eleven went to Gethsemane where Jesus prayed. Jesus was then betrayed and arrested (*Matthew 26:47-56*) and Jesus was taken first to Annas and then taken to Caiaphas, the high priest (*John 18:13-14*). Jesus was tried before the Council (*Matthew 26:59-66*) and was mocked and beaten (*Matthew 26:67-68*). During that evening, but after midnight, on April 1, A.D. 33, Peter denied Jesus three times (*Matthew 26:69-75*).

According to the requirements of the *Mishnah*, (*Tractate Sanhedrin 4.1*), this trial of Jesus was illegal because trials for both capital and non-capital cases should be held during the daytime. *Matthew 26:65-66* says:

> Then the high priest tore his robes and said, "He has blasphemed! What further need do we have of witnesses? Behold, you have now heard the blasphemy; what do you think?" They answered, "He deserves death!"

Again according to the *Mishnah,* this verdict was illegal since, in capital cases a verdict of acquittal might be reached on the same day as the trial, but a verdict of conviction should not be given until the following day. Since all of these events of the trial took place during the early morning hours of April 1, again this trial of Jesus was illegal. Also Leviticus 21:10 says that the high priest should not tear his clothes. The reason for the haste in carrying out Jesus' trial was due to the fact that trials were not permitted on a Sabbath or on a festival day, so they could not delay in carrying out the trial. Accordingly, for the Sanhedrin to carry out a legal trial of Jesus, they would have had to wait until Sunday, April 3, to begin the trial. But this was exactly what they did not want to do as stated in *Mark 14:26* where the chief priests and scribes said: "Not during the festival, lest there be a riot of the people." Also we can see the hand of God at work, since Jesus was to fulfill the law of the Passover lamb and accordingly must die at twilight on the fourteenth day of the first month of the Jewish year (*Leviticus 23:5*). Also Jesus arose from the tomb on the first Sunday after the Passover Feast which was the time for the First Fruits Offering (*Leviticus 23:9-14*). Jesus was the first fruit of God's plan for the salvation of man.

Had the Jewish leaders been questioned concerning the legality of their trial, they would have probably said that the trial and conviction of Jesus took place before Pilate and that their trial was only an informal hearing to determine if Jesus should be taken to Pilate for trial. However, unknown to them, these Jewish leaders were playing a part in God's plan for the salvation of all mankind by allowing His Son to suffer death for the sins of those who would accept Him as Savior.

> Then when Judas, who had betrayed Him, saw that He had been condemned, he felt remorse and returned the thirty pieces of silver to the chief priests and elders, saying, "I have sinned by betraying innocent blood." But they said, "What is that to us? See to that yourself!" And he threw the pieces of silver into the temple sanctuary and departed; and he went away and hanged himself. The chief priests took the pieces of silver and said, "It is not lawful to put them into the temple treasury, since it is the price of blood." And they conferred together and with the money bought the Potter's Field as a burial place for strangers. For this reason that field has been called the Field of Blood to this day (Matthew 27:3-8).

This was in fulfillment of Jeremiah 19:1-13 and Zechariah 11:12,13. Jeremiah 19:4 speaks of shedding the blood of the innocent and Zechariah 11:12,13 says:

> I said to them, "If it is good in your sight, give me my wages; but if not, never mind!" So they weighed out thirty shekels of silver as my wages. Then the LORD said to me, "Throw it to the potter, that magnificent price at which I was valued by them." So I took the thirty shekels of silver and threw them to the potter in the house of the LORD.

Thus, the Jewish leaders valued the Son of God at thirty shekels of silver and these thirty shekels went to the potter in payment for his field after Judas threw them into the sanctuary. More than four hundred years before Jesus' death, Zechariah predicted the details of Judas' receiving thirty pieces of silver and its exact deposition.

The *Mishnah, Tractate Bekhoroth* (Firstlings) *8:7* says:

> The five selas due for the (First born) son should be paid in Tyrian coinage; the thirty due for the slave (that was gored by an ox) and the fifty due from the violator and the seducer, and the hundred due from him that has brought an evil name, and all are to be paid according to the value of the shekels of the sanctuary, in Tyrian coinage.

The primary element of the Tyrian coinage was the Shekel of Tyre (see *Figure 2.7*). The above reference appears to prescribe this coin for use in the Temple and was therefore probably the coin that was given to Judas. This coin weighed about 14 grams (our Kennedy half dollar weighs 11.5 grams) and had the highest silver content of any of the silver coins circulating in the Middle East during New Testament times which probably explains why it was selected as the Temple coin. On the obverse of this coin was the head of Heracles and on the reverse of this coin was an eagle standing on the prow of a ship. The reverse also bore the Greek inscription which can be translated Tyre the Holy and Secure. Each of these coins were also dated by Greek letters that appear above the club on the reverse of the coins. These dates indicate that this type of coin was struck continuously for 191 years with the first year bearing the Greek letter A (year 1) and was minted in 126 B.C. It is believed, beginning in 18 B.C. with year 109 (PH), the Shekel of Tyre was actually minted in Jerusalem (*Meshorer, Vol. 2*, page 8). Coins from this period were found around Jerusalem rather than around Tyre, and the coins ceased to be minted in A.D. 66 at the beginning of the Jewish War against Rome. At the same time a silver coin of the same weight and metallic composition was issued as an autonomous Jewish shekel in Jerusalem. These coins bore the Hebrew inscription "Jerusalem the Holy" paralleling "Tyre the Holy" of the Shekel of Tyre.

Obverse   Reverse
Shekel of Tyre
The coin pictured is dated PM
or Year 140 of the Tyrian Era or A.D. 14-15
Figure 2.7

The chief priests and elders then took Jesus to Pilate, the Roman governor, for trial. *John 18:28* says:

They led Jesus therefore from Caiaphas into the Praetorium, and it was early; and they themselves did not enter into the Praetorium in order that they might not be defiled, but might eat the Passover.

Many have associated the Praetorium with the Antonia, a fortress located immediately north and adjacent to the Temple Mount (see *Figure 2.8)*; however, the term "Praetorium" only indicates the Roman governor's residence. Herod I ruled from his palace on the west side of the city of Jerusalem (see *Figure 2.8*) as undoubtedly did his son Archelaus. When the Roman governor took control of Judea, it would be natural for them to make Herod's palace the Jerusalem headquarters for the governor whose primary residence was in Caesarea. Herod's palace in Jerusalem was very strongly fortified with three towers, one of which remains to this day. *Mark 15:16* says: "And the soldiers took Him away into the palace (that is, the Praetorium), and they called together the whole Roman cohort." Thus, the Praetorium was probably Herod I's palace rather than the Antonia (*Schurer, Vol. I*, page 361). Then *Luke 12:4-7* says:

> And Pilate said to the chief priests and the multitudes, "I find no guilt in this man." But they kept on insisting saying, "He stirs up the people, teaching all over Judea, starting from Galilee, even as far as this place." But when Pilate heard it, he asked whether the man was a Galilean. And when he learned that He belonged to Herod's jurisdiction, he sent Him to Herod, who himself also was in Jerusalem.

Herod would have been Herod Antipas, the tetrarch of Galilee (*Luke 3:1*) and a son of Herod I. Herod Antipas' Jerusalem residence may have been the Old Hasmonean palace located west of the Temple Mount (See *Figure 2.8*). When Jesus refused to speak, Herod Antipas, after treating Jesus with contempt, returned Jesus to Pilate. *Luke 23:13-16* then says:

> And Pilate summoned the chief priests and the scribes and the people, and said to them, "You brought this man to me as one who incites the people to rebellion and behold, having examined Him before you, I have found

no guilt in this man regarding the changes which you made against Him. No, nor has Herod, for he sent Him back to us, and behold, nothing deserving death has been done by Him. I will therefore punish Him and release Him." However, the chief priests and the multitude kept calling out "Crucify, Crucify Him!" Herod offered to release Jesus or Barabbas and the crowd chose Barabbas. Finally, because of the pressure of the crowd Pilate sentenced Jesus to be crucified.

John 19:17 then says: " They took Jesus, therefore, and He went out, bearing His own cross, to the place called the Place of a Skull, which is called in Hebrew, Golgotha." Today there are two popular sites for Golgotha. One is the site marked by the Church of the Holy Sepulcher and the other is the Garden Tomb outside the present wall enclosing the Old City of Jerusalem. The site of the Holy Sepulcher is favored by most archaeologists as the correct site, although the Garden Tomb gives a much better idea of how the *site* must have looked in Jesus' day. The procession probably would have left by the Gennath Gate and then preceded along the city wall to Golgotha. In Jerusalem, today, there is the famous Via Dolorosa leading from the site of the Antonia to the Church of the Holy Sepulcher. However, if the Praetorium was at Herod's palace, this obviously could not have been the route that Jesus followed. The probable route that Jesus followed during the final hours of His ministry is indicated in *Figure 2.8.*

Number	Event	Place	Approximate Time
1	Last Supper	Mount Zion	8:30 PM, Thursday
2	Jesus Prays	Gethsemane	11:00 PM, Thursday
3	Jesus Arrested	Gethsemane	12:00 PM, Thursday
4	Jesus Taken To Annas	Mount Zion	1:00 AM, Friday
5	Trial Before Caiaphas	Mount Zion	5:00 AM, Friday
6	Jesus Taken To Pilate	Herod I's Palace	6:00 AM, Friday
7	Jesus Taken To Herod	Hasmonean Palace	6:30 AM, Friday
8	Trial Before Pilate	Herod I's Palace	7:00 AM, Friday
9	Crucifixion	Golgotha	8:00 AM- 3:00 PM Friday
10	Burial	Golgotha	5:00 PM, Friday
11	Resurrection	Golgotha	5:00 AM, Sunday

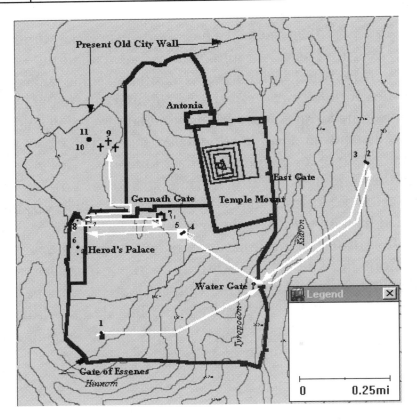

Jesus' Final Hours
Figure 2.8

After Jesus' crucifixion, *John 19:41-42* says:

> Now in the place where He was crucified there was a garden, and in the garden a new tomb, in which no one had yet been laid. Therefore on account of the Jewish day of preparation, because the tomb was nearby, they laid Jesus there.

Thus, Jesus was buried in a garden tomb at Golgotha. This was before sunset on Friday on April 1, A.D. 33, probably about 5:00 P.M.

Resurrection and Ascension

Jesus remained in the tomb for three days counting inclusively. Part of Nisan 14 was the first day; all of Nisan 15 was the second day; and part of Nisan 16 was the third day. Then before dawn on Nisan 16, Sunday, April 3, A.D. 33. Jesus was resurrected (*Matthew 28:2-4*), Jesus then appeared to Mary Magdalene (*Luke 24:10-11*), to Peter (*Luke 24:34*) and to the two disciples on the road to Emmaus (*Luke 24:13-34*) on Sunday, April 3 prior to sunset. Then after sunset on Nisan 17, but still on Sunday, April 3, Jesus appeared to ten of the apostles in Jerusalem (Luke 24:36-43). Then, after eight days, counting inclusively, Jesus appears to the eleven apostles, including Thomas, on Sunday, April 10, A.D. 33.

Next Jesus appeared to the disciples at the Sea of Tiberius (*John 21:1-23*). No exact date is given in the New Testament for this event other than the fact that it occurred prior to Jesus' Ascension which occurred forty days after the Resurrection. It appears that the apostles were still in Jerusalem at the time of Jesus' appearance to all eleven apostles on Sunday, April 10. They probably left for Galilee shortly after this appearance of Jesus, and they would have arrived in Galilee before the next Sabbath which was April 16. They may have spent the next two weeks resting with families and friends. Then about Sunday,

May 1, A.D. 33, according to *John 21:1-2*, Jesus manifested Himself again to the disciples at the Sea of Tiberias. *John 21:2* indicates that at this appearance Peter, Thomas, Nathanael, James and John and two other disciples were present. This appearance probably took place at the small town of Ginnesaret where both Peter and the sons of Zebedee probably kept their boats. At this meeting Jesus probably told these apostles to get the other apostles, who had also returned to Galilee (*Matthew 28:16*), and meet Him later that day on the nearby hilltop. At this second appearance of Jesus in Galilee, *Matthew 28:18* says:

> And Jesus came up and spoke to them saying, "All authority has been given to Me in heaven and on earth. Go therefore and make disciples of all the nations, baptizing them in the name of the Father and the Son and the Holy Spirit, teaching them to observe all that I command you; and lo, I am with you always, even to the end of the age.

The disciples would have probably left the next day for Jerusalem and would have arrived in Jerusalem about Friday, May 6. Thus, they would have been in Jerusalem to witness Jesus' Ascension into Heaven on Thursday, May 12, A.D. 33, forty days after Jesus' Resurrection (*Acts 1:3*). *Acts 1:12* indicates that the Ascension took place on Mount Olivet just east of Jerusalem.

The date of these two appearances of Jesus to his disciples in Galilee, as well as the dates for two other verses in chapter 21 of John, are designated in Table 2.4 as Level of Confidence II while the other events in this chapter are designated as Level of Confidence I. Level of Confidence I dates are dates that the author believes have a high probability of being exactly correct since they are supported by clear chronological information given in Scripture. Level of Confidence II dates represent the author's best estimate of the date of the given event; however these dates have a lower probability of being exactly correct because they may depend on interpolation between Level of Confidence I dates and may involve the interpretation of less clear Bible passages. Level of Confidence II dates may also depend more heavily on extra-Biblical ancient sources. The date for Jesus' appearances in Galilee are consistent with all the information given in the four Gospels and due to the travel time involved between Jerusalem and Galilee must be at least near the exact date; however, they can only be termed probable dates for the occurrences of these events.

Thus, from the record of the four Gospels and using the calendars of *Appendix D* we have determined that Jesus was crucified from about 8:00 A.M. until 3:00 P.M. on April 1, A.D. 33 in terms of our Gregorian calendar. Using this date for Christ's crucifixion, we have also been able to determine the exact date for almost all of the other events of the final week of Jesus' earthly ministry. The paramount significance of Jesus' death, burial and resurrection is indicated by the detailed chronological information given for these events and by the amount of space these events receive in the four Gospels. Using the dates for Christ's crucifixion and resurrection as benchmarks, in the next chapter we shall determine the date of Jesus' birth.

Another Approach

However, before we leave the dating of the final days of Jesus' earthly ministry, there is another approach to dating these events that needs to be discussed because it is frequently found in New Testament commentaries. In this approach, since *Matthew 26:17, Mark 14:12* and *Luke 22:7* all indicate that preparations for the Last Supper were made on Nisan 14, it is assumed that the Last Supper took place on Nisan 15 at the regular time of the Passover Feast. With this assumption, since Jesus' Last Supper took place on a Thursday, we would be looking for a year in which Nisan 15 began on a Thursday rather than on a Friday as we did in our previous approach. Again examining the calendars of *Appendix D*, we find that during this period, Nisan 15 began on a Thursday in A.D. 27, A.D. 30 and A.D. 44. The date A.D. 27 would be too early since John the Baptist's ministry preceded Jesus'. Likewise, A.D. 44 would be too late because it would require a much longer earthly ministry of Jesus than that indicated in the Gospels. Thus we are led to the year A.D. 30 which is widely accepted as the year of Christ's death and resurrection. Why wouldn't this dating be as acceptable as the one previously given? The problem with this dating is that it causes serious contradictions within the Scriptures. *Matthew 26:5* relates: "And they were saying, 'Not during the festival, lest a riot occur among the people.'" Would the chief priests and elders have said this on Nisan 14 and then turned around and had Jesus crucified on Nisan 15, the most holy day of the festival? Also *John 19:31* says:

> The Jews therefore, because it was the day of preparation, so that the bodies should not remain on the cross on the Sabbath (for that Sabbath was a high day), asked Pilate that their legs might be broken and that they might be taken away.

If it was important not to have the bodies remain on the cross on the Sabbath, wouldn't it have been even more important not to have the bodies on the cross during the Passover Feast on Nisan 15? Also *John 19:14* says: "Now it was the day of preparation for the Passover, it was about the sixth hour, and he said to the Jews, 'Behold you King.'" Thus, John says that it was the day of preparation for the Passover, Nisan 14, rather than the day of the Passover Feast, Nisan 15, when Jesus was crucified.

Finally, John, in his Gospel, mentions three different Passover Feasts during Jesus' earthly ministry. If Jesus had been crucified in

A.D. 30, the final Passover (*John 11:55*) would have occurred in A.D. 30, the second Passover (*John 6:4*) would have occurred in A.D. 29 and the first Passover (*John 2:13*) would have occurred in A.D. 28, but this would be before the fifteenth year of Tiberius which was shown to correspond to calendar year A.D. 29 when John the Baptist began his ministry (*Luke 3:1-2*). Thus, Jesus would be well into his ministry before John the Baptist even began his ministry. Thus this alternate approach contradicts the clear teaching of Scripture and therefore cannot be accepted.

	Table 2.4 **Jesus' Final Days** **A.D. 33**			
Event Sequence Number	Event (Scripture References)	Location of Event	Gregorian Date	Level of Confidence*
368	Jesus Arrives at Bethany (Jn 12:1)	Bethany	Monday March 28, AD 33	I
369	Jesus Anointed by Mary (Jn 12:2-8) (Mt 26:6-13) (Mk 14:3-9)	Bethany	Monday March 28, AD 33	I
370	Multitude Came to See Jesus & Lazarus (Jn 12:9)	Bethany	Monday March 28, AD 33	I
371	Plot Against Jesus & Lazarus (Jn 12:10-11)	Bethany	Tuesday March 29, AD 33	I
372	The Triumphal Entry (Jn 12:12-19) (Mt 21:1-11) (Mk 11:1-11) (Lk 19:28-40)	Jerusalem	Tuesday March 29, AD 33	I
373	Jesus Weeps Over Jerusalem (Lk 19:41-44)	Jerusalem	Tuesday March 29, AD 33	I
374	Greeks "We wish to see Jesus" (Jn 12:20-22)	Jerusalem	Tuesday March 29, AD 33	I
375	"He Who Loves His Life Loses It" (Jn 12:23-26)	Jerusalem	Tuesday March 29, AD 33	I

Event Sequence Number	Event (Scripture References)	Location of Event	Gregorian Date	Level of Confidence*
376	Voice Out of Heaven (Jn 12:27-36)	Jerusalem	Tuesday March 29, AD 33	I
377	Many Don't Believe in Jesus (Jn 12:37-50)	Jerusalem	Tuesday March 29, AD 33	I
378	Cursing of the Fig Tree (Mk 11:12-14) (Mt 21:18-22)	Bethany	Wednesday March 30, AD 33	I
379	Cleansing of the Temple (Lk 19:45-46) (Mt 21:12-13) (Mk 11:15-17)	Jerusalem	Wednesday March 30, AD 33	I
380	Jesus Heals the Blind & Lame (Mt 21:14)	Temple Jerusalem	Wednesday March 30, AD 33	I
381	Children Crying "Hosanna to the Son of David" (Mt 21:15-17)	Temple Jerusalem	Wednesday March 30, AD 33	I
382	Religious Leaders Seek to Kill Jesus (Mk 11:18-19, Lk 19:47-48)	Jerusalem	Wednesday March 30, AD 33	I
383	Withered Fig Tree (Mk 11:20-26)	Bethany	Thursday March 31, AD 33	I
384	Jesus' Authority Questioned (Mk 11:27-33) (Mt 21:23-27) (Lk 20:1-8)	Jerusalem	Thursday March 31, AD 33	I

* Level of Confidence in Date   Level I = Highly Probable   Level II = Probable

Event Sequence Number	Event (Scripture References)	Location of Event	Gregorian Date	Level of Confidence*
385	Parable of the Two Sons (Mt 21:28-32)	Jerusalem	Thursday March 31, AD 33	I
386	Parable of the Wicked Husbandman (Mt 21:33-46) (Mk 12:1-12) (Lk 20:9-19)	Jerusalem	Thursday March 31, AD 33	I
387	Parable of the Marriage Feast (Mt 22:1-14)	Jerusalem	Thursday March 31, AD 33	I
388	Question On Tribute to Caesar (Mt 22:15-22) (Mk 12:13-17) (Lk 20:20-26)	Jerusalem	Thursday March 31, AD 33	I
389	Question Concerning the Resurrection (Mt 22:23-33) (Mk 12:18-27) (Lk 20:27-40)	Jerusalem	Thursday March 31, AD 33	I
390	The Greatest Commandment (Mt 22:34-40) (Mk 12:28-34)	Jerusalem	Thursday March 31, AD 33	I
391	Jesus Not David's Son (Mt 22:41-46) (Mk 12:35-37) (Lk 20:41-44)	Jerusalem	Thursday March 31, AD 33	I
392	Warning to Scribes & Pharisees (Mt 23:1-36) (Mk 12:38-40) (Lk 20:45-47)	Jerusalem	Thursday March 31, AD 33	I

* Level of Confidence in Date   Level I = Highly Probable   Level II = Probable

Event Sequence Number	Event (Scripture References)	Location of Event	Gregorian Date	Level of Confidence*
393	Lament Over Jerusalem (Mt 23:37-39)	Jerusalem	Thursday March 31, AD 33	I
394	Comments On the Widow's Gift (Mk 12:41-44) (Lk 21:1-4)	Jerusalem	Thursday March 31, AD 33	I
395	Prediction of Destruction of Temple (Mt 24:1-2) (Mk 13:1-2) (Luke 21:5-6)	Jerusalem	Thursday March 31, AD 33	I
396	Signs Before the End (Mt 24:3-8) (Mk 13:3-8) (Lk 21:7-11)	Mount of Olives	Thursday March 31, AD 33	I
397	Coming Resurrection (Mt 24:9-14) (Mk 13:9-13) (Lk 21:12-19)	Mount of Olives	Thursday March 31, AD 33	I
398	Jerusalem to Be Destroyed (Mt 24:15-22) (Mk 13:14-20) (Lk 21:20-24)	Mount of Olives	Thursday March 31, AD 33	I
399	False Christ & False Prophets (Mt 24:23-28) (Mk 13:21-23)	Mount of Olives	Thursday March 31, AD 33	I
400	Signs of Jesus' Second Coming (Mt 24:29-31) (Mk 13:24-27) (Lk 21:25-28)	Mount of Olives	Thursday March 31, AD 33	I

* Level of Confidence in Date   Level I = Highly Probable   Level II = Probable

Event Sequence Number	Event (Scripture References)	Location of Event	Gregorian Date	Level of Confidence*
401	Parable of the Fig Tree (Mt 24:32-36) (Mk 13:28-32) (Lk 21:29-33)	Mount of Olives	Thursday March 31, AD 33	I
402	Second Coming Like Days of Noah (Mt 24:37-44)	Mount of Olives	Thursday March 31, AD 33	I
403	Parable of Faithful & Wicked Steward (Mt 24:45-51) (Lk 21:34-36) (Mk 13:33-37)	Mount of Olives	Thursday March 31, AD 33	I
404	Parable of Ten Virgins (Mt 25:1-13)	Mount of Olives	Thursday March 31, AD 33	I
405	Parable of the Talents (Mt 25:14-30)	Mount of Olives	Thursday March 31, AD 33	I
406	The Judgment (Mt 25:31-46)	Mount of Olives	Thursday March 31, AD 33	I
407	Days Teaching in Temple, Nights on Olivet (Lk 21:37-38)	Jerusalem	March 29-31, AD 33	I
408	Jesus Predicts His Crucifixion (Mt 26:1-2)	Mount of Olives	Thursday March 31, AD 33	I
409	Priests & Scribes Seek to Kill Jesus (Mt 26:3-5),(Mk 14:1-2) (Lk 22:1-2)	Jerusalem	Thursday March 31, AD 33	I

* Level of Confidence in Date   Level I = Highly Probable   Level II = Probable

Event Sequence Number	Event (Scripture References)	Location of Event	Gregorian Date	Level of Confidence*
410	Judas Bargains to Betray Jesus (Mt 26:14-16) (Mk 14:10-11) (Lk 22:3-6)	Jerusalem	Thursday March 31, AD 33	I
411	Peter & John Prepare the Last Supper (Mt 26:17-19) (Mk 14:12-16) (Lk 22:7-13)	Jerusalem	Thursday March 31, AD 33	I
412	Last Supper (Mt 26:20-29) (Mk 14:17-25) (Lk 22:14-38) (Jn 13:1-17:26)	Jerusalem	Thursday March 31, AD 33	I
413	Journey to Mount of Olives (Mt 26:30) (Mk 14:26) (Lk 22:39) (Jn 18:1)	Jerusalem	Thursday March 31, AD 33	I
414	Jesus Said:"You Will All Fall Away" (Mt 26:31-35) (Mk 14:27-31)	Jerusalem	Thursday March 31, AD 33	I
415	Jesus Prays in Gethsemane (Mt 26:36-46) (Mk 14:32-42) (Lk 22:40-46)	Mount of Olives	Thursday March 31, AD 33	I
416	Jesus' Betrayal & Arrest (Mt 26:47-56, Mk 14:43-52) (Lk 22:47-53) (Jn 18:2-12)	Mount of Olives	Thursday, March 31	I
417	Jesus Taken To Annas (Jn 18:13-14)	Jerusalem	Thursday, March 31	I

* Level of Confidence in Date   Level I = Highly Probable   Level II = Probable

Event Sequence Number	Event (Scripture References)	Location of Event	Gregorian Date	Level of Confidence*
418	Peter's First Denial of Jesus (Jn 18:15-18)	Jerusalem	Thursday, March 31	I
419	Jesus' Hearing Before Annas (Jn 18:19-23)	Jerusalem	Thursday, March 31	I
420	Jesus Sent to Caiaphas (Jn 18:24, Mt 26:57) (Mk 14:53-54) (Lk 22:54a)	Jerusalem	Thursday, March 31 AD 33	I
421	Jesus' Trial Before Caiaphas (Mt 26:59-68) (Mk 14:55-64) (Lk 22:66-71)	Jerusalem	Friday April 1, AD 33	I
422	Jesus Mocked & Beaten (Mt 26:67-68) (Mk 14:65) (Lk 22:63-65)	Jerusalem	Friday April 1, AD 33	I
423	Peter's Denial of Jesus (Jn 18: 25-27) (Mt 26: 58, 69-75) (Mk 14:66-72) (Lk 22:54b-62)	Jerusalem	Friday April 1, AD 33	I
424	Jesus Delivered to Pilate (Jn 18:28) (Mt 27:1-2) (Mk 15:1) (Lk 23:1)	Jerusalem	Friday April 1, AD 33	I
425	Judas Returns Thirty Pieces of Silver (Mt 27:3-10)	Jerusalem	Friday April 1, AD 33	I

* Level of Confidence in Date   Level I = Highly Probable   Level II = Probable

Event Sequence Number	Event (Scripture References)	Location of Event	Gregorian Date	Level of Confidence*
426	Jesus Hearing Before Pilate (Lk 23:2-6) (Mt 27:11-14) (Mk 15:2-5) (Jn 18:29-38a)	Jerusalem	Friday April 1, AD 33	I
427	Jesus Sent to Herod Antipas (Lk 23:7-12)	Jerusalem	Friday April 1, AD 33	I
428	Pilate Declares Jesus Innocent (Lk 23:13-16) (Jn 18:38b)	Jerusalem	Friday April 1, AD 33	I
429	Barabbas or Jesus to be Released (Mt 27:15-26a) (Mk 15:6-15a) (Lk 23:17-25a) (Jn 18:39-40)	Jerusalem	Friday April 1, AD 33	I
430	Crown of Thorns & Abuse of Jesus (Mt 27:27-31a) (Mk 15:16-20a) (Jn 19:1-3)	Jerusalem	Friday April 1, AD 33	I
431	Pilate Says: "Behold the Man" (Jn 19:4-12)	Jerusalem	Friday April 1, AD 33	I
432	Pilate Delivers Jesus to be Crucified (Jn 19:13-16) (Mt 27:26b) (Mk 15:15b) (Lk 23:25b)	Jerusalem	Friday April 1, AD 33	I

* Level of Confidence in Date   Level I = Highly Probable   Level II = Probable

Event Sequence Number	Event (Scripture References)	Location of Event	Gregorian Date	Level of Confidence*
433	Jesus Lead to Golgotha (Jn 19:17) (Lk 23:26a, 27-32) (Mt 27:31b) (Mk 15:20b)	Jerusalem	Friday April 1, AD 33	I
434	Simon Bears Jesus' Cross (Mt 27:32, Mk 15:21, Lk 23:26b)	Jerusalem	Friday April 1, AD 33	I
435	Jesus is Crucified (Jn 19:18) (Mt 27:33-36) (Mk 15:22-25) (Lk 23:33-37)	Jerusalem	Friday April 1, AD 33	I
436	Inscription on the Cross (Jn 19:19-22) (Mt 27:37) (Mk 15:26) (Lk 23:38)	Jerusalem	Friday April 1, AD 33	I
437	Soldiers Divide Jesus' Garments (Jn 19:23,24) (Mt 27:35) (Mk 15:24) (Lk 23:34)	Jerusalem	Friday April 1, AD 33	I
438	"Woman Behold Your Son" (Jn 19:25-27)	Jerusalem	Friday April 1, AD 33	I
439	Jesus Mocked on the Cross (Lk 23:35-36, Mt 27:38-43) (Mk 15:27-32)	Jerusalem	Friday April 1, AD 33	I

* Level of Confidence in Date   Level I = Highly Probable   Level II = Probable

Event Sequence Number	Event (Scripture References)	Location of Event	Gregorian Date	Level of Confidence*
440	The Two Robbers (Lk 23:39-43, Mt 27:44)	Jerusalem	Friday April 1, AD 33	I
441	The Death of Jesus (Jn 19:28-30) (Mt 27:45-54) (Mk 15:33-39) (Lk 23:44-48)	Jerusalem	Friday April 1, AD 33	I
442	Witnesses to the Crucifixion (Mt 27:55-56) (Mk 15:40-41) (Lk 23:49)	Jerusalem	Friday April 1, AD 33	I
443	Jesus' Side Pierced (Jn 19:31-37)	Jerusalem	Friday April 1, AD 33	I
444	Burial of Jesus (Jn 19:38-42) (Mt 27:57-61) (Mk 15:42-47) (Lk 23:50-56)	Jerusalem	Friday April 1, AD 33	I
445	The Guard for the Tomb (Mt 27:62-66)	Jerusalem	Friday April 1, AD 33	I
446	Resurrection (Mt 28:2-4)	Jerusalem	Sunday April 3, AD 33	I
447	The Women at the Tomb (Lk 24:1-8) (Mt 28:1, 5-8) (Mk 16:1-8) (Jn 20:1)	Jerusalem	Sunday April 3, AD 33	I

* Level of Confidence in Date   Level I = Highly Probable   Level II = Probable

Event Sequence Number	Event (Scripture References)	Location of Event	Gregorian Date	Level of Confidence*
448	Jesus Appears to Women (Mt 28:9-10)	Jerusalem	Sunday April 3, AD 33	I
449	The Report of the Guards (Mt 28:11-15)	Jerusalem	Sunday April 3, AD 33	I
450	Women Report to Apostles (Lk 24:9-11, Jn 20:2)	Jerusalem	Sunday April 3, AD 33	I
451	Peter & John Run to Tomb (Jn 20:3-10, Lk 24:12)	Jerusalem	Sunday April 3, AD 33	I
452	Jesus Appears to Mary Magdalene (Jn 20:11-18, Mk 16:9-11)	Jerusalem	Sunday April 3, AD 33	I
453	Jesus Appears to Peter (Lk 24:34)	Jerusalem	Sunday April 3, AD 33	I
454	Jesus Appears on Road to Emmaus (Lk 24:13-35, Mk 16:12-13)	Road to Emmaus	Sunday April 3, AD 33	I
455	Jesus Appears to Ten Apostles (Lk 24:36-43, Jn 20:19-23)	Jerusalem	Sunday April 3, AD 33	I
456	Jesus Appears to Eleven Apostles (Jn 20:24-29, Mk 16:14-18)	Jerusalem	Sunday April 11, AD 33	I
457	Many Other Signs Performed by Jesus During His Ministry (Jn 20:30-31)	Judea, Galilee& Samaria	AD 31 to AD 33	II

* Level of Confidence in Date   Level I = Highly Probable   Level II = Probable

Event Sequence Number	Event (Scripture References)	Location of Event	Gregorian Date	Level of Confidence*
458	Jesus Appears at Sea of Tiberius (Jn 21:1-23)	Genne-saret, Galilee	Sunday May 1 AD 33,	II
459	Jesus Appears to the Eleven in Galilee (Mt 28:16-20)	Hepta-pegen	Sunday May 1, AD 33	II
460	Apostle John Writing the Gospel of John (Jn 21:24)	Ephesus, Asia	AD 65	II
461	Jesus Did Many Other Things (Jn 21:25)	Judea & Galilee	AD 31 to AD 33	II
462	Jesus' Final Words Before His Ascension (Lk 24:44-49) (Acts 1:4-8)	Near Bethany, Judea	Thursday May 12, AD 33	I
463	Ascension (Mk 16:19) (Lk 24:50-51) (Acts 1:9-11)	Bethany	Thursday May 12, AD 33	I
464	Apostles Return to Upper Room (Lk 24:52) (Acts 1:12-13)	Mount Zion, Jerusalem	Thursday May 12, AD 33	I
465	Disciples Continually in the Temple (Lk 24:53)	Jerusalem	Beginning May 12, AD 33	I
466	Apostles Preach Everywhere (Mk 16:20)	Mediter-rean Area	Beginning May 22, AD 33	I

* Level of Confidence in Date   Level I = Highly Probable   Level II = Probable

3

Jesus' Birth and Childhood

In contrast with the extensive coverage given to Jesus' death and resurrection in all four Gospels, only Matthew and Luke discuss the birth of Jesus. And, although Jesus' crucifixion and resurrection were commemorated from the beginning of the Church, there is no indication in the New Testament that the birth of Jesus was celebrated by the Apostolic Church. Also, subsequent to New Testament times, the early church fathers were not even in agreement as to the year of Jesus' birth. *Table 3.1* lists the years of Jesus' birth according to a number of early Christian writers from the second century A.D. onward as given by Jack Finegan in *Handbook of Biblical Chronology*.

Some of the early Christian writers gave an exact date for the birth of Jesus. Clement of Alexandria in *Stromata*, circa A.D. 194, indicates that the birth of Christ took place 194 years, 1 month and 13 days before the death of Commodus. The Roman emperor Commodus died on December 31, A.D. 192 (Julian) which, Jack Finegan shows, implies that Christ was born on November 18, 3 B.C.(Julian). Clement of Alexandria also indicates in *Stromata* that some other

	Table 3.1 Years of Jesus' Birth			
Source	Reference	Year of Source	Year Given for Birth of Jesus	Equivalent Year
Alogi	Epiphanius' *Panarion* (*Finegan*, p. 228)	A.D. 180	40th Year of Augustus [a]	4 B.C.
Irenaeus	*Against Heresies* (*Finegan*, p. 222)	A.D. 180	41st Year of Augustus [a]	3 B.C.
Clement of Alexandria	*Stromata* (*Finegan*, p. 223)	A.D. 194	28th Year of Augustus [b]	3 B.C.
Tertullian	An Answer to the Jews (*Finegan*, p. 224)	A.D. 198	28 years after the death of Cleopatra	3 B.C.
Julius Africanus	*Chronographies* (*Finegan*, p. 225)	A.D. 226	Olympiad 194,2	3/2 B.C.
Origen	*Homilies on Luke* (*Finegan*, p. 225)	A.D. 231	41st Year of Augustus [a]	3 B.C.
Hippolytus of Thebes	fragment (*Finegan*, p. 228)	A.D. 234	42nd Year of Augustus [a]	2 B.C.
Hippolytus of Thebes	another fragment (*Finegan*, p.228)	A.D. 234	43rd Year of Augustus [a]	1 B.C.
Eusebius	*The History of the Church* (*Eusebius*, p. 49)	A.D. 325	42nd Year of Augustus [a]	2 B.C.
Epiphanius	*Panarion* (*Finegan*, p. 227)	A.D. 357	Consuls - Octavian XIII (Augusto) & Silvano	2 B.C.
Dionysius Exiguus	*Letter to Pope John I* (*Finegan*, p. 132)	A.D. 525	A.U.C. 754 (From foundation of the city-Rome)	1 B.C.
a From 43 BC, the year following the Death of Julius Caesar b Alexandrian Era				

groups place the birth of Jesus on April 19 or 20 and some on May 20. Epiphanius in *Pararion*, written in A.D. 357, indicates that a group called the Alogi (not Logos) in c. A.D. 180 gave the date of the conception of Jesus as either May 21 or June 20. If Jesus' conception took place on May 21, then His birth would have taken place about forty weeks later or on about February 25. If the conception was on June 20, then the birth would have been about March 27. The date that Epiphanius himself accepted was equivalent to January 6, 2 B.C. (Julian). The earliest extant reference to the celebration of December 25 as the date of Jesus' birth is found in a Roman city calendar for the year A.D. 354 edited by Filocalus.

Thus, there is no agreement in the earliest surviving testimony of the church fathers concerning the day, the month or even the year of Jesus' birth. However, collectively, these early Christian writers believed that Jesus was born sometime between 4 B.C. and 1 B.C. It is significant that these dates for the birth of Jesus by the Church fathers seem to contradict the dating of Josephus for the death of Herod I who ruled Judea at the birth of Jesus (Matthew 2:1). Josephus indicates that Herod I died in early 4 B.C. and, based on this dating of the death of Herod I, many modern Bible scholars have placed the birth of Jesus in 5 B.C. or earlier. However, the exact date of Jesus' birth appears to have been lost by the early church. Thus, we have a much more difficult task to determine this date than was the case for determining the dates of Christ's crucifixion and resurrection which were recorded in the New Testament in terms of the Jewish feast day of Passover. However, there are a number of clues given in the New Testament as to the time of Jesus' birth.

John the Baptist's Birth

We shall first investigate the date of the birth of John the Baptist. Since John the Baptist was 5 to 6 months older than Jesus, if we can determine the date of birth of John the Baptist, it will give us a good indication of the date of birth of Jesus. We know that John the Baptist was 5 to 6 months older than Jesus because *Luke 1:36* tells us that the angel said to Mary, "And behold, even your relative Elizabeth has also conceived a son in her old age, and she who was called barren is now in her sixth month." This verse indicates that at the time of Jesus' conception, Elizabeth was already in her sixth month so that the conception of John the Baptist had occurred five to six months earlier and therefore John was 5 to 6 months older than Jesus.

It has already been noted in Chapter 2, based on Luke 3:1, that John the Baptist began his ministry in the fifteenth year of the reign of Tiberius Caesar and it has been shown that the fifteenth year of Tiberius corresponded to the calendar year A.D. 29. Also, *Luke 3:23a* says, "And when He began His ministry, Jesus Himself was about thirty years of age." Thirty years of age seems to be the age of full maturity in Bible times. Thirty was the age required to enter the Levitical priesthood (Numbers 4:2-3). There are also a number of Old Testament personages that began their work at age thirty: Joseph was thirty years old when he assumed the position of second to Pharaoh (Genesis 41:46), David was thirty when he became king (*2 Samuel 5:4*) and Ezekiel was thirty when he was called as a prophet (Ezekiel 1:1). Thus, both Jesus and John the Baptist were probably at least thirty years old when they began their ministry.

If both Jesus and John the Baptist began their ministries on or near their thirtieth birthday, then John the Baptist would have had a ministry of only about six months since John's ministry ended shortly after Jesus' ministry began (Mark 1:14) and he was only five to six months older than Jesus. However the Scriptures suggest a much longer ministry for John the Baptist since his teachings had spread throughout the Middle East. Thus Acts 18:24-26 says:

> Now a certain Jew named Apollos, an Alexandrian by birth, an eloquent man, came to Ephesus; and he was mighty in the Scriptures. This man had been instructed in the way of the Lord; and being fervent in spirit, he was speaking and teaching accurately the things concerning Jesus, being acquainted only with the baptism of John; and he began to speak out boldly in the synagogue. But when Priscilla and Aquila heard him, they took him aside and explained to him the way of God more accurately.

Thus John the Baptist probably began his ministry on or near his thirtieth birthday while Jesus began his ministry near his thirty-first birthday. If John the Baptist's thirtieth birthday occurred in A.D. 29, then Table 3.2 indicates his age on his birthday for each calendar year until his birth.

The first chapter of Luke gives us another clue as to the date of the birth of John the Baptist. Luke 1.5 says: "In the days of Herod, king of Judea, there was a certain priest named Zacharias, of the division of Abijah; and he had a wife from the daughters of Aaron, and her name was Elizabeth." Thus, we learn that Zacharias, the father of John the Baptist, was of the priestly division of Abijah. Then Luke 1:23-25 says:

> When the days of his priestly service were ended, he went back home. After these days Elizabeth his wife became pregnant, and she kept herself in seclusion for five months, saying, "This is the way the Lord has dealt with me in the days when He looked with favor upon me, to take away my disgrace among men."

Thus, we learn that shortly after the service of the priestly division of

Table 3.2 Age of John the Baptist on His Birthday					
Year	**Age**	**Year**	**Age**	**Year**	**Age**
A.D. 29	30	A.D. 18	19	A.D. 7	8
A.D. 28	29	A.D. 17	18	A.D. 6	7
A.D. 27	28	A.D. 16	17	A.D. 5	6
A.D. 26	27	A.D. 15	16	A.D. 4	5
A.D. 25	26	A.D. 14	15	A.D. 3	4
A.D. 24	25	A.D. 13	14	A.D. 2	3
A.D. 23	24	A.D. 12	13	A.D. 1	2
A.D. 22	23	A.D. 11	12	1 B.C.	1
A.D. 21	22	A.D. 10	11	2 B.C.	birth
A.D. 20	21	A.D. 9	10		
A.D. 19	20	A.D. 8	9		

Abijah was completed, the conception of John the Baptist took place. Byzantine tradition indicates that Elizabeth brought her infant son, John the Baptist, to a cave in En Kerem in order to save him from the murderous Herod (Murphy-O'Connor page 208). Since En Kerem is located only about four miles from the site of the Temple, this would suggest that the home of Zacharias and Elizabeth was located not far from Jerusalem and near to Bethlehem. From *Table 3.2* we know that John the Baptist was born in Julian calendar year 2 B.C. Therefore the conception of John the Baptist took place forty weeks earlier or between March 27, 3 B.C. and March 26, 2 B.C. (Julian), forty weeks prior to the interval of his birth from January 1, 2 B.C. to December 31, 2 B.C.(Julian). If we knew when the Division of Abijah served during the period between March 27, 3 B.C. and March 26, 2 B.C. (Julian), we would have a good indication of when the conception of John the Baptist took place and hence when he was born.

Chapter 24 of the book of Chronicles records that David divided the descendants of Aaron into twenty-four divisions according to their fathers' households. The order in which these divisions served was assigned by lot and the division of Abijah was the eighth division (1 Chronicles 24:10). Table 3.3 gives the names of each division and their division number which indicates their order of service.

Josephus in *Antiquities of the Jews, 7:15.7*, page 208, indicates that these divisions each served in turn for one week from Sabbath to Sabbath and that these same 24 divisions remained until Josephus' time (A.D. 37-c.100). Each division served from noon on one Sabbath until noon on the next Sabbath so that each division would have its regular service once every 24 weeks. However, at feast times all the divisions served, but this did not disturb the regular order of service of the divisions. We know this because in the *Mishnah,* Tractate Sukkah *5:7*, a distinction is made in the sharing of the offerings between the divisions whose regular service included the feast day and the priests of the other divisions who were also serving. Thus, for any period of continuous service of the priestly divisions, if we can determine the priestly division serving on one known date, then we can determine the priestly division serving on any other date by computing the number of weeks separating the two dates. If this number of weeks is divided by 24 and the fractional remainder is zero, then the same division would be serving on the two dates. Otherwise, the fractional remainder would indicate how many priestly divisions separates the divisions serving on the two dates.

Table 3.3 Priestly Divisions (*1 Chronicles 24*)			
Name	**Division #**	**Name**	**Division #**
Jehoiarib	1	Huppah	13
Jedaiah	2	Jeshebeab	14
Harim	3	Bilgah	15
Seorim	4	Immer	16
Malchijah	5	Hezir	17
Mijamin	6	Happizzez	18
Hakkoz	7	Pethahiah	19
Abijah	8	Jehezkel	20
Jeshua	9	Jachim	21
Shecaniah	10	Gamul	22
Eliashib	11	Delaiah	23
Jakim	12	Maaziah	24

Thus, we need to know which division was serving on some known date during the first century of the Christian Era. The *Babylonian Talmud* appears to provide this information. Both Tractate Arakin 12b and Tractate Taaneth 29a indicate that the first division, the Division of Jehoiarib, was serving at the destruction of both the first and second temple. In Tractate Arakin 12b, the statement that the Division of Jehorarib was serving at the destruction of the Second Temple is questioned by Rabbi Judah (A.D. 165-200).

However, his argument is based on Ezra 2:36-39 which states that only members of four priestly families returned to Jerusalem after the Babylonian Exile [Jeshua, Immer, Pashkur (also Immer) and Harim]. Therefore, Rabbi Judah concluded that a division called Jehoiarib could not have served at the time of the destruction of the Second Temple because this was not one of the returning divisions. However, we know from Luke 1:5 that Zacharias served in the Division called Abijah in the Second Temple and Abijah was not one of the four returning divisions either. Also we have the testimony of Josephus that the same twenty-four priestly divisions continued to serve until his day (A.D. 37-c. 100), *Antiquities 7.15.7, page 208.* Josephus' testimony is significant since he was himself a priest and a member of the Division of Jehoiarib, *Life 1.1,* page 1. Apparently on the return from exile, the four returning priestly divisions were again divided into twenty-four divisions, which assumed the names and order of service given in chapter 24 of 1 Chronicles. Thus, the Division of Jehoiarib could have been serving at the time of the destruction of the Second Temple.

Tractate Taanith 29a of the *Babylonian Talmud*, page 154, as translated by Rev. Dr. J. Rabbinowitz says:

> It is reported that the day on which the First Temple was destroyed was the eve of the ninth of Ab, a Sunday, and in a year following the Sabbatical year, and the *Mishmar* of the family Jehoiarib were on duty and the Levites were chanting the Psalms standing on the Duchan, and what Psalm did they recite?- [The Psalm] containing the verse, *And He hath brought upon them their own iniquities, and will cast off in their own evil (Psalm 94:23).* And hardly had they had time to say, *'The Lord our God will cut them off,'* when the heathens came and

captured them. The same thing too happened in the Second Temple.

As with Tractate Arakin 12b, subsequent discussion in Tractate Taanith 29a indicate the sentence "The same thing too happened in the Second Temple." applies to the whole paragraph. Thus, Tractate Taanith 29a indicates that the day on which both the First and Second Temple were destroyed, was the eve of the ninth of Ab, a Sunday, in a year following a Sabbatical year, and that the first priestly division, the Division of Jehoiarib was serving. If we can accept this statement from Taanith 29a, we will have the required known date of service of one of the priestly divisions since the year of the destruction of the Second Temple is firmly established as A.D. 70.   Also, if the symmetries between the destruction of the First and Second Temple proved to be true, it would certainly be remarkable. However, we must check these claims against the Jewish calendars to see if this statement can be verified.   Our primary interest will be in the destruction of the Second Temple; however, we shall also consider the First Temple's destruction as well.

In considering the statement from Taanith 29a, we must remember that the Jewish day begins at sunset so that we have night first and then the daylight hours as the last part of the day. Thus the eve of the Jewish Sunday would actually occur on our Saturday. When we examine the calendar of Appendix D for A.D. 70, we find that Ab 9 does indeed begin on a Saturday and therefore does confirm Taanith 29a for the destruction of the Second Temple.

However, does this statement actually also apply to the destruction of the First Temple? Many Bible scholars place the destruction of the First Temple in 587 B.C. (Aharoni, page 162). It is not necessary to construct the entire calendar for 587 B.C. to determine the day of the week of Ab 9. Instead we shall just use Goldstine's *Tables of New and Full Moons from 1001 B.C. to A.D.*

1651 to determine the Julian date of Ab 9, 587 B.C. We shall then compute the Julian Day Number for that date using the Tables of Appendix B. The Julian Day Number of a given date is simply the number of days from January 1, 4713 B.C. to the given date. January 1, 4713 B.C. is a more or less arbitrary early date selected by John Hershel in A.D. 1583 to define the Julian Day Number. Since the days of the week repeat every seven days, if the Julian Day Number is divided by 7, the fractional remainder of the answer indicates the day of the week for the given date (see Appendix B).

To demonstrate the method we shall first use it to determine the day of the week for August 2, A.D. 70, the Gregorian date of the destruction of Second Temple, which has already been determined to be Saturday by reference to the calendars of Appendix D. From Appendix B we determine that the Julian Day Number for August 2, A.D. (Gregorian) is 1,746,841.

$$1,746,841 \div 7 = 249,548.71$$

Thus the remainder is .71 which according to Appendix B indicates that Ab 9, A.D. 70 began on a Saturday which is the same result that we obtained using the calendar of Appendix D.

For the destruction of the First Temple, if the year was 587 B.C., Goldstine's Tables indicate the Ab 9 corresponds to the Julian date July 27. The Julian Day Number for July 27, 587 B.C. (Julian) is 1,507,229.

$$1,507,229 \div 7 = 215,318.42$$

Thus the fractional remainder is .42 (3/7), which, according to the table of Appendix B, indicates that this date fell on a Thursday and not on a Saturday as required by Taanith 29a. However, some Bible scholars consider the year of the destruction of the First Temple to be

586 B.C. The Julian Day Number for Ab 9, 586 B.C. [July 17, 586 B.C. (Julian)] is 1,507,576.

$$1,507,576 \div 7 = 215,368$$

Thus the fractional remainder is zero which would indicate that the date would fall on a Monday, again not meeting the requirement of Taanith 29a. However, if we try 588 B.C. as the year of the destruction of the First Temple, the Julian Day Number for Ab 9, 588 B.C. [August 9, 588 B.C.(Julian)] is 1,506,874.

$$1,506,874 \div 7 = 215,267.71$$

Thus the fractional remainder is .71 which would indicate that Ab 9, 588 B.C. did fall on a Saturday and therefore would meet the requirements of Taanith 29a. E.W. Faulstich in *History, Harmony and the Hebrew Kings* concluded that 588 B.C. is the year of the destruction of the First Temple based on a similar calendar analysis.

There is another requirement given in Tannith 29a for the day of the destruction of both the First and the Second Temple. Both events must occur in a year following a Sabbatical year. Leviticus 25:3,4 says:

> Six years you shall sow your field, and six years you shall prune your vineyard and gather in its crop, but during the seventh year the land shall have a sabbath rest, a sabbath to the LORD; you shall not sow your field nor prune your vineyard.

Thus every seventh year was to be a Sabbatical year. If the year prior to the destruction of both the First and Second Temple were Sabbatical years and the First Temple was destroyed in 588 B.C., then 589 B.C. would be a Sabbatical year as would be A.D. 69. If both of these years are Sabbatical years, then the number of years separating them should be a multiple of seven. However, 589 B.C. is separated from 1 B.C. by 588 years and A.D. 69 would be another 69 years so 589 B.C. and A.D. 69 are separated by 588 + 69 = 657 years. 657 ÷ 7 = 93.857. Therefore, 589 B.C. and A.D. 69 cannot both be Sabbatical years. Since it seems much more likely that the writers of the Talmud would have extra-Biblical information concerning the destruction of the Second Temple than for the destruction of the First Temple, we must conclude that all the information of Taanith 29a applies only to the destruction of the Second Temple. Since the day and the month of the destruction of both temples were very similar, it was probably assumed that all the details of the destruction of the Second Temple also applied to the destruction of the First Temple.

Thus, it does appear that the first priestly division, the Division of Jehoiarib, did begin their service at noon, August 2, A.D. 70 (Gregorian) just hours before the Second Temple was destroyed by fire. Using this information we shall be able to determine when Zacharias' division, the Division of Abijah, served during the indicated period of the conception of John the Baptist from March 25, 3 B.C. to March 24, 2 B.C. (Gregorian). Looking at the calendars of Appendix D for 3 B.C., we see that March 25, 3 B.C. (Gregorian) fell on a Wednesday so the priestly division serving on that date began their service on Saturday, March 21, 3 B.C. (Gregorian). To determine which priestly division was serving on that date we could just use the calendars of Appendix D and actually count the number of weeks separating March 21, 3 B.C. and August 2, A.D. 70 and then divide that number of weeks by 24. If the answer was a whole number, that is the fractional remainder was zero, the same two divisions would have been serving on the two dates. Otherwise, the fractional remainder would indicate which division was serving on March 21, 3 B.C. However, counting all those weeks would be a rather tedious task and might be subject to error. Therefore, instead we shall compute the Julian Day Number for the two dates using the tables of Appendix B and then find the difference of these two numbers which would be the number of days separating the two dates. Since the twenty-four divisions each serve for seven days in turn and 24×7=168 days, therefore every 168 days the divisions repeat themselves. The results for our particular dates are recorded in Table 3.4.

Table 3.4 Determination of the Division Serving on March 21, 3 B.C.(Gregorian)	
Gregorian Date	Julian Day Number
August 2, A.D. 70	1,746,841
March 21, 3 B.C.	1,720,409
Difference (Number of Days Between Dates)	26,432
Difference ÷ 168	157.33 = 157 8/24

Thus, the division that began its service on March 21, 3 B.C. would be the division that began its service 8 divisions before the first division, the Division of Jehoiarib. This would be the 17th division, Hezir. Therefore, eight weeks after that division began its service, the first division, Jehoiarib began its service again on May 16, 3 B.C. and seven weeks later, the eighth division, the Division of Abijah began its service. Then, a week later, on July 11, 3 B.C. (Gregorian), Zacharias and his division completed their service and he returned home, and the conception of John the Baptist may have taken place shortly thereafter. However, Zacharias would have served a second time during the indicated time of John the Baptist's conception. Twenty-four weeks after Zacharias' division completed its service on July 11, 3 B.C. (Gregorian), they would have completed another week of service on Saturday, December 26, 3 B.C. (Gregorian).

Since the conception of John the Baptist occurred shortly after the priestly Division of Abijah completed their service between March 25, 3 B.C. and March 24, 2 B.C., then his conception would have taken place about July 11, 3 B.C. (Gregorian) or December 26, 3 B.C. (Gregorian). Forty weeks after these dates or on April 17, 2 B.C. or October 2, 2 B.C. would be the indicated dates of birth of John the Baptist. Since Luke 1:36 says that Elizabeth was in her sixth month when Jesus was conceived, then if John the Baptist was born on April 17, 2 B.C., then Jesus would have been born from about September 12, 2 B.C. to October 11, 2 B.C., five months and one day to six months after the birth of John using the Jewish calendar. If John the Baptist was born on December 26, then Jesus would have been born from about February 29, 1 B.C. to March 20, 1 B.C. Thus the date of Jesus' birth is narrowed to two periods of about one month each, neglecting for the moment such factors as the variation in the lengths of pregnancies.

Jesus' Birth

In his Gospel, Luke attempts to give us another clue as to the date of Jesus' birth when in Luke 2:1-2 he says, "In those days Caesar Augustus issued a decree that a census should be taken of the Roman world. (This was the first census that took place while Quirinius was governor of Syria.)" Unfortunately, no historical record outside of this passage from Luke mentions Quirinius' governorship of Syria at this time. This does not mean that Luke was mistaken concerning Quirinius being governor.   It merely reflects the sparseness of historical data concerning the Middle East for this period. In general if the information is not available in the New Testament or in the works of the Jewish historian Josephus, it probably is not available.

Josephus does, however, in *Antiquities, 17.5.3*, page 457, indicate that shortly before the death of Herod I, Varus came to replace Saturninus as governor of Syria. Josephus also says that shortly after the arrival of Varus, Herod I executed several Jewish priests on the eve of an eclipse of the moon. Since Herod I was alive at the time of the birth of Jesus and John the Baptist, this eclipse could not have occurred prior to 2 B.C. However, there was no eclipse of the moon visible from Judea in 2 B.C. and the next such eclipse occurred on the night of January 7 and 8, 1 B.C. (see Table 3.5, page 130). If this was the eclipse of the moon shortly before the death of Herod I, then Varus would have arrived in the closing months of 2 B.C. Since Luke tells us that Quirinius was governor of Syria when Jesus was born, Quirinius must have served as governor of Syria in 2 B.C. prior to the arrival of Varus. Therefore, John the Baptist must have been born about April 17, 2 B.C., and not October 2, 2 B.C., because, if John the Baptist was born on the latter date, then Jesus would have been born between February 29, 1 B.C. and March 28, 1 B.C. and Varus would have been governor of Syria rather than Quirinius. Thus John the Baptist must have been born about April 17, 2 B.C. and Jesus must have been born from about September 12, 2 B.C. to October 11, 2 B.C.

Ernest Martin in *"The Birth of Christ Recalculated,"* page 101, gives a reasonable explanation as to why Quirinius was serving as governor of Syria in 2 B.C. The year 2 B.C. was the year that Augustus was given the title Pater Patrae (Father of the Country) by the Roman Senate. This probably involved a major celebration and both Saturninus and Varus would have wanted to be in Rome. Therefore, Quirinius probably served as governor of Syria so Saturninus could leave Syria early and Varus, his regular replacement, could leave Rome late.

The birth of Jesus is discussed in only three places in the New Testament: in Matthew 1:18-25, in Luke 1:26-2:20 and in Revelation 12:1-6. In Revelation 12:1-6, John says:

> A great sign appeared in heaven: a woman clothed with the sun, and the moon under her feet, and on her head a crown of twelve stars; and she was with child; and she cried out, being in labor and in pain to give birth. Then another sign appeared in heaven: and behold, a great red dragon having seven heads and ten horns, and on his heads were seven diadems. And his tail swept away a third of the stars of heaven and threw them to the earth. And the dragon stood before the woman who was about to give birth, so that when she gave birth he might devour her child. And she gave birth to a son, a male child, who is to rule all the nations with a rod of iron; and her child was caught up to God and to His throne. Then the woman fled into the wilderness where she had a place prepared by God, so that there she would be nourished for one thousand two hundred and sixty days.

This great sign certainly appears to refer to the birth of Jesus. The women gave birth to a Son who is to rule all nations and then the Son was caught up to God. This great sign was in heaven and involved the sun and the moon and the stars, which suggests that the sign involves a constellation of stars together with the sun and the moon. The only constellation that fits the conditions of the sign is the constellation Virgo (the Virgin). The constellation Virgo is the

Jewish constellation Betulah which also means virgin. Virgo is one of the twelve zodiac constellations which are located along the ecliptic which is the apparent path of the sun as it moves among the stars due to the annual revolution of the earth around the sun. Only the zodiac constellations could be clothed by the sun in the sense that the sun would be contained within the constellation and Virgo is the only one of these constellations that is a woman. Before the constellation Virgo is the constellation Draco, the Dragon. Figure 3.1 shows Virgo and Draco in the Autumn skies.

The sun spends approximately 30 days in the region of each of the twelve zodiac constellations each year. However, Revelation 12:1-6 also requires that the moon should be under the woman's feet. Since the moon revolves around the earth every 29.5 days, its apparent position among the stars changes approximately 12 degree from one night until the next. So, for the 30 days that the sun would be in Virgo (clothing the woman), the moon would be immediately under Virgo's feet only one night. Thus if Revelation 12 does give a sign for the birth of Jesus, it will indicate an exact date!

To determine this date a computer program, *The Sky*, version 4, from Software Bisque, © 1984-1996 was used to reproduce the skies of New Testament times. Using this computer program, the sun was found to be in Virgo with the moon immediately under Virgo's feet during 2 B.C. on September 27 (Gregorian) and on that day the moon would only be visible at Jerusalem (and Bethlehem) for a few minutes immediately after sunset. We know that Jesus was born that day after sunset because in Luke 2:11 the shepherd, "keeping watch over their flocks by night", were told by an angel, "For today in the city of David there has been born for you a Savior who is Christ the Lord." Since the Jewish day began at sunset, Jesus was born between sunset and the time that night that the angels appeared to the shepherds. Thus Revelation 12:1-6 indicates that Jesus was born on September 27, 2 B.C. and if this sign was to be visible in Judea at the

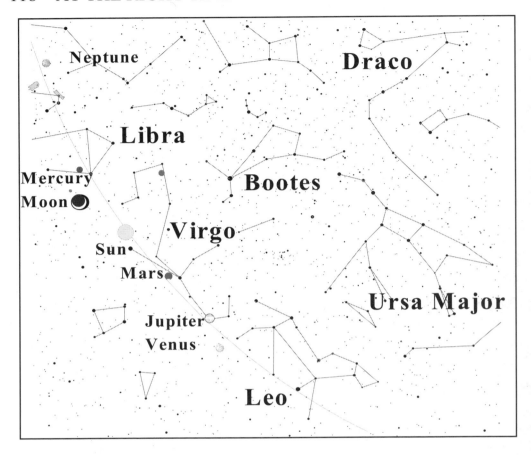

Virgo Clothed in the Sun
With the Moon Under Her Feet
September 27, 2 B.C. (Gregorian)
Figure 3.1

time of Jesus' birth, the birth would have occurred about 6:30 P.M. local Jerusalem time. Ernest Martin in *The Birth of Christ Recalculated,* 1980 used a similar approach to date the birth of Christ; however, since he believed that the birth of Christ took place in 3 B.C., he found a different date.

Admittedly, this determination of the exact date of Jesus' birth does depend on interpreting Revelation 12:1-6 as a heavenly sign of

Jesus' birth which is not the usual interpretation given for this Scripture. However, the heavenly sign does fit the circumstances of Jesus' birth extremely well. The woman may not just represent Mary, but all the faithful children of God. Romans 9:8 says, "That is, it is not the children of the flesh who are the children of God, but the children of the promise are regarded as descendants." Thus when Revelation 12:6 says, "And the woman fled into the wilderness where she had a place prepared by God, so that she might be nourished for one thousand two hundred and sixty days," this could refer to the Christian community leaving Jerusalem, shortly before its destruction in A.D. 70, and fleeing to Pella, a city of the Decapolis east of the Jordan River (see Eusebius 5.4, page 111). This interpretation fits well with Revelation 12:15-16 which says, "And the serpent poured water like a river out of his mouth after the woman, so that he might cause her to be swept away with the flood. And the earth helped the woman, and the earth opened its mouth and drank up the river which the dragon poured out of his mouth." The river that the Dragon (Devil) poured out of his mouth was a figure for the attacking Roman armies. However, the Rift Valley, which contains the Jordan River, was a natural barrier which stopped the pursuit of the Roman forces (figuratively, drank the river).

Even more striking is the fact that September 27, 2 B.C. falls right within the interval for Jesus' birth, from September 12, 2 B.C. to October 2, 2 B.C., determined independently from the weeks of priestly service of Zacharias' division, Abijah. Thus the two independent determinations of the date of the birth of Jesus support each other. When we examine the calendars of Appendix D, we discover another amazing fact concerning September 27, 2 B.C. (Gregorian). At sunset that day, began the first day of the seventh Jewish month, Tishri 1, which was the Day of Trumpets! Leviticus 23:23-25 says,

> And again the Lord spoke to Moses, saying, "Speak to the sons of Israel, saying, 'In the seventh month on the first of the month, you shall have a rest, a reminder by the blowing of trumpets, a holy convocation. You shall not do any laborious work, but you shall present an offering by fire to the Lord.'"

For all of the other five observances commanded in Leviticus 23, the event being commemorated is given: The Sabbath commemorates the day God rested after Creation. The Passover Feast commemorates God's deliverance of the of the children of Israel from bondage in Egypt. The Day of Pentecost commemorates the harvest. The Day of Atonement commemorates atonement for sin and the Feast of Booths commemorates the children of Israel living in booths during the Exodus. But what did the Day of Trumpets commemorate? Its purpose is not stated in Scripture, but it appears that its purpose was to commemorate the birth of Jesus! The sounding of a trumpet is definitely associated with Jesus' second coming (1 Thessalonians 4:16 and 1 Corinthians 15:51,52). Thus, without knowing it, the Jewish community may have been celebrating the birth of Jesus on Tishri 1, Rosh Hashanah (the New Year), for more than 3200 years. Although Exodus 12:2, referring to the month of the Passover Feast, says, "This month shall be the beginning of months for you, it is to be the first month of the year to you.", under the current Jewish calendar Tishri 1, the Day of Trumpets and probably Jesus' birthday, is the first day of the new Jewish year.

Again looking at the calendar of Appendix D for 2 B.C., we see that the indicated date of the birth of John the Baptist, April 17, 2 B.C. (Gregorian), is the day of the Passover Feast. Jesus was crucified on the afternoon of the Day of Preparation for the Passover as the Lamb of God who takes away the sins of the world and, if John the Baptist was born during daylight hour on April 17, 2 B.C., he would have been born on the Day of Preparation for the Passover Feast. This may symbolize John the Baptist's connection with Jesus' mission to bring salvation to mankind. Thus, in the probable dates for the birth of both Jesus and John the Baptist, we see the marvelous hand of God at work.

We now turn to the Gospel of Matthew where the coming of the magi (the wise men) is recorded. Matthew 2:1-2 says, " Now after Jesus was born in Bethlehem of Judea in the days of Herod the king, magi from the east arrived in Jerusalem, saying, 'Where is He who has been born King of the Jews? For we saw His star in the east and have come to worship Him.'" In this Scripture we are told that the magi came from the east to worship the new King of the Jews. We are also told that they followed a star, but which star did they follow and why did they follow it? What brought the magi to Jerusalem?

The magi were some of the leading astronomers of their day, and they were highly regarded as wise men in the ancient world. They were not kings, but they did serve as advisors to kings, especially the kings of Persia. Magi were mentioned in the book of Daniel. Daniel 2:1-2 says:

> Now in the second year of the reign of Nebuchadnezzar, Nebuchadnezzar had dreams; and his spirit was troubled and his sleep left him. Then the king gave orders to call in the magicians, the conjurers, the sorcerers and the Chaldeans to tell the king his dreams. So they came in and stood before the king.

In the Greek version of the Old Testament, the Septuagint, the word translated magician in the New American Standard Bible (NASB) version of Daniel 2:2 was the same Greek word translated magi in Matthew 2:1. The magicians, conjurers, sorcerers and Chaldeans are referred to collectively as wise men in Daniel 2:12 and, when they could not tell Nebuchadnezzar his dream, he ordered that all the wise men be killed.   However, when Daniel was able to tell Nebuchadnezzar his dream and its interpretation, he made Daniel ruler of all the wise men of Babylon including the magi (Daniel 2:48). Thus there was a connection between the magi and the prophet Daniel. Daniel 9:25 says, "So you are to know and discern that from the issuing of a decree to restore and rebuild Jerusalem until Messiah the Prince there will be seven weeks and sixty-two weeks; it will be built again, with plaza and moat, even in times of distress." For a discussion of this prophecy see Appendix E. It is possible that Daniel's prophecy concerning the coming of the Messiah was handed down among the magi from the time of Daniel. Actually, the belief in the imminent coming of a world ruler from Judea was widely held at that time through out the Middle East and beyond.. Thus the magi probably knew something of the prophecies concerning the coming of the Messiah, but what did they see in the sky at that particular time that sent them to Jerusalem?

The magi were astronomers and astrologers and they would have been watching the stars and the planets in the night skies. The stars are so far away that their relative position to one another remains essentially fixed from night to night and year to year. However, since the planets are relatively close to the earth and since they also revolve around the sun, they appear to be moving among the fixed stars from night to night. This movement is reflected in their name since the word planet is derived from a Greek word meaning wanderer. One of the things the magi would be particularly watching for would be conjunctions. A conjunction occurs when two planets or a planet and a major star come close together. Since our investigation has indicated that the birth of Jesus took place in 2 B.C., we shall be looking at the night skies during 2 and 3 B.C., since Herod I ordered that all the male children, two years old and under, be killed according to the time which he had ascertained from the magi

(Matthew 2:16). Again we shall be using the computer program *The Sky*. The results of this investigation is truly remarkable.

The spectacular display begins on August 10, 3 B.C. (Gregorian) when the planet Jupiter rose as a morning star in conjunction with the planet Venus. Since these two planets are the brightest objects in the sky other than the sun and the moon, this conjunction would have certainly gotten the attention of the magi. This was followed on August 30, 3 B.C. by a conjunction of Venus and Mercury. Then Jupiter, the king planet, moved into conjunction with Regulus, the king star, on September 7, 3 B.C. and remained in conjunction with Regulus with a separation of less than 1 degree until September 17, 3 B.C.(See Figure 3.2).   Jupiter moved into conjunction with Regulus again on February 13, 2 B.C. and remained in conjunction with a separation of less than one degree until February 20, 2 B.C. Finally Jupiter moved into conjunction with Regulus for a third time on April 30, 2 B.C. and remained in conjunction with a separation of less than one degree until May 11, 2 B.C.

In Genesis 49:8-9 Jacob speaking prophetically says:

> "Judah, your brothers shall praise you; your hand shall be on the neck of your enemies; your father's sons shall bow down to you. Judah is a lion's whelp; from the prey, my son, you have gone up. He couches, he lies down as a lion, and as a lion, who dares rouse him up? The scepter shall not depart from Judah, nor the ruler's staff from between his feet, until Shiloh comes, and to him shall be the obedience of the peoples."

The king star, Regulus, is part of the constellation Leo, the lion, and Regulus is located in the area of the two front feet of Leo. Shiloh is a Hebrew word meaning "to whom it belongs." David, of the tribe

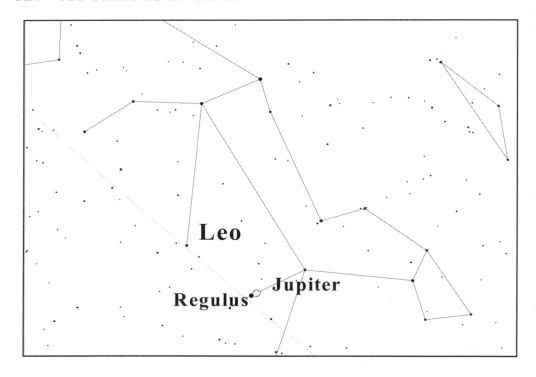

Conjunction Between
Jupiter and Regulus
Figure 3.2

of Judah, became king in fulfilment of this prophecy and a descendent of Judah ruled until the time of Herod I who was an Idumean. The scepter departed Judah when Herod I became king and it was during Herod I's reign that Jesus was born and Shiloh came!

Next comes the most spectacular event in this heavenly display. On June 16, 2 B.C.(Gregorian), Jupiter and Venus again came into conjunction and at their closest approach would have a separation of only one half minute of arc which to the naked eye would make the two planets appear as a single brilliant star of a magnitude of - 4.4. This would be the most spectacular planetary conjunction visible in the Near East between 12 B.C. and A.D. 7 (Sinnoth, *Computing the Star of Bethlehem,* Sky and Telescope,

December 1986). Again this conjunction took place in Leo the Lion (see Figure 3.3). And if this was not enough to convince the magi that the long awaited King of the Jews had come, on August 25, 2 B.C. (Gregorian), there occurred a massing of four of the five planets visible to the naked eye: Jupiter, Venus, Mars and Mercury with Jupiter and Mars in close conjunction in the constellation Leo. But even after the magi were convinced that the King had been born, it would take time to make the journey to Jerusalem. If the magi came from Babylon, they would have had to travel about 900 miles. When Ezra, who was sent by King Artaxerxes, traveled from Babylon to Jerusalem, the trip took him four months. If the magi came from Persia, the distance would be even greater.

But what was the Star of Bethlehem that led the magi? Some have suggested that the Star of Bethlehem was a miraculous phenomenon such as the Shekinah Light that accompanied the children of Israel during the Exodus. Such a light could have certainly stood over the house where the Christ Child was, but why wasn't it seen by anyone but the magi? The Shekinah Light was seen by everyone and there was no doubt among the people that something special was going on. Since the Star of Bethlehem seems to have been only seen by the professional astronomers, the magi, it would be more likely that the Star of Bethlehem was an unusual astronomical phenomenon which would be noticed by the magi, but not noticed by anyone else. The one object which was involved in almost all the spectacular conjunctions preceding the birth of Christ was the planet Jupiter. In the latter part of 2 B.C., Jupiter would have been seen in the eastern skies, starting as a morning star, and moving further westward each morning leading the magi to Jerusalem and Bethlehem. After the magi talked to Herod, Matthew 2:9-10 says:

> After hearing the king, they went their way; and the star, which they had seen in the east, went on before them

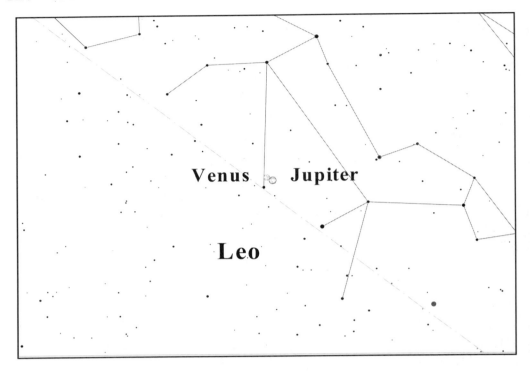

Conjunction of Jupiter and Venus
June 16, 2 B.C. (Gregorian)
Figure 3.3

until it came and stood over the place where the Child
was. When they saw the star, they rejoiced exceedingly
with great joy.

On the morning of December 23, 2 B.C. (Gregorian) or December 25,
2 B.C. (Julian), an observer in Jerusalem would see Jupiter located
right over Bethlehem (see Figure 3.4). When the magi saw this, they
rejoiced because it seemed to confirm what Herod had told them, that
the new King would be born in Bethlehem. And where was the
planet Jupiter? It was with the Virgin, in the constellation Virgo.
Since Matthew 2:11 uses the Greek word Paidion, which is translated
Child, for Jesus when the magi came, while Luke 2:16 uses the Greek

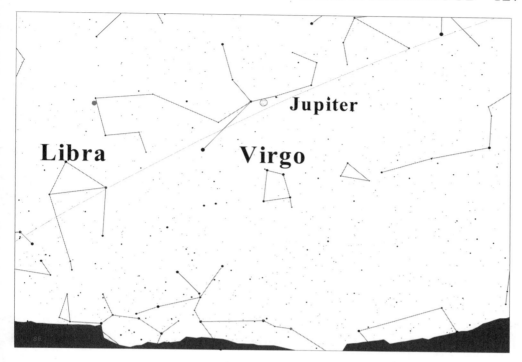

Jupiter Standing Over
Bethlehem
Looking South from Jerusalem
Figure 3.4

word Brephos, which is translated baby, for Jesus when the shepherds came, some have concluded that Jesus was a year or more old when the magi came. However, Luke 1:59 uses the same Greek word paidion, which is translated child, for John the Baptist when he was circumcised, one week after his birth. Therefore Jesus was probably about two months old when the magi came, "after Jesus was born in Bethlehem". These spectacular astronomical events of 3 and 2 B.C. do seem to support 2 B.C. as being the correct year for Jesus' birth. The fact that astronomical signs probably played an important role in bringing the magi to Bethlehem should not be taken as support for the use of astrology in predicting human affairs.   Astrology is condemned in the Bible and is a misuse of God's heavenly signs.

Many other explanations have been proposed for the Star of Bethlehem.   For example, in 1606 the great astronomer Kepler suggested that the star of Bethlehem was associated with the conjunctions of the planets Jupiter and Saturn that occurred in 6 and 7 B.C. The closest approach of the planets in these conjunctions was only one degree while the conjunction of June 17, 2 B.C. of Jupiter and Venus had a separation of only one half of one minute of arc and thus was more than 100 times closer.   Why were Kepler and many others led to believe that these less spectacular conjunctions were associated with the Star of Bethlehem?   The main reason that many scholars have placed the birth of Jesus earlier than 2 B.C. is because Josephus, the Jewish historian, placed the death of Herod I in 4 B.C., and since the New Testament indicates that Herod I was alive at the time of Jesus' birth, they conclude that Jesus could not have been born earlier than 4 B.C.

In *Antiquities* 17.8.1, page 464, Josephus states that when Herod I died, he had reigned 34 years since he had caused Antigonus to be slain and 37 years since he was declared king by the Romans. In Antiquities 14.16.4, page 396, Josephus indicates that Jerusalem fell and Antigonus was captured when Marcus Agrippa and Caninius Gallius were consuls of Rome, which corresponds to the year 37 B.C. (See Table 2.2). If 37 B.C. was year 1 of Herod I reign, then 4 B.C. would be year 34. *Antiquities* 14.14.5, page 391, indicates that Herod was made king by the Romans when Caius Domithis Colvinus was consul for the second time and Caius Asinius Pollio (the first time) or 40 B.C. If 40 B.C. was year 1 of the reign of Herod I from his being made king by the Romans, then again year 37 would correspond to 4 B.C. However, as we have seen, this date for the death of Herod I is in conflict with the date for the birth of Jesus and John the Baptist indicated by the New Testament.

However, Josephus does give other information concerning the death of Herod I which may prove to be more reliable. In *Antiquities*, 17.6.4, page 462, Josephus says:

> But Herod deprived Matthias of the high priesthood, and burnt the other Matthias, who had raised the sedition, with his companions, alive. And that very night there was an eclipse of the moon.

This event occurred shortly before the death of Herod I. Table 3.5 indicates all the lunar eclipses, visible in Judea, that occurred from 8 B.C. through 1 B.C.

Many scholars have thought that the eclipse of March 11, 4 B.C. (Gregorian) was the eclipse associated with the death of Herod I; however, as pointed out by Ernest Martin in *The Birth of Christ Recalculated,* there was not enough time between that eclipse of the moon and the next Jewish Passover Feast to accommodate all the events Josephus indicated took place during this period. After Herod executed the Jewish priests, his condition worsened and he sent for physicians and underwent a number of treatments, including a trip to Callirhoe, which was some twenty-five miles from Jericho, to bathe in the warm springs there. After several treatments, Herod returned to Jericho. This travel and treatment probably took several weeks to complete. Then, convinced that his death was near, Herod devised a plan so that the nation would mourn when he died. Herod commanded that all the principal men of the Jewish nation should come to him, under penalty of death it they did not obey. He had all these men shut up in the hippodrome and told his sister, Salome, and her husband to order the death of these principal men in his name as soon as he died. Fortunately, Salome and her husband did not carry out Herod's plan. However, sending messengers throughout the nation and allowing time for the arrival of these principal men would

| | | | Date of Next | |
Year	Date of Eclipse (Gregorian)	Type of Eclipse	Passover (Gregorian)	Days Between
8 BC	November 16	partial	April 12, 7BC	147
7 BC	no eclipse			
6 BC	no eclipse			
5 BC	March 21	total	April 19, 5BC	29
5 BC	September 13/14	total	April 9, 4BC	208
4 BC	March 11	partial	April 9, 4BC	29
3 BC	no eclipse			
2 BC	no eclipse			
1 BC	January 7/8	total	April 6, 1BC	90
1 BC	December 27	partial	March 26, AD.	89

Table 3.5
Lunar Eclipses Visible in Judea
8 B.C. through 1 B.C.

have taken several weeks. Also, prior to his death, Herod received permission from Augustus Caesar to punish Antipater, Herod's son, with death if he so desired. Shortly thereafter Herod had his son executed. Herod then drew up a new will and then five days after he had executed his son, Herod I died.

Arrangements were then made for a large state funeral for Herod which took considerable preparation and the funeral itself probably occupied several days since the body was buried in the Herodium, which was a fortress about twenty miles from Jericho and the body may have been carried there by dignitaries on foot. After the funeral and after a seven-day mourning period, Archelaus, another of Herod I's sons, took control of Herod's palace in Jerusalem, but did not assume the title of king without Augustus Caesar's approval. However, rioting broke out and finally Archelaus sent his whole army to suppress it. As a result thousands of Jews were killed and the Passover Feast was suspended. Thus the events that occurred between the eclipse prior to the death of Herod I and the next Passover Feast appear to require a period of about three months rather than the twenty-nine days available between the eclipse of March 11, 4 B.C. and the next Passover Feast. On the other hand, the ninety days from the eclipse of the moon on January 7/8, 1 B.C. until the next Passover Feast fits the events nicely.

Another fact that would make it unlikely that the eclipse of March 11, 4 B.C. would be the eclipse of the moon associated with Herod's execution of the Jewish priests shortly before his death is revealed by the calendars of Appendix D. The daylight hours of March 11, 4 B.C. fell on the Jewish day of Adar 15. Esther 9:20-22 says:

> Then Mordecai recorded these events, and he sent letters to all the Jews who were in all the provinces of King Ahasuerus, both near and far, obliging them to celebrate the fourteenth day of the month Adar, and the fifteenth day of the same month, annually, because on those days the Jews rid themselves of their enemies, and it was a month which was turned for them from sorrow into gladness and from mourning into a holiday; that they should make them days of feasting and rejoicing and sending portions of food to one another and gifts to the poor.

Adar 15 was the last day of the Jewish festival of Purim which is not mentioned in the New Testament, but was celebrated by the Jews in

New Testament times (see Josephus, *Antiquities*, 10.6.16, page 306). It seems unlikely that Herod, a foreign ruler, would have chosen a festival day when the Jews were celebrating their deliverance from Haman, a foreign ruler, to execute a group of popular Jewish priests.

There is one final area of evidence that bears on the question of the year of Herod I's death. Many of the coins issued in the Holy Land during this period were dated and thus may indicate when Herod I died. Most of the coins of Herod I were not dated and they offer no clue as to the year of his death. However, most of the coin of his sons, Antipas and Philip were dated and they seem to indicate that they began their rule in 4 B.C. which may be the basis of Josephus' dating of Herod's death. However, the earliest of these coins which has been found was dated year 5 which would correspond to A.D. 1. Why would a new ruler, anxious to establish his authority, wait five years to start issuing his coins?

Archelaus issued coin, but none of his coins were dated. However Archelaus rule was a short one and, in *The Wars of the Jews*, 2.7.3, page 604, Josephus says:

> And now Archelaus took possession of his ethnarchy, and used not the Jews only, but the Samaritans also, barbarously; and this out of his resentment of their old quarrels with him. Whereupon they both sent ambassadors against him to Caesar; and in the ninth year of his government he was banished to Vienna, a city of Gaul.

Archelaus was replaced by the Roman governor Coponius and Coponius issued coins, the earliest of which was dated year 36 of Augustus (see Figure 3.5). But what regnal years for Augustus was Coponius using? Most numismatists assume that Coponius was using the Alexandrian regnal dates so that the dating of these coins would agree with Josephus' dating of the death of Herod I. However, why would a Roman governor of Judea use the Alexandrian regnal

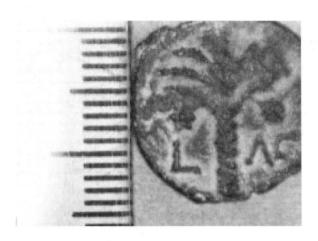

Judean Coin Issued Under the Roman Governor Coponius
(Dated Year 36 of Augustus)
Figure 3.5

years which is based on the year Augustus captured Alexandra? It would seem more appropriate to base Augustus' regnal years on the year he was given supreme power over the empire and received the title of Augustus. This occurred on February 15, 27 B.C. (Julian). Table 3.6 shows the regnal years of Augustus with year 1 equal to 27 B.C. Using these regnal years, the 36th year of Augustus would be A.D. 9. If Herod I died early in 1 B.C., that would be Archelaus' first year of reign and A.D. 8 would be his ninth year of reign when he was deposed by Augustus. This would fit well with Coponius issuing coins in Judea in A.D. 9. This dating of the coins of the Roman governors of Judea is also supported by the fact that the last coin issued by the Roman governors under Augustus was dated year 41,

			Table 3.6		
		Years of Reign of Augustus Caesar			
		With the Year He received the Title Augustus Being Year 1			

Year of Reign	Julian Calendar Year	Year of Reign	Julian Calendar Year	Year of Reign	Julian Calendar Year
1	27 BC	15	13 BC	29	AD 2
2	26 BC	16	12 BC	30	AD 3
3	25 BC	17	11 BC	31	AD 4
4	24 BC	18	10 BC	32	AD 5
5	23 BC	19	9 BC	33	AD 6
6	22 BC	20	8 BC	34	AD 7
7	21 BC	21	7 BC	35	AD 8
8	20 BC	22	6 BC	36	AD 9
9	19 BC	23	5 BC	37	AD 10
10	18 BC	24	4 BC	38	AD 11
11	17 BC	25	3 BC	39	AD 12
12	16 BC	26	2 BC	40	AD 13
13	15 BC	27	1 BC	41	AD 14
14	14 BC	28	AD 1		

which according to Table 3.6 corresponds to the year A.D. 14. Augustus Caesar died on August 19, A.D. 14 (Julian).

Although the evidence of the coins is not completely clear, they too seem to support the eclipse of January 7, 1 B.C. (Gregorian) being the eclipse of the moon that occurred shortly before the death of Herod I. However, the most important reason that the eclipse of

4 B.C. could not have been the eclipse of the moon shortly before the death of Herod I, is that the information given in the Gospels indicates that Jesus was born in 2 B.C. and that Herod I died after the birth of Jesus.

Thus we have established the date of birth of Jesus as September 27, 2 B.C.(Gregorian) according to our calendar and Tishri 1, the Day of Trumpets, according to the Jewish calendar. The date of birth of John the Baptist was found to be April 17, 2 B.C. according to our calendar and Nisan 14 according to the Jewish calendar. Although there is a considerable amount of evidence supporting these dates, they cannot be considered as certain as the dates for Jesus' crucifixion and resurrection and therefore they have been assigned a Level of Confidence of II. We shall now proceed to date the other events associated with Jesus' birth and childhood.

Other Events

In the sixth month of Elizabeth's pregnancy, the angel Gabriel visited Mary to announce the coming birth of Jesus (Luke 11:26-38) This was also probably the date of the conception of Jesus because the angel said to Mary, "Your relative Elizabeth has also conceived." If Jesus was born on September 27, 2 B.C., forty weeks prior to that date would be December 21, 3 B.C. (Gregorian) which would be the date of the conception of Jesus and the Annunciation to Mary. December 21 is the exact date of the winter solstice, the date the sun comes forth in the sense that from that date onward the hours of daylight increase each day until the summer solstice. We would expect the birth of Jesus to be without complications so that the time from conception to birth would be 40 weeks. If the conception of John the Baptist occurred on July 11, 3 B.C. or on the 1st day of the

5th Jewish month (see calendar of Appendix D) and the Annunciation occurred on December 21, 3 B.C. or on the 16th day of the 10th Jewish month, then at the time of the Annunciation, Elizabeth would have been pregnant for five months and sixteen days according to the Jewish calendar and therefore would indeed be in her sixth month in accordance with the words of the angel Gabriel (Luke 1:36).

Then Luke 1:39,40 says, " Now at this time Mary arose and went with haste to the hill country, to a city of Judah, and entered the house of Zacharias and greeted Elizabeth." Mary would have probably left Nazareth the next Sunday, December 27, 3 B.C. to visit Elizabeth. As a devout Jew, Mary would have probably wanted to leave on a Sunday to avoid spending the Sabbath on the road. The journey would have taken about six days, so Mary would have arrived about January 1, A.D. 2 B.C. which would be the date of the "Magnificat" (Luke 1:46-56). Mary stayed with Elizabeth about three months and then returned to her home (Luke 1:56). Three Jewish months from January 1, 2 B.C. would be March 31, 2 B.C., so Mary probably left on Sunday, April 4, 2 B.C. before the Passover Feast and before the birth of John the Baptist. This is suggested by the fact that in Luke's Gospel, Mary's departure (Luke 1:56) proceeds the birth of John the Baptist (Luke 1:57). Since John the Baptist's mission was to prepare the way for the Christ, it seems more appropriate that he be born before sunset on April 17, 2 B.C. or on the Jewish day Nisan 14, the Day of Preparation for the Passover Feast. Then eight days later, counting inclusively, on Saturday, April 24, 2 B.C. John the Baptist was circumcised. At that time John the Baptist received his name and Zacharias was again able to speak and Zacharias gave the "Benedictus" (Luke 1:57-79).

It was probably on Mary's return to Nazareth that she was found to be with child (Matthew 1:18). If Mary departed from the home of Zacharias on April 4, 2 B.C., then she would have arrived at Nazareth about six days later on Friday, April 9, 2 B.C. When Joseph found out that Mary was pregnant, he planned to put her away secretly. However, probably on Sunday, April 11, 2 B.C. Matthew 1:20 says:

> But when he had considered this, behold, an angel of the Lord appeared to him in a dream, saying, "Joseph, son of David, do not be afraid to take Mary as your wife; for the Child who has been conceived in her is of the Holy Spirit.

Then Joseph took Mary as his wife.

Later Joseph and Mary left Nazareth and went to Bethlehem to register for a census while Quirinius was governor of Syria (Luke 2:1-5). They probably left Nazareth about Sunday, September, 19, 2 B.C. and arrived in Bethlehem about Friday, September 24. The only housing they could find was in a stable. Then in the evening of Monday, September 27, 2 B.C. (Gregorian) Luke 2:7 says:

> And she gave birth to her firstborn son; and she wrapped Him in cloths, and laid Him in a manger, because there was no room for them in the inn.

At sunset on September 27, 2 B.C. was the beginning of Tishri 1 on the Jewish calendar which was the Day of Trumpets. That very night angels appeared to shepherds in the region and Luke 2:10-14 says:

> But the angel said to them, "Do not be afraid; for behold, I bring you good news of great joy which will be for all the people; for today in the city of David there has been born for you a Savior, who is Christ the Lord. "This will be a sign for you: you will find a baby wrapped in cloths and lying in a manger." And

suddenly there appeared with the angel a multitude of the heavenly host praising God and saying, "Glory to God in the highest, And on earth peace among men with whom He is pleased."

Eight days later, on Tuesday, October 5, 2 B.C., Jesus was circumcised and received His name, Jesus (Hebrew Yeshua), which means "Yahweh saves." This was in accordance with the instructions of the angel Gabriel. Next Luke 2:22 says, " And when the days for their purification according to the law of Moses were completed, they brought Him up to Jerusalem to present Him to the Lord." Leviticus 12:2-4 requires when a women bore a male child, she would be considered unclean for forty days and would then be purified. Forty days after the birth of Jesus, counting inclusively, would be Marheshvan 10 and the daylight hours of that Jewish day would be on Saturday, November 6, 2 B.C. Luke 2:24 indicates that the purification offering was a pair of turtledoves or two young pigeons. Leviticus 12:8 say, "But if she cannot afford a lamb, then she shall take two turtledoves or two young pigeons, the one for a burnt offering and the other for a sin offering; and the priest shall make atonement for her, and she will be clean." The fact that Mary and Joseph could not afford the regular offering suggests that they were of modest financial means. On the same day, November 6, 2 B.C., two witnesses, Simeon and Anna, gave testimony that Jesus was the promised Messiah. All these events took place on the Temple Mount.

Then Luke 2:39 says, " When they had performed everything according to the Law of the Lord, they returned to Galilee, to their own city of Nazareth." At this point Luke is speaking in general terms and covers the next twelve years of Jesus' life in two verses; however, Matthew gives us further details concerning the first few months of Jesus' earthly life. As we have seen, probably on about December 24 (Julian), or December 22 (Gregorian), the magi arrived at Jerusalem saying, "Where is He who is born King of the Jews?" Herod I sent the magi to Bethlehem. The next morning, December 25 (Julian), while observing the skies from Jerusalem, the magi saw the planet Jupiter standing directly over Bethlehem which seemed to confirm Herod's direction and they rejoiced exceedingly. That day they brought their gifts to the Christ Child and then departed for their own country by another way, having been warned by God in a dream not to return to Herod. That night Joseph was also warned in a dream by an angel and arose probably after midnight on December 24, 2 B.C.(Gregorian) and took Jesus and Mary and departed for Egypt to await Herod I's death. Herod would have probably expected the magi to return to him on Sunday, December 24 (Gregorian), and when they did not return by Monday, December 25 (Gregorian), he knew they had tricked him; therefore, that day he sent his troops to slaughter the male children of Bethlehem.

The events recorded in Josephus indicate that Herod I probably died about six weeks after the eclipse of the moon of January 7 and 8, 1 B.C. or about February 11, 1 B.C.(Gregorian) Then Matthew 2:19-23 says:

> But when Herod died, behold, an angel of the Lord appeared in a dream to Joseph in Egypt, and said, "Get up, take the Child and His mother, and go into the land of Israel; for those who sought the Child's life are dead." So Joseph got up, took the Child and His mother, and came into the land of Israel. But when he heard that Archelaus was reigning over Judea in place of his father Herod, he was afraid to go there. Then after being warned by God in a dream, he left for the regions of Galilee,(Matthew 2:23) and came and lived in a city called Nazareth. This was to fulfill what was spoken through the prophets: "He shall be called a Nazarene."

Thus Joseph, Mary and Jesus probably departed Egypt about Sunday, February 13, 1 B.C. and the return journey to Jerusalem would probably take about three weeks. This would bring them very close to the time of the Passover Feast which was to be celebrated that year on April 6th. Normally they would have gone to Jerusalem to attend the Passover Feast; however, having been warned in a dream by God, Joseph apparently went directly to Galilee without stopping in Jerusalem. Josephus tell us that this first Passover after the death of Herod I was the Passover Feast when rioting broke out and Archelaus sent his army against the people and killed 3,000 people and the Passover Feast was canceled (*Antiquities* 17.9, page 465). Thus God warned Joseph to avoid exposing his family to the dangers of the Passover of 1 B.C.

The last event mentioned in the New Testament concerning this early period of Jesus' life was His visit to Jerusalem with his parents to attend the Passover Feast when he was twelve years old (Luke 2:41-51). Jesus would have celebrated His twelfth birthday on Tishri 1, A.D. 11 from sunset Thursday, September 15, to sunset Friday, September 16. The next Passover Feast would be celebrated on March 24, A.D. 12. This feast would have ended at sunset on Saturday, March 31. Thus Joseph and Mary would have probably left Jerusalem on Sunday, April 1, A.D. 12. They did not discover that Jesus was missing until that evening. It would take another day to return to Jerusalem, so Mary and Joseph would have arrived back in Jerusalem Monday evening, April 2. They did not find Jesus in the Temple with the teachers until the third day, Tuesday, April 3, 12 A.D.

Thus we have been able to date all the events recorded in the New Testament concerning Jesus' birth and early childhood, and again we see the marvelous hand of God ordering the events in the life of His Son, Jesus.

Table 3.7
Jesus' Birth and Childhood

Event Sequence Number	Event (Scripture Reference)	Location of Event	Gregorian Date	Level * of Confidence
1	The Word Was With God (John 1:1-5)	Heaven	In The Beginning	I
2	Genealogy Of Jesus The Christ (Matthew 1:1-17) (Luke 3:23b-38)	Asia Minor	The Beginning To 2 B.C.	I
3	Angel Appears To Zacharias (Luke 1:5-22)	Jerusalem	Wednesday July 8 3 B.C.	II
4	Conception Of John The Baptist (Luke 1:23-25)	Hill Country of Judea	Saturday July 11 3 B.C.	II
5	Angel Visits Mary (Luke 1:26-38)	Nazareth, Galilee	Monday Dec 21 3 B.C.	II
6	Conception Of Jesus (Luke 1:36)	Nazareth, Galilee	Monday Dec 21 3 B.C.	II
7	Mary Departs To Visit Elizabeth (Luke 1:39)	Nazareth, Galilee	Sunday Dec 27 3 B.C.	II
8	Mary Greets Elizabeth (Luke 1:40-55)	Hill Country of Judea	Friday Jan 1 3 B.C.	II

* Level of Confidence in Date   Level I = Highly Probable   Level II = Probable

Event Sequence Number	Event (Scripture Reference)	Location of Event	Gregorian Date	Level* of Confidence
9	Mary Departs for Nazareth (Luke 1:56)	Hill Country of Judea	Sunday Mar 28 2 B.C.	II
10	Mary Found To Be With Child (Matthew 1:18)	Nazareth, Galilee	Friday April 9 2 B.C.	II
11	Angel Appears To Joseph (Matthew 1:19-25)	Nazareth, Galilee	Sunday April 11 2 B.C.	II
12	Birth of John The Baptist (Luke 1:57,58)	Hill Country of Judea	Saturday April 17 2 B.C.	II
13	John The Baptist Circumcised (Luke 1:59-79)	Hill Country of Judea	Saturday April 24 2 B.C.	II
13a	John Grows Up in Desert (Luke 1:80)	Judea	2 BC to AD 29	II
14	Birth of Jesus (Luke 2:1-7)	Bethle-hem	Monday Sept 27 2 B.C.	II
15	Angels Appear To Shepherds (Luke 2:8-20)	Bethle-hem	Monday Sept 27 2 B.C.	II
16	Jesus Circumcised (Luke 2:21)	Bethle-hem	Tuesday Oct 5 2 B.C.	II
17	Jesus Presented At The Temple (Luke 2:22-38)	Jerusalem	Saturday Nov 6 2 B.C.	II

* Level of Confidence in Date   Level I = Highly Probable   Level II = Probable

Event Sequence Number	Event (Scripture Reference)	Location of Event	Gregorian Date	Level* of Confidence
18	Magi Arrive In Jerusalem (Matthew 2:1-8)	Jerusalem	Friday Dec 22 2 B.C.	II
19	Magi Worship Jesus (Matthew 2:9-11)	Bethle-hem	Saturday Dec 23 2 B.C.	II
20	Magi Depart By Another Way (Matthew 2:12)	Bethle-hem	Sunday Dec 24 2 B.C.	II
21	Jesus' Family Flees To Egypt (Matthew 2:13-15)	Bethle-hem	Sunday Dec 24 2 B.C.	II
22	Herod I Has Babies Slaughtered (Matthew 2:16-18)	Bethle-hem	Monday Dec 25 2 B.C.	II
23	Angel Tells Joseph of Herod I's Death (Matthew 2:19-20)	Egypt	Friday Feb 18 1 B.C.	II
24	Jesus & Family Depart For Nazareth (Matthew 2:21-23, Luke 2:39)	Egypt	Sunday Feb 20 1 B.C.	II
25	Jesus Grows Up (Luke 2:40)	Nazareth	1 B.C.- A.D. 12	II
26	Jesus Left In Jerusalem (Luke 2:41-44)	Jerusalem	Sunday April 1 A.D. 12	II
27	Joseph & Mary Return For Jesus (Luke 2:45)	Judea	Monday April 2 A.D. 12	II

* Level of Confidence in Date   Level I = Highly Probable   Level II = Probable

Event Sequence Number	Event (Scripture Reference)	Location of Event	Gregorian Date	Level* of Confidence
28	Jesus Found In Temple (Luke 2:46-50)	Jerusalem	Tuesday April 3 A.D. 12	II
29	Jesus Increases In Wisdom & Stature (Luke 2:51,52)	Nazareth	A.D. 12- A.D. 30	II

* Level of Confidence in Date   Level I = Highly Probable   Level II = Probable

4

Jesus' First Year of Ministry

Luke 3:23a says, "And when He began His ministry, Jesus Himself was about thirty years of age." This verse was discussed in Chapter 3 and it was concluded that both Jesus and John the Baptist had probably reached their thirtieth birthday before they began their ministry because that was considered the age of full maturity in Bible times. It was the age at which men entered the Levitical priesthood and it was also the age when a number of Old Testament personages began their work. John the Baptist probably received his call on or near his thirtieth birthday in the fifteenth year of Tiberius Caesar (Luke 3:1), which in chapter 3 was shown to probably be the Day of Preparation for the Passover. Thus John the Baptist would have received his call about Nisan 14, A.D. 29 or about April 15, A.D. 29 (Gregorian). This would be a particularly good time for John the Baptist to begin his ministry in the districts of the Jordan because large numbers of Jewish pilgrims would soon be returning home through the Jordan River Valley after attending the Passover Feast in Jerusalem. In A.D. 29 the Passover Feast ended on Sunday, April 22.

Jesus Begins His Ministry

Jesus' thirtieth birthday would have been on Tishri 1, the Day of Trumpets, in A.D. 29.   This Jewish day would have begun at sunset on September 25 according to our Gregorian calendar. However, apparently to allow time for John the Baptist to carry out his preparatory ministry, in chapter 3 we found that Jesus may have began His ministry nearer His thirty-first birthday beginning on September 15, A. D. 30. The first clearly dated event during Jesus' earthly ministry is the celebration of the Passover Feast recorded in John 2:13 in A. D. 31. In order to obtain an indication of the date that Jesus began His ministry with His baptism by John, we must work backward from the known date of this first Passover Feast. Table 4.1 summarizes the events prior to this Passover Feast as recorded in the Gospel of John. The other Gospels do not discuss this period of Jesus' ministry except for mentioning Jesus' baptism by John.

Jesus would have probably arrived in Jerusalem about two weeks prior to the beginning of the Passover Feast. This is indicated by the fact that when Jesus arrived just six days before the Passover Feast, John 11:55-56 says:

> Now the Passover of the Jews was near, and many went
> up to Jerusalem out of the country before the Passover
> to purify themselves. So they were seeking for Jesus,
> and were saying to one another as they stood in the
> temple, "What do you think; that He will not come to the
> feast at all?"

Thus the many who went up to Jerusalem for the Passover Feast had arrived more than six days before the feast and they expected Jesus to be there. The Gregorian date of the Passover Feast of A.D. 31, the first during Jesus' earthly ministry, was March 25. Therefore, Jesus

Table 4.1 Events Prior To The First Passover Feast Recorded in the Gospel of John	
Events	**Scripture**
John the Baptist Witnesses To The Priests and Levites	John 1:19,20
John the Baptist Witnesses That Jesus Is The Son of God	John 1:29-34
Andrew and Another Disciple Follow Jesus	John 1:35-39
Andrew Calls Simon Peter	John 1:40-42
Jesus Calls Philip	John 1:43,44
Philip Calls Nathanael	John 1:45-51
Wedding of Cana	John 2:1-11
Jesus Departs to Capernaum	John 2:12
Jesus Departs to Jerusalem	John 2:13
Jesus Cleanses the Temple	John 2:14-17
Jews Ask For A Sign	John 2:18-22
Jesus in Jerusalem for the Passover Feast	John 2:23-25

would have probably departed Capernaum for Jerusalem about Sunday March 9, A.D. 31. If Jesus took the usual route of Jewish pilgrims from Galilee to Jerusalem, He would have followed the main north south route through Galilee going east of Mount Tabor and, about five miles south of Nain, He would have turned east through the Harod Valley, passing by Beth Shan. When Jesus reached the Jordan River Valley, He would turn south until He reached the road to Jericho. Then He would have turned west and would have gone on to Jerusalem (see Figure 4.1). The distance would have been about 125 miles and traveling twenty-five miles per day, the journey would

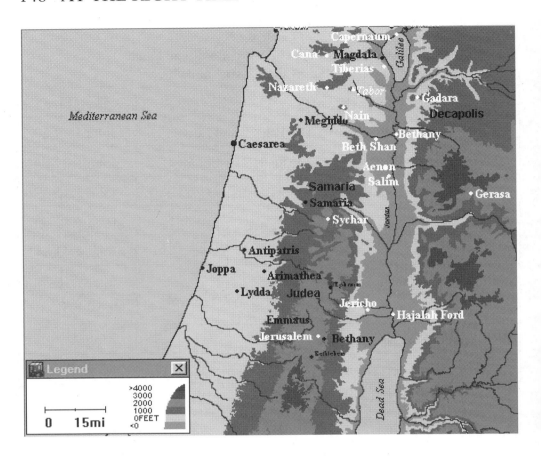

Journey From Capernaum To Jerusalem
Figure 4.1

have taken about five days. The direct route through Samaria would have been about 110 miles and might have only taken four days.

If Jesus took the longer route through the Jordan River Valley and arrived in Jerusalem on Thursday, March 13, A.D. 31, the next day would be the Day of Preparation for the Sabbath. Jesus went to the Temple that day and John 2:14-16 says:

> And He found in the temple those who were selling oxen and sheep and doves, and the money changers seated at

their tables. And He made a scourge of cords, and drove them all out of the temple, with the sheep and the oxen; and He poured out the coins of the money changers and overturned their tables; and to those who were selling the doves He said, "Take these things away; stop making My Father's house a place of business."

Thus, on Friday, March 14, A.D. 31, Jesus first cleansed the Temple. Following Jesus' cleansing of the Temple, John 2:18-22 says:

> The Jews then said to Him, "What sign do You show us as your authority for doing these things?" Jesus answered them, "Destroy this temple, and in three days I will raise it up." The Jews then said, "It took forty-six years to build this temple, and will You raise it up in three days?" But He was speaking of the temple of His body. So when He was raised from the dead, His disciples remembered that He said this; and they believed the Scripture and the word which Jesus had spoken.

Some have taken this statement of the Jews that it took forty-six years to build this temple as a means of dating this incident. Josephus in *Antiquities*, 15.11.1, page 423, indicates that Herod I began work on rebuilding the Temple in the eighteenth year of his reign or in 20 B.C. Forty-six years from 20 B.C., counting inclusively, would be A.D. 26. Thus the current phase of the building program on the Temple had been completed five years prior to this incident. The Jews said that it had taken forty-six years to build the Temple, but this statement does not necessarily mean that they had just completed the work. Actually, the construction of the Temple continued almost to the time of its destruction in A.D. 70. However, this construction was carried out under several different administrations and therefore was probably carried out in a number of separate building projects.

Prior to Jesus' departure to Jerusalem, John 2:12 says, "After this He went down to Capernaum, He and His mother, and His brothers and His disciples; and there they stayed for a few days." This would have been the last few days of February and the first week of March. It was probably at this time that Jesus moved with His family to Capernaum. Matthew 4:13 says, "And leaving Nazareth, He came and settled in Capernaum, which is by the sea, in the region of Zebulun and Naphtali."

Wedding At Cana

Prior to going to Capernaum, John 2:1-3 says:

> On the third day there was a wedding in Cana of Galilee, and the mother of Jesus was there; and both Jesus and His disciples were invited to the wedding. When the wine ran out, the mother of Jesus said to Him, "They have no wine."

According to the Mishnah, Tractate Ketuboth (Marriage Deeds), 1.1, page 245, a virgin should be married on a Wednesday and a widow on a Thursday. Since more virgins were married than widows, the wedding of Cana probably took place on a Wednesday. Allowing two weeks for the few days' stay in Capernaum (John 2:12) and travel time, the wedding at Cana probably started on Wednesday, February 19, A.D. 31. Some commentators have pointed out that wedding feasts might last as long as a week, so it is possible that this wedding feast started a week earlier. However, in view of the modest means of the bridegroom, since the wine ran out, a one or two-day feast seems more likely.

Witness of John the Baptist

Prior to the wedding at Cana, John indicated that Jesus was at Bethany beyond the Jordan where Jesus had been baptized by John the Baptist (John 1:28). The traditional site for Bethany beyond the Jordan is the Hajalah Ford of the Jordan River, just north of the Dead Sea (see Figure 4.1). However, since John 2:1 indicates that the wedding of Cana took place on the third day from Jesus' departure from Bethany beyond the Jordan, this Bethany is probably located on the east bank of the Jordan River near the Sea of Galilee (see Figure 4.1). The wedding at Cana was on the third day and this day was Wednesday, February 19, A.D. 31. Then, counting inclusively, Jesus and His disciples departed Bethany beyond the Jordan on Monday, February 17, A.D. 31. On the day of His departure, Jesus called Philip and Philip called Nathanael (John 1:43-45). It was only about twenty-five miles to Nazareth; however, Jesus and His disciples probably got a late start since time was taken to call Philip and Nathanael. Therefore, they probably didn't arrive in Nazareth until Tuesday, February 18. After Jesus and His disciples arrived in Nazareth, they probably found out about the wedding and at that time Jesus and His disciples were invited. John 2:1-2 says, "On the third day there was a wedding in Cana of Galilee, and the mother of Jesus was there; and both Jesus and His disciples were invited to the wedding." Since prior to their encounter in Bethany beyond the Jordan, His disciples did not seem to know Him, it seems unlikely that they all had been previously invited to the same wedding.

The day prior to Jesus' departure from Bethany beyond the Jordan, Andrew and another disciple, probably John the Apostle, followed Jesus and spent the day with Him. This would have been Sunday, February 16. Probably the same Gregorian day, after sunset, Andrew called His brother, Simon Peter. The day prior to that, Saturday, February 15, John the Baptist bore witness that Jesus was the Son of God. On the day prior to that, February 14, the priests and Levities arrived to question John the Baptist and he confessed, "I am not the Christ." The fact that the priest and Levities arrived on a Friday, confirms that the Wedding of Cana was indeed for a virgin on a Wednesday because if it had been for a widow on a Thursday, then the priests and Levities would have arrived on a Saturday which is highly unlikely because of the Sabbath travel restrictions of Judaism. All these events are listed in Figure 4.2 together with their dates of occurrence in terms of both the Gregorian calendar and the Jewish calendar.

	midnight	midnight	midnight	midnight
Gregorian Calendar	Friday February 14 John's Witness To Priests & Levites	Saturday February 15 John's Witness That Jesus Is The Son of God	Sunday February 16 Andrew & Another Disciple Follow Jesus	Monday February 17 Jesus Calls Philip & Philip Calls Nathanael
Jewish Calendar	6th Day Adar 5	7th Day Adar 6	1st Day Adar 7	2nd Day Adar 8
	sunset	sunset	sunset	sunset

Jesus At Bethany Beyond the Jordan
(John 1:19-51)
Figure 4.2

Baptism of Jesus

Thus Jesus' first appearance in the Gospel of John is on Saturday, February 15, A.D. 31 (Gregorian). On seeing Jesus, John

1:32 says, " John testified saying, 'I have seen the Spirit descending as a dove out of heaven, and He remained upon Him.'" John was referring to the baptism of Jesus (Mt 3:16, Mk 1:10, and Luke 3:22). Thus, the baptism of Jesus took place before February 15, A.D. 31, but how long before? If Luke 3:23a, which says, "And when He began His ministry, Jesus Himself was about thirty years of age," is taken to mean that He had not yet reached His thirty-first birthday, then Jesus would have begun His ministry prior to September 15 (Tishri 1), A.D. 30. If this were the case, there would have been a break of almost four months between the completion of Jesus' temptations and the first event in His ministry recorded in John's Gospel. However, if the Greek word *hosei*, which is translated about, would allow Jesus to be thirty-one, which is probably the case, then the traditional date for Jesus' baptism of January 6 (Julian) becomes an interesting possibility. This day was called the Epiphany (the Manifestation) by the early church, and was celebrated by the churches in the East as both the date of Jesus' birth and His baptism. It is mentioned by Clement of Alexandria in *Stromata (Miscellaneous)*, I 21, written about A.D. 194, as one of the dates celebrated for the baptism of Jesus. Thus, the celebration of January 6 can be traced back almost to the time when the Apostles were still alive. The early church apparently assumed that Jesus was baptized on His birthday since the same date was celebrated as the anniversary of both events. It is possible that some of the Apostles and possibly some of the other Galilean disciples witnessed Jesus' baptism; however, it is very unlikely that any of them were present at His birth. If we take January 6 (Julian) as the date of Jesus' baptism, then Jesus began His ministry according to our Gregorian Calendar on Saturday, January 4, A.D. 31.

Temptation of Jesus

Immediately after His baptism, Jesus was led into the wilderness by the Holy Spirit for forty days to be tempted by the devil (Mt 4:1-11, Mk 1:12,13, Lk 4:1-13). Forty days from Jesus' baptism, counting inclusively, brings us to Wednesday, February 12, A.D. 31. Probably the day after His temptation, Jesus returned to the vicinity of Bethany beyond the Jordan on Thursday, February 13 and located a place to stay nearby (within a Sabbath day's journey). Then on Saturday, February 15, A.D. 31, Jesus would have been identified as the Son of God by John the Baptist. Thus there would be no gap between Jesus' temptation and Jesus' meeting His first disciples.

However, some objections might be raised to this dating of the baptism of Jesus. First, would Jesus have been physically able to begin His ministry immediately after fasting for forty days? Certainly such a fast would be debilitating; however, Matthew 4:11 says, "Then the devil left Him; and behold, angels came and began to minister to Him." Thus, through the ministry of these angels, Jesus could have continued His ministry immediately. Another question that might be raised is, would January temperatures permit baptism in the Jordan River? The Sea of Galilee and the Jordan River in this area are both about 700 feet below sea level which would tend to moderate the winter temperature. The presence of John the Baptist and his disciples at Bethany beyond the Jordan and the question asked by the priests and Levities in John 1:25, both suggest that he was baptizing in this place in February. John 1:25 says, "They asked him, and said to him, 'Why then are you baptizing, if you are not the Christ, nor Elijah, nor the Prophet?'" If John baptized there in February, then Jesus could have been baptized there in January. Thus the traditional date of January 6 (Julian) or January 4, (Gregorian) for the baptism of Jesus provides a good fit with the earliest recorded events of Jesus' ministry contained in the first and second chapter of John's Gospel.

Nicodemus Comes To Jesus

Returning now to the first Passover Feast during Jesus' earthly ministry mentioned in John 2:13, we shall move forward with our chronology. John 2:23 says, "Now when He was in Jerusalem at the Passover, during the feast, many believed in His name, observing His signs which He was doing." This event can be exactly dated since the Passover Feast lasted from Nisan 15 through Nisan 21. In A.D. 31, those Jewish dates would correspond to the period from sunset on Tuesday, March 25 until sunset on Tuesday, April 1. The next event recorded in the Gospel of John is the coming of Nicodemus to Jesus (John 3:1-12). This probably occurred immediately after the end of the Passover Feast about Wednesday evening, April 2, A.D. 31.

Jesus' Disciples Baptizing

John 3:22 then says,   "After these things Jesus and His disciples came into the land of Judea, and there He was spending time with them and baptizing." Jesus apparently left Jerusalem, but stayed in Judea. Jesus was teaching, and His disciples were baptizing (John 4:2). Jesus and His disciples probably returned to the Jordan River, possibly at the Hajalah Ford opposite Jericho. Jesus probably remained there until the time of the Day of Pentecost which in A.D. 31 was celebrated on Sunday, May 18. Probably sometime shortly before that date, John the Baptist's disciples came to Aenon near Salim (see Figure 4.1), where John was baptizing, and reported to John that Jesus was baptizing and all were coming to Him. John the Baptist replied, "He must increase, but I must decrease (John 3:30)." This event probably took place about Wednesday, May 7, A.D. 31. About Sunday, May 11, Jesus and his disciples probably returned to Jerusalem to attend the Feast of Pentecost. The New Testament does not mention Jesus attending this feast, but we can be sure that Jesus did attend the Feast of Pentecost which was also called the Feast of Weeks, since Deuteronomy 16:16 says:

> " Three times in a year all your males shall appear before the LORD your God in the place which He chooses, at the Feast of Unleavened Bread and at the Feast of Weeks and at the Feast of Booths, and they shall not appear before the LORD empty-handed."

Return To Galilee

It was probably about Wednesday, May 14, A.D. 31, just before the Feast of Pentecost, that John the Baptist was arrested by Herod Antipas since Matthew and Mark indicate that when Jesus heard that John the Baptist was in custody, He withdrew into Galilee (Mt 4:12, Mk 1:14). Thus, after the arrest of John the Baptist, Jesus probably departed in haste from Jerusalem immediately after the Feast of Pentecost on about Monday, May 19, A.D. 31.

John, in his Gospel, indicates that Jesus took the direct route to Galilee through Samaria (see Figure 4.1). At the sixth hour (5:00 to 6:00 P.M. since John is using Roman time, see Chapter 1), probably on the second day after His departure or on Tuesday, May 20, A.D. 31, Jesus and His disciples reached the outskirts of a city of Samaria called Sychar (John 4:5,6). At that time Jesus met the Samaritan woman at Jacob's Well. When Jesus' disciples returned from the city where they went to buy food, they marveled that Jesus was speaking to this woman. These were probably new disciples from Judea because Matthew, Mark and Luke indicate that Jesus called Peter, Andrew, James and John to full-time discipleship in Galilee after Jesus arrived there. Judas Iscariot may have been one of these Judean disciples because Iscariot means a man from Keriott. Keriott was probably the Judean city of that name near Hebron. Judas Iscariot seemed to have been the only non-Galilean among the Twelve. Jesus spent part of two days with the Samaritans, probably Tuesday, May 20 and Wednesday, May 21. He then probably departed for Galilee on Wednesday, May 21.

Jesus In Cana

Jesus and His disciples probably passed through Nazareth on His return to Galilee, but apparently did not stop for the Sabbath because the next town mentioned by John in His Gospel is Cana. John 4:44 says, "For Jesus Himself testified that a prophet has no honor in his own country." This verse indicates that Jesus knew that He would be rejected by the people of Nazareth, and He probably didn't want to begin this phase of His ministry with a rejection; therefore, Jesus went on to Cana where He was more likely to be well received because of His first miracle of turning water into wine at the wedding of Cana. Luke seems to indicate that Jesus began this phase of His Galilean ministry in Nazareth; however, both Matthew and Mark place Jesus' visit to Nazareth later in Jesus' Galilean ministry. Jesus would have arrived in Nazareth about Thursday, May 22, where He may have spent the night. Then the next morning Jesus and His disciples would have gone on to Cana, arriving the same day, Friday, May 23, A.D. 31 since the distance is only about eight miles.

Jesus spent the Sabbath, May 24, in Cana and at least part of the next week since there must have been sufficient time for the news of Jesus' arrival to have reached Capernaum and for a royal official to travel to Cana (John 4:46-54). If Jesus spoke in the synagogue at Cana on Saturday, May 24, then news of Jesus' arrival would have probably reached Capernaum by Sunday evening, May 25. The royal official would have probably left Capernaum the next morning, and he would have reached Cana Monday evening, May 26, where Jesus told him that his son lives. Then John 4:51-53 says:

As he was now going down, his slaves met him, saying that his son was living. So he inquired of them the hour when he began to get better. Then they said to him, "Yesterday at the seventh hour the fever left him." So the father knew that it was at that hour in which Jesus said to him, "Your son lives"; and he himself believed and his whole household.

Thus the royal official spoke to Jesus during the seventh Roman hour or from 6:00 to 7:00 P.M. on Monday, May 26 and he would have met his slaves the next day, Tuesday, May 27, A.D. 31.

Galilean Ministry

John 5:1 says, "After these things there was a feast of the Jews, and Jesus went up to Jerusalem." Since Jesus had just attended the Feast of Pentecost, this would have probably been the Feast of Booths, which in A.D. 31 began on September 18. Some have suggested that this was another Passover Feast; however, in three other instances of the Passover Feast in John's Gospel, he mentioned it by name, it seems unlikely that this was a Passover Feast. In his Gospel John seems to be using the Passover Feasts to indicate the various years of Jesus' ministry. Jesus would have probably wanted to be in Jerusalem for the Day of Trumpets, September 5, A.D. 31 and for the Day of Atonement, September 14, so Jesus would have probably left Galilee for Jerusalem about Sunday, August 24, A.D. 31. Thus, this portion of Jesus' Galilean ministry would have lasted about three months from May 22 until August 24.

However, the synoptic Gospels (Matthew, Mark and Luke) give us more details concerning this portion of Jesus' ministry. After Jesus' visit to Cana mentioned in John 4:46, He probably made His way to the Sea of Galilee. Mark 1:16-20 says:

> As He was going along by the Sea of Galilee, He saw Simon and Andrew, the brother of Simon, casting a net in the sea; for they were fishermen. And Jesus said to them, "Follow Me, and I will make you become fishers of men." Immediately they left their nets and followed Him. Going on a little farther, He saw James the son of Zebedee, and John his brother, who were also in the boat mending the nets. Immediately He called them; and they left their father Zebedee in the boat with the hired servants, and went away to follow Him.

These events probably took place about Thursday, May 29. In John 1:40-42, Simon Peter and Andrew had previously met Jesus, but apparently did not accompany Him to Jerusalem for the Passover Feast. John 2:13 says, "The Passover of the Jews was near, and Jesus went up to Jerusalem." Only Jesus is mentioned as going up to Jerusalem in this verse, whereas in the previous verses in this chapter of John both Jesus and His disciples are mentioned. Although these men had previously followed Jesus, it was at this time that Jesus called the brothers Peter and Andrew and the brothers James and John to be full-time disciples. Then Mark 1:21,22 says:

> They went into Capernaum; and immediately on the Sabbath He entered the synagogue and began to teach. They were amazed at His teaching; for He was teaching them as one having authority, and not as the scribes.

This would have probably taken place on Saturday, May 31. During the synagogue service Jesus healed a man with an unclean spirit. Immediately after the service, Jesus, Simon Peter, Andrew, James and John went to Simon Peter's house where Jesus healed Simon's mother-in-law (Mark 1:29-31). After sunset, the same Roman day, but the first day of the week according to Jewish reckoning, they brought to Jesus many who were ill and those who were demon possessed and He healed them. The next day, Sunday June 1, Mark 1:35-38 says:

> In the early morning, while it was still dark, Jesus got up, left the house, and went away to a secluded place, and was praying there. Simon and his companions searched for Him; they found Him, and said to Him, "Everyone is looking for You." He said to them, "Let us go somewhere else to the towns nearby, so that I may preach there also; for that is what I came for."

Mark 1:39 then indicates that Jesus went into the synagogues throughout all Galilee, preaching and casting out demons. This verse describes Jesus' ministry in Galilee from early June until the end of August.

Sermon on the Mount

Then Matthew 5:1 says, " When Jesus saw the crowds, He went up on the mountain; and after He sat down, His disciples came to Him." At that time Jesus preached the Sermon on the Mount which is recorded in Chapter 5, 6 and 7 of the Gospel of Matthew. This event probably took place on Sunday, June 8, A.D. 31. Luke presents some of the teachings of this sermon in the 6th chapter of his Gospel; however, Matthew is our primary reference for this sermon. The Sermon on the Mount may be the first event of Matthew's Gospel that he actually witnessed. The church fathers identify Matthew as the tax collector of Matthew 9:9 (see Chapter 8). As a tax collector Matthew would have been literate since he would have had to prepare reports on his collections. It seems reasonable that when Matthew heard the wisdom of Jesus' teaching, he would have taken detailed notes on the sermon. The Sermon on the Mount is one of five major discourses recorded in Matthew's Gospel. The other four discourses were: Jesus' Instructions To the Twelve (10:5-42), The Parables of the Kingdom (13:1-53), The Kingdom of God (18:1-35) and The Discourse on the Mount of Olives (24:1-26:5). Matthew probably took notes during all these major discourses. Reading the Sermon on the Mount makes it clear that this sermon is not the invention of some unknown church writer, as many liberal scholars claim, but it is clearly the revolutionary teachings of the Son of God!

Galilean Ministry Continues

Then Matthew 8:1-2 says, "When Jesus came down from the mountain, large crowds followed Him. And a leper came to Him and bowed down before Him, and said, 'Lord, if You are willing, You can make me clean.'" Jesus healed the leper and told him to say nothing to anyone, but show himself to the priest in accordance with the law of Moses. However, the leper proclaimed his healing, and Jesus could no longer enter cities because of the crowds (Mark 1:40-45). This event probably also took place on Sunday, June 8, A.D. 31.

Several days later, about Wednesday, June 11, Mark 2:1 reports, "When He had come back to Capernaum several days afterward, it was heard that He was at home." Jesus had previously moved to Capernaum (Matthew 4:13) and this town was now His home and the center for His Galilean ministry. On that day Jesus healed the centurion's servant (Matthew 8:5-13) and the next day, Thursday, June 12, Jesus healed the paralytic that was lowered through the roof (Mark 2:2-12). On the same day, Thursday, June 12, Jesus probably called Matthew (Matthew 9:9). That evening Jesus had dinner with Matthew (Levi) and Matthew's friends, many of whom were also tax collectors and possibly other employees of the Herodian government. The Pharisees criticized Jesus for eating with tax collectors and sinners. Jesus said, "It is not those who are healthy who need a physician, but those who are sick; I did not come to call the righteous, but sinners (Mark 2:17b)."

Probably the next day, Friday, June 13, the disciples of John came to Jesus. Mark 2:18-19 says:

> John's disciples and the Pharisees were fasting; and they came and said to Him, "Why do John's disciples and the disciples of the Pharisees fast, but Your disciples do not fast?" And Jesus said to them, "While the bridegroom is with them, the attendants of the bridegroom cannot fast, can they? So long as they have the bridegroom with them, they cannot fast.

At this same time Mark 2:22 says:

> No one puts new wine into old wineskins; otherwise the wine will burst the skins, and the wine is lost and the skins as well; but one puts new wine into fresh wineskins.

Thus, Jesus was saying that Christianity should not be made to conform to the ritualistic forms of the teaching of the Pharisees or of John the Baptist. Next Mark 2:23, 24 says:

> And it happened that He was passing through the grainfields on the Sabbath, and His disciples began to make their way along while picking the heads of grain. The Pharisees were saying to Him, "Look, why are they doing what is not lawful on the Sabbath?"

This event probably took place on Saturday, June 14, A.D. 31. This is about as late as this event could have taken place since the wheat harvest in Galilee ends about the middle of June. The field may have already been harvested and the disciples were picking the heads of grain that were left by the harvesters, but it still could have not been much later. Luke 6:1 also records this event and in many of the ancient Greek manuscripts of Luke 6:1, the word deuteroproto (second-first) appears modifying the word Sabbath. Thus the King James version of Luke 6:1 says:

> And it came to pass on the second sabbath after the first, that he went through the corn fields; and his disciples plucked the ears of corn, and did eat, rubbing them in their hands.

This Greek word is not used elsewhere in the New Testament and some have suggested that it refers to the second Sabbath after the Passover. However, since Jesus attended the Passover Feast in A.D. 31 (John 2:13), and the Passover Feast didn't end until April 1st, Jesus could not be walking through a grain field in Galilee on April 5th, the second Sabbath after the Passover. However, this is the second Sabbath since the brothers Peter and Andrew and James and John began their full-time ministry; and this may provide a simple explanation of the use of this Greek word that has puzzled Bible scholars. If this explanation of the use of this Greek word is correct, it would confirm the compression of the chronology of this portion of Jesus' Galilean ministry. Since these events were some of the first experiences of the Apostles after they were called to full-time discipleship, they may have been particularly vivid in their memories and thus often used in their preaching.

The next event recorded in Mark's Gospel is the healing of the man with a withered hand on another Sabbath (Mark 3:1-5). This event is probably the last event recorded in the Gospels prior to Jesus' departure to attend the Feast of Booths. There is a noticeable hardening of the position of the Pharisees. After this event Mark 3:6 says, "The Pharisees went out and immediately began conspiring with the Herodians against Him, as to how they might destroy Him."Thus, the Pharisees, representing the religious leaders, and the Herodians, representing the political leaders, conspired how they could eliminate Jesus. This event probably took place on Sunday, August 24, A.D. 31, the day Jesus departed Capernaum to attend the Feast of Booths in Jerusalem (John 5:1) as previously noted.

If Jesus departed for Jerusalem on Sunday, August 24, then after a journey of five days he would have arrived in Jerusalem about Thursday, August 28. Probably the next Sabbath, August 30, Jesus healed the man at the pool called Bethesda (John 5:2-13). Again Jesus encountered opposition because He healed on the Sabbath. It was probably on the same day Jesus said in John 5:19, "Truly, truly, I say to you, the Son can do nothing of Himself, unless it is something He sees the Father doing; for whatever the Father does, these things the Son also does in like manner."

Return to Galilee

Shortly after Thursday, September 26, A.D. 31, the last day of the Feast of Booths, Jesus probably departed Jerusalem to return to Galilee. He probably left Jerusalem about Sunday October 5 and He would have arrived in Galilee about Thursday, October 9. He would have probably returned to Capernaum which was the center for His Galilean ministry. Then Mark 3:7-8 says, " Jesus withdrew to the sea with His disciples; and a great multitude from Galilee followed; and also from Judea, and from Jerusalem, and from Idumea, and beyond the Jordan, and the vicinity of Tyre and Sidon, a great number of people heard of all that He was doing and came to Him." As Jesus neared the end of His first year of ministry, His fame had reached throughout Judea and Galilee and the surrounding area. Apparently to address such large groups of people, Jesus often taught from a boat with the people seated on the shore. As we shall see in Mark 6:53, the boats of Peter and Andrew and of the father of James and John were probably moored at Gennesaret (see Figure 4.3), about two miles west of Capernaum on the Sea of Galilee. Therefore, Gennesaret was probably the site of much of Jesus' teaching. Then Mark 3:13-19 says:

> And He went up on the mountain and summoned those whom He Himself wanted, and they came to Him. And He appointed twelve, so that they would be with Him and that He could send them out to preach, and to have authority to cast out the demons. And He appointed the twelve: Simon (to whom He gave the name Peter), and James, the son of Zebedee, and John the brother of James (to them He gave the name Boanerges, which means, "Sons of Thunder"); and Andrew, and Philip, and Bartholomew, and Matthew, and Thomas, and James the son of Alphaeus, and Thaddaeus, and Simon the Zealot; and Judas Iscariot, who betrayed Him.

This event probably happened about Sunday, December 21, A.D. 31. The traditional site for this event is a hill (mountain) near the town of Heptapegon which overlooks the northern end of the Sea of Galilee west of Capernaum (see Figure 4.3). The traditional site for the Sermon on the Mount is also on this same mountain. This site is marked by the ruins of a fourth century A.D. church and is mentioned

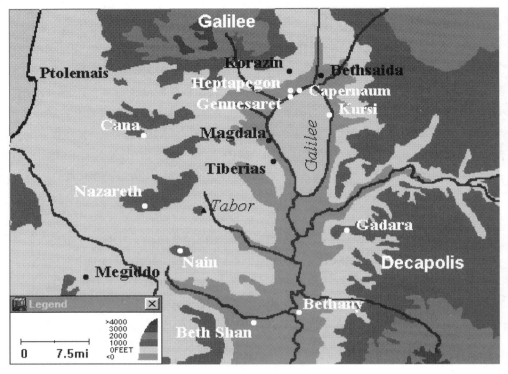

Return To Galilee
Figure 4.3

by Egeria, a fourth century nun traveling in the Holy Land about A.D. 381.

Probably the next day, Monday, December 22, A,D. 31, Jesus rebuked the scribes who said that He cast out demons by Beelzebul, the ruler of demons (Mark 3:22-30). Then later that day, Jesus' mother and brothers sought to take Jesus into custody, thinking He had lost His senses (Mark 3:21). Jesus says in Mark 3:35, "For whoever does the will of God, he is My brother and sister and mother." Then Luke 7:11-17 says:

Soon afterwards He went to a city called Nain; and His

disciples were going along with Him, accompanied by a large crowd. Now as He approached the gate of the city, a dead man was being carried out, the only son of his mother, and she was a widow; and a sizeable crowd from the city was with her. When the Lord saw her, He felt compassion for her, and said to her, "Do not weep." And He came up and touched the coffin; and the bearers came to a halt. And He said, "Young man, I say to you, arise!" The dead man sat up and began to speak. And Jesus gave him back to his mother. Fear gripped them all, and they began glorifying God, saying, "A great prophet has arisen among us!" and, "God has visited His people!" This report concerning Him went out all over Judea and in all the surrounding district.

The town of Nain is located southwest of the Sea of Galilee (see Figure 4.3). This event probably happened about Wednesday, December 24, A.D. 31. After a short stay in Nain, Jesus probably returned to Capernaum.

Beginning in chapter 4, Mark records Jesus telling the parable of the Sower and the Soils as He is teaching in Galilee. Afterwards, Jesus' disciples ask Him to explain the parable. This event probably took place about Sunday, December 28, A.D. 31. At this time Jesus said in Mark 4:21b, "A lamp is not brought to be put under a basket, is it, or under a bed? Is it not brought to be put on the lampstand?"

Then Mark 4:35,36 says:

On that day, when evening came, He said to them, "Let us go over to the other side." Leaving the crowd, they took Him along with them in the boat, just as He was; and other boats were with Him.

Jesus and His disciples probably left from Gennesaret where Peter and James seemed to have kept their boats.   During that night Jesus calmed the storm on the Sea of Galilee. Mark and Luke then say that they came to the other side of the Sea of Galilee into the country of the Gerasenes. The city of Gerasa was located about thirty-five miles southeast of the Sea of Galilee and was one of the important cities of the Decapolis (see Figure 4.1). Apparently in New Testament times this area was associated with the City of Gerasa, and therefore Mark and Luke used this city to identify the area to their readers. However, Matthew 8:28 identifies this area as the country of the Gadarenes. The City of Gadara is located about six miles from the southeastern end of the Sea of Galilee (see Figure 4.3). The largest harbor on the Sea of Galilee has been found opposite Gadara; and since there does not seem to have been any other city between Gadara and the Sea of Galilee, this harbor appears to have been the harbor of Gadara. Figure 4.4 shows an ancient coin minted in Gadara   picturing a boat.

Thus, Mark and Luke identify the site of the exorcism of the demoniac with the city of Gerasa while Matthew identifies this area with the city of Gadara. Gerasa was larger and probably better known, but a more distant city than Gadara. At any rate, the site of this exorcism would be on the southeast coast of the Sea of Galilee opposite both Gadara and Gerasa (see Figure 4.1). The traditional site for this event is at Kursi (see Figure 4.3) which is located on the eastside of the Sea of Galilee; however, since all three synoptic Gospels identify this event with cities opposite the southeast end of the Sea of Galilee, it seems more likely that this event took place in that area rather than the traditional site. This event would have probably taken place on Monday, December 29, A.D. 31.Then Mark 5:21-23 says:

> When Jesus had crossed over again in the boat to the
> other side, a large crowd gathered around Him; and so
> He stayed by the seashore.   One of the synagogue

officials named Jairus came up, and on seeing Him, fell at His feet and implored Him earnestly, saying, "My little daughter is at the point of death; please come and lay Your hands on her, so that she will get well and live."

Ancient Coin of Gadara
Inscription
Can Be Translated
Of Pompey's Gadara
Figure 4.4

Jesus and His disciples would have probably returned to Gennesaret where Peter kept his boat. Jairus was probably the ruler of the synagogue at Capernaum; although it is possible he was from one of the smaller towns in the region. Jesus went home with Jarius. On the way, Jesus was touched by a woman with a hemorrhage and the women was healed immediately (Matthew 9:20-22). Then word came that Jairus' daughter was dead. However, in Mark 5:36b Jesus says, "Do not be afraid any longer, only believe." Then Jesus went to Jairus' house and raised his daughter from the dead. This event probably took place on Monday, December 29, A.D. 31. Then Matthew 9:27-30 says:

As Jesus went on from there, two blind men followed

Him, crying out, "Have mercy on us, Son of David!"
When He entered the house, the blind men came up to
Him, and Jesus said to them, "Do you believe that I am
able to do this?" They said to Him, "Yes, Lord." Then He
touched their eyes, saying, "It shall be done to you
according to your faith." And their eyes were opened.
And Jesus sternly warned them: "See that no one knows
about this!"

This event also took place on Monday, December 29, A.D. 31. The
next day, Tuesday, December 30, a demon-possessed, mute man was
brought to Jesus. He cast out the demon, and the mute man spoke
(Matthew 9:32,33).

Next Jesus returned to Nazareth with His disciples and Mark
6:1-3 says:

Jesus went out from there and came into His hometown;
and His disciples followed Him. When the Sabbath
came, He began to teach in the synagogue; and the many
listeners were astonished, saying, "Where did this man
get these things, and what is this wisdom given to Him,
and such miracles as these performed by His hands? "Is
not this the carpenter, the son of Mary, and brother of
James and Joses and Judas and Simon? Are not His
sisters here with us?" And they took offense at Him.

This event probably took place on Saturday, January 3, A.D. 32, and
this would be the last event in Jesus' first year of ministry that is
recorded in the New Testament.

	Table 4.2 **Jesus' First Year of Ministry**			
Event Sequence Number	**Event (Scripture Reference)**	**Location of Event**	**Gregorian Date**	**Level of Confidence***
30	Calling of John the Baptist (Luke 3:1-6) (Jn 1:6-8)	Wilderness of Judea	Sunday, April 15, A.D. 31	II
31	John the Baptist Preaching (Mt 3:1-12, Mk 1:1-8, Lk 3:7-18)	Jordan River Valley	April AD 29 Until June AD 31	II
32	Baptism of Jesus (Mt 3:13-17, Mk 1:9-11, Lk 3:21-23a,Jn 1:9-18)	Bethany beyond the Jordan	Saturday, Jan 4, AD 31	II
33	Jesus Fasting for Forty Days (Mt 4:1-2, Mk 1:12-13a, Lk 4:1-2)	Wilderness near Jordan	Jan 4 to Feb 12, AD 31	II
34	Temptation of Jesus (Mt 4:3-11, Mk 1:13b, Lk 4:3-13)	Wilderness Jerusalem Mountain	Wednesday, Feb 12, AD 31	II
35	John the Baptist Witness To the Priests and Levites (Jn 1:19-28)	Bethany beyond the Jordan	Friday, Feb 14, AD 31	II
36	John the Baptist Witness That Jesus Is the Son of God (John 1:29-34)	Bethany beyond the Jordan	Saturday, Feb 15, AD 31	II
37	Andrew and Another Disciple Follow Jesus (Jn 1:35-40)	Bethany beyond the Jordan	Sunday, Feb 16. AD 31	II
38	Andrew Calls Simon Peter (Jn 1:41-42)	Bethany beyond the Jordan	Sunday, Feb 16, AD 31	II

* Level of Confidence in Date   Level I = Highly Probable Level II = Probable

Event Sequence Number	Event (Scripture Reference)	Location of Event	Gregorian Date	Level of Confidence*
39	Jesus Calls Philip (Jn 1:43-44)	Bethany beyond the Jordan	Monday, Feb 17, AD 31	II
40	Philip Calls Nathanael (Jn 1:45-51)	Bethany beyond the Jordan	Monday, Feb 17, AD 31	II
41	The Wedding At Cana (Jn 2:1-11)	Cana, Galilee	Wednesday, Feb 19, AD 31	II
42	Jesus Departs to Capernaum (Jn 2:12a)	Cana, Galilee	Sunday, Mar 2, AD 31	II
43	Jesus Moves To Capernaum (Mt 4:13-16)	Capernaum Galilee	Monday, Mar 3 AD 31	II
44	Jesus Stays A Few Days In Capernaum (Jn 2:12b)	Capernaum Galilee	Mar 2-9 AD 31	II
45	Jesus Departs To Jerusalem (Jn 2:13)	Capernaum Galilee	Sunday, Mar 9 AD 31	II
46	Jesus Cleanses the Temple (Jn 2:14-17)	Jerusalem	Friday, Mar 14, AD 31	II
47	"Destroy This Temple And In Three Days I Will Raise It Up" (Jn 2:18-22)	Jerusalem	Friday, Mar 14, AD 31	II
48	Many Believe During the Feast (Jn 2:23-25)	Jerusalem	Mar 23 - Apr 2, AD31	I

* Level of Confidence in Date   Level I = Highly Probable Level II = Probable

Event Sequence Number	Event (Scripture Reference)	Location of Event	Gregorian Date	Level of Confidence*
49	Nicodemus Visits Jesus (Jn 3:1-2)	Jerusalem	Wednesday, Apr 2, AD 31	II
50	"Unless Born of Water & Spirit Cannot Enter Kingdom" (Jn 3:3-15)	Jerusalem	Wednesday, Apr 2, AD 31	II
51	"For God So Loved the World" (Jn 3:16-21)	Jerusalem	Wednesday, Apr 2, AD 31	II
52	Jesus Spends Time in Judea And Disciples Baptizing (Jn 3:22)	Jordan River, Judea	Apr 6 - May 11, AD 31	II
53	John the Baptist, "He Must Increase, I Must Decrease" (Jn 3:23-36)	Aenon near Salim	Wednesday, May 7, AD 31	II
54	John the Baptist Arrested (Mt 4:12a, Mt 14:3-5, Mk 1:14a, Mk 6:14-29 Luke 3:19-20)	Aenon near Salim	Wednesday, May 14, AD31	II
55	Jesus Departs for Galilee (Jn 4:1-3, Mt 4:12b, Mk 1:14b Lk 4:14)	Jerusalem	Monday, May 19. AD 31	II
56	Jesus Meets the Samaritan Women (Jn 4:4-38)	Sychar, Samaria	Tuesday, May 20, AD 31	II
57	Jesus Spends Two Days With the Samaritans (Jn 4:39-42)	Sychar, Samaria	May 20 - 21, AD 31	II

* Level of Confidence in Date   Level I = Highly Probable Level II = Probable

Event Sequence Number	Event (Scripture Reference)	Location of Event	Gregorian Date	Level of Confidence*
58	Jesus Departs Sychar (Jn 4:43)	Sychar, Samaria	Wednesday, May 21, AD 31	II
59	Prophet Has No Honor In His Own Country (Jn 4:44-45)	Galilee	Thursday, May 22, AD 31	II
60	Jesus Arrives In Cana (Jn 4:46a)	Cana, Galilee	Friday, May 23, AD 31	II
61	Royal Official's Son Healed (Jn 4:46b-50)	Cana, Galilee	Monday, May 26, AD 31	II
62	Receives News of Son's Healing (Jn 4:51-54)	Galilee	Tuesday, May 27, AD 31	II
63	Jesus Preaches in Galilee (Mt 4:17, Mk 1:14c-15, Lk 4: 15)	Galilee	May 22 - May 29, AD31	II
64	Jesus Calls Peter, Andrew, James & John (Mk 1:16-20, Mt 4:18-22, Lk 5:1-11)	Gennesaret Galilee	Thursday, May 29, AD 31	II
65	Jesus Heals Man with Unclean Spirit in Synagogue on Sabbath (Mk 1:21-28, Lk 4:31-37)	Capernaum Galilee	Saturday, May 31, AD 31	II
66	Jesus Heals Peter's Mother-in-law (Mk 1:29-31, Mt 8:14-15 Lk 4:38-39)	Capernaum Galilee	Saturday, May 31, AD 31	II

* Level of Confidence in Date   Level I = Highly Probable Level II = Probable

Event Sequence Number	Event (Scripture Reference)	Location of Event	Gregorian Date	Level of Confidence*
67	Jesus Heals All After Sabbath (Mk 1:32-34, Mt 8:16-17, Lk 4:40-41)	Capernaum Galilee	Saturday, May 31, AD 31	II
68	Jesus Departs to a Lonely Place (Mk 1:35-38, Lk 4:42-43)	Near Capernaum	Sunday, June 1, AD 31	II
69	Jesus Ministry in Galilee (Mk 1:39, Mt 4:23-25, Lk 4:44)	Galilee	June 1-8, AD 31	II
70	Jesus Teaches on the Mountain (Mt 5:1-2, Lk 6:17-18a)	Hepta-pegon, Galilee	Sunday, June 8, AD 31	II
71	The Beatitudes (Mt 5:3-12, Lk 6:20-23)	Hepta-pegon, Galilee	Sunday, June 8, AD 31	II
72	"You Are the Salt of the Earth" (Mt 5:13)	Hepta-pegon, Galilee	Sunday, June 8, AD 31	II
73	"You Are the Light of the World" (Mt 5:14-16)	Hepta-pegon, Galilee	Sunday, June 8, AD 31	II
74	Jesus Came to Fulfill the Law (Mt 5:17-19)	Hepta-pegon, Galilee	Sunday, June 8, AD 31	II
75	Righteousness Must Surpass That of Scribes & Pharisees (Mt 5:20)	Hepta-pegon, Galilee	Sunday, June 8, AD 31	II
76	Being Angry with Your Brother Makes You Guilty (Mt 5:21-22)	Hepta-pegon, Galilee	Sunday, June 8, AD 31	II

* Level of Confidence in Date   Level I = Highly Probable   Level II = Probable

Event Sequence Number	Event (Scripture Reference)	Location of Event	Gregorian Date	Level of Confidence*
77	Leave Offering and Be Reconciled with Your Brother (Mt 5:23-24)	Hepta-pegon, Galilee	Sunday, June 8, AD 31	II
78	Make Friends Quickly with Your Opponent at Law (Mt 5:25-26)	Hepta-pegon, Galilee	Sunday, June 8, AD 31	II
79	To Lust is to Commit Adultery (Mt 5:27-28)	Hepta-pegon, Galilee	Sunday, June 8, AD 31	II
80	Better Part of Body Parish Than Whole Body Go To Hell (Mt 5:29-30)	Hepta-pegon, Galilee	Sunday, June 8, AD 31	II
81	Teaching on Divorce (Mt 5:31-32)	Hepta-pegon, Galilee	Sunday, June 8, AD 31	II
82	Make No Oath At All (Mt 5:33-37)	Hepta-pegon, Galilee	Sunday, June 8, AD 31	II
83	Do Not Resist Evil (Mt 5:38-41, Lk 6:29)	Hepta-pegon, Galilee	Sunday, June 8, AD 31	II
84	Give To Him That Asks (Mt 5:42, Lk 6:30)	Hepta-pegon, Galilee	Sunday, June 8, AD 31	II
85	Love Your Enemies (Mt 5:43-47, Lk 6:27-35)	Hepta-pegon, Galilee	Sunday, June 8, AD 31	II
86	Be Perfect As Your Heavenly Father Is Perfect (Mt 5:48, Lk 6:36)	Hepta-pegon, Galilee	Sunday, June 8, AD 31	II

* Level of Confidence in Date   Level I = Highly Probable Level II = Probable

Event Sequence Number	Event (Scripture Reference)	Location of Event	Gregorian Date	Level of Confidence*
87	Beware of Practicing Your Righteousness Before Men (Mt 6:1)	Hepta-pegon, Galilee	Sunday, June 8, AD 31	II
88	Give Alms In Secret (Mt 6:2-4)	Hepta-pegon, Galilee	Sunday, June 8, AD 31	II
89	To Pray Go Into Your Inner Room (Mt 6:5-8)	Hepta-pegon, Galilee	Sunday, June 8, AD 31	II
90	The Lord's Prayer (Mt 6:9-13)	Hepta-pegon, Galilee	Sunday, June 8, AD 31	II
91	If You Forgive Transgressions God will Forgive You (Mt 6:14-15)	Hepta-pegon, Galilee	Sunday, June 8, AD 31	II
92	Fast in Secret (Mt 6:16-18)	Hepta-pegon, Galilee	Sunday, June 8, AD 31	II
93	Lay Up Treasures in Heaven (Mt 6:19-21)	Hepta-pegon, Galilee	Sunday, June 8, AD 31	II
94	The Eye Is the Lamp of the Body (Mt 6:22-23)	Hepta-pegon, Galilee	Sunday, June 8, AD 31	II
95	No One Can Serve Two Masters (Mt 6:24)	Hepta-pegon, Galilee	Sunday, June 8, AD 31	II
96	Do Not Be Anxious (Mt 6:25-34)	Hepta-pegon, Galilee	Sunday, June 8, AD 31	II

* Level of Confidence in Date   Level I = Highly Probable Level II = Probable

Event Sequence Number	Event (Scripture Reference)	Location of Event	Gregorian Date	Level of Confidence*
97	The Woes (Lk 6:24-26)	Hepta-pegon, Galilee	Sunday, June 8, AD 31	II
98	Do Not Judge (Mt 7:1-5, Lk 6:37,41,42)	Hepta-pegon, Galilee	Sunday, June 8, AD 31	II
99	Give and It Will Be Given To You (Lk 6:38)	Hepta-pegon, Galilee	Sunday, June 8, AD 31	II
100	Blind Guiding the Blind (Lk 6:39)	Hepta-pegon, Galilee	Sunday, June 8, AD 31	II
101	A Pupil Is Not Above His Teacher (Lk 6:40)	Hepta-pegon, Galilee	Sunday, June 8, AD 31	II
102	Don't Give What Is Holy To Dogs (Mt 7:6)	Hepta-pegon, Galilee	Sunday, June 8, AD 31	II
103	Ask And It Shall Be Given (Mt 7:7-11)	Hepta-pegon, Galilee	Sunday, June 8, AD 31	II
104	The Golden Rule (Mt 7:12, Lk 6:31)	Hepta-pegon, Galilee	Sunday, June 8, AD 31	II
105	Enter By the Narrow Gate (Mt 7:13-14)	Hepta-pegon, Galilee	Sunday, June 8, AD 31	II
106	Know False Prophets By Their Fruit (Mt 7:15-20, Lk 6:43-45)	Hepta-pegon, Galilee	Sunday, June 8, AD 31	II

* Level of Confidence in Date   Level I = Highly Probable Level II = Probable

Event Sequence Number	Event (Scripture Reference)	Location of Event	Gregorian Date	Level of Confidence*
107	Not Everyone Who Says Lord Lord Will Enter the Kingdom (Mt 7:21-23, Lk 6:46)	Hepta-pegon, Galilee	Sunday, June 8, AD 31	II
108	House Built On the Rock (Mt 7:24-25, Lk 6:47-48)	Hepta-pegon, Galilee	Sunday, June 8, AD 31	II
109	House Built On the Sand (Mt 7:26-27, Lk 6:49)	Hepta-pegon, Galilee	Sunday, June 8, AD 31	II
110	Multitude Amazed By His Teaching (Mt 7:28-29)	Hepta-pegon, Galilee	Sunday, June 8, AD 31	II
111	Jesus Comes Down From the Mountain (Mt 8:1)	Hepta-pegon, Galilee	Sunday, June 8, AD 31	II
112	Jesus Heals a Leper (Mt 8:2-4, Mk 1:40-45, Lk 5:12-16)	Hepta-pegon, Galilee	Sunday, June 8, AD 31	II
113	Jesus Heals the Centurion's Son (Mt 8:5:-13, Lk 7:1-10)	Capernaum Galilee	Wednesday, June 11, AD 31	II
114	Jesus Heals the Paralytic (Mk 2:1-12, Mt 9:2-8, Lk 5:17-26)	Capernaum Galilee	Thursday, June 12, AD 31	II
115	Jesus Teaches by the Seashore (Mk2:13)	Near Capernaum	Thursday, June 12, AD 31	II
116	Calling of Matthew (Levi) (Mt 9:9, Mk 2:14, Lk 5:27-28)	Near Capernaum	Thursday, June 12, AD 31	II

* Level of Confidence in Date   Level I = Highly Probable Level II = Probable

Event Sequence Number	Event (Scripture Reference)	Location of Event	Gregorian Date	Level of Confidence*
117	Matthew Gives a Reception for Jesus (Mt 9:10-13, Mk 2:15-17 Lk 5:29-32)	Capernaum Galilee	Thursday, June 12, AD 31	II
118	John the Baptist's Disciples Question Jesus on Fasting (Mt 9:14-17, Mk 2:18-22, Lk 5:33-39)	Capernaum Galilee	Friday, June 13, AD 31	II
119	Picking Grain on the Sabbath (Mk 2:23-28, Mt 12:1-8, Lk 6:1-5)	Near Capernaum Galilee	Saturday, June 14, AD 31	II
120	Healing the Man With the Withered Hand (Mk 3:1-6, Mt 12:9-13, Lk 6:6-11)	Capernaum Galilee	Saturday, August 23, AD 31	II
121	Pharisees Council To Destroy Jesus (Mt 12:14)	Capernaum Galilee	Sunday, August 24, AD 31	II
122	Jesus Heals Many (Mt 12:15-21)	Galilee	Sunday, August 24 AD 31	II
123	Jesus Heals Man at the Pool of Bethesda (Jn 5:1-9)	Jerusalem	Saturday, August 30, AD 31	II
124	Jesus Answers Question Concerning Sabbath Healing (Jn 5:10-47)	Jerusalem	Saturday, August 30, AD 31	II
125	Jesus Heals the Multitude By the Sea (Mk 3:7-12, Lk 6:18b-19)	Gennesaret Galilee	Thursday, November 6 AD 31	II

* Level of Confidence in Date   Level I = Highly Probable Level II = Probable

Event Sequence Number	Event (Scripture Reference)	Location of Event	Gregorian Date	Level of Confidence*
126	Jesus Goes To Mountain To Pray (Lk 6:12)	Near Hepta-pegon	Night Dec 21/22 AD 31	II
127	Jesus Chooses the Twelve (Mk 3:13-19, Lk 6:13-16)	Near Hepta-pegon	Sunday, Dec 21, AD 31	II
128	Jesus Raises the Widow of Nain's Son (Lk 7:11-17)	Nain, Galilee	Wednesday, Dec 24, AD 31	II
129	The Supporting Women (Lk 8:1-3)	Galilee	Sunday, Dec 28, AD 31	II
130	Jesus Can't Eat For the Multitude (Mk3:20)	Capernaum Galilee	Sunday, Dec 28, AD 31	II
131	Jesus' Family Wants To Take Him Into Custody (Mk 3:21)	Capernaum Galilee	Sunday, Dec 28, AD 31	II
132	Jesus Heals Demon-Possessed Man (Mt 12:22-23)	Capernaum Galilee	Sunday, Dec 28, AD 31	II
133	Jesus Refutes Scribes Who Claim His Works From Satan (Mk 3:22-30, Mt 12:24-29)	Capernaum Galilee	Sunday, Dec 28, AD 31	II
134	"He Who Is Not With Me Is Against Me" (Mt 12:30)	Capernaum Galilee	Sunday, Dec 28, AD 31	II

* Level of Confidence in Date   Level I = Highly Probable Level II = Probable

Event Sequence Number	Event (Scripture Reference)	Location of Event	Gregorian Date	Level of Confidence*
135	Unpardonable Sin (Mt 12:31-32)	Capernaum Galilee	Sunday, Dec 28, AD 31	II
136	By You Words You Shall Be Judged (Mt 12:33-37)	Capernaum Galilee	Sunday, Dec 28, AD 31	II
137	Scribes & Pharisees Desire a Sign (Mt 12:38-45)	Capernaum Galilee	Sunday, Dec 28, AD 31	II
138	Who Are My Mother & My Brothers (Mt 12:46-50, Mk 3:31-35 Lk 8:19-21)	Capernaum Galilee	Sunday, Dec 28, AD 31	II
139	Jesus' Parable of the Sower (Mk 4:1-9, Mt 13:1-9, Lk 8:4-8)	Gennesaret Galilee	Sunday, Dec 28, AD 31	II
140	Reason For Speaking in Parables (Mk 4:10-12, Mt 13:10-17)	Gennesaret Galilee	Sunday, Dec 28, AD 31	II
141	Explanation of the Parable of the Sower (Mk 4:13-20, Mt 13:18-23, Lk 8:9-15)	Gennesaret Galilee	Sunday, Dec 28, AD 31	II
142	Parable of the Lamp (Lk 8:16-18)	Gennesaret Galilee	Sunday, Dec 28, AD 31	II
143	Hidden to be Revealed (Mk 4:21-22)	Gennesaret Galilee	Sunday, Dec 28, AD 31	II

* Level of Confidence in Date   Level I = Highly Probable   Level II = Probable

Event Sequence Number	Event (Scripture Reference)	Location of Event	Gregorian Date	Level of Confidence*
144	Whoever Has Shall Be Given (Mk 4:23-25)	Gennesaret Galilee	Sunday, Dec 28, AD 31	II
145	Parable of the Growth of a Seed (Mk 4:26-29)	Gennesaret Galilee	Sunday, Dec 28, AD 31	II
146	Parable of the Tares (Mt 13:24-30)	Gennesaret Galilee	Sunday, Dec 28, AD 31	II
147	Parable of the Mustard Seed Mk 4:30-32, Mt 13:31-32, Lk 13:18-19)	Gennesaret Galilee	Sunday, Dec 28, AD 31	II
148	Parable of the Leaven (Mt 13:33, Lk 13:20-21)	Gennesaret Galilee	Sunday, Dec 28, AD 31	II
149	Jesus' Use of Parables (Mk 4:33-34, Mt 13:34-35)	Gennesaret Galilee	Sunday, Dec 28, AD 31	II
150	Explanation of the Parable of the Tares (Mt 13: 36-43)	Gennesaret Galilee	Sunday, Dec 28, AD 31	II
151	Parable of Hidden Treasure (Mt 13:44)	Gennesaret Galilee	Sunday, Dec 28, AD 31	II
152	Parable of the Pearl of Great Price (Mt 13:45-46)	Gennesaret Galilee	Sunday, Dec 28, AD 31	II
153	Parable of the Drag Net (Mt 13:47-50)	Gennesaret Galilee	Sunday, Dec 28, AD 31	II

* Level of Confidence in Date   Level I = Highly Probable Level II = Probable

Event Sequence Number	Event (Scripture Reference)	Location of Event	Gregorian Date	Level of Confidence*
154	Disciples Say They Understand (Mt 13:51-52)	Gennesaret Galilee	Sunday, Dec 28, AD 31	II
155	Jesus Gives Orders to Depart to Other Side of Sea of Galilee (Mt 8:18)	Gennesaret Galilee	Sunday, Dec 28, AD 31	II
156	"Foxes Have Holes, But the Son of Man Has Nowhere" (Mt 8:19-20, Lk 9:57-58)	Gennesaret Galilee	Sunday, Dec 28, AD 31	II
157	"Let the Dead Bury the Dead" (Mt 8:21-22, Lk 9:59-60)	Gennesaret Galilee	Sunday, Dec 28, AD 31	II
158	Jesus & Disciples Depart by Boat (Mk 4:35-36, Mt 8:23,Lk 8:22)	Gennesaret Galilee	Sunday, Dec 28, AD 31	II
159	Jesus Calms the Storm (Mk 4:37-41, Mt 8:24-27, Lk 8:23-25)	Sea of Galilee	Sunday, Dec 28, AD 31	II
160	Jesus Healed the Gerasene Demoniac (Mk 5:1-13, Mt 8:28-32, Lk 8:26-33)	SE Shore Sea of Galilee	Monday, Dec 29, AD 31	II
161	People From City Ask Jesus To Leave (Mk 5:14-17, Mt 8:33-34, Lk 8:34-37)	SE Shore Sea of Galilee	Monday, Dec 29, AD 31	II
162	Jesus Sends Former Demoniac Home (Mk 5:18-19, Lk 8:38-39a)	SE Shore Sea of Galilee	Monday, Dec 29, AD 31	II

* Level of Confidence in Date   Level I = Highly Probable Level II = Probable

Event Sequence Number	Event (Scripture Reference)	Location of Event	Gregorian Date	Level of Confidence*
163	Former Demoniac Praises Jesus (Mk 5:20, Lk 8:39b)	Decapolis	After Dec 29, AD 31	II
164	Jesus Cross Sea of Galilee Again (Mk 5:21, Mt 9:1, Lk 8:40)	Sea of Galilee	Monday, Dec 29, AD 31	II
1645	Jairus Asks Jesus to Heal His Daughter (Mk 5:22-24, Mt 9:18-19, Lk 8:41-42)	Gennesaret Galilee	Monday, Dec 29, AD 31	II
166	Jesus Heals Woman With Hemorrhage (Mk 5:25-34, Mt 9:20-22, Lk 8:43-48)	Near Gennesaret Galilee	Monday, Dec 29, AD 31	II
167	Jesus Raises Jairus' Daughter (Mk 5:35-43, Mt 9:23-26, Lk 8:49-56)	Capernaum Galilee	Monday, Dec 29, AD 31	II
168	Jesus Heals Two Blind Men (Mt 9:27-31)	Near Capernaum Galilee	Monday Dec 29, AD 31	II
169	Jesus Heals the Dumb Demoniac (Mt 9:32-34)	On Way to Nazareth	Tuesday, Dec 30, AD 31	II
170	Jesus Teaches in Synagogue in Nazareth (Mk 6:1-6, Mt 13:53-58, Lk 4:16-30)	Nazareth, Galilee	Saturday, Jan 3, AD 32	II

* Level of Confidence in Date   Level I = Highly Probable Level II = Probable

5

Jesus' Second Year of Ministry

Jesus ended His first year of ministry in His hometown of Nazareth. Following His visit to Nazareth, Mark 6:6b says, "And He was going around the villages teaching." This teaching probably occupied a period of about six weeks which would fill the gap between Jesus' visit to Nazareth and the next event recorded in the Gospels. Mark 6:7-9 says:

> And He summoned the twelve and began to send them out in pairs, and gave them authority over the unclean spirits; and He instructed them that they should take nothing for their journey, except a mere staff--no bread, no bag, no money in their belt-- but to wear sandals; and He added, "Do not put on two tunics."

This preaching and healing mission of the twelve probably began about Sunday, February 15, A.D. 32 and probably lasted about one month. In fact, Jesus may have told the twelve to meet Him at Gennesaret, where the Apostles probably kept their boats, immediately after the next full moon which would have occurred on

Saturday, March 13, A.D. 32. A return of the twelve at that time would fit well with the subsequent events recorded in the four Gospels.

Feeding the 5000

Returning to the Gospel of John, the next event that can be exactly dated is found in chapter 6. Chapter 6 begins abruptly after the close of chapter 5 which found Jesus in Jerusalem attending a feast of the Jews (the Feast of Booths). This abrupt beginning of chapter 6 may suggest that John assumes that his readers would also be reading the synoptic Gospels which would supply the intervening details. John 6:1-4 says:

> After these things Jesus went away to the other side of the Sea of Galilee (or Tiberias). A large crowd followed Him, because they saw the signs which He was performing on those who were sick. Then Jesus went up on the mountain, and there He sat down with His disciples. Now the Passover, the feast of the Jews, was near.

From a chronological standpoint this is a very important Scripture passage because it enables us to date the Feeding of the 5000 together with the surrounding events. Generally, with the exception of the events of Jesus' final days, these are the only events that appear in all four Gospels. Therefore, this Scripture supplies a key benchmark for tying the chronologies of the four Gospels together. This Passover Feast would have been the Passover Feast of A. D. 32 which was celebrated on the evening of Sunday, April 11. We shall date the Feeding of the 5000 and the surrounding events by working backward from the known date of the Passover Feast.

We know that Jesus attended this Passover Feast because it is commanded by Deuteronomy 16:16. In order to arrive in Jerusalem two weeks before the beginning of this feast, Jesus would have departed Capernaum about Sunday, March 21, A.D. 32. Since the Passover Feast was at hand when Jesus and His disciples departed to the other side of the Sea of Galilee, this event probably took place during the week preceding Jesus' departure from Capernaum. The twelve had just returned from their mission of preaching and healing. Mark 6:30-34 says:

> The apostles gathered together with Jesus; and they reported to Him all that they had done and taught. And He said to them, "Come away by yourselves to a secluded place and rest a while." (For there were many people coming and going, and they did not even have time to eat.) They went away in the boat to a secluded place by themselves. The people saw them going, and many recognized them and ran there together on foot from all the cities, and got there ahead of them. When Jesus went ashore, He saw a large crowd, and He felt compassion for them because they were like sheep without a shepherd; and He began to teach them many things.

Assuming the Apostles began their return from their mission of preaching and healing on Sunday, March 14, the day following the night of the full moon, and allowing three days for all of them to return to Gennesaret, then the departure to the other side of the Sea of Galilee would have taken place on Wednesday, March 17. Jesus and His disciples apparently sailed near the shore so the people on the shore could recognize them and many of these people followed them by walking along the seashore. Luke 9:10 adds that the lonely place was near Bethsaida, so they were sailing along the north shore of the Sea of Galilee from Gennesaret to near Bethsaida (see Figure 5.1, page 192). It was at this site near Bethsaida that the Feeding of the 5000 took place on Wednesday, March 17, A.D. 32.

Jesus Walks on the Water

Then John 6:15 says, "So Jesus, perceiving that they were intending to come and take Him by force to make Him king, withdrew again to the mountain by Himself alone." The Jewish people believed that the Messiah would be a worldly king who would secure political freedom for the nation of Israel. Since the Passover Feast commemorates God's deliverance of the nation of Israel from slavery in Egypt, expectation for Messianic deliverance was heightened as Passover time approached.

That evening the disciples got into their boats and began their return to Gennesaret leaving Jesus on the mountain (John 6:16-17). It was already dark and a strong wind was blowing. John 6:19 tells us that the disciples were rowing, which indicates that the wind was coming from the west so that they could not use their sail. After the disciples had rowed about three or four miles, they saw Jesus walking on the sea (John 6:19). At Peter's request, Jesus invited Peter to join Him in walking on the sea. However, when Peter began to sink because of his fear, Jesus caught him. Then Jesus got into the boat and the boat was miraculously at Gennesaret which is about five miles from Bethsaida, possibly carried by a great swell associated with the sudden stopping of the wind (Mark 6:51). This event took place during the fourth watch (3:00-6:00 A.M.) and it would now be Thursday, March 18, A.D. 32. Matthew 14:34 and Mark 6:53 both say that they landed at Gennesaret (see Figure 5.1) and moored to shore even though they were returning to Capernaum (John 6:17). This detail is important because it probably indicates that Gennesaret was where the Apostles kept their boats. In New Testament times almost the entire coast of the Sea of Galilee was occupied with small villages and almost every mooring space would be taken. Therefore, even though Peter lived in Capernaum (Mark 1:24-29), he apparently had to keep his boat at Gennesaret. Several important events of the Gospels took place at Peter's mooring site.

Jesus Teaches in Capernaum

The multitude followed Jesus and found Him on Thursday, March 18, A.D. 32 in Capernaum. .Then John 6:28-29 says:

> Therefore they said to Him, "What shall we do, so that we may work the works of God?" Jesus answered and said to them, "This is the work of God, that you believe in Him whom He has sent."

The multitude then asked for a sign and spoke of the manna received in the wilderness. In John 6:51 Jesus says, "I am the living bread that came down out of heaven; if anyone eats of this bread, he will live forever; and the bread also which I will give for the life of the world is My flesh."John 6:59 indicates that these sayings were taught in the synagogue in Capernaum. Jesus was probably taking part in one of the regular synagogue services. Hendricks in *The Gospel of John*, page 244, indicates that synagogue services were held on Monday, Thursday and Saturday which would be consistent with Jesus teaching in the synagogue on a Thursday. John 6:66 indicates that as a result of this teaching, many of Jesus' followers withdrew. Then Jesus asked the twelve if they wanted to go away also. John 6:68-69 says, "Simon Peter answered Him, 'Lord, to whom shall we go? You have words of eternal life. We have believed and have come to know that You are the Holy One of God.'"

After observing the Sabbath in Capernaum, Jesus probably departed on Sunday, March 28, A.D. 32, for Jerusalem to celebrate the Passover Feast. The four Gospels do not record any of the events that took place during this visit to Jerusalem. However, because

Deuteronomy 16:16 requires that all males Jews attend the three major Jewish feasts in Jerusalem, we can be sure that Jesus attended this Passover Feast. Also, since the journey from Capernaum to Jerusalem took a week each way, Jesus probably stayed in Judea until after the celebration of the Day of Pentecost which in A.D. 32 was celebrated on Sunday, June 13. After the Day of Pentecost, Jesus would have probably departed Jerusalem on Sunday, June 20, and He would have arrived in Capernaum about Thursday, June 24.

While Jesus was teaching in Capernaum, the Pharisees and scribes questioned Him about His disciples eating without ceremonially washing their hands. They said that Jesus' disciples were not walking according to the tradition of the elders. In Mark 7:7-8 Jesus answers them by quoting Isaiah 29:13, "'BUT IN VAIN DO THEY WORSHIP ME, TEACHING AS DOCTRINES THE PRECEPTS OF MEN.' 'Neglecting the commandment of God, you hold to the tradition of men.'" This encounter probably took place about Monday, June 28, A.D. 32.

Jesus Departs to Tyre

At this point in His ministry, Jesus realized that the pressure of the crowds was preventing Him from providing needed teaching to His disciples; therefore, He decided to withdraw from Galilee and go to Tyre. Mark 7:24 says, "Jesus got up and went away from there to the region of Tyre. And when He had entered a house, He wanted no one to know of it; yet He could not escape notice."

Jesus' route from Capernaum to Tyre is not recorded in the Gospels; however, because Jesus was attempting to get away from the Jewish crowds, He would have probably traveled east along the Sea of Galilee and crossed over the northern branch of the Jordan River into the Tetrarchy of Philip. Jesus and His disciples would have then traveled north through the Huleh Basin to the vicinity of Caesarea Philippi and then turned west and traveled to the vicinity of Tyre (see

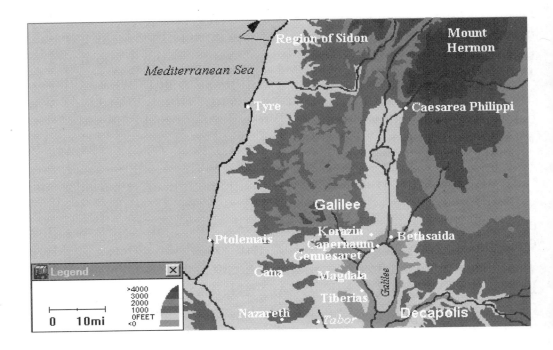

Jesus' Journey to Tyre
Figure 5.1

Figure 5.1). This route would have been through a less populated and primarily Gentile area compared to the alternate route of traveling west from Capernaum through Galilee to the coastal highway and then north to Tyre. Jesus and His disciples probably left Capernaum early in the morning since He was attempting to escape notice, about Tuesday, June 29. They would have probably avoided the large cities of Caesarea Philippi and Tyre.

Taking their time, Jesus and His disciples would have probably arrived in the region of Tyre about Thursday, July 1, since the journey from Capernaum to Tyre was only about fifty miles. Mark 7:24b indicates that in the region of Tyre Jesus entered a house. This may have been the home of a Jewish disciple of Jesus who had heard Jesus teaching in Galilee or Jerusalem. Jesus apparently stayed there for several days probably including the Sabbath on July 3. It may have been on Sunday, July 4, A.D. 32 that the Syrophoenician women learned of Jesus' presence from Jewish friends that had attended the synagogue service. She probably went to Jesus immediately to get Him to heal her demon possessed daughter. After testing the Syrophoenician women's faith, Jesus healed her daughter.

Jesus Departs Tyre

Then Mark 7:31 says, "Again He went out from the region of Tyre, and came through Sidon to the Sea of Galilee, within the region of Decapolis." Thus Jesus and His disciples left Tyre and headed north to the region of Sidon probably leaving early Monday, July 5 and arriving in the vicinity of Sidon later that same day. At this location He may have finally been far enough away from the site of His ministry to escape notice. Jesus probably spent a couple of weeks there teaching His disciples and then retraced His route back to the Sea of Galilee. However, Mark 7:31, quoted above, says that they returned to the Sea of Galilee in the region of Decapolis. This is the opposite side of the Sea of Galilee from that where Jesus carried out most of His ministry and is the area in which Jesus had earlier healed the Gerasene demoniac. Thus when Jesus and His disciples reached the vicinity of the Sea of Galilee, instead of turning west to Capernaum, they apparently continued south, along the east shore of the Sea of Galilee, into the region of the Decapolis. However, Jesus probably sent some of His disciples back to Gennesaret to pick up a boat with instructions to meet Him in the Decapolis because Jesus left the Decapolis by boat (Mark 8:10). As soon as Jesus reached the vicinity of the Sea of Galilee people would begin to recognize Him and a crowd would begin to follow Him. Jesus would have probably arrived in the Decapolis about Tuesday, July 20, A.D. 32. Then Mark 7:32-35 says:

They brought to Him one who was deaf and spoke with difficulty, and they implored Him to lay His hand on him. Jesus took him aside from the crowd, by himself, and put His fingers into his ears, and after spitting, He touched his tongue with the saliva; and looking up to heaven with a deep sigh, He said to him, "Ephphatha!" that is, "Be opened!" And his ears were opened, and the impediment of his tongue was removed, and he began speaking plainly.

Feeding of the 4000

After healing this man, Matthew 15:29 says that Jesus went up on a mountain and a great multitude came to Him bringing the lame, the crippled, the blind, the dumb and many others and Jesus healed them. Then Matthew 15:32 says:

And Jesus called His disciples to Him, and said, "I feel compassion for the people, because they have remained with Me now three days and have nothing to eat; and I do not want to send them away hungry, for they might faint on the way."

The feeding of the 4000 then took place. The three days mentioned in this verse would be Tuesday, July 20, Wednesday, July 21, and Thursday, July 22. Therefore the feeding of the 4000 would have taken place about Thursday, July 22.

Jesus at Magadan

Jesus and His disciples then entered the boat crossed over the Sea of Galilee to the region of Magadan (Matthew 15:39) or

Dalmanutha (Mark 8:10). Magadan may have been the town of Magdala, the hometown of Mary of Magdala, which is located on the western shore of the Sea of Galilee and Dalmanutha must have been another designation for the same region (see Figure 5.1).

Jesus and His disciples probably spent the Sabbath at Magadan and it was there, probably on Sunday, July 25, that the Pharisees and Sadducees came up and tested Jesus, asking Him to show them a sign from heaven. In Matthew 16:4, Jesus answers them saying, "'An evil and adulterous generation seeks after a sign; and a sign will not be given it, except the sign of Jonah.' And He left them and went away." This sign of Jonah is a veiled reference to Jesus' death, burial and resurrection. Jesus and His disciples then departed the same day to the other side of the Sea of Galilee. While in route, Matthew 16:6 says, "And Jesus said to them, 'Watch out and beware of the leaven of the Pharisees and Sadducees.'" However, the disciples had forgotten to take bread with them and they misunderstood this teaching until Jesus told them He was not speaking about bread and then they understood He was speaking of the teaching of the Pharisees and Sadducees.

Jesus in Bethsaida

And they came to Bethsaida. And they brought a blind man to Jesus and implored Him to touch him. Taking the blind man by the hand, He brought him out of the village; and after spitting on his eyes and laying His hands on him, He asked him, "Do you see anything?" And he looked up and said, "I see men, for I see them like trees, walking around." Then again He laid His hands on his eyes; and he looked intently and was restored, and began to see everything clearly. And He sent him to his home, saying, "Do not even enter the village" (Mark 8:22-26).

Thus the destination of Jesus and His disciples on the other side of the Sea of Galilee was Bethsaida (see Figure 5.1). It was at Bethsaida that Jesus healed a blind man, probably on Monday, July 26, A.D. 32.

Peter's Confession

> Jesus went out, along with His disciples, to the villages of Caesarea Philippi; and on the way He questioned His disciples, saying to them, "Who do people say that I am?" They told Him, saying, "John the Baptist; and others say Elijah; but others, one of the prophets." And He continued by questioning them, "But who do you say that I am?" Peter answered and said to Him, "You are the Christ." And He warned them to tell no one about Him (Mark 8:27-30).

Jesus departed the vicinity of Bethsaida on Monday, July 26, A.D. 32, but probably didn't arrive in the vicinity of Caesarea Philippi until Tuesday, July 27 and it was probably on that date that Peter made his great confession. After Peter's confession, Jesus warned the disciples concerning His upcoming passion. Then Matthew 16:22-23 says:

> Peter took Him aside and began to rebuke Him, saying, "God forbid it, Lord! This shall never happen to You." But He turned and said to Peter, "Get behind Me, Satan! You are a stumbling block to Me; for you are not setting your mind on God's interests, but man's."

Thus, probably on the same day, Tuesday, July 27, A.D. 32, Peter was commended by Jesus for his great confession and rebuked for trying to prevent Jesus from carrying out God's plan for the salvation of mankind.

This discourse was concluded with Mark 9:1 which says, "And Jesus was saying to them, 'Truly I say to you, there are some of those who are standing here who will not taste death until they see the kingdom of God after it has come with power.'" Some have seen this verse as a reference to Jesus' Second Coming in which case either Jesus was mistaken concerning His prediction or some of Jesus' disciples who were present on July 27, A.D. 32 are still alive. Neither of these alternatives are acceptable, therefore Jesus must not have been speaking of His Second Coming. In Matthew 12:28 Jesus said, "But if I cast out demons by the Spirit of God, then the Kingdom of God has come upon you." Since Jesus did cast out demons by the Spirit of God, the kingdom of God had come during Jesus' earthly ministry; however, it had not yet come in power in the sense that very few had accepted Jesus as Lord and Savior. However, in the lifetime of many of those present on July 27, A.D. 32, the Holy Spirit did come in power with many hundreds of thousands of believers.

Transfiguration of Jesus

Six days later, Jesus took with Him Peter and James and John, and brought them up on a high mountain by themselves. And He was transfigured before them; and His garments became radiant and exceedingly white, as no launderer on earth can whiten them. Elijah appeared to them along with Moses; and they were talking with Jesus. Peter said to Jesus, "Rabbi, it is good for us to be here; let us make three tabernacles, one for You, and one for Moses, and one for Elijah." For he did not know what to answer; for they became terrified. Then a cloud formed, overshadowing them, and a voice came out of the cloud, "This is My beloved Son, listen to Him!" All at once they looked around and saw no one with them anymore, except Jesus alone (Mark 9:2-9).

Counting inclusively six days from Peter's great confession on July 27, brings us to Sunday, August 1, as the date of Jesus' transfiguration. One of the traditional sites for the transfiguration is Mount Tabor which is located in the valley of Jezreel southwest of the Sea of Galilee (see Figure 5.1). However, Luke 9:37 says, "On the next day, when they came down from the mountain, a large crowd met Him." Immediately before the transfiguration, Jesus and His disciples were in the vicinity of Caesarea Philippi where apparently Jesus left the other disciples. After the transfiguration, Jesus returned to these other disciples in one day. It would have been more than a one day journey to return to the vicinity of Caesarea Philippi from Mount Tabor. However, Mount Herman is located within a day's journey of Caesarea Philippi (see Figure 5.1). Also Matthew 17:1 describes the Mount of the Transfiguration as a very high mountain. Mount Tabor rises only 1690 feet above sea level while Mount Herman rises 9100 feet above sea level.

Jesus and Peter, James and John would have returned to the vicinity of Caesarea Philippi on Monday, August 2. On the journey down the mountain, Jesus told these disciples not to relate this experience to anyone until the Son of Man should rise from the dead, but the disciples didn't understand. Then Matthew 17:10-13 says:

> And His disciples asked Him, "Why then do the scribes say that Elijah must come first?" And He answered and said, "Elijah is coming and will restore all things; but I say to you that Elijah already came, and they did not recognize him, but did to him whatever they wished. So also the Son of Man is going to suffer at their hands." Then the disciples understood that He had spoken to them about John the Baptist.

Demoniac Boy Cured

When they came to the crowd, a man came up to Jesus, falling on his knees before Him and saying, "Lord, have mercy on my son, for he is a lunatic and is very ill; for he often falls into the fire and often into the water. I brought him to Your disciples, and they could not cure him." And Jesus answered and said, "You unbelieving and perverted generation, how long shall I be with you? How long shall I put up with you? Bring him here to Me." And Jesus rebuked him, and the demon came out of him, and the boy was cured at once. Then the disciples came to Jesus privately and said, "Why could we not drive it out?" And He said to them, "Because of the littleness of your faith; for truly I say to you, if you have faith the size of a mustard seed, you will say to this mountain, 'Move from here to there,' and it will move; and nothing will be impossible to you" (Matthew 17:14-20).

Following the transfiguration and the casting out of the demon from the boy, Jesus and His disciples departed the region of Caesarea Philippi and returned to Galilee. They went about Galilee in secret and He was teaching His disciples (Mark 9:30-32). Jesus repeatedly told His disciples of His upcoming passion, but they were unable at that time to receive this teaching. They believed Jesus was the long awaited Messiah who would restore the worldly kingdom of Israel and they could not accept Jesus' death before He had established that worldly kingdom. However, at this stage of His ministry, Jesus was more concerned with teaching His disciples than with preaching to the multitude so for a period of several days Jesus and His disciples moved about Galilee avoiding the larger cities.

Jesus Returns to Capernaum

Then about Thursday, August 12, A.D. 32, Jesus and His disciples returned to Capernaum. Mark 9:33-35 says:

> They came to Capernaum; and when He was in the house, He began to question them, "What were you discussing on the way?" But they kept silent, for on the way they had discussed with one another which of them was the greatest. Sitting down, He called the twelve and said to them, "If anyone wants to be first, he shall be last of all and servant of all."

Jesus and His disciples probably spent the next Sabbath, August 14, and the following week in Capernaum. The collectors of the temple tax probably saw Jesus and His disciples in the synagogue, so the next day, Sunday, August 15, Matthew 17:24-27 says:

> When they came to Capernaum, those who collected the two-drachma tax came to Peter and said, "Does your teacher not pay the two-drachma tax?" He said, "Yes." And when he came into the house, Jesus spoke to him first, saying, "What do you think, Simon? From whom do the kings of the earth collect customs or poll-tax, from their sons or from strangers?" When Peter said, "From strangers," Jesus said to him, "Then the sons are exempt. However, so that we do not offend them, go to the sea and throw in a hook, and take the first fish that comes up; and when you open its mouth, you will find a shekel. Take that and give it to them for you and Me."

As discussed in Chapter 2, the shekel which Jesus mentioned would have been the Shekel of Tyre (see Figure 2.7, page 79) which was required for payment of the Temple tax. The Shekel of Tyre was a tetradrachma (four drachma) coin and since the Temple tax was a two drachma tax, this shekel would pay the tax for both Jesus and Peter. In this incident Jesus demonstrates that He was truly God in the form of man. He seemed to have supernatural knowledge of Peter's conversation with the collectors of the temple tax and was able to supply the shekel needed to pay the tax supernaturally. If we accept John 1:1 which says, "In the beginning was the Word, and the Word was with God, and the Word was God," then we should have no problem with Jesus being able to supernaturally supply the temple tax. However, those that don't accept the deity of Jesus, can't accept the miracles of Jesus recorded in the Gospels.

Feast of Booths

The next event that can be specifically dated in the Gospels is found in John 7:2-10 which says:

Now the feast of the Jews, the Feast of Booths, was near. Therefore His brothers said to Him, "Leave here and go into Judea, so that Your disciples also may see Your works which You are doing. For no one does anything in secret when he himself seeks to be known publicly. If You do these things, show Yourself to the world." For not even His brothers were believing in Him. So Jesus said to them, "My time is not yet here, but your time is always opportune. The world cannot hate you, but it hates Me because I testify of it, that its deeds are evil. Go up to the feast yourselves; I do not go up to this feast because My time has not yet fully come." Having said these things to them, He stayed in Galilee. But when His brothers had gone up to the feast, then He Himself also went up, not publicly, but as if, in secret.

The festivals around the Feast of Booths began with the Day of Trumpets which, in A.D. 32, began at sunset on Wednesday, September 22. Jesus' brothers would have probably left on Sunday, September 12 and would have probably arrived in Jerusalem on Thursday, September 16. Jesus may have waited until Sunday, September 19, to depart. He probably took the direct route through Samaria and thus could have arrived on Wednesday, September 22, with the Day of Trumpets beginning that day at sunset. This event occurred during the period when Jesus was avoiding crowds so He could teach His disciples which would explain why His brothers were encouraging Him to be more public with His ministry. However, Jesus didn't reveal Himself at the Feast of Booths until the middle of the feast (John 7:14). This would have probably been Sunday, October 10, A.D. 32 when Jesus began teaching in public. Then John 7:37-39 says:

> Now on the last day, the great day of the feast, Jesus stood and cried out, saying, "If anyone is thirsty, let him come to Me and drink. He who believes in Me, as the Scripture said, 'From his innermost being will flow rivers of living water.'" But this He spoke of the Spirit, whom those who believed in Him were to receive; for the Spirit was not yet given, because Jesus was not yet glorified.

The last day of the Feast of Booth was Tishri 22, which in A.D. 32 began at sunset on Wednesday, October 13, with the convocation occurring during the daylight hours of October 14. Thus, this event would have taken place on Thursday, October 14. During the feast the chief priests and Pharisees sent the temple guard to arrest Jesus, but they returned without Him. Then John 7:45-52 says:

> The officers then came to the chief priests and Pharisees,

and they said to them, "Why did you not bring Him?" The officers answered, "Never has a man spoken the way this man speaks." The Pharisees then answered them, "You have not also been led astray, have you? No one of the rulers or Pharisees has believed in Him, has he? But this crowd which does not know the Law is accursed." Nicodemus (he who came to Him before, being one of them) said to them, "Our Law does not judge a man unless it first hears from him and knows what he is doing, does it?" They answered him, "You are not also from Galilee, are you? Search, and see that no prophet arises out of Galilee."

Woman Caught in Adultery

Then John 7:53-8:,2 says, "Everyone went to his home. But Jesus went to the Mount of Olives. Early in the morning He came again into the temple, and all the people were coming to Him; and He sat down and began to teach them." This would have been Friday, October 15, A.D. 32. At this time the scribes and Pharisees brought to Jesus a woman caught in adultery and said to Him, "Now the Law of Moses commanded us to stone such women, what then do You say (John 8:5)?" To the Jewish leaders this seemed like the perfect trap for Jesus. If Jesus said they should follow the law of Moses and stone the woman, then He would be advocating breaking the Roman law that said only the Roman governor had the power to condemn someone to death. However, if Jesus said, "Don't stone her," He would be contradicting the Law of Moses. John 8:6-9 says:

They were saying this, testing Him, so that they might have grounds for accusing Him. But Jesus stooped down and with His finger wrote on the ground. But when they persisted in asking Him, He straightened up, and said to them, "He who is without sin among you, let him be the first to throw a stone at her." Again He stooped down and wrote on the ground. When they heard it, they began to go out one by one, beginning with the older ones, and He was left alone, and the woman, where she was, in the center of the court.

Thus, Jesus was able to avoid the trap of the scribes and Pharisees and deliver the sinful woman. This incident shows that Jesus is willing to forgive a repentant sinner while still rejecting the sinful act. Jesus told the woman, "From now on, sin no more (John 8:11b)."

Light of the World

Later, probably on the same day, Jesus was teaching in the area of the treasury of the Temple and John 8:12-19says:

Then Jesus again spoke to them, saying, "I am the Light of the world; he who follows Me will not walk in the darkness, but will have the Light of life." So the Pharisees said to Him, "You are testifying about Yourself; Your testimony is not true." Jesus answered and said to them, "Even if I testify about Myself, My testimony is true, for I know where I came from and where I am going; but you do not know where I come from or where I am going. You judge according to the flesh; I am not judging anyone. But even if I do judge, My judgment is true; for I am not alone in it, but I and the Father who sent Me. Even in your law it has been written that the testimony of two men is true. I am He who testifies about Myself, and the Father who sent Me testifies about Me." So they were saying to Him, "Where is Your Father?" Jesus answered, "You know neither Me nor My Father; if you knew Me, you would know My Father also."

Jesus said in John 5:34a, "But the witness which I receive is not from man." Since the Holy Spirit had not yet been sent, the only qualified witnesses were God and Jesus Himself. At this same time Jesus said, "I go away and you shall seek me, and shall die in your sins, where I am you can not come (John 8:21)." At this time Jesus also said, "If you abide in My words, then you are truly disciples of Mine and you shall know the truth and the truth shall make you free (John 8:31,32)." The majority of the Jews rejected Jesus' words and tried to stone Him, but Jesus hid Himself and went out of the Temple.

Blind Man Healed

In chapter 9 of the Gospel of John is recorded Jesus' healing of a blind man. John 9:14 says, "Now it was a Sabbath on the day when Jesus made the clay and opened his eyes." This would have been Saturday, October 16, A.D. 32. The Pharisees questioned the former blind man concerning how he had received his sight. Some of the Pharisees claimed that Jesus was not from God because He had healed the blind man on the Sabbath. They asked the former blind man what he though and he said, "He is a prophet." The Pharisees did not believe the man had been blind until after they talked to his parents. Then the Pharisees called the former blind man back a second time and tried to get him to reject Jesus. When he wouldn't, they, "put him out," which was probably a form of excommunication from the Temple. When Jesus heard that the former blind man had been put out of the Temple, He found him and Jesus revealed that He was the Son of Man (Messiah) and the former blind man worshiped Jesus. Then John 9:39-41 says:

And Jesus said, "For judgment I came into this world, so

that those who do not see may see, and that those who see may become blind." Those of the Pharisees who were with Him heard these things and said to Him, "We are not blind too, are we?" Jesus said to them, "If you were blind, you would have no sin; but since you say, 'We see,' your sin remains.".

Probably on that same day Jesus taught the Parable of the Sheepfold. John 10:1-4 says:

"Truly, truly, I say to you, he who does not enter by the door into the fold of the sheep, but climbs up some other way, he is a thief and a robber. But he who enters by the door is a shepherd of the sheep. To him the doorkeeper opens, and the sheep hear his voice, and he calls his own sheep by name and leads them out. When he puts forth all his own, he goes ahead of them, and the sheep follow him because they know his voice."

Probably the next day, Sunday, October 17, A.D. 32, Jesus departed Jerusalem for Galilee.

Seventy Sent

The next event that can be exactly dated is found in John 10:22-23 which says:

At that time the Feast of the Dedication took place at Jerusalem; it was winter, and Jesus was walking in the temple in the portico of Solomon.

The Feast of Dedication in A.D. 32 began on Tuesday, December 14. Jesus' departure from Galilee for this visit to Jerusalem is probably recorded in Luke 9:51-56 which says:

> When the days were approaching for His ascension, He was determined to go to Jerusalem; and He sent messengers on ahead of Him, and they went and entered a village of the Samaritans to make arrangements for Him. But they did not receive Him, because He was traveling toward Jerusalem. When His disciples James and John saw this, they said, "Lord, do You want us to command fire to come down from heaven and consume them?" But He turned and rebuked them, and said, "You do not know what kind of spirit you are of; for the Son of Man did not come to destroy men's lives, but to save them." And they went on to another village.

Possibly as a result of this incident, Jesus sent out seventy disciples in teams of two to prepare the way for Him. These thirty-five teams would have visited all the town Jesus would pass through on His way to Jerusalem. The teams visiting the towns nearest Jerusalem would have taken about five days to reach their destination and five days to return, so allowing four days at their town, this operation would have required at least two weeks.

Thus Jesus probably departed Galilee about Sunday, November 7, A.D. 32. That first day was probably spent in Galilee. The next day Jesus probably sent messengers ahead to Samaria. It would have been on Monday, November 8, that the Samaritans refused to receive Jesus and James and John suggested that they command fire from heaven to come down to destroy that village. The seventy was probably sent out about Wednesday, November 10, and probably returned about Thursday, November 25. Then Luke 10:17-20 says:

> The seventy returned with joy, saying, "Lord, even the demons are subject to us in Your name." And He said to

them, "I was watching Satan fall from heaven like lightning. Behold, I have given you authority to tread on serpents and scorpions, and over all the power of the enemy, and nothing will injure you. Nevertheless do not rejoice in this, that the spirits are subject to you, but rejoice that your names are recorded in heaven."

It is interesting to note from the calendar for A.D. 32 that the new month, Kislev, began on Saturday, November 20. Thus, Jesus may have instructed the seventy to begin their return journey to Him before the beginning of the new month. Thus the disciples could gauge their time by watching the phases of the moon. When the new moon was approaching, they knew they must return to Jesus. Probably on the same day that Jesus addressed the seventy about Thursday, November 25, Luke 10:25-29 says:

And a lawyer stood up and put Him to the test, saying, "Teacher, what shall I do to inherit eternal life?" And He said to him, "What is written in the Law? How does it read to you?" And he answered, "YOU SHALL LOVE THE LORD YOUR GOD WITH ALL YOUR HEART, AND WITH ALL YOUR SOUL, AND WITH ALL YOUR STRENGTH, AND WITH ALL YOUR MIND; AND YOUR NEIGHBOR AS YOURSELF." And He said to him, "You have answered correctly; DO THIS AND YOU WILL LIVE." But wishing to justify himself, he said to Jesus, "And who is my neighbor?"

In answer to this question, Jesus told the parable on the Good Samaritan. The next event recorded in Luke's Gospel is found in Luke 10:38-42 which says:

Now as they were traveling along, He entered a village;

and a woman named Martha welcomed Him into her home. She had a sister called Mary, who was seated at the Lord's feet, listening to His word. But Martha was distracted with all her preparations; and she came up to Him and said, "Lord, do You not care that my sister has left me to do all the serving alone? Then tell her to help me." But the Lord answered and said to her, "Martha, Martha, you are worried and bothered about so many things; but only one thing is necessary, for Mary has chosen the good part, which shall not be taken away from her."

Jesus is still on His way to Jerusalem, but we know from John 11:1 that Mary and Martha live in Bethany, right outside Jerusalem. Therefore this event probably took place about Thursday, December 9, A.D. 32 when Jesus and His disciples had arrived in the vicinity of Jerusalem just before the Feast of the Dedication.

Feast of the Dedication

At this point Luke records a number of events that apparently occurred during this visit to Jerusalem to attend the Feast of the Dedication. Some of these events parallel events recorded in Matthew either earlier or later in Jesus' ministry. It is possible that some of these events may reflect an editing by Luke of material from Matthew; however, it is also possible that these events reflect a repetition of illustrations and teachings by Jesus for emphasis and because His audience was continually changing. Luke 11:1 says:

It happened that while Jesus was praying in a certain place, after He had finished, one of His disciples said to Him, "Lord, teach us to pray just as John also taught his disciples."

In response to this request, Jesus taught His disciples the Lord's Prayer (Luke 11:2-4). Then Jesus told the parable of the Persistent Friend (Luke 11:5-8) and said, "So I say to you, ask, and it will be given to you; seek, and you will find; knock, and it will be opened to you (Luke 11:9)." At the same time Jesus also said (Luke 11:13), "If you then, being evil, know how to give good gifts to your children, how much more will your heavenly Father give the Holy Spirit to those who ask Him?" These things probably happened on Friday, December 10, A.D. 32, on the way from Bethany to Jerusalem.

The next event recorded in Luke's Gospel probably occurred on Sunday, December 19, during the Feast of Dedication. Luke 11:14-16 says:

> And He was casting out a demon, and it was mute; when the demon had gone out, the mute man spoke; and the crowds were amazed. But some of them said, "He casts out demons by Beelzebul, the ruler of the demons." Others, to test Him, were demanding of Him a sign from heaven.

Jesus answered these detractors by pointing out that Satan's kingdom is not divided against itself so Beelzebul would not cast out other demons. Then Jesus said (Luke 11:20), "But if I cast out demons by the finger of God, then the kingdom of God has come upon you." Jesus indicated His power over Satan by pointing out that when a stronger man (Jesus) attacks a strong man (Satan), then the possessions of the strong man (sinners) are plundered. Then Jesus said (Luke 11:23), "He who is not with Me is against Me; and he who does not gather with Me, scatters." Thus, Jesus says we must either accept Him as Savior and Lord or we are lost. Then Luke 11:26-27 says:

> While Jesus was saying these things, one of the women

in the crowd raised her voice and said to Him, "Blessed
is the womb that bore You and the breasts at which You
nursed." But He said, "On the contrary, blessed are those
who hear the word of God and observe it."

Our salvation does not depend on our ancestry, but on hearing and
following the word of God. Then Luke 11:29-32 says:

As the crowds were increasing, He began to say, "This
generation is a wicked generation; it seeks for a sign,
and yet no sign will be given to it but the sign of Jonah.
For just as Jonah became a sign to the Ninevites, so will
the Son of Man be to this generation. The Queen of the
South will rise up with the men of this generation at the
judgment and condemn them, because she came from the
ends of the earth to hear the wisdom of Solomon; and
behold, something greater than Solomon is here. The
men of Nineveh will stand up with this generation at the
judgment and condemn it, because they repented at the
preaching of Jonah; and behold, something greater than
Jonah is here."

Then Jesus told the Parable of the Lamp and the Parable of the Eye.
On the same day, Jesus was invited to have lunch with a
Pharisee. Jesus surprised His host by not ceremonially washing His
hands before the meal. Then Jesus said to those gathered at the
Pharisee's house (Luke 11:39b), "Now you Pharisees clean the
outside of the cup and of the platter; but inside of you, you are full of
robbery and wickedness." Then Jesus proceeded to pronounce three
woes against the Pharisees and also three woes against the lawyers.
After this the scribes and Pharisees became very hostile toward Jesus
and plotted against Him.
The multitude continued to follow Jesus, and in Luke 12:1

Jesus warned His disciples to beware of the leaven of the Pharisees which was hypocrisy. Then Jesus said in Luke 12:4-5:

> "I say to you, My friends, do not be afraid of those who kill the body and after that have no more that they can do. But I will warn you whom to fear: fear the One who, after He has killed, has authority to cast into hell; yes, I tell you, fear Him!"

After that Jesus gave encouragement and advise to His disciples concerning the coming persecution (Luke 12:6-12). Then someone in the crowd said, "Teacher, tell my brother to divide the family inheritance with me," but Jesus refused. After that Jesus told the Parable of the Rich Fool. Jesus also cautioned His disciples about being anxious about their life. He then told them the Parable of the Faithful Stewards. Then in Luke 12:41 Peter said, "Lord, are You addressing this parable to us, or to everyone else as well?" In His answer Jesus said in Luke 12:48b, "From everyone who has been given much, much will be required; and to whom they entrusted much, of him they will ask all the more." Then in Luke 12:49-51 Jesus says:

> "I have come to cast fire upon the earth; and how I wish it were already kindled! But I have a baptism to undergo, and how distressed I am until it is accomplished! Do you suppose that I came to grant peace on earth? I tell you, no, but rather division; for from now on five members in one household will be divided, three against two and two against three."

Again Jesus is saying He must be either accepted or rejected. This would bring division in the family especially in the Jewish community of Jesus' day. Then Jesus turned to the multitude and condemned them because they recognized the signs indicating future weather, but they would not recognize the signs of the coming of the Kingdom of God. Then some of those present reported to Jesus concerning the Galileans whose blood Pilate had mingled with their sacrifices. We know nothing about this incident from sources other than this passage of Luke; however, it probably occurred during the Passover Feast, while the Galileans were sacrificing their lambs because that is the only time men other than priests were directly involved in the sacrifices and thus could have their blood mingled with that of the sacrifices. At that time, it was widely believed that involvement in a calamity was caused by the sin of the people involved. In answer to this report Jesus said in Luke 13:2b-3, "Do you suppose that these Galileans were greater sinners than all other Galileans because they suffered this fate? I tell you, no, but unless you repent, you will all likewise perish." Jesus made similar remarks concerning the fall of the tower of Siloam. Then He told the Parable of the Fig Tree which warned His hearers that they only had a limited time to accept Jesus as Lord and Savior. All of these events probably took place during the Feast of Dedication on Sunday, December 19, A.D. 32.

Then on the next day, Monday, December 20, Jesus was walking in the Temple in the portico of Solomon, which would probably have been in the outer courts of the Temple area on the east side of the Temple Mount (see Figure 5.2). John 10:24-29 says:

> The Jews then gathered around Him, and were saying to Him, "How long will You keep us in suspense? If You are the Christ, tell us plainly." Jesus answered them, "I told you, and you do not believe; the works that I do in My Father's name, these testify of Me. But you do not believe because you are not of My sheep. My sheep hear My voice, and I know them, and they follow Me; and I give eternal life to them, and they will never

perish; and no one will snatch them out of My hand. My Father, who has given them to Me, is greater than all; and no one is able to snatch them out of the Father's hand. I and the Father are one." The Jews picked up stones again to stone Him.

These Jews had no problem understanding that Jesus was claiming to be the Christ although this fact seems to have escaped many liberal Bible scholars. Then John 10:32-33 says, "Jesus answered them, 'I showed you many good works from the Father; for which of them are you stoning Me?' The Jews answered Him, 'For a good work we do not stone You, but for blasphemy; and because You, being a man, make Yourself out to be God.'" Jesus eluded these Jews and probably early the next morning He returned to Galilee.

The next event recorded in John's Gospel places Jesus beyond the Jordan where John the Baptist was baptizing. However, the synoptic Gospels record some additional events that took place in Galilee, so Jesus probably returned to Galilee for a short time and spent the remainder of His second year of ministry there.

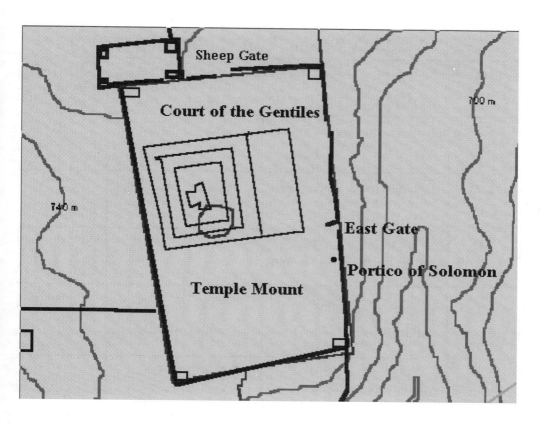

Temple Mount
Figure 5.2

Table 5.1 Jesus' Second Year of Ministry				
Event Sequence Number	Event (Scripture Reference)	Location of Event	Gregorian Date	Level of Confidence*
171	Jesus Teaching in the Villages (Mt 9:35)	Galilee	June 8-Feb 15, A.D. 32	II
172	Harvest Plentiful, Workers Few (Mt 9:36-38)	Galilee	Wednesday Feb 11, A.D. 32	II
173	Jesus Sends Out the Twelve (Mt 10:1-4, Mk 6:7, Lk 9:1,2)	Galilee	Sunday Feb 15, A.D. 32	II
174	Jesus' Instructions to the Twelve (Mt 10:5-15, Mk 6:8-11, Lk 9:3-6)	Galilee	Sunday Feb 15, A.D. 32	II
175	Be Shrewd as Serpents, Innocent as Doves (Mt 10:16)	Galilee	Sunday Feb 15, A.D. 32	II
176	Jesus Foretells Persecution of Twelve (Mt 10:17-23)	Galilee	Sunday Feb 15, A.D. 32	II
177	Fear Him Who Can Destroy Body & Send Soul To Hell (Mt 10:24-28)	Galilee	Sunday Feb 15, A.D. 32	II
178	He Who Confesses Me, I Will Confess (Mt 10:29-33)	Galilee	Sunday Feb 15, A.D. 32	II
179	I Didn't Come To Bring Peace (Mt 10:34-39)	Galilee	Sunday Feb 15, A.D. 32	II

*Level of Confidence in Date   Level I = Highly Probable   Level II = Probable

Event Sequence Number	Event (Scripture Reference)	Location of Event	Gregorian Date	Level of Confidence*
180	He Who Receives You, Receives Me (Mt 10:40-42)	Galilee	Sunday, Feb 15, A.D. 32	II
181	Jesus Departs to Teach & Preach (Mt 11:1)	Galilee	Sunday, Feb 15, A.D. 32	II
182	Twelve Preaching & Healing (Mk 6:12-13)	Galilee	Feb 15-Mar 13, A.D. 32	II
183	John the Baptist Sends Messenger (Mt 11:2-6, Lk 7:18-23)	Galilee	Wednesday Feb 25, A.D. 32	II
184	Jesus Praises John the Baptist (Mt 11:7-19, Lk 7:24-35)	Galilee	Wednesday Feb 25, A.D. 32	II
185	Jesus Anointed by Women of the City (Lk 7:36-50)	Galilee	Wednesday Feb 25, A.D. 32	II
186	Death of John the Baptist (Mk 6:27-29, Mt 14:6-12)	Machaerus Peraea	Wednesday Mar 3, A.D. 32	II
187	Jesus Reproaches the Unrepentant Cities (Mt 11:20-24, Lk 10:13-15)	Galilee	Wednesday Mar 10, A.D. 32	II
188	Jesus Gives Thanks for the Simplicity of the Gospel (Mt 11:25-27, Lk 10:21-24)	Galilee	Wednesday Mar 10, A.D. 32	II
189	My Yoke Is Easy & My Load Is Light (Mt 11:28-30)	Galilee	Wednesday Mar 10, A.D. 32	II

*Level of Confidence in Date   Level I = Highly Probable   Level II = Probable

Event Sequence Number	Event (Scripture Reference)	Location of Event	Gregorian Date	Level of Confidence*
190	Herod Thinks John the Baptist Has Risen (Mk 6:14-16, Mt 14:1-2, Lk 9:7-9)	Galilee	Thursday, Mar 11, A.D. 31	II
191	The Twelve Report on Their Mission (Mk 6:30, Lk 9:10a)	Gennesaret Galilee	Wednesday Mar 17 A.D. 32	II
192	Jesus & Disciples Depart to a Lonely Place (Mk 6:31-32, Jn 6:1, Mt 14:13, Lk 9:10b)	Gennesaret Galilee	Wednesday Mar 17, A.D. 32	II
193	Feeding the 5000 (Mk 6:33-44, Jn 6:2-13, Mt 14:14-21, Lk 9:11-17)	Near Bethsaida, Galilee	Wednesday Mar 17, A.D. 32	II
194	People Intend To Make Jesus King (Jn 6:14-15)	Near Bethsaida, Galilee	Wednesday Mar 17, A.D. 32	II
195	Disciples Depart by Boat (Mk 6:45, Mt 14:22, Jn 6:16-17)	Near Bethsaida, Galilee	Wednesday Mar 17, A.D. 32	II
196	Jesus Went Up the Mountain To Pray (Mk 6:46-47, Mt 14:23)	Near Bethsaida Galilee	Wednesday Mar 17, A.D. 32	II
197	Jesus Walks on the Water (Mk 6:48-50, Mt 14:24-27, Jn 6:18-21a)	Sea of Galilee	Thursday Mar 18, A.D. 32	II
198	Peter Walks on the Water (Mt 14:28-31)	Sea of Galilee	Thursday Mar 18, A.D. 32	II

*Level of Confidence in Date   Level I = Highly Probable   Level II = Probable

Event Sequence Number	Event (Scripture Reference)	Location of Event	Gregorian Date	Level of Confidence*
199	Jesus Enters the Boat and Arrives at Gennesaret (Mk 6:51-53, Mt 14:32-34, Jn 6:21b)	Gennesaret Galilee	Thursday Mar 18, A.D. 32	II
200	Jesus Heals At Gennesaret (Mk 6:54-56, Mt 14:35-36)	Gennesaret Galilee	Thursday Mar 18, A.D. 32	II
201	Multitude Follow Jesus to Capernaum (Jn 6:22-25)	Capernaum Galilee	Thursday Mar 18, A.D. 32	II
202	The Work of God (Jn 6:26-29)	Capernaum Galilee	Thursday Mar 18, A.D. 32	II
203	All the Father Gives Comes to Me (Jn 6:30-40)	Capernaum Galilee	Thursday Mar 18, A.D. 32	II
204	He Who Eats My Flesh & Drinks My Blood Abides in Me (Jn 6:41-58)	Capernaum Galilee	Thursday Mar 18, A.D. 32	II
205	Many Disciples Withdraw From Jesus (Jn 6:59-66)	Capernaum Galilee	Thursday Mar 18, A.D. 32	II
206	Peter Says, "To Whom Shall We Go" (Jn 6:67-69)	Capernaum Galilee	Thursday Mar 18, A.D. 32	II
207	Jesus Foretells One of the Twelve Would Betray Him (Jn 6:70-71)	Capernaum Galilee	Thursday Mar 18, A.D. 32	II
208	Question Concerning the Tradition of the Elders (Mk 7:1-5, Mt 15:1-2)	Capernaum Galilee	Monday Jun 28, A.D. 32	II

*Level of Confidence in Date   Level I = Highly Probable   Level II = Probable

Event Sequence Number	Event (Scripture Reference)	Location of Event	Gregorian Date	Level of Confidence*
209	Invalidating the Word of God By Their Traditions (Mk 7:6-13, Mt 15:3-9)	Capernaum Galilee	Monday June 28, A.D. 32	II
210	Man is Not Defiled From Without, but From Within (Mk 7:14-16, Mt 15:10-11)	Capernaum Galilee	Monday June 28, A.D. 32	II
211	Pharisees Offended By Jesus' Teaching (Mt 15:12-14)	Capernaum Galilee	Monday June 28, A.D. 32	II
212	Jesus Explains His Teaching (Mk 7:17-23, Mt 15:15-20)	Capernaum Galilee	Monday June 28, A.D. 32	II
213	Jesus & Disciples Depart for Tyre (Mk 7:24a, Mt 15:21)	Capernaum Galilee	Monday June 28, A.D. 32	II
214	Jesus Heals the Daughter of the Syrophoenician Women (Mk 7:24b-30, Mt 15:22-28)	Tyre, Phoenicia	Sunday July 4, A.D. 32	II
215	Jesus Departs Tyre for Sidon & Sea of Galilee and Decapolis (Mk 7:31, Mt 15:29a)	Tyre, Phoenicia	Monday July 5, A.D. 32	II
216	Jesus Heals Deaf & Dumb Man (Mk 7:32-37)	Decapolis Near Sea of Galilee	Tuesday July 20, A.D. 32	II
217	Jesus Heals Many On A Mountain (Mt 15:29b-31)	Decapolis Near Sea of Galilee	Tuesday July 20, A.D. 32	II
218	Feeding of the 4000 (Mk 8:1-9, Mt 15:32-38)	Decapolis Near Sea of Galilee	Thursday July 22, A.D. 32	II

*Level of Confidence in Date   Level I = Highly Probable   Level II = Probable

Event Sequence Number	Event (Scripture Reference)	Location of Event	Gregorian Date	Level of Confidence*
219	Jesus Departs to Magadan (Dalmanutha) (Mk 8:10, Mk 15:39)	Decapolis Near Sea of Galilee	Thursday July 22, A.D. 32	II
220	Pharisees & Sadducees Ask Jesus for a Sign (Mk 8:11, Mt 16:1)	Magadan Galilee	Sunday July 25, A.D. 32	II
221	Can Discern Signs of Weather, But Not Signs of the Times (Mt 16:2-3)	Magadan Galilee	Sunday July 25, A.D. 32	II
222	No Sign But the Sign of Jonah (Mk 8:12-13, Mt 16:4)	Magadan Galilee	Sunday July 25, A.D. 32	II
223	Beware of the Leaven of the Pharisees (Mk 8:14-21, Mt 16:5-12)	On Sea of Galilee	Sunday July 25, A.D. 32	II
224	Jesus Heals a Blind Man (Mk 8:22-26)	Bethsaida Galilee	Monday July 26, A.D. 32	II
225	Peter's Confession of Christ (Mk 8:27-30, Mt 16:13-17)	Near Caesarea Philippi	Tuesday July 27, A.D. 32	II
226	Peter Will Be Given The Keys To the Kingdom (Mt 16:18-20)	Near Caesarea Philippi	Tuesday July 27, A.D. 32	II
227	Jesus Foretells His Passion (Mk 8:31, Mt 16:21)	Near Caesarea Philippi	Tuesday July 27, A.D. 32	II

*Level of Confidence in Date   Level I = Highly Probable   Level II = Probable

Event Sequence Number	Event (Scripture Reference)	Location of Event	Gregorian Date	Level of Confidence*
228	Jesus Tells Peter, "Get Behind Me Satan" (Mk 8:32-33, Mt 16:22-23, Lk 9:18-20)	Near Caesarea Philippi	Tuesday July 27, A.D. 32	II
229	Let Him Deny Himself & Take Up His Cross & Follow Me (Mt 16:24)	Near Caesarea Philippi	Tuesday July 27, A.D. 32	II
230	What Will a Man Give In Exchange for His Soul (Mk 8:34-38, Mt 16:25-27), Lk 9:21-26)	Near Caesarea Philippi	Tuesday July 27, A.D. 32	II
231	Some Will Not Taste Death Until Kingdom Comes in Power (Mk 9:1, Mt 16:28, Lk 9:27)	Near Caesarea Philippi	Tuesday July 27, A.D. 32	II
232	Transfiguration of Jesus (Mk 9:2-8, Mt 17:1-8, Lk 9:28-36a)	Mount Hermon	Sunday August 1, A.D. 32	II
233	Not To Tell of Transfiguration Until He Had Risen From Dead (Mk 9:9, Mt 17:9, Lk 9:36b)	Slope of Mount Hermon	Monday August 2, A.D. 32	II
234	Disciples Discuss Meaning of Risen From the Dead (Mk 9:10)	Slope of Mount Hermon	Monday August 2, A.D. 32	II
235	Jesus Said, "Elijah Has Come" (Mk 9:11-13, Mt 17:10-13)	Slope of Mount Hermon	Monday August 2, A.D. 32	II
236	Jesus Heals Demoniac Boy (Mk 9:14-27, Mt 17:14-18, Lk 9:37-43)	Near Caesarea Philippi	Monday August 2, A.D. 32	II

*Level of Confidence in Date   Level I = Highly Probable   Level II = Probable

Event Sequence Number	Event (Scripture Reference)	Location of Event	Gregorian Date	Level of Confidence*
237	Disciples Ask Why They Could Not Cast It Out (Mk 9:28-29, Mt 17:19-21)	Near Caesarea Philippi	Monday August 2, A.D. 32	II
238	Jesus & Disciples Begin Going Through Galilee (Mk 9:30)	Galilee	Wednesday August 4, A.D. 32	II
239	Jesus Foretells His Passion (Mk 9:31-32, Mt 17:22-23, Lk 9:44-45)	Galilee	Wednesday August 4. A.D..32	II
240	Jesus & Disciples Return to Capernaum (Mk 9:33a, Mt 17:24a)	Capernaum Galilee	Thursday August 12, ADD. 32	II
241	Which of the Disciples Was the Greatest? (Mk 9:33b-37, Mt 18:1-4, Lk 9:46-48)	Capernaum Galilee	Thursday August 12, A.D. 32	II
242	He Who Is Not Against Us, Is For Us (Mk 9:38-41, Lk 9:49-50)	Capernaum Galilee	Thursday August 12, A.D. 32	II
243	Stumbling Blocks (Mk 9:42-50, Mt 18:5-11	Capernaum Galilee	Thursday August 12, A.D. 32	II
244	Parable of the Lost Sheep (Mt 18:12-14)	Capernaum Galilee	Thursday August 12, A.D. 32	II
245	Restoring a Brother That Sins (Mt 18:15-17)	Capernaum Galilee	Thursday August 12, A.D. 32	II
246	Whatever You Bind, Will Have Been Bound In Heaven (Mt 18:18)	Capernaum Galilee	Thursday August 12, A.D. 32	II

*Level of Confidence in Date   Level I = Highly Probable   Level II = Probable

Event Sequence Number	Event (Scripture Reference)	Location of Event	Gregorian Date	Level of Confidence*
247	If Two Agree, Ask and It Shall Be Done (Mt 18:19-20)	Capernaum Galilee	Thursday August 12, A.D. 32	II
248	Should Jesus Pay the Temple Tax? (Mt 17:24b-27)	Capernaum Galilee	Sunday August 15, A.D. 32	II
249	Jesus' Brothers Say, "Show Yourself" (Jn 7:1-9)	Capernaum Galilee	Wednesday Sept 8, A.D. 32	II
250	Jesus Departs To Attend Feast of Booths (Jn 7:10)	Capernaum Galilee	Sunday Sept 19, A.D. 32	II
251	Jews Seek Jesus At Feast of Booths (Jn 7:11-13)	Jerusalem	Sept 16- Oct 10, A.D. 32	I
252	Jesus Begins Teaching in Middle of Feast (Jn 7: 14-24)	Jerusalem	Sunday Oct 10, A.D. 32	I
253	Many Believe Jesus (Jn7:25-31)	Jerusalem	Sunday Oct 10, A.D. 32	I
254	Officers Sent to Seize Jesus (Jn7:32)	Jerusalem	Thursday Oct 14, A.D. 32	I
255	You Shall Seek Me and Not Find Me (Jn 7:33-36)	Jerusalem	Thursday Oct 14, A.D. 32	I
256	If Thirsty Come To Me To Drink (Jn 7:37-39)	Jerusalem	Thursday Oct 14, A.D. 32	I

*Level of Confidence in Date   Level I = Highly Probable   Level II = Probable

Event Sequence Number	Event (Scripture Reference)	Location of Event	Gregorian Date	Level of Confidence*
257	Division Over Jesus In The Multitude (Jn 7:40-44)	Jerusalem	Thursday Oct 14, A.D. 32	I
258	Officers Return Without Jesus (Jn 7:45-49)	Jerusalem	Thursday Oct 14, A.D. 32`	I
259	Nicodemus, "Our Law Does Not Judge a Man Without First Hearing From Him, Does It?" (Jn 7:50-52)	Jerusalem	Thursday Oct 14, A.D.32	I
260	Jesus Spends the Night on the Mount of Olives (Jn 7:53-8:1)	Mount of Olives	Oct 14- Oct 15, A.D. 52	I
261	Adulterous Woman Brought To Jesus (Jn 8:2-11)	Jerusalem	Friday Oct 15, A.D. 32	I
262	I Am the Light of the World (Jn 8:12)	Jerusalem	Friday Oct 15, A.D. 32	I
263	Pharisees "You Are Bearing Witness to Yourself" (Jn 8:13-20)	Jerusalem	Friday Oct 15, A.D. 32	I
264	Jesus, "I Go Away and You Shall Seek Me" (Jn 8: 21-30)	Jerusalem	Friday Oct 15, A.D. 32	I
265	You Shall Know the Truth, and the Truth Shall Make You Free (Jn 8:31-32)	Jerusalem	Friday Oct 15, A.D. 32	I
266	You Are Doing the Deeds of Your Father (Jn 8:33-47)	Jerusalem	Friday Oct 15, A.D. 32	I

*Level of Confidence in Date   Level I = Highly Probable   Level II = Probable

Event Sequence Number	Event (Scripture Reference)	Location of Event	Gregorian Date	Level of Confidence*
267	If Anyone Keeps My Words, He Shall Never See Death (Jn 8:48-59)	Jerusalem	Friday Oct 15, A.D. 32	I
268	Jesus Heals the Man Born Blind (Jn 9:1-12)	Jerusalem	Saturday Oct 16, A.D. 32	I
269	Pharisees Question Former Blind Man (Jn 9:13-17)	Jerusalem	Saturday Oct 16, A.D. 32	I
270	Parents of Former Blind Man Questioned (Jn 9:18-23)	Jerusalem	Saturday Oct 16, A.D. 32	I
271	Former Blind Man Put Out of the Temple (Jn 9: 24-34)	Jerusalem	Saturday Oct 16, A.D. 32	I
272	Former Blind Man Worships Jesus (Jn 9:35-41)	Jerusalem	Saturday Oct 16, A.D. 32	I
273	Parable of the Good Shepherd (Jn 10:1-18)	Jerusalem	Saturday Oct 16, A.D. 32	I
274	Division Among the Jews Concerning Jesus (Jn 10:19-21)	Jerusalem	Saturday Oct 16, A.D. 32	I
275	Samaritan Village Does Not Receive Jesus (Lk 9:51-56)	Samaria	Monday Nov 8, A.D. 32	II
276	The Son of Man Has Nowhere to Lay His Head (Lk 9:57-58)	Galilee	Tuesday Nov 9, A.D. 32	II

*Level of Confidence in Date   Level I = Highly Probable   Level II = Probable

Event Sequence Number	Event (Scripture Reference)	Location of Event	Gregorian Date	Level of Confidence*
277	Allow the Dead to Bury Their Own Dead (Lk 9:59-60)	Galilee	Tuesday Nov 9, A.D. 32	II
278	No One Looking Back Is Fit For the Kingdom of God (Lk 9:61-62)	Galilee	Monday Nov 8, A.D. 32	II
279	Jesus Sends Out the Seventy (Lk 10:1-12)	Galilee	Wednesday Nov 10, A.D. 32	II
280	Woes to the Cities of Galilee (Lk 10: 13-16)	Galilee	Wednesday Nov 10, A.D. 32	II
281	Seventy Return With Joy (Lk 10: 17-20)	Galilee	Thursday Nov 25, A.D. 32	II
282	Lawyer Tests Jesus (Lk 10:25-29)	Galilee	Thursday Nov 25, A.D. 32	II
283	Parable of the Good Samaritan (Lk 10:30-37)	Galilee	Thursday Nov 25, A.D. 32	II
284	Dinner With Mary & Martha (Lk 10:38-42)	Bethany Judea	Thursday Dec 9, A.D. 32	II
285	Lord, Teach Us To Pray (Lk 11:1-4)	Jerusalem	Sunday Dec 19, A.D. 32	II
286	Parable of the Persistent Friend At Midnight (Lk 11:5-8)	Jerusalem	Sunday Dec 19, A.D. 32	II

*Level of Confidence in Date   Level I = Highly Probable   Level II = Probable

Event Sequence Number	Event (Scripture Reference)	Location of Event	Gregorian Date	Level of Confidence*
287	Prayers Will Be Answered (Lk 11:9-13)	Jerusalem	Sunday Dec 19, A.D. 32	II
288	Jesus Accused of Healing By Beelzebul (Lk 11:14-23)	Jerusalem	Sunday Dec 19, A.D. 32	II
289	Parable of the Unclean Spirit (Lk 11:24-26)	Jerusalem	Sunday Dec 19, A.D. 32	II
290	Blessed Are Those That Hear and Observe the Word of God (Lk 11:27-28)	Jerusalem	Sunday Dec 19, A.D. 32	II
291	No Sign But the Sign of Jonah (Lk 11:29-30)	Jerusalem	Sunday Dec 19, A.D. 32	II
292	Queen of the South Shall Condemn This Generation (Lk 11: 31)	Jerusalem	Sunday Dec 19, A.D. 32	II
293	Men of Nineveh Shall Condemn This Generation (Lk 11:32)	Jerusalem	Sunday Dec 19, A.D. 32	II
294	Eye Is The Lamp of the Body (Lk 11:33-36)	Jerusalem	Sunday Dec 19, A.D. 32	II
295	Jesus Has Lunch With a Pharisee (Lk 11:37)	Jerusalem	Sunday Dec 19, A.D. 32	II
296	Woe To the Pharisees (Lk 11:38-44)	Jerusalem	Sunday Dec 19, A.D. 32	II

*Level of Confidence in Date   Level I = Highly Probable   Level II = Probable

Event Sequence Number	Event (Scripture Reference)	Location of Event	Gregorian Date	Level of Confidence*
297	Woe To The Lawyers (Lk 11:45-52)	Jerusalem	Sunday Dec 19, A.D. 32	II
298	Scribes & Pharisees Become Very Hostile (Lk 11:53-54)	Jerusalem	Sunday Dec 19, A.D. 32	II
299	Fear Nothing But God (Lk 12:1-12)	Jerusalem	Sunday Dec 19, A.D. 32	II
300	Beware of Greed (Lk 12: 13-15)	Jerusalem	Sunday Dec 19, A.D. 32	II
301	Parable of the Rich Fool (Lk 12:16-21)	Jerusalem	Sunday Dec 19, A.D. 32	II
302	Where Your Treasure, There Will Your Heart Be Also (Lk 12:22-34)	Jerusalem	Sunday Dec 19, A.D. 32	II
303	Faithfully Await the Master's Return (Lk 12:35-48)	Jerusalem	Sunday Dec 19, A.D. 32	II
304	I Come To Cast Fire Upon the Earth (Lk 12:49-53)	Jerusalem	Sunday Dec 19, A.D. 32	II
305	Galileans Killed By Pilate (Lk 13: 1-3)	Jerusalem	Sunday Dec 19, A.D. 32	II
306	Tower of Siloam (Lk 13: 4-5)	Jerusalem	Sunday Dec 19, A.D. 32	II

*Level of Confidence in Date   Level I = Highly Probable   Level II = Probable

Event Sequence Number	Event (Scripture Reference)	Location of Event	Gregorian Date	Level of Confidence*
307	Parable of the Fig Tree (Lk 13:6-9)	Jerusalem	Sunday Dec 19, A.D. 32	II
308	I and the Father Are One (Jn 10:22-39)	Jerusalem	Monday Dec 20, A.D. 32	II

*Level of Confidence in Date   Level I = Highly Probable   Level II = Probable

6

Jesus' Final Months of Ministry

Jesus' third year of earthly ministry began on January 5, A.D. 33 and end with Jesus' ascension on May 12, A.D. 33. In Chapter 2, Jesus' Final Days, we have already considered the events of Jesus' ministry from His arrival At Bethany on March 20, A.D. 33 until His ascension. In this chapter, we will consider the events of Jesus' third year of ministry prior to His arrival at Bethany. At the close of the previous chapter, Jesus had just left Jerusalem after attending the Feast of the Dedication. Then Luke 13:10-17 says:

And He was teaching in one of the synagogues on the Sabbath. And there was a woman who for eighteen years had a sickness caused by a spirit; and she was bent double, and could not straighten up at all. When Jesus saw her, He called her over and said to her, "Woman, you are freed from your sickness." And He laid His hands on her; and immediately she was made erect again and began glorifying God. But the synagogue official, indignant because Jesus had healed on the Sabbath, began saying to the crowd in response, "There are six days in which work should be done; so come during them and get healed, and not on the Sabbath day." But the Lord answered him and said, "You hypocrites, does not each of you on the Sabbath untie his ox or his donkey from the stall and lead him away to water him? And this woman, a daughter of Abraham as she is, whom Satan has bound for eighteen long years, should she not have been released from this bond on the Sabbath day?" As He said this, all His opponents were being humiliated; and the entire crowd was rejoicing over all the glorious things being done by Him.

Since Luke speaks of a multitude being present, this must have been one of the larger synagogues in Galilee and therefore probably in one of the larger cities. This event probably took place on Saturday, January 8, A.D. 33. On the same day Jesus probably told the two similes concerning the kingdom of God: like a mustard seed (Luke 13:19) and like leaven (Luke 13:21).

Jesus Traveling Through Galilee

At this point Luke 13:22 says, "And He was passing through from one city and village to another, teaching, and proceeding on His way to Jerusalem." Jesus probably started toward Jerusalem about Sunday, January 9. He probably followed the route through eastern Galilee, traveling along the western shore side of the Sea of Galilee. During this journey, probably about Wednesday, January 12, A.D. 33, Luke 13:23-27 says:

And someone said to Him, "Lord, are there just a few who are being saved?" And He said to them, "Strive to enter through the narrow door; for many, I tell you, will seek to enter and will not be able. Once the head of the house gets up and shuts the door, and you begin to stand outside and knock on the door, saying, 'Lord, open up to us!' then He will answer and say to you, 'I do not know where you are from.' Then you will begin to say, 'We ate and drank in Your presence, and You taught in our streets'; and He will say, 'I tell you, I do not know where you are from; DEPART FROM ME, ALL YOU EVILDOERS.'"

On the same day some Pharisees came to Jesus and said, "Go away and depart from here, for Herod wants to kill you (Luke 13:31)." Jesus responded to this threat in Luke 13:32-33 which says, "And He said to them, Go and tell that fox, 'Behold, I cast out demons and perform cures today and tomorrow, and the third day I reach My goal' Nevertheless I must journey on today and tomorrow and the next day; for it cannot be that a prophet would perish outside of Jerusalem."

On the next Sabbath Jesus is probably still in Galilee, and on that day Luke 14:1 tells us that Jesus was invited to the home of one of the leaders of the Pharisees. This was probably the lunch time meal served after the morning synagogue service. There was a man with dropsy present at the meal. The Pharisees had probably invited this man to see if Jesus would heal him on the Sabbath. Luke 14:3-6 says:

And Jesus answered and spoke to the lawyers and Pharisees, saying, "Is it lawful to heal on the Sabbath, or not?" But they kept silent. And He took hold of him and healed him, and sent him away. And He said to them, "Which one of you will have a son or an ox fall into a well, and will not immediately pull him out on a Sabbath day?"And they could make no reply to this.

Then Jesus told a parable concerning taking the places of honor at a wedding feast and in Luke 14:11-14 Jesus says:

> "For everyone who exalts himself will be humbled, and he who humbles himself will be exalted." And He also went on to say to the one who had invited Him, "When you give a luncheon or a dinner, do not invite your friends or your brothers or your relatives or rich neighbors, otherwise they may also invite you in return and that will be your repayment. But when you give a reception, invite the poor, the crippled, the lame, the blind, and you will be blessed, since they do not have the means to repay you; for you will be repaid at the resurrection of the righteous."

Then one of those that were reclining at the table with Jesus said, "Blessed is everyone who shall eat bread in the kingdom of God." In response Jesus told the Parable of the Great Banquet as a warning to those that did not accept Him. In Luke 14:24 Jesus says, "For I tell you, none of those men who were invited shall taste of my dinner." Thus Israel, as God's chosen people, were invited to be part of the kingdom of God, but, if they do not accept the Messiah that God sent, they will not be part of that kingdom.

On the next day, Sunday, January 16, A.D. 33, Jesus was still traveling through Galilee and great multitudes were going along with Him (Luke 14:25). Jesus said to the multitude, "If anyone comes to Me, and does not hate his own father and mother and wife and children and brothers and sisters, yes, and even his own life, he cannot be My disciple. Whoever does not carry his own cross and come after Me cannot be My disciple." Jesus is saying that if we want to be Jesus' disciples, we must give Jesus first place in our lives and be willing to pay the cost of discipleship (carry our own cross). Then Jesus told the parables of the Builder of a Tower, the King

Preparing for War and the Tasteless Salt.

Among the multitude that were traveling along with Jesus were many tax collectors and others that were considered to be sinners which caused the Pharisees and scribes to grumble. In response to their grumbling, Jesus told three important parables concerning God's joy over repentant sinners (Luke 15:4-32). These were: the Parable of the Lost Sheep, the Parable of the Lost Coin and the Parable of the Lost Son. At the same time Jesus told the Parable of the Unrighteous Steward (Luke 16:1-13). Then Jesus said (Luke 16:13), "No servant can serve two masters; for either he will hate the one and love the other, or else he will be devoted to one and despise the other. You cannot serve God and wealth." Luke 16:14 says that the Pharisees, who were lovers of money, scoffed at Jesus and Jesus rebuked them. Then Jesus told the Parable of the Rich Man and Lazarus, and He addressed His disciples concerning forgiveness, faith and faithfulness.

Probably the next day, Monday, January 17, A.D. 33, Jesus was passing between Samaria and Galilee (Luke 17:11) and He healed ten lepers. Then the Pharisees questioned Jesus concerning when the Kingdom of God was coming. Luke 17:20b-21 says, "He answered them and said, 'The kingdom of God is not coming with signs to be observed; nor will they say, "Look, here it is!" or, "There it is!" For behold, the kingdom of God is in your midst.'" Then Jesus spoke to His disciples concerning His Second Coming and in Luke 17:24-25 said, "For just like the lightning, when it flashes out of one part of the sky, shines to the other part of the sky, so will the Son of Man be in His day. But first He must suffer many things and be rejected by this generation."

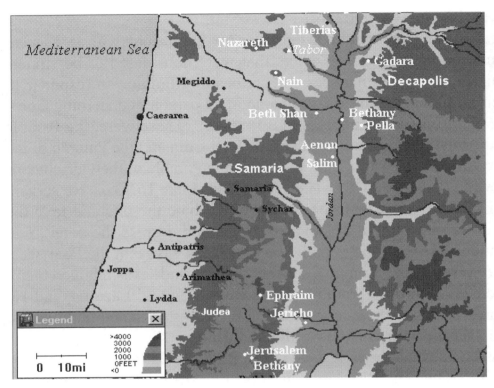

Jesus' Journeys to Jerusalem
Figure 6.1

Jesus At Bethany Beyond the Jordan

Probably the next day, Tuesday, January 18, A.D. 33, Jesus and His disciples arrived at Bethany

> And He went away again beyond the Jordan to the place where John was first baptizing, and He was staying there. Many came to Him and were saying, "While John performed no sign, yet everything John said about this man was true." Many believed in Him there.

We shall see that Jesus and His disciples spent almost a month at Bethany beyond the Jordan. Bethany beyond the Jordan was probably located where the road between Beth Shan and Pella crossed the Jordan River (see Figure 6.1). This Bethany would be located on the east side of the Jordan River hence its name, Bethany beyond the Jordan. The exact location of this site has not been found, but it can be inferred from the travel times in John 11:1-40 and John 1:19-2:2. Matthew 19:1-2 says:

> When Jesus had finished these words, He departed from Galilee and came into the region of Judea beyond the Jordan; and large crowds followed Him, and He healed them there.

This is probably the same visit to Bethany beyond the Jordan that was recorded in John 10:40. Matthew 19:3 says, "Some Pharisees came to Jesus, testing Him and asking, "Is it lawful for a man to divorce his wife for any reason at all?" In His answer (Matthew 19:9) Jesus said, "And I say to you, whoever divorces his wife, except for immorality, and marries another woman commits adultery." This encounter probably took place about Wednesday, February 2, A.D. 33, since it would have taken time before the Pharisees would have known that Jesus was staying at Bethany beyond the Jordan. After Jesus' discussion with the Pharisees, Matthew 19:10-11 says, "The disciples said to Him, 'If the relationship of the man with his wife is like this, it is better not to marry.' But He said to them, 'Not all men can accept this statement, but only those to whom it has been given.'" The next event is recorded in Matthew 19:13-15:

> Then some children were brought to Him so that He might lay His hands on them and pray; and the disciples rebuked them. But Jesus said, "Let the children alone, and do not hinder them from coming to Me; for the

kingdom of heaven belongs to such as these." After laying His hands on them, He departed from there.

This event probably took place on February 15, A.D. 33, which we shall see was the same day that the messengers arrived bringing news of the illness of Lazarus. John 11:1-6 says:

Raising of Lazarus

Now a certain man was sick, Lazarus of Bethany, the village of Mary and her sister Martha. It was the Mary who anointed the Lord with ointment, and wiped His feet with her hair, whose brother Lazarus was sick. So the sisters sent word to Him, saying, "Lord, behold, he whom You love is sick." But when Jesus heard this, He said, "This sickness is not to end in death, but for the glory of God, so that the Son of God may be glorified by it." Now Jesus loved Martha and her sister and Lazarus. So when He heard that he was sick, He then stayed two days longer in the place where He was.

But when did Jesus raise Lazarus from the dead? John in His Gospel does not directly relate this event to one of the Jewish feast days; however, the Talmud, Tractate Sanhedrin 43a, as translated into English by Jacob Shachter, may provide a clue to the date of this event. In this tractate, on page 281, it says:

On the eve of the Passover Yeshu was hanged. For forty days before the execution took place, a herald went forth and cried, "He is going forth to be stoned because he has practiced sorcery and enticed Israel to apostasy. Anyone who can say anything in his favor, let him come forward and plead on his behalf." But since nothing was brought forward in his favor he was hanged on the eve of the Passover.

Yeshu is a Hebrew form of the name Jesus. This section of the Talmud indicates that for forty days prior to Jesus' execution on the eve of the Passover, a herald sought witnesses for Jesus' trial. Since Jesus was executed on April 1, A.D. 33 (Gregorian), forty days prior to that date, counting inclusively, would be Monday, February 21, A.D. 33. In chapter 11 of John's Gospel it is related that after Jesus raised Lazarus, that the Pharisees were told. Then John 11:47-53 says:

> Therefore the chief priests and the Pharisees convened a council, and were saying, "What are we doing? For this man is performing many signs. If we let Him go on like this, all men will believe in Him, and the Romans will come and take away both our place and our nation." But one of them, Caiaphas, who was high priest that year, said to them, "You know nothing at all, nor do you take into account that it is expedient for you that one man die for the people, and that the whole nation not perish." Now he did not say this on his own initiative, but being high priest that year, he prophesied that Jesus was going to die for the nation, and not for the nation only, but in order that He might also gather together into one the children of God who are scattered abroad. So from that day on they planned together to kill Him.

At this council the chief priests and Pharisees decided to kill Jesus. If we can accept the testimony of the Talmud, it was probably also on this day that the herald was sent forth to collect witnesses for Jesus' trial. If this council took place on Monday, February 21, then Jesus probably raised Lazarus on Sunday, February 20, A.D. 33. Working backward from this date, since John 11:39 says that Lazarus had been dead for four days when he was raised, Lazarus must have died on Thursday, February 17. The day Jesus departed from Bethany beyond the Jordan, Jesus in John 11:14 says, "Lazarus is dead." Therefore, Jesus could not have departed before February 17, the day of Lazarus' death. However, Jesus waited two days before he departed, probably waiting until Lazarus' death. If Jesus departed on February 17, these two days which Jesus waited would have been February 15 and 16. On February 15 the messengers would have arrived with news of Lazarus' sickness. Since the trip to Bethany outside of Jerusalem took Jesus three days, assuming they stopped for the Sabbath, the messengers were probably sent out by Mary and Martha on Sunday, February 13, and would have arrived on the third day, Tuesday, February 15. Table 6.1 summarizes the dates of the events associated with the raising of Lazarus.

The distance between the Bethany, which is two miles outside Jerusalem, and the site, where the road from Beth Shan to Pella crosses the Jordan River, is about 65 miles. Thus the messengers, traveling about 25 miles per day, would reach Jesus on the third day. This would seem to confirm the general location of Bethany beyond the Jordan(see Figure 6.1). Also, as pointed out in chapter 4, this location is also consistent with Jesus leaving Bethany beyond the Jordan on day one and attending a wedding at Cana of Galilee on the third day (John 2:1).

Jesus in Ephraim

Then John 11:54 says, "Therefore Jesus no longer continued to walk publicly among the Jews, but went away from there to the country near the wilderness, into a city called Ephraim; and there He stayed with the disciples." Ephraim was located about fifteen miles north of Jerusalem (see Figure 6.1). It was from Ephraim that Jesus

Table 6.1 **Events Associated with the Raising of Lazarus** **February A.D. 33**						
Sun	Mon	Tue	Wed	Thu	Fri	Sat
13 Message Sent to Jesus	14	15 Message Arrives, Jesus Waits	16 Jesus Waits	17 Lazarus Dies, Jesus Departs	18	19
20 Jesus Raises Lazarus	21 Council Plans to Kill Jesus	22	23	24	25	26

began His last journey to Jerusalem. Therefore the events of Matthew, Mark and Luke that occur during Jesus' final journey to Jerusalem begin from Ephraim. Matthew 20:17-19 says:

> As Jesus was about to go up to Jerusalem, He took the twelve disciples aside by themselves, and on the way He said to them, "Behold, we are going up to Jerusalem; and the Son of Man will be delivered to the chief priests and scribes, and they will condemn Him to death, and will hand Him over to the Gentiles to mock and scourge and crucify Him, and on the third day He will be raised up."

In chapter 2 we saw that Jesus arrived at Bethany six days before the Passover Feast of A.D. 33, on Monday, March 28. Since Ephraim is only about fifteen miles from Jerusalem, Jesus probably spent the Sabbath there in seclusion with His disciples and then left for

Jerusalem on Sunday, March 27, going by the way of Jericho. This was not the shortest route to Jerusalem, but Jesus still had ministries to perform. Also in Jericho He would meet the main route of the Jewish pilgrims who would be coming to Jerusalem for the Passover Feast. Then Luke 18:35-43 says:

Jesus in Jericho

> As Jesus was approaching Jericho, a blind man was sitting by the road begging. Now hearing a crowd going by, he began to inquire what this was. They told him that Jesus of Nazareth was passing by. And he called out, saying, "Jesus, Son of David, have mercy on me!" Those who led the way were sternly telling him to be quiet; but he kept crying out all the more, "Son of David, have mercy on me!" And Jesus stopped and commanded that he be brought to Him; and when he came near, He questioned him, "What do you want Me to do for you?" And he said, "Lord, I want to regain my sight!" And Jesus said to him, "Receive your sight; your faith has made you well." Immediately he regained his sight and began following Him, glorifying God; and when all the people saw it, they gave praise to God.

The trip from Ephraim to Jericho is only about eleven miles, so Jesus and His disciples would have probably arrived in Jericho around noon time, and Luke 19:1-10 says:

> He entered Jericho and was passing through. And there was a man called by the name of Zaccheus; he was a chief tax collector and he was rich. Zaccheus was trying to see who Jesus was, and was unable because of the crowd, for he was small in stature. So he ran on ahead

and climbed up into a sycamore tree in order to see Him, for He was about to pass through that way. When Jesus came to the place, He looked up and said to him, "Zaccheus, hurry and come down, for today I must stay at your house." And he hurried and came down and received Him gladly. When they saw it, they all began to grumble, saying, "He has gone to be the guest of a man who is a sinner." Zaccheus stopped and said to the Lord, "Behold, Lord, half of my possessions I will give to the poor, and if I have defrauded anyone of anything, I will give back four times as much." And Jesus said to him, "Today salvation has come to this house, because he, too, is a son of Abraham. For the Son of Man has come to seek and to save that which was lost."

At this time Jesus told the parable of the ten slaves who were each given ten minas to invest while their master, a nobleman went to receive his kingdom. The slaves that invested their lord's money and made more were commended, but the one that hide his minas was condemned. Jesus then went with Zaccheus to his home where Jesus eat the evening meal. The next morning Jesus and His disciples departed Jericho and probably arrived in Bethany about noon on Monday, March 28, A.D. 33. This brings us to Jesus' final days that were already discussed in chapter 2.

Thus, we have followed Jesus ministry through all four Gospels and we have found that, rather than being inconsistent or contradictory as many liberal scholars claim, the Gospels are completely consistent and supplement each other beautifully. In the tables at the end of this chapter we have dated each event that occurred during the final months of Jesus' ministry. We shall now turn to the book of Acts to follow the events that occurred after Jesus' resurrection and particularly the growth of Christ's Church which had its beginning on the Day of Pentecost in A.D. 33.

Table 6.2 Jesus' Final Months of Ministry				
Event Sequence Number	Event (Scripture Reference)	Location of Event	Gregorian Date	Level* of Confidence
309	Jesus Heals the Stooped Woman (Lk 13:10-17)	Galilee	Saturday Jan 8, A.D. 33	II
310	Simile of the Mustard Seed (Lk 13:18-19)	Galilee	Saturday Jan 8, A.D. 33	II
311	Simile of the Leaven (Lk 13: 20-21)	Galilee	Saturday Jan 8, A.D. 33	II
312	Are Just a Few Being Saved? (Lk 13:22-30)	Galilee	Wednesday Jan 12, A.D. 33	II
313	Pharisees' Warning (Lk 13:31-33)	Galilee	Wednesday Jan 12, A.D. 33	II
314	Lament Over Jerusalem (Lk 13:34-35)	Galilee	Wednesday Jan 12, A.D. 33	II
315	Healing the Man with Dropsy (Lk 14:1-6)	Galilee	Saturday Jan 15, A.D. 33	II
316	Parable of the Guests at a Feast (Lk 14:7-11)	Galilee	Saturday Jan 15, A.D. 33	II
317	When You Give a Reception, Invite the Poor (Lk 14:12-14)	Galilee	Saturday Jan 15, A.D. 33	II

* Level of Confidence in Date   Level I = Highly Probable   Level II = Probable

Event Sequence Number	Event (Scripture Reference)	Location of Event	Gregorian Date	Level* of Confidence
358	Caiaphas, "It Is Expedient That One Should Die for the People" (Jn 11:48-52)	Jerusalem	Monday Feb 21, A.D. 33	II
359	From That Day On They Planned To Kill Jesus (Jn 11:53)	Jerusalem	Monday Feb 21, A.D. 33	II
360	Jesus Departs to Ephraim (Jn 11:54)	Bethany Near Jerusalem	Monday Feb 21 A.D.33	II
361	Many Seek Jesus Before the Passover Feast (Jn 11:55-57)	Jerusalem	Mar 20- Mar 27 A.D. 33	II
362	Jesus Foretells His Passion and Resurrection (Mt 20:17-19, Mk 10:32-34, Lk 18:31-34)	On Road To Jericho	Sunday Mar 27, A.D. 33	II
363	James & John Ask to be First In Jesus' Kingdom (Mt 20:20-23, Mk 10:35-40)	On Road To Jericho	Sunday Mar 27, A.D. 33	II
364	Whosoever Wishes To Be First Shall Be Your Slave (Mt 20:24-28, Mk 10:41-45)	On Road To Jericho	Sunday Mar 27, A.D. 33	II
365	Jesus Heals Two Blind Men (Mt 20:29-34, Mk 10:46-52, (Lk 18:35-43)	Jericho, Judea	Sunday Mar 27, A.D. 33	II
366	Salvation for Zaccheus (Lk 19:1-10)	Jericho, Judea	Sunday Mar 27, A.D. 33	II
367	Parable of the Minas (Lk 19:11-27)	Jericho, Judea	Sunday Mar 27, A.D. 33	II

* Level of Confidence in Date   Level I = Highly Probable   Level II = Probable

7

The Acts

The book of Acts opens with a reference to a first account concerning what Jesus did and taught until He was taken up (His Ascension). This would be a reference to a Gospel and since both the Gospel of Luke and the Acts are addressed to Theophilus, it appears that these two books have a common author. The testimony of the earliest Christian writers identify this common author as Luke the physician and companion of the Apostle Paul. Luke's authorship of these two books will be discussed in more detail in chapter 8, the Authors and Dates of the New Testament Books.

Post-Resurrection Appearances

Acts 1:3 speaks of a period of forty days of Jesus' post-resurrection appearances. These appearances would begin with Jesus' first appearance after His resurrection which was to Mary Magdalene (John 20:14), on His resurrection day, Sunday, April 3, A.D. 33 (Gregorian). Jesus also appeared on the same Jewish day to Peter (Luke 24:35) and to the two disciples on the road to Emmaus (Luke 24:13). Forty days (counting inclusively) from Jesus' day of resurrection brings us to Thursday, May 12, A.D. 33 as the date of Jesus' Ascension. Table 7.1 summarizes the fifteen post-resurrection appearances of Jesus recorded in the New Testament. Most of these appearances are recorded in the four Gospels and have already been discussed in chapter 2.

Paul, in 1 Corinthians 15:5-8, lists five post-resurrection appearances of Jesus, most of which parallel appearances reported in the Gospel; however, 1 Corinthians 15:6 says, "After that He appeared to more than five hundred brethren at one time, most of whom remain until now, but some have fallen asleep." In Table 7.1 this appearance of Jesus is correlated with the appearance to the eleven Apostles on a mountain in Galilee reported in Matthew 28:16-20. This correlation is suggested by John 21:1-23. In these verses from the Gospel of John, Jesus appears to seven of the disciples at the Sea of Tiberias (Sea of Galilee) apparently prior to His appearance to the eleven disciples on the mountain. During this appearance, Jesus probably told the seven disciples to meet Him on the mountain with the rest of the eleven Apostles. The seven disciples probably told, not only the other Apostles that were not present, but also some of Jesus' other followers in Galilee of their meeting with Jesus and of the upcoming meeting with Jesus on the mountain. Word of this upcoming meeting with Jesus would have probably spread quickly so when Jesus appeared on the mountain there was gathered a group of more than five hundred brethren. If this was the case, it would explain Matthew 28:17 which says, "When they saw Him, they worshiped Him; but some were doubtful." All of the eleven Apostles had seen the risen Lord at least twice before this appearance on the mountain, and the Gospels indicate that they had believed. Thus, in Matthew 28:17 it would be strange if some of the Apostles were doubtful; however, it would not be surprising if some of the more than five hundred brethren doubted that Jesus had really risen from the dead. Why didn't Matthew make this clearer in his Gospel?

Table 7.1 Post-Resurrection Appearances of Jesus			
Appearance	**Location**	**Gregorian Date**	**Scripture**
1 To Mary Magdalene	Garden Tomb	4 / 3 / 33	John 20:11-17 Matt 28:9-10 Mark 16:9
2 To Peter	Jerusalem	4 / 3 / 33	Luke 24:34 1 Cor 15:5a
3 To Cleopas & Another Disciple	Road to Emmaus	4 / 3 / 33	Luke 24:13-31
4 To the Apostles (less Thomas) and Other Disciples	Jerusalem	4 / 3 / 33	John 20:19-23 Luke 24:36-49 1 Cor 15:5b
5 To the Eleven Apostles	Jerusalem	4 / 10 / 33	John 20:26-29
6 To Peter, Thomas, Nathanael, James & John &Two Others	By Sea of Tiberias	5 / 1 / 33	John 21:1-23
7 To More Than Five Hundred Brethren -Including the Apostles	Mountain Galilee	5 / 1 / 33	Matt 28:16-20 1 Cor 15:6
8 To James (Brother of Jesus)	Not Given	5 / 1 / 33	1 Cor 15:7
9 To Eleven Apostles At Jesus' Ascension	Near Bethany	5 / 12 / 33	Luke 24:50,51 Act 1:4-7
10 To Paul	Near Damascus	10 / 26 / 33	Act 9:3-8 1 Cor 15:8
11 To Ananias	Damascus	10 / 28 / 33	Act 9:10-16
12 To Paul	Jerusalem	3 / 4 / 36	Act 22:17-21
13 To Paul	Corinth	3 / 27 / 50	Act 18:9,10
14 To Paul	Jerusalem	6 / 18 /57	Act 23:11
15 To Apostle John	Patmos	A.D. 66	Rev 1:10-19

Possibly because he had reached the end of the scroll on which he was writing his Gospel and he didn't have room to say any more.

The mountain in Galilee on which Jesus appeared was probably the same mountain on which Jesus commissioned His twelve Apostles (Luke 6:12-16) which is traditionally located near Heptapegon (see Figure 4.3, page 166). This site is near Gennesaret where Peter probably kept his boat, and Gennesaret was probably the site of Jesus' appearance by the Sea of Tiberias. Other traditions place the site of Jesus' appearance on Mount Tabor, but there is nothing in the New Testament to support that location.

After Jesus' ascension, Acts 1:12 says, "Then they returned to Jerusalem from the mount called Olivet, which is near Jerusalem, a Sabbath day's journey away." A Sabbath day's journey was 2000 cubits or about 1000 yards. Measuring 2000 cubits from the wall of Jerusalem would bring you to Bethphage from where Jesus began His Triumphal Entry into Jerusalem. Bethphage was considered to be the city limits of Jerusalem since the outer limits of the city included the pastor lands surrounding the city (Numbers 35:4). However, since Luke 25:50 says that Jesus led them out as far as Bethany on the occasion of His Ascension, the site of the Ascension must have been further up the slope of the Mount of Olives north of Bethphage. This site would be near the summit of the Mount of Olives and overlooking the village of Bethany, but still about a Sabbath days' journey from the wall of Jerusalem. The traditional site of the Ascension is lower on the Mount of Olives and is marked by the Church of the Ascension which is now a mosque .

When the Apostles returned from the Mount of Olives, they went to the upper room which is traditionally located on the western hill of Jerusalem which is currently called Mount Zion. Acts 1:14 says, "These all with one mind were continually devoting themselves to prayer, along with the women, and Mary the mother of Jesus, and with His brothers." Then, about Sunday, May 15, A.D. 33, Peter stood up in the midst of the gathering of about 120 disciples and proposed the selection of a replacement for Judas to fill his office of Apostle. Mathias was selected by lot from two men that were put forward by the disciples from the men who had been with Jesus since His baptism by John the Baptist.

Pentecost

> When the day of Pentecost had come, they were all together in one place. And suddenly there came from heaven a noise like a violent rushing wind, and it filled the whole house where they were sitting. And there appeared to them tongues as of fire distributing themselves, and they rested on each one of them. And they were all filled with the Holy Spirit and began to speak with other tongues, as the Spirit was giving them utterance (Acts 2:1-4).

While the Temple still stood, Pentecost was celebrated on the eighth Sunday after the Passover Feast (see Appendix C). Thus, in A.D. 33, Pentecost would have been celebrated on Sunday, May 22. Act 2:2 says that the noise filled the whole house where they were sitting. This house may have been the same house that contained the upper room where the Apostles were staying; although the exact location of the house is not specified.

Who were the they that "were all together" in Acts 2:1 and received the Holy Spirit? Some have said that the antecedent of this pronoun "they" would be the first previously mentioned noun which would be the apostles of Act 1:26. However, in this section of Acts, the pronoun "they" is repeatedly used beginning with Acts 1:23. The "they" in Acts 1:23 appears to refer to the one hundred and twenty brethren that Peter is addressing. If the one hundred and twenty brethren did not participate in the selection of the replacement for Judas Iscariot, why did Peter raise this question before them? Thus, the "they" in Acts 1:23, Acts 1:24, and Acts 1:26 all refer to the one hundred and twenty; therefore, when "they" is used again in the next verse, Act 2:1, without a clear indication of a change in antecedent, the antecedent of the "they" in Acts 2:1 must still be the one hundred and twenty brethren. All Christians were to receive the Holy Spirit, normally at the time of their baptism (Act 2:38); however, these one hundred and twenty brethren had already been baptized in the name of Jesus (John 4:1-4) prior to Jesus' resurrection and the sending of the Holy Spirit. Therefore, they had not previously received the Holy Spirit which did not come until this Pentecost Sunday.

The result of the brethren receiving the Holy Spirit was that they began to speak in foreign languages that they had not learned Acts 2:5-10 says:

> Now there were Jews living in Jerusalem, devout men from every nation under heaven. And when this sound occurred, the crowd came together, and were bewildered because each one of them was hearing them speak in his own language. They were amazed and astonished, saying, "Why, are not all these who are speaking Galileans? And how is it that we each hear them in our own language to which we were born? Parthians and Medes and Elamites, and residents of Mesopotamia, Judea and Cappadocia, Pontus and Asia, Phrygia and Pamphylia, Egypt and the districts of Libya around Cyrene, and visitors from Rome, both Jews and proselytes, Cretans and Arabs--we hear them in our own tongues speaking of the mighty deeds of God."

Most of the crowd were amazed, but some mocked and said the brethren were just full of new wine. Then Peter stood up, with the other eleven apostles, and used the keys of the kingdom of God which had been given him. Peter preached to the crowd Jesus' death and resurrection as fulfilment of God's plan for the salvation of mankind in accordance with the Old Testament prophets. Then Acts 2:36-42 says:

> "Therefore let all the house of Israel know for certain that God has made Him both Lord and Christ-this Jesus whom you crucified." Now when they heard this, they were pierced to the heart, and said to Peter and the rest of the apostles, "Brethren, what shall we do?" Peter said to them, "Repent, and each of you be baptized in the name of Jesus Christ for the forgiveness of your sins; and you will receive the gift of the Holy Spirit. For the promise is for you and your children and for all who are far off, as many as the Lord our God will call to Himself." And with many other words he solemnly testified and kept on exhorting them, saying, "Be saved from this perverse generation!" So then, those who had received his word were baptized; and that day there were added about three thousand souls. They were continually devoting themselves to the apostles' teaching and to fellowship, to the breaking of bread and to prayer.

Where in Jerusalem could three thousand people be baptized and by whom were they baptized? In Jerusalem there were numerous ritual baths (mikvahs) where Jewish worshipers purified themselves by total immersion before entering the Temple precincts (see John 11:55 & Acts 21:26). These ritual baths are a likely site for the baptisms. If only the apostles baptized the 3000 converts and each confession of Jesus and baptism took two minutes, then the 3000 conversion to Christianity would have taken over eight hours. However, if all of the 120 brethren took part, all the conversions could have been accomplished in less than one hour. Thus it appears likely that the brethren assisted the apostles.

The 3000 people who received the word and were baptized, together with the original 120 disciples of Jesus, formed the beginning of the Jerusalem Church which was the first congregation of Christ's Church.

Dating the Remainder of Acts

As we examine the remainder of the book of Acts two things are apparent: First, there are fewer feast days mentioned in the book of Acts than we found in the Gospel of John, so it will not be possible to assign exact dates to as many events in Acts as was possible for the Gospels. Second, the book of Acts records events that took place over a much longer period of time than the events recorded in the Gospels. In fact, all the events of the Gospels, with the exception of the introduction of John and the events concerning Jesus' birth and early childhood of Matthew and Luke, took place during a period of less than two and one half years. In contrast the book of Acts covers a period of about thirty years. Thus, in general, it will not be possible to date the events of the book of Acts as exactly as it was possible to date the events of the Gospels.

However, several passages in the New Testament do provide precise chronological information concerning the events of the book of Acts and these passages will provide the key to unlocking the chronology of this book. A remarkable passage in Paul's letter to the Galatians provides us with a basic chronological structure to Paul's early ministry which in turn gives us a terminus date for the early chapters of the book of Acts and a chronological structure for the entire book. In Galatians 1:15-2:5 Paul says:

> But when God, who had set me apart even from my mother's womb and called me through His grace, was pleased to reveal His Son in me so that I might preach Him among the Gentiles, I did not immediately consult

with flesh and blood, nor did I go up to Jerusalem to those who were apostles before me; but I went away to Arabia, and returned once more to Damascus.

Then three years later I went up to Jerusalem to become acquainted with Cephas, and stayed with him fifteen days. But I did not see any other of the apostles except James, the Lord's brother. (Now in what I am writing to you, I assure you before God that I am not lying.) Then I went into the regions of Syria and Cilicia. I was still unknown by sight to the churches of Judea which were in Christ; but only, they kept hearing, "He who once persecuted us is now preaching the faith which he once tried to destroy." And they were glorifying God because of me.

Then after an interval of fourteen years I went up again to Jerusalem with Barnabas, taking Titus along also. It was because of a revelation that I went up; and I submitted to them the gospel which I preach among the Gentiles, but I did so in private to those who were of reputation, for fear that I might be running, or had run, in vain. But not even Titus, who was with me, though he was a Greek, was compelled to be circumcised. But it was because of the false brethren secretly brought in, who had sneaked in to spy out our liberty which we have in Christ Jesus, in order to bring us into bondage. But we did not yield in subjection to them for even an hour, so that the truth of the gospel would remain with you.

The events recorded by Paul in this passage from Galatians can be correlated with the events recorded in the book of Acts. Thus, the phrase, "was pleased to reveal His Son to me," refers to Paul's encounter with the risen Christ on the road to Damascus (Acts 9:3-5). The phrase, "then three years later I went up to Jerusalem to become acquainted with Cephas," refers to the visit of Paul to Jerusalem recorded in Acts 9:26-30. Finally, the phrase, "then, after an interval of fourteen years, I went up again to Jerusalem with Barnabas," refers to the Council of Jerusalem recorded in Acts 15:1-29. Thus, if we can determine the year in which the Council of Jerusalem took place, we can determine the year of Paul's conversion to Christianity and the year of his first post-conversion visit to Jerusalem. Also knowing the year of Paul's conversion will give us a terminus for the events recorded in the first eight chapters of the book of Acts.

In order to determine the year in which the Council of Jerusalem took place, we must follow Paul on his second missionary journey, which started after Paul and Barnabas returned from the Council of Jerusalem, looking for an event that can be dated. We find such an event in Acts 18:12-13 which says, "But while Gallio was proconsul of Achaia, the Jews with one accord rose up against Paul and brought him before the judgment seat, saying, 'This man persuades men to worship God contrary to the law.'" Finegan, in his *Handbook of Biblical Chronology*, page 319, dates the arrival of Gallio for his proconsulship of Achaia to May or June of A.D. 51. His dating of Gallio's arrival is based on an inscription found on a stone in Delphi which mentions Gallio as proconsul and is dated to the first half of A.D. 52. Since proconsuls were normally appointed for a one-year term and were not required to leave Rome for their post until the middle of April, a proconsul serving in Achaia in the first half of A.D. 52 would have probably arrived at his post late in the previous spring. Paul was probably brought before Gallio shortly after Gallio had arrived in Corinth since the Jews would have probably preferred to bring their false charges before a proconsul without personal knowledge of the situation. If Paul appeared before Gallio during June of A.D. 51, that would be during the Jewish month of Sivan. Prior to appearing before Gallio, Acts 18:11 says, "And he settled there a year and six months, teaching the word of God among them." A year and six months prior to the Jewish month of Sivan, A.D. 51, counting inclusively, brings us to the Jewish month of Shebat (see calendars of Appendix D). This month of Shebat began on January 11, A.D. 50 and ended on February 9, A.D. 50.

This time for Paul's arrival at Corinth is further supported by Acts 18:1-3 which says:

> After these things he left Athens and went to Corinth.
> And he found a Jew named Aquila, a native of Pontus,
> having recently come from Italy with his wife Priscilla,
> because Claudius had commanded all the Jews to leave
> Rome. He came to them, and because he was of the same
> trade, he stayed with them and they were working, for by
> trade they were tent-makers.

Orosius, in his *Seven Books of History Against the Pagans,* written in A.D. 416-17, says that Claudius expelled the Jews from Rome in his ninth year of reign. The ninth year of Claudius would correspond to the year A.D. 49 and so if Paul's arrival in Corinth near the end of January, A.D. 50, then Aquila and Priscilla would have indeed recently come from Italy. If we note carefully the time between Paul's departure from Antioch, Syria, on his second missionary journey, until his arrival at Corinth, which we shall do later in this chapter, we find that the time elapsed was approximately thirty-seven weeks. Since we have shown that Paul arrived in Corinth near the end of January A.D. 50, he must have left Antioch about May, A.D. 49. However, Acts 15:35-36 says:

> But Paul and Barnabas stayed in Antioch, teaching and
> preaching with many others also, the word of the Lord.
> After some days Paul said to Barnabas, "Let us return

and visit the brethren in every city in which we proclaimed the word of the Lord, and see how they are."

Thus, the Council of Jerusalem took place some days prior to Paul's departure on his second missionary journey. The trip from Antioch to Jerusalem was more than 300 miles, and the preferred mode of travel would be by sea. However, Acts 15:3 says, "Therefore, being sent on their way by the church, they were passing through both Phoenicia and Samaria, describing in detail the conversion of the Gentiles, and were bringing great joy to all the brethren." Thus, Paul and Barnabas must have taken the overland route to Jerusalem which passed through Phoenicia and Samaria (see Figure 7.1). This suggests that Paul and Barnabas must have left Antioch during the winter of A.D. 48/49 before sea travel on the Mediterranean Sea was safe. Sea travel on the Mediterranean was considered safe from mid March until mid November (see Act 27:9-10). Thus the Council of Jerusalem would have taken place near the beginning of A.D. 49.

Knowing approximately when the Council of Jerusalem took place and using the information from Paul's letter to the Galatians we can now develop a chronology for the first part of Paul's ministry. In Galatians 2:1 Paul says, "Then after an interval of fourteen years I went up again to Jerusalem with Barnabas, taking Titus along also." Since Paul speaks of again going up to Jerusalem, the fourteen years must be measured from his previously mentioned visit to Jerusalem in Galatians 1:18. Thus Paul went up to get acquainted with Peter fourteen years prior to the Council of Jerusalem. Since the Council of Jerusalem took place near the beginning of A.D. 49, from Appendix D, we can see that it must have taken place during the Jewish year that began April 1, A.D. 48. Counting, inclusively, fourteen Jewish years prior to that year brings us to the Jewish year from March 27, A.D. 35 to March 15, A.D. 36, which would be the year that Paul went up to Jerusalem to become acquainted with Peter.

Galatians 1:18 says, "Then three years later I went up to

Jerusalem to become acquainted with Cephas, and stayed with him fifteen days." Prior to this verse, Paul spoke of when God had revealed His Son to him which was when Paul met Jesus on the road to Damascus, and it was from this incident that Paul is counting the three years. Thus, counting inclusively, three years prior to the year when Paul went up to Jerusalem to become acquainted with Peter, would be the Jewish year from March 18, A.D. 33 until March 8, A.D. 34 and this would be the year of Paul's heavenly vision and his conversion to Christianity. This, of course, was also the year of Jesus' crucifixion and resurrection. Thus, Paul, as a student of Gamaliel studying in Jerusalem, must have seen Jesus during His earthly ministry. However, it was not until Jesus made a miraculous appearance to Paul on the road to Damascus that Paul realized that Jesus was the Messiah. In 2 Corinthians 5:16 Paul says, "Therefore from now on we recognize no one according to the flesh; even though we have known Christ according to the flesh, yet now we know Him in this way no longer." This verse suggests that Paul did see Jesus during His earthly ministry.

Some have suggested that the journey to Jerusalem of Galatians 2:1 was not to attend the Council of Jerusalem, but rather was the journey to Jerusalem by Barnabas and Saul (Paul) to bring the relief offering which is recorded in Acts 11:27-30. However, in Chapter 1 and 2 of Galatians, Paul is not recording all his visits to Jerusalem but rather all incidents where he spent time with the other apostles to show that his apostleship came directly from Jesus and did not depend on the other apostles. This is clearly shown by the fact the during the relief visit to Jerusalem, Peter was imprisoned by Herod Agrippa I and that imprisonment can be exactly dated to the Passover Feast of A.D. 44 which was celebrated on March 31. Fourteen Years before that date would bring us to A.D. 31 for the year Paul came to Jerusalem to become acquainted with Peter which would be in the beginning of Jesus' earthly ministry rather than after it. Thus the journey recorded in Galatians 2:1 was to the Council of Jerusalem.

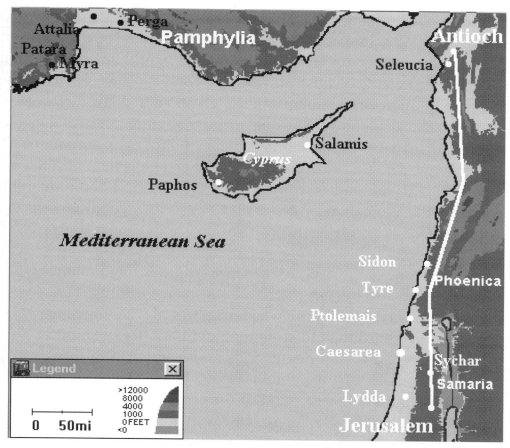

Paul & Barnabas Attend
Council at Jerusalem
Figure 7.1

Thus, we know that Paul received his heavenly vision and converted to Christianity in the Jewish year from March 18, A.D. 33 until April 5, A.D. 34; but when during that year did these events take place? Since a number of events recorded in the first eight chapters of Acts took place prior to Paul's heavenly vision, this event must have taken place later during the year rather than earlier in the year. Prior to his conversion to Christianity, Paul was a very zealous Pharisee and persecutor of Christ's Church. As a zealous Pharisee,

Paul would have wanted to be in Jerusalem for the three major Jewish feasts. However, immediately after the completion of the Feast of Booths which ended on October 3, A.D. 33, would be an ideal time for Paul to depart. Thus, allowing a couple of weeks to make preparation for the trip, Paul may have left about Sunday, October 16, A.D. 33. This departure date would avoid the summer heat and would permit the arrival at Damascus before the winter rainy season. With this terminus date for the events in the first eight chapters of Acts, we shall return to the end of chapter 2 of Acts to date the remaining events in these chapters. Acts 2:43-48 describes conditions in the early Church:

> Everyone kept feeling a sense of awe; and many wonders and signs were taking place through the apostles. And all those who had believed were together and had all things in common; and they began selling their property and possessions and were sharing them with all, as anyone might have need. Day by day continuing with one mind in the temple, and breaking bread from house to house, they were taking their meals together with gladness and sincerity of heart, praising God and having favor with all the people. And the Lord was adding to their number day by day those who were being saved.

Healing of the Lame Beggar

Then Acts 3:1-8 gives a specific example of one of the wonders performed by the apostles:

> Now Peter and John were going up to the temple at the ninth hour, the hour of prayer. And a man who had been lame from his mother's womb was being carried along,

whom they used to set down every day at the gate of the temple which is called Beautiful, in order to beg alms of those who were entering the temple. When he saw Peter and John about to go into the temple, he began asking to receive alms. But Peter, along with John, fixed his gaze on him and said, "Look at us!" And he began to give them his attention, expecting to receive something from them. But Peter said, "I do not possess silver and gold, but what I do have I give to you: In the name of Jesus Christ the Nazarene--walk!" And seizing him by the right hand, he raised him up; and immediately his feet and his ankles were strengthened. With a leap he stood upright and began to walk; and he entered the temple with them, walking and leaping and praising God.

This healing of the lame beggar took place at the Beautiful Gate at the entrance to the temple; however, it is not completely clear whether this is the gate to the Temple Mount, which is the enclosure upon which the Temple was built, or a gate leading into the courts surrounding the Temple itself. Since Peter and John are going up to the temple at the hour of prayer it appears that they may be entering the courts surrounding the Temple itself. Although Josephus, the Jewish historian, and the rabbinical writings do not mention a gate of the temple called Beautiful, they do have special praise for the west gate leading out of the Court of the Women and this is probably the Beautiful Gate of Matthew 3:2 (see Figure 7.2). This event probably took place about a week after the great outpouring of the Holy Spirit on the Day of Pentecost or Sunday, May 29, A.D. 33. After leaving the courts around the Temple, but still on the Temple Mount, Peter and John went to Solomon's Portico (see Figure 7.2), and they were followed by the healed beggar and a large crowd. Peter preached the Gospel message to this crowd of Jewish worshipers; however, his message was interrupted by the temple officials that came and arrested Peter, John and the beggar. Nevertheless, many that heard the message, believed and the number of men came to about 5000.

The next day, Monday, May 30, A.D. 33 Peter, John and the beggar were brought before the rulers and elders of the Temple. Then Acts 4:7-12 says:

> When they had placed them in the center, they began to inquire, "By what power, or in what name, have you done this?" Then Peter, filled with the Holy Spirit, said to them, "Rulers and elders of the people, if we are on trial today for a benefit done to a sick man, as to how this man has been made well, let it be known to all of you and to all the people of Israel, that by the name of Jesus Christ the Nazarene, whom you crucified, whom God raised from the dead-by this name this man stands here before you in good health. He is the STONE WHICH WAS REJECTED by you, THE BUILDERS, but WHICH BECAME THE CHIEF CORNER stone. And there is salvation in no one else; for there is no other name under heaven that has been given among men by which we must be saved."

Because the entire city recognized that a great miracle had taken place, the temple officials didn't feel that they could punish the apostles. However, they ordered the apostles not to speak to anyone about Jesus. However, Acts 4:19-20 say, "But Peter and John answered and said to them, 'Whether it is right in the sight of God to give heed to you rather than to God, you be the judge; for we cannot stop speaking about what we have seen and heard.'" The tribunal threatened Peter and John again and then released them. That same day Peter and John returned to their companions, probably in the upper room where the apostles were staying (Acts 1:13) and reported

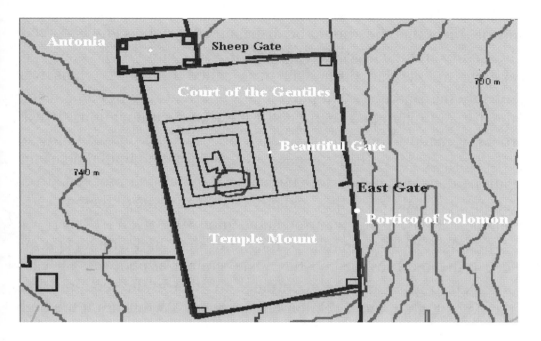

Temple Mount
Figure 7.2

all that the chief priests and the elders had said to them. Then Acts 4:31 says, "And when they had prayed, the place where they had gathered together was shaken, and they were all filled with the Holy Spirit and began to speak the word of God with boldness."

Life in the Early Church

Acts 4:32-35 again summarizes the activity of the early Jerusalem church which involved the sharing of property among this group of believers and the apostles giving witness to the resurrection of Jesus with great power. Then two examples are given of the selling of property and the laying of the proceeds of the sale at the apostles' feet that they might be distributed to each as any had need. The first example is recorded in Acts 4:36-37 and involved Joseph, a Levite of Cyprian birth, who was called Barnabas. This was probably the Barnabas that played an important role in Paul's early ministry and may have been one of the first such donations. It was probably made about June 15, A.D. 33. The second example of giving property involved Ananas and Sapphira who both died as the result of their pretending to have contributed all the proceeds from their property sale when they actually held back some of the proceeds. This incident probably occurred about June 30, A.D. 33.

Acts 5:12-16 then tells of the many signs and wonders taking place at the hands of the apostles. The number of believers in Jesus continued to grow and they continued to meet in the section of the Temple Mount known as Solomon's portico. At this point the high priest and the members of his sect, the Sadducees, rose up and arrested the apostles. This probably occurred about Thursday, July 14, A.D. 33. However, an angel released them during the night and told the apostles, "Go your way, stand and speak to the people in the temple the whole message of this Life." The next day the Jewish rulers were perplexed to learn that the apostles were missing from their prison cell. Then word came that they were preaching in the temple precincts and the captain of the temple guard went with his officers and brought the apostles to the Council. Then Acts 5:27-29 says:

> When they had brought them, they stood them before the Council. The high priest questioned them, saying, "We gave you strict orders not to continue teaching in this name, and yet, you have filled Jerusalem with your teaching and intend to bring this man's blood upon us." But Peter and the apostles answered, "We must obey God rather than men."

The apostles answer greatly angered the Council and they wanted to kill the apostles; however, Gamaliel, a respected teacher of the law, addressed the Council and advised caution in dealing with the apostles. The apostles were therefore flogged and then released. This event happened the day after the apostles were arrested or about Friday, July 15.

At this point a complaint arose concerning discrimination against the Hellenistic Jewish widows in the daily distribution of food. To solve this problem, the apostles asked the congregation to select seven men to handle this distribution. The men selected were Stephen, Philip, Prochorus, Nicanor, Timon, Parmenas and Nicolas. This event probably took place on July 28, A.D. 33. In addition to their duties of distributing food, at least some of these men also became evangelists.

Stoning of Stephen

And Stephen, full of grace and power, was performing great wonders and signs among the people. But some men from what was called the Synagogue of the Freedmen, including both Cyrenians and Alexandrians, and some from Cilicia and Asia, rose up and argued with Stephen. But they were unable to cope with the wisdom and the Spirit with which he was speaking. Then they secretly induced men to say, "We have heard him speak blasphemous words against Moses and against God." And they stirred up the people, the elders and the scribes, and they came up to him and dragged him away and brought him before the Council. They put forward false witnesses who said, "This man incessantly speaks against this holy place and the Law; for we have heard him say that this Nazarene, Jesus, will destroy this place and alter the customs which Moses handed down to us."

> And fixing their gaze on him, all who were sitting in the Council saw his face like the face of an angel (Acts 6:8-15).

These opponents of Stephen were from a Jewish synagogue where apparently Stephen was preaching and teaching. A trial was conducted before the Council and after his accusers were heard, the high priest asked Stephen if these things were true. Stephen in his defense give a review of the entire history of the Jews. Then in Acts 7:51-53 Stephen said:

> "You men who are stiff-necked and uncircumcised in heart and ears are always resisting the Holy Spirit; you are doing just as your fathers did. Which one of the prophets did your fathers not persecute? They killed those who had previously announced the coming of the Righteous One, whose betrayers and murderers you have now become; you who received the law as ordained by angels, and yet did not keep it."

Stephen was speaking under the influence of the Holy Spirit and was actually giving God's rebuke to those people. Then in Acts 7:56 Stephen said, "Behold, I see the heavens opened up and the Son of Man standing at the right hand of God." When Stephen said this, those gathered in the Council chamber rushed upon him and drove him out of the city, probably into the Kidron Valley, and stoned him. This event took place about August 12, A.D. 33.

Following the stoning of Stephen, a great persecution of the church began in Jerusalem. As a result of this persecution, the Jerusalem Church was scattered through the region of Judea and Samaria except for the apostles. Why were the apostles able to remain in Jerusalem while the rest of the church was scattered? This point is not explained in Scripture, but it may have something to due with the fact that they were living together in the upper room (see Act 1:13). If this was the same upper room as that in which Jesus celebrated His Last Supper, then we saw in chapter 2 that this upper room may have been in a building in the Essence community which was one of the three primary Jewish sects at this time (see Josephus, *Antiquities*, 13.5.9). If this was the case, then the Essence community, who were quite independent of the Temple authorities, might have protected the apostles. Saul, who would later be called Paul, seems to have been one of the leaders in carrying out this persecution.

Philip's Ministry

Among those who were scattered because of this persecution was Philip, another member of the seven. Acts 8:5-8 says:

> Philip went down to the city of Samaria and began proclaiming Christ to them. The crowds with one accord were giving attention to what was said by Philip, as they heard and saw the signs which he was performing. For in the case of many who had unclean spirits, they were coming out of them shouting with a loud voice; and many who had been paralyzed and lame were healed. So there was much rejoicing in that city.

Philip probably arrived in Samaria about Thursday, August 18, A.D. 33. When the apostles in Jerusalem heard that the Samaritans had received the word of God, they sent Peter and John to Samaria that they might receive the Holy Spirit The Samaritans were not accepted by the Jewish Temple authorities in Jerusalem because of their lack of racial purity even though the Samaritans did accept the Jewish Scriptures. Normally the Holy Spirit was received at the time of baptism (Acts 2:38); however, to avoid a split in Christ's Church between Jewish Christians and Samaritan Christians, God did not send the Holy Spirit to the Samaritan Church until Peter and John laid their hands on the Samaritans that had already been baptized in the name of the Lord Jesus. Thus God showed the connection between the church in Jerusalem and the church in Samaria. They were all part of Christ's Church. This event probably took place about Thursday, September 8, A.D. 33.

In the city of Samaria there was a sorcerer named Simon who believed in Christ and was baptized. When Simon saw the Holy Spirit being received when the apostles laid their hands on the Samaritans, he offered the apostles money if he could receive this power. Peter rebuked Simon for his offer. Then about Sunday, September 11, A.D. 33, Peter and John returned to Jerusalem. On their way back to Jerusalem they preached in many Samaritan villages. After Peter and John had left the city of Samaria, probably during the night of Sunday, September 11, Acts 8:26-38 says:

> But an angel of the Lord spoke to Philip saying, "Get up and go south to the road that descends from Jerusalem to Gaza." (This is a desert road.) So he got up and went; and there was an Ethiopian eunuch, a court official of Candace, queen of the Ethiopians, who was in charge of all her treasure; and he had come to Jerusalem to worship, and he was returning and sitting in his chariot, and was reading the prophet Isaiah. Then the Spirit said to Philip, "Go up and join this chariot." Philip ran up and heard him reading Isaiah the prophet, and said, "Do you understand what you are reading?" And he said, "Well, how could I, unless someone guides me?" And he invited Philip to come up and sit with him. Now the passage of Scripture which he was reading was this: "HE WAS LED AS A SHEEP TO SLAUGHTER; AND AS

A LAMB BEFORE ITS SHEARER IS SILENT, SO HE DOES NOT OPEN HIS MOUTH. IN HUMILIATION HIS JUDGMENT WAS TAKEN AWAY; WHO WILL RELATE HIS GENERATION? FOR HIS LIFE IS REMOVED FROM THE EARTH."   The eunuch answered Philip and said, "Please tell me, of whom does the prophet say this? Of himself or of someone else?" Then Philip opened his mouth, and beginning from this Scripture he preached Jesus to him. As they went along the road they came to some water; and the eunuch said, "Look! Water! What prevents me from being baptized?" And Philip said, "If you believe with all your heart, you may." And he answered and said, "I believe that Jesus Christ is the Son of God." And he ordered the chariot to stop; and they both went down into the water, Philip as well as the eunuch, and he baptized him.

Philip probably left the city of Samaria on Monday, September 12, A.D. 33, and would have arrived in Jerusalem on Tuesday, September 13 later in the day. The next morning, Wednesday, September 14 Philip probably met the Ethiopian eunuch on the desert road to Gaza (see Figure 7.3). Philip was snatched away by the Holy Spirit and the eunuch went on his way rejoicing. Philip found himself in Azotus on the Mediterranean coast and then proceeded up the coast preaching the Gospel in all the cities until he reached Caesarea where Acts 21:8 indicates he eventually made his home.

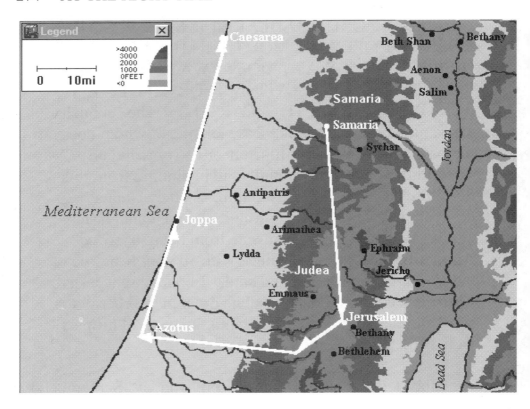

Philip's Ministry
Figure 7.3

Conversion of Paul

In chapter 9 of the book of Acts, Saul (Paul) departs Jerusalem to go to Damascus to bring back bound any members of the Way. As previously discussed, his departure probably occurred shortly after the end of the Feast of Booths on October 3, A.D. 33. Saul probably went to the high priest to obtain letters to the synagogues of Damascus to arrest any members of the Way about Wednesday, October 5, A.D. 33 and he probably departed about Sunday, October 16. Since there is no mention of horses or chariots in this narrative,

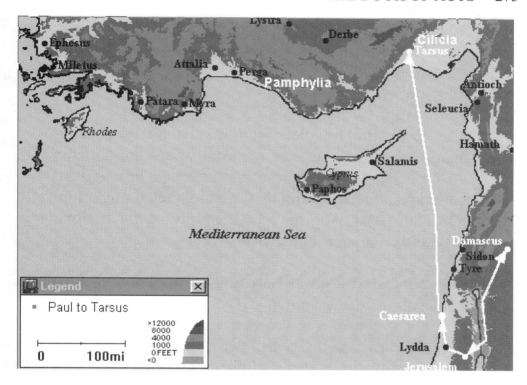

Paul's Journey to Damascus
Figure 7.4

Saul and his party were probably traveling on foot. By Friday, October 21, A.D. 33, Saul and his party would have reached the vicinity of the sea of Galilee where they may have stopped for the Sabbath. Saul and his party probably departed this area on Sunday, October 23 and would have been probably been approaching Damascus on Wednesday, October 26, A.D. 33 (see Figure 7.4). Then Acts 9:3-9 says:

> As he was traveling, it happened that he was approaching Damascus, and suddenly a light from heaven flashed around him; and he fell to the ground and heard a voice saying to him, "Saul, Saul, why are

you persecuting Me?" And he said, "Who are You, Lord?" And He said," I am Jesus whom you are persecuting, but get up and enter the city, and it will be told you what you must do."

The men who traveled with him stood speechless, hearing the voice but seeing no one. Saul got up from the ground, and though his eyes were open, he could see nothing; and leading him by the hand, they brought him into Damascus. And he was three days without sight, and neither ate nor drank.

Saul (Paul) confessed Jesus as Lord and he probably repented of his sinful persecution of the church. If God's plan of salvation only involves belief, confession and repentance, why didn't Jesus tell Paul to just "invite Him into his heart." which is widely represented as God's plan of salvation today? However, this was not what Jesus said. Rather, Jesus told Saul to rise up and enter the city and it would be told what he must do. It was three days later that Ananias, a devout Christian living in Damascus, came to Saul at the direction of Jesus. The most detailed account of Ananias' visit to Saul is found in Acts 22:12-16 which says:

"And a certain Ananias, a man who was devout by the standard of the Law, and well spoken of by all the Jews who lived there, came to me, and standing near said to me, 'Brother Saul, receive your sight!' And at that very time I looked up at him. And he said, 'The God of our fathers has appointed you to know His will and to see the Righteous One and to hear an utterance from His mouth. For you will be a witness for Him to all men of what you have seen and heard. Now why do you delay? Get up and be baptized, and wash away your sins, calling on His name.'"

If Saul had been saved on the road to Damascus, why was he still in his sins and still needing to have them washed away? Obviously Saul was not saved on the road to Damascus. This Scripture indicates that he did not receive salvation until he had believed, repented, confessed Jesus and was baptized . Thus baptism is an integral part of God's plan of salvation. In fact, in all the instances where the details of the salvation of an individual is recorded in the New Testament after Jesus' resurrection, baptism was an integral part of that salvation. These instances include the salvation of the 3000 on Pentecost (Acts 2:38), those in the city of Samaria (Acts 8:11), the Ethiopian eunuch (Acts 8:38), Saul (Paul) in Damascus (Acts 9:18), Cornelius and friends (Act 10:48), Lydia and her household (Acts 16:15), the Philippian Jailer and household (Acts 16:33), Crispus and the Corinthian (Acts 18:8) and the twelve at Ephesus (Act 19:5).

It is sometimes pointed out that Peter's message in Acts 3:11-26 following the healing of a lame beggar in the Temple area did not mention baptism; however, Acts 4:1-4 says:

> As they were speaking to the people, the priests and the captain of the temple guard and the Sadducees came up to them, being greatly disturbed because they were teaching the people and proclaiming in Jesus the resurrection from the dead. And they laid hands on them and put them in jail until the next day, for it was already evening. But many of those who had heard the message believed; and the number of the men came to be about five thousand.

Peter did not mention baptism in this message because he was interrupted by the temple officials. However, there is no reason to believe that baptism was not a part of the salvation of these 5000 men as it was for all the other instances given in the book of Acts where the message was completed. Nowhere in the New Testament was anyone seeking salvation ever told to "just invite Jesus into their heart" or "to pray the sinners' prayer."

If this widely followed plan of salvation is not found in the New Testament, where did it come from? Actually its roots can be traced to John Calvin, the great Reformation leader, and to many of the other leaders of that movement. One of the points of contention in the Reformation was the Roman Catholic dogma that all unbaptized children dying in infancy were condemned to eternal damnation because of Adam's sin. Philip Schaff, *The History of the Church,* Volume VIII, page 556, says:

> Calvin offers an escape from the horrible dogma of infant damnation by denying the necessity of water baptism for salvation, and by making salvation dependent on sovereign election alone, which may work regeneration without baptism, as in the case of the Old Testament saints and the thief on the cross.

However, it is not necessary to deny the role of baptism in God's plan of salvation to establish that children dying in infancy are not condemned to eternal damnation. Matthew 19:16-17 says:

> And someone came to Him and said, "Teacher, what good thing shall I do that I may obtain eternal life?" And He said to him, "Why are you asking Me about what is good? There is only One who is good; but if you wish to enter into life, keep the commandments."

Thus, Jesus said to this man, if he keep the commandments, he would obtain eternal life. Of course, for an adult, this would be impossible for Romans 3:23 says, "for all have sinned and fall short of the glory of God." However, for an infant that has not reached the age of accountability, they have not sinned and therefore have kept the commandments. This is confirmed by the fact that immediately before these verses Matthew 19:13-14 says:

> Then some children were brought to Him so that He might lay His hands on them and pray; and the disciples rebuked them. But Jesus said, "Let the children alone, and do not hinder them from coming to Me; for the kingdom of heaven belongs to such as these."

However, as an adult, the Apostle Paul, received salvation in the same manner as every other convert to Christianity in the New Testament after the outpouring of the Holy Spirit on Pentecost: by belief, confession, repentance and baptism. This was God's plan of salvation communicated by the apostles under the guidance of the Holy Spirit. None of these elements of the plan of salvation are works by which the recipient earns his or her salvation, especially baptism which is performed on the recipient not by the recipient. In John 14:15 Jesus says, "If you love Me, you will keep My commandments." Jesus commands baptism. In Matthew 28:19-20 Jesus says:

> "Go therefore and make disciples of all the nations, baptizing them in the name of the Father and the Son and the Holy Spirit, teaching them to observe all that I commanded you; and lo, I am with you always, even to the end of the age."

If Jesus says that all His disciples should be baptized, who can say that baptism is not essential? Does Jesus have any optional commandments? We should stop trying to figure out the mechanism of salvation and humbly submit to the commandments of God. The

Apostle Peter, under the guidance of the Holy Spirit, on Pentecost Sunday said to a believing multitude (Acts 2:38), "Repent, and each of you be baptized in the name of Jesus Christ for the forgiveness of your sins; and you will receive the gift of the Holy Spirit." This is God's plan of salvation and cannot be improved upon by the wisdom of man!

Paul's Early Ministry

Saul's (Paul's) heavenly vision on the road to Damascus occurred about Wednesday, October 26, A.D. 33 as previously seen and, according to Acts 22:6, the time was about noontime. Then, three days later, Ananias visited Saul. Counting inclusively, this would be Friday, October 28, A.D. 33 when Saul was baptized and washed his sins away. Saul only spent a few days in Damascus, but immediately began to proclaim Jesus in the synagogues of Damascus according to Acts 9:19b-21. Galatians 1:17 tells us that Saul then left Damascus and went away to Arabia which is probably a reference to the Nabatean Kingdom, and then returned to Damascus. Galatians 1:18 says, "Then three years later I went up to Jerusalem to become acquainted with Cephas, and stayed with him fifteen days." This would be the visit to Jerusalem described in Acts 9:23. Three Jewish years, counting inclusively, after the year of Paul's heavenly vision would be the Jewish year from March 27, A.D. 35 until March 15, A.D. 36. There is no clear indication when during this year that Saul departed Damascus; however, since there is no mention of any festivals occurring during this visit to Jerusalem, it probably didn't occur early in the Jewish year. Since summer travel on foot in this area is difficult because of the heat, Saul probably returned to Damascus in the fall of A.D. 35 and, after preaching in the synagogues, Acts 9:22-25 says:

But Saul kept increasing in strength and confounding the

Jews who lived at Damascus by proving that this Jesus is the Christ. When many days had elapsed, the Jews plotted together to do away with him, but their plot became known to Saul. They were also watching the gates day and night so that they might put him to death; but his disciples took him by night and let him down through an opening in the wall, lowering him in a large basket.

Further details of this incident are given in 2 Corinthians 11:32-33 which says:

In Damascus the ethnarch under Aretas the king was guarding the city of the Damascenes in order to seize me, and I was let down in a basket through a window in the wall, and so escaped his hands.

2 Corinthians 11:32 indicates that the Jews had enlisted the aid of the ethnarch of the city that had been appointed by the Nabatean king Aretas. Nabatean control of Damascus at this time seems to be supported by Josephus who in *Antiquities*, 18.5.1 reports that King Aretas IV of Nabatea moved militarily against Herod Antipas because Herod had divorced Aretas' daughter to marry his brother Philip's wife (Matthew 14:3-4). This military action probably took place in the territory of Gamalitis since Josephus also indicates that Aretas had a territorial dispute with Herod Antipas over this region. Also, Josephus indicates that Herod Antipas' army was destroyed by the treachery of some of the people from the former tetrarchy of Philip which included Gamalitis. Since Damascus is located near Gamalitis, it may have been the base from which Aretas launched his attack on the forces of Herod Antipas or a least must have been under Nabatean control before the attack was launched. When Herod Antipas' army was defeated, he complained to the Roman emperor,

Tiberius Caesar, who sent orders to Vitellius, the governor of Syria, to make war on Aretas. However, while Vitellius was advancing on Petra, King Aretas capital, he received news that Tiberius had died so Vitellius returned to Syria to await orders from the new emperor. Tiberius died on March 16, A.D. 37 (Julian) and Vitellius received word of Tiberius death while in Jerusalem during the Passover Feast, April 17 until April 24, A.D. 37. Thus Aretas' attack on the forces of Herod Antipas probably took place in A.D. 36. It was probably earlier during that same year that Paul was let down in a basket through a window in the wall of Damascus and thus escaped the ethnarch under Aretas. Thus, after spending many days in Damascus, Saul left for Jerusalem about February 6, A.D. 36. The journey would have taken about two weeks so he would have arrived in Jerusalem about February 20. Galatians 1:18 indicated that Saul only spent fifteen days there getting acquainted Peter. Acts 9:26-30 gives us considerably more details of this visit:

> When he came to Jerusalem, he was trying to associate with the disciples; but they were all afraid of him, not believing that he was a disciple. But Barnabas took hold of him and brought him to the apostles and described to them how he had seen the Lord on the road, and that He had talked to him, and how at Damascus he had spoken out boldly in the name of Jesus. And he was with them, moving about freely in Jerusalem, speaking out boldly in the name of the Lord. And he was talking and arguing with the Hellenistic Jews; but they were attempting to put him to death. But when the brethren learned of it, they brought him down to Caesarea and sent him away to Tarsus.

Saul would have departed Jerusalem about March 5, A.D. 36 and would have arrived in Caesarea about March 7. Saul would have spent a few days in Caesarea arranging for sea travel and would have probably departed Caesarea for Tarsus about the middle of March when sea travel on the Mediterranean Sea was again safe. Although Paul had probably planned to celebrate the Passover Feast in Jerusalem, which occurred that year on March 29, because of the threat on his life, he had to leave before the feast. Then Acts 9:31 says "So the church throughout all Judea and Galilee and Samaria enjoyed peace, being built up; and going on in the fear of the Lord and in the comfort of the Holy Spirit, it continued to increase." This period of peace for the church would have begun with the departure of Saul from Jerusalem and ended with the execution the Apostle James, the brother of John, by King Agrippa I, which is recorded Acts 12:1-2. We shall consider the death of James now because this event can be exactly dated and will give us a terminus date for the remaining events in chapters 9,10 and 11.

Death of James the Brother of John

> Now about that time Herod the king laid hands on some
> who belonged to the church in order to mistreat them.
> And he had James the brother of John put to death with
> a sword (Acts 12:1-2).

We know that this is King Herod Agrippa I because he was the first king of Judea after King Herod I, who ruled at the time of Jesus' birth and died shortly thereafter. Of the other rulers that succeeded Herod I, Archelaus was an ethnarch and Herod Antipas and Philip were tetrarches. Shortly after this Feast of Unleavened Bread, Acts 12:23 indicates that King Herod Agrippa I died and Josephus and the coins of King Agrippa I indicate he died in A.D. 44. Thus we know that this Feast of Unleavened Bread was the one that took place from March 31 until April 7, A.D. 44. James, the brother of John, was probably executed about Friday, March 25, A.D. 44, just before the. beginning of the feast.

Relief Offering for Jerusalem

Working backwards from this known date we can date the events of chapters 10 and 11 and the latter part of chapter 9. Acts 11:27-30 says:

> Now at this time some prophets came down from Jerusalem to Antioch. One of them named Agabus stood up and began to indicate by the Spirit that there would certainly be a great famine all over the world. And this took place in the reign of Claudius. And in the proportion that any of the disciples had means, each of them determined to send a contribution for the relief of the brethren living in Judea. And this they did, sending it in charge of Barnabas and Saul to the elders.

The prophets would have probably remained in Jerusalem until after the Feast of Booths, which ended on October 13 in the year A.D. 43, since the Christians in Jerusalem were still practicing Jews. Then they would have traveled overland to Antioch since the period of safe sea travel on the Mediterranean had passed. They probably made several stops on the way and probably arrived in Antioch about the middle of December. At the next meeting of the church, probably about Sunday, December 20, A.D. 43, Agabus prophesied a great famine. This famine we are told took place in the reign of Claudius. Claudius was emperor of Rome from A.D. 41 until A.D. 54. Allowing about a month to make the collection and prepare for the journey, Barnabas and Saul probably departed Antioch about February 1, A.D. 44. They probably hastened to Jerusalem and the journey of more than 300 miles probably took them about four weeks.

Thus, Barnabas and Saul would have arrived in Jerusalem about February 25, A.D. 44, immediately prior to the Passover Feast. The famine had probably not started yet because the church at Antioch was sending the relief offering based on the prophesy of Agabus rather than the existence of a famine.However, Josephus in *Antiquities,* 20.2.5, in the next chapter after he describes the death of King Herod Agrippa I in A.D. 44, tells of Helena, the queen of Adiabene, coming to Jerusalem and finding a famine.

Church Established At Antioch

Prior to the famine relief visit Acts 11:19-26 says:

> So then those who were scattered because of the persecution that occurred in connection with Stephen made their way to Phoenicia and Cyprus and Antioch, speaking the word to no one except to Jews alone. But there were some of them, men of Cyprus and Cyrene, who came to Antioch and began speaking to the Greeks also, preaching the Lord Jesus. And the hand of the Lord was with them, and a large number who believed turned to the Lord. The news about them reached the ears of the church at Jerusalem, and they sent Barnabas off to Antioch. Then when he arrived and witnessed the grace of God, he rejoiced and began to encourage them all with resolute heart to remain true to the Lord; for he was a good man, and full of the Holy Spirit and of faith. And considerable numbers were brought to the Lord.
>
> And he left for Tarsus to look for Saul; and when he had found him, he brought him to Antioch. And for an entire year they met with the church and taught considerable numbers; and the disciples were first called Christians in

Antioch.

An entire year before the prophesy of Agabus would be December of A.D. 42. Again, Barnabas would have probably left after the end of the Feast of Booths on September 24, A.D. 42. Barnabas probably departed Jerusalem about Sunday, October 6, A.D. 42. Since Antioch was the first Gentile Christian Church, Barnabas would have probably only stopped for the Sabbaths and would have probably arrived about October 31, A.D. 42. Barnabas probably spent most of November A.D. 42 preaching in Antioch. Then about November 23, Barnabas probably departed for Tarsus to look for Saul. The journey to Tarsus would have taken about two weeks and, after finding Saul, they both returned to Antioch, arriving about December 25, A.D. 42 to begin a full year of ministry in Antioch.

Antioch is the first Gentle Christian Church mentioned in the New Testament. Some of the disciples that were dispersed as a result of the persecution of the church that arose after the stoning of Stephen in A.D. 33 went to Antioch. They apparently started a Christian Church in Antioch or at least preached the word in the synagogue, but initially only to Jewish believers. Then later, some of the scattered disciples, men from Cyprus and Cyrene, came to Antioch and began speaking to the Greeks also. This first Gentile Christian Church was probably established about July 1, A.D. 40. Acts 11:26 tells us that the disciples were first called Christians at Antioch. It was probably not until the summer of A.D. 42, after the church had grown, that news of the Gentle Christian Church at Antioch reached Jerusalem.

Peter's Early Ministry

It was probably in A.D. 39, the year before the establishment of the first Gentile Christian Church, that Peter was teaching through out Judea. Acts 9:32-35 says:

Now as Peter was traveling through all those regions, he came down also to the saints who lived at Lydda. There he found a man named Aeneas, who had been bedridden eight years, for he was paralyzed. Peter said to him, "Aeneas, Jesus Christ heals you; get up and make your bed." Immediately he got up. And all who lived at Lydda and Sharon saw him, and they turned to the Lord.

If this event took place in A.D. 39, it would have taken place six years after the establishment of Christ's Church in Jerusalem on Pentecost Sunday in A.D. 33 and there would be many groups of Jewish Christians throughout Judea. Peter would have probably remained in Jerusalem until after Pentecost since he was a practicing Jew. Pentecost was celebrated in A.D. 39 on May 15. Since Peter probably made several stops before reaching Lydda, Peter probably arrived there about June 2. Possibly the next Sunday, June 5, Peter found Aeneas and healed him. Word of this healing would have traveled quickly through the Christian community. It was probably the next week that Dorcas died in Joppa (see Figure 7.5), and they sent for Peter. The journey from Lydda to Joppa would have only taken one day. Thus, about June 16, A.D. 39, Peter would have arrived in Joppa and raised Dorcas from the dead. Acts 9:43 says, "And Peter stayed many days in Joppa with a tanner named Simon." It was now the time of the heat of the summer and it would be very pleasant living in Joppa on the shores of the Mediterranean Sea.

Conversion of Cornelius

Now there was a man at Caesarea named Cornelius, a centurion of what was called the Italian cohort, a devout man and one who feared God with all his household, and gave many alms to the Jewish people and prayed to God

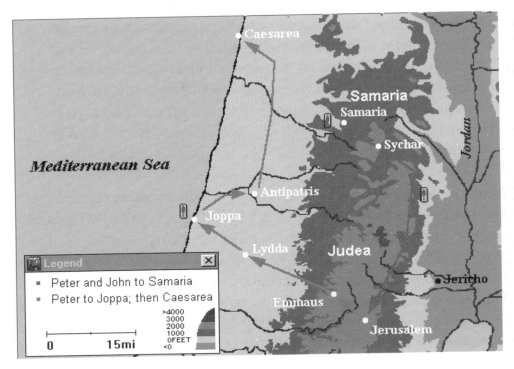

Peter's Early Ministry
Figure 7.5

continually. About the ninth hour of the day he clearly saw in a vision an angel of God who had just come in and said to him, "Cornelius!" And fixing his gaze on him and being much alarmed, he said, "What is it, Lord?" And he said to him, "Your prayers and alms have ascended as a memorial before God. "Now dispatch some men to Joppa and send for a man named Simon, who is also called Peter; he is staying with a tanner named Simon, whose house is by the sea"(Acts 10:1-6).

Immediately after the angelic visit, Cornelius dispatched two servants and one of his soldiers to bring Simon Peter. This event probably took place about July 31, A.D. 39. This delegation from

Cornelius probably traveled several hours after sunset, since they were approaching Joppa by the sixth hour (11:00 to 12:00 noon). At this same time Peter went up on the housetop to pray, and he had a vision of a sheet-like object being lowered from heaven. On this sheet were all kinds of animals and insects; some, and possibly all of which, were considered unclean by Leviticus 11. A voice said to him, "Arise, Peter, kill and eat." But Peter refused, saying he had never eaten anything unclean. But the voice said, "What God has cleansed, no longer consider unholy." The same thing happened three times in Peter's vision and then the object was taken away. As Peter was trying to figure out what the vision meant, the men from Cornelius arrived and were calling out if Simon Peter lived there. The Spirit told Peter of the men and said, "But arise, go downstairs, and accompany them without misgivings; for I have sent them Myself." The next day Peter, with some of the Jewish brethren from Joppa, returned to Cornelius at Caesarea. When Peter and the group arrived, a large group of Cornelius' friends and relatives were waiting in his house for them. Then Acts 10:25-33 says:

> When Peter entered, Cornelius met him, and fell at his feet and worshiped him. But Peter raised him up, saying, "Stand up; I too am just a man." As he talked with him, he entered and found many people assembled. And he said to them, "You yourselves know how unlawful it is for a man who is a Jew to associate with a foreigner or to visit him; and yet God has shown me that I should not call any man unholy or unclean. That is why I came without even raising any objection when I was sent for. So I ask for what reason you have sent for me." Cornelius said, "Four days ago to this hour, I was praying in my house during the ninth hour; and behold, a man stood before me in shining garments, and he said, 'Cornelius, your prayer has been heard and your alms

have been remembered before God. Therefore send to Joppa and invite Simon, who is also called Peter, to come to you; he is staying at the house of Simon the tanner by the sea.' So I sent for you immediately, and you have been kind enough to come. Now then, we are all here present before God to hear all that you have been commanded by the Lord."

Peter and his group arrived at Cornelis house during the ninth hour on the second day after their departure from Joppa. Since the distance from Joppa to Caesarea is about 32 miles and, if they traveled ten hours the first day and six hours the second day, they would be traveling at about two miles per hour, which is a reasonable rate of travel for a group of men traveling on foot. Peter preached Jesus to the assembled group and Acts 10:44-48 says:

> While Peter was still speaking these words, the Holy Spirit fell upon all those who were listening to the message. All the circumcised believers who came with Peter were amazed, because the gift of the Holy Spirit had been poured out on the Gentiles also. For they were hearing them speaking with tongues and exalting God. Then Peter answered, "Surely no one can refuse the water for these to be baptized who have received the Holy Spirit just as we did, can he?" And he ordered them to be baptized in the name of Jesus Christ. Then they asked him to stay on for a few days.

As was the case for the first Samaritan believers, these first Gentile believers did not receive the Holy Spirit in the usual way at baptism, so that God could show the Jewish believer that He also welcomed Gentile believers into His church. Thus, Christ's Church was expanded from its initial Jewish congregations to include all repentant believers that are obedient to the commands of Jesus.

After this experience, Acts 11:2 indicates that Peter returned to Jerusalem, and he was criticized for having fellowship with Gentiles. Peter probably returned to Jerusalem for the Feast of Booths and Peter's defense of his inviting Gentiles into Christ's Church probably took place just after that feast. So Peter probably defended his actions before the church in Jerusalem on about Monday, September 26, A.D. 39. Peter explained all that had happened and then Acts 11:18 says, "When they heard this, they quieted down and glorified God, saying, 'Well then, God has granted to the Gentiles also the repentance that leads to life.'" We have now dated all the events of chapters 9, 10 and 11 of Acts so that we can return to the beginning of chapter 12 of Acts and move forward.

Peter Delivered From Prison

Acts 12:1-2 indicates that King Herod Agrippa began to persecute the church, and that he executed the Apostle James, the brother of John, the first of the apostles to be martyred. This probably occurred about Friday, March 25, A.D. 44. Then Acts 12:3 says, "When he saw that it pleased the Jews, he proceeded to arrest Peter also. Now it was during the days of Unleavened Bread." Peter would have probably met with the other Christians in Jerusalem for the observance of the Lord's Supper on the first day of the week and this is a likely time for Peter's arrest. Thus Peter was probably arrested on Sunday, April 3, during the Feast of Unleavened Bread in A.D. 44. Then Acts 12:4-7 says:

> When he had seized him, he put him in prison, delivering him to four squads of soldiers to guard him, intending after the Passover to bring him out before the people. So Peter was kept in the prison, but prayer for

> him was being made fervently by the church to God. On the very night when Herod was about to bring him forward, Peter was sleeping between two soldiers, bound with two chains, and guards in front of the door were watching over the prison. And behold, an angel of the Lord suddenly appeared and a light shone in the cell; and he struck Peter's side and woke him up, saying, "Get up quickly." And his chains fell off his hands.

Therefore, Peter was delivered from prison by an angel on the night of the Jewish day following the end of the Feast of Unleavened Bread or on Thursday, April 7, A.D. 44. After being delivered, Peter went to the home of Mary, the mother of John Mark, where many were gathered praying for Peter. After telling them of his release he departed Jerusalem. When King Herod Agrippa I learned of Peter's escape, he examined the guards and had them executed.

Death of Herod Agrippa I

After this event Herod Agrippa I left Jerusalem and returned to his primary residence at Caesarea (Acts 12:19). While in Caesarea, Herod Agrippa I addressed a gathering and the people called him a god. Then Acts 12:23 says "And immediately an angel of the Lord struck him because he did not give God the glory, and he was eaten by worms and died." Josephus, *Antiquities,* 19.8.2, page 523, also records this same incident. Josephus indicates that the occasion for the gathering was a festival to honor Caesar, probably on his birthday. The Caesar during Herod Agrippa's reign was Claudius. Suetonius in *The Twelve Caesars,* page 162, indicates that Claudius' birthday was August 1 (Julian) and, using the tables of Appendix A, this would indicate that this festival probably started on July 30, A.D. 44. (Gregorian). Josephus indicates that on the second day of the festival the group was gathered in the theater early in the morning and King Agrippa I came on the stage dressed in a wonderful silver garment which reflected the morning sunlight and surprised his audience. Josephus, as did Acts 12:22, indicates that the audience proclaimed Herod Agrippa a god and he did not rebuke them. Josephus also said at that time a severe pain arose in his belly and after five days he died. Therefore, King Herod Agrippa I was probably stricken on Sunday, July 31 and died five days later, counting inclusively, on Thursday, August 4, A.D. 44.

Barnabas and Saul
Return to Antioch

The death of King Herod Agrippa I probably ended this period of persecution of the church. Acts 12:24-25 says, "But the word of the Lord continued to grow and to be multiplied. And Barnabas and Saul returned from Jerusalem when they had fulfilled their mission, taking along with them John, who was also called Mark." Barnabas and Saul had arrived during this period of persecution at Passover time. Being practicing Jews, normally they would have probably stayed for the Feast of Pentecost which in A.D. 44 was celebrated on May 22. However, since the leaders of the church were being arrested and since a group of Jews had previously sought to kill Saul, Barnabas and Saul probably returned to Antioch immediately after completing their mission on about Sunday, April 10. Barnabas and Saul took John Mark with them. Since Colossians 4:10 indicates that Mark was Barnabas' cousin, there is a good chance that Barnabas and Saul were staying with Mary, the mother of John Mark, in Jerusalem.

Paul's First Missionary Journey

Now there were at Antioch, in the church that was there, prophets and teachers: Barnabas, and Simeon who was called Niger, and Lucius of Cyrene, and Manaen who had been brought up with Herod the tetrarch, and Saul. While they were ministering to the Lord and fasting, the Holy Spirit said, "Set apart for Me Barnabas and Saul for the work to which I have called them." Then, when they had fasted and prayed and laid their hands on them, they sent them away (Acts 13:1-3).

After being commissioned by the church at Antioch, Syria, Barnabas and Saul departed for Cyprus by ship. It was probably in the spring of A.D. 45 when they left, after sea travel on the Mediterranean Sea was safe. They probably left Antioch after the Passover time which was celebrated by the first-century A.D. church as the time of Jesus' death, burial and resurrection. This would be a reasonable time for "ministering to the Lord and fasting." Thus, it was probably during the Easter celebration about Sunday April 23, A.D. 45, that the Holy Spirit commanded that Barnabas and Saul be set apart. After a couple of weeks of preparation, Barnabas and Saul probably departed Antioch about May 8, A.D. 45. According to Acts 13:4, Barnabas and Saul went down to Seleucia, the seaport of Antioch, and probably departed the next day according to arrangements previously made.

They would have arrived at Salamis, Cyprus about May 11, A.D. 45. Acts 4:36 indicates that Barnabas was originally from Cyprus. Barnabas and Saul also took John Mark with them as a helper. Acts 13:5 says that when they reached Salamus they began to proclaim the word of God in the synagogues of the Jews. They probably began their ministry on Cyprus by preaching in one of the synagogues of Salamus on Saturday, May 13, A.D. 45. Barnabas and Saul probably spent about three months preaching the Gospel in Cyprus, traveling some ninety miles from Salamus on the eastern end of the island to Paphos on the western end (see Figure 7.6).

It was probably about August 6, A.D. 45, that Sergius Paulus, the proconsul, summoned Barnabas and Saul that he might hear the word of God. Then Acts 13:8-12 says:

> But Elymas the magician (for so his name is translated) was opposing them, seeking to turn the proconsul away from the faith. But Saul, who was also known as Paul, filled with the Holy Spirit, fixed his gaze on him, and said, "You who are full of all deceit and fraud, you son of the devil, you enemy of all righteousness, will you not cease to make crooked the straight ways of the Lord? Now, behold, the hand of the Lord is upon you, and you will be blind and not see the sun for a time." And immediately a mist and a darkness fell upon him, and he went about seeking those who would lead him by the hand. Then the proconsul believed when he saw what had happened, being amazed at the teaching of the Lord.

From this point on in the Acts, Saul is referred to by his Greek name, Paul, and he seems to be given precedence over Barnabas since Paul's name is mentioned first.

Acts 13:13 says, "Now Paul and his companions put out to sea from Paphos and came to Perga in Pamphylia; but John left them and returned to Jerusalem." Paul and Barnabas probably departed Cyprus about August 21, A.D. 45 and at the latest in late fall before sea travel became dangerous. Paul and Barnabas probably arrived in Perga about August 23, A.D. 45; however, they did not stay in Perga, but went on to Pisidian Antioch. The trip to Pisidian Antioch would have taken about five days and leaving Perga on Monday, August 28, they would have arrived in Antioch on Friday, September 1. Then on the next Sabbath, September 2, they attended services at the synagogue in Antioch. After the Law and Prophets were read the leader of the synagogue invited Paul and Barnabas to speak a word of exhortation. Paul rose and preached a sermon recorded in Acts 13:16-41 which demonstrated from the law and prophets that Jesus was the promised

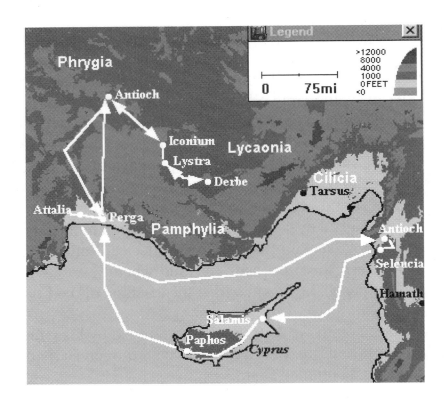

Paul's First Missionary Journey
Figure 7.6

Messiah. Paul's message was well received and the people begged that these things might be spoken of again on the next Sabbath. Then Acts 13:44-46 says:

> The next Sabbath nearly the whole city assembled to hear the word of the Lord. But when the Jews saw the crowds, they were filled with jealousy and began contradicting the things spoken by Paul, and were blaspheming. Paul and Barnabas spoke out boldly and

said, "It was necessary that the word of God be spoken to you first; since you repudiate it and judge yourselves unworthy of eternal life, behold, we are turning to the Gentiles."

The Gentiles rejoiced at what Paul said and apparently Paul and Barnabas had a fairly lengthy ministry in Pisidian Antioch since Acts 13:49 says, "And the word of the Lord was being spread through the whole region."Paul's second sermon would have been delivered on Saturday, September 9, A.D. 45. Several months later, Acts 13:50-51 says:

> But the Jews incited the devout women of prominence and the leading men of the city, and instigated a persecution against Paul and Barnabas, and drove them out of their district. But they shook off the dust of their feet in protest against them and went to Iconium.

It was probably about Sunday, December 10, A.D. 45, that the Jews drove Paul and Barnabas out of Pisidian Antioch. The journey to Iconium probably took about four days, so it was probably on Saturday, December 16, A.D. 45 that Paul and Barnabas taught in the synagogue of Iconium. Acts 14:1-7 says:

> In Iconium they entered the synagogue of the Jews together, and spoke in such a manner that a large number of people believed, both of Jews and of Greeks. But the Jews who disbelieved stirred up the minds of the Gentiles and embittered them against the brethren. Therefore they spent a long time there speaking boldly with reliance upon the Lord, who was testifying to the word of His grace, granting that signs and wonders be done by their hands. But the people of the city were

> divided; and some sided with the Jews, and some with the apostles. And when an attempt was made by both the Gentiles and the Jews with their rulers, to mistreat and to stone them, they became aware of it and fled to the cities of Lycaonia, Lystra and Derbe, and the surrounding region; and there they continued to preach the gospel.

Since Paul and Barnabas spent a long time in Iconium, it was probably about Thursday, June 7, A.D. 46, that they became aware o the plot to have them killed. Therefore, they probably left Iconium that night and it was probably about Sunday, June 10, A.D. 46, tha they arrived at Lystra. June 6, A.D. 46 was the night of the full moon and thus. on June 7 there would be almost a full moon which woulc aid them in night travel.

At Lystra Paul healed a lame man who had never walked whicl caused the people of the city to believe that Paul and Barnabas wer the Greek gods, Hermes and Zeus. The priest of the Temple of Zeu: brought oxen and garlands and wanted to offer them in sacrifice tc Paul and Barnabas. However, Paul and Barnabas refused these sacrifices, telling the people they were just ordinary men the same a: they were. Then they preached to the people concerning the one true God, but they were hardly able to restrain the crowd from offering sacrifices (Acts 14:18). However, the next verse, Acts 14:19 says "But Jews came from Antioch and Iconium, and having won over the crowds, they stoned Paul and dragged him out of the city, supposing him to be dead." Since there was considerable travel and commerce among Antioch, Iconium and Lystra, it probably didn't take long fo news that Paul and Barnabas were preaching in Lystra to reacl Antioch and Iconium. Apparently Jews from both Antioch anc Iconium came to Lystra to continue their persecution of the evangelists. It was probably on about Sunday, July 1, A.D. 46 tha Paul was stoned and left for dead.

However, Paul was not dead, but arose and again entered the city. The next day Paul and Barnabas departed Lystra for Derbe. The miraculous recovery of Paul from this stoning probably made a deep impression on the people of Lystra as well as on the Jews that instigated the stoning. There is no report of any further persecution of Paul and Barnabas on this missionary journey. Paul and Barnabas probably spent the next three months in Derbe since Acts 14:21-22 says, "After they had preached the gospel to that city and had made many disciples, they returned to Lystra and to Iconium and to Antioch, strengthening the souls of the disciples, encouraging them to continue in the faith, and saying, 'Through many tribulations we must enter the kingdom of God.'" Paul and Barnabas probably spent July, August and September in Derbe. Then they spent November A.D. 46 in Lystra, December A.D. 46 in Iconium and January, A.D. 47 in Pisidian Antioch. Apparently, churches were established in each of these cities, and Paul and Barnabas appointed elders for each church. Then Acts 14:24-28 says:

> They passed through Pisidia and came into Pamphylia. When they had spoken the word in Perga, they went down to Attalia. From there they sailed to Antioch, from which they had been commended to the grace of God for the work that they had accomplished. When they had arrived and gathered the church together, they began to report all things that God had done with them and how He had opened a door of faith to the Gentiles. And they spent a long time with the disciples.

Paul and Barnabas probably arrived at Perga, about February, 13, A.D. 47 and remained there until sea travel on the Mediterranean started again about the middle of March. Paul and Barnabas had not stopped at Perga to preach the Gospel on their initial visit to the city, possibly because the city didn't have a Jewish synagogue. However, their experience during this missionary journey had shown them that the people of the synagogue were not always the most responsive to the Gospel. Therefore, on their return visit, they may have felt more free to go directly to the Gentiles. Paul and Barnabas probably arrived bach in Antioch of Syria and called the church together to report on their work on about Sunday, April 7, A.D. 47.

Council at Jerusalem

Paul and Barnabas probably spent the next eighteen months ("a long time"- Acts 14:28) ministering to the church a Antioch. It was probably near the end of A.D. 48 that the Judaizers arrived in Antioch. These Judaizers, being zealous for the Law, could be expected to place great importance on attending the three major Jewish feasts celebrated in Jerusalem that were commanded by the Law. Therefore, they would not have left Jerusalem until after the Feast of Booths which ended on October 17, A.D. 48. Since it is now approaching the time when sea travel would be unsafe, they probably traveled overland to Antioch, Syria. Traveling overland would probably also be less expensive since they could probably rely on the hospitality of Christians and Jews along the way for most of their food and lodging. However, the trip overland would have taken at least four weeks (300 miles) so the Judaizers probably didn't arrive in Antioch until about Thursday, November 26, A.D. 48. Allowing several weeks for the dispute over their teachings and the decision to send Paul and Barnabas to Jerusalem and another four weeks of travel time, it was probably about Sunday, January 24, A.D. 49 when Paul and Barnabas were received by the Church in Jerusalem.

Then Acts 15:5 says, "But some of the sect of the Pharisees who had believed stood up, saying, 'It is necessary to circumcise them and to direct them to observe the Law of Moses.'" Thus, the issue of whether all Christians must also convert to Judaism was raised before the church. To answer this question, a special meeting of the apostles and elders of the church was held. Then Acts 15:7-11 says:

> After there had been much debate, Peter stood up and said to them, "Brethren, you know that in the early days God made a choice among you, that by my mouth the Gentiles would hear the word of the gospel and believe. And God, who knows the heart, testified to them giving them the Holy Spirit, just as He also did to us; and He made no distinction between us and them, cleansing their hearts by faith. Now therefore why do you put God to the test by placing upon the neck of the disciples a yoke which neither our fathers nor we have been able to bear? But we believe that we are saved through the grace of the Lord Jesus, in the same way as they also are."

Peter's statement silenced the council of apostles and elders, and then Barnabas and Paul related the signs and wonders God had done through them among the Gentiles. Then James, the Lord's brother, said in Acts 15:19-20:

> "Therefore it is my judgment that we do not trouble those who are turning to God from among the Gentiles, but that we write to them that they abstain from things contaminated by idols and from fornication and from what is strangled and from blood."

Thus, the unity between the Jewish and the Gentile arms of Christ's Church was preserved. This meeting of the Apostles and the elders of the Church of Jerusalem probably took place about Monday, January 25, A. D. 49. This decision was written in the form of a letter to the churches in Antioch, Syria and Cilicia and was sent with Judas and Silas who accompanied Peter and Barnabas back to Antioch of

Syria. It was probably about a month later, on Sunday, February 28, A.D. 49, that the letter was delivered to the congregation at Antioch. Then Paul and Barnabas stayed in Antioch, preaching and teaching.

Paul' Second Missionary Journey

> After some days Paul said to Barnabas, "Let us return and visit the brethren in every city in which we proclaimed the word of the Lord, and see how they are." Barnabas wanted to take John, called Mark, along with them also. But Paul kept insisting that they should not take him along who had deserted them in Pamphylia and had not gone with them to the work. And there occurred such a sharp disagreement that they separated from one another, and Barnabas took Mark with him and sailed away to Cyprus. But Paul chose Silas and left, being committed by the brethren to the grace of the Lord. And he was traveling through Syria and Cilicia, strengthening the churches (Acts 15:36-41).

Thus, Paul began his second missionary journey. Since Barnabas and Mark departed first by sea, they must have departed after mid-March and probably after Easter. Easter was celebrated at the time of the Jewish Passover Feast which in A.D. 49 was celebrated on Sunday, April 15. Thus, Paul and Silas would have departed Antioch, Syria, about May 17, A.D. 49, and traveled overland through Syria and Cilicia. There must have been Christian Churches in Syria other than Antioch and in Cilicia because the letter from the Jerusalem apostles and elders was addressed to the brethren in Antioch and Syria and Cilicia. There may have been a Christian Church at Tarsus, Paul's birth place, since Paul spent a period of time there after his conversion to Christianity. However, there is no direct reference to a church there in the New Testament. Then Acts 16:1-5 says:

> Paul came also to Derbe and to Lystra. And a disciple
> was there, named Timothy, the son of a Jewish woman
> who was a believer, but his father was a Greek, and he
> was well spoken of by the brethren who were in Lystra
> and Iconium. Paul wanted this man to go with him; and
> he took him and circumcised him because of the Jews
> who were in those parts, for they all knew that his father
> was a Greek. Now while they were passing through the
> cities, they were delivering the decrees which had been
> decided upon by the apostles and elders who were in
> Jerusalem, for them to observe. So the churches were
> being strengthened in the faith, and were increasing in
> number daily.

Paul and Silas probably reached Derbe about June 18, A.D. 49,
staying there for two Sundays and then departing Derbe about June
28 and arriving in Lystra in the evening of the next day. They may
have spent two Sundays with the church at Lystra and then departed
for Iconium on about July 12 and again arrived on the evening of the
next day. At Lystra Paul met Timothy who was the son of a Jewish
woman, who was a believer, and a Greek man. Paul wanted to take
Timothy with him and since Paul may have often staying at Jewish
homes he circumcised Timothy, who was already a Christian, to make
him more acceptable to his Jewish hosts. Timothy and possibly his
mother followed Paul and Silas to Iconium and it was probably there
that Timothy was circumcised. Paul, Silas and Timothy probably left
Iconium about July 28, A.D. 49, and probably didn't reach Pisidian
Antioch until the next week. They would have spent the next two
Sundays in Antioch strengthening the church. Then Acts 16:6-8 says:

> They passed through the Phrygian and Galatian region,

having been forbidden by the Holy Spirit to speak the word in Asia; and after they came to Mysia, they were trying to go into Bithynia, and the Spirit of Jesus did not permit them; and passing by Mysia, they came down to Troas. A vision appeared to Paul in the night: a man of Macedonia was standing and appealing to him, and saying, "Come over to Macedonia and help us." When he had seen the vision, immediately we sought to go into Macedonia, concluding that God had called us to preach the gospel to them.

Paul and his companions probably left Pisidian Antioch about August 16, A.D. 49, and arrived at Troas (see Figure 7.7) about September 3, A.D. 49. Paul probably saw the vision of a man of Macedonia during the early morning of Sunday, September 5, A.D. 49. It was there at Troas that the first of the "we passages" begin; thus it may be that Luke, the author of the Acts, joined Paul and his party there. The fact that Luke's presence is not explicitly mentioned would be in keeping with the modesty of the Gospel writers. At this point Paul and his companions immediately sought passage to Macedonia. Acts 16:11 indicates that the trip from Troas to Neapolis, Macedonia, only took two days so they must have traveled about sixty miles a day, but of course the ship would be sailing twenty-four hours a day. Paul and his companions probably departed Troas about September 7 and arrived at Neapolis on September 8. Probably the next day, Paul and his companions left Neapolis for the larger city of Philippi and arrived there the same day. Then Acts 16:13-16 says:

> And on the Sabbath day we went outside the gate to a riverside, where we were supposing that there would be a place of prayer; and we sat down and began speaking

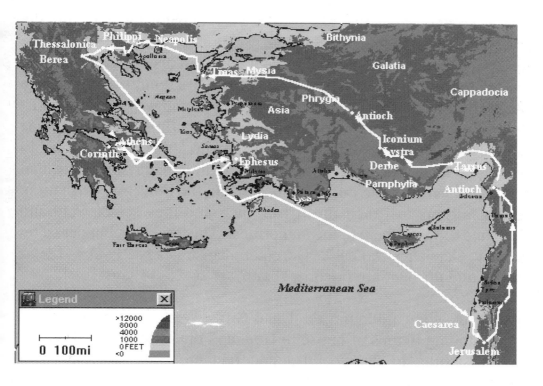

Paul's Second Missionary Journey
Figure 7.7

to the women who had assembled. A woman named Lydia, from the city of Thyatira, a seller of purple fabrics, a worshiper of God, was listening; and the Lord opened her heart to respond to the things spoken by Paul. and when she and her household had been baptized, she urged us, saying, "If you have judged me to be faithful to the Lord, come into my house and stay." And she prevailed upon us.

This Sabbath would be September 11, A.D. 49, and Lydia and her family were Paul's first converts to Christianity in Macedonia and in Europe. Paul and his companions spent several weeks in Philippi. As they were going to the place of prayer outside the gate on the riverside, possibly the next Sabbath, September 18, A.D. 49, a slave girl, having a spirit of divination, met Paul and his companions. She started following them saying, "These men are bond-servants of the Most High God, who are proclaiming to you the way of salvation." And she continued this for many days and finally Paul became annoyed and exorcized the spirit in the slave-girl. This probably happened about October 2, A.D. 49. Without the spirit that had possessed her, the slave-girl no longer had the power of divination, so her masters lost their profit from her, and they seized Paul and Silas and brought them to the authorities. This probably happened on Sunday, October 3, A.D. 49. The chief magistrates had Paul and Silas beaten and thrown into prison. Then Acts 16:25-34 says:

> But about midnight Paul and Silas were praying and singing hymns of praise to God, and the prisoners were listening to them; and suddenly there came a great earthquake, so that the foundations of the prison house were shaken; and immediately all the doors were opened and everyone's chains were unfastened. When the jailer awoke and saw the prison doors opened, he drew his sword and was about to kill himself, supposing that the prisoners had escaped. But Paul cried out with a loud voice, saying, "Do not harm yourself, for we are all here!" and he called for lights and rushed in, and trembling with fear he fell down before Paul and Silas, and after he brought them out, he said, "Sirs, what must I do to be saved?" They said, "Believe in the Lord Jesus, and you will be saved, you and your household." And they spoke the word of the Lord to him together with all who were in his house. And he took them that very hour of the night and washed their wounds, and immediately he was baptized, he and all his household. And he

brought them into his house and set food before them, and rejoiced greatly, having believed in God with his whole household.

Clearly there was more to the word of the Lord than just belief in Jesus, and when the Philippian jailer and his household heard this word, they were immediately baptized. Also, this verse is not a justification for infant baptism because in the New Testament only believers were baptized. Acts 16:34 above says that the jailer believed with his whole household. Thus, the household could not have included a baby since a baby couldn't believe.

When morning came, the chief magistrates of the city sent word to release Paul and Silas. However, Paul demanded that the magistrates themselves come and release them because they had beaten them in public without a trial, men who were Romans. When the magistrates heard this they were afraid and came and asked Paul and Silas to leave. After probably spending the night at Lydia's house and encouraging the new converts at Philippi, Paul and Silas probably left the next day, October 5, A.D. 49.

Paul in Thessalonica

Now when they had traveled through Amphipolis and Apollonia, they came to Thessalonica, where there was a synagogue of the Jews. And according to Paul's custom, he went to them, and for three Sabbaths reasoned with them from the Scriptures, explaining and giving evidence that the Christ had to suffer and rise again from the dead, and saying, "This Jesus whom I am proclaiming to you is the Christ (Acts 17:1-3)."

The journey to Thessalonica would have taken at least a week so that the three Sabbaths Paul spent there were probably October 16, October 23, and October 30, A.D. 49. Some of the Jews and a great number of the God-fearing Greek men and women joined Paul and Silas. However, the non-believing Jews stirred up a mob against Paul and Silas and therefore they were sent by night to Berea. The uproar probably occurred on Monday, November 1, A.D. 49, and Paul and Silas left that night.

Paul in Berea

> The brethren immediately sent Paul and Silas away by night to Berea, and when they arrived, they went into the synagogue of the Jews. Now these were more noble-minded than those in Thessalonica, for they received the word with great eagerness, examining the Scriptures daily to see whether these things were so. Therefore many of them believed, along with a number of prominent Greek women and men. But when the Jews of Thessalonica found out that the word of God had been proclaimed by Paul in Berea also, they came there as well, agitating and stirring up the crowds. Then immediately the brethren sent Paul out to go as far as the sea; and Silas and Timothy remained there. Now those who escorted Paul brought him as far as Athens; and receiving a command for Silas and Timothy to come to him as soon as possible, they left (Acts 17:10-15).

Paul and Silas would have arrived in Berea about November 3, A.D. 49, and they probably spent the next six weeks preaching there. The Jews of the synagogue of Berea received the word with great eagerness and many of them believed along with a number of prominent Greek women and men. However, eventually the Jews at

Thessalonica learned that Paul was preaching in Berea and they came and again stirred up a mob against Paul. Apparently the persecution was primarily directed against Paul, so he was sent on to Athens, and Silas and Timothy remained behind to work with the new church at Berea. Paul would have left Berea about December 14, A.D. 49, and would have reached the sea by December 15. Allowing a couple of days to find a ship bound for Athens and about a week sailing time, Paul probably arrived in Athens about December 24, A.D. 49. Paul's stay in Athens must have been at least a month, since he sent instructions back with those who conducted him to Athens for Silas and Timothy to join him as soon as possible. It would have taken a few days to arrange passage back, another week to sail back and then a couple of days to reach Berea. Therefore, those that escorted Paul to Athens would not have reached Berea until about January 7, A.D. 50. It would have taken another two weeks for the return journey; therefore they would not have reached Paul in Athens until about January 21. However, 1 Thessalonians 3:1-5 says:

> Therefore when we could endure it no longer, we thought it best to be left behind at Athens alone, and we sent Timothy, our brother and God's fellow worker in the gospel of Christ, to strengthen and encourage you as to your faith, so that no one would be disturbed by these afflictions; for you yourselves know that we have been destined for this. For indeed when we were with you, we kept telling you in advance that we were going to suffer affliction; and so it came to pass, as you know. For this reason, when I could endure it no longer, I also sent to find out about your faith, for fear that the tempter might have tempted you, and our labor would be in vain.

Thus apparently only Timothy returned to Paul in Athens about January 21, since when he left, Paul was again alone. Timothy apparently brought news of persecution of the church at Thessalonica and therefore, Paul sent him to Thessalonica probably with a letter to strengthen the church. Silas had probably remained with the church at Berea which may have also been experiencing persecution. It is only some time later that both Silas and Timothy would join Paul in Corinth. By the time Timothy arrived, Paul had probably already decided to leave Athens not finding that city particularly receptive to the Gospel.

While Paul was in Athens he taught in the synagogue and in the market place. On the basis of teaching in the market place he was invited to address the Areopagus , a court that once met on the hill of Ares (Ares was the Greek god of war). Acts 17:22,23 says:

> So Paul stood in the midst of the Areopagus and said, "Men of Athens, I observe that you are very religious in all respects. For while I was passing through and examining the objects of your worship, I also found an altar with this inscription, 'TO AN UNKNOWN GOD.' Therefore what you worship in ignorance, this I proclaim to you."

Paul then taught them concerning the one true God and the coming judgement with Jesus as the Judge. Paul received a mixed response to his message, but some said, "We shall hear from you again concerning this." Also there were several that joined Paul and believed including Dionysius the Areopagite and a women named Damaris and others. Paul probably appeared before the Areopagus about January 5, A.D. 50. Paul probably left Athens about January 25, A.D. 50, after sending Timothy to Thessalonica. Paul would have arrived in Corinth about Friday, January 28, A.D. 50. The next day, Saturday, January 29, Paul probably attended the synagogue in Corinth and it was probably there that he met Aquila and Priscilla. Since Paul and Aquila had the same trade, Paul was invited to live with them and work in their tent-making business. Then Acts 18:4-11 says:

> And he was reasoning in the synagogue every Sabbath and trying to persuade Jews and Greeks. But when Silas and Timothy came down from Macedonia, Paul began devoting himself completely to the word, solemnly testifying to the Jews that Jesus was the Christ. But when they resisted and blasphemed, he shook out his garments and said to them, "Your blood be on your own heads! I am clean. From now on I will go to the Gentiles." Then he left there and went to the house of a man named Titius Justus, a worshiper of God, whose house was next to the synagogue. Crispus, the leader of the synagogue, believed in the Lord with all his household, and many of the Corinthians when they heard were believing and being baptized. And the Lord said to Paul in the night by a vision, "Do not be afraid any longer, but go on speaking and do not be silent; for I am with you, and no man will attack you in order to harm you, for I have many people in this city." And he settled there a year and six months, teaching the word of God among them.

Silas and Timothy probably arrived at Corinth about March 17, A.D. 50, and after that time, Paul was able to devote himself completely to the preaching of the word rather than working through the week as a tent-maker to support himself. It appears that Silas and Timothy brought an offering with them. Philippians 4:15-16 says, "You yourselves also know, Philippians, that at the first preaching of the gospel, after I left Macedonia, no church shared with me in the matter of giving and receiving but you alone; for even in Thessalonica you sent a gift more than once for my needs." Thus, Timothy may have found a gift waiting for Paul when he arrived in Thessalonica. This seems to be confirmed in 2 Corinthians 11:8-9 which says, "I robbed other churches by taking wages from them to serve you; and when I was present with you and was in need, I was not a burden to anyone; for when the brethren came from Macedonia they fully supplied my need, and in everything I kept myself from being a burden to you, and will continue to do so." When Silas and Timothy arrived from Macedonia, they apparently brought good news concerning the faithfulness of the church in Thessalonica. It was at that time that Paul wrote 1 Thessalonians and sent it to them with one of the brethren.

However, by this time resistance to the Gospel had already arose in the synagogue; so Paul moved his ministry from the synagogue to the house of Titius Justus, which was located next to the synagogue. Paul apparently converted a number of the members of the synagogue to Christianity including the leader of the synagogue Crispus. In 1 Corinthians 1:14 Paul says, "I thank God that I baptized none of you except Crispus and Gaius." Crispus is probably the leader of the synagogue and Gaius is further identified in Romans 16:23a which says, "Gaius, host to me and to the whole church, greets you." Thus, Gaius and Titius Justus must be the same person. Thus Crispus and Titius Justus must have been Paul' first converts in Corinth and were baptized before the arrival of Silas and Timothy. Therefore they were baptized by Paul himself. Probably shortly after the arrival of Silas and Timothy, Jesus encouraged Paul in a vision. This vision probably occurred about March 26, A.D. 50. Paul continued preaching and teaching in Corinth for a year and six months. Since Luke probably got this information from Paul, since this is not one of the "we sections" of Acts, Paul was probably using the Jewish calendar. If Paul arrived in Corinth on January 28, A.D. 50 or on Sebat 17, A.D. 50, a year and six months after that date counting inclusively, would bring us to the month of Sivan, which in A.D. 51 began on May 27 and ended on June 26, which would be just about the time of the arrival of the new proconsul of Achaia, Gallio, as indicated by a stone inscription found in Delphi which was discussed earlier in this chapter. Acts 18:12-16 say:

> But while Gallio was proconsul of Achaia, the Jews with one accord rose up against Paul and brought him before the judgment seat, saying, "This man persuades men to worship God contrary to the law." But when Paul was about to open his mouth, Gallio said to the Jews, "If it were a matter of wrong or of vicious crime, O Jews, it would be reasonable for me to put up with you; but if there are questions about words and names and your own law, look after it yourselves; I am unwilling to be a judge of these matters." And he drove them away from the judgment seat.

Paul was probably brought before Gallio about June 14, A.D. 51. Then Acts 18:18 says, "Paul, having remained many days longer, took leave of the brethren and put out to sea for Syria, and with him were Priscilla and Aquila. In Cenchrea he had his hair cut, for he was keeping a vow." Paul probably did not leave Corinth until the spring of A.D. 52, because Acts 18:18 says that they remained many days in Corinth after Paul appeared before Gallio and after October 2, the time of the fast (Day of Atonement), he would have faced a dangerous voyage on the Mediterranean returning to Antioch, Syria. If they delayed their departure until spring, they probably remained in Corinth to celebrate Easter there. Then Paul and his companions probably left Cenchrea, the Aegean seaport near Corinth about April 17, A.D. 52. Romans 16:1 commends Phoebe, a deaconess of the church at Cenchrea, to the church at Rome. People from Cenchrea may have been converted by Paul in Corinth and started a church, or some of the Corinthian Christians may have moved to Cenchrea and started a Christian Church there.

The voyage from Cenchrea to Ephesus would have probably taken about two weeks; so Paul and his companions probably arrived at Ephesus about May 2, A.D. 52. Paul left Priscilla and Aquila at Ephesus. On the Sabbath, May 4. A.D. 52, Paul taught in the synagogue, and Acts 18:20 says that the people of the synagogue asked Paul to stay a long time, but he declined their invitation. However, Paul said he would return again, if God wills, and then he departed Ephesus. Later that year Paul did return to Ephesus. Paul probably departed Ephesus about May 15 and would have arrived at Caesarea, Samaria about June 13, A.D. 52. Paul probably attended worship services at Caesarea on June 15 and 16 and then returned to Antioch, Syria.

Paul's Third Missionary Journey

Then Acts 18:23 says, "And having spent some time there, he left and passed successively through the Galatian region and Phrygia, strengthening all the disciples." Having spent some time in Antioch, Syria, Paul then began his third missionary journey (see Figure 7.8, page 317). Paul probably left Antioch about September 16, A.D. 52, which would avoid the summer heat and, since he was heading for Ephesus, would avoid traveling through the mountainous regions in winter, which would have been difficult.

The journey to Derbe was about 300 miles; so Paul probably arrived there about October 11, A.D. 52. He would have probably spent about two weeks there and then departed about October 21. Paul would have spent the next two weekends at Lystra departing from there about November 4. He would have probably spent the next two weekends in Iconium, departing November 18. Then Paul probably proceeded to Pisidian Antioch, spending the next two weekends there, and departing December 2, A.D. 52. Paul then passed through the Roman province of Asia and arrived at Ephesus about December 19, A.D. 52.

While Paul was passing through the Galatian region and Phrygia, Acts 18:24-28 says:

> Now a Jew named Apollos, an Alexandrian by birth, an eloquent man, came to Ephesus; and he was mighty in the Scriptures. This man had been instructed in the way of the Lord; and being fervent in spirit, he was speaking and teaching accurately the things concerning Jesus, being acquainted only with the baptism of John; and he began to speak out boldly in the synagogue. But when Priscilla and Aquila heard him, they took him aside and explained to him the way of God more accurately.

What was lacking in Apollos' preaching? The only thing mentioned is that he was only acquainted with the baptism of John. Thus, Christian baptism was not part of Apollos' preaching, and Priscilla and Aquila recognized the importance of this omission, as did Luke who included this incident in the Acts. Priscilla and Aquila probably heard Apollos in Ephesus about September 28, A.D. 52. Then, prior to Paul's arrival, Apollos left Ephesus for Corinth. Then Acts 19:1-7 says:

> It happened that while Apollos was at Corinth, Paul passed through the upper country and came to Ephesus, and found some disciples. He said to them, "Did you receive the Holy Spirit when you believed?" And they said to him, "No, we have not even heard whether there is a Holy Spirit." And he said, "Into what then were you baptized?" And they said, "Into John's baptism." Paul said, "John baptized with the baptism of repentance, telling the people to believe in Him who was coming after him, that is, in Jesus." When they heard this, they were baptized in the name of the Lord Jesus. And when

Paul had laid his hands upon them, the Holy Spirit came on them, and they began speaking with tongues and prophesying. There were in all about twelve men.

Again, Luke includes this incident to point out the importance of baptism in God's plan of salvation. These men had believed, but they had not been baptized in the name of the Lord Jesus and had not received the gift of the Holy Spirit. When Paul laid his hands on them, probably when he baptized them, they received the gift of the Holy Spirit. When Paul learned that these twelve disciples had not received the Holy Spirit, his question to them was, "Into what then were you baptized?" Prior to their baptism were these twelve disciples in the faith? Paul, in 2 Corinthians 13:5, says, "Test yourselves to see if you are in the faith; examine yourselves! Or do you not recognize this about yourselves, that Jesus Christ is in you-unless indeed you fail the test?" If you are in the faith then the Holy Spirit dwells in you. On Pentecost, Acts 2:38 says, "Peter said to them, 'Repent, and each of you be baptized in the name of Jesus Christ for the forgiveness of your sins; and you will receive the gift of the Holy Spirit.'" Obviously, baptism is an important part of God's plan of salvation. These twelve disciples were probably the nucleus of the Christian Church at Ephesus. Then Acts 19:8-10 says:

And he entered the synagogue and continued speaking out boldly for three months, reasoning and persuading them about the kingdom of God. But when some were becoming hardened and disobedient, speaking evil of the Way before the people, he withdrew from them and took away the disciples, reasoning daily in the school of Tyrannus. This took place for two years, so that all who lived in Asia heard the word of the Lord, both Jews and Greeks.

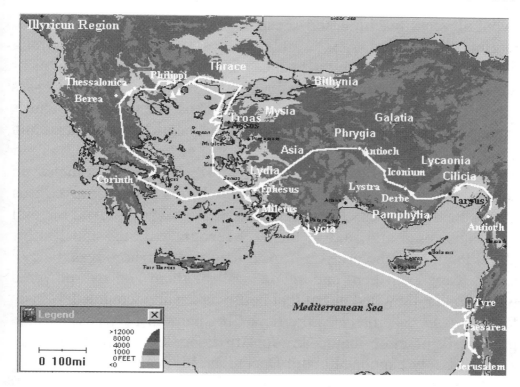

Paul's Third Missionary Journey
Figure 7.8

Paul initially taught in the synagogue at Ephesus, where he was invited to speak during his brief stop there on his return from his second missionary journey. He probably began his teaching and preaching there on about Saturday, December 21, A.D. 52, and continued for three months. Paul probably started in the tenth Jewish month, Tebeth, so three months, counting inclusively, brings us to the twelfth month, Adar. Thus Paul probably left the synagogue about February 22, A.D. 53. This, was the beginning of a period of two years teaching in the school of Tyrannus. Since Luke is probably using inclusive counting, this could represent a period of slightly more than one year up to two full years. However, since Acts 20:31 says that Paul spent three years at Ephesus, he must have spent nearly two full years teaching and preaching in the school of Tyrannus. During this period Acts 19:11-12 says, "God was performing extraordinary miracles by the hands of Paul, so that handkerchiefs or aprons were even carried from his body to the sick, and the diseases left them and the evil spirits went out." Thus, the validity of Paul's ministry was confirmed by the miraculous healings of diseases and exorcisms of evil spirits

It was probably about November 18, A.D. 54, that the seven sons of Sceva attempted an exorcism of a demon in the name of Jesus whom Paul preaches. However, Acts 19:15-16 says, "And the evil spirit answered and said to them, 'I recognize Jesus, and I know about Paul, but who are you?' And the man, in whom was the evil spirit, leaped on them and subdued all of them and overpowered them, so that they fled out of that house naked and wounded." Also, later in A.D. 54, many of the new Christians in Ephesus that had previously practice magic, brought their books and burned them. This probably happened about December 13, A.D. 54. Thus Paul's ministry was blessed and there was great growth in the church at Ephesus. Then Acts 19:21-22 says:

> Now after these things were finished, Paul purposed in the spirit to go to Jerusalem after he had passed through Macedonia and Achaia, saying, "After I have been there, I must also see Rome." And having sent into Macedonia two of those who ministered to him, Timothy and Erastus, he himself stayed in Asia for a while.

This event, as we shall see in a moment, took place just before Passover time in the spring of A.D. 55. Then Acts 19:23-26 says:

> About that time there occurred no small disturbance concerning the Way. For a man named Demetrius, a silversmith, who made silver shrines of Artemis, was

bringing no little business to the craftsmen; these he gathered together with the workmen of similar trades, and said, "Men, you know that our prosperity depends upon this business. You see and hear that not only in Ephesus, but in almost all of Asia, this Paul has persuaded and turned away a considerable number of people, saying that gods made with hands are no gods at all."

The Temple of Artemis, which was located at Ephesus, was one of the seven wonders of the ancient world, and Demetrius and the other craftsmen were employed in making shrines of Artemis. As a result of Demetrius' speech, an angry crowd formed and rushed to the city's theater dragging Gaius and Aristarchus, Paul's traveling companions, since apparently they could not find Paul. Paul wanted to go into the theater and address the crowd, but his disciples would not let him. For about two hours the crowd cried, "Great is Artemis of the Ephesians!" Finally the city clerk was able to quiet the crowd and said in Acts 19:38, "So then, if Demetrius and the craftsmen who are with him have a complaint against any man, the courts are in session and proconsuls are available; let them bring charges against one another. Then the clerk dismissed the assembly. This riot probably occurred shortly after Pentecost of A.D. 55 about June 1.

To obtain the chronological details of this period of Paul's ministry, we must use Paul's letters as well as the account given in the book of Acts. Paul's first letter to the Corinthians seem to reflect the same situation given in Acts 19:21-22, which we have just cited. 1 Corinthians 16:5-9 says:

But I will come to you after I go through Macedonia, for I am going through Macedonia; and perhaps I will stay with you, or even spend the winter, so that you may send me on my way wherever I may go. For I do not wish to see you now just in passing; for I hope to remain with you for some time, if the Lord permits. But I will remain in Ephesus until Pentecost; for a wide door for effective service has opened to me, and there are many adversaries.

Thus, Paul dispatched Timothy and Erastus to Corinth with a letter, and this letter is First Corinthians of the New Testament. The easiest way to reach Corinth from Ephesus was by sea, but sea travel did not become safe until the middle of March. Therefore, Timothy and Erastus probably stayed in Ephesus until after the Passover and Easter observance and then left for Corinth by sea about April 6, A.D. 55. The fact that Paul wrote First Corinthians at Passover time is also suggested by 1 Corinthians 5:7 which says, "Clean out the old leaven so that you may be a new lump, just as you are in fact unleavened. For Christ our Passover also has been sacrificed."

Paul was planning to stay at Ephesus until Pentecost, May 23, A.D. 55, and then go first to Macedonia and then to Corinth, possibly spending the winter of A.D. 55/56 in Corinth. However, when Timothy got to Corinth, he found that there were some serious problems in the church there. Therefore, after a short visit in Corinth, Timothy must have returned to Ephesus to report to Paul. As a result of this information, Paul apparently changed his plans and, instead of going to Macedonia first, he went directly to Corinth from Ephesus. This change in plans is reflected in 2 Corinthians 1:15-16 which says, "In this confidence I intended at first to come to you, so that you might twice receive a blessing; that is, to pass your way into Macedonia, and again from Macedonia to come to you, and by you to be helped on my journey to Judea." The fact that Paul actually did make this visit to Corinth seems to be confirmed in 2 Corinthians 13:1 where, speaking of an upcoming visit to Corinth, Paul says, "This is the third time I am coming to you. EVERY FACT IS TO BE CONFIRMED BY THE TESTIMONY OF TWO OR THREE

WITNESSES."   However, Paul did not return directly from Macedonia to Corinth because in 2 Corinthians 2:1-3 Paul says:

> But I determined this for my own sake, that I would not come to you in sorrow again. For if I cause you sorrow, who then makes me glad but the one whom I made sorrowful? This is the very thing I wrote you, so that when I came, I would not have sorrow from those who ought to make me rejoice; having confidence in you all that my joy would be the joy of you all. For out of much affliction and anguish of heart I wrote to you with many tears; not so that you would be made sorrowful, but that you might know the love which I have especially for you.

Thus, in A.D. 55, when Paul had completed his Macedonian ministry, instead of returning to Corinth, Paul wrote them another letter which he sent by Titus. Then Paul returned to the Roman province of Asia (see Figure 7.8. page 317). Apparently Paul had arranged for Titus to meet him in Troas because 2 Corinthians 2:12-13 says, "Now when I came to Troas for the gospel of Christ and when a door was opened for me in the Lord, I had no rest for my spirit, not finding Titus my brother; but taking my leave of them, I went on to Macedonia." Evidently, Paul was waiting at Troas for Titus to return by sea from Corinth. However, when Titus hadn't arrived by the middle of November, the end of safe sea travel, Paul knew that Titus would be returning to him by land. Therefore, probably in early December A.D. 55, Paul left Troas and traveled by land to Macedonia since he was anxious to learn the Corinthian Church's response to his letter. Then 2 Corinthian 7:5-7 says:

> For even when we came into Macedonia our flesh had no rest, but we were afflicted on every side: conflicts

> without, fears within. But God, who comforts the depressed, comforted us by the coming of Titus; and not only by his coming, but also by the comfort with which he was comforted in you, as he reported to us your longing, your mourning, your zeal for me; so that I rejoiced even more.

It is now probably January A.D. 56, and Paul sends Titus and two other brothers back to Corinth to complete the collection for the saints in Jerusalem and sends with them another letter which is the New Testament's Second Corinthians. Paul wants them to complete the collection before he returns to Corinth (2 Corinthians 9:1-3), therefore, it would be some time before he returns to Corinth.

We now return to the Acts. When we left that narrative, Demetrius, a silversmith, had just stirred up a riot in Ephesus against Paul's teachings. Then Acts 20:1-6 says:

> After the uproar had ceased, Paul sent for the disciples, and when he had exhorted them and taken his leave of them, he left to go to Macedonia. When he had gone through those districts and had given them much exhortation, he came to Greece. And there he spent three months, and when a plot was formed against him by the Jews as he was about to set sail for Syria, he decided to return through Macedonia. And he was accompanied by Sopater of Berea, the son of Pyrrhus, and by Aristarchus and Secundus of the Thessalonians, and Gaius of Derbe, and Timothy, and Tychicus and Trophimus of Asia. But these had gone on ahead and were waiting for us at Troas. We sailed from Philippi after the days of Unleavened Bread, and came to them at Troas within five days; and there we stayed seven days.

In these verses Luke only gives us a brief summary of Paul's activities during this period while more details are provided by Paul's two letters to the Corinthians. However, it is important that Acts 20:3 says that Paul spent three months in Greece and then departed from Philippi after the days of Unleavened Bread. Since Titus was sent to Corinth about January A.D. 56 with the Second Corinthian letter, there would not be time for the collection to be made and for Paul to spend three months in Greece and then depart immediately after the days of Unleavened Bread of A.D. 56. Thus, Paul did not depart Philippi until after the Easter celebration of A.D. 57. Therefore, Paul must have spent the year of A.D. 56 in ministries in and around Macedonia which are not recorded in the book of Acts. For example, Romans 15:18-19 says, "For I will not presume to speak of anything except what Christ has accomplished through me, resulting in the obedience of the Gentiles by word and deed, in the power of signs and wonders, in the power of the Spirit; so that from Jerusalem and round about as far as Illyricum I have fully preached the gospel of Christ." There is no mention in the Acts of Paul preaching in Illyricum, but this could very well have taken place in this silent year of A.D. 56. Paul's letter to the Romans was probably written from Corinth in early A.D. 57 during Paul's third and final visit to that city. After Paul left Philippi and arrived in Troas, Acts 20:7-12 says:

> On the first day of the week, when we were gathered together to break bread, Paul began talking to them, intending to leave the next day, and he prolonged his message until midnight. There were many lamps in the upper room where we were gathered together. And there was a young man named Eutychus sitting on the window sill, sinking into a deep sleep; and as Paul kept on talking, he was overcome by sleep and fell down from the third floor and was picked up dead. But Paul went down and fell upon him, and after embracing him,

he said, "Do not be troubled, for his life is in him." When he had gone back up and had broken the bread and eaten, he talked with them a long while until daybreak, and then left. They took away the boy alive, and were greatly comforted.

Since Paul stayed in Troas for seven days before they gathered on the first day of the week to break bread, that is to celebrate the Lord's Supper, counting inclusively, Paul must have arrived at Troas on a Monday. Since the trip from Macedonia took five days (Acts 20:6), they must have departed the Macedonian port on a Thursday. The Feast of Unleavened Bread in A.D. 57 did not technically end until sunset on Thursday, April 12; however, the Gentile Christian Church at Philippi would be celebrating the Feast of Unleavened Bread as an Easter celebration which would probably end on Sunday, April 8. Since Paul was hoping to arrive in Jerusalem by Pentecost (Acts 20:16), he would have left Philippi as soon as possible after the completion of the Easter celebration by the church at Philippi. Thus, Paul and Luke, since this is one of the "we passages" of Acts, probably departed Neapolis on Thursday, April 12, A.D. 57. Since the passage from Neapolis to Troas took five days, they arrived at Troas on Monday, April 16, and Eutychus was raised from the dead shortly after midnight on April 23, A.D. 57. That same day Paul and his companions departed Troas.

Probably the ship that Paul and his companions were traveling on was a small coastal sailing vessel that stayed near to the shore. This would account for the five days' travel time between Neapolis and Troas whereas in Acts 16:11 the trip from Troas to Neapolis only took two days. In Acts 16:11, they went straight across the Aegean Sea, so the distance would be shorter than if they had to stay near the shore. Apparently this small sailing ship was available for Paul's exclusive use. Paul's disciples probably thought traveling on such a vessel would be safer than booking passage on a larger commercial ship where the Jews, who were plotting against Paul, could also book passage.

Luke provides an interesting detail of the next leg of Paul's journey. Acts 20:13-14 says, "But we, going ahead to the ship, set sail for Assos, intending from there to take Paul on board; for so he had arranged it, intending himself to go by land. And when he met us at Assos, we took him on board and came to Mitylene." Various reasons have been suggested why Paul traveled this portion of the journey by land, but probably he wanted to visit someone on the road between Troas and Assos, because apparently the ship arrived at Assos first and they had to wait for Paul. If Paul just wanted to remain in Troas to be sure that Eutychus was all right, it would have been quicker for Paul to have delayed the departure of his ship since it seems to be at his disposal. Since Assos is twenty miles from Troas, they probably picked up Paul the next day, May 1, A.D. 57, and Paul probably spent the night with the friends he visited. That same day they passed Mitylene and the following day, May 2, they reached Chios. The next day, May 3, they crossed over to Samos and on the next day, May 4, they reached Miletus. Then Acts 20:17-18 says:

> For Paul had decided to sail past Ephesus so that he would not have to spend time in Asia; for he was hurrying to be in Jerusalem, if possible, on the day of Pentecost. From Miletus he sent to Ephesus and called to him the elders of the church.

Here again Paul seems to be in command of the ship since if it was a commercial vessel Paul could not have decided not to stop at Ephesus. Paul arrived at Miletus on about Friday, May 4. Paul probably sent the ship up to Ephesus to pick up the elders on Monday, May 7. They would have probably arrived at Ephesus that evening and returned from Ephesus on Wednesday, May 9. The next day Paul spoke to the elders of Ephesus and after a tearful parting that same day, Paul and his party departed Miletus and set a straight course to Cos. The next day, Friday, May 11, they sailed past Rhodes and on to Patara of Lycia (see Figure 7.8, page 317).

At Patara Paul and his companions left their small coastal sailing vessel and obtained passage on a larger commercial vessel. It would probably take a few days to make arrangements for the ship, so they probably departed about Tuesday, May 15, A.D. 57. The four hundred-mile trip to Syria would take about eight days; thus they probably arrived about Tuesday, May 22, landing at Tyre. Acts 21:4 says, "After looking up the disciples, we stayed there seven days; and they kept telling Paul through the Spirit not to set foot in Jerusalem." Thus, they left Tyre on about Monday, May 28. Later that same day they arrived at Ptolemais. Then Acts 21:8-11 says:

> On the next day we left and came to Caesarea, and entering the house of Philip the evangelist, who was one of the seven, we stayed with him. Now this man had four virgin daughters who were prophetesses. As we were staying there for some days, a prophet named Agabus came down from Judea. And coming to us, he took Paul's belt and bound his own feet and hands, and said, "This is what the Holy Spirit says: 'In this way the Jews at Jerusalem will bind the man who owns this belt and deliver him into the hands of the Gentiles.'"

Paul and his companions left Ptolemais the next day, May 29, and arrived in Caesarea the same day. In Caesarea they stayed in the home of Philip the evangelist. It is now already after the Day of Pentecost which was celebrated on Sunday, May 27, in A.D. 57. Therefore, Paul was no longer hastening to get to Jerusalem and therefore they stayed with Philip for some days. The prophet Agabus was probably in Jerusalem for Pentecost although the text only says that he came from Judea. Agabus probably arrived in Caesarea about June 8, possibly hearing of Paul's arrival, and may have made his prophesy concerning Paul's arrest in Jerusalem on Sunday, June 10.

Paul Arrested in Jerusalem

After these days we got ready and started on our way up to Jerusalem. Some of the disciples from Caesarea also came with us, taking us to Mnason of Cyprus, a disciple of long standing with whom we were to lodge. After we arrived in Jerusalem, the brethren received us gladly. And the following day Paul went in with us to James, and all the elders were present (Acts 21:15-18).

Paul and those with him probably left Caesarea on Tuesday, June 12, and may have gone as far as Lydda and then stopped there for the weekend. They would have continued on their journey on Monday and would have arrived in Jerusalem on Tuesday, June 19, A.D. 57. The next day, Wednesday, June 20, A.D. 57, Paul and his companions met with James and the elders of the church of Jerusalem. At this meeting Paul reported on his work with the Gentiles and the leaders of the Jerusalem Christian Church glorified God for this work. Then these leaders related a problem to Paul. They said that in the Jerusalem church there were many thousands of Jews that believed, but were all still zealous for the Law. These Jews had heard that Paul was teaching all the Jews among the Gentiles to forsake the Law. Therefore, they proposed that Paul participate with four men that were undertaking a vow so that Paul could demonstrate that he was still a practicing Jew. Therefore, the next day, Thursday, June 21, Paul purified himself along with the men and went into the Temple and gave notice when the days of purification would be completed and the sacrifices would be offered for the men. Then

Acts 21:27-28:

> When the seven days were almost over, the Jews from Asia, upon seeing him in the temple, began to stir up all the crowd and laid hands on him, crying out, "Men of Israel, come to our aid! This is the man who preaches to all men everywhere against our people and the Law and this place; and besides he has even brought Greeks into the temple and has defiled this holy place."

The seven days from when Paul first went up to the Temple, counting inclusively, would have been completed on Wednesday, June 27. However, Luke says when the seven days were almost completed Paul was attacked by the Asian Jews in the Temple. Therefore, this event must have happened before Wednesday, June 27. The phrase "when the seven days were almost over" might suggest Monday or Tuesday as the day of the attack. However, the attack must have occurred on Sunday, June 24, the fifth day after the purification, in order to be consistent with later statements by Paul. At the time Paul was attacked in the Temple he was not engaged in any activity connected with his participation with the four men who had taken a vow, so accommodating the church leaders played no role in his being beaten by the Jews or arrested by the Romans. Rather, Paul was arrested in accordance with God's plan that he might be a witness to Judea and to the courts of Rome. Paul was rescued from the Jews by the commander of the Roman cohort stationed in the Antonia located next to the Temple mount. The Roman commander took Paul into custody and ordered that he be bound with two chains. Before being brought into the barracks (Antonia), Paul asked and received permission to address the crowd. Then Paul made a speech to the Jews that is recorded in Acts 22:1-21. The crowd listened until Paul related his heavenly vision in Acts 22:21 which says, "And He said to me, 'Go! For I will send you far away to the Gentiles.'" The

Jews at this point shouted, "Away with such a fellow from the earth for he should not be allowed to live!" and they made a great commotion and the commander ordered Paul to be brought into the Antonia (see Figure 7.2, page 267).

Paul was probably in the Court of the Gentiles in the northern part of the Temple Mount when he was attacked by the Asian Jews. He was probably dragged out the northern gate of the Temple Mount right in front of the Antonia and this gate was closed, shutting out the murderous crowd from the Temple precincts. Once the commander had gotten Paul into the Antonia, he decided to examine him by scourging. Scourging was a method of torture using a scourge, which was a whip consisting of leather thongs studded with pieces of metal or bone. However, Acts 22:25 says, "But when they stretched him out with thongs, Paul said to the centurion who was standing by, 'Is it lawful for you to scourge a man who is a Roman and uncondemned?'" The centurion brought this information to the commander and, after he discussed Paul's Roman citizenship with him, the scourging was not carried out.

The next day, Monday, June 25, the Roman commander brought Paul before an assembly of the Jewish council, the Sanhedrin. Paul tried to address the assembly, but the high priest, Ananias, had him slapped in the mouth. When Paul saw that he would not be able to present his case, Acts 23:6 says, "But perceiving that one group were Sadducees and the other Pharisees, Paul began crying out in the Council, 'Brethren, I am a Pharisee, a son of Pharisees; I am on trial for the hope and resurrection of the dead!'" This was a true statement because he was preaching the resurrected Christ. However, this was an issue that divided the Sadducees, who did not believe in the resurrection of the dead, and the Pharisees who did. Thus, a violent discussion developed within the council and the commander had to order his troops to remove Paul from the assembly by force. Then Acts 23:11 says, "But on the night immediately following, the Lord stood at his side and said, 'Take courage; for as you have solemnly witnessed to My cause at Jerusalem, so you must witness at Rome also.'" Assuming Paul's vision occurred before midnight, this vision would have occurred on Monday, June 25, A.D. 57.

Paul Imprisoned in Caesarea

Then Acts 23:12 says, "When it was day, the Jews formed a conspiracy and bound themselves under an oath, saying that they would neither eat nor drink until they had killed Paul." The next day would be Tuesday, June 26. However, the son of Paul's sister learned of the ambush planned by the Jews and he told Paul. Paul had the centurion take the boy to the commander and repeat his story. When the commander learned of the plot, he wrote a letter to the Roman governor concerning Paul and sent Paul and the letter with a large detachment of soldiers to the governor at Caesarea. The soldiers were gathered during the third hour of the night. The sun would have set in Jerusalem about 7:00 P.M. And the night time hours would only be about fifty minutes long during June; therefore the third hour would be from about 8:40 P.M. to 9:30 P.M. Thus Paul and his military escort probably left Jerusalem about 10:00 P.M., Tuesday, June 26, A.D. 57. That night they traveled as far as Antipatris, a distance of about 35 miles. At this point the two hundred foot soldiers accompanying Paul returned to Jerusalem and Paul proceeded on to Caesarea with the seventy horsemen. Thus, they probably arrived at Caesarea late in the day on Wednesday, June 27, A.D. 57. When they arrived at Caesarea, the soldiers turned Paul and the letter over to Governor Felix. After he had read the letter, he asked Paul what province he was from. When Paul answered Cilicia, Felix said he would hear his case as soon as his accusers had arrived.

Then Acts 24:1 says, "After five days the high priest Ananias came down with some elders, with an attorney named Tertullus, and they brought charges to the governor against Paul." Five days after

Paul's arrival in Caesarea would be Sunday, July 1. All of these events are shown in the calendar of Figure 7.9. When Paul's accusers arrived, he was summoned and a hearing was held before Felix. First Tertullus presented the case against Paul and then Paul was asked to make his defense.

June A.D. 57						
Sun	Mon	Tue	Wed	Thu	Fri	Sat
17	18	19 Paul Arrives at Jerusalem	20 Paul Meets with James	21 Paul Goes to Temple with Four with Vow	22	21
24 Attack on Paul in Temple	25 Paul Before the Sanhedrin	26 Paul Sent to Caesarea	27 Paul Arrives in Caesarea	28	29	30
July A.D. 57						
1 Paul's Accusers Arrive at Caesarea	2	3	4	5	6	7

Paul's Visit to Jerusalem
His Subsequent Attacked, Arrested And
Imprisonment in Jerusalem and Caesarea
Figure 7.9

Acts 24:10-11 says:

When the governor had nodded for him to speak, Paul responded: "Knowing that for many years you have been a judge to this nation, I cheerfully make my

> defense, since you can take note of the fact that no
> more than twelve days ago I went up to Jerusalem to
> worship."

Twelve days before Sunday, July 1, counting inclusively, would be Wednesday, June 20, the day Paul met with James and the elders of the church of Jerusalem. But, Acts 21:18 indicates that Paul met with James and the elders the day following his arrival in Jerusalem, so why would Paul say he arrived that day? Paul probably arrived in Jerusalem late in the day because he was traveling that day and if he arrived on Tuesday, June 19 after sunset, it would already be the next Jewish day. Thus for Paul, using the Jewish reckoning of time, he would have arrived and met with James the same day, while for Luke and for us, using the Roman reckoning of time where the day begins at midnight, they would have met with James the next day. Thus Paul's statement before Felix establishes some of the details concerning his arrival on June 19. This statement also requires that the attack on Paul in the Temple precincts took place on the fourth day after Paul first went up to the Temple with the four men who were under a vow. This instance also shows that inclusive counting was used because without inclusive counting it would be impossible to fit all the events in the indicated period of time.

After Paul had presented his defense, Acts 24:22 says, "But Felix, having a more exact knowledge about the Way, put them off, saying, 'When Lysias the commander comes down, I will decide your case.'" Paul was kept in custody, but his friends were allowed to visit him and minister to him. Then Acts 24:24-26 says:

> But some days later Felix arrived with Drusilla, his wife
> who was a Jewess, and sent for Paul and heard him
> speak about faith in Christ Jesus. But as he was
> discussing righteousness, self-control and the judgment
> to come, Felix became frightened and said, "Go away

for the present, and when I find time I will summon you." At the same time too, he was hoping that money would be given him by Paul; therefore he also used to send for him quite often and converse with him.

It was probably late in A.D. 57 that Felix invited Paul to speak to his wife, Drusilla, and himself about faith in Christ Jesus. This meeting may have taken place about December 14, A.D. 57, after the Feast of the Dedication. Drusilla was the youngest daughter of King Herod Agrippa I and was Felix's third wife. She had been married to Azizus, king of the small kingdom of Enesa in Syria, but Felix convinced her to marry him (Josephus, *Antiquities,* 20.7.2). In his message Paul did not try to flatter his captor, but spoke of righteousness, self-control and the coming judgment, which was what Felix and Drusilla needed to hear. Felix apparently realized his position because he became frightened; however, he didn't accept Jesus as his Lord and Savior. Rather he postponed a decision by sending Paul away. Although he often spoke with Paul, there is no indication that he ever became a Christian.

Then Acts 24:27 says, "But after two years had passed, Felix was succeeded by Porcius Festus, and wishing to do the Jews a favor, Felix left Paul imprisoned." Since Luke is using inclusive counting, after two years could be either A.D. 58 or A.D. 59, depending on when Festus arrived. Any time between June 21, A.D. 58 and June 20, A.D. 59 would be considered after two years using inclusive counting. However, since Judea was an important assignment and since Felix was being replaced for cause, it is quite likely that Festus did arrive before June 21 and therefore in A.D. 59 probably around June 6, A.D. 59.

The ship bringing Festus landed directly in Caesarea, but apparently Festus was anxious to learn about conditions in Jerusalem since that had been the source of complaints about Felix. Festus departed Caesarea after three days or on June 8 and would have probably arrived in Jerusalem about June 9 since he would be traveling by chariot or horseback. Probably the next day, June 10, the Jewish leaders brought charges against Paul. These leaders wanted Paul to be brought to Jerusalem so that they might have him ambushed on the way. However, Festus said he was returning soon to Caesarea and Paul's accusers could accompany him, and he would hear Paul's case as soon as he got back to Caesarea. Therefore, about June 17, not more then ten days after he arrived, Festus left Jerusalem and arrived in Caesarea about June 18. Acts 25:6-12 says:

> After he had spent not more than eight or ten days among them, he went down to Caesarea, and on the next day he took his seat on the tribunal and ordered Paul to be brought. After Paul arrived, the Jews who had come down from Jerusalem stood around him, bringing many and serious charges against him which they could not prove, while Paul said in his own defense, "I have committed no offense either against the Law of the Jews or against the temple or against Caesar." But Festus, wishing to do the Jews a favor, answered Paul and said, "Are you willing to go up to Jerusalem and stand trial before me on these charges?" But Paul said, "I am standing before Caesar's tribunal, where I ought to be tried. I have done no wrong to the Jews, as you also very well know. "If, then, I am a wrongdoer and have committed anything worthy of death, I do not refuse to die; but if none of those things is true of which these men accuse me, no one can hand me over to them. I appeal to Caesar." Then when Festus had conferred with his council, he answered, "You have appealed to Caesar, to Caesar you shall go."

Thus, on about June 19, A.D. 59, Paul appealed to Caesar and Festus agreed to send him to Caesar. A few days later King Agrippa II and his sister Bernice arrived at Caesarea, probably about June 26. King Agrippa II was the son of King Agrippa I, who had executed James the brother of John and imprisoned Peter shortly before Agrippa I's death in A.D. 44. Festus probably welcomed the visit of King Agrippa since Festus was unfamiliar with local conditions and customs in this province. King Agrippa had been educated in Rome and of course was anxious to be friendly with the imperial representative. After some time, probably about June 30, A.D. 59, Festus discussed Paul's case with Agrippa. Then Acts 25:22 says, "Then Agrippa said to Festus, "I also would like to hear the man myself." "Tomorrow," he said, "you shall hear him." The next day, July 31, A.D. 59, Paul appeared before King Agrippa II and Bernice and made his defense. At the conclusion of this defense Acts 26:32 says, "And Agrippa said to Festus, 'This man might have been set free if he had not appealed to Caesar.'" It would appear, based on this response of Agrippa to Paul's case, that Festus' letter to the emperor concerning Paul would have stated his case in fairly favorable terms.

Paul's Journey to Rome

Subsequent events in the Acts indicate that Paul was not immediately sent to Rome probably because he would require a military escort, which would not be justified for one prisoner. Acts 27:1 says, "When it was decided that we would sail for Italy, they proceeded to deliver Paul and some other prisoners to a centurion of the Augustan cohort named Julius." Thus, it was probably the end of August, about August 24, A.D. 59 that Paul finally left Caesarea. The next day they arrived at Sidon (see Figure 7.10) and Paul was allowed to visit his friends there and receive care. The ship probably

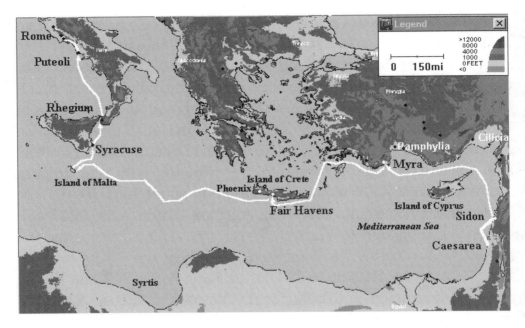

Paul's Journey to Rome
Figure 7.10

spent several days there discharging and loading cargo and then departed about August 31.

Ocean Passages for the World published by the British Navy speaking of the period from May to September says, "Over the whole of the Eastern Mediterranean, other than the Aegean Sea, the prevailing winds are NW'ly throughout this period, and particularly persistent in July and August and East of the 20th meridian, where winds from directions other than between N and W are uncommon. This of course is a modern work, published in 1973, but prevailing winds have probably not changed since ancient times. Since Paul's ship was sailing east of the 20th meridian, it would be faced with northwest winds. Since a sailing vessel, especially in ancient times, cannot sail directly into the wind, it was necessary for Paul's ship to sail north along the coast of Syria and then west along the coast of Cilicia and Pamphylai (see 7.10). Then Act 27:4-8 says:

From there we put out to sea and sailed under the shelter of Cyprus because the winds were contrary. When we had sailed through the sea along the coast of Cilicia and Pamphylia, we landed at Myra in Lycia. There the centurion found an Alexandrian ship sailing for Italy, and he put us aboard it. When we had sailed slowly for a good many days, and with difficulty had arrived off Cnidus, since the wind did not permit us to go farther, we sailed under the shelter of Crete, off Salmone; and with difficulty sailing past it we came to a place called Fair Havens, near which was the city of Lasea.

Thus they could not take the direct route across the Mediterranean that Paul had taken when he was coming to Jerusalem and sailing with the wind. The almost 500-mile trip from Sidon to Myria in Lycia probably took about eighteen days with Paul's ship arriving about September 17, A.D. 59. Allowing a couple of days for making arrangements for another ship and that ship departing, they probably left Myria about September 21, A.D. 59. They were sailing northeast and during this passage they were apparently sailing almost into the wind. After many days, probably about September 30 they reached Cnidus, and the wind would not let them go any further on their northwestern course. They therefore turned south and with difficulty sailed around the eastern end of Crete and sailed as far as Fair Havens. Paul's ship probably arrived at Fair Havens about October 9, A.D. 59. Then Acts 27:9-11 says:

When considerable time had passed and the voyage was now dangerous, since even the fast was already over, Paul began to admonish them, and said to them, "Men, I perceive that the voyage will certainly be with damage and great loss, not only of the cargo and the ship, but also of our lives." But the centurion was more

persuaded by the pilot and the captain of the ship than
by what was being said by Paul.

The fast was the Day of Atonement, which in A.D. 59 was celebrated
on October 3, A.D. 59. Paul's advise was not accepted because the
pilot and the captain of the ship thought they could reach Phoenix, a
harbor further west along the south coast of Crete which would be a
better winter harbor than Fair Havens. Then Acts 27:13-20 says:

> When a moderate south wind came up, supposing that
> they had attained their purpose, they weighed anchor
> and began sailing along Crete, close inshore. But before
> very long there rushed down from the land a violent
> wind, called Euraquilo; and when the ship was caught in
> it and could not face the wind, we gave way to it and let
> ourselves be driven along. Running under the shelter of
> a small island called Clauda, we were scarcely able to
> get the ship's boat under control. After they had hoisted
> it up, they used supporting cables in undergirding the
> ship; and fearing that they might run aground on the
> shallows of Syrtis, they let down the sea anchor and in
> this way let themselves be driven along. The next day
> as we were being violently storm-tossed, they began to
> jettison the cargo; and on the third day they threw the
> ship's tackle overboard with their own hands. Since
> neither sun nor stars appeared for many days, and no
> small storm was assailing us, from then on all hope of
> our being saved was gradually abandoned.

They undergirded the ship with supporting cables and let down sea
anchors to slow down the ship because they were afraid the storm
might drive the ship aground on the shallows of Syrtis which are
located along the coast of North Africa (see Figure 7.10, page 336).

The ship continued to be driven by the storm until the fourteenth night, October 25, A.D. 59, when the sailors realized they were near land. To prevent them from running aground, the sailors cast out four anchors from the stern of the ship. The next morning they sailed the ship into a bay and tried to ground it near the sandy beach. However, they struck a reef and were grounded further out from shore and the ship was breaking up due to the pounding of the waves. The soldiers were ready to kill the prisoners to prevent their escape, but were stopped by Julius, the centurion. Therefore, all who could swim left first, and then the remaining people followed supported by planks and other wreckage from the ship. There were 276 persons on board and they all reached shore safely in accordance with an earlier shipboard prophecy by Paul. The shipwreck probably occurred about Sunday, October 26, A.D. 59.

After they had landed, they found that they were on the Island of Malta only 150 miles off the coast of Italy and they had been driven almost 600 miles by the storm. To add to the problems of those shipwrecked, it was cold and raining. However, the natives were very helpful and they started a fire for them. As Paul was gathering sticks and placing them on the fire, a viper that was in the sticks that Paul picked up bit him on the hand. When the natives of the island saw this, they thought Paul must have been a murderer and even though he had survived the shipwreck, was still to suffer death for his crimes. However, when Paul was unaffected by the snake bite, they thought he must be a god.

The leading man of the island, Publius, owned land near the site of the shipwreck, and he entertained Paul and his companions for three days. During this time, Publius' father was sick with a recurrent fever and dysentery and Paul healed him. After this, everyone on the island that had diseases came to Paul and were cured. Paul and his companions probably stayed with Pulius October 28, 29 and 30. Because of Paul's healing of the sick, Paul and his companions were treated with great respect and, when they departed, all their needs were provided. Then Acts 28:11-16 says:

> At the end of three months we set sail on an Alexandrian ship which had wintered at the island, and which had the Twin Brothers for its figurehead. After we put in at Syracuse, we stayed there for three days. From there we sailed around and arrived at Rhegium, and a day later a south wind sprang up, and on the second day we came to Puteoli. There we found some brethren, and were invited to stay with them for seven days; and thus we came to Rome. And the brethren, when they heard about us, came from there as far as the Market of Appius and Three Inns to meet us; and when Paul saw them, he thanked God and took courage. When we entered Rome, Paul was allowed to stay by himself, with the soldier who was guarding him.

Paul was shipwrecked on Malta about October 26, A.D. 59, which was early in the eighth Jewish month. Paul spent three months on Malta, which would be the eighth, ninth and tenth Jewish months. It would be easy for them to keep track of the Jewish months by watching the phases of the moon. The tenth Jewish month in A.D. 60 ended on January 21. Pliny the Elder in *Natural History,* 2, 122, says that navigation began to be resumed on about February 8 while other ancient sources place the date of resumption later. However, it may have varied from year to year depending on local conditions. The Alexandrian ship was probably anxious to get its cargo to Italy and probably left Malta about February 11, A.D. 60. This ship probably reached Syracuse about Friday, February 13. They spent three days at Syracuse, probably unloading part of their cargo, and then departed on Sunday, February 15. Later that day, they arrived in Rhegium in southern Italy. The next day a favorable south wind sprang up and the following day, Tuesday, February 17, they reached Puteoli, Italy.

In Puteoli they found brethren and were invited to stay with them. They spent seven days in Puteoli, possibly while Julius made arrangements for their journey to Rome, but more likely simply as an accommodation by Julius so Paul could spend Saturday and Sunday with these Christian brethren. At any rate Paul spent seven days in Puteoli and departed for Rome on Monday, February 23, and reached the Market of Appius on Friday, February 27 where Paul was met by some brethren from the church at Rome.   These brethren had probably heard of Paul's arrival in Italy from travelers passing through Puteoli and came out to meet him.   They also met some brethren from Rome at a hamlet Tres Tabernae (Three Inns) as they proceeded along the Appian Way. The whole group probably arrived in Rome about Wednesday, March 3, A.D. 60. When Paul reached Rome, he was not put into a prison but was allowed to stay in his own rented quarters with a soldier to guard him.

Paul in Rome

As soon as Paul was settled, he arranged a meeting with the Jewish leaders in Rome. This meeting took place on the third day after his arrival in Rome, on Tuesday March 5, A.D. 60. Paul explained his situation to the Jewish leaders and they said that they had not heard anything about him from Judea; however, they said this sect (Christianity) was spoken against everywhere. At an agreed upon time the Jews came to Paul again, and he testified to them concerning the kingdom of God. Some of the Jews were persuaded, but others apparently rejected the Gospel and as they left Paul quoted Isaiah 6:9-10 to them.

Then Acts 28:30-31 says, "And he stayed two full years in his own rented quarters and was welcoming all who came to him, preaching the kingdom of God, and teaching concerning the Lord Jesus Christ with all openness, unhindered." Paul arrived in Rome about March 3, A.D. 60 and his first full Jewish year in Rome would have ended February 21, A.D. 61, and his second full year in Rome would have ended March 12, A.D. 62. Luke ends the Acts at this point. Why did Luke stop at this point? We cannot be sure, but the answer may be as simple as it was at this point, after spending two years with Paul in Rome, that Luke completed his writing of the Gospel of Luke and had written about all the events in Acts that had happened up to that time. Therefore, Luke chose to stop the Acts at this point, having traced the growth of Christ' Church from Jerusalem to the political capital of his world, Rome. Also the Christian community would be anxious to receive this work.

What was the ultimate outcome of Paul's trial in Rome? Many New Testament commentaries postulate that Paul was released after a first hearing before the Emperor Nero and that Paul made a fourth missionary journey to Span and to Crete. Then they postulate that Paul returned again to Rome and was then condemned and executed by Nero. However, there is really nothing in the New Testament to support this view. In Romans 15:28 Paul said he planned to visit Spain after he visited Rome; however, at that time he did not know he would come to Rome as a prisoner. Also, during Paul's missionary journeys, he often had to change his plans. As for his visit to Crete, although it is not mentioned in the Acts, it fits well into the journeys reflected in Paul's letters between his departure from Ephesus in A.D. 55 and his departure from Greece in A.D. 57. On the other hand, there is considerable evidence that Paul never left Rome.

Eusebius (c.A.D. 264-340) in *The History of The Church*, 2.25.1, as translated by G. A. Williamson, quotes the Roman Tertullian (c A.D. 160-221) as follows:

> Study your records: there you will find that Nero was the first to persecute this teaching when, after subjugating the entire East, in Rome especially he

treated everyone with savagery. That such a man was author of our chastisement fills us with pride. For anyone who knows him can understand that anything not supremely good would never have been condemned by Nero.

Eusebius then continues:

So it came about that this man, the first to be heralded as a conspicuous fighter against God, was led on to murder the apostles. It is recorded that in his reign Paul was beheaded in Rome itself, and Peter likewise was crucified, and the record is confirmed by the fact that the cemeteries there are still called by the names of Peter and Paul, and equally so by the churchman named Gaius, who was living while Zephyrinus was Bishop of Rome (c A.D. 200). In his published *Dialogue with Proclus,* the leader of the Phrygian heretics, Gaius had this to say about the place where the remains of the two apostles have been reverently laid:

I can point out the monuments of the victorious apostles. If you will go as far as the Vatican or the Ostian Way, you will find the monuments of those who founded this church.

Thus, Eusebius, quoting earlier sources, affirms that both Paul and Peter met their death at the hands of Nero who reigned from A.D. 54 to 68. But when during Nero's reign were they executed? We shall obtain an important clue as to when their death occurred in the writings of the Roman historian Tacitus (c.A.D. 55-120). In describing the great fire that burned half of the city of Rome in A.D.

64, Tacitus, writing in *The Annals of Imperial Rome*, chapter 14, page 365, as translated by Michael Grant, says:

> But neither human resources, nor imperial munificence, nor appeasement of the gods, eliminated sinister suspicions that the fire had been instigated. To suppress this rumor, Nero fabricated scapegoats - and punished with every refinement the notoriously depraved Christians (as they are popularly called).   Their originator, Christ, had been executed in Tiberius' reign by the governor of Judea, Pontius Pilatus. But in spite of this temporary setback the deadly superstition had broken out afresh, not only in Judea (where the mischief had started) but even in Rome.   All degraded and shameful practices collect and flourish in the capital.
>
> First, Nero had self-acknowledged Christians arrested. Then, on their information, a number of others were condemned-not so much for incendiarism as for anti-social tendencies.   Their deaths were made farcical. Dressed in wild animals' skins, they were torn to pieces by dogs, or crucified, or made into torches to be ignited after dark as substitutes for daylight. Nero provided his Garden for the spectacle, and exhibited displays in the Circus, at which he mingled with the crowd - or stood in a chariot, dressed as a charioteer. Despite their guilt as Christians, and the ruthless punishment it deserved, the victims were pitied. For it was felt that they were being sacrificed to one man's brutality rather than to the national interest.

Tacitus' statement concerning the persecution of the Christians as scapegoats that started after the burning of Rome in July A.D. 64

indicates that this persecution probably began in the second half of A.D. 64. But how did Nero know about the Christians? It seems most likely that he learned about Christianity by presiding over the trial of one of their leaders, the Apostle Paul, which must have taken place before the fire of July, A.D. 64. It would be incredible that such a wicked man, the personification of the antichrist, would have released Paul. Also Tacitus indicates that the Christians were already notorious when Nero selected them as his scapegoat for the fire, which again would suggest that Paul was condemned to death before the fire in A.D. 64. Since the letters of Paul and Peter indicate a period of increasing tension and danger in Rome following the two years of the Acts which ended in A.D. 62 when Paul preached "with all openness, unhindered," Paul probably met his death during the first half of A.D. 64.

Peter's letters indicate that he was in Rome late in A.D. 63 and in A.D. 64 and therefore was probably one of the first Christians martyred under Nero's persecution after the burning of Rome in July A.D. 64. Therefore he probably met his death late in A.D. 64; thus, early writers said that Paul and Peter died at the same time.

In the book of Acts we have traced the growth of Christ's Church from His Ascension on Thursday, May 12, A.D. 33, until Paul completed his second year as a prisoner in Rome about March 12, A.D. 62. All of the events of Acts are summarized in Table 7.2.

	Table 7.2			
	The Acts			
Event Sequence Number	Event (Scripture Reference)	Location of Event	Gregorian Date	Level* of Confidence
467	Post- Resurrection Appearances (Acts 1:3)	Judea & Galilee	4/3/33 to 5/12/33	I
468	Jesus' Final Words Before His Ascension (Acts 1:4-8)	Near Bethany, Judea	Thursday May 12, AD 33	I
469	Ascension (Mk 16:19) (Lk 24:50-51) (Acts 1:9-11)	Near Bethany, Judea	Thursday May 12, AD 33	I
470	Apostles Return to Upper Room (Acts 1:12-13) (Lk 24:52)	Mount Zion, Jerusalem	Thursday May 12, AD 33	I
471	The Apostles, the Women & Jesus' Family Continually Devote Themselves to Prayer (Acts 1:14)	Jerusalem	May 12 to May 22, A.D. 33	I
472	Matthias Chosen to Replace Judas Iscariot (Acts 1:15-26)	Jerusalem	Sunday May 15, AD 33	II
473	The Coming of the Holy Spirit On Pentecost (Acts 2:1-13)	Jerusalem	Sunday May 22, AD 33	I
474	Peter's Pentecost Sermon (Acts 2:14-36)	Jerusalem	Sunday May 22, AD 33	I
475	Peter's Audience Said, "What Shall We Do?" (Acts 2:37)	Jerusalem	Sunday May 22, AD 33	I

*Level of Confidence in Date   Level I = Highly Probable   Level II = Probable

Event Sequence Number	Event (Scripture Reference)	Location of Event	Gregorian Date	Level* of Confidence
476	Peter Says, "Repent and Be Baptized" (Acts 2:38-40)	Jerusalem	Sunday May 22, AD 33	I
477	3000 Souls Added to the Church (Acts 2:41)	Jerusalem	Sunday May 22, AD 33	I
478	Fellowship of the Jerusalem Church (Acts 2:42-47)	Jerusalem	May 22 to August 12, AD 33	I
479	Peter Healing of a Lame Beggar (Acts 3:1-10)	Beautiful Gate, Jerusalem	Sunday May 29, AD 33	II
480	Peter Preaching about Jesus (Acts 3:11-26)	Portico of Solomon, Jerusalem	Sunday May 29, AD 33	II
481	Peter, John & Beggar Arrested (Acts 4:1-3)	Portico of Solomon, Jerusalem	Sunday May 29, AD33	II
482	Many, Including 5000 Men, Believe (Acts 4:4)	Portico of Solomon, Jerusalem	Sunday May 29, AD33	II
483	Trial Before Temple Rulers & Elders (Acts 4:5-22)	Jerusalem	Monday May 30, AD 33	II
484	Disciples Pray & Meeting Place Shaken (Acts 4:23-31)	Jerusalem	Monday May 30, AD 33	II
485	Disciples Share Everything & Apostles Witness (Acts 4:32-35)	Jerusalem	May 22 to August 12,, AD 33	II

*Level of Confidence in Date   Level I = Highly Probable   Level II = Probable

Event Sequence Number	Event (Scripture Reference)	Location of Event	Gregorian Date	Level* of Confidence
486	Barnabas Donates Money From The Sale of Land (Acts 4:36-37)	Jerusalem	Wednesday June 15, AD 33	II
487	Death of Ananias & Sapphira (Acts 5:1-11)	Jerusalem	Thursday June 30, AD 33	II
488	Many Signs & Wonders Taking Place at the Hands of Apostles (Acts 5:12-16)	Jerusalem	May 30 to August 12, AD 33	II
489	High Priest & Sadducees Arrest Apostles (Acts 5:17-18)	Jerusalem	Thursday July 14, AD 33	II
490	Apostles Released By An Angel (Acts 5:19-20)	Jerusalem	Friday July 15, AD 33	II
491	Apostles Return to the Temple to Preach (Acts 5:21a)	Jerusalem	Friday July 15, AD 33	II
492	Missing Apostles Perplex Guards & Chief Priests (Acts 5:21b-24)	Jerusalem	Friday July 15, AD 33	II
493	Apostles Again Appear Before the Council (Acts 5:25-33))	Jerusalem	Friday July 15, AD 33	II
494	Gamaliel Counsels Caution (Acts 5:34-39)	Jerusalem	Friday July 15, AD 33	II
495	Apostles Flogged & Released (Acts 5:40)	Jerusalem	Friday July 15, AD 33	II

*Level of Confidence in Date   Level I = Highly Probable   Level II = Probable

Event Sequence Number	Event (Scripture Reference)	Location of Event	Gregorian Date	Level* of Confidence
496	Apostles Rejoice & Continue Preaching Jesus (Acts 5:41-42)	Jerusalem	Friday July 15, AD 33	II
497	Complaints Hellenistic Widows Were Overlooked (Acts 6:1)	Jerusalem	July 17 to July 28, AD 33	II
498	Seven Chosen to Distribute Food to the Widows (Acts 6:2-6)	Jerusalem	Thursday July 28, AD 33	II
499	Christ's Church in Jerusalem Continues to Grow (Acts 6:7)	Jerusalem	July 28 to August 12, AD 33	II
500	Synagogue Jews Argue With Stephen (Acts 6:8-10)	Jerusalem	July 28 to August 12, AD 33	II
501	False Charges Brought Against Stephen Before the Council (Acts 6:11-15)	Jerusalem	Friday August 12, AD 33	II
502	Stephen's Defense Before the Council (Acts 7:1-54)	Jerusalem	Friday August 12, AD 33	II
503	Stephen Sees the Glory of God & Jesus (Acts 7:55-56)	Jerusalem	Friday August 12, AD 33	II
504	Stephen Is Stoned (Acts 7:57-60)	Jerusalem	Friday August 12, AD 33	II
505	Church Scattered Due to Persecution (Acts 8:1)	Jerusalem	Aug 12 to Sept 23, AD 33	II

*Level of Confidence in Date   Level I = Highly Probable   Level II = Probable

Event Sequence Number	Event (Scripture Reference)	Location of Event	Gregorian Date	Level* of Confidence
506	Stephen Buried & Lamented (Acts 8:2)	Jerusalem	Friday, August 12, AD 33	II
507	Saul Ravages the Church (Acts 8:3)	Jerusalem	Aug 12 to Sept 23, AD 33	II
508	Philip Preaches in Samaria (Acts 8:4-8)	City of Samaria, Samaria	Thursday August 18, AD 33	II
509	Simon the Sorcerer Believes (Acts 8:9-13)	City of Samaria, Samaria	Thursday Sept 1, AD 33	II
510	Peter & John Go to Samaria (Acts 8:14-17)	City of Samaria, Samaria	Monday Sept 5, AD 33	II
511	Simon Tries to Buy the Power to Bestow the Holy Spirit (Acts 8:18-24)	City of Samaria, Samaria	Thursday Sept 8, AD 33	II
512	Peter & John Return to Jerusalem (Acts 8:25)	City of Samaria, Samaria	Sunday Sept 11, AD 33	II
513	Philip Witnesses to the Ethiopian Eunuch (Acts 8:26-39)	Road to Gaza	Wednesday Sept 14, AD 33	II
514	Philip Preaches From Azotus to Caesarea (Acts 8:40)	Coastal Judea	Sept 14 to Sept 30, AD 33	II
515	Saul Ask High Priest For Letters to Arrest Christians in Damascus (Acts 9:1-2)	Jerusalem	Wednesday Sept 14, AD 33	II

*Level of Confidence in Date   Level I = Highly Probable   Level II = Probable

Event Sequence Number	Event (Scripture Reference)	Location of Event	Gregorian Date	Level* of Confidence
516	Paul's Heavenly Vision on the Road to Damascus (Acts 9:3-9)	Near Damascus	Wednesday Oct 26, AD 33	II
517	Ananias Sent to Saul (Acts 9:10-16)	Damascus	Friday Oct 28, AD 33	II
518	Ananias Restores Saul's Vision & Baptizes Saul (Acts 9:17-19a)	Damascus	Friday Oct 28, AD 33	II
519	Saul Proclaims Jesus in the Synagogues of Damascus (Acts 9:19b-21)	Damascus	Saturday Oct 29, AD 33	II
520	Paul Escape Damascus in a Basket (Acts 9:22-25)	Damascus	Wednesday Feb 6, AD 36	II
521	Barnabas Introduces Saul to the Apostles (Acts 9:26-27)	Jerusalem	Wednesday Feb 27, AD 36	II
522	Saul Speaks Freely in Jerusalem (Acts 9:28)	Jerusalem	Feb 27 to Mar 4, AD 36`	II
523	Hellenistic Jews Plan to Kill Saul (Acts 9:29)	Jerusalem	Tuesday Mar 4. AD 36	II
524	Saul Sent to Caesarea to Depart for Tarsus (Acts 9:30)	Jerusalem	Wednesday Mar 5, AD 36	II
525	Church Increases During a Period of Peace (Acts 9:31)	Judea, Galilee & Samaria	Mar AD 36 to Mar AD42	II

*Level of Confidence in Date   Level I = Highly Probable   Level II = Probable

Event Sequence Number	Event (Scripture Reference)	Location of Event	Gregorian Date	Level* of Confidence
526	Peter Heals Aeneas (Acts 9:32-35)	Lydda, Judea	Sunday June 5, AD 39	II
527	Peter Raises Dorcas from the Dead (Acts 9:36-43)	Joppa, Judea	Thursday June 16, AD 39	II
528	Cornelius' Vision of an Angel (Acts 10:1-8)	Caesarea, Samaria	Sunday July 31, AD 39	II
529	Peter's Vision Concerning Uncleanness (Acts 10:9-16)	Joppa, Judea	Monday Aug 1, AD 39	II
530	Cornelius' Servant's Arrive (Acts 10:17-23a)	Joppa, Judea	Monday August 1, AD 39	II
531	Peter Departs with Cornelius' Servants (Acts 10:23b)	Joppa, Judea	Tuesday August 2, AD 39	II
532	Peter Presents the Gospel to Those Gathered with Cornelius (Acts 10:24-43)	Caesarea, Samaria	Wednesday August 3, AD 39	II
533	Holy Spirit Fell o All Who Were Gathered to Hear Peter (Acts 10:44-46)	Caesarea, Samaria	Wednesday August 3, AD 39	II
534	Peter Baptized All Who Were Gathered At Cornelius' House (Acts 10:47-48)	Caesarea, Samaria	Wednesday August 3, AD 39	II
535	Peter Explains His Taking the Word to the Gentiles (Acts 11:1-18)	Jerusalem	Monday Sept 26, AD 39	II

*Level of Confidence in Date   Level I = Highly Probable   Level II = Probable

Event Sequence Number	Event (Scripture Reference)	Location of Event	Gregorian Date	Level* of Confidence
536	Gospel Preached to Greeks At Antioch (Acts 11:19-21)	Antioch, Syria	Sunday July 1, AD 40	II
537	Jerusalem Church Sends Barnabas to Antioch (Acts 11:22-24)	Antioch, Syria	Monday Oct 6, AD 42	II
538	Barnabas Gets Saul and Brings Him to Antioch (Acts 11:25-26)	Antioch, Syria	Thursday Dec 25, AD 42	II
539	Agabus Foretells Worldwide Famine (Acts 11:27-28)	Antioch, Syria	Sunday Dec 20, AD 43	II
540	Offering Sent to Jerusalem with Barnabas & Saul (Acts 11:29-30)	Antioch, Syria	Monday Feb 1, AD 44	II
541	Herod Agrippa I Puts James the Brother of John to Death (Acts 12:1-2)	Jerusalem	Friday March 25, AD 44	II
542	Herod Agrippa I Puts Peter In Prison (Acts 12:3-5)	Jerusalem	Sunday April 3, AD 44	II
543	Angel Releases Peter From Prison (Acts 12:6-11)	Jerusalem	Thursday April 7, AD 44	I
544	Peter Goes to the Home of John Mark (Acts 12:12-17)	Jerusalem	Thursday April 7, AD 44	I
545	Herod Agrippa I Executes Peter's Guards (Acts 12:18-19a)	Jerusalem	Friday April 6, AD 44	II

*Level of Confidence in Date   Level I = Highly Probable   Level II = Probable

Event Sequence Number	Event (Scripture Reference)	Location of Event	Gregorian Date	Level* of Confidence
546	Herod Agrippa I Dies (Acts 12:19b-23)	Caesarea, Samaria	Thursday August 4, AD 44	II
547	Growth & Multiplication of the Word of Lord (Acts 12:24)	Judea, Samaria & Galilee	AD 44	II
548	Barnabas & Saul Depart Jerusalem to Return to Antioch (Acts 12:25)	Jerusalem	Monday April 11, AD 44	II
549	Barnabas & Saul Set Apart By the Direction of the Holy Spirit (Acts 13:1-3)	Antioch, Syria	Sunday April 23, AD 45	II
550	Barnabas & Saul Depart for Cyprus (Acts 13: 4-5)	Antioch, Syria	Monday May 8, AD 45	II
551	Paul Curses Elymas, the Magician (Acts 13:6-12)	Paphos, Cyprus	Sunday August 6, AD 45	II
552	Paul & His Companions Depart Paphos to Perga, Pamphylia (Acts 13:13a)	Paphos, Cyprus	Monday August 21, AD 45	II
553	John Mark Returns to Jerusalem (Acts 13:13b)	Perga, Pamphy-lia	Thursday August 24, AD 45	II
554	Paul & Barnabas Depart for Pisidian Antioch (Acts 13:14a)	Perga, Pamphy-lia	Monday August 28, AD 45	II
555	Paul Preaches in Synagogue in Pisidian Antioch (Acts 13:14b-41)	Pisidian Antioch	Saturday Sept 2, AD 45	II

*Level of Confidence in Date   Level I = Highly Probable   Level II = Probable

Event Sequence Number	Event (Scripture Reference)	Location of Event	Gregorian Date	Level* of Confidence
556	Paul Invited to Speak at the Synagogue the Next Sabbath (Acts 13:42)	Pisidian Antioch	Saturday Sept 2, AD 45	II
557	Many Jews & Proselyte Follow Paul & Barnabas (Acts 13:43)	Pisidian Antioch	Saturday Sept 2, AD 45	II
558	Nearly the Whole City Assembles in Synagogue to Hear the Word (Acts 13:44)	Pisidian Antioch	Saturday Sept 9, AD 45	II
559	Jews Contradict the Things Said By Paul (Acts 13:45)	Pisidian Antioch	Saturday Sept 9, AD 45	II
560	Paul & Barnabas Turn to Gentiles (Acts 13:46-48)	Pisidian Antioch	Saturday Sept 9, AD 45	II
561	The Word of the Lord Spread Through the Whole Region (Acts 13:49)	Pisidia	Sept 9 to Dec 10, AD 45	II
562	Jews Instigate a Persecution of Paul and Barnabas (Acts 13:50)	Pisidian Antioch	Sunday Dec 10, AD 45	II
563	Paul & Barnabas Depart for Iconium (Acts 13:51-52)	Pisidian Antioch	Sunday Dec 10, AD 45	II
564	Paul & Barnabas Preach in Synagogue & Many Believe (Acts 14:1)	Iconium. Galatia	Saturday Dec 23, AD 45	II
565	Disbelieving Jews Speak Against the Gospel (Acts 14:2)	Iconium, Galatia	Saturday Dec 23, AD 45	II

*Level of Confidence in Date   Level I = Highly Probable   Level II = Probable

Event Sequence Number	Event (Scripture Reference)	Location of Event	Gregorian Date	Level* of Confidence
566	Paul & Barnabas Spend a Long Time There Speaking Boldly (Acts 14:3)	Iconium, Galatia	12/23/45 to 6/7/46	II
567	Gentiles & Jews Attempt to Stone Paul & Barnabas (Acts 14:4-5)	Iconium, Galatia	Thursday June 7, AD 46	II
568	Paul & Barnabas Depart For Lycaonia (Acts 14:6-7)	Iconium, Galatia	Thursday June 7, AD 46	II
569	Paul Heals a Lame Man (Acts 14:8-10)	Lystra, Lycaonia	Sunday June 10, AD 46	II
570	People Think Paul & Barnabas Are Gods (Acts 14:11-18)	Lystra, Lycaonia	Sunday June 10, AD 46	II
571	Paul Is Stoned (Acts 14:19-20a)	Lystra, Lycaonia	Sunday July 1, AD 46	II
572	Paul & Barnabas Depart For Derbe (Acts 14:20b)	Lystra, Lycaonia	Monday July 1, AD 46	II
573	Paul & Barnabas Make Many Disciples (Acts 14:21a)	Derbe, Lycaonia	July to Sept, AD 46	II
574	Paul & Barnabas Return to Lystra, Iconium & Antioch (Acts 14:21b-23)	Lycaonia and Pisidia	Nov 46 to Jan 47	II
575	Paul & Barnabas Preach in Perga (Acts 14:24-25a)	Perga, Pamphy-lia	Feb & Mar, AD 47	II

*Level of Confidence in Date   Level I = Highly Probable   Level II = Probable

Event Sequence Number	Event (Scripture Reference)	Location of Event	Gregorian Date	Level* of Confidence
576	Paul & Barnabas Depart Attalia (Acts 14:25b-26)	Attalia, Pamphy-lia	Wednesday Mar 20, AD 47	II
577	Paul & Barnabas Report to the Church at Antioch (Acts 14:27)	Antioch, Syria	Sunday April 7, AD 47	II
578	Paul & Barnabas Spend a Long Time with the Disciples (Acts 14:28)	Antioch, Syria	Apr 47 to Dec 48	II
579	Judaizers Teach That Circumcision Is Necessary (Acts 15:1)	Antioch, Syria	Sunday Dec 6, AD 48	II
580	Paul & Barnabas Debate With Judaizers (Acts 15:2a)	Antioch, Syria	Dec 6 to Dec 20, AD 48	II
581	Paul & Barnabas Sent to Jerusalem (Acts 15:2b-3a)	Antioch, Syria	Monday Dec 20, AD 48	II
582	Paul & Barnabas Pass Through Phoenicia & Samaria (Acts 15:3b)	Syria	Jan 2 to Jan 17, AD 49	II
583	Paul & Barnabas Report to the Church of Jerusalem (Acts 15:4)	Jerusalem	Sunday January 24, AD 49	II
584	Christian Pharisees Say Gentile Christians Must Be Circumcised (Acts 15:5)	Jerusalem	Sunday Jan 24, AD 49	II
585	Apostles & Elders of Jerusalem Church Consider the Question (Acts 15:6-12)	Jerusalem	Monday Jan 25, AD 49	II

*Level of Confidence in Date   Level I = Highly Probable   Level II = Probable

Event Sequence Number	Event (Scripture Reference)	Location of Event	Gregorian Date	Level* of Confidence
586	Judgment of James (Acts 15:13-21)	Jerusalem	Monday Jan 25, AD 49	II
587	Letter Sent to the Gentile Churches with Judas & Silas (Acts 15:22-29)	Jerusalem	Monday Feb 1, AD 49	II
588	Paul, Barnabas, Judas & Silas Depart for Antioch (Acts 15:30a)	Jerusalem	Monday Feb 1, AD 49	II
589	Paul & Barnabas Deliver the Letter to the Church at Antioch (Acts 15:30b-31	Antioch, Syria	Sunday Feb 28, AD 49	II
590	Judas & Silas Preach to the Church at Antioch (Acts 15:32)	Antioch, Syria	Feb 28 to Apr 12, AD 49	II
591	Judas & Others Return to Jerusalem But Silas Remains (Acts 15:33-34)	Antioch, Syria	Monday April 12, AD 49	II
592	Paul & Barnabas Teaching & Preaching in Antioch (Acts 15:35)	Antioch, Syria	Feb 28 to Apr 19, AD 49	II
593	Paul Proposes Returning to Cities Previously Visited (Acts 15:36)	Antioch, Syria	Monday Apr 19, AD 49	II
594	Dispute With Barnabas Over Taking John Mark (Acts 15:37-38)	Antioch, Syria	Monday Apr 19, AD 49	II
595	Barnabas Takes John Mark and Departs for Cyrus (Acts 15:39)	Antioch, Syria	Wednesday Apr 28, AD 49	II

*Level of Confidence in Date   Level I = Highly Probable   Level II = Probable

Event Sequence Number	Event (Scripture Reference)	Location of Event	Gregorian Date	Level* of Confidence
596	Paul Takes Silas and Departs Through Syria & Cilicia (Acts 15:40-41)	Antioch, Syria	Monday May 17, AD 49	II
597	Paul Selects Timothy as an Assistant (Acts 16:1-3)	Lystra, Lycaonia	Sunday July 25, AD 49	II
598	Paul Delivers Jerusalem Decree and Churches are Strengthened (Acts 16:4-5)	Lycaonia & Pisidia	June 18 to Aug 16, AD 49	II
599	Paul and Companions Travel Though Phrygia, Galatia & Mysia (Acts 16:6-8)	Phrygia, Galatia, Mysia	Aug 16 to Sept 3, AD 49	II
600	Paul's Vision To Go Macedonia (Acts 16:9-10)	Troas, Mysia	Sunday Sept 5, AD 49	II
601	Paul and Party Depart to Philippi, Macedonia (Acts 16:11-12)	Troas, Mysia	Tuesday Sept 7, AD 49	II
602	Lydia & Household Believe & Are Baptized (Acts 16:13-15)	Philippi, Mace-donia	Saturday Sept 11, AD 49	II
603	Paul Exorcizes a Slave Girl (Acts 16:16-18)	Philippi, Mace-donia	Saturday Oct 2, AD 49	II
604	Paul & Silas Arrested & Beaten (Acts 16:19-23a)	Philippi, Mace-donia	Sunday Oct 3, AD 49	II
605	Paul & Silas Thrown in Prison (Acts 16:23b-24)	Philippi, Mace-donia	Sunday Oct 3, AD 49	II

*Level of Confidence in Date   Level I = Highly Probable   Level II = Probable

Event Sequence Number	Event (Scripture Reference)	Location of Event	Gregorian Date	Level* of Confidence
606	Earthquake Releases Paul & Silas (Acts 16:25-26)	Philippi, Macedonia	Monday Oct 4, AD 49	II
607	Philippian Jailer Converted to Christianity (Acts 16:27-34)	Philippi, Macedonia	Monday Oct 4, AD 49	II
608	Officials Release Paul & Silas (Acts 16:35-39)	Philippi, Macedonia	Monday Oct 4, AD 49	II
609	After Encouraging Lydia & the Brethren They Depart (Acts 16:40)	Philippi, Macedonia	Tuesday, Oct 5, AD 49	II
610	Paul Preaches in Synagogue in Thessalonica (Acts 17:1-4)	Thessalonica	Saturday Oct 15, AD 49	II
611	Jews Seek Paul & Seize Jason (Acts 17:5-9)	Thessalonica	Monday Nov 1, AD 49	II
612	Paul & Silas Depart to Berea (Acts 17:10a)	Thessalonica	Monday Nov 1, AD 49	II
613	Paul Preaches in the Synagogue & Many Believe (Acts 17:10b-12)	Berea, Macedonia	Saturday Nov 6, AD 49	II
614	Jews From Thessalonica Stir Up Persecution Against Paul & Silas (Acts 17:13)	Berea, Macedonia	Tuesday Dec 14, AD 49	II
615	Paul Sent to Athens (Acts 17:14-15)	Berea, Macedonia	Tuesday Dec 14, AD 49	II

*Level of Confidence in Date   Level I = Highly Probable   Level II = Probable

Event Sequence Number	Event (Scripture Reference)	Location of Event	Gregorian Date	Level* of Confidence
616	Paul Preaches in Athens (Acts 17:16-18)	Athens, Greece	12/24/49 to 1/21/50	II
617	Paul Preaches to the Areopagus (Acts 17:19-34)	Athens, Greece	Wednesday Jan 5, AD 50	II
618	Paul Departs for Corinth (Acts 18:1)	Athens, Greece	Tuesday Jan 25, AD 50	II
619	Paul Meets Aquila & Priscilla (Acts 18:2-3)	Corinth, Greece	Saturday Jan 29, AD 50	II
620	Paul Reasons in Synagogue Every Sabbath (Acts 18:4)	Corinth, Greece	Jan 29 to Mar 26, AD 50	II
621	Silas & Timothy Arrive & Paul Preaches Full-time (Acts 18:5)	Corinth, Greece	Thursday Mar 17, AD 50	II
622	Paul Moves Ministry to the House of Titius Justus (Acts 18:6-8)	Corinth, Greece	Saturday Mar 26, AD 50	II
623	The Lord Appears to Paul in a Vision (Acts 18:9-10	Corinth, Greece	Sunday Mar 27, AD 50	II
624	Paul Teaching for Eighteen Months (Acts 18:11)	Corinth, Greece	1/28/50 to 6/11/51	II
625	Jews Bring Paul Before Gallio (Acts 18:12-17)	Corinth, Greece	Wednesday June 14, AD 51	II

*Level of Confidence in Date   Level I = Highly Probable   Level II = Probable

Event Sequence Number	Event (Scripture Reference)	Location of Event	Gregorian Date	Level* of Confidence
626	Paul Departs Greece For Syria (Acts 18:18)	Cenchrea, Greece	Wednesday Apr 17, AD 52	II
627	Paul Preaches in the Synagogue at Ephesus (Acts 18:19-20)	Ephesus, Asia	Saturday May 4, AD 52	II
628	Paul Departs for Caesarea (Acts 18:21-22a)	Ephesus, Asia	Wednesday May 15, AD 52	II
629	Paul Departs to Antioch (Acts 18:22b-23a)	Caesarea, Samaria	Tuesday June 18, AD 52	II
630	Paul Departs for Galatia & Phrygia (Acts 18:23b)	Antioch, Syria	Monday Sept 16, AD 52	II
631	Apollos Instructed By Priscilla & Aquila (Acts 18:24-28)	Ephesus, Asia	Saturday Sept 28, AD 52	II
632	About Twelve Disciples Receive the Holy Spirit (Acts 19:1-7)	Ephesus, Asia	Friday Dec 20, AD 52	II
633	Paul Preaches in the Synagogue (Acts 19:8)	Ephesus, Asia	Saturday Dec 21, AD 52	II
634	Paul Moves Ministry to School of Tyrannus (Acts 19:9-12)	Ephesus, Asia	Saturday Feb 22, AD 53	II
635	Jewish Exorcists Overpowered by an Evil Spirit (Acts 19:13-17)	Ephesus, Asia	Wednesday Nov 18, AD 54	II

*Level of Confidence in Date   Level I = Highly Probable   Level II = Probable

Event Sequence Number	Event (Scripture Reference)	Location of Event	Gregorian Date	Level* of Confidence
636	Books of Magic Burnt (Acts 19:18-20)	Ephesus, Asia	Sunday Dec 13, AD 54	II
637	Paul Sends Timothy & Eratus to Macedonia (Acts 19:21-22)	Ephesus, Asia	Tuesday April 6, AD 55	II
638	Demetrius, a Silversmith, Arouses the City Against Paul (Act 19:23-41)	Ephesus, Asia	Tuesday June 1, AD 55	II
639	Paul Departs to Macedonia (Acts 20:1)	Ephesus, Asia	Thursday June 3, AD 55	II
640	Paul Visits the Churches in Macedonia & Surrounding Area (Acts 20:2a)	Macedonia	AD 55 to AD 56	II
641	Paul Visits Greece (Acts 20:2b-3a)	Greece	12/15/56 to 2/12/57	II
642	Paul Departs to Macedonia (Acts 20:3b)	Greece	Monday Feb 12, AD 57	II
643	Paul's Traveling Companions Depart by Sea for Troas (Acts 20:4-5)	Greece	Wednesday Mar 28, AD 57	II
644	Paul & Luke Depart for Troas (Acts 20:6)	Philippi, Macedonia	Thursday Apr 12, AD 57	II
645	Eutychus Raised From the Dead (Acts 20:7-12)	Troas, Mysia	Monday Apr 30, AD 57	II

*Level of Confidence in Date   Level I = Highly Probable   Level II = Probable

Event Sequence Number	Event (Scripture Reference)	Location of Event	Gregorian Date	Level* of Confidence
646	Paul Departs for Assos by Land (Acts 20:13-14)	Troas, Mysia	Monday Apr 30, AD 57	II
647	Paul & Companions Arrive at Miletus (Acts 20:15-16)	Miletus, Asia	Thursday May 3, AD 57	II
648	Paul Speaks to the Elders from Ephesus (Acts 20:17-38)	Miletus, Asia	Thursday May 10, AD 57	II
649	Paul & Companions Depart for Patara (Acts 21:1)	Miletus, Asia	Thursday May 10, AD 57	II
650	Paul & Companions Depart for Phoenicia (Acts 21:2)	Patara, Lycia	Tuesday May 15, AD 57	II
651	Paul & Companions Spend Seven Days at Tyre (Acts 21:3-6)	Tyre, Phoenicia	May 23 to May 28, AD 57	II
652	Paul & Companions Depart for Ptolemais (Acts 21:7)	Tyre, Phoenicia	Monday May 28, AD 57	II
653	Paul & Companions Arrive at Caesarea (Acts 21:8a)	Caesarea, Samaria	Tuesday May 29, AD 57	II
654	Paul & Companions Stay with Philip the Evangelist (Acts 21:8b-9)	Caesarea, Samaria	May 29 to June 12, AD 57	II
655	Agabus Prophesies Paul's Arrest By the Gentiles (Acts 21:10-14)	Caesarea, Samaria	Sunday June 10, AD 57	II

*Level of Confidence in Date   Level I = Highly Probable   Level II = Probable

Event Sequence Number	Event (Scripture Reference)	Location of Event	Gregorian Date	Level* of Confidence
656	Paul & Companions Depart for Jerusalem (Acts 21:15-16)	Caesarea, Samaria	Tuesday June 12, AD 57	II
657	Paul Meets with Church Leaders of Jerusalem (Acts 21:17-25)	Jerusalem	Wednesday June 20, AD 57	II
658	Paul Visits the Temple to Make Arrangements for an Offering (Acts 21:26)	Jerusalem	Thursday June 21, AD 57	II
659	Paul Visits the Temple Again and is Attacked (Acts 21:27-30)	Jerusalem	Sunday June 24, AD 57	II
660	Roman Officer Arrests Paul (Acts 21:31-36)	Jerusalem	Sunday June 24, AD 57	II
661	Paul Asks Permission to Address the Crowd (Acts 21:37-40)	Jerusalem	Sunday June 24, AD 57	II
662	Paul Addresses the Crowd (Acts 22:1-21)	Jerusalem	Sunday June 24, AD 57	II
663	Paul Brought into the Barracks (Acts 22:22-24a)	Jerusalem	Sunday June 24, AD 57	II
664	Paul Escapes Scourging Because He is a Roman Citizen (Acts 22:24b-29)	Jerusalem	Sunday June 24, AD 57	II
665	Paul Appears Before the Jewish Council (Acts 22:30-23:10)	Jerusalem	Monday June 25, AD 57	II

*Level of Confidence in Date   Level I = Highly Probable   Level II = Probable

Event Sequence Number	Event (Scripture Reference)	Location of Event	Gregorian Date	Level* of Confidence
666	The Lord Stands at Paul's Side & Encourages Him (Acts 23:11)	Jerusalem	Monday June 25, AD 57	II
667	Paul Learns of a Conspiracy to Kill Him From His Nephew (Acts 23:12-16)	Jerusalem	Tuesday June 26, AD 57	II
668	Commander Sends Paul to Caesarea (Acts 23:17-24)	Jerusalem	Tuesday June 26, AD 57	II
669	Commander Sends A Letter to Governor Felix with Paul (Acts 23:25-30)	Jerusalem	Tuesday June 26, AD 57	II
670	Paul Taken As Far As Antipatris By Night (Acts 23:31-32)	Antipatris Samaria	Wednesday June 27, AD 57	II
671	Paul Arrives at Caesarea (Acts 23:33-35)	Caesarea, Samaria	Wednesday June 27, AD 57	II
672	Paul Accused By the High Priest, Ananias, Tertullus & Elders (Acts 24:1-9)	Caesarea, Samaria	Sunday July 1, AD 57	II
673	Paul's Defense Before Governor Felex (Acts 24:10-21)	Caesarea, Samaria	Sunday July 1, AD 57	II
674	Felix Postpones Judgment in Paul's Case (Acts 24:22-23)	Caesarea, Samaria	Sunday July 1, AD 57	II
675	Paul Preaches to Felix (Acts 24:24-26)	Caesarea, Samaria	Friday Dec 14, AD 57	II

*Level of Confidence in Date   Level I = Highly Probable   Level II = Probable

Event Sequence Number	Event (Scripture Reference)	Location of Event	Gregorian Date	Level* of Confidence
676	After Two Years Festus Arrives to Replace Felix (Acts 24:27)	Caesarea, Samaria	Friday June 6, AD 59	II
677	Jews Bring Charges Against Paul to Festus (Acts 25:1-5)	Jerusalem	Tuesday June 10, AD 59	II
678	Paul's Hearing Before Festus (Acts 25:6-10)	Caesarea, Samaria	Thursday June 19, AD 59	II
679	Paul Appeals to Caesar (Acts 25:11-12)	Caesarea, Samaria	Thursday June 19, AD 59	II
680	Festus Tells King Agrippa About Paul's Case (Acts 25:13-22)	Caesarea, Samaria	Wednesday July 30, AD 59	II
681	Paul's Hearing Before King Agrippa (Acts 25:23-26:29)	Caesarea, Samaria	Thursday July 31, AD 59	II
682	Agrippa Thinks Paul Innocent, But Must Go To Caesar (Acts 26:30-31)	Caesarea, Samaria	Thursday July 31, AD 59	II
683	Centurion Departs with Paul to Sidon (Acts 27:1-3)	Caesarea, Samaria	Tuesday Aug 24, AD 59	II
684	Centurion Departs with Paul to Myra (Acts 27:4-5)	Sidon, Phoenicia	Sunday Aug 31, AD 59	II
685	Centurion with Paul Departs to Fair Havens (Acts 27:6-8)	Myra, Lycia	Sunday Sept 21, AD 59	II

*Level of Confidence in Date   Level I = Highly Probable   Level II = Probable

Event Sequence Number	Event (Scripture Reference)	Location of Event	Gregorian Date	Level* of Confidence
686	Paul Warns of Danger of Continuing the Voyage (Acts 27:9-12)	Fair Havens, Crete	Thursday Oct 9, AD 59	II
687	Centurion with Paul Departs Fair Havens (Acts 27:13)	Fair Havens, Crete	Sunday Oct 12, AD 59	II
688	Violent Wind, Called Euraquilo, Catches the Ship (Acts 27:14-20)	Off Island of Crete	Sunday Oct 12, AD 59	II
689	Paul Told All Would Be Saved (Acts 27:21-26)	Adriatic Sea	Saturday Oct 25, AD 59	II
690	Sailors Attempt to Abandon the Ship (Acts 27:27-32)	Adriatic Sea	Saturday Oct 25, AD 59	II
691	Ship Is Wrecked But All the Passengers & Crew are Saved (Acts 27:33-28:1)	Island of Malta	Sunday Oct 26, AD 59	II
692	Paul Bitten By a Viper But Suffers No Harm (Acts 28:2-6)	Island of Malta	Sunday Oct 26, AD 59	II
693	Paul Heals All On The Island With Diseases (Acts 28:7-10)	Island of Malta	10/28/59 to 2/10/60	II
694	Paul & Companions Depart for Syracuse (Acts 28:11-12)	Island of Malta	Wednesday Feb 11, AD 60	II
695	Paul & Companions Depart for Puteoli (Acts 28:13)	Syracuse, Sicily	Sunday Feb 15, AD 60	II

*Level of Confidence in Date   Level I = Highly Probable   Level II = Probable

Event Sequence Number	Event (Scripture Reference)	Location of Event	Gregorian Date	Level* of Confidence
696	Paul Spends Seven Days With Brethren (Acts 28:14)	Puteoli, Italy	Feb 17 to Feb 23, AD 60	II
697	Paul Meets Brethren On Road to Rome (Acts 28:15)	Market of Appius	Friday Feb 27, AD 60	II
698	Paul Arrives at Rome (Acts 28:16)	Rome	Wednesday Mar 3, AD 60	II
699	Paul Explains His Case to the Jews of Rome (Acts 28:17-22)	Rome	Friday Mar 5, AD 60	II
700	Paul Presents the Gospel to the Jews of Rome (Acts 28:23-29)	Rome	Tuesday Mar 9, AD 60	II
701	Paul Spends Two Years Preaching & Teaching in Rome (Acts 28:30-31)	Rome	3/3/60 to 3/12/62	II
702	Introduction to Luke's Gospel (Luke 1:1-4)	Rome	AD 60	II
703	Introduction to the Acts (Acts 1:1-2)	Rome	AD 61	II

*Level of Confidence in Date   Level I = Highly Probable   Level II = Probable

8

Authors and Years
of
The New Testament Books

In this chapter we shall discuss the authors of each of the books of the New Testament and the probable year in which each book was completed. In the introduction of this book I have already discussed the authors of the four Gospels and the book of Acts because it was important to show that these books reflected the eyewitness testimony of the Apostles who were directly called by Jesus. However, for completeness, I shall again briefly discuss the authors of these books. In this chapter we shall undertake a difficult task. None of the books of the New Testament were explicitly dated by their authors and several do not even mention the name of the author. How then shall we accomplish this task of determining the author and year of completion of each of these books?

If we were to only rely on the internal evidence of the New Testament, we would face an impossible task; however, the New Testament is not some unknown document just recently unearthed in some remote archaeological dig. Rather, it is a collection of books that have been known and preserved by the church since the time of their composition. The initial recipients of the New Testament books knew who their authors were and it seems reasonable to believe that they would have appreciated the importance of these books and would therefore have carefully preserved them and the identity of their authors. Therefore, the testimony of the church fathers provide an important source of information concerning the authors and time of completion of the books of the New Testament. However, since the testimony of the church fathers does not possess the same level of certitude as the New Testament Scriptures, it must be carefully evaluated and made subordinate to the internal testimony of the New Testament Scriptures themselves.

Jesus, speaking to His eleven Apostles in Acts 1:8, said: "But you shall receive power when the Holy Spirit has come upon you; and you shall be My witnesses both in Jerusalem, and in all Judea and Samaria, and even to the remotest part of the earth." In this verse, was Jesus speaking figuratively and was this prophecy fulfilled by Peter's visit to Rome and his and the other Apostle's ministries in the Mediterranean area? I think not. Rather, its fulfilment is taking place even today when the eyewitness testimony of the Apostles is reaching even to the remotest part of the world through the words of the New Testament. It is important that the New Testament records the eyewitness testimony of Jesus' apostles.

Paul also wrote a major portion of the New Testament and, in Act 26:16, Paul recalled Jesus' words to him: "But arise, and stand on your feet; for this purpose I have appeared to you, to appoint you a minister and to witness not only to the things which you have seen, but also to the things in which I will appear to you." Thus Paul, as well as Jesus' original eleven Apostles, were eyewitnesses to Jesus' teaching. These twelve men, together with two of Jesus' half-brothers, James and Jude, who had known Jesus all their life, were selected to be Jesus' primary witnesses. This was the belief of the early church fathers and no book became a part of the New Testament canon unless it was believed to reflect the testimony of these primary witnesses. Thus Luke 1:1-3 says:

> In as much as many have under taken to compile an
> account of the things accomplished among us, just as
> they were handed down to us by those who from the
> beginning were eyewitnesses and servants of the word,
> it seemed fitting for me as well, having investigated
> everything carefully from the beginning, to write it out
> for you in consecutive order, most excellent Theophilus.

If the New Testament is the Word of God, wouldn't God have guided the church in the preservation and canonization of the books of the New Testament? The New Testament does reflect the testimony of Jesus' primary witnesses although this testimony may have been recorded by companions to the Apostles, as was the case for Mark (Gospel), Luke (Gospel & Acts), Tertius (Romans) and Silvanus (1 Peter).

Matthew

Papias, in *The Sayings of the Lord Explained* (c. A.D. 135) in a fragment preserved by Eusebius in his *The History of The Church* (3.34.16, page 152), as translated by G.A. Williamson said: "Matthew compiled the *Sayings* in the Aramaic language, and everyone translated them as well as he could." Irenaeus, writing between A.D. 182 and A.D. 188 in *Against Heresies,* said: "Matthew also used a written Gospel among the Hebrews in their own dialect." Both of these men were only one generation removed from the time when some of the Apostles still lived and therefore were in a position to know the identity of the author of the first Gospel. It was the testimony of all the early Christian writers that the Apostle Matthew, the former tax collector, was the author of the Gospel of Matthew and, during the early history of the Church, this book was the most often quoted and probably given the greatest respect of all the New Testament books.

It was not until the nineteenth century that some scholars began to question the testimony of the church fathers concerning Matthew's authorship of the first Gospel. This questioning was not based on the discovery of new objective evidence, but rather appears to be caused by the rejection of all the miracles recorded in the New Testament. These scholars may have reasoned that if all the miraculous events of the New Testament were not true, then it would be more reasonable to attribute these writings, which claimed that the miracles were true, to later church writers rather than to the Apostles who were eyewitnesses and went to their death for proclaiming their faith. However, if Jesus is the "only begotten Son" of God (John 3:16), then why wouldn't He be able to perform miracles? Some have questioned the testimony of the church fathers that Matthew wrote his Gospel originally in Hebrew on the basis that the Greek version of Matthew does not appear to be a translation of an Aramaic work. However, there is no reason why Matthew, as probably the most educated of Jesus' original twelve apostles, could not have been bilingual, as clearly the Apostle Paul was. Thus, as soon as the Greek-speaking Gentiles became a significant part of the Church, Matthew could have produced a Greek version of his Gospel. As the original author of the book, he would feel free to provide more than just a word for word translation of his original work, which may account for any lack of Aramaic characteristics in the Greek text of Matthew.

As was indicated in chapter 4 of this book, Matthew's composition of his Gospel probably began with notes he took during Jesus' Sermon on the Mount in A.D. 31. There are four other major discourses of Jesus recorded in Matthew's Gospel: Instructions to the Twelve (9:35-11:1), Teaching in Parables (13:1-50), Teachings Concerning the Kingdom (18:1-19:2) and Teachings Concerning the End Time (24:1-26:2). These five discourses contain one third of the verses of this Gospel and were probably all based on notes that Matthew took while Jesus spoke. Certainly one of the primary purposes of Matthew in writing his Gospel was to preserve these words of Jesus. After Jesus' death, resurrection and ascension and the Pentecost experience, there is no reason to believe that Matthew would have delayed writing his Gospel. In Matthew 24:35 Jesus says, "Heaven and earth will pass away, but My words will not pass away." If Jesus' words were not to pass away, why would Matthew have waited thirty or forty years to write them down as many New Testament scholars claim? Thus Matthew, with the guidance of the Holy Spirit, probably completed his Aramaic version of his Gospel in A.D. 33. After the report of Paul and Barnabas in January A.D. 49 at the Council of Jerusalem, which indicated that many Greek-speaking Gentiles were accepting the gospel message, Matthew may have undertaken the preparation of a Greek version of his Gospel which he would have probably completed in A.D. 49. Matthew may have had assistance in this effort as Peter and Paul sometimes did; however, since Matthew appears to be the primary scribe of Jesus' ministry, there is no reason to believe that he was not capable of preparing the Greek version of his Gospel himself.

Eusebius (c AD 264-340) in *The History of the Church,* 3.24.5 page 132, says, "Matthew had begun by preaching to the Hebrews; and when he made up his mind to go to others too, he committed his own gospel to writing in his native tongue, so that for those with whom he was no longer present, the gap left by his departure was filled by what he wrote." Matthew undoubtedly left a copy of his Gospel with the church at Jerusalem when he departed and this may have been the first time many in that church had heard of his writing a Gospel. However, it seems unlikely that Matthew would have waited until he was ready to depart to undertake the task of writing his Gospel which must have taken several months to complete. Thus, Matthew's Aramaic version may have received wider circulation after his departure from Jerusalem; however, it was probably written years before that time.

What about the "Synoptic Problem?" If you accept the testimony of the church fathers as to when and by whom the Gospels were written, there is no synoptic problem. It is only when you completely reject this testimony and assume that Matthew's Gospel was based on Mark's that you have a synoptic problem.

Mark

Eusebius, ibid. 2.14.5, page 88, summarizes the witness of the church fathers concerning Mark's Gospel as follows:

> So brightly shone the light of true religion on the minds of Peter's hearers that, not satisfied with a single hearing or with the oral teaching of the divine message, they resorted to appeals of every kind to induce Mark (whose gospel we have), as a follower of Peter, to leave them in writing a summary of the instructions they had received by word of mouth, nor did they let him go till they had persuaded him, and thus became responsible for the writing of what is known as the Gospel according to Mark. It is said that, on learning by revelation of the spirit what had happened, the apostle was delighted at their enthusiasm and authorized the reading of the book in the churches. Clement quotes the story in *Outline Book VI*, and his statement is confirmed by Bishop Papias of Hierapolis, who also points out that Mark is mentioned by Peter in his first epistle, which he is said to have composed in Rome itself, as he himself indicates when he speaks of the city figuratively as Babylon: "The church in Babylon, chosen like yourselves, send you greetings, and so does my son Mark."

Eusebius, quoting earlier authorities, indicates that Peter and Mark were together in Rome prior to Mark's writing of his Gospel. But when were Peter and Mark together in Rome? In A.D. 44, immediately after the Passover Feast, Peter was released from prison by an angel and departed Jerusalem. However, it is apparent that Mark did not accompany Peter because Acts 12:25 says "And Barnabas and Saul returned from Jerusalem when they had fulfilled their mission, taking along with them John, who was also called Mark." Thus in A.D. 44 Mark accompanied Barnabas and Paul not Peter. Mark then accompanied Barnabas and Paul on their first missionary journey; however, Mark left Paul and Barnabas in the late summer of A.D. 45 and returned to Jerusalem. Peter next appears in the Acts at the Council of Jerusalem in A.D. 49. Thus, both Peter and Mark had returned to Jerusalem after the death of Herod Agrippa I, and they might possibly have gone to Rome together some time between A.D. 45 and A.D. 48. However, Acts 12:24 speaking of the church at Jerusalem says, "But the word of the Lord continued to grow and to be multiplied." Thus, this was a period of growth for the church in Judea, and since Peter was primarily concerned with bringing the Gospel to the circumcised (Galatians 2:7), he would have probably spent this period of time in Judea.

Following the Council of Jerusalem, Acts 15:22 says that Judas and Silas accompanied Paul and Barnabas back to Antioch of Syria with the letter from the Apostles and elders of the Church at Jerusalem. If Peter had accompanied them, he would certainly have been mentioned. Later in A.D. 49 Barnabas and Mark depart Antioch for Cyprus, so Mark must have returned to Antioch with Paul and Barnabas. In Galatians 2:11 Paul speaks of opposing Cephas (Peter) at Antioch. This would indicate that Peter had left Judea and visited Antioch during one of the periods when Paul was there. There is no indication that Peter was in Antioch before the Council of Jerusalem and he did not return with Paul and Barnabas after the Council of Jerusalem. Therefore, the only time for Peter's visit to Antioch recorded in Galatians 2:11 would be between Paul's second and third missionary journeys or in A.D. 52.

Paul departed on his third missionary journey in September A.D. 52 traveling overland. However, if Peter planned to go to Rome, he would have probably wanted to travel by sea since that would have been much easier than traveling overland. Therefore, Peter probably didn't leave Antioch until the time of safe sea travel in the spring of A.D. 53. Thus, Peter probably was in Rome in A.D. 53 and therefore arrived there before Paul. Peter probably spent about a year there, departing in A.D. 54. Peter's extensive travels during this period are indicated by 1 Corinthians 1:12 which says that some of the brethren at Corinth were saying, "I am of Cephas (Peter)" and it was indicated in Chapter 7 that 1 Corinthians was written by Paul in A.D. 55. This would probably indicate a visit to Corinth by Peter subsequent to Paul's first visit to Corinth in A.D. 50 and 51 because during Paul's first visit to Corinth there was no indication of any contact by the Corinthians with Peter.

Peter probably left Rome in A.D. 54 leaving Mark behind. Thus Mark probably completed his Gospel in Rome in A.D. 55. It appears that Mark had a copy of Matthew's Gospel with him, probably the Greek version, since he generally reports the same events in his Gospel as appears in Matthew's Gospel except that he begins with the baptism of John, which is probably where Peter's preaching began since this is where Peter first encountered Jesus. However, Mark was recording the Gospel as presented by Peter and therefore revised the order of some of the events to reflect Peter's preaching. The greater vividness of Mark's Gospel probably also reflects Peter's preaching. It would not be surprising that the primary spokesman of Jesus' Apostles would be a vivid speaker. Also the emphasis on what Jesus did as opposed to what He said, probably also reflects Peter's preaching. It is fortunate because Matthew seems primarily concerned with recording the words of Jesus while Mark gives us a more action oriented account. Thus, through Mark's

Gospel many additional details of Jesus' ministry as presented in the preaching of Peter are preserved.

Luke and the Acts

Eusebius, ibid., 3.4.6 page 109, says:

> Luke, by birth an Antiochene and by profession a physician, was for a long period a companion of Paul and was closely associated to the other apostles as well. So he has left us examples of the fine art of healing souls which he learnt from them in two divinely inspired books, the Gospel and the Acts of the Apostles.

This was Eusebius' summary of the testimony of the church fathers.

The book of Acts indicates by the "we passage" of Acts 20:6 that Luke accompanied Paul when he returned to Jerusalem in A.D. 57 and apparently remained in the Judean area during Paul's two-year imprisonment at Caesarea since he also accompanied Paul to Rome (Acts 27:1). During these two years Luke probably often met with the Apostles and probably collected the material for his Gospel; however, he probably didn't finish writing his Gospel until after he and Paul had reached Rome in A.D. 60. Both Luke's Gospel and the Acts were addressed to Theophilus, who was probably a Roman official. There is no mention of a Theophilus in the detailed description of the events at Caesarea and it is much more likely that there would be a Roman official associated with the well established church in Rome than in Caesarea where no Christian church is mentioned. The introductions to both the Gospel and the Acts indicate that these two books are two volumes of a single work. Thus, since Acts couldn't have been completed until after A.D. 62, since events of that year are recorded in it, it seems likely that both volumes were written in Rome during the two years of Paul's imprisonment there recorded in the Acts.

Luke acknowledges that there were other gospels before his (Luke 1:1-3). Luke probably brought a copy of Matthew's Gospel with him from Judea and he could have obtained a copy of Mark's Gospel from the church at Rome. Mark may have been in Rome at the time that Paul and Luke arrived; but in Second Timothy Paul asks Timothy to pick up Mark and bring him to Rome. We shall see that Second Timothy was probably written in A.D. 63. However, Mark could have been in Rome and was subsequently sent to Ephesus on some mission for Paul. In 2 Timothy 4:11 Paul says, "Only Luke is with me. Pick up Mark and bring him with you, for he is useful to me for service." This verse suggests a much different attitude by Paul toward Mark than was reflected in Acts 15:36-39, where Paul refused to take Mark on his second missionary journey, which would suggest that Paul must have spent some time with Mark subsequent to his second missionary journey in A.D. 49-52. At any rate, Luke probably used Matthew's and Mark's Gospels as a guide in preparing his Gospel while incorporating all the additional material he had collected during his time in Judea. Luke probably completed his Gospel in A.D. 61 and then continued on with the Acts which was probably completed early in A.D. 62 and which included Paul's experiences up to that time.

John

Eusebius, ibid, 3.24.5, page 132, in discussing the order in which the Gospels were written, says:

And when Mark and Luke had now published their gospels, John, we are told, who hitherto had relied entirely on the spoken word, took to writing for the following reason. The three gospels already written were in general circulation and copies had come into John's hands. He welcomed them, we are told, and confirmed their accuracy, but remarked that the narrative only lacked the story of what Christ had done first of all at the beginning of his mission.

Thus, we have Eusebius' summary of the testimony of the church fathers concerning the writing of the Gospel of John. Of course John, in his Gospel, does much more than just add what Jesus did first of all, but this statement is consistent with the modesty displayed by the Apostle John in his New Testament writings. Assuming Luke's Gospel was first circulated in connection with the Acts which was probably completed in A.D. 62, John couldn't have completed his Gospel until A.D. 63.

However, in John 21:18 Jesus said to Peter, "Truly, truly, I say to you, when you were younger, you used to gird yourself and walk wherever you wished; but when you grow old, you will stretch out your hands and someone else will gird you, and bring you where you do not wish to go." It is unlikely that Jesus explained this statement at the time He made it, since this would leave Peter with a death sentence hanging over him. However, if John wrote his gospel after the death of Peter, then he would understand this saying of Jesus and thus John 21:19 says, "Now this He said, signifying by what kind of death he would glorify God. And when He had spoken this, He said to him, 'Follow Me!'" Therefore, John probably completed his Gospel after he had received word of the death of Peter and Paul, both of whom died under the persecution of the church by Nero. As indicated in chapter 7, Paul was probably executed by Nero in A.D. 64 before the burning of Rome in July, and Peter was probably one of the early martyrs in the persecution that followed the burning of Rome. Therefore, the Gospel of John was completed by the Apostle John, the son of Zebedee, probably in A.D. 65.

Through the Gospel of John, we have a much fuller picture of the ministry of Jesus, and through his inclusion of the many feast days, we are given a great deal more chronological data concerning this ministry. Some have suggested that John wrote his Gospel near the close of the first century A.D. God could have invigorated a ninety year-old Apostle John to be able to write his Gospel then, but why would he have waited once the other Gospels were written and he saw the need for a fourth Gospel? The fact that John reported that Jesus predicted the destruction of the Temple of Jerusalem does not necessitate that the Gospel was written after its destruction in A.D. 70. If Old Testament prophets could predict future events, which they certainly did, there is no reason that the Son of God could not have predicted the destruction of the Temple. Hebrews 11:6 says, "And without faith it is impossible to please Him, for he who comes to God must believe that He is and that He is a rewarder of those who seek Him." It seems unlikely that those that do not believe the Bible will be its most trustworthy interpreters.

We now come to the letters of the New Testament attributed to Paul. Of these letters Eusebius, ibid., 3.3.3, page 108, summarizing the testimony of the church fathers concerning these letters, says:

> Paul on the other hand was obviously and unmistakably the author of fourteen epistles, but we must not shut our eyes to the fact that some authorities have rejected the Epistle to the Hebrews, pointing out that the Roman Church denies that it was the work of Paul.

However, Eusebius, after reviewing all the evidence of the church fathers available to him, concludes that all fourteen of the letters attributed to Paul, including Hebrews, were "obviously and unmistakably" written by the Apostle Paul. We shall discuss the witness of the church fathers concerning Hebrews when we arrive at that book in this chapter.

Romans

The Apostle Paul is identified as the author of this letter in Romans 1:1. Romans 15:25-26 says, "But now, I am going to Jerusalem serving the saints. For Macedonia and Achaia have been pleased to make a contribution for the poor among the saints in Jerusalem." The reference to the gift which Macedonia and Achaia had already made for the saints at Jerusalem would seem to identify the time of this letter as immediately prior to Paul's departure to Jerusalem at the close of his third missionary journey, which our discussion in chapter 7 of the chronology of Acts places in A.D. 57. Roman 16:23a says, "Gaius, host to me and to the whole church, greets you" and 1 Corinthians 1:14-15 says, "*I* thank God that I baptized none of you except Crispus and Gaius, so that no one would say you were baptized in my name." This is probably the same Gaius, and thus the letter to the Romans was probably written from Corinth during the three months spent by Paul in Greece referenced in Acts 20:2-3.

1 Corinthians

1 Corinthians 1:1 identifies the Apostle Paul as the author of this letter. 1 Corinthians 16:5-9 says:

> But I will come to you after I go through Macedonia, for I am going through Macedonia; and perhaps I will stay with you, or even spend the winter, so that you may send me on my way wherever I may go. For I do not wish to see you now just in passing; for I hope to remain with you for some time, if the Lord permits. But I will remain in Ephesus until Pentecost; for a wide door for

effective service has opened to me, and there are many adversaries.

These verses from 1 Corinthians seem to describe the same situation as Acts 19:21-22 which, during Paul's second visit to Ephesus, says:

> Now after these things were finished, Paul purposed in the spirit to go to Jerusalem after he had passed through Macedonia and Achaia, saying, "After I have been there, I must also see Rome." And having sent into Macedonia two of those who ministered to him, Timothy and Erastus, he himself stayed in Asia for a while.

Thus in accordance with the chronology of the book of Acts discussed in chapter 7, 1 Corinthians can be dated to the spring of A.D. 55 (see page 320).

2 Corinthians

2 Corinthians 1:1 identifies the Apostle Paul as the author of this letter and in chapter 7 it was shown that this book was probably written in A.D. 56 (see page 322).

Galatians

The Apostle Paul is identified as the author of this letter in Galatians 1:1. Galatians 2:1-2 says:

> Then after an interval of fourteen years I went up again to Jerusalem with Barnabas, taking Titus along also. It

> was because of a revelation that I went up; and I submitted to them the gospel which I preach among the Gentiles, but I did so in private to those who were of reputation, for fear that I might be running, or had run, in vain.

As discussed in chapter 7, these verses refer to the Council at Jerusalem that was shown to have taken place in January A.D. 49 so that this letter could not have been written until after that date. Galatians seems to address two problems: first Paul's authority as an apostle seems to have been questioned, and second was the question of whether circumcision and following the Jewish law was necessary for the Gentile Christians. This sounds like the same questions raised by the Judaizers that came to Antioch of Syria and precipitated the Council of Jerusalem. Some of these same Judaizers or other Jews with similar ideas may have also visited the Galatian churches at about the same time they came to Antioch. Therefore, when Paul returned from the Council of Jerusalem, he received word of this problem in the Galatian church. Paul could have answered the question concerning the Old Testament Law by simply sending a copy of the letter from the Apostles and elders of Jerusalem; however, this would seem to prove Paul's subordination to the Apostles in Jerusalem. Paul didn't want his authority to be dependent on the Apostles of Jerusalem since he had been called by the risen Lord to be the Apostle to the Gentiles. Therefore, in A.D. 49, just after his return from the Council of Jerusalem and while he was still in Antioch, Paul probably wrote the Galatian letter which defended his apostleship and directly argued why it was neither necessary or desirable for the Gentile Christians to place themselves under the Old Testament Law. Paul mentions the Council of Jerusalem in his letter and the conclusion of the Council; however, he did not include the letter from the Jerusalem church with the Galatian letter.

Later in A.D. 49, Paul left on his second missionary journey accompanied by Silas, the representative of the Jerusalem church. Acts 16:4 says, "Now while they were passing through the cities, they were delivering the decrees which had been decided upon by the apostles and elders who were in Jerusalem, for them to observe." Thus, Paul answered the questions raised by the Judaizers in his letter to the Galatians based on his own apostolic authority and then when he visited the Galatian church he was able to show them the letter from the church of Jerusalem to show that they were in agreement with him. Thus Paul not only answered the question concerning circumcision of Gentile Christians, but also maintained his authority as an apostle in the Galatian letter which was written in A.D. 49.

Ephesians, Colossians and Philemon

These three letters are discussed together because the great similarity of the people and situation suggest that all three letters were written by the same person at about the same time. The Apostle Paul is identified as the author in the first verse of each letter. Ephesians 6:21-22 says, "But that you also may know about my circumstances, how I am doing, Tychicus, the beloved brother and faithful minister in the Lord, will make everything known to you. I have sent him to you for this very purpose, so that you may know about us, and that he may comfort your hearts." Similarly, Colossians 4:7-14 says:

> As to all my affairs, Tychicus, our beloved brother and faithful servant and fellow bond-servant in the Lord, will bring you information. For I have sent him to you for this very purpose, that you may know about our circumstances and that he may encourage your hearts; and with him Onesimus, our faithful and beloved brother, who is one of your number. They will inform you about the whole situation here. Aristarchus, my

fellow prisoner, sends you his greetings; and also Barnabas' cousin Mark (about whom you received instructions; if he comes to you, welcome him); and also Jesus who is called Justus; these are the only fellow workers for the kingdom of God who are from the circumcision, and they have proved to be an encouragement to me. Epaphras, who is one of your number, a bondslave of Jesus Christ, sends you his greetings, always laboring earnestly for you in his prayers, that you may stand perfect and fully assured in all the will of God. For I testify for him that he has a deep concern for you and for those who are in Laodicea and Hierapolis. Luke, the beloved physician, sends you his greetings, and also Demas.

Also, Philemon 23 and 24 says, "Epaphras, my fellow prisoner in Christ Jesus, greets you, as do Mark, Aristarchus, Demas, Luke, my fellow workers." Finally, Onesimus is the subject of this letter to Philemon, and Timothy is mentioned in both Philemon and Colossians. Thus, the same people are with Paul in all three letters, and Tychicus seems to be the carrier of all three letters. Therefore, it appears that all three letters were written at about the same time, but when were they written?

It is clear from these letters that Paul is a prisoner and has been a prisoner for an extended period of time. The only extended periods of imprisonments of Paul recorded in the book of Acts were those at Caesarea and Rome. When Paul departed Greece for Jerusalem, Acts 20:4 says, "And he was accompanied by Sopater of Berea, the son of Pyrrhus, and by Aristarchus and Secundus of the Thessalonians, and Gaius of Derbe, and Timothy, and Tychicus and Trophimus of Asia." Thus, we have Aristarchus, Timothy, Tychicus as well as Luke, all accompanying Paul to Jerusalem and also being mentioned in these letters. This would suggest that the imprisonment of Paul referenced in these three letters was that at Caesarea since Acts 27:1-2 indicates that only Aristarchus and Luke accompanied Paul to Rome. If these letters were written during Paul's Caesarea imprisonment during A.D. 57 and 58, then they were probably written in A.D. 58, which would allow time for news of Paul's arrest to reach the Province of Asia and for Epaphras to come to Paul. Also Onesimus did not come with Paul, but apparently spent some time with him prior to the letters being written.

Philippians

Philippians 1:1 identifies the Apostle Paul with Timothy as the authors of this letter. However, since Paul uses the singular pronoun, I, throughout the letter, it is clear that he is the primary author of this letter. Philippians 1:12-14 says, "Now I want you to know, brethren, that my circumstances have turned out for the greater progress of the gospel, so that my imprisonment in the cause of Christ has become well known throughout the whole praetorian guard and to everyone else, and that most of the brethren, trusting in the Lord because of my imprisonment, have far more courage to speak the word of God without fear." Thus, Philippians was also written during one of Paul's two extended imprisonments. The reference to the praetorian guard would fit well with either his Caesarean or Roman imprisonment; however, the brethren speaking the word of God without fear seems to fit the imprisonment in Rome better since there was an active Christian church in Rome, but nothing is mentioned concerning the church in Caesarea. Also Philippians 4:22 says, "All the saints greet you, especially those of Caesar's household." Caesar's household is in Rome, not in Caesarea. Therefore the letter to the Philippians was probably written from Rome.

Philippians 2:25-26 says, "But I thought it necessary to send to you Epaphroditus, my brother and fellow worker and fellow soldier, who is also your messenger and minister to my need;

because he was longing for you all and was distressed because you had heard that he was sick." Thus, sufficient time must have passed for the Philippians to hear that Paul had been transferred to Rome, for Epaphioditus to come to Paul with a relief offering from the church at Philippi, for Epaphioditus to become sick to the point of death (Philippians 2:27), for news of his sickness to reach Philippi, and for their concern to get back to Paul. Thus, a considerable time must have passed since Paul first arrived in Rome. Also, Paul's case seems to be about ready to be heard because Paul, speaking of Timothy in Philippians 2:23-24 says, "Therefore I hope to send him immediately, as soon as I see how things go with me; and I trust in the Lord that I myself also will be coming shortly." Thus, this letter appears to have been written after the period of Paul's imprisonment in Rome described in the Acts which ended in A.D. 62, since at that time Paul had no indication of the resolution of his case. However, Paul still expects to be released although he realizes that might not be the case, and therefore in Philippians 2:17 says, "But even if I am being poured out as a drink offering upon the sacrifice and service of your faith, I rejoice and share my joy with you all." Thus, this letter from the Apostle Paul to the Philippian church was probably written about A.D. 63 from Rome.

1 Thessalonians

Paul, along with Silvanus (Silas) and Timothy, are identified as the authors of this letter in 1 Thessalonians 1:1. Since this letter closely parallels and supplements the information given in the Acts, it is possible to date this letter with considerable precision. Paul in 1 Thessalonians 3:1-2 says:

Therefore when we could endure it no longer, we thought it best to be left behind at Athens alone, and we

sent Timothy, our brother and God's fellow worker in
the gospel of Christ, to strengthen and encourage you as
to your faith.

This statement correlates with the information given in the Acts. In
the 17th chapter of Acts, Paul was preaching in the synagogue of
Thessalonica and Acts 17:4 says, "And some of them were persuaded
and joined Paul and Silas, along with a large number of the
God-fearing Greeks and a number of the leading women." This was
the beginning of the church at Thessalonica. However, the Jews
formed a mob and accused some of the new Christians before the city
authorities of disturbing the peace. Paul was sent to Berea, but the
Jews from Thessalonica followed and therefore Paul was taken to
Athens. From Athens Paul sent word that Silas and Timothy should
join him. According to the 1 Thessalonians letter, at least Timothy
did join Paul; however, apparently Paul sent Timothy immediately
back to visit the Thessalonica church. In chapter 7 it was indicated
that Silas and Timothy did not rejoin Paul until March of A.D. 50, by
which time Paul had moved on to the city of Corinth. It was shortly
after the arrival of Silas and Timothy in Corinth with an offering
from the Thessalonians church that Paul wrote 1 Thessalonians in the
name of the three evangelists in A.D. 50.

2 Thessalonians

Again, Paul, along with Silvanus and Timothy, are identified
as the authors of this letter in verse 1:1, and 2 Thessalonians 3:17
says, "I, Paul, write this greeting with my own hand, and this is a
distinguishing mark in every letter; this is the way I write." This
letter seems to have been written to warn the Thessalonians church
against false messages or letters claiming to be from Paul that say
that Jesus has already returned. Possibly Paul had already heard of
the circulation of such false messages. Since the same workers are

with Paul, this letter was probably written later during Paul's ministry in Corinth during his second missionary journey, probably in A.D. 51.

1 Timothy

The Apostle Paul is identified as the author of this letter in 1 Timothy 1:1. Timothy first appears in Acts 16:1, where Paul adds him to his evangelistic team during Paul's second missionary journey in July of A.D. 49. A clue as to when this letter was written is given in 1 Timothy 1:3-4 which says:

> As I urged you upon my departure for Macedonia, remain on at Ephesus so that you may instruct certain men not to teach strange doctrines, nor to pay attention to myths and endless genealogies, which give rise to mere speculation rather than furthering the administration of God which is by faith.

Thus, prior to writing this letter, Paul had departed Ephesus leaving Timothy behind to instruct certain men. In Acts 20:1, during Paul's third missionary journey, Paul departs Ephesus for Macedonia and Timothy had been with Paul in Ephesus. However, Acts 19:22, referring to Paul, says, "And having sent into Macedonia two of those who ministered to him, Timothy and Erastus, he himself stayed in Asia for a while." Apparently Timothy returned to Ephesus before Paul departed and thus could have been left behind in Ephesus at that time. Since Paul did not spend an extended period of time in Ephesus during his first two missionary journeys, this departure from Ephesus during Paul's third missionary journey must be the one referred to in 1 Timothy.

In 1 Corinthians 16:8-9 Paul says, "But I will remain in Ephesus until Pentecost; for a wide door for effective service has opened to me, and there are many adversaries." Thus, as indicated in chapter 7, Paul stayed in Ephesus until Pentecost of A.D. 55, so that there was time for Timothy to return to Ephesus. 1 Timothy was probably written in A.D. 55 from Macedonia some time after Paul's departure from Ephesus and his visit to Corinth. We infer this from the fact that 2 Corinthians 1:15-16 suggests that when Paul departed Ephesus he went to Corinth first and then to Macedonia. However, 1 Timothy mentions only Macedonia, which suggests that Paul was in Macedonia when he wrote the letter.

2 Timothy

2 Timothy 1:1 identifies the Apostle Paul as the author of this letter. Although 1 Timothy gives no indication that Paul was a prisoner, 2 Timothy 1:8 says, "Therefore do not be ashamed of the testimony of our Lord or of me His prisoner, but join with me in suffering for the gospel according to the power of God." Also Paul says in 2 Timothy 4:6-8, "For I am already being poured out as a drink offering, and the time of my departure has come. I have fought the good fight, I have finished the course, I have kept the faith; in the future there is laid up for me the crown of righteousness, which the Lord, the righteous Judge, will award to me on that day; and not only to me, but also to all who have loved His appearing." These verses place Paul in prison and near the end of his life. Since there is a strong tradition that Paul died in Rome, being executed by Emperor Nero, this letter was probably written from Rome. The fact that this letter was written from Rome is also supported by 2 Timothy 1:16-17 that says, "The Lord grant mercy to the house of Onesiphorus, for he often refreshed me and was not ashamed of my chains; but when he was in Rome, he eagerly searched for me and found me –"

The time of writing this letter appears to be late in the

imprisonment of Paul in Rome. The fact that Onesiphorus often refreshed Paul suggests that he ministered to Paul over a period of time, probably over several visits to Rome. Also the statement that the time of his departure has come suggests he feels he will soon be executed, which is much different than Paul's condition at the end of the Acts in A.D. 62 when he was teaching concerning the Lord Jesus Christ with all openness, unhindered in a rented house. Thus, Paul's second letter to Timothy must have been written after A.D. 62.

One final clue is given as to the time of Paul's writing of this letter. In 2 Timothy 4:13 Paul says, "When you come bring the cloak which I left at Troas with Carpus, and the books, especially the parchments." Paul must have left this cloak at Troas in A.D. 57 when he was on his way to Jerusalem. It is easy to understand why Paul would have left his heavy cloak as he was heading for the milder climate of Judea, but why would he have waited six years to retrieve it? While Paul was imprisoned in Caesarea, he was held in the Praetorium, Herod I's former palace, which undoubtedly was heated during the winter. During the first two years of Paul's imprisonment in Rome, Paul was staying in a rented house which again would have been heated. However, in 2 Timothy, conditions seems to have changed and now Paul is anticipating the need for a cloak. This suggests that 2 Timothy was written from an unheated prison cell, as opposed to a rented house, probably in the summer of A.D. 63 while sea travel was still possible.

Titus

The Apostle Paul is identified as the author of this letter in Titus 1:1. Titus 1:5 says, "For this reason I left you in Crete, that you would set in order what remains and appoint elders in every city as I directed you." Since the Acts does not mention any ministry of Paul in Crete, many Bible scholars have postulated that Titus was written during a fourth missionary journey of Paul which took place after he was initially released by Nero shortly after the close of the book of Acts. However, there is really no support for a fourth missionary journey for Paul in the New Testament. Romans 15:22-25 says:

> For this reason I have often been prevented from coming to you; but now, with no further place for me in these regions, and since I have had for many years a longing to come to you whenever I go to Spain--for I hope to see you in passing, and to be helped on my way there by you, when I have first enjoyed your company for a while-- but now, I am going to Jerusalem serving the saints."

Would Paul had said that he had no further place to go in these regions if he had not visited Crete, which is the largest island of this area lying off the coast of Greece? It seems more likely that Paul had just come from Crete when he arrived in Corinth in A.D. 57. It should be noted that Titus was with Paul in Macedonia when he wrote 2 Corinthians and sent it with Titus to Corinth. However, when Paul wrote Romans from Corinth in the spring of A.D. 57, Titus was not among those sending greetings from Corinth. Therefore, after Titus delivered 2 Corinthians, he must have returned to Paul in Macedonia and then Paul and Titus went to Crete, where Titus was left while Paul preceded on to Corinth. Thus Paul probably wrote both Romans and Titus early in A.D. 57.

But doesn't Paul's plans to visit Spain in Romans 15:24 require him to make a fourth missionary journey? Not at all. Paul often had to change his plans as can be clearly seen from his letters. When Paul wrote his letter to the Romans, he did not expect to come to Rome as a prisoner. Thus from Paul's letters, we can reconstruct the details of his activities during this period which were not recorded in the Acts, and there is no need to postulate a fourth missionary journey for Paul to account for Paul's letter to Titus.

Hebrews

Hebrews and the letters of John (1,2 &3 John) are the only letters in the New Testament where the author is not identified within the text of the letters. However, Clement of Rome, writing in the first century A.D., appears to be drawing on Hebrews, which would indicate an early date for the composition of this letter. Eusebius in *The History of the Church*, ibid.,6.14.2, page 254, writing concerning Clement of Alexandria (c A.D. 150-215) says, "The Epistle to the Hebrews he attributes to Paul, but says that it was written for the Hebrews in their own language, and then accurately translated by Luke and published for the Greek readers." As quoted at the beginning of this discussion of Paul's letters in this chapter, Eusebius himself accepted Hebrews as the work of Paul, but he points out that the Roman Church denied Paul was its author. Ultimately, Hebrews was included in the canon of the New Testament and Paul was accepted as its author.

Many today do not accept Paul as the author of Hebrews, raising many objections. They say that the style of this letter is too different from the other letters written by Paul to have been his work. However, to what other letter that Paul wrote to a Hebrew audience, probably in Aramaic, are they comparing Hebrews? The book of Acts clearly indicates that Paul did adapt his message to the particular audience he was addressing. Thus, Paul's message to the members of the synagogue of Piscidia Antioch of Acts 13:16-41 was quite different from his message to the Areopagus of Athens of Acts 17:23-31. Greek was probably Paul's second language. Therefore it would not be surprising that his Greek would be rugged while his Aramaic and Hebrew polished. Paul was certainly capable of writing the letter to the Hebrews since he was brought up in Jerusalem and educated under Gamaliel (Acts 23:3). But why and to whom was this letter written?

The only name that has been ascribed to this letter is to the

Hebrews, and the contents certainly support such an intended audience. Most commentaries on Hebrews identify the intended audience of this letter as some unspecified group of Jewish Christians in Rome. Certainly there were Jews within the church of Rome, who were undoubtedly the people that started the church: however, these Jewish Christians probably soon became a minority in the church at Rome. Thus, who was this group of Jewish Christians in Rome that would warrant the preparation of such a major work as Hebrews? Those who propose such a destination for Hebrews usually gloss over the identity of this group.

If we want to find a large group of Jewish Christians, where would we look? In the first century A.D. certainly the place to look would be in Judea. In Acts 21:20b James and the elders of the church at Jerusalem said, "You see, brother, how many thousands there are among the Jews of those who have believed, and they are all zealous for the Law." Thus Judea is the natural designation for this letter. Hebrews 13:24 says, "Greet all of your leaders and all the saints. Those from Italy greet you." The natural interpretation of this greeting would be that the origin of the letter was Italy and that those from Italy were sending their greeting. Some have contended that the letter was sent to Rome and that former residents of Italy were sending their greeting. However, since this is the only greeting in the letter, it would be strange indeed that the only ones sending greetings would be the former residents of Italy. If this letter was not written from Italy, surely not all the people of that Christian community were former residents of Italy, so why wouldn't they also have sent greetings? The obvious answer is that the letter was sent from Italy.

But if Paul was the author of this letter, why didn't he indicate his authorship in the first verse as he did in his other letters? Clement of Alexandria (c A.D. 150-215), preserved by Eusebius, ibid., 6.14.1 page 254, suggests that Paul did not give his name because the Hebrews were prejudiced against him and because in writing to the Hebrews he was working outside of his province as Apostle to the

Gentiles. However, I would like to suggest another possible reason for Paul omitting his name. Hebrews 13:23 says, "Take notice that our brother Timothy has been released, with whom, if he comes soon, I will see you." If Paul is still in prison when this letter is sent, as I believe was the case, then the inclusion of the name of the notorious prisoner Paul in the letter might place the bearer of the letter in danger. What Paul may be saying in Hebrews 13:23 is that Timothy, who is with him having recently been released from prison, will bring the letter. If Timothy comes to the Hebrews quickly and then returns to Paul, Paul would be able to see the Hebrews through Timothy. This somewhat cryptic note would be in harmony with Paul concealing his identity as the writer of the letter and the fact that he is a prisoner.

We last heard of Timothy in 2 Timothy, which we have deduced was probably written in the summer of A.D. 63. In that letter Paul requested Timothy to come to him before winter, which Timothy apparently did. However, after arriving in Rome, Timothy was apparently also arrested, but apparently was released and now Paul is sending him to Judea with the letter to the Hebrews. By now it is probably early in A.D. 64, and Paul probably died later that same year. Therefore, it is uncertain if Timothy could have returned before Paul's execution. Paul may have purposely sent Timothy to Judea for his safety.

Thus, probably early in A.D. 64, Paul wrote the letter to the Hebrews, which was sent to the church in Jerusalem by the hand of Timothy. This may explain why the letter was accepted as written by Paul in the eastern church, but questioned by the western church. The letter would be better known by those who received it than by the church of the city from which it was sent since at this time Paul was probably in prison and the church may not have had very much contact with him. In Romans 9:1-5 Paul says:

I am telling the truth in Christ, I am not lying, my

conscience testifies with me in the Holy Spirit, that I have great sorrow and unceasing grief in my heart. For I could wish that I myself were accursed, separated from Christ for the sake of my brethren, my kinsmen according to the flesh, who are Israelites, to whom belongs the adoption as sons, and the glory and the covenants and the giving of the Law and the temple service and the promises, whose are the fathers, and from whom is the Christ according to the flesh, who is over all, God blessed forever. Amen.

This was Paul's concern for the salvation of his fellow Jews in A.D. 57 and now seven years later as he faces death, he is still concerned for his Jewish brethren. Therefore, it is not surprising that his last great letter would be Hebrews, addressed to the church in Judea. In writing to the church in Judea it would be natural for Paul to write this letter in his and their own language as Clement of Alexandria suggested. This letter would have arrived only two years before the time of the Jewish War with Rome and the departure of the Christians from Jerusalem so initially this letter didn't get wide circulation especially in the Gentile Christian churches.

James

The author of this letter is identified as James in James 1:1 which says, "James, a bond-servant of God and of the Lord Jesus Christ, to the twelve tribes who are dispersed abroad: Greetings." The author of this letter is apparently of such stature that further identification was deemed unnecessary. This suggests that the letter was either the work of James, the son of Zebedee (Matthew 4:21) or James, the half brother of Jesus (Matthew 13:55). After discussing the death of James, the half brother of Jesus, Eusebius, ibid., 2.23.21, page 103, says:

Such is the story of James, to whom is attributed the first of the 'general' epistles.   Admittedly its authenticity is doubted, since few early writers refer to it, any more than to 'Jude's', which is also one of the seven called general.   But the fact remains that these two, like the others, have been regularly used in very many churches.

Thus, James was accepted into the canon of the New Testament on the basis of it being the work of the Apostle James, the Lord's half brother.

At the time of his death in A.D. 44, James, the son of Zebedee, together with Peter were probably the leaders of the Jerusalem church. This was probably why Herod Agrippa I selected them for execution. However, when James, the son of Zebedee, was executed (Acts 12:1) and Peter left Jerusalem, speaking of Peter, Acts 12:17 says, "But motioning to them with his hand to be silent, he described to them how the Lord had led him out of the prison. And he said, 'Report these things to James and the brethren.' Then he left and went to another place." Thus, at this time, James, the half brother of Jesus, became the primary leader of the Jerusalem church, and thus, the letter of James would have probably been written after A.D. 44. Since there is no indication in James' letter of any conflict between the Jewish Christians, to which this letter is addressed, and the Gentile Christians over the Gentile Christians following the law of Moses, it appears that this letter was written prior to the Council of Jerusalem in A.D. 49. Thus allowing three years for the leadership of James to be generally recognized, this letter was probably written about A.D. 47.   In A.D. 49 the leadership of James is clearly indicated in that he made the final judgment at the Council of Jerusalem (Acts 15:19).

As a letter addressed to the Jewish Christian Church, James was probably originally written by James in Aramaic and only later translated into Greek. This would explain why the letter was not widely circulated among the Gentile Christian Churches that ultimately became dominant within the Church. If it had not been widely circulated within the Gentile Christian Churches, this would explain why it was not quoted by the early writers of the Gentile church and therefore why its authenticity was doubted. However, the church fathers, who were in the best position to judge the authenticity of this letter, ultimately accepted it into the canon of the New Testament as the work of the Apostle James, the half brother of Jesus.

1 Peter

1 Peter 1:1 says, "Peter, an apostle of Jesus Christ, to those who reside as aliens, scattered throughout Pontus, Galatia, Cappadocia, Asia, and Bithynia, who are chosen-" Thus the Apostle Peter is identified as the author of this letter. Eusebius, ibid., 3.3.1, page 108, says, "Of Peter one epistle, known as his first, is accepted, and this the early fathers quote freely, as undoubtedly genuine, in their own writings" Thus the Apostle Peter seems to have been recognized as the author of this letter from the earliest times. 1 Peter 5:12-13 says:

> Through Silvanus, our faithful brother (for so I regard him), I have written to you briefly, exhorting and testifying that this is the true grace of God. Stand firm in it! She who is in Babylon, chosen together with you, sends you greetings, and so does my son, Mark.

Peter says that he is writing to the Greek speaking churches through Silvanus, probably the Silas that was the companion of Paul and a former member of the Jerusalem Church sent to Antioch, Syria after the Council of Jerusalem, who wrote the letter at Peter's dictation. This could explain the classical form of the Greek of this letter which was the product of an uneducated fisherman from Galilee. Of course God could have given Peter the ability to write this letter without assistance, but instead Silvanus was chosen to do the writing. The Mark that is mentioned is probably John Mark, who was also a companion of Paul. Peter had known Mark from the early days of the Christian Church in Jerusalem.

The use of the name Babylon is probably a veiled reference to the city of Rome. Revelation 17:5 speaks of the woman called Babylon and Revelation 17:18 says, "The woman whom you saw is the great city, which reigns over the kings of the earth." Thus, clearly the Babylon of Revelation 17 was the city of Rome. Therefore, probably the city from which greetings are sent in 1 Peter 5:13 is also Rome. It is apparently a time that requires secrecy in correspondence. Both Silas and Mark are present in Rome at the time 1 Peter is written and we have previously noted that 2 Timothy 4:11 says, "Only Luke is with me. Pick up Mark and bring him with you, for he is useful to me for service." Thus 1 Peter was probably written by the Apostle Peter from Rome after the arrival of Mark near the end of A.D. 63.

2 Peter

2 Peter 1:1 says, "Simon Peter, a bond-servant and apostle of Jesus Christ, to those who have received a faith of the same kind as ours, by the righteousness of our God and Savior, Jesus Christ:" Thus, this letter identifies its author as the Apostle Peter. Eusebius, ibid,. 3.3.1, page 108, says, "But the second Petrine epistle we have been taught to regard as uncanonical; many, however, have thought it valuable and have honored it with a place among the other Scriptures." 2 Peter was among the most disputed of the books that ultimately became a part of the New Testament canon. One of the reasons that this book was questioned was because of the difference in the style of the Greek used in 1 Peter and 2 Peter. However, since

Peter indicated that he wrote 1 Peter through Silvanus, there is no reason that Peter could not have had a different writer for 2 Peter, which could account for the difference in style between the two letters. The impending persecution that seems to cast a shadow over 1 Peter has now arrived so that 2 Peter 1:13-14 says:

> I consider it right, as long as I am in this earthly dwelling, to stir you up by way of reminder, knowing that the laying aside of my earthly dwelling is imminent, as also our Lord Jesus Christ has made clear to me.

In 2 Peter no names are mentioned, again indicating a need for even greater secrecy.

2 Peter 3:1-2 says, "This is now, beloved, the second letter I am writing to you in which I am stirring up your sincere mind by way of reminder, that you should remember the words spoken beforehand by the holy prophets and the commandment of the Lord and Savior spoken by your apostles." If the first letter to which Peter is referring is 1 Peter, then the destination of 2 Peter is again the churches in northern Asia minor. At any rate the time seems to be shortly after the writing of 1 Peter probably early in A.D. 64. 2 Peter 3:15-16 says:

> Therefore, beloved, since you look for these things, be diligent to be found by Him in peace, spotless and blameless, and regard the patience of our Lord as salvation; just as also our beloved brother Paul, according to the wisdom given him, wrote to you, as also in all his letters, speaking in them of these things, in which are some things hard to understand, which the untaught and unstable distort, as they do also the rest of the Scriptures, to their own destruction.

The reference to Paul speaking to them of these things seems to imply that the Apostle Paul is still alive when 2 Peter was written. Since it was shown that Paul was probably executed by Nero prior to the burning of Rome in July A.D. 64, this again would indicate that 2 Peter was written early in A.D. 64.

1 John, 2 John & 3 John

The author of these three letters are not identified in any of these letters. Eusebius, ibid., 3.24.16, page 134, speaking of the Apostle John says, "Of John's writings, besides the gospel, the first of the epistles has been accepted as unquestionably his by scholars both of the present and of a much earlier period: the other two are disputed." However, ultimately, all three of these letters were accepted into the canon of the New Testament on the basis that they were all the work of the Apostle John.

John probably wrote these three letters after he wrote his Gospel and before he wrote the Revelation. These letters are closely connected with John's Gospel and were probably all written during A.D. 65, the same year that John wrote his Gospel.

Jude

Clement of Alexandria (c A.D. 150-215) in fragments from Cassiodorus recorded in *The Ante-Nicene Fathers,* Volume 2, page 573, says, "Jude, who wrote the Catholic Epistle, the brother of the son of Joseph, and very religious, whilst knowing the near relationship of the Lord, yet did not say that he himself was His brother. But what said he? 'Jude, a servant of Jesus Christ,' - of Him as Lord, but 'the brother of James.'" Thus Clement of Alexandria, citing the first verse of Jude, identifies the author of Jude as Jude, the half brother of Jesus. When James, also the half brother of Jesus, was executed by the Jews in A.D. 62, his brother Jude would be the natural choice to replace James as the head of the Christian Church at Jerusalem. Thus, this letter would probably be dated after A.D. 62.

Jude reflects the same theme that was discussed in the second chapter of 2 Peter. 2 Peter 2:1 says, "But false prophets also arose among the people, just as there will also be false teachers among you, who will secretly introduce destructive heresies, even denying the Master who bought them, bringing swift destruction upon themselves." Thus, 2 Peter speaks of future false teachers. However, Jude 1:4 says, "For certain persons have crept in unnoticed, those who were long beforehand marked out for this condemnation, ungodly persons who turn the grace of our God into licentiousness and deny our only Master and Lord, Jesus Christ." Thus, in Jude the false teachers have already crept in, and thus, Jude is describing a later condition than 2 Peter, which was dated in A.D. 64.

Some scholars have claimed that 2 Peter was based on Jude. However, Jude 17-18 says:

> But you, beloved, ought to remember the words that were spoken beforehand by the apostles of our Lord Jesus Christ, that they were saying to you, "In the last time there will be mockers, following after their own ungodly lusts."

Thus, Jude is quoting 2 Peter, not 2 Peter quoting Jude. Note also that Jude is testifying that 2 Peter is the word of the apostles of our Lord Jesus Christ. There is no special mention of persecution of the church in Judea; therefore the persecution which followed the burning of Rome had not yet reached the churches of the east which would suggest a date of A.D. 65, the same year that John's letters were probably written.

Revelation

Revelation 1:4a says, "John to the seven churches that are in Asia:" and Revelation 1:9 says "I, John, your brother and fellow partaker in the tribulation and kingdom and perseverance which are in Jesus, was on the island called Patmos because of the word of God and the testimony of Jesus." Thus, the author of Revelation is identified as John and the place of the revelation was identified as the island of Patmos off the coast of the Roman Province of Asia (see Figure 8.1). Patmos was probably also the place of composition of the book. The destination of this book was the seven churches of Asia. These seven churches are further identified in Revelation 1:10-11 which says, "I was in the Spirit on the Lord's day, and I heard behind me a loud voice like the sound of a trumpet, saying, 'Write in a book what you see, and send it to the seven churches: to Ephesus and to Smyrna and to Pergamum and to Thyatira and to Sardis and to Philadelphia and to Laodicea.'"

Origen (c185-254), in his commentary on the Gospel of John, Book V preserved by Eusebius in *The History of the Church, 6.25.10, page 265, says:*

> Need I say anything about the man who leant back on Jesus' breast, John? He left a single gospel, though he confessed that he could write so many that the whole world would not hold them. He also wrote the Revelation, but was ordered to remain silent and not write the utterances of the seven thunders."

The Apostle John's authorship of the Revelation was also attested by Justin Martyr (c100-165), Clement of Alexandria (c150-215) and Hippolytus (c170-235).

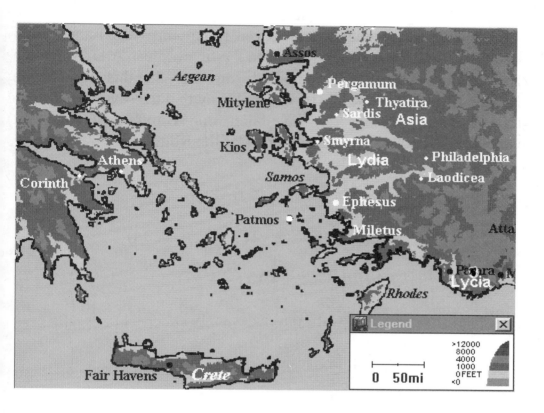

Seven Churches of Asia
Island of Patmos
Figure 8.1

Revelation 17:3, in describing John's vision of the great harlot, says, "And he carried me away in the Spirit into a wilderness; and I saw a woman sitting on a scarlet beast, full of blasphemous names, having seven heads and ten horns." Then in Revelation 17:9-10 the angel interpreting this vision says, "Here is the mind which has wisdom. The seven heads are seven mountains on which the woman sits, and they are seven kings; five have fallen, one is, the other has not yet come; and when he comes, he must remain a little while." Then Revelation 17:18 says, "The woman whom you saw is the great city, which reigns over the kings of the earth." Thus the women in the vision is a city that sits on seven mountains (hills) and which reigns over the kings of the world. In the first century A.D., when the Revelation was written, there could be no doubt that this city must be Rome. But Revelation 17:10 goes on to say that the seven heads also represents "seven kings, five have fallen, one is, and the other has not yet come." The first seven emperors of the Roman empire were:

1. Julius Caesar (46-44 B.C.)

2. Augustus Caesar (27 B.C. -A.D. 14)

3. Tiberius Caesar (A.D. 14-37)

4. Gaius (Caligula) Caesar (A.D. 37-41)

5. Claudius Caesar (A.D. 41-54)

6. Nero Caesar (A.D. 54-68)

7. Galba Caesar (A.D. 68-69)

At the time that John received his vision, five of the kings associated with the women seated on the beast (Rome) had fallen and one is. Thus the king of the Roman empire at the time John received his vision was the sixth king, Nero. Nero was emperor from AD 54 to AD 68; however, Revelation was written during a time of persecution of the church, which did not begin until after the burning of Rome which took place in July A.D. 64. It would have taken a little while before the persecution of Christ's Church reached the provinces, so Revelation was probably written about A.D. 66. Nero Caesar committed suicide on June 9, A.D. 68 (Julian). The Roman emperor

Nero was succeeded by Galba who was assassinated on January 15, A.D. 69(Julian), after reigning for only 6 months, which fulfilled the last part of Revelation 17:10 (the other has not yet come; but when he does come, he must remain for a little while). Thus Revelation 17:10 seems to indicate that John received his vision about A.D. 66.

However, Eusebius, ibid., 5.8.9, page 211, cites Irenaeus (cA..D.. 130-200), who says concerning the book of Revelation:

> "Such then is the case: this number is found in all good and early copies and confirmed by the very people who saw John face to face, and reason teaches us that the number of the Beast's name is shown according to Greek numerical usage by the letters in it....I for one dare not risk making any positive assertion regarding the name of the antichrist. Had there been a need for his name to be openly announced at the present time, it would have been stated by the one who saw the revelation. For it was not seen along time back, but almost in my own lifetime, at the end of Domitian's reign.

Thus, Irenaeus believed that John's revelation took place near the end of the reign of Domitian, which ended in A.D. 96. However, Irenaeus was writing some eighty years after the reign of Domitian, and he doesn't give any specific source for this information. Tradition indicates that the Apostle John lived to a great age and may have been martyred during the persecution under Domitian. Therefore, Irenaeus may have assumed that the revelation also came during the reign of Domitian. However, that assumption seems to contradict Chapter 17 of Revelation that indicates that John received his revelation during the reign of the sixth king of Rome, Nero. Who wrote the books of the New Testament was much more important than when they were written. Therefore, knowledge of the authors of the New Testament books was much more carefully preserved than information concerning exactly when they were written. Thus, Irenaeus could have correct information concerning who wrote the Revelation, but may have been mistaken as to when it was written.

Table 8.1 lists the books of the New Testament in the order that they appear in our Bible together with the author and date of completion of each book. Table 8.2 lists the books of the New Testament in the order that they were written together with the author and date of completion of each book.

We have now identified the authors and determined the year of completion of each of the books of the New Testament and have come to the end of this volume. However, this is more of a beginning rather than the end of a journey. Hopefully, many will continue the task of refining the results presented here, recognizing that the New Testament, as the Word of God, is a limitless storehouse of knowledge to guide men and women in this life and in the eternity beyond.

Table 8.1
Author & Year of Completion
For the New Testament Books

Book	Author	Year Completed
Matthew	Apostle Matthew	AD 33a AD 49b
Mark	Mark - Companion of Peter	AD 54
Luke	Luke - Companion of Paul	AD 61
John	Apostle John	AD 65
Acts	Luke - Companion of Paul	AD 62
Romans	Apostle Paul	AD 57
1 Corinthians	Apostle Paul	AD 55
2 Corinthians	Apostle Paul	AD 56
Galatians	Apostle Paul	AD 49
Ephesians	Apostle Paul	AD 58
Philippians	Apostle Paul	AD 63
Colossians	Apostle Paul	AD 58
1 Thessalonians	Apostle Paul	AD 50
2 Thessalonians	Apostle Paul	AD 51
1 Timothy	Apostle Paul	AD 55
2 Timothy	Apostle Paul	AD 63
Titus	Apostle Paul	AD 57
Philemon	Apostle Paul	AD 58
Hebrews	Apostle Paul	AD 64a
James	James - Jesus' Half Brother	AD 47a
1 Peter	Apostle Peter	AD 63
2 Peter	Apostle Peter	AD 64
1 John	Apostle John	AD 65
2 John	Apostle John	AD 65
3 John	Apostle John	AD 65
Jude	Jude - Jesus' Half Brother	AD 65
Revelation	Apostle John	AD 66

a - Aramaic Version

b - Greek Version

Table 8.2 Author & Year of Completion For the New Testament Books Ordered By Year of Completion		
Book	**Author**	**Year Completed**
Matthew	Apostle Matthew	AD 33a AD 49b
James	James - Jesus' Half Brother	AD 47a
Galatians	Apostle Paul	AD 49
1 Thessalonians	Apostle Paul	AD 50
2 Thessalonians	Apostle Paul	AD 51
Mark	Mark - Companion of Peter	AD 54
1 Corinthians	Apostle Paul	AD 55
1 Timothy	Apostle Paul	AD 55
2 Corinthians	Apostle Paul	AD 56
Titus	Apostle Paul	AD 57
Romans	Apostle Paul	AD 57
Ephesians	Apostle Paul	AD 58
Colossians	Apostle Paul	AD 58
Philemon	Apostle Paul	AD 58
Luke	Luke - Companion of Paul	AD 61
Acts	Luke - Companion of Paul	AD 62
Philippians	Apostle Paul	AD 63
2 Timothy	Apostle Paul	AD 63
1 Peter	Apostle Peter	AD 63
Hebrews	Apostle Paul	AD 64a
2 Peter	Apostle Peter	AD 64
John	Apostle John	AD 65
1 John	Apostle John	AD 65
2 John	Apostle John	AD 65
3 John	Apostle John	AD 65
Jude	Jude - Jesus' Half Brother	AD 65
Revelation	Apostle John	AD 66

a - Aramaic Version

b - Greek Version

Appendix A

Conversion From the Julian
to the Gregorian Calendar

In many references ancient dates are given in terms of the Julian Calendar, introduced under Julius Caesar in 46 B.C.; however, in this book the Gregorian Calendar, introduced under Pope Gregory XIII in A.D. 1582, is used since this is the calendar in common use today. The Julian Calendar is based on a 365¼ day year with every fourth year a leap year with 366 days. However, this calendar resulted in a year which averaged about 11¼ minutes too long compared to the actual length of the year as determined by the earth's revolution around the sun so that in 128 years the cumulative error was about 24 hours or one day. In order to correct for this error, the Gregorian Calendar was introduced which was just like the Julian Calendar except that centesimal years (years ending in 00) are made leap years only if they are evenly divisible by 400. Thus under the Gregorian Calendar A.D. 1300, A.D. 1400 and A.D. 1500 would be regular years with 365 days and A.D. 1600 would be a leap year with 366 days.

The Gregorian Calendar was not adopted in the United States, then a British colony, until 1752. After the adoption of the Gregorian Calendar it has been customary to restate the dates of events that took place under the Julian Calendar to their corresponding date under the

Gregorian Calendar. Thus, George Washington was born on February 11 according to the Julian calendar; however, his birthday is now celebrated on February 22 according to the Gregorian Calendar. Thus, in dating the events of the New Testament, I have used the Gregorian Calendar and converted any dates given in terms of the Julian Calendar to the Gregorian Calendar since that is the calendar we use today.

In order to facilitate this conversion, I have supplied Table 1 of this appendix, which gives the correction to be applied to the Julian date to obtain the Gregorian date. From this table we can see that in A.D. 1752 when the United States adopted the Gregorian Calendar, it was necessary to add 11 days to the Julian date to obtain the Gregorian date. Thus, George Washington's birthday, which was February 11 (Julian), became February 22 (Gregorian). When the Gregorian Calendar was adopted in the United States, the day following September 2, 1752 (Julian) was designated September 14, 1752 (Gregorian).

Table 1 is easily constructed since changes in the correction factor only occur at centesimal years (years ending in 00), which are not evenly divisible by 400 and then the correction factor increases by one. Table 1 extends from 2101 B.C. to A.D. 2100 so that almost any Julian dates encountered can be converted. Note that since there is no year zero in either the Julian or the Gregorian calendars, in order that the usual rule for determining leap years can be applied to B.C. years, these years must be converted to astronomical years by subtracting the B.C. year number from one. Thus the year 1 B.C. becomes (1-1 BC) or the astronomical year 0, which is a leap year since it is evenly divisible by 4 and 400. The next leap year would be 5 B.C. or astronomical year -4 (1-5 BC). Also note that for New Testament times the correction factor for converting Julian dates into Gregorian dates is minus two days. Thus Julius Caesar was assassinated on March 15, 44 B.C. (Julian) or March 13, 44 B.C. (Gregorian).

Table 1 Correction Factor to be Applied to Julian Dated To Obtain the Corresponding Gregorian Date	
Julian Date	Correction Factor (Days)
February 29, 2101 B.C. to February 28, 1901 B.C.	-17
February 29, 1901 B.C. to February 28, 1801 B.C.	-16
February 29, 1801 B.C. to February 28, 1701 B.C.	-15
February 29, 1701 B.C. to February 28, 1501 B.C.	-14
February 29, 1501 B.C. to February 28, 1401 B.C.	-13
February 29, 1401 B.C. to February 28, 1301 B.C.	-12
February 29, 1301 B.C. to February 28, 1101 B.C.	-11
February 29, 1101 B.C. to February 28, 1001 B.C.	-10
February 29, 1001 B.C. to February 28, 901 B.C.	-9
February 29, 901 B.C. to February 28, 701 B.C.	-8
February 29, 701 B.C. to February 28, 601 B.C.	-7
February 29, 601 B.C. to February 28, 501 B.C.	-6
February 29, 501 B.C. to February 28, 301 B.C.	-5
February 29, 301 B.C. to February 28, 201 B.C.	-4
February 29, 201 B.C. to February 28, 101 B.C.	-3
February 29, 101 B.C. to February 28, A.D. 100.	-2
February 29, A.D. 100 to February 28, A.D. 200	-1
February 29, A.D. 200 to February 28, A.D. 300	0
February 29, A.D. 300 to February 28, A.D. 500	+1
February 29, A.D. 500 to February 28, A.D. 600	+2
February 29, A.D. 600 to February 28, A.D. 700	+3
February 29, A.D. 700 to February 28, A.D. 900	+4
February 29, A.D. 900 to February 28, A.D. 1000	+5
February 29, A.D. 1000 to February 28, A.D. 1100	+6
February 29, A.D. 1100 to February 28, A.D. 1300	+7
February 29, A.D. 1300 to February 28, A.D. 1400	+8
February 29, A.D. 1400 to February 28, A.D. 1500	+9
February 29, A.D. 1500 to February 28, A.D. 1700	+10
February 29, A.D. 1700 to February 28, A.D. 1800	+11
February 29, A.D. 1800 to February 28, A.D. 1900	+12
February 29, A.D. 1900 to February 28, A.D. 2100	+13

Appendix B

Julian Day Number*

To facilitate some calendar calculations the Julian Day Number was introduced by Sir John Herschel in 1849 as a refinement of a system proposed by J. J. Scaliger in 1583. The Julian Day Number for a given date is the number of days that separates that date, using the Julian Calendar, from January 1, 4713 B.C. (Julian). The Julian Day Number is defined in terms of the Julian Calendar to simplify the construction of the tables used in its calculation; however, these tables can also be used in the determination of the Julian Day Number for Gregorian dates by applying the correction factors given in Appendix A.

The Julian Day Numbers are useful in determining the number of days between any two dates which is found by simply calculating the difference between the Julian Day Numbers for the two dates. Also, if the Julian Day Number of a given date is divided by 7, the fractional remainder of the answer indicates the day of the week. Thus we have the following relationship:

Fractional Remainder When Julian Day Number is ÷ 7	0	.14	.28	.42	.56	.71	.85
Day of the Week	Mon	Tue	Wed	Thu	Fri	Sat	Sun

* The method used in this appendix for determining the Julian Day Number is based on the method given by O. L. Harvey on page 3 of *Calendar Conversion by Way of the Julian Day Number,* American Philosophical Society, Independence Square, Philadelphia 1983.

To better understand the Julian Day Number we shall compute the Julian Day Number for January 1, 1996 (Gregorian) without using the tables of this appendix. First we must convert this date to a Julian date by using the correction factors from Appendix A. Since the correction factors of Appendix A are designed for the conversion of Julian dates to Gregorian dates, we must change the sign of the correction factor to convert Gregorian dates to Julian dates. Thus, using Appendix A, the tabulated value is + 13 so the correction factor is - 13. Therefore, January 1, 1996 (Gregorian) becomes December 19, 1995 (Julian). Sir Herschel defined the fixed starting point on his counting of days as noon January 1, 4713 B.C. Therefore, January 1, 4713 B.C. (Julian) is only a half day and January 2, 4713 B.C. (Julian) is the first full day and January 1, 4713 B.C. (Julian) is the zero day.

In counting the number of days that have elapsed, it will be convenient to introduce the astronomical year. For A.D. years the astronomical year number is the same as the A.D. year number, but for B.C. years, the astronomical year is defined as one minus the B.C. year. Thus 4713 B.C. is the astronomical year 1- 4713 = - 4712. Using the astronomical year will simplify our counting of years since the astronomical year corresponding to 1 B.C. equal 1-1 = 0. Thus we have a year zero. Also, the rule that a year is a leap year if it is exactly divisible by 4 holds for all years if astronomical years are used, while this rule only hold for A.D. years for our regular calendar. Thus year 4713 B.C. is a leap year since - 4712 ÷ 4 = -1178. However, since January 2, 4713 is day one under Sir Herschel's counting, there will only be 365 days in this first year even though it is a leap year.

To compute the number of days that elapsed from January 1, 4713 B.C. (Julian) until December 19, 1995 (Julian), we shall first determine the number of complete years that have elapsed and multiply the number of regular years by 365 and multiply the number of leap years by 366. Prior to astronomical year zero (1 B.C.) until

4713 B.C., there are 4712 ÷ 4 = 1178 leap years and 4712 - 1178 = 3534 regular years. However, because of Herschel's definition, astronomical year -4712 (4713 B.C.) although a leap year, only adds 365 days to our count. Thus:

Before Astronomical Year 0 (1 B.C.)

$$
\begin{array}{rcl}
\text{For year } -4712 & = & 365 \text{ days} \\
366 \times 1177 & = & 430{,}782 \text{ days} \\
365 \times 3534 & = & 1{,}289{,}910 \text{ days}
\end{array}
$$

For Astronomical Year 0 (1 B.C.)

$$
\text{Year } 0 \qquad = \qquad 366 \text{ days}
$$

After Astronomical Year 0 (1 B.C.)

$$
\begin{array}{rcl}
366 \times 498 & = & 182{,}268 \text{ days} \\
365 \times 1494 & = & 545.310 \text{ days} \\
\text{For } 1993 \ \& \ 1994 & = & 730 \text{ days} \\
\text{For } 1995 & = & \underline{353 \text{ days}}
\end{array}
$$

Julian Day Number   2,450,084 days

The years 1993, 1994 and 1995 were not leap years, but 1992 was a leap year. Therefore, after 1 B.C. there were 1992 ÷ 4 = 498 leap years and 1992 - 498 = 1494 regular years. In 1995 from January 1 (Julian) until December 19 (Julian) , there were 353 days.

Thus the Julian Day Number for December 19, 1995 (Julian) and for January 1, 1996 (Gregorian) is 2,450, 084. If this date is divided by 7, the fractional remainder is zero, which according to the table above indicates that January 1, 1996 (Gregorian) fell on a Monday which agrees with the calendar for 1996.

The direct computation of the Julian Day Number is a simple, but tedious task; however, in 1983 O. L. Harvey introduced a table similar to Table 1 of this appendix, which greatly simplifies this computation. There are five steps in the computation of the Julian Day Number using Table 1:

1. Convert the year of the given date to the astronomical year by subtracting the year number from one if a B.C. year. For A.D. years, the astronomical and the A.D. year number are the same.

2. Convert the astronomical year to a Scaliger Year (SY) by adding 4712 to the astronomical year. Thus SY for January 1, 1996 would be $1996 + 4712 = 6708$.

3 If the month is January or February, subtract 1 from SY.

4. From Table 1 record the number of days for entries of SY that total the required Scaliger year. Thus for SY = 6707 (reduced by 1 since the month is January) the days for SY = 6000, SY = 700 and SY = 7 are recorded.

5. Also , from Table 1, the days for the month of the given date and the day of the month of the given date are recorded. If the date is a Gregorian date, record the correction factor from Table 1 of Appendix A with the opposite sign. The sum of all these days is the Julian Day Number of the given date.

Thus for January 1, 1996 (Gregorian) we have:

$$
\begin{array}{rr}
 & 1996 \text{ (astronomical year)} \\
 & +\underline{4712} \\
SY = & 6708 \\
\text{month Jan.} & \underline{-1} \\
 & 6707
\end{array}
$$

$$6000 = 2,191,559$$
$$700 = 255,675$$
$$7 = 2,556$$
$$\text{Jan.} = 306$$
$$1 = 1$$
$$\text{Gregorian Correction G} = \underline{-13}$$

Julian Day Number   2,450,084

This is the same Julian Day Number for this date that we obtained directly without using Table 1.

As a second example of the use of Table 1, consider the date of the destruction of the First Temple on the seventh day of the fifth Jewish month (2 Kings 25:8) generally believed to be in 587 B.C. From Goldstine's Tables, the first day of the fifth month of 587 B.C. (astronomical year -586) would be July 19 (Julian), the day following the new moon. Thus the seventh day of that month would begin on July 25 and the daylight hours of that Jewish day would be July 26, 587 B.C. (Julian).

The Julian Day Number for July 26, 587 B.C. (Julian) would be:

$$- 586 \text{ (astronomical year)}$$
$$+\underline{4712}$$
$$4126$$
$$4000 = 1,461,059$$
$$100 = 36,525$$
$$26 = 9,496$$
$$\text{July} = 122$$
$$26 = \underline{26}$$

Julian Day Number = 1,507,228

Thus the Julian Day Number of July 26, 587 B.C. (Julian) is 1,507,228.

Table 1							
Table for Computing Julian Day Number							
SY	Days	SY	Days	SY	Days	Months	Days
8000	2,922,059	77	28,124	38	13,879	Mar	0
7000	2,556,809	76	27,759	37	13,514	Apr	31
6000	2,191,559	75	27,363	36	13,149	May	61
5000	1,826,309	74	27,028	35	12,783	Jun	92
4000	1,461,059	73	26,663	34	12,418	July	122
3000	1,095,809	72	26,298	33	12,053	Aug	153
2000	730,559	71	25,932	32	11,688	Sept	184
1000	365.250	70	25,567	31	11,322	Oct	214
900	328,725	69	25,202	30	10,957	Nov	245
800	292,200	68	24,837	29	10,592	Dec	275
700	255,675	67	24,471	28	10,227	Jan*	306
600	219,150	66	24,106	27	9,861	Feb*	337
500	182,625	65	23,741	26	9,496	*If January or	
400	146,100	64	23,376	25	9,131	February subtract	
300	109,575	63	23,010	24	8,766	1 year from the	
200	73,050	62	22,645	23	8,400	Scaliger Year	
100	36,525	61	22,280	22	8,035	(SY).	
99	36,159	60	21,915	21	7,670		
98	35,794	59	21,549	20	7,305		
97	35,429	58	21,184	19	6,939		
96	35,064	57	20,819	18	6,574		
95	34,698	56	20,454	17	6,209		
94	34,333	55	20,088	16	5,844		
93	33,968	54	19,723	15	5,478		
92	33,603	53	19,358	14	5,113		
91	33,237	52	18,993	13	4,748		
90	32,872	51	18,627	12	4,383		
89	32,507	50	18,262	11	4,017		
88	32,142	49	17,897	10	3,652		
87	31,776	48	17,532	9	3,287		
86	31,411	47	17,166	8	2,922		
85	31,046	46	16,801	7	2,556		
84	30,681	45	16,436	6	2,191		
83	30,315	44	16,071	5	1,826		
82	29,950	43	15,705	4	1,461		
81	29,585	42	15,340	3	1,095		
80	29,220	41	14,975	2	730		
79	28,854	40	14,610	1	365		
78	28,489	39	14,244	0	0		

Appendix C

Jewish Festivals

In this appendix all the Jewish festivals mentioned in the New Testament shall be discussed. All of these festivals were commanded by the Old Testament with the exception of the Feast of Dedication. Exodus 23:14-17 says:

> "Three times a year you shall celebrate a feast to Me. You shall observe the Feast of Unleavened Bread; for seven days you are to eat unleavened bread, as I commanded you, at the appointed time in the month Abib, for in it you came out of Egypt. And none shall appear before Me empty-handed. Also you shall observe the Feast of the Harvest of the first fruits of your labors from what you sow in the field; also the Feast of the Ingathering at the end of the year when you gather in the fruit of your labors from the field. Three times a year all your males shall appear before the Lord GOD."

Thus, the Old Testament Law required every male Jew to appear before the Lord in Jerusalem for the Feast of Passover (Feast of Unleavened Bread), the Feast of Pentecost (Feast of the Harvest), and for the Feast of Booths (Feast of the Ingathering). Jesus, being blameless under the Law, certainly attended each of these feasts during His earthly ministry. Associated with these major feasts there were certain specific observances. Associated with the Passover Feast were the sacrificing of the Passover lamb, the Passover meal, and the First Fruits offering. Associated with the Feast of Booths were the Day of Trumpets, the Day of Atonement and the Feast of Booths. There were many other festivals celebrated by the first century A.D. Jewish community, but in this appendix we shall only be concerned with those festivals that are mentioned in the New Testament.

Passover Sacrifice

Now the LORD said to Moses and Aaron in the land of Egypt, "This month shall be the beginning of months for you; it is to be the first month of the year to you. Speak to all the congregation of Israel, saying, 'On the tenth of this month they are each one to take a lamb for themselves, according to their fathers' households, a lamb for each household. Now if the household is too small for a lamb, then he and his neighbor nearest to his house are to take one according to the number of persons in them; according to what each man should eat, you are to divide the lamb. Your lamb shall be an unblemished male a year old; you may take it from the sheep or from the goats. You shall keep it until the fourteenth day of the same month, then the whole assembly of the congregation of Israel is to kill it at twilight.'" (Exodus 12:1-5)

While in captivity in Egypt the children of Israel probably used the Egyptian lunar calendar. However, the first month of the Egyptian calendar was in the summer, corresponding to the time the

Nile River overflowed its banks which was the basis for the Egyptian agricultural system. The exodus from Egypt took place in the spring (Passover time) which was probably in the eighth Egyptian month; however, God told Moses and Aaron that the lunar month of the Exodus was to be their first month of the year. At twilight on the fourteenth day of that month they were to sacrifice a lamb. Initially, the first month was called Abib, but after the Babylonian captivity the Jewish community changed the names of their calendar months to correspond to those used in the Babylonian calendar. Thus in New Testament times the first Jewish month was called Nisan.

The blood of the Passover lamb was applied to the lintel and the two doorposts of the houses of the children of Israel in Egypt to save them from the death of their firstborn. The shedding of Jesus' blood on the cross delivered us from spiritual death and separation from God. 1 Corinthians 5:7 says, "Clean out the old leaven so that you may be a new lump, just as you are in fact unleavened. For Christ our Passover also has been sacrificed."

Passover Feast

"'In the first month, on the fourteenth day of the month at twilight is the LORD'S Passover. Then on the fifteenth day of the same month there is the Feast of Unleavened Bread to the LORD; for seven days you shall eat unleavened bread. On the first day you shall have a holy convocation; you shall not do any laborious work. But for seven days you shall present an offering by fire to the LORD. On the seventh day is a holy convocation; you shall not do any laborious work.'" (Leviticus 23:5-8)

During the evening of the fifteenth day of the first Jewish month, the Passover Feast was eaten. Since the Jewish day began at sunset, the Passover Feast was eaten shortly after the beginning of the fifteenth day. However, Jesus celebrated His last Passover Feast of His earthly ministry during the evening of the fourteenth day of the first Jewish month because He was to die on the cross later that same Jewish day as the Lamb of God who takes away the sins of the world, as discussed in Chapter 2. The Passover Feast was celebrated for seven days, which, counting inclusively, would be Nisan 15 through 21. A convocation was held on both Nisan 15 and Nisan 21, and no laborious work could be done on either of these days. During Jesus' Last Supper as He celebrated the Passover Feast with His Apostles, Jesus used the bread and the third cup (the cup of redemption) of the Passover Feast to institute the Christian Communion Service. Thus, on the first day of the week, the New Testament Church gathered to break bread (celebrate the communion) in remembrance of Jesus' sacrificial death on a cross (Acts 20:7). Just as the Passover Feast commemorated God's deliverance of the children of Israel from slavery in Egypt, the Christian communion service commemorates Jesus' death on the cross that delivers us from slavery to sin.

First Fruits Offering

Then the LORD spoke to Moses, saying, "Speak to the sons of Israel and say to them, 'When you enter the land which I am going to give to you and reap its harvest, then you shall bring in the sheaf of the first fruits of your harvest to the priest. He shall wave the sheaf before the LORD for you to be accepted; on the day after the sabbath the priest shall wave it. Now on the day when you wave the sheaf, you shall offer a male lamb one year old without defect for a burnt offering to the LORD. Its grain offering shall then be two-tenths of an ephah of fine flour mixed with oil, an offering by fire to the LORD for a soothing aroma, with its drink offering, a fourth of a hin of wine. Until this same day, until you have brought in the offering of your God, you shall eat neither bread nor roasted grain nor new growth. It is to be a perpetual statute throughout your generations in all your dwelling places'" (Leviticus 23:9-14).

The First Fruits offering was the beginning of the harvest observances. Barley would have been the first of the grain harvest, and the first sheaf of this harvest was to be a wave offering on the day following the first Sabbath after the Passover Feast. Thus, in A.D. 33, when the Passover Feast was celebrated on Friday, April 1 (Gregorian), then the First Fruits Offering was celebrated on Sunday, April 3, which was the day Jesus arose from the grave, the first fruit of the Kingdom of God! Thus, the First Fruits Offering anticipated Jesus' resurrection by almost fifteen centuries, and Jesus fulfilled the Old Testament Law by being the first fruit of God's New Covenant. Later, under the leadership of the Pharisees, the Sabbath in Leviticus 23:11 was interpreted as the Passover Feast and the First Fruits Offering was celebrated on the day following the Passover Feast or on Nisan 16. However, while the Temple still stood, the First Fruits Offerings were brought on the day following the first Sabbath after the Passover Feast.

Pentecost

"'You shall also count for yourselves from the day after the sabbath, from the day when you brought in the sheaf of the wave offering; there shall be seven complete sabbaths. You shall count fifty days to the day after the seventh sabbath; then you shall present a new grain offering to the LORD.'" (Leviticus 23:15-16)

The Greek name Pentecost for this feast refers to the inclusive counting of fifty days from the day after the Sabbath, when the First Fruits Offering was made. This feast was also called the Feast of Weeks because seven Sabbaths and weeks were counted from the First Fruits Offering until the observance of Pentecost. The current Jewish calendar, which was introduced under the rabbinical patriarch Hillel II in A.D. 358/9, celebrated Pentecost fifty days after the day following the Passover Feast. Since under the current calculated Jewish calendar Nisan always has 30 days, Pentecost is celebrated on the fixed date of Sivan 6. Clearly this does not satisfy the requirements of Leviticus 23:16 which says, "You shall count fifty days to the day after the seventh Sabbath." If you counted fifty days starting with the day after the Passover Feast, you would not reach the day after the seventh Sabbath unless the Passover Feast happened to occur on a Sabbath. Hillel II's calendar was introduced shortly after the Christian Church gained political acceptance during the reign of Constantine I (A.D. 307-337). Possibly these changes were influenced by the fact that the Christian community was using the Jewish calendar to show that Jesus did in fact fulfil the Old Testament Law.

Pentecost commemorated the first harvest by the nation of Israel in the Promised Land, and this day was also the occasion of God's first harvest under the New Covenant when on Pentecost Sunday in A.D. 33 there were added three thousand souls to the Kingdom of God (Acts 2:41). The first Sunday following the Passover Feast would be the occasion of the First Fruits Offering and on the seventh Sunday after that offering Pentecost was celebrated.

Day of Trumpets

Again the LORD spoke to Moses, saying, "Speak to the sons of Israel, saying, 'In the seventh month on the first of the month you shall have a rest, a reminder by blowing of trumpets, a holy convocation. You shall not do any laborious work, but you shall present an offering by fire to the LORD'" (Leviticus 23:23-25).

The first day of the seventh month, Tishri 1, was celebrated as the Day of Trumpets with a holy convocation and a day of rest and featured the blowing of trumpets. But what did the Day of Trumpets commemorate? The Old Testament Scripture does not say, but we saw in Chapter 3 that Tishri 1 was probably the day of Jesus' birth! Thus again Jesus fulfilled and gave new meaning to the Old Testament Law. There may also be an allusion to Jesus' second coming in this Jewish festival. 1 Corinthians 15:51-52 says:

Behold, I tell you a mystery; we will not all sleep, but we will all be changed, in a moment, in the twinkling of an eye, at the last trumpet; for the trumpet will sound, and the dead will be raised imperishable, and we will be changed.

Day of Atonement

The LORD spoke to Moses, saying, "On exactly the tenth day of this seventh month is the day of atonement; it shall be a holy convocation for you, and you shall humble your souls and present an offering by fire to the LORD. You shall not do any work on this same day, for it is a day of atonement, to make atonement on your behalf before the LORD your God. If there is any person who will not humble himself on this same day, he shall be cut off from his people. As for any person who does any work on this same day, that person I will destroy from among his people. You shall do no work at all. It is

to be a perpetual statute throughout your generations in all your dwelling places. It is to be a sabbath of complete rest to you, and you shall humble your souls; on the ninth of the month at evening, from evening until evening you shall keep your sabbath."
(Leviticus 23:26-32)

The tenth day of the seventh month, Tishri 10, was the Day of Atonement when atonement was made for the sins of the children of Israel. It was only on the Day of Atonement that the high priest entered the Holy of Holies of the Temple to atone for his own sins and those of the nation of Israel. However, Christ's death on the cross atoned for the sins of all who would accept Him as Lord and Savior. Hebrew 9:24-28 says:

For Christ did not enter a holy place made with hands, a mere copy of the true one, but into heaven itself, now to appear in the presence of God for us; nor was it that He would offer Himself often, as the high priest enters the holy place year by year with blood that is not his own. Otherwise, He would have needed to suffer often since the foundation of the world; but now once at the consummation of the ages He has been manifested to put away sin by the sacrifice of Himself. And inasmuch as it is appointed for men to die once and after this comes judgment, so Christ also, having been offered once to bear the sins of many, will appear a second time for salvation without reference to sin, to those who eagerly await Him.

Jesus was God's atoning sacrifice that took away the sins of those who accept Him and are eagerly awaiting His return. Jesus died on Nisan 14 at the time that the Passover lamb was to be sacrificed;

however, Hebrews 9:27 makes reference to the judgment, which may indicate that the final fulfilment of the Day of Atonement on Tishri 10 may be the Judgment Day.

Feast of Booths

'"On exactly the fifteenth day of the seventh month, when you have gathered in the crops of the land, you shall celebrate the feast of the LORD for seven days, with a rest on the first day and a rest on the eighth day. Now on the first day you shall take for yourselves the foliage of beautiful trees, palm branches and boughs of leafy trees and willows of the brook, and you shall rejoice before the LORD your God for seven days. You shall thus celebrate it as a feast to the LORD for seven days in the year. It shall be a perpetual statute throughout your generations; you shall celebrate it in the seventh month. You shall live in booths for seven days; all the native-born in Israel shall live in booths, so that your generations may know that I had the sons of Israel live in booths when I brought them out from the land of Egypt. I am the LORD your God'" (Leviticus 23:39-43).

The Feast of Booths commemorates the time of the Exodus from Egypt. During this time in the history of the children of Israel God's presence was revealed by a pillar of cloud by day and a pillar of fire by night (Exodus 13:21). The final fulfilment of this feast day may be revealed in Revelation 21:22-23 which says, speaking of the New Jerusalem:

I saw no temple in it, for the Lord God the Almighty and the Lamb are its temple. And the city has no need of the sun or of the moon to shine on it, for the glory of God has illumined it, and its lamp is the Lamb.

Thus, the Feast of Booths may ultimately looks forward to the day when those whose names are written in the Lamb's Book of Life will join God and His only begotten Son, Jesus, in heaven.

Feast of Dedication (Hanukkah)

The Feast of Dedication commemorates the cleansing of the Temple by Judas Maccabaeus in 164 B.C. after it had been defiled by Antiochus Epiphanes, and therefore there is no Old Testament Scripture commanding this feast. However, John 10:22 indicates that Jesus did attend this feast. The feast was celebrated for eight days beginning on Kislev 25. 2 Maccabees 10:5-6, as translated by Sir Lancelot Brenton, says:

> Now upon the same day that the strangers profaned the temple, on the very same day it was cleansed again, even the five and twentieth of the same month which is Kislev. And they kept eight days with gladness, as in the feast of the tabernacles, remembering that not long afore they had held the feast of tabernacles when as they wandered in the mountains and dens like beasts.

Since this feast was not commanded by the Old Testament Law, it would not find fulfilment in the coming of the Messiah. The seven other festivals mentioned in the New Testament are listed in Table 1, together with their dates of celebration and the events they commemorate as indicated by both the Old and New Testaments.

Table 1 Jewish Festivals		
Jewish Festival Date	**To Commemorate Old Testament**	**To Commemorate New Testament**
Sacrifice of the Passover Lamb Nisan 14	The Lambs Whose Blood Saved Israel From the Death of Their First Born in Egypt (Exodus 12:1-14)	Jesus' Death on the Cross To Save Us From Spiritual Death (1 Corinthians 5:7)
Passover Feast Nisan 15	Israel's Deliverance From Slavery In Egypt (Exodus 12:15-20)	Our Deliverance From Slavery To Sin (Acts 3:11-26)
First Fruits Offering First Sunday After Passover	The Beginning of the First Grain Harvest In the Promised Land (Leviticus 23:9-14)	Jesus' Resurrection The First Fruit of the Kingdom of God (Acts 2:22-24)
Pentecost Eighth Sunday After Passover	The First Grain Harvest in the Promised Land (Leviticus 23:15-21)	The First Harvest of The Kingdom of God (Acts 2:41)
Day of Trumpets Tishri 1	Not Revealed (Leviticus 23:23-25)	Jesus Birth on Tishri 1, 2 B.C. (Luke 2:1-7)
Day of Atonement Tishri 10	Atonement For Sin (Leviticus 23:26-32)	Judgment Day (Revelation 20:11-15)
Feast of Booths Tishri 15-22	God's Dwelling With the Children of Israel During Their Wandering in the Wilderness (Leviticus 23:39-44)	Heaven (Revelation 21:9-27)

Appendix D

The Jewish Calendars
10 B.C. to A.D. 70

The Jewish calendars of this appendix are based on the tables prepared by Herman H. Goldstine, *New and Full Moons, 1001 B.C. to A.D. 1651,* published by the American Philosophical Society, Independence Square, Philadelphia 1973. However, since the calendars of this appendix are based on the Gregorian calendar while Goldstine used the Julian calendar in the construction of his tables, it was necessary to convert Goldstine's dates for the new moons to the Gregorian calendar. This was easily accomplished for the period 10 B.C. to A.D. 70 by subtracting two days from the dates given in Goldstine's tables (see Appendix A). Thus the date for the first new moon for astronomical year -9 (10 B.C.) is given in Goldstine's tables as January 5 (Julian) and the Gregorian date for this new moon would be January 3.

The Jewish month, during New Testament times, began with the Jewish day, when the thin crescent of the new moon was first sighted and reported to the Jewish court controlling the calendar by two credible witnesses. The new moon occurs at the exact instant when the celestial longitude of the sun and the moon are equal. Celestial longitude is the angular distance from the spring (vernal) equinox measured eastward along the ecliptic to the circle that passes through the celestial body at right angles to the ecliptic. At the time of the new moon, the moon would generally be above or below the sun because the orbit of the moon around the earth is tilted about 5° to the plane of the earth's orbit around the sun.   In those rare instances when the moon is in the plane of the earth's orbit around the sun at the time of the new moon, an eclipse of the sun occurs. In an eclipse of the sun, the moon blocks the light of the sun from reaching an area on the earth's surface.   It is possible for the moon to completely block the light from the sun for an area on the earth and thus produce a total eclipse of the sun because the moon's angular diameter is approximately the same as that of the sun (about 0.5 degrees). This near equality in the apparent size of the sun and the moon is due to the fact that although the sun's diameter is about 400 times as larger as that of the moon, it is also about 400 times as far away as the moon. At the instant of the new moon, none of the illumination of the moon would be visible from the earth (see Figure 1.1 of chapter 1) However, as the moon continues to revolve around the earth, a thin crescent of the illuminated side of the moon becomes visible.

The question of how soon after the instant of the new moon a crescent of the new moon becomes visible continues to be the subject of research. Of course, this visibility depends on the observation conditions and the visual acuity of the observer. This thin crescent would not be visible until the sun has set and the moon will be setting shortly thereafter, so the crescent of the new moon will only be visible for a few minutes immediately after sunset. The modern naked eye record for detecting the new moon is 15.4 hours after the instant of the new moon. This record was set by Julius Schmidt on September 14, 1871. Thus, if the instant of the new moon occurred shortly after midnight, it is possible that someone might see the less than eighteen hour old crescent moon at sunset on the same day that the new moon occurred; however, this would be an extremely rare sighting. Table 1 gives the number of hours from the instant of the occurrence of the new moon until sunset that day and until sunset the next day. The values are given for a 7:00 P.M. sunset, which would be in the month of June when the latest sunset occurs and for a 5:00 P.M. sunset, which would occur in the month of December when the earliest sunset occurs. Because the latitude of Jerusalem is less than that for most of the United States, the sunsets there are neither as late nor as early as those of most of the United States.

The moon is constantly moving along its orbit around the earth so that the longer the time from the instant of the new moon until the sunset, the greater will be the separation between the sun and the moon. Since a sighting of the crescent of a new moon less than 20 hours after the instant of the new moon is very rare, in general the crescent of the new moon will not be seen until after the sunset of the next day following the instant of the new moon. Therefore, in the construction of the calendars of this appendix, it is assumed that the sighting of the new moon would not occur until the day following the occurrence of the new moon. Thus, the crescent moon at sunset would be at least 18 hours old. Seeing an 18 hour old new moon would be a rare occurrence, but to establish the beginning of a new month only two creditable witnesses were required, and there would have probably been hundreds of thousands of observers since the entire population of Judea would have been interested in the establishment of the beginning of the new month. Also, much of the area of Judea was a desert with practically no air or light pollution. However, in order that the uncertainty due to this factor can be evaluated on a case by case basis, the local Jerusalem time of each new moon is footnoted below the calendar. Bad observation conditions (e.g. cloudy weather over the entire area) might also preclude the seeing of the new moon at its proper time. However, such conditions would only cause a one day error in the beginning of the month, and this error should be corrected in the determination of the start of the next month based on new observations. Thus, there would be no cumulative errors in the calendar.

Table 1 — Hours From New Moon Until Sunset				
Time of New Moon	June (Sunset 7:00 PM)		December (Sunset 5:00 PM)	
	Hours Until Sunset on Day of New Moon	Hours Until Sunset the Next Day	Hours Until Sunset on Day of New Moon	Hours Until Sunset the Next Day
Midnight	19	43	17	41
1:00 AM	18	42	16	40
2:00 AM	17	41	15	39
3:00 AM	16	40	14	38
4:00 AM	15	39	13	37
5:00 AM	14	38	12	36
6:00 AM	13	37	11	35
7:00 AM	12	36	10	34
8:00 AM	11	35	9	33
9:00 AM	10	34	8	32
10:00 AM	9	33	7	31
11:00 AM	8	32	6	30
Noon	7	31	5	29
1:00 PM	6	30	4	28
1:00 PM	5	29	3	27
3:00 PM	4	28	2	26
4:00 PM	3	27	1	25
5:00 PM	2	26		24
6:00 PM	1	25		23
7:00 PM		24		22
8:00 PM		23		21
9:00 PM		22		20
10:00 PM		21		19
11:00 PM		20		18

In his tables Goldstine gives the times of the new moons for an observer at Babylon. Therefore, it was necessary to adjust these times for the difference in longitude between Jerusalem and Babylon. This correction was -39 minutes. Thus, Goldstine's table gives the time of the new moon on January 13, A.D. 1 (Julian) as 14:09 hours (2:09 PM) Babylon local time. In the calendar of this appendix for A.D. 1, footnote a. indicates that this new moon occurred at 13:30 hours (1:30 PM) Jerusalem local time on January 11 (Gregorian). The date reflects the subtraction of two days to convert the Julian date given by Goldstine to the Gregorian date used in this appendix. The time correction of -39 minutes was obtained as follows:

The longitude of Jerusalem is 35.13 degrees east. Since 360 degrees of longitude equals 24 hours of time, one hour equals 15 degrees. Since Jerusalem is 35.13 degrees east of Greenwich, England, its local time would be 35.13 ÷ 15 = 2.34 hours or 2 hours and 21 minutes later than Greenwich local time. Thus when it is 2:21 P.M. at Jerusalem, it would be 12:00 noon at Greenwich. In Goldstein's tables Babylon is assumed to have a longitude of 45 degrees east; so Babylon local time would be 45 ÷ 15 = 3 hours later than Greenwich local time. Therefore, to convert the times of the new moons given in Goldstine's tables to Jerusalem local time, we must subtract 39 minutes (2^h21^m - 3^h00^m = - 39^m) from the times given in Goldstine's tables.

In the construction of the calendars of this appendix, it was also necessary to consider the introduction of a thirteenth month into the Jewish calendar periodically so that the seasons would occur at the proper time. Josephus, in *Antiquities,* 3.10.5(248), indicates that on the fourteenth day of the first Jewish month (Nisan) the sun must be in the constellation Aries. Thus, the position of the sun was determined at the close of the twelfth Jewish month, Adar. If the sun would reach the constellation Aries by the fourteenth of the next lunar month, then the next month would be the month of Nisan, the first month of a new year. However, if the sun would not yet reached the constellation Aries by the fourteenth of the next lunar month, then a thirteenth month, called Second Adar, was intercalated into the calendar for that Jewish year. In this case the new year would not begin until after the end of Second Adar.

The apparent path of the sun among the stars during the year, due to the earth's revolving around the sun, is called the ecliptic. The intersection of the ecliptic with the celestial equator as the sun moves north of the celestial equator is called the spring (vernal) equinox and the sun reaches this position about March 20 for the Gregorian calendar with some variation due to leap years. From 10 B.C. to A.D. 70, the position of the spring equinox was very near the western edge of the constellation Aries. Therefore, if the sun was in Aries on Nisan 1, then the Passover Feast on Nisan 15 would always be celebrated after the time when the sun reaches the spring equinox.

The fact that the Passover Feast was always celebrated after the time that the sun reached the spring equinox was used to establish the date on which Easter was celebrated. In A.D. 325 at the Council of Nicaea, it was ordained that Easter should be celebrated on the first Sunday after the first full moon following the spring equinox and this practice has continued until today. Thus, Easter can be celebrated as early as March 22 and as late as April 25.

Anatolius, a Bishop of Laodicea, traces the practice of starting the month of Nisan so that the Passover Feast will always be celebrated after the spring equinox back to the Hasmonean ruler of Judea, Judas Aristobulus I (died 105 B.C.). These writings of Bishop Anatolius were preserved by Eusebius in *The History of the Church*, 7.32.18, page 323.

Since the spring equinox was located near the western edge of the constellation Aries during the first century A.D., if the celestial longitude of the sun indicates that it has passed the spring equinox, then the sun would be in the constellation Aries. At the time of the new moon the celestial longitude of the sun and the moon are equal, and in his tables Goldstine gives the celestial longitudes of the new and full moons. Thus, by using this celestial longitude data for the full moons, it is possible to determine whether the sun had reached Aries by the fourteenth day of the next Jewish month and thus whether or not a thirteenth month must be intercalated into the calendar. This was the method used in the construction of the calendars of this appendix.

In the Talmud, Sanhedrin 11b, it is stated that their rabbis taught that a thirteenth month could be intercalated for three reasons: on account of the premature state of the corn crops (barley), the premature state of the fruit trees, or on account of the Tekufah. The Jewish year was divided into four tekufoth or seasons. The tekufah involved with the intercalation of the thirteenth month was the Tekufah of Nisan which began when the sun entered the constellation Aries. This section of the Talmud goes on to state that according to their rabbinical teaching, any two of these reasons can justify intercalation, but not one alone. However, this section of the Talmud also states that Rabban Simeon Gamaliel (probably the Gamaliel mentioned in Acts 5:34 & Acts 22:3) said that on account of the tekufah a thirteenth month could be intercalated. The question is then asked whether Gamaliel meant a month could be intercalated on the basis of the tekufah alone or that the tekufah would be one of two reasons and it is concluded that the question remains undecided.

Obviously, if the intercalation was based on the state of the crops rather than the astronomical phenomenon of the sun being in Aries, we could not determine when the intercalation took place. However, in general the crops advancement would follow the progression of the season as indicated by the position of the sun, so that an intercalation based on the position of the sun would insure the availability of the crops for the offerings. It should also be noted that the first fruits offering associated with the Passover Feast required only a few sheaths of barley which could probably be obtained from the Jericho area where the crops would be advanced several weeks beyond the crops around Jerusalem due to the much lower elevation of Jericho. Thus, Gamaliel's statement probably does mean that the intercalation was made on the basis of the tekufah alone and the lateness of the crops was probably used simply to explain the need for intercalating a thirteenth month to the people who might not understand the astronomical basis for the intercalation. However, the Sanhedrin court probably did retain the prerogative to intercalate or not which would introduce another source of uncertainty concerning the Jewish calendar of New Testament times.

In the following collection of calendars, the regular Gregorian calendars are given for each year from 10 B.C. to A.D. 70. Superimposed on these Gregorian calendars are the Jewish calendar for each year. The name and number of the Jewish month is indicated in parentheses under the Gregorian month. This Jewish month is the month of the Jewish day that begins on the first day of the Gregorian month. The Jewish day number is indicated in parentheses under the Gregorian day number. The Jewish day number indicates the Gregorian day on which that Jewish day begins. Since the Jewish day begins at sunset on one Gregorian day and ends at sunset on the next Gregorian day, each Jewish day occupies part of two Gregorian days. Therefore, it is important to remember that the Jewish day numbers recorded on these calendars appear on the Gregorian day when the Jewish day begins.

10 B.C.

January
(Tebeth 10)

S	M	T	W	T	F	S
		1	2	3	4	5
		(28)	(29)	(30a)	(1)	(2)
6	7	8	9	10	11	12
(3)	(4)	(5)	(6)	(7)	(8)	(9)
13	14	15	16	17	18	19
(10)	(11)	(12)	(13)	(14)	(15)	(16)
20	21	22	23	24	25	26
(17)	(18)	(19)	(20)	(21)	(22)	(23)
27	28	29	30	31		
(24)	(25)	(26)	(27)	(28)		

April
(Adar II 13)

S	M	T	W	T	F	S
		1	2	3	4	5	6
	(29d)	(1)	(2)	(3)	(4)	(5)
7	8	9	10	11	12	13
(6)	(7)	(8)	(9)	(10)	(11)	(12)
14	15	16	17	18	19	20
(13)	(14)	(15)	(16)	(17)	(18)	(19)
21	22	23	24	25	26	27
(20)	(21)	(22)	(23)	(24)	(25)	(26)
28	29	30				
(27)	(28)	(29e)				

February
(Shebat 11)

S	M	T	W	T	F	S
					1	2
					(29b)	(1)
3	4	5	6	7	8	9
(2)	(3)	(4)	(5)	(6)	(7)	(8)
10	11	12	13	14	15	16
(9)	(10)	(11)	(12)	(13)	(14)	(15)
17	18	19	20	21	22	23
(16)	(17)	(18)	(19)	(20)	(21)	(22)
24	25	26	27	28		
(23)	(24)	(25)	(26)	(27)		

May
(Iyyar 2)

S	M	T	W	T	F	S
			1	2	3	4
			(1)	(2)	(3)	(4)
5	6	7	8	9	10	11
(5)	(6)	(7)	(8)	(9)	(10)	(11)
12	13	14	15	16	17	18
(12)	(13)	(14)	(15)	(16)	(17)	(18)
19	20	21	22	23	24	25
(19)	(20)	(21)	(22)	(23)	(24)	(25)
26	27	28	29	30	31	
(26)	(27)	(28)	(29)	(30f)	(1)	

March
(Adar 12)

S	M	T	W	T	F	S
					1	2
					(28)	(29)
3	4	5	6	7	8	9
(30c)	(1)	(2)	(3)	(4)	(5)	(6)
10	11	12	13	14	15	16
(7)	(8)	(9)	(10)	(11)	(12)	(13)
17	18	19	20	21	22	23
(14)	(15)	(16)	(17)	(18)	(19)	(20)
24	25	26	27	28	29	30
(21)	(22)	(23)	(24)	(25)	(26)	(27)
31						
(28)						

June
(Sivan 3)

S	M	T	W	T	F	S
						1
						(2)
2	3	4	5	6	7	8
(3)	(4)	(5)	(6)	(7)	(8)	(9)
9	10	11	12	13	14	15
(10)	(11)	(12)	(13)	(14)	(15)	(16)
16	17	18	19	20	21	22
(17)	(18)	(19)	(20)	(21)	(22)	(23)
23	24	25	26	27	28	29
(24)	(25)	(26)	(27)	(28)	(29g)	(1)
30						
(2)						

Passover Lamb Sacrificed — Nisan 14
Feast of First Fruits — 1st Sunday after Nisan 15

Feast of Unleavened Bread — Nisan 15-21
Pentecost — 8th Sunday after Nisan 15

Time of New Moon (Jerusalem) — a23:33 b15:55 c4:58 d15:00 e22:56 f5:54 g12.53

10 B.C.

July
(Tammuz 4)

S	M	T	W	T	F	S
	1	2	3	4	5	6
	(3)	(4)	(5)	(6)	(7)	(8)
7	8	9	10	11	12	13
(9)	(10)	(11)	(12)	(13)	(14)	(15)
14	15	16	17	18	19	20
(16)	(17)	(18)	(19)	(20)	(21)	(22)
21	22	23	24	25	26	27
(23)	(24)	(25)	(26)	(27)	(28)	(29h)
28	29	30	31			
(1)	(2)	(3)	(4)			

August
(Ab 5)

S	M	T	W	T	F	S
				1	2	3
				(5)	(6)	(7)
4	5	6	7	8	9	10
(8)	(9)	(10)	(11)	(12)	(13)	(14)
11	12	13	14	15	16	17
(15)	(16)	(17)	(18)	(19)	(20)	(21)
18	19	20	21	22	23	24
(22)	(23)	(24)	(25)	(26)	(27)	(28)
25	26	27	28	29	30	31
(29)	(30i)	(1)	(2)	(3)	(4)	(5)

September
(Elul 6)

S	M	T	W	T	F	S
1	2	3	4	5	6	7
(6)	(7)	(8)	(9)	(10)	(11)	(12)
8	9	10	11	12	13	14
(13)	(14)	(15)	(16)	(17)	(18)	(19)
15	16	17	18	19	20	21
(20)	(21)	(22)	(23)	(24)	(25)	(26)
22	23	24	25	26	27	28
(27)	(28)	(29j)	(1)	(2)	(3)	(4)
29	30					
(5)	(6)					

October
(Tishri 7)

S	M	T	W	T	F	S
		1	2	3	4	5
		(7)	(8)	(9)	(10)	(11)
6	7	8	9	10	11	12
(12)	(13)	(14)	(15)	(16)	(17)	(18)
13	14	15	16	17	18	19
(19)	(20)	(21)	(22)	(23)	(24)	(25)
20	21	22	23	24	25	26
(26)	(27)	(28)	(29)	(30k)	(1)	(2)
27	28	29	30	31		
(3)	(4)	(5)	(6)	(7)		

November
(Marheshvan 8)

S	M	T	W	T	F	S
					1	2
					(8)	(9)
3	4	5	6	7	8	9
(10)	(11)	(12)	(13)	(14)	(15)	(16)
10	11	12	13	14	15	16
(17)	(18)	(19)	(20)	(21)	(22)	(23)
17	18	19	20	21	22	23
(24)	(25)	(26)	(27)	(28)	(29)	(30m)
24	25	26	27	28	29	30
(1)	(2)	(3)	(4)	(5)	(6)	(7)

December
(Kislev 9)

S	M	T	W	T	F	S
1	2	3	4	5	6	7
(8)	(9)	(10)	(11)	(12)	(13)	(14)
8	9	10	11	12	13	14
(15)	(16)	(17)	(18)	(19)	(20)	(21)
15	16	17	18	19	20	21
(22)	(23)	(24)	(25)	(26)	(27)	(28)
22	23	24	25	26	27	28
(29)	(30n)	(1)	(2)	(3)	(4)	(5)
29	30	31				
(6)	(7)	(8)				

Day of Trumpets — Tishri 1
Feast of Booths — Tishri 15-22

Day of Atonement — Tishri 10
Feast of Dedication — 8 days beginning Kislev 25

Time of the New Moon — h20:46   i6:23   j18:29   k9:37   m3:47   n23:38

9 B.C.

January
(Tebeth 10)

S	M	T	W	T	F	S
			1	2	3	4
			(9)	(10)	(11)	(12)
5	6	7	8	9	10	11
(13)	(14)	(15)	(16)	(17)	(18)	(19)
12	13	14	15	16	17	18
(20)	(21)	(22)	(23)	(24)	(25)	(26)
19	20	21	22	23	24	25
(27)	(28)	(29a)	(1)	(2)	(3)	(4)
26	27	28	29	30	31	
(5)	(6)	(7)	(8)	(9)	(10)	

April
(Nisan 1)

S	M	T	W	T	F	S
			1	2	3	4
			(11)	(12)	(13)	(14)
5	6	7	8	9	10	11
(15)	(16)	(17)	(18)	(19)	(20)	(21)
12	13	14	15	16	17	18
(22)	(23)	(24)	(25)	(26)	(27)	(28)
19	20	21	22	23	24	25
(29d)	(1)	(2)	(3)	(4)	(5)	(6)
26	27	28	29	30		
(7)	(8)	(9)	(10)	(11)		

February
(Shebat 11)

S	M	T	W	T	F	S
						1
						(11)
2	3	4	5	6	7	8
(12)	(13)	(14)	(15)	(16)	(17)	(18)
9	10	11	12	13	14	15
(19)	(20)	(21)	(22)	(23)	(24)	(25)
16	17	18	19	20	21	22
(26)	(27)	(28)	(29)	(30b)	(1)	(2)
23	24	25	26	27	28	29
(3)	(4)	(5)	(6)	(7)	(8)	(9)

May
(Iyyar 2)

S	M	T	W	T	F	S
					1	2
					(12)	(13)
3	4	5	6	7	8	9
(14)	(15)	(16)	(17)	(18)	(19)	(20)
10	11	12	13	14	15	16
(21)	(22)	(23)	(24)	(25)	(26)	(27)
17	18	19	20	21	22	23
(28)	(29e)	(1)	(2)	(3)	(4)	(5)
24	25	26	27	28	29	30
(6)	(7)	(8)	(9)	(10)	(11)	(12)
31						

March
(Adar 12)

S	M	T	W	T	F	S
1	2	3	4	5	6	7
(10)	(11)	(12)	(13)	(14)	(15)	(16)
8	9	10	11	12	13	14
(17)	(18)	(19)	(20)	(21)	(22)	(23)
15	16	17	18	19	20	21
(24)	(25)	(26)	(27)	(28)	(29)	(30c)
22	23	24	25	26	27	28
(1)	(2)	(3)	(4)	(5)	(6)	(7)
29	30	31				
(8)	(9)	(10)				

June
(Sivan 3)

S	M	T	W	T	F	S
	1	2	3	4	5	6
	(14)	(15)	(16)	(17)	(18)	(19)
7	8	9	10	11	12	13
(20)	(21)	(22)	(23)	(24)	(25)	(26)
14	15	16	17	18	19	20
(27)	(28)	(29)	(30f)	(1)	(2)	(3)
21	22	23	24	25	26	27
(4)	(5)	(6)	(7)	(8)	(9)	(10)
28	29	30				
(11)	(12)	(13)				

Passover Lamb Sacrificed — Nisan 14

Feast of First Fruits — 1st Sunday after Nisan 15

Feast of Unleavened Bread — Nisan 15-21

Pentecost — 8th Sunday after Nisan 15

Time of New Moon (Jerusalem) — a19:04 b12:04 c2:13 d13:25 e22:28 f6:11

9 B.C..

July
(Tammuz 4)

S	M	T	W	T	F	S
			1	2	3	4
			(14)	(15)	(16)	(17)
5	6	7	8	9	10	11
(18)	(19)	(20)	(21)	(22)	(23)	(24)
12	13	14	15	16	17	18
(25)	(26)	(27)	(28)	(29g)	(1)	(2)
19	20	21	22	23	24	25
(3)	(4)	(5)	(6)	(7)	(8)	(9)
26	27	28	29	30	31	
(10)	(11)	(12)	(13)	(14)	(15)	

October
(Tishri 7)

S	M	T	W	T	F	S
				1	2	3
				(18)	(19)	(20)
4	5	6	7	8	9	10
(21)	(22)	(23)	(24)	(25)	(26)	(27)
11	12	13	14	15	16	17
(28)	(29j)	(1)	(2)	(3)	(4)	(5)
18	19	20	21	22	23	24
(6)	(7)	(8)	(9)	(10)	(11)	(12)
25	26	27	28	29	30	31
(13)	(14)	(15)	(16)	(17)	(18)	(19)

August
(Ab 5)

S	M	T	W	T	F	S
						1
						(16)
2	3	4	5	6	7	8
(17)	(18)	(19)	(20)	(21)	(22)	(23)
9	10	11	12	13	14	15
(24)	(25)	(26)	(27)	(28)	(29h)	(1)
16	17	18	19	20	21	22
(2)	(3)	(4)	(5)	(6)	(7)	(8)
23	24	25	26	27	28	29
(9)	(10)	(11)	(12)	(13)	(14)	(15)
30	31					
(16)	(17)					

November
(Marheshvan 8)

S	M	T	W	T	F	S
1	2	3	4	5	6	7
(20)	(21)	(22)	(23)	(24)	(25)	(26)
8	9	10	11	12	13	14
(27)	(28)	(29)	(30k)	(1)	(2)	(3)
15	16	17	18	19	20	21
(4)	(5)	(6)	(7)	(8)	(9)	(10)
22	23	24	25	26	27	28
(11)	(12)	(13)	(14)	(15)	(16)	(17)
29	30					
(18)	(19)					

September
(Elul 6)

S	M	T	W	T	F	S
		1	2	3	4	5
		(18)	(19)	(20)	(21)	(22)
6	7	8	9	10	11	12
(23)	(24)	(25)	(26)	(27)	(28)	(29)
13	14	15	16	17	18	19
(30i)	(1)	(2)	(3)	(4)	(5)	(6)
20	21	22	23	24	25	26
(7)	(8)	(9)	(10)	(11)	(12)	(13)
27	28	29	30			
(14)	(15)	(16)	(17)			

December
(Kislev 9)

S	M	T	W	T	F	S
		1	2	3	4	5
		(20)	(21)	(22)	(23)	(24)
6	7	8	9	10	11	12
(25)	(26)	(27)	(28)	(29)	(30m)	(1)
13	14	15	16	17	18	19
(2)	(3)	(4)	(5)	(6)	(7)	(8)
20	21	22	23	24	25	26
(9)	(10)	(11)	(12)	(13)	(14)	(15)
27	28	29	30	31		
(16)	(17)	(18)	(19)	(20)		

Day of Trumpets — Tishri 1

Day of Atonement — Tishri 10

Feast of Booths — Tishri 15-22

Feast of Dedication — 8 days beginning Kislev 25

Time of the New Moon — g13:26 h21:05 i6:04 j17:18 k7:21 m0:04

8 B.C.

January (Tebeth 10)

S	M	T	W	T	F	S
					1	2
					(21)	(22)
3	4	5	6	7	8	9
(23)	(24)	(25)	(26)	(27)	(28)	(29a)
10	11	12	13	14	15	16
(1)	(2)	(3)	(4)	(5)	(6)	(7)
17	18	19	20	21	22	23
(8)	(9)	(10)	(11)	(12)	(13)	(14)
24	25	26	27	28	29	30
(15)	(16)	(17)	(18)	(19)	(20)	(21)
31						
(22)						

February (Shebat 11)

S	M	T	W	T	F	S
	1	2	3	4	5	6
	(23)	(24)	(25)	(26)	(27)	(28)
7	8	9	10	11	12	13
(29)	(30b)	(1)	(2)	(3)	(4)	(5)
14	15	16	17	18	19	20
(6)	(7)	(8)	(9)	(10)	(11)	(12)
21	22	23	24	25	26	27
(13)	(14)	(15)	(16)	(17)	(18)	(19)
28						
(20)						

March (Adar 12)

S	M	T	W	T	F	S
	1	2	3	4	5	6
	(21)	(22)	(23)	(24)	(25)	(26)
7	8	9	10	11	12	13
(27)	(28)	(29)	(30c)	(1)	(2)	(3)
14	15	16	17	18	19	20
(4)	(5)	(6)	(7)	(8)	(9)	(10)
21	22	23	24	25	26	27
(11)	(12)	(13)	(14)	(15)	(16)	(17)
28	29	30	31			
(18)	(19)	(20)	(21)			

April (Nisan 1)

S	M	T	W	T	F	S
					1	2
					(4)	(5)
3	4	5	6	7	8	9
(6)	(7)	(8)	(9)	(10)	(11)	(12)
10	11	12	13	14	15	16
(13)	(14)	(15)	(16)	(17)	(18)	(19)
17	18	19	20	21	22	23
(20)	(21)	(22)	(23)	(24)	(25)	(26)
24	25	26	27	28	29	30
(27)	(28)	(29)	(30d)	(1)	(2)	(3)

May (Iyyar 2)

S	M	T	W	T	F	S
1	2	3	4	5	6	7
(4)	(5)	(6)	(7)	(8)	(9)	(10)
8	9	10	11	12	13	14
(11)	(12)	(13)	(14)	(15)	(16)	(17)
15	16	17	18	19	20	21
(18)	(19)	(20)	(21)	(22)	(23)	(24)
22	23	24	25	26	27	28
(25)	(26)	(27)	(28)	(29)	(30e)	(1)
29	30	31				
(2)	(3)	(4)				

June (Sivan 3)

S	M	T	W	T	F	S
			1	2	3	4
			(5)	(6)	(7)	(8)
5	6	7	8	9	10	11
(9)	(10)	(11)	(12)	(13)	(14)	(15)
12	13	14	15	16	17	18
(16)	(17)	(18)	(18)	(20)	(21)	(22)
19	20	21	22	23	24	25
(23)	(24)	(25)	(26)	(27)	(28)	(29f)
26	27	28	29	30		
(1)	(2)	(3)	(4)	(5)		

Passover Lamb Sacrificed — Nisan 14
Feast of First Fruits — 1ˢᵗ Sunday after Nisan 15

Feast of Unleavened Bread — Nisan 15-21
Pentecost — 8ᵗʰ Sunday after Nisan 15

Time of New Moon (Jerusalem) — a18:26   b12:53   c6:07   d21:19   e10:12   f20:50

8 B.C.

July
(Tammuz 4)

S	M	T	W	T	F	S
				1	2	3
				(25)	(26)	(27)
4	5	6	7	8	9	10
(28)	(29)	(30g)	(1)	(2)	(3)	(4)
11	12	13	14	15	16	17
(5)	(6)	(7)	(8)	(9)	(10)	(11)
18	19	20	21	22	23	24
(12)	(13)	(14)	(15)	(16)	(17)	(18)
25	26	27	28	29	30	31
(19)	(20)	(21)	(22)	(23)	(24)	(25)

October
(Tishri 7)

S	M	T	W	T	F	S
					1	2
					(29)	(30j)
3	4	5	6	7	8	9
(1)	(2)	(3)	(4)	(5)	(6)	(7)
10	11	12	13	14	15	16
(8)	(9)	(10)	(11)	(12)	(13)	(14)
17	18	19	20	21	22	23
(15)	(16)	(17)	(18)	(19)	(20)	(21)
24	25	26	27	28	29	30
(22)	(23)	(24)	(25)	(26)	(27)	(28)
31						
(29k)						

August
(Ab 5)

S	M	T	W	T	F	S
1	2	3	4	5	6	7
(26)	(27)	(28)	(29h)	(1)	(2)	(3)
8	9	10	11	12	13	14
(4)	(5)	(6)	(7)	(8)	(9)	(10)
15	16	17	18	19	20	21
(11)	(12)	(13)	(14)	(15)	(16)	(17)
22	23	24	25	26	27	28
(18)	(19)	(20)	(21)	(22)	(23)	(24)
29	30	31				
(25)	(26)	(27)				

November
(Kislev 9)

S	M	T	W	T	F	S
	1	2	3	4	5	6
	(1)	(2)	(3)	(4)	(5)	(6)
7	8	9	10	11	12	13
(7)	(8)	(9)	(10)	(11)	(12)	(13)
14	15	16	17	18	19	20
(14)	(15)	(16)	(17)	(18)	(19)	(20)
21	22	23	24	25	26	27
(21)	(22)	(23)	(24)	(25)	(26)	(27)
28	29	30				
(28)	(29)	(30m)				

September
(Elul 6)

S	M	T	W	T	F	S
			1	2	3	4
			(28)	(29i)	(1)	(2)
5	6	7	8	9	10	11
(3)	(4)	(5)	(6)	(7)	(8)	(9)
12	13	14	15	16	17	18
(10)	(11)	(12)	(13)	(14)	(15)	(16)
19	20	21	22	23	24	25
(17)	(18)	(19)	(20)	(21)	(22)	(23)
26	27	28	29	30		
(24)	(25)	(26)	(27)	(28)		

December
(Tebeth 10)

S	M	T	W	T	F	S
			1	2	3	4
			(1)	(2)	(3)	(4)
5	6	7	8	9	10	11
(5)	(6)	(7)	(8)	(9)	(10)	(11)
12	13	14	15	16	17	18
(12)	(13)	(14)	(15)	(16)	(17)	(18)
19	20	21	22	23	24	25
(19)	(20)	(21)	(22)	(23)	(24)	(25)
26	27	28	29	30	31	
(26)	(27)	(28)	(29n)	(1)	(2)	

Day of Trumpets — Tishri 1
Feast of Booths — Tishri 15-22

Day of Atonement — Tishri 10
Feast of Dedication — 8 days beginning Kislev 25

Time of the New Moon — g5:46 h13:49 i22:01 j7:16 k18:12 m7:01 n21:33

7 B.C.

January
(Shebat 11)

S	M	T	W	T	F	S
						1
						(3)
2	3	4	5	6	7	8
(4)	(5)	(6)	(7)	(8)	(9)	(10)
9	10	11	12	13	14	15
(11)	(12)	(13)	(14)	(15)	(16)	(17)
16	17	18	19	20	21	22
(18)	(19)	(20)	(21)	(22)	(23)	(24)
23	24	25	26	27	28	29
(25)	(26)	(27)	(28)	(29)	(30a)	(1)
30	31					
(2)	(3)					

April
(Nisan 1)

S	M	T	W	T	F	S
					1	2
					(4)	(5)
3	4	5	6	7	8	9
(6)	(7)	(8)	(9)	(10)	(11)	(12)
10	11	12	13	14	15	16
(13)	(14)	(15)	(16)	(17)	(18)	(19)
17	18	19	20	21	22	23
(20)	(21)	(22)	(23)	(24)	(25)	(26)
24	25	26	27	28	29	30
(27)	(28)	(29)	(30d)	(1)	(2)	(3)

February
(Adar 12)

S	M	T	W	T	F	S
		1	2	3	4	5
		(4)	(5)	(6)	(7)	(8)
6	7	8	9	10	11	12
(9)	(10)	(11)	(12)	(13)	(14)	(15)
13	14	15	16	17	18	19
(16)	(17)	(18)	(19)	(20)	(21)	(22)
20	21	22	23	24	25	26
(23)	(24)	(25)	(26)	(27)	(28)	(29)
27	28					
(30b)	(1)					

May
(Iyyar 2)

S	M	T	W	T	F	S
1	2	3	4	5	6	7
(4)	(5)	(6)	(7)	(8)	(9)	(10)
8	9	10	11	12	13	14
(11)	(12)	(13)	(14)	(15)	(16)	(17)
15	16	17	18	19	20	21
(18)	(19)	(20)	(21)	(22)	(23)	(24)
22	23	24	25	26	27	28
(25)	(26)	(27)	(28)	(29)	(30e)	(1)
29	30	31				
(2)	(3)	(4)				

March
(Adar II 13)

S	M	T	W	T	F	S
		1	2	3	4	5
		(2)	(3)	(4)	(5)	(6)
6	7	8	9	10	11	12
(7)	(8)	(9)	(10)	(11)	(12)	(13)
13	14	15	16	17	18	19
(14)	(15)	(16)	(17)	(18)	(19)	(20)
20	21	22	23	24	25	26
(21)	(22)	(23)	(24)	(25)	(26)	(27)
27	28	29	30	31		
(28)	(29c)	(1)	(2)	(3)		

June
(Sivan 3)

S	M	T	W	T	F	S
			1	2	3	4
			(5)	(6)	(7)	(8)
5	6	7	8	9	10	11
(9)	(10)	(11)	(12)	(13)	(14)	(15)
12	13	14	15	16	17	18
(16)	(17)	(18)	(18)	(20)	(21)	(22)
19	20	21	22	23	24	25
(23)	(24)	(25)	(26)	(27)	(28)	(29f)
26	27	28	29	30		
(1)	(2)	(3)	(4)	(5)		

Passover Lamb Sacrificed — Nisan 14
Feast of First Fruits — 1st Sunday after Nisan 15

Feast of Unleavened Bread — Nisan 15-21
Pentecost — 8th Sunday after Nisan 15

Time of New Moon (Jerusalem) —   a13:25   b6:04   c22:49   d14:44   e5:01   f17:20

7 B.C..

July
(Tammuz 4)

S	M	T	W	T	F	S
					1	2
					(6)	(7)
3	4	5	6	7	8	9
(8)	(9)	(10)	(11)	(12)	(13)	(14)
10	11	12	13	14	15	16
(15)	(16)	(17)	(18)	(19)	(20)	(21)
17	18	19	20	21	22	23
(22)	(23)	(24)	(25)	(26)	(27)	(28)
24	25	26	27	28	29	30
(29)	(30g)	(1)	(2)	(3)	(4)	(5)
31						
(6)						

October
(Tishri 7)

S	M	T	W	T	F	S
						1
						(9)
2	3	4	5	6	7	8
(10)	(11)	(12)	(13)	(14)	(15)	(16)
9	10	11	12	13	14	15
(17)	(18)	(19)	(20)	(21)	(22)	(23)
16	17	18	19	20	21	22
(24)	(25)	(26)	(27)	(28)	(29j)	(1)
23	24	25	26	27	28	29
(2)	(3)	(4)	(5)	(6)	(7)	(8)
30	31					
(9)	(10)					

August
(Ab 5)

S	M	T	W	T	F	S
	1	2	3	4	5	6
	(7)	(8)	(9)	(10)	(11)	(12)
7	8	9	10	11	12	13
(13)	(14)	(15)	(16)	(17)	(18)	(19)
14	15	16	17	18	19	20
(20)	(21)	(22)	(23)	(24)	(25)	(26)
21	22	23	24	25	26	27
(27)	(28)	(29h)	(1)	(2)	(3)	(4)
28	29	30	31			
(5)	(6)	(7)	(8)			

November
(Marheshvan 8)

S	M	T	W	T	F	S
		1	2	3	4	5
		(11)	(12)	(13)	(14)	(15)
6	7	8	9	10	11	12
(16)	(17)	(18)	(19)	(20)	(21)	(22)
13	14	15	16	17	18	19
(23)	(24)	(25)	(26)	(27)	(28)	(29k)
20	21	22	23	24	25	26
(1)	(2)	(3)	(4)	(5)	(6)	(7)
27	28	29	30			
(8)	(9)	(10)	(11)			

September
(Elul 6)

S	M	T	W	T	F	S
				1	2	3
				(9)	(10)	(11)
4	5	6	7	8	9	10
(12)	(13)	(14)	(15)	(16)	(17)	(18)
11	12	13	14	15	16	17
(19)	(20)	(21)	(22)	(23)	(24)	(25)
18	19	20	21	22	23	24
(26)	(27)	(28)	(29)	(30i)	(1)	(2)
25	26	27	28	29	30	
(3)	(4)	(5)	(6)	(7)	(8)	

December
(Kislev 9)

S	M	T	W	T	F	S
				1	2	3
				(12)	(13)	(14)
4	5	6	7	8	9	10
(15)	(16)	(17)	(18)	(19)	(20)	(21)
11	12	13	14	15	16	17
(22)	(23)	(24)	(25)	(26)	(27)	(28)
18	19	20	21	22	23	24
(29)	(30m)	(1)	(2)	(3)	(4)	(5)
25	26	27	28	29	30	31
(6)	(7)	(8)	(9)	(10)	(11)	(12)

Day of Trumpets — Tishri 1
Feast of Booths — Tishri 15-22

Day of Atonement — Tishri 10
Feast of Dedication — 8 days beginning Kislev 25

Time of the New Moon — g3:59   h13:45   i23:26   j9:35   k20:22   m7:51

6 B.C.

January
(Tebeth 10)

S	M	T	W	T	F	S
1	2	3	4	5	6	7
(13)	(14)	(15)	(16)	(17)	(18)	(19)
8	9	10	11	12	13	14
(20)	(21)	(22)	(23)	(24)	(25)	(26)
15	16	17	18	19	20	21
(27)	(28)	(29a)	(1)	(2)	(3)	(4)
22	23	24	25	26	27	28
(5)	(6)	(7)	(8)	(9)	(10	(11)
29	30	31				
(12)	(13)	(14)				

April
(Nisan 1)

S	M	T	W	T	F	S
						1
						(14)
2	3	4	5	6	7	8
(15)	(16)	(17)	(18)	(19)	(20)	(21)
9	10	11	12	13	14	15
(22)	(23)	(24)	(25)	(26)	(27)	(28)
16	17	18	19	20	21	22
(29d)	(1)	(2)	(3)	(4)	(5)	(6)
23	24	25	26	27	28	29
(7)	(8)	(9)	(10)	(11)	(12)	(13)
30						
(14)						

February
(Shebat 11)

S	M	T	W	T	F	S
			1	2	3	4
			(15)	(16)	(17)	(18)
5	6	7	8	9	10	11
(19)	(20)	(21)	(22)	(23)	(24)	(25)
12	13	14	15	16	17	18
(26)	(27)	(28)	(29)	(30b)	(1)	(2)
19	20	21	22	23	24	25
(3)	(4)	(5)	(6)	(7)	(8)	(9)
26	27	28				
(10)	(11)	(12)				

May
(Iyyar 2)

S	M	T	W	T	F	S
	1	2	3	4	5	6
	(15)	(16)	(17)	(18)	(19)	(20)
7	8	9	10	11	12	13
(21)	(22)	(23)	(24)	(25)	(26)	(27)
14	15	16	17	18	19	20
(28)	(29)	(30e)	(1)	(2)	(3)	(4)
21	22	23	24	25	26	27
(5)	(6)	(7)	(8)	(9)	(10)	(11)
28	29	30	31			
(12)	(13)	(14)	(15)			

March
(Adar 12)

S	M	T	W	T	F	S
			1	2	3	4
			(13)	(14)	(15)	(16)
5	6	7	8	9	10	11
(17)	(18)	(19)	(20)	(21)	(22)	(23)
12	13	14	15	16	17	18
(24)	(25)	(26)	(27)	(28)	(29)	(30c)
19	20	21	22	23	24	25
(1)	(2)	(3)	(4)	(5)	(6)	(7)
26	27	28	29	30	31	
(8)	(9)	(10)	(11)	(12)	(13)	

June
(Sivan 3)

S	M	T	W	T	F	S
				1	2	3
				(16)	(17)	(18)
4	5	6	7	8	9	10
(19)	(20)	(21)	(22)	(23)	(24)	(25)
11	12	13	14	15	16	17
(26)	(27)	(28)	(29f)	(1)	(2)	(3)
18	19	20	21	22	23	24
(4)	(5)	(6)	(7)	(8)	(9)	(10)
25	26	27	28	29	30	
(11)	(12)	(13)	(14)	(15)	(16)	

Passover Lamb Sacrificed — Nisan 14

Feast of First Fruits — 1st Sunday after Nisan 15

Feast of Unleavened Bread — Nisan 15-21

Pentecost — 8th Sunday after Nisan 15

Time of New Moon (Jerusalem) — a20:08 b9:28 c0:00 d15:22 e6:52 f21:48

6 B.C.

July
(Tammuz 4)

S	M	T	W	T	F	S
						1
						(17)
2	3	4	5	6	7	8
(18)	(19)	(20)	(21)	(22)	(23)	(24)
9	10	11	12	13	14	15
(25)	(26)	(27)	(28)	(29)	(30g)	(1)
16	17	18	19	20	21	22
(2)	(3)	(4)	(5)	(6)	(7)	(8)
23	24	25	26	27	28	29
(9)	(10)	(11)	(12)	(13)	(14)	(15)
30	31					
(16)	(17)					

October
(Tishri 7)

S	M	T	W	T	F	S
1	2	3	4	5	6	7
(20)	(21)	(22)	(23)	(24)	(25)	(26)
8	9	10	11	12	13	14
(27)	(28)	(29)	(30j)	(1)	(2)	(3)
15	16	17	18	19	20	21
(4)	(5)	(6)	(7)	(8)	(9)	(10)
22	23	24	25	26	27	28
(11)	(12)	(13)	(14)	(15)	(16)	(17)
29	30	31				
(18)	(19)	(20)				

August
(Ab 5)

S	M	T	W	T	F	S
		1	2	3	4	5
		(18)	(19)	(20)	(21)	(22)
6	7	8	9	10	11	12
(23)	(24)	(25)	(26)	(27)	(28)	(29)
13	14	15	16	17	18	19
(30h)	(1)	(2)	(3)	(4)	(5)	(6)
20	21	22	23	24	25	26
(7)	(8)	(9)	(10)	(11)	(12)	(13)
27	28	29	30	31		
(14)	(15)	(16)	(17)	(18)		

November
(Marheshvan 8)

S	M	T	W	T	F	S
			1	2	3	4
			(21)	(22)	(23)	(24)
5	6	7	8	9	10	11
(25)	(26)	(27)	(28)	(29k)	(1)	(2)
12	13	14	15	16	17	18
(3)	(4)	(5)	(6)	(7)	(8)	(9)
19	20	21	22	23	24	25
(10)	(11)	(12)	(13)	(14)	(15)	(16)
26	27	28	29	30		
(17)	(18)	(19)	(20)	(21)		

September
(Elul 6)

S	M	T	W	T	F	S
					1	2
					(19)	(20)
3	4	5	6	7	8	9
(21)	(22)	(23)	(24)	(25)	(26)	(27)
10	11	12	13	14	15	16
(28)	(29i)	(1)	(2)	(3)	(4)	(5)
17	18	19	20	21	22	23
(6)	(7)	(8)	(9)	(10)	(11)	(12)
24	25	26	27	28	29	30
(13)	(14)	(15)	(16)	(17)	(18)	(19)

December
(Kislev 9)

S	M	T	W	T	F	S
					1	2
					(22)	(23)
3	4	5	6	7	8	9
(24)	(25)	(26)	(27)	(28)	(29m)	(1)
10	11	12	13	14	15	16
(2)	(3)	(4)	(5)	(6)	(7)	(8)
17	18	19	20	21	22	23
(9)	(10)	(11)	(12)	(13)	(14)	(15)
24	25	26	27	28	29	30
(16)	(17)	(18)	(19)	(20)	(21)	(22)
31						
(23)						

Day of Trumpets — Tishri 1
Feast of Booths — Tishri 15-22

Day of Atonement — Tishri 10
Feast of Dedication — 8 days beginning Kislev 25

Time of the New Moon — g11:45 h0:48 i13:08 j0:54 k12:06 m22:50

5 B.C.

January
(Tebeth 10)

S	M	T	W	T	F	S
	1	2	3	4	5	6
	(24)	(25)	(26)	(27)	(28)	(29)
7	8	9	10	11	12	13
(30a)	(1)	(2)	(3)	(4)	(5)	(6)
14	15	16	17	18	19	20
(7)	(8)	(9)	(10)	(11)	(12)	(13)
21	22	23	24	25	26	27
(14)	(15)	(16)	(17)	(18)	(19)	(20)
28	29	30	31			
(21)	(22)	(23)	(24)			

April
(Nisan 1)

S	M	T	W	T	F	S
	1	2	3	4	5	6
	(26)	(27)	(28)	(29d)	(1)	(2)
7	8	9	10	11	12	13
(3)	(4)	(5)	(6)	(7)	(8)	(9)
14	15	16	17	18	19	20
(10)	(11)	(12)	(13)	(14)	(15)	(16)
21	22	23	24	25	26	27
(17)	(18)	(19)	(20)	(21)	(22)	(23)
28	29	30				
(24)	(25)	(26)				

February
(Shebat 11)

S	M	T	W	T	F	S
				1	2	3
				(25)	(26)	(27)
4	5	6	7	8	9	10
(28)	(29b)	(1)	(2)	(3)	(4)	(5)
11	12	13	14	15	16	17
(6)	(7)	(8)	(9)	(10)	(11)	(12)
18	19	20	21	22	23	24
(13)	(14)	(15)	(16)	(17)	(18)	(19)
25	26	27	28	29		
(20)	(21)	(22)	(23)	(24)		

May
(Iyyar 2)

S	M	T	W	T	F	S
			1	2	3	4
			(27)	(28)	(29)	(30e)
5	6	7	8	9	10	11
(1)	(2)	(3)	(4)	(5)	(6)	(7)
12	13	14	15	16	17	18
(8)	(9)	(10)	(11)	(12)	(13)	(14)
19	20	21	22	23	24	25
(15)	(16)	(17)	(18)	(19)	(20)	(21)
26	27	28	29	30	31	
(22)	(23)	(24)	(25)	(26)	(27)	

March
(Adar 12)

S	M	T	W	T	F	S
					1	2
					(25)	(26)
3	4	5	6	7	8	9
(27)	(28)	(29)	(30c)	(1)	(2)	(3)
10	11	12	13	14	15	16
(4)	(5)	(6)	(7)	(8)	(9)	(10)
17	18	19	20	21	22	23
(11)	(12)	(13)	(14)	(15)	(16)	(17)
24	25	26	27	28	29	30
(18)	(19)	(20)	(21)	(22)	(23)	(24)
31						
(25)						

June
(Sivan 3)

S	M	T	W	T	F	S
						1
						(28)
2	3	4	5	6	7	8
(29f)	(1)	(2)	(3)	(4)	(5)	(6)
9	10	11	12	13	14	15
(7)	(8)	(9)	(10)	(11)	(12)	(13)
16	17	18	19	20	21	22
(14)	(15)	(16)	(17)	(18)	(19)	(20)
23	24	25	26	27	28	29
(21)	(22)	(23)	(24)	(25)	(26)	(27)
30						
(28)						

Passover Lamb Sacrificed — Nisan 14
Feast of First Fruits — 1st Sunday after Nisan 15

Feast of Unleavened Bread — Nisan 15-21
Pentecost — 8th Sunday after Nisan 15

Time of New Moon (Jerusalem) — a9:19   b19:58   c:7:13   d19:21   e8:26   f22:27

5 B.C.

July
(Tammuz 4)

S	M	T	W	T	F	S
	1	2	3	4	5	6
	(29)	(30g)	(1)	(2)	(3)	(4)
7	8	9	10	11	12	13
(5)	(6)	(7)	(8)	(9)	(10)	(11)
14	15	16	17	18	19	20
(12)	(13)	(14)	(15)	(16)	(17)	(18)
21	22	23	24	25	26	27
(19)	(20)	(21)	(22)	(23)	(24)	(25)
28	29	30	31			
(26)	(27)	(28)	(29)			

October
(Marheshvan 8)

S	M	T	W	T	F	S
		1	2	3	4	5
		(2)	(3)	(4)	(5)	(6)
6	7	8	9	10	11	12
(7)	(8)	(9)	(10)	(11)	(12)	(13)
13	14	15	16	17	18	19
(14)	(15)	(16)	(17)	(18)	(19)	(20)
20	21	22	23	24	25	26
(21)	(22)	(23)	(24)	(25)	(26)	(27)
27	28	29	30	31		
(28)	(29)	(30k)	(1)	(2)		

August
(Ab 5)

S	M	T	W	T	F	S
				1	2	3
				(30h)	(1)	(2)
4	5	6	7	8	9	10
(3)	(4)	(5)	(6)	(7)	(8)	(9)
11	12	13	14	15	16	17
(10)	(11)	(12)	(13)	(14)	(15)	(16)
18	19	20	21	22	23	24
(17)	(18)	(19)	(20)	(21)	(22)	(23)
25	26	27	28	29	30	31
(24)	(25)	(26)	(27)	(28)	(29i)	(1)

November
(Kislev 9)

S	M	T	W	T	F	S
					1	2
					(3)	(4)
3	4	5	6	7	8	9
(5)	(6)	(7)	(8)	(9)	(10)	(11)
10	11	12	13	14	15	16
(12)	(13)	(14)	(15)	(16)	(17)	(18)
17	18	19	20	21	22	23
(19)	(20)	(21)	(22)	(23)	(24)	(25)
24	25	26	27	28	29	30
(26)	(27)	(28)	(29m)	(1)	(2)	(3)

September
(Tishri 7)

S	M	T	W	T	F	S
1	2	3	4	5	6	7
(2)	(3)	(4)	(5)	(6)	(7)	(8)
8	9	10	11	12	13	14
(9)	(10)	(11)	(12)	(13)	(14)	(15)
15	16	17	18	19	20	21
(16)	(17)	(18)	(19)	(20)	(21)	(22)
22	23	24	25	26	27	28
(23)	(24)	(25)	(26)	(27)	(28)	(29)
29	30					
(30j)	(1)					

December
(Tebeth 10)

S	M	T	W	T	F	S
1	2	3	4	5	6	7
(4)	(5)	(6)	(7)	(8)	(9)	(10)
8	9	10	11	12	13	14
(11)	(12)	(13)	(14)	(15)	(16)	(17)
15	16	17	18	19	20	21
(18)	(19)	(20)	(21)	(22)	(23)	(24)
22	23	24	25	26	27	28
(25)	(26)	(27)	(28)	(29)	(30n)	(1)
29	30	31				
(2)	(3)	(4)				

Day of Trumpets — Tishri 1
Feast of Booths — Tishri 15-22

Day of Atonement — Tishri 10
Feast of Dedication — 8 days beginning Kislev 25

Time of the New Moon — g13:20 h4:51 i20:32 j11:39 k1:33 m13:58 n1:04

Gregorian

4 B.C.

January
(Shebat 11)

S	M	T	W	T	F	S
			1	2	3	4
			(5)	(6)	(7)	(8)
5	6	7	8	9	10	11
(9)	(10)	(11)	(12)	(13)	(14)	(15)
12	13	14	15	16	17	18
(16)	(17)	(18)	(19)	(20)	(21)	(22)
19	20	21	22	23	24	25
(23)	(24)	(25)	(26)	(27)	(28)	(29a)
26	27	28	29	30	31	
(1)	(2)	(3)	(4)	(5)	(6)	

February
(Adar 12)

S	M	T	W	T	F	S
						1
						(7)
2	3	4	5	6	7	8
(8)	(9)	(10)	(11)	(12)	(13)	(14)
9	10	11	12	13	14	15
(15)	(16)	(17)	(18)	(19)	(20)	(21)
16	17	18	19	20	21	22
(22)	(23)	(24)	(25)	(26)	(27)	(28)
23	24	25	26	27	28	
(29b)	(1)	(2)	(3)	(4)	(5)	

March
(Adar II 13)

S	M	T	W	T	F	S
						1
						(6)
2	3	4	5	6	7	8
(7)	(8)	(9)	(10)	(11)	(12)	(13)
9	10	11	12	13	14	15
(14)	(15)	(16)	(17)	(18)	(19)	(20)
16	17	18	19	20	21	22
(21)	(22)	(23)	(24)	(25)	(26)	(27)
23	24	25	26	27	28	29
(28)	(29)	(30c)	(1)	(2)	(3)	(4)
30	31					
(5)	(6)					

April
(Nisan 1)

S	M	T	W	T	F	S
		1	2	3	4	5
		(7)	(8)	(9)	(10)	(11)
6	7	8	9	10	11	12
(12)	(13)	(14)	(15)	(16)	(17)	(18)
13	14	15	16	17	18	19
(19)	(20)	(21)	(22)	(23)	(24)	(25)
20	21	22	23	24	25	26
(26)	(27)	(28)	(29d)	(1)	(2)	(3)
27	28	29	30			
(4)	(5)	(6)	(7)			

May
(Iyyar 2)

S	M	T	W	T	F	S
				1	2	3
				(8)	(9)	(10)
4	5	6	7	8	9	10
(11)	(12)	(13)	(14)	(15)	(16)	(17)
11	12	13	14	15	16	17
(18)	(19)	(20)	(21)	(22)	(23)	(24)
18	19	20	21	22	23	24
(25)	(26)	(27)	(28)	(29)	(30e)	(1)
25	26	27	28	29	30	31
(2)	(3)	(4)	(5)	(6)	(7)	(8)

June
(Sivan 3)

S	M	T	W	T	F	S
1	2	3	4	5	6	7
(9)	(10)	(11)	(12)	(13)	(14)	(15)
8	9	10	11	12	13	14
(16)	(17)	(18)	(19)	(20)	(21)	(22)
15	16	17	18	19	20	21
(23)	(24)	(25)	(26)	(27)	(28)	(29f)
22	23	24	25	26	27	28
(1)	(2)	(3)	(4)	(5)	(6)	(7)
29	30					
(8)	(9)					

Passover Lamb Sacrificed — Nisan 14
Feast of First Fruits — 1st Sunday after Nisan 15

Feast of Unleavened Bread — Nisan 15-21
Pentecost — 8th Sunday after Nisan 15

Time of New Moon (Jerusalem) — a11:16   b20:54   c6:20   d16:01   e2:36   f14:40

4 B,C.

July
(Tammuz 4)

S	M	T	W	T	F	S
		1	2	3	4	5
		(10)	(11)	(12)	(13)	(14)
6	7	8	9	10	11	12
(15)	(16)	(17)	(18)	(19)	(20)	(21)
13	14	15	16	17	18	19
(22)	(23)	(24)	(25)	(26)	(27)	(28)
20	21	22	23	24	25	26
(29)	(30g)	(1)	(2)	(3)	(4)	(5)
27	28	29	30	31		
(6)	(7)	(8)	(9)	(10)		

October
(Tishri 7)

S	M	T	W	T	F	S
		1	2	3	4	
		(13)	(14)	(15)	(16)	
5	6	7	8	9	10	11
(17)	(18)	(19)	(20)	(21)	(22)	(23)
12	13	14	15	16	17	18
(24)	(25)	(26)	(27)	(28)	(29)	(30j)
19	20	21	22	23	24	25
(1)	(2)	(3)	(4)	(5)	(6)	(7)
26	27	28	29	30	31	
(8)	(9)	(10)	(11)	(12)	(13)	

August
(Ab 5)

S	M	T	W	T	F	S
					1	2
					(11)	(12)
3	4	5	6	7	8	9
(13)	(14)	(15)	(16)	(17)	(18)	(19)
10	11	12	13	14	15	16
(20)	(21)	(22)	(23)	(24)	(25)	(26)
17	18	19	20	21	22	23
(27)	(28)	(29h)	(1)	(2)	(3)	(4)
24	25	26	27	28	29	30
(5)	(6)	(7)	(8)	(9)	(10)	(11)
31						
(12)						

November
(Marheshvan 8)

S	M	T	W	T	F	S
						1
						(14)
2	3	4	5	6	7	8
(15)	(16)	(17)	(18)	(19)	(20)	(21)
9	10	11	12	13	14	15
(22)	(23)	(24)	(25)	(26)	(27)	(28)
16	17	18	19	20	21	22
(29)	(30k)	(1)	(2)	(3)	(4)	(5)
23	24	25	26	27	28	29
(6)	(7)	(8)	(9)	(10)	(11)	(12)
30						
(13)						

September
(Elul 6)

S	M	T	W	T	F	S
	1	2	3	4	5	6
	(13)	(14)	(15)	(16)	(17)	(18)
7	8	9	10	11	12	13
(19)	(20)	(21)	(22)	(23)	(24)	(25)
14	15	16	17	18	19	20
(26)	(27)	(28)	(29)	(30i)	(1)	(2)
21	22	23	24	25	25	27
(3)	(4)	(5)	(6)	(7)	(8)	(9)
28	29	30				
(10)	(11)	(12)				

December
(Kislev 9)

S	M	T	W	T	F	S
	1	2	3	4	5	6
	(14)	(15)	(16)	(17)	(18)	(19)
7	8	9	10	11	12	13
(20)	(21)	(22)	(23)	(24)	(25)	(26)
14	15	16	17	18	19	20
(27)	28()	(29m)	(1)	(2)	(3)	(4)
21	22	23	24	25	26	27
(5)	(6)	(7)	(8)	(9)	(10)	(11)
28	29	30	31			
(12)	(13)	(14)	(15)			

Day of Trumpets — Tishri 1
Feast of Booths — Tishri 15-22

Day of Atonement — Tishri 10
Feast of Dedication — 8 days beginning Kislev 25

Time of the New Moon — g5:15 h21:43 i15:20 j8:41 k0:39 m14:44

3 B.C.

January (Tebeth 10)						
S	M	T	W	T	F	S
				1	2	3
				(16)	(17)	(18)
4	5	6	7	8	9	10
(19)	(20)	(21)	(22)	(23)	(24)	(25)
11	12	13	14	15	16	17
(26)	(27)	(28)	(29)	(30a)	(1)	(2)
18	19	20	21	22	23	24
(3)	(4)	(5)	(6)	(7)	(8)	(9)
25	26	27	28	29	30	31
(10)	(11)	(12)	(13)	(14)	(15)	(16)

April (Nisan 1)						
S	M	T	W	T	F	S
			1	2	3	4
			(18)	(19)	(20)	(21)
5	6	7	8	9	10	11
(22)	(23)	(24)	(25)	(26)	(27)	(28)
12	13	14	15	16	17	18
(29)	(30d)	(1)	(2)	(3)	(4)	(5)
19	20	21	22	23	24	25
(6)	(7)	(8)	(9)	(10)	(11)	(12)
26	27	28	29	30		
(13)	(14)	(15)	(16)	(17)		

February (Shebat 11)						
S	M	T	W	T	F	S
1	2	3	4	5	6	7
(17)	(18)	(19)	(20)	(21)	(22)	(23)
8	9	10	11	12	13	14
(24)	(25)	(26)	(27)	(28)	(29b)	(1)
15	16	17	18	19	20	21
(2)	(3)	(4)	(5)	(6)	(7)	(8)
22	23	24	25	26	27	28
(9)	(10)	(11)	(12)	(13)	(14)	(15)

May (Iyyar 2)						
S	M	T	W	T	F	S
					1	2
					(18)	(19)
3	4	5	6	7	8	9
(20)	(21)	(22)	(23)	(24)	(25)	(26)
10	11	12	13	14	15	16
(27)	(28)	(29e)	(1)	(2)	(3)	(4)
17	18	19	20	21	22	23
(5)	(6)	(7)	(8)	(9)	(10)	(11)
24	25	26	27	28	29	30
(12)	(13)	(14)	(15)	(16)	(17)	(18)
31						
(19)						

March (Adar 12)						
S	M	T	W	T	F	S
1	2	3	4	5	6	7
(16)	(17)	(18)	(19)	(20)	(21)	(22)
8	9	10	11	12	13	14
(23)	(24)	(25)	(26)	(27)	(28)	(29c)
15	16	17	18	19	20	21
(1)	(2)	(3)	(4)	(5)	(6)	(7)
22	23	24	25	26	27	28
(8)	(9)	(10)	(11)	(12)	(13)	(14)
29	30	31				
(15)	(16)	(17)				

June (Sivan 3)						
S	M	T	W	T	F	S
	1	2	3	4	5	6
	(20)	(21)	(22)	(23)	(24)	(25)
7	8	9	10	11	12	13
(26)	(27)	(28)	(29f)	(1)	(2)	(3)
14	15	16	17	18	19	20
(4)	(5)	(6)	(7)	(8)	(9)	(10)
21	22	23	24	25	26	27
(11)	(12)	(13)	(14)	(15)	(16)	(17)
28	29	30				
(18)	(19)	(20)				

Passover Lamb Sacrificed — Nisan 14
Feast of First Fruits — 1st Sunday after Nisan 15

Feast of Unleavened Bread — Nisan 15-21
Pentecost — 8th Sunday after Nisan 15

Time of New Moon (Jerusalem) —   a2:54 b13:18 c22:12 d6:07 e13:52 f22:35

3 B.C.

July
(Tammuz 4)

S	M	T	W	T	F	S
			1	2	3	4
			(21)	(22)	(23)	(24)
5	6	7	8	9	10	11
(25)	(26)	(27)	(28)	(29)	(30g)	(1)
12	13	14	15	16	17	18
(2)	(3)	(4)	(5)	(6)	(7)	(8)
19	20	21	22	23	24	25
(9)	(10)	(11)	(12)	(13)	(14)	(15)
26	27	28	29	30	31	
(16)	(17)	(18)	(19)	(20)	(21)	

October
(Tishri 7)

S	M	T	W	T	F	S
				1	2	3
				(24)	(25)	(26)
4	5	6	7	8	9	10
(27)	(28)	(29)	(30j)	(1)	(2)	(3)
11	12	13	14	15	16	17
(4)	(5)	(6)	(7)	(8)	(9)	(10)
18	19	20	21	22	23	24
(11)	(12)	(13)	(14)	(15)	(16)	(17)
25	26	27	28	29	30	31
(18)	(19)	(20)	(21)	(22)	(23)	(24)

August
(Ab 5)

S	M	T	W	T	F	S
						1
						(22)
2	3	4	5	6	7	8
(23)	(24)	(25)	(26)	(27)	(28)	(29h)
9	10	11	12	13	14	15
(1)	(2)	(3)	(4)	(5)	(6)	(7)
16	17	18	19	20	21	22
(8)	(9)	(10)	(11)	(12)	(13)	(14)
23	24	25	26	27	28	29
(15)	(16)	(17)	(18)	(19)	(20)	(21)
30	31					
(22)	(23)					

November
(Marheshvan 8)

S	M	T	W	T	F	S
1	2	3	4	5	6	7
(25)	(26)	(27)	(28)	(29)	(30k)	(1)
8	9	10	11	12	13	14
(2)	(3)	(4)	(5)	(6)	(7)	(8)
15	16	17	18	19	20	21
(9)	(10)	(11)	(12)	(13)	(14)	(15)
22	23	24	25	26	27	28
(16)	(17)	(18)	(19)	(20)	(21)	(22)
29	30					
(23)	(24)					

September
(Elul 6)

S	M	T	W	T	F	S
		1	2	3	4	5
		(24)	(25)	(26)	(27)	(28)
6	7	8	9	10	11	12
(29)	(30i)	(1)	(2)	(3)	(4)	(5)
13	14	15	16	17	18	19
(6)	(7)	(8)	(9)	(10)	(11)	(12)
20	21	22	23	24	25	26
(13)	(14)	(15)	(16)	(17)	(18)	(19)
27	28	29	30			
(20)	(21)	(22)	(23)			

December
(Kislev 9)

S	M	T	W	T	F	S
		1	2	3	4	5
		(25)	(26)	(27)	(28)	(29m)
6	7	8	9	10	11	12
(1)	(2)	(3)	(4)	(5)	(6)	(7)
13	14	15	16	17	18	19
(8)	(9)	(10)	(11)	(12)	(13)	(14)
20	21	22	23	24	25	26
(15)	(16)	(17)	(18)	(19)	(20)	(21)
27	28	29	30	31		
(22)	(23)	(24)	(25)	(26)		

Day of Trumpets — Tishri 1
Feast of Booths — Tishri 15-22

Day of Atonement — Tishri 10
Feast of Dedication — 8 days beginning Kislev 25

Time of the New Moon — g9:20   h22:52   i15:08   j9:20   k4:08   m22:09

Gregorian

2 B.C.

January
(Tebeth 10)

S	M	T	W	T	F	S
					1	2
					(27)	(28)
3	4	5	6	7	8	9
(29)	(30a)	(1)	(2)	(3)	(4)	(5)
10	11	12	13	14	15	16
(6)	(7)	(8)	(9)	(10)	(11)	(12)
17	18	19	20	21	22	23
(13)	(14)	(15)	(16)	(17)	(18)	(19)
24	25	26	27	28	29	30
(20)	(21)	(22)	(23)	(24)	(25)	(26)
31						
(27)						

April
(Adar II 13)

S	M	T	W	T	F	S
				1	2	3
				(28)	(29d)	(1)
4	5	6	7	8	9	10
(2)	(3)	(4)	(5)	(6)	(7)	(8)
11	12	13	14	15	16	17
(9)	(10)	(11)	(12)	(13)	(14)	(15)
18	19	20	21	22	23	24
(16)	(17)	(18)	(19)	(20)	(21)	(22)
25	26	27	28	29	30	
(23)	(24)	(25)	(26)	(27)	(28)	

February
(Shebat 11)

S	M	T	W	T	F	S
	1	2	3	4	5	6
	(28)	(29)	(30b)	(1)	(2)	(3)
7	8	9	10	11	12	13
(4)	(5)	(6)	(7)	(8)	(9)	(10)
14	15	16	17	18	19	20
(11)	(12)	(13)	(14)	(15)	(16)	(17)
21	22	23	24	25	26	27
(18)	(19)	(20)	(21)	(22)	(23)	(24)
28						
(25)						

May
(Nisan 1)

S	M	T	W	T	F	S
						1
						(29)
2	3	4	5	6	7	8
(30e)	(1)	(2)	(3)	(4)	(5)	(6)
9	10	11	12	13	14	15
(7)	(8)	(9)	(10)	(11)	(12)	(13)
16	17	18	19	20	21	22
(14)	(15)	(16)	(17)	(18)	(19)	(20)
23	24	25	26	27	28	29
(21)	(22)	(23)	(24)	(25)	(26)	(27)
30	31					
(28)	(29f)					

March
(Adar 12)

S	M	T	W	T	F	S
	1	2	3	4	5	6
	(26)	(27)	(28)	(29c)	(1)	(2)
7	8	9	10	11	12	13
(3)	(4)	(5)	(6)	(7)	(8)	(9)
14	15	16	17	18	19	20
(10)	(11)	(12)	(13)	(14)	(15)	(16)
21	22	23	24	25	26	27
(17)	(18)	(19)	(20)	(21)	(22)	(23)
28	29	30	31			
(24)	(25)	(26)	(27)			

June
(Sivan 3)

S	M	T	W	T	F	S
		1	2	3	4	5
		(1)	(2)	(3)	(4)	(5)
6	7	8	9	10	11	12
(6)	(7)	(8)	(9)	(10)	(11)	(12)
13	14	15	16	17	18	19
(13)	(14)	(15)	(16)	(17)	(18)	(19)
20	21	22	23	24	25	26
(20)	(21)	(22)	(23)	(24)	(25)	(26)
27	28	29	30			
(27)	(28)	(29g)	(1)			

Passover Lamb Sacrificed — Nisan 14
Feast of First Fruits — 1st Sunday after Nisan 15

Feast of Unleavened Bread — Nisan 15-21
Pentecost — 8th Sunday after Nisan 15

Time of New Moon (Jerusalem) — a14:17 b3:48 c14:34 d23:02 e6:08 f12:57 g20:41

2 B.C.

July
(Tammuz 4)

S	M	T	W	T	F	S
				1	2	3
				(2)	(3)	(4)
4	5	6	7	8	9	10
(5)	(6)	(7)	(8)	(9)	(10)	(11)
11	12	13	14	15	16	17
(12)	(13)	(14)	(15)	(16)	(17)	(18)
18	19	20	21	22	23	24
(19)	(20)	(21)	(22)	(23)	(24)	(25)
25	26	27	28	29	30	31
(26)	(27)	(28)	(29)	(30h)	(1)	(2)

October
(Tishri 7)

S	M	T	W	T	F	S
					1	2
					(5)	(6)
3	4	5	6	7	8	9
(7)	(8)	(9)	(10)	(11)	(12)	(13)
10	11	12	13	14	15	16
(14)	(15)	(16)	(17)	(18)	(19)	(20)
17	18	19	20	21	22	23
(21)	(22)	(23)	(24)	(25)	(26)	(27)
24	25	26	27	28	29	30
(28)	(29)	(30k)	(1)	(2)	(3)	(4)
31						
(5)						

August
(Ab 5)

S	M	T	W	T	F	S
1	2	3	4	5	6	7
(3)	(4)	(5)	(6)	(7)	(8)	(9)
8	9	10	11	12	13	14
(10)	(11)	(12)	(13)	(14)	(15)	(16)
15	16	17	18	19	20	21
(17)	(18)	(19)	(20)	(21)	(22)	(23)
22	23	24	25	26	27	28
(24)	(25)	(26)	(27)	(28)	(29i)	(1)
29	30	31				
(2)	(3)	(4)				

September
(Elul 6)

S	M	T	W	T	F	S
			1	2	3	4
			(5)	(6)	(7)	(8)
5	6	7	8	9	10	11
(9)	(10)	(11)	(12)	(13)	(14)	(15)
12	13	14	15	16	17	18
(16)	(17)	(18)	(19)	(20)	(21)	(22)
19	20	21	22	23	24	25
(23)	(24)	(25)	(26)	(27)	(28)	(29)
26	27	28	29	30		
(30j)	(1)	(2)	(3)	(4)		

September
(Elul 6)

S	M	T	W	T	F	S
			1	2	3	4
			(5)	(6)	(7)	(8)
5	6	7	8	9	10	11
(9)	(10)	(11)	(12)	(13)	(14)	(15)
12	13	14	15	16	17	18
(16)	(17)	(18)	(19)	(20)	(21)	(22)
19	20	21	22	23	24	25
(23)	(24)	(25)	(26)	(27)	(28)	(29)
26	27	28	29	30		
(30j)	(1)	(2)	(3)	(4)		

December
(Kislev 9)

S	M	T	W	T	F	S
			1	2	3	4
			(7)	(8)	(9)	(10)
5	6	7	8	9	10	11
(11)	(12)	(13)	(14)	(15)	(16)	(17)
12	13	14	15	16	17	18
(18)	(19)	(20)	(21)	(22)	(23)	(24)
19	20	21	22	23	24	25
(25)	(26)	(27)	(28)	(29)	(30n)	(1)
26	27	28	29	30	31	
(2)	(3)	(4)	(5)	(6)	(7)	

ay of Trumpets — Tishri 1
east of Booths — Tishri 15-22

Day of Atonement — Tishri 10
Feast of Dedication — 8 days beginning Kislev 25

ime of the New Moon —   h6:19   i18:31   j9:35   k3:18   m22:47   n18:23

Gregorian

1 B.C.

January
(Tebeth 10)

S	M	T	W	T	F	S
						1
						(8)
2	3	4	5	6	7	8
(9)	(10)	(11)	(12)	(13)	(14)	(15)
9	10	11	12	13	14	15
(16)	(17)	(18)	(19)	(20)	(21)	(22)
16	17	18	19	20	21	22
(23)	(24)	(25)	(26)	(27)	(28)	(29)
23	24	25	26	27	28	29
(30a)	(1)	(2)	(3)	(4)	(5)	(6)
30	31					

April
(Nisan 1)

S	M	T	W	T	F	S
						1
						(10)
2	3	4	5	6	7	8
(11)	(12)	(13)	(14)	(15)	(16)	(17)
9	10	11	12	13	14	15
(18)	(19)	(20)	(21)	(22)	(23)	(24)
16	17	18	19	20	21	22
(25)	(26)	(27)	(28)	(29d)	(1)	(2)
23	24	25	26	27	28	29
(3)	(4)	(5)	(6)	(7)	(8)	(9)
30						
(10)						

February
(Shebat 11)

S	M	T	W	T	F	S
		1	2	3	4	5
		(9)	(10)	(11)	(12)	(13)
6	7	8	9	10	11	12
(14)	(15)	(16)	(17)	(18)	(19)	(20)
13	14	15	16	17	18	19
(21)	(22)	(23)	(24)	(25)	(26)	(27)
20	21	22	23	24	25	26
(28)	(29)	(30b)	(1)	(2)	(3)	(4)
27	28	29				
(5)	(6)	(7)				

May
(Iyyar 2)

S	M	T	W	T	F	S
		1	2	3	4	5	6
		(11)	(12)	(13)	(14)	(15)	(16)
7	8	9	10	11	12	13
(17)	(18)	(19)	(20)	(21)	(22)	(23)
14	15	16	17	18	19	20
(24)	(25)	(26)	(27)	(28)	(29)	(30e)
21	22	23	24	25	26	27
(1)	(2)	(3)	(4)	(5)	(6)	(7)
28	29	30	31			
(8)	(9)	(10)	(11)			

March
(Adar 12)

S	M	T	W	T	F	S
			1	2	3	4
			(8)	(9)	(10)	(11)
5	6	7	8	9	10	11
(12)	(13)	(14)	(15)	(16)	(17)	(18)
12	13	14	15	16	17	18
(19)	(20)	(21)	(22)	(23)	(24)	(25)
19	20	21	22	23	24	25
(26)	(27)	(28)	(29c)	(1)	(2)	(3)
26	27	28	29	30	31	
(4)	(5)	(6)	(7)	(8)	(9)	

June
(Sivan 3)

S	M	T	W	T	F	S
				1	2	3
				(12)	(13)	(14)
4	5	6	7	8	9	10
(15)	(16)	(17)	(18)	(19)	(20)	(21)
11	12	13	14	15	16	17
(22)	(23)	(24)	(25)	(26)	(27)	(28)
18	19	20	21	22	23	24
(29f)	(1)	(2)	(3)	(4)	(5)	(6)
25	26	27	28	29	30	
(7)	(8)	(9)	(10)	(11)	(12)	

Passover Lamb Sacrificed — Nisan 14
Feast of First Fruits — 1st Sunday after Nisan 15

Feast of Unleavened Bread — Nisan 15-21
Pentecost — 8th Sunday after Nisan 15

Time of New Moon (Jerusalem) — a12:10 b2:49 c14:10 d22:57 e6:14 f13:05

July
(Tammuz 4)

S	M	T	W	T	F	S
						1
						(13)
2	3	4	5	6	7	8
(14)	(15)	(16)	(17)	(18)	(19)	(20)
9	10	11	12	13	14	15
(21)	(22)	(23)	(24)	(25)	(26)	(27)
16	17	18	19	20	21	22
(28)	(29g)	(1)	(2)	(3)	(4)	(5)
23	24	25	26	27	28	29
(6)	(7)	(8)	(9)	(10)	(11)	(12)
30	31					
(13)	(14)					

October
(Tishri 7)

S	M	T	W	T	F	S
1	2	3	4	5	6	7
(17)	(18)	(19)	(20)	(21)	(22)	(23)
8	9	10	11	12	13	14
(24)	(25)	(26)	(27)	(28)	(29)	(30j)
15	16	17	18	19	20	21
(1)	(2)	(3)	(4)	(5)	(6)	(7)
		23	24	25	26	27	28
(8)	(9)	(10)	(11)	(12)	(13)	(14)
29	30	31				
(15)	(16)	(17)				

August
(Ab 5)

S	M	T	W	T	F	S
		1	2	3	4	5
		(15)	(16)	(17)	(18)	(19)
6	7	8	9	10	11	12
(20)	(21)	(22)	(23)	(24)	(25)	(26)
13	14	15	16	17	18	19
(27)	(28)	(29)	(30h)	(1)	(2)	(3)
20	21	22	23	24	25	26
(4)	(5)	(6)	(7)	(8)	(9)	(10)
27	28	29	30	31		
(11)	(12)	(13)	(14)	(15)		

November
(Marheshvan 8)

S	M	T	W	T	F	S
			1	2	3	4
			(18)	(19)	(20)	(21)
5	6	7	8	9	10	11
(22)	(23)	(24)	(25)	(26)	(27)	(28)
12	13	14	15	16	17	18
(29k)	(1)	(2)	(3)	(4)	(5)	(6)
Elul	20	21	22	23	24	25
	(8)	(9)	(10)	(11)	(12)	(13)
26	27	28	29	30		
(14)	(15)	(16)	(17)	(18)		

September
(Elul 6)

S	M	T	W	T	F	S
					1	2
					(16)	(17)
3	4	5	6	7	8	9
(18)	(19)	(20)	(21)	(22)	(23)	(24)
10	11	12	13	14	15	16
(25)	(26)	(27)	(28)	(29i)	(1)	(2)
17	18	19	20	21	22	23
(3)	(4)	(5)	(6)	(7)	(8)	(9)
24	25	26	27	28	29	30
(10)	(11)	(12)	(13)	(14)	(15)	(16)

December
(Kislev 9)

S	M	T	W	T	F	S
					1	2
					(19)	(20)
3	4	5	6	7	8	9
(21)	(22)	(23)	(24)	(25)	(26)	(27)
10	11	12	13	14	15	16
(28)	(29)	(30m)	(1)	(2)	(3)	(4)
17	18	19	20	21	22	23
(5)	(6)	(7)	(8)	(9)	(10)	(11)
24	25	26	27	28	29	30
(12)	(13)	(14)	(15)	(16)	(17)	(18)
31						
(19)						

Day of Trumpets — Tishri 1
Feast of Booths — Tishri 15-22

Day of Atonement — Tishri 10
Feast of Dedication — 8 days beginning Kislev 25

Time of the New Moon —   g20:34   h5:13   i16:05   j5:45   k22:30   m17:40

A.D. 1

January
(Tebeth 10)

S	M	T	W	T	F	S
	1	2	3	4	5	6
	(20)	(21)	(22)	(23)	(24)	(25)
7	8	9	10	11	12	13
(26)	(27)	(28)	(29)	(30a)	(1)	(2)
14	15	16	17	18	19	20
(3)	(4)	(5)	(6)	(7)	(8)	(9)
21	22	23	24	25	26	27
(10)	(11)	(12)	(13)	(14)	(15)	(16)
28	29	30	31			
(17)	(18)	(19)	(20)			

April
(Nisan 1)

S	M	T	W	T	F	S
1	2	3	4	5	6	7
(21)	(22)	(23)	(24)	(25)	(26)	(27)
8	9	10	11	12	13	14
(28)	(29)	(30d)	(1)	(2)	(3)	(4)
15	16	17	18	19	20	21
(5)	(6)	(7)	(8)	(9)	(10)	(11)
22	23	24	25	26	27	28
(12)	(13)	(14)	(15)	(16)	(17)	(18)
29	30					
(19)	(20)					

February
(Shebat 11)

S	M	T	W	T	F	S
				1	2	3
				(21)	(22)	(23)
4	5	6	7	8	9	10
(24)	(25)	(26)	(27)	(28)	(29)	(30b)
11	12	13	14	15	16	17
(1)	(2)	(3)	(4)	(5)	(6)	(7)
18	19	20	21	22	23	24
(8)	(9)	(10)	(11)	(12)	(13)	(14)
25	26	27	28			
(15)	(16)	(17)	(18)			

May
(Iyyar 2)

S	M	T	W	T	F	S
		1	2	3	4	5
		(21)	(22)	(23)	(24)	(25)
6	7	8	9	10	11	12
(26)	(27)	(28)	(29e)	(1)	(2)	(3)
13	14	15	16	17	18	19
(4)	(5)	(6)	(7)	(8)	(9)	(10)
20	21	22	23	24	25	26
(11)	(12)	(13)	(14)	(15)	(16)	(17)
27	28	29	30	31		
(18)	(19)	(20)	(21)	(22)		

March
(Adar 12)

S	M	T	W	T	F	S
				1	2	3
				(19)	(20)	(21)
4	5	6	7	8	9	10
(22)	(23)	(24)	(25)	(26)	(27)	(28)
11	12	13	14	15	16	17
(29c)	(1)	(2)	(3)	(4)	(5)	(6)
18	19	20	21	22	23	24
(7)	(8)	(9)	(10)	(11)	(12)	(13)
25	26	27	28	29	30	31
(14)	(15)	(16)	(17)	(18)	(19)	(20)

June
(Sivan 3)

S	M	T	W	T	F	S
					1	2
					(23)	(24)
3	4	5	6	7	8	9
(26)	(26)	(27)	(28)	(29)	(30f)	(1)
10	11	12	13	14	15	16
(2)	(3)	(4)	(5)	(6)	(7)	(8)
17	18	19	20	21	22	23
(9)	(10)	(11)	(12)	(13)	(14)	(15)
24	25	26	27	28	29	30
(16)	(17)	(18)	(19)	(20)	(21)	(22)

Passover Lamb Sacrificed — Nisan 14
Feast of First Fruits — 1st Sunday after Nisan 15

Feast of Unleavened Bread — Nisan 15-21
Pentecost — 8th Sunday after Nisan 15

Time of New Moon (Jerusalem) —   a13:30   b7:49   c23:18   d11:47   e22:48   f7:07

A.D. 1

July						
(Tammuz 4)						
S	M	T	W	T	F	S
1	2	3	4	5	6	7
(23)	(24)	(25)	(26)	(27)	(28)	(29g)
8	9	10	11	12	13	14
(1)	(2)	(3)	(4)	(5)	(6)	(7)
15	16	17	18	19	20	21
(8)	(9)	(10)	(11)	(12)	(13)	(14)
22	23	24	25	26	27	28
(15)	(16)	(17)	(18)	(19)	(20)	(21)
29	30	31				
(22)	(23)	(24)				

October						
(Tishri 7)						
S	M	T	W	T	F	S
	1	2	3	4	5	6
	(27)	(28)	(29j)	(1)	(2)	(3)
7	8	9	10	11	12	13
(4)	(5)	(6)	(7)	(8)	(9)	(10)
14	15	16	17	18	19	20
(11)	(12)	(13)	(14)	(15)	(16)	(17)
21	22	23	24	25	26	27
(18)	(19)	(20)	(21)	(22)	(23)	(24)
28	29	30	31			
(25)	(26)	(27)	(28)			

August						
(Ab 5)						
S	M	T	W	T	F	S
			1	2	3	4
			(25)	(26)	(27)	(28)
5	6	7	8	9	10	11
(29h)	(1)	(2)	(3)	(4)	(5)	(6)
12	13	14	15	16	17	18
(7)	(8)	(9)	(10)	(11)	(12)	(13)
19	20	21	22	23	24	25
(14)	(15)	(16)	(17)	(18)	(19)	(20)
26	27	28	29	30	31	
(21)	(22)	(23)	(24)	(25)	(26)	

November						
(Marheshvan 8)						
S	M	T	W	T	F	S
				1	2	3
				(29)	(30k)	(1)
4	5	6	7	8	9	10
(2)	(3)	(4)	(5)	(6)	(7)	(8)
11	12	13	14	15	16	17
(9)	(10)	(11)	(12)	(13)	(14)	(15)
18	19	20	21	22	23	24
(16)	(17)	(18)	(19)	(20)	(21)	(22)
25	26	27	28	29	30	
(23)	(24)	(25)	(26)	(27)	(28)	

September						
(Elul 6)						
S	M	T	W	T	F	S
						1
						(27)
2	3	4	5	6	7	8
(28)	(29)	(30i)	(1)	(2)	(3)	(4)
9	10	11	12	13	14	15
(5)	(6)	(7)	(8)	(9)	(10)	(11)
16	17	18	19	20	21	22
(12)	(13)	(14)	(15)	(16)	(17)	(18)
23	24	25	26	27	28	29
(19)	(20)	(21)	(22)	(23)	(24)	(25)
30						
(26)						

December						
(Kislev 9)						
S	M	T	W	T	F	S
						1
						(29m)
2	3	4	5	6	7	8
(1)	(2)	(3)	(4)	(5)	(6)	(7)
9	10	11	12	13	14	15
(8)	(9)	(10)	(11)	(12)	(13)	(14)
16	17	18	19	20	21	22
(15)	(16)	(17)	(18)	(19)	(20)	(21)
23	24	25	26	27	28	29
(22)	(23)	(24)	(25)	(26)	(27)	(28)
30	31					
(29)	(30n)					

Day of Trumpets — Tishri 1
Feast of Booths — Tishri 15-22

Day of Atonement — Tishri 10
Feast of Dedication — 8 days beginning Kislev 25

Time of the New Moon — g13:36 h21:04 i5:26 j15:34 k4:13 m19:38 n13:12

A.D. 2

January
(Shebat 11)

S	M	T	W	T	F	S
		1	2	3	4	5
		(1)	(2)	(3)	(4)	(5)
6	7	8	9	10	11	12
(6)	(7)	(8)	(9)	(10)	(11)	(12)
13	14	15	16	17	18	19
(13)	(14)	(15)	(16)	(17)	(18)	(19)
20	21	22	23	24	25	26
20()	21()	(22)	(23)	(24)	(25)	(26)
27	28	29	30	31		
(27)	(28)	(29)	(30a)	(1)		

February
(Adar 12)

S	M	T	W	T	F	S
					1	2
					(2)	(3)
3	4	5	6	7	8	9
(4)	(5)	(6)	(7)	(8)	(9)	(10)
10	11	12	13	14	15	16
(11)	(12)	(13)	(14)	(15)	(16)	(17)
17	18	19	20	21	22	23
(18)	(19)	(20)	(21)	(22)	(23)	(24)
24	25	26	27	28		
(25)	(26)	(27)	(28)	(29)		

March
(Adar 12)

S	M	T	W	T	F	S
					1	2
					(30b)	(1)
3	4	5	6	7	8	9
(2)	(3)	(4)	(5)	(6)	(7)	(8)
10	11	12	13	14	15	16
(9)	(10)	(11)	(12)	(13)	(14)	(15)
17	18	19	20	21	22	23
(16)	(17)	(18)	(19)	(20)	(21)	(22)
24	25	26	27	28	29	30
(23)	(24)	(25)	(26)	(27)	(28)	(29c)
31						
(1)						

April
(Nisan 1)

S	M	T	W	T	F	S
	1	2	3	4	5	6
	(2)	(3)	(4)	(5)	(6)	(7)
7	8	9	10	11	12	13
(8)	(9)	(10)	(11)	(12)	(13)	(14)
14	15	16	17	18	19	20
(15)	(16)	(17)	(18)	(19)	(20)	(21)
21	22	23	24	25	26	27
(22)	(23)	(24)	(25)	(26)	(27)	(28)
28	29	30				
(29)	(30d)	(1)				

May
(Iyyar 2)

S	M	T	W	T	F	S
			1	2	3	4
			(2)	(3)	(4)	(5)
5	6	7	8	9	10	11
(6)	(7)	(8)	(9)	(10)	(11)	(12)
12	13	14	15	16	17	18
(13)	(14)	(15)	(16)	(17)	(18)	(19)
19	20	21	22	23	24	25
(20)	(21)	(22)	(23)	(24)	(25)	(26)
26	27	28	29	30	31	
(27)	(28)	(29e)	(1)	(2)	(3)	

June
(Sivan 3)

S	M	T	W	T	F	S
						1
						(4)
2	3	4	5	6	7	8
(5)	(6)	(7)	(8)	(9)	(10)	(11)
9	10	11	12	13	14	15
(12)	(13)	(14)	(15)	(16)	(17)	(18)
16	17	18	19	20	21	22
(19)	(20)	(21)	(22)	(23)	(24)	(25)
23	24	25	26	27	28	29
(26)	(27)	(28)	(29)	(30f)	(1)	(2)
30						
(3)						

Passover Lamb Sacrificed — Nisan 14
Feast of First Fruits — 1st Sunday after Nisan 15

Feast of Unleavened Bread — Nisan 15-21
Pentecost — 8th Sunday after Nisan 15

Time of New Moon (Jerusalem) —   a7:35   b1:21   c17:29   d7:29   e19:16   f5:06

A.D. 2

July (Tammuz 4)						
S	M	T	W	T	F	S
	1	2	3	4	5	6
	(4)	(5)	(6)	(7)	(8)	(9)
7	8	9	10	11	12	13
(10)	(11)	(12)	(13)	(14)	(15)	(16)
14	15	16	17	18	19	20
(17)	(18)	(19)	(20)	(21)	(22)	(23)
21	22	23	24	25	26	27
(24)	(25)	(26)	(27)	(28)	(29g)	(1)
28	29	30	31			
(2)	(3)	(4)	(5)			

October (Tishri 7)						
S	M	T	W	T	F	S
		1	2	3	4	5
		(8)	(9)	(10)	(11)	(12)
6	7	8	9	10	11	12
(13)	(13)	(15)	(16)	(17)	(18)	(19)
13	14	15	16	17	18	19
(20)	(21)	(22)	(23)	(24)	(25)	(26)
20	21	22	23	24	25	26
(27)	(28)	(29j)	(1)	(2)	(3)	(4)
27	28	29	30	31		
(5)	(6)	(7)	(8)	(9)		

August (Ab 5)						
S	M	T	W	T	F	S
				1	2	3
				(6)	(7)	(8)
4	5	6	7	8	9	10
(9)	(10)	(11)	(12)	(13)	(14)	(15)
11	12	13	14	15	16	17
(16)	(17)	(18)	(19)	(20)	(21)	(22)
18	19	20	21	22	23	24
(23)	(24)	(25)	(26)	(27)	(28)	(29h)
25	26	27	28	29	30	31
(1)	(2)	(3)	(4)	(5)	(6)	(7)

November (Marheshvan 8)						
S	M	T	W	T	F	S
					1	2
					(10)	(11)
3	4	5	6	7	8	9
(12)	(13)	(14)	(15)	(16)	(17)	(18)
10	11	12	13	14	15	16
(19)	(20)	(21)	(22)	(23)	(24)	(25)
17	18	19	20	21	22	23
(26)	(27)	(28)	(29)	(30k)	(1)	(2)
24	25	26	27	28	29	30
(3)	(4)	(5)	(6)	(7)	(8)	(9)

September (Elul 6)						
S	M	T	W	T	F	S
1	2	3	4	5	6	7
(8)	(9)	(10)	(11)	(12)	(13)	(14)
8	9	10	11	12	13	14
(15)	(16)	(17)	(18)	(19)	(20)	(21)
15	16	17	18	19	20	21
(22)	(23)	(24)	(25)	(26)	(27)	(28)
22	23	24	25	26	27	28
(29)	(30i)	(1)	(2)	(3)	(4)	(5)
29	30					
(6)	(7)					

December (Kislev 9)						
S	M	T	W	T	F	S
1	2	3	4	5	6	7
(10)	(11)	(12)	(13)	(14)	(15)	(16)
8	9	10	11	12	13	14
(17)	(18)	(19)	(20)	(21)	(22)	(23)
15	16	17	18	19	20	21
(24)	(25)	(26)	(27)	(28)	(29m)	(1)
22	23	24	25	26	27	28
(2)	(3)	(4)	(5)	(6)	(7)	(8)
29	30	31				
(9)	(10)	(11)				

Day of Trumpets — Tishri 1

Feast of Booths — Tishri 15-22

Day of Atonement — Tishri 10

Feast of Dedication — 8 days beginning Kislev 25

Time of the New Moon — g13:40   h21:52   i6:41   j16:51   k4:45   m18:22

A.D. 3

January
(Tebeth 10)

S	M	T	W	T	F	S
			1	2	3	4
			(12)	(13)	(14)	(15)
5	6	7	8	9	10	11
(16)	(17)	(18)	(19)	(20)	(21)	(22)
12	13	14	15	16	17	18
(23)	(24)	(25)	(26)	(27)	(28)	(29)
19	20	21	22	23	24	25
(30a)	(1)	(2)	(3)	(4)	(5)	(6)
26	27	28	29	30	31	
(7)	(8)	(9)	(10)	(11)	(12)	

April
(Nisan 1)

S	M	T	W	T	F	S
		1	2	3	4	5
		(13)	(14)	(15)	(16)	(17)
6	7	8	9	10	11	12
(18)	(19)	(20)	(21)	(22)	(23)	(24)
13	14	15	16	17	18	19
(25)	(26)	(27)	(28)	(29)	(30d)	(1)
20	21	22	23	24	25	26
(2)	(3)	(4)	(5)	(6)	(7)	(8)
27	28	29	30			
(9)	(10)	(11)	(12)			

February
(Shebat 11)

S	M	T	W	T	F	S
						1
						(13)
2	3	4	5	6	7	8
(14)	(15)	(16)	(17)	(18)	(19)	(20)
9	10	11	12	13	14	15
(21)	(22)	(23)	(24)	(25)	(26)	(27)
16	17	18	19	20	21	22
(28)	(29)	(30b)	(1)	(2)	(3)	(4)
23	24	25	26	27	28	
(5)	(6)	(7)	(8)	(9)	(10)	

June
(Sivan 3)

S	M	T	W	T	F	S
1	2	3	4	5	6	7
(14)	(15)	(16)	(17)	(18)	(19)	(20)
8	9	10	11	12	13	14
(21)	(22)	(23)	(24)	(25)	(26)	(27)
15	16	17	18	19	20	21
(28)	(29f)	(1)	(2)	(3)	(4)	(5)
22	23	24	25	26	27	28
(6)	(7)	(8)	(9)	(10)	(11)	(12)
29	30					
(13)	(14)					

March
(Adar 12)

S	M	T	W	T	F	S
						1
						(11)
2	3	4	5	6	7	8
(12)	(13)	(14)	(15)	(16)	(17)	(18)
9	10	11	12	13	14	15
(19)	(20)	(21)	(22)	(23)	(24)	(25)
16	17	18	19	20	21	22
(26)	(27)	(28)	(29c)	(1)	(2)	(3)
23	24	25	26	27	28	29
(4)	(5)	(6)	(7)	(8)	(9)	(10)
30	31					

June
(Sivan 3)

S	M	T	W	T	F	S
1	2	3	4	5	6	7
(14)	(15)	(16)	(17)	(18)	(19)	(20)
8	9	10	11	12	13	14
(21)	(22)	(23)	(24)	(25)	(26)	(27)
15	16	17	18	19	20	21
(28)	(29f)	(1)	(2)	(3)	(4)	(5)
22	23	24	25	26	27	28
(6)	(7)	(8)	(9)	(10)	(11)	(12)
29	30					
(13)	(14)					

Passover Lamb Sacrificed — Nisan 14
Feast of First Fruits — 1st Sunday after Nisan 15

Feast of Unleavened Bread — Nisan 15-21
Pentecost — 8th Sunday after Nisan 15

Time of New Moon (Jerusalem) — a9:24 b1:27 c17:58 d10:15 e1:24 f14:48

A.D. 3

July
(Tammuz 4)

S	M	T	W	T	F	S
		1	2	3	4	5
		(15)	(16)	(17)	(18)	(19)
6	7	8	9	10	11	12
(20)	(21)	(22)	(23)	(24)	(25)	(26)
13	14	15	16	17	18	19
(27)	(28)	(29)	(30g)	(1)	(2)	(3)
20	21	22	23	24	25	26
(4)	(5)	(6)	(7)	(8)	(9)	(10)
27	28	29	30	31		
(11)	(12)	(13)	(14)	(15)		

October
(Tishri 7)

S	M	T	W	T	F	S
			1	2	3	4
			(19)	(20)	(21)	(22)
5	6	7	8	9	10	11
(23)	(24)	(25)	(26)	(27)	(28)	(29)
12	13	14	15	16	17	18
(30j)	(1)	(2)	(3)	(4)	(5)	(6)
19	20	21	22	23	24	25
(7)	(8)	(9)	(10)	(11)	(12)	(13)
26	27	28	29	30	31	
(14)	(15)	(16)	(17)	(18)	(19)	

August
(Ab 5)

S	M	T	W	T	F	S
					1	2
					(16)	(17)
3	4	5	6	7	8	9
(18)	(19)	(20)	(21)	(22)	(23)	(24)
10	11	12	13	14	15	16
(25)	(26)	(27)	(28)	(29h)	(1)	(2)
17	18	19	20	21	22	23
(3)	(4)	(5)	(6)	(7)	(8)	(9)
24	25	26	27	28	29	30
(10)	(11)	(12)	(13)	(14)	(15)	(16)
31						
(17)						

November
(Marheshvan 8)

S	M	T	W	T	F	S
						1
						(20)
2	3	4	5	6	7	8
(21)	(22)	(23)	(24)	(25)	(26)	(27)
9	10	11	12	13	14	15
(28)	(29k)	(1)	(2)	(3)	(4)	(5)
16	17	18	19	20	21	22
(6)	(7)	(8)	(9)	(10)	(11)	(12)
23	24	25	26	27	28	29
(13)	(14)	(15)	(16)	(17)	(18)	(19)
30						
(20)						

September
(Elul 6)

S	M	T	W	T	F	S
	1	2	3	4	5	6
	(18)	(19)	(20)	(21)	(22)	(23)
7	8	9	10	11	12	13
(24)	(25)	(26)	(27)	(28)	(29i)	(1)
14	15	16	17	18	19	20
(2)	(3)	(4)	(5)	(6)	(7)	(8)
21	22	23	24	25	25	27
(9)	(10)	(11)	(12)	(13)	(14)	(15)
28	29	30				
(16)	(17)	(18)				

December
(Kislev 9)

S	M	T	W	T	F	S
	1	2	3	4	5	6
	(21)	(22)	(23)	(24)	(25)	(26)
7	8	9	10	11	12	13
(27)	(28)	(29)	(30m)	(1)	(2)	(3)
14	15	16	17	18	19	20
(4)	(5)	(6)	(7)	(8)	(9)	(10)
21	22	23	24	25	26	27
(11)	(12)	(13)	(14)	(15)	(16)	(17)
28	29	30	31			
(18)	(19)	(20)	(21)			

Day of Trumpets — Tishri 1

Feast of Booths — Tishri 15-22

Day of Atonement — Tishri 10

Feast of Dedication — 8 days beginning Kislev 25

Time of the New Moon —   g2:24   h12:46   i22:39   j8:44   k19:19   m6:27

A.D. 4

January
(Tebeth 10)

S	M	T	W	T	F	S
				1	2	3
				(22)	(23)	(24)
4	5	6	7	8	9	10
(25)	(26)	(27)	(28)	(29a)	(1)	(2)
11	12	13	14	15	16	17
(3)	(4)	(5)	(6)	(7)	(8)	(9)
18	19	20	21	22	23	24
(10)	(11)	(12)	(13)	(14)	(15)	(16)
25	26	27	28	29	30	31
(17)	(18)	(19)	(20)	(21)	(22)	(23)

April
(Nisan 1)

S	M	T	W	T	F	S
				1	2	3
				(25)	(26)	(27)
4	5	6	7	8	9	10
(28)	(29)	(30d)	(1)	(2)	(3)	(4)
11	12	13	14	15	16	17
(5)	(6)	(7)	(8)	(9)	(10)	(11)
18	19	20	21	22	23	24
(12)	(13)	(14)	(15)	(16)	(17)	(18)
25	26	27	28	29	30	
(19)	(20)	(21)	(22)	(23)	(24)	

February
(Shebat 11)

S	M	T	W	T	F	S
1	2	3	4	5	6	7
(24)	(25)	(26)	(27)	(28)	(29)	(30b)
8	9	10	11	12	13	14
(1)	(2)	(3)	(4)	(5)	(6)	(7)
15	16	17	18	19	20	21
(8)	(9)	(10)	(11)	(12)	(13)	(14)
22	23	24	25	26	27	28
(15)	(16)	(17)	(18)	(19)	(20)	(21)
29						
(22)						

May
(Iyyar 2)

S	M	T	W	T	F	S
						1
						(25)
2	3	4	5	6	7	8
(26)	(27)	(28)	(29)	(30e)	(1)	(2)
9	10	11	12	13	14	15
(3)	(4)	(5)	(6)	(7)	(8)	(9)
16	17	18	19	20	21	22
(10)	(11)	(12)	(13)	(14)	(15)	(16)
23	24	25	26	27	28	29
(17)	(18)	(19)	(20)	(21)	(22)	(23)
30	31					
(24)	(25)					

March
(Adar 12)

S	M	T	W	T	F	S
	1	2	3	4	5	6
	(23)	(24)	(25)	(26)	(27)	(28)
7	8	9	10	11	12	13
(29c)	(1)	(2)	(3)	(4)	(5)	(6)
14	15	16	17	18	19	20
(7)	(8)	(9)	(10)	(11)	(12)	(13)
21	22	23	24	25	26	27
(14)	(15)	(16)	(17)	(18)	(19)	(20)
28	29	30	31			
(21)	(22)	(23)	(24)			

June
(Sivan 3)

S	M	T	W	T	F	S
		1	2	3	4	5
		(26)	(27)	(28)	(29f)	(1)
6	7	8	9	10	11	12
(2)	(3)	(4)	(5)	(6)	(7)	(8)
13	14	15	16	17	18	19
(9)	(10)	(11)	(12)	(13)	(14)	(15)
20	21	22	23	24	25	26
(16)	(17)	(18)	(19)	(20)	(21)	(22)
27	28	29	30			
(23)	(24)	(25)	(26)			

Passover Lamb Sacrificed — Nisan 14
Feast of First Fruits — 1st Sunday after Nisan 15

Feast of Unleavened Bread — Nisan 15-21
Pentecost — 8th Sunday after Nisan 15

Time of New Moon (Jerusalem) — a18:10 b6:42 c20:20 d11:02 e2:23 f17:38

A.D. 4

		July (Tammuz 4)				
S	M	T	W	T	F	S
				1	2	3
				(27)	(28)	(29)
4	5	6	7	8	9	10
(30g)	(1)	(2)	(3)	(4)	(5)	(6)
11	12	13	14	15	16	17
(7)	(8)	(9)	(10)	(11)	(12)	(13)
18	19	20	21	22	23	24
(14)	(15)	(16)	(17)	(18)	(19)	(20)
25	26	27	28	29	30	31
(21)	(22)	(23)	(24)	(25)	(26)	(27)

		October (Marheshvan 8)				
S	M	T	W	T	F	S
					1	2
					(1)	(2)
3	4	5	6	7	8	9
(3)	(4)	(5)	(6)	(7)	(8)	(9)
10	11	12	13	14	15	16
(10)	(11)	(12)	(13)	(14)	(15)	(16)
17	18	19	20	21	22	23
(17)	(18)	(19)	(20)	(21)	(22)	(23)
24	25	26	27	28	29	30
(24)	(25)	(26)	(27)	(28)	(29)	(30k)
31						
(1)						

		August (Ab 5)				
S	M	T	W	T	F	S
1	2	3	4	5	6	7
(28)	(29h)	(1)	(2)	(3)	(4)	(5)
8	9	10	11	12	13	14
(6)	(7)	(8)	(9)	(10)	(11)	(12)
15	16	17	18	19	20	21
(13)	(14)	(15)	(16)	(17)	(18)	(19)
22	23	24	25	26	27	28
(20)	(21)	(22)	(23)	(24)	(25)	(26)
29	30	31				
(27)	(28)	(29)				

		November (Kislev 9)				
S	M	T	W	T	F	S
	1	2	3	4	5	6
	(2)	(3)	(4)	(5)	(6)	(7)
7	8	9	10	11	12	13
(8)	(9)	(10)	(11)	(12)	(13)	(14)
14	15	16	17	18	19	20
(15)	(16)	(17)	(18)	(19)	(20)	(21)
21	22	23	24	25	26	27
(22)	(23)	(24)	(25)	(26)	(27)	(28)
28	29	30				
(29m)	(1)	(2)				

		September (Elul 6)				
S	M	T	W	T	F	S
			1	2	3	4
			(30i)	(1)	(2)	(3)
5	6	7	8	9	10	11
(4)	(5)	(6)	(7)	(8)	(9)	(10)
12	13	14	15	16	17	18
(11)	(12)	(13)	(14)	(15)	(16)	(17)
19	20	21	22	23	24	25
(18)	(19)	(20)	(21)	(22)	(23)	(24)
26	27	28	29	30		
(25)	(26)	(27)	(28)	(29k)		

		December (Tebeth 10)				
S	M	T	W	T	F	S
			1	2	3	4
			(3)	(4)	(5)	(6)
5	6	7	8	9	10	11
(7)	(8)	(9)	(10)	(11)	(12)	(13)
12	13	14	15	16	17	18
(14)	(15)	(16)	(17)	(18)	(19)	(20)
19	20	21	22	23	24	25
(21)	(22)	(23)	(24)	(25)	(26)	(27)
26	27	28	29	30	31	
(28)	(29)	(30n)	(1)	(2)	(3)	

Day of Trumpets — Tishri 1
Feast of Booths — Tishri 15-22

Day of Atonement — Tishri 10
Feast of Dedication — 8 days beginning Kislev 25

Time of the New Moon —   g8:13   h21:56   i10:54   j23:14   k10:56   m21:52   n8:30

A.D. 5

January
(Shebat 11)

S	M	T	W	T	F	S
						1
						(4)
2	3	4	5	6	7	8
(5)	(6)	(7)	(8)	(9)	(10)	(11)
9	10	11	12	13	14	15
(12)	(13)	(14)	(15)	(16)	(17)	(18)
16	17	18	19	20	21	22
(19)	(20)	(21)	(22)	(23)	(24)	(25)
23	24	25	26	27	28	29
(26)	(27)	(28)	(29a)	(1)	(2)	(3)
30	31					
(4)	(5)					

April
(Nisan 1)

S	M	T	W	T	F	S
					1	2
					(6)	(7)
3	4	5	6	7	8	9
(8)	(9)	(10)	(11)	(12)	(13)	(14)
10	11	12	13	14	15	16
(15)	(16)	(17)	(18)	(19)	(20)	(21)
17	18	19	20	21	22	23
(22)	(23)	(24)	(25)	(26)	(27)	(28)
24	25	26	27	28	29	30
(29)	(30d)	(1)	(2)	(3)	(4)	(5)

February
(Adar 12)

S	M	T	W	T	F	S
		1	2	3	4	5
		(6)	(7)	(8)	(9)	(10)
6	7	8	9	10	11	12
(11)	(12)	(13)	(14)	(15)	(16)	(17)
13	14	15	16	17	18	19
(18)	(19)	(20)	(21)	(22)	(23)	(24)
20	21	22	23	24	25	26
(25)	(26)	(27)	(28)	(29)	(30b)	(1)
27	28					
(2)	(3)					

May
(Iyyar 2)

S	M	T	W	T	F	S
1	2	3	4	5	6	7
(6)	(7)	(8)	(9)	(10)	(11)	(12)
8	9	10	11	12	13	14
(13)	(14)	(15)	(16)	(17)	(18)	(19)
15	16	17	18	19	20	21
(20)	(21)	(22)	(23)	(24)	(25)	(26)
22	23	24	25	26	27	28
(27)	(28)	(29e)	(1)	(2)	(3)	(4)
29	30	31				
(5)	(6)	(7)				

March
(Adar II 13)

S	M	T	W	T	F	S
		1	2	3	4	5
		(4)	(5)	(6)	(7)	(8)
6	7	8	9	10	11	12
(9)	(10)	(11)	(12)	(13)	(14)	(15)
13	14	15	16	17	18	19
(16)	(17)	(18)	(19)	(20)	(21)	(22)
20	21	22	23	24	25	26
(23)	(24)	(25)	(26)	(27)	(28)	(29c)
27	28	29	30	31		
(1)	(2)	(3)	(4)	(5)		

June
(Sivan 3)

S	M	T	W	T	F	S
			1	2	3	4
			(8)	(9)	(10)	(11)
5	6	7	8	9	10	11
(12)	(13)	(14)	(15)	(16)	(17)	(18)
12	13	14	15	16	17	18
(19)	(20)	(21)	(22)	(23)	(24)	(25)
19	20	21	22	23	24	25
(26)	(27)	(28)	(29)	(30f)	(1)	(2)
26	27	28	29	30		
(3)	(4)	(5)	(6)	(7)		

Passover Lamb Sacrificed — Nisan 14
Feast of First Fruits — 1st Sunday after Nisan 15

Feast of Unleavened Bread — Nisan 15-21
Pentecost — 8th Sunday after Nisan 15

Time of New Moon (Jerusalem) — a18:51 b5:30 c16:52 d5:13 e18:35 f9:00

A.D. 5

July
(Tammuz 4)

S	M	T	W	T	F	S
					1	2
					(8)	(9)
3	4	5	6	7	8	9
(10)	(11)	(12)	(13)	(14)	(15)	(16)
10	11	12	13	14	15	16
(17)	(18)	(19)	(20)	(21)	(22)	(23)
17	18	19	20	21	22	23
(24)	(25)	(26)	(27)	(28)	(29)	(30g)
24	25	26	27	28	29	30
(1)	(2)	(3)	(4)	(5)	(6)	(7)
31						
(8)						

October
(Tishri 7)

S	M	T	W	T	F	S
						1
						(11)
2	3	4	5	6	7	8
(12)	(13)	(14)	(15)	(16)	(17)	(18)
9	10	11	12	13	14	15
(19)	(20)	(21)	(22)	(23)	(24)	(25)
16	17	18	19	20	21	22
(26)	(27)	(28)	(29j)	(1)	(2)	(3)
23	24	25	26	27	28	29
(4)	(5)	(6)	(7)	(8)	(9)	(10)
30	31					
(11)	(12)					

August
(Ab 5)

S	M	T	W	T	F	S
	1	2	3	4	5	6
	(9)	(10)	(11)	(12)	(13)	(14)
7	8	9	10	11	12	13
(15)	(16)	(17)	(18)	(19)	(20)	(21)
14	15	16	17	18	19	20
(22)	(23)	(24)	(25)	(26)	(27)	(28)
21	22	23	24	25	26	27
(29h)	(1)	(2)	(3)	(4)	(5)	(6)
28	29	30	31			
(7)	(8)	(9)	(10)			

November
(Marheshvan 8)

S	M	T	W	T	F	S
		1	2	3	4	5
		(13)	(14)	(15)	(16)	(17)
6	7	8	9	10	11	12
(18)	(19)	(20)	(21)	(22)	(23)	(24)
13	14	15	16	17	18	19
(25)	(26)	(27)	(28)	(29)	(30k)	(1)
20	21	22	23	24	25	26
(2)	(3)	(4)	(5)	(6)	(7)	(8)
27	28	29	30			
(9)	(10)	(11)	(12)			

September
(Elul 6)

S	M	T	W	T	F	S
				1	2	3
				(11)	(12)	(13)
4	5	6	7	8	9	10
(14)	(15)	(16)	(17)	(18)	(19)	(20)
11	12	13	14	15	16	17
(21)	(22)	(23)	(24)	(25)	(26)	(27)
18	19	20	21	22	23	24
(28)	(29)	(30i)	(1)	(2)	(3)	(4)
25	26	27	28	29	30	
(5)	(6)	(7)	(8)	(9)	(10)	

December
(Kislev 9)

S	M	T	W	T	F	S
				1	2	3
				(13)	(14)	(15)
4	5	6	7	8	9	10
(16)	(17)	(18)	(19)	(20)	(21)	(22)
11	12	13	14	15	16	17
(23)	(24)	(25)	(26)	(27)	(28)	(29)
18	19	20	21	22	23	24
(30m)	(1)	(2)	(3)	(4)	(5)	(6)
25	26	27	28	29	30	31
(7)	(8)	(9)	(10)	(11)	(12)	(13)

Day of Trumpets — Tishri 1
Feast of Booths — Tishri 15-22

Day of Atonement — Tishri 10
Feast of Dedication — 8 days beginning Kislev 25

Time of the New Moon — g0:21　h16:17　i804　j22:57　k12:18　m0:05

A.D. 6

January
(Tebeth 10)

S	M	T	W	T	F	S
1	2	3	4	5	6	7
(14)	(15)	(16)	(17)	(18)	(19)	(20)
8	9	10	11	12	13	14
(21)	(22)	(23)	(24)	(25)	(26)	(27)
15	16	17	18	19	20	21
(28)	(29a)	(1)	(2)	(3)	(4)	(5)
22	23	24	25	26	27	28
(6)	(7)	(8)	(9)	(10)	(11)	(12)
29	30	31				
(13)	(14)	(15)				

February
(Shebat 11)

S	M	T	W	T	F	S
			1	2	3	4
			(16)	(17)	(18)	(19)
5	6	7	8	9	10	11
(20)	(21)	(22)	(23)	(24)	(25)	(26)
12	13	14	15	16	17	18
(27)	(28)	(29b)	(1)	(2)	(3)	(4)
19	20	21	22	23	24	25
(5)	(6)	(7)	(8)	(9)	(10)	(11)
26	27	28				
(12)	(13)	(14)				

March
(Adar 12)

S	M	T	W	T	F	S
			1	2	3	4
			(15)	(16)	(17)	(18)
5	6	7	8	9	10	11
(19)	(20)	(21)	(22)	(23)	(24)	(25)
12	13	14	15	16	17	18
(26)	(27)	(28)	(29)	(30c)	(1)	(2)
19	20	21	22	23	24	25
(3)	(4)	(5)	(6)	(7)	(8)	(9)
26	27	28	29	30	31	
(10)	(11)	(12)	(13)	(14)	(15)	

April
(Nisan 1)

S	M	T	W	T	F	S
						1
						(16)
2	3	4	5	6	7	8
(17)	(18)	(19)	(20)	(21)	(22)	(23)
9	10	11	12	13	14	15
(24)	(25)	(26)	(27)	(28)	(29d)	(1)
16	17	18	19	20	21	22
(2)	(3)	(4)	(5)	(6)	(7)	(8)
23	24	25	26	27	28	29
(9)	(10)	(11)	(12)	(13)	(14)	(15)
30						
(16)						

May
(Iyyar 2)

S	M	T	W	T	F	S
	1	2	3	4	5	6
	(17)	(18)	(19)	(20)	(21)	(22)
7	8	9	10	11	12	13
(23)	(24)	(25)	(26)	(27)	(28)	(29)
14	15	16	17	18	19	20
(30e)	(1)	(2)	(3)	(4)	(5)	(6)
21	22	23	24	25	26	27
(7)	(8)	(9)	(10)	(11)	(12)	(13)
28	29	30	31			
(14)	(15)	(16)	(17)			

June
(Sivan 3)

S	M	T	W	T	F	S
				1	2	3
				(18)	(19)	(20)
4	5	6	7	8	9	10
(21)	(22)	(23)	(24)	(25)	(26)	(27)
11	12	13	14	15	16	17
(28)	(29f)	(1)	(2)	(3)	(4)	(5)
18	19	20	21	22	23	24
(6)	(7)	(8)	(9)	(10)	(11)	(12)
25	26	27	28	29	30	
(13)	(14)	(15)	(16)	(17)	(18)	

Passover Lamb Sacrificed — Nisan 14
Feast of First Fruits — 1st Sunday after Nisan 15

Feast of Unleavened Bread — Nisan 15-21
Pentecost — 8th Sunday after Nisan 15

Time of New Moon (Jerusalem) — a10:37 b20:19 c5:35 d14:50 e0:40 f11:51

A.D. 6

July (Tammuz 4)						
S	M	T	W	T	F	S
						1 (19)
2 (20)	3 (21)	4 (22)	5 (23)	6 (24)	7 (25)	8 (26)
9 (27)	10 (28)	11 (29)	12 (30g)	13 (1)	14 (2)	15 (3)
16 (4)	17 (5)	18 (6)	19 (7)	20 (8)	21 (9)	22 (10)
23 (11)	24 (12)	25 (13)	26 (14)	27 (15)	28 (16)	29 (17)
30	31					

October (Tishri 7)						
S	M	T	W	T	F	S
1 (22)	2 (23)	3 (24)	4 (25)	5 (26)	6 (27)	7 (28)
8 (29)	9 (30j)	10 (1)	11 (2)	12 (3)	13 (4)	14 (5)
15	16	17	18	19	20	21
22 (6)	23 (7)	24 (8)	25 (9)	26 (10)	27 (11)	28 (12)
29 (13)	30 (14)	31 (15)	(16)	(17)	(18)	(19)
(20)	(21)	(22)				

August (Ab 5)						
S	M	T	W	T	F	S
		1 (20)	2 (21)	3 (22)	4 (23)	5 (24)
6 (25)	7 (26)	8 (27)	9 (28)	10 (29h)	11 (1)	12 (2)
13 (3)	14 (4)	15 (5)	16 (6)	17 (7)	18 (8)	19 (9)
20 (10)	21 (11)	22 (12)	23 (13)	24 (14)	25 (15)	26 (16)
27 (17)	28 (18)	29 (19)	30 (20)	31 (21)		

November (Marheshvan 8)						
S	M	T	W	T	F	S
			1 (23)	2 (24)	3 (25)	4 (26)
5 (27)	6 (28)	7 (29k)	8 (1)	9 (2)	10 (3)	11 (4)
12 (5)	13 (6)	14 (7)	15 (8)	16 (9)	17 (10)	18 (11)
19 (12)	20 (13)	21 (14)	22 (15)	23 (16)	24 (17)	25 (18)
26 (19)	27 (20)	28 (21)	29 (22)	30 (23)		

September (Elul 6)						
S	M	T	W	T	F	S
					1 (22)	2 (23)
3 (24)	4 (25)	5 (26)	6 (27)	7 (28)	8 (29)	9 (30i)
10 (1)	11 (2)	12 (3)	13 (4)	14 (5)	15 (6)	16 (7)
17 (8)	18 (9)	19 (10)	20 (11)	21 (12)	22 (13)	23 (14)
24 (15)	25 (16)	26 (17)	27 (18)	28 (19)	29 (20)	30 (21)

December (Kislev 9)						
S	M	T	W	T	F	S
					1 (24)	2 (25)
3 (26)	4 (27)	5 (28)	6 (29)	7 (30m)	8 (1)	9 (2)
10 (3)	11 (4)	12 (5)	13 (6)	14 (7)	15 (8)	16 (9)
17 (10)	18 (11)	19 (12)	20 (13)	21 (14)	22 (15)	23 (16)
24 (17)	25 (18)	26 (19)	27 (20)	28 (21)	29 (22)	30 (23)
31 (24)						

Day of Trumpets — Tishri 1
Feast of Booths — Tishri 15-22

Day of Atonement — Tishri 10
Feast of Dedication — 8 days beginning Kislev 25

Time of the New Moon — g1:06 h16:42 i10:07 j4:03 k21:03 m12:14

A.D. 7

January
(Tebeth 10)

S	M	T	W	T	F	S
	1	2	3	4	5	6
	(25)	(26)	(27)	(28)	(29)	(30a)
7	8	9	10	11	12	13
(1)	(2)	(3)	(4)	(5)	(6)	(7)
14	15	16	17	18	19	20
(8)	(9)	(10)	(11)	(12)	(13)	(14)
21	22	23	24	25	26	27
(15)	(16)	(17)	(18)	(19)	(20)	(21)
28	29	30	31			
(22)	(23)	(24)	(25)			

February
(Shebat 11)

S	M	T	W	T	F	S
				1	2	3
				(26)	(27)	(28)
4	5	6	7	8	9	10
(29b)	(1)	(2)	(3)	(4)	(5)	(6)
11	12	13	14	15	16	17
(7)	(8)	(9)	(10)	(11)	(12)	(13)
18	19	20	21	22	23	24
(14)	(15)	(16)	(17)	(18)	(19)	(20)
25	26	27	28			
(21)	(22)	(23)	(24)			

March
(Adar 12)

S	M	T	W	T	F	S
				1	2	3
				(25)	(26)	(27)
4	5	6	7	8	9	10
(28)	(29c)	(1)	(2)	(3)	(4)	(5)
11	12	13	14	15	16	17
(6)	(7)	(8)	(9)	(10)	(11)	(12)
18	19	20	21	22	23	24
(13)	(14)	(15)	(16)	(17)	(18)	(19)
25	26	27	28	29	30	31
(20)	(21)	(22)	(23)	(24)	(25)	(26)

April
(Adar II 13)

S	M	T	W	T	F	S
1	2	3	4	5	6	7
(27)	(28)	(29)	(30d)	(1)	(2)	(3)
8	9	10	11	12	13	14
(4)	(5)	(6)	(7)	(8)	(9)	(10)
15	16	17	18	19	20	21
(11)	(12)	(13)	(14)	(15)	(16)	(17)
22	23	24	25	26	27	28
(18)	(19)	(20)	(21)	(22)	(23)	(24)
29	30					
(25)	(26)					

May
(Nisan 1)

S	M	T	W	T	F	S
		1	2	3	4	5
		(27)	(28)	(29e)	(1)	(2)
6	7	8	9	10	11	12
(3)	(4)	(5)	(6)	(7)	(8)	(9)
13	14	15	16	17	18	19
(10)	(11)	(12)	(13)	(14)	(15)	(16)
20	21	22	23	24	25	26
(17)	(18)	(19)	(20)	(21)	(22)	(23)
27	28	29	30	31		
(24)	(25)	(26)	(27)	(28)		

June
(Iyyar 2)

S	M	T	W	T	F	S
					1	2
					(29f)	(1)
3	4	5	6	7	8	9
(2)	(3)	(4)	(5)	(6)	(7)	(8)
10	11	12	13	14	15	16
(9)	(10)	(11)	(12)	(13)	(14)	(15)
17	18	19	20	21	22	23
(16)	(17)	(18)	(19)	(20)	(21)	(22)
24	25	26	27	28	29	30
(23)	(24)	(25)	(26)	(27)	(28)	(29)

Passover Lamb Sacrificed — Nisan 14
Feast of First Fruits — 1st Sunday after Nisan 15

Feast of Unleavened Bread — Nisan 15-21
Pentecost — 8th Sunday after Nisan 15

Time of New Moon (Jerusalem) —   a1:22   b12:33   c22:00   d6:09   e13:41   f21:39

A.D. 7

July
(Sivan 3)

S	M	T	W	T	F	S
1	2	3	4	5	6	7
(30g)	(1)	(2)	(3)	(4)	(5)	(6)
8	9	10	11	12	13	14
(7)	(8)	(9)	(10)	(11)	(12)	(13)
15	16	17	18	19	20	21
(14)	(15)	(16)	(17)	(18)	(19)	(20)
22	23	24	25	26	27	28
(21)	(22)	(23)	(24)	(25)	(26)	(27)
29	30	31				
(28)	(29h)	(1)				

October
(Tishri 7)

S	M	T	W	T	F	S
	1	2	3	4	5	6
	(3)	(4)	(5)	(6)	(7)	(8)
7	8	9	10	11	12	13
(9)	(10)	(11)	(12)	(13)	(14)	(15)
14	15	16	17	18	19	20
(16)	(17)	(18)	(19)	(20)	(21)	(22)
21	22	23	24	25	26	27
(23)	(24)	(25)	(26)	(27)	(28)	(29k)
28	29	30	31			
(1)	(2)	(3)	(4)			

August
(Ab 5)

S	M	T	W	T	F	S
			1	2	3	4
			(2)	(3)	(4)	(5)
5	6	7	8	9	10	11
(6)	(7)	(8)	(9)	(10)	(11)	(12)
12	13	14	15	16	17	18
(13)	(14)	(15)	(16)	(17)	(18)	(19)
19	20	21	22	23	24	25
(20)	(21)	(22)	(23)	(24)	(25)	(26)
26	27	28	29	30	31	
(27)	(28)	(29)	(30i)	(1)	(2)	

November
(Marheshvan 8)

S	M	T	W	T	F	S
				1	2	3
				(5)	(6)	(7)
4	5	6	7	8	9	10
(8)	(9)	(10)	(11)	(12)	(13)	(14)
11	12	13	14	15	16	17
(15)	(16)	(17)	(18)	(19)	(20)	(21)
18	19	20	21	22	23	24
(22)	(23)	(24)	(25)	(26)	(27)	(28)
25	26	27	28	29	30	
(29)	(30m)	(1)	(2)	(3)	(4)	

September
(Elul 6)

S	M	T	W	T	F	S
						1
						(3)
2	3	4	5	6	7	8
(4)	(5)	(6)	(7)	(8)	(9)	(10)
9	10	11	12	13	14	15
(11)	(12)	(13)	(14)	(15)	(16)	(17)
16	17	18	19	20	21	22
(18)	(19)	(20)	(21)	(22)	(23)	(24)
23	24	25	26	27	28	29
(25)	(26)	(27)	(28)	(29)	(30j)	(1)
30						

December
(Kislev 9)

S	M	T	W	T	F	S
						1
						(5)
2	3	4	5	6	7	8
(6)	(7)	(8)	(9)	(10)	(11)	(12)
9	10	11	12	13	14	15
(13)	(14)	(15)	(16)	(17)	(18)	(19)
16	17	18	19	20	21	22
(20)	(21)	(22)	(23)	(24)	(25)	(26)
23	24	25	26	27	28	29
(27)	(28)	(29)	(30n)	(1)	(2)	(3)
30	31					

Day of Trumpets — Tishri 1
Feast of Booths — Tishri 15-22

Day of Atonement — Tishri 10
Feast of Dedication — 8 days beginning Kislev 25

Time of the New Moon — g7:11   h19:14   i10:19   j3:52   k22:43   m17:26   n10:42

A.D. 8

January (Tebeth 10)						
S	M	T	W	T	F	S
		1	2	3	4	5
		(6)	(7)	(8)	(9)	(10)
6	7	8	9	10	11	12
(11)	(12)	(13)	(14)	(15)	(16)	(17)
13	14	15	16	17	18	19
(18)	(19)	(20)	(21)	(22)	(23)	(24)
20	21	22	23	24	25	26
(25)	(26)	(27)	(28)	(29)	(30a)	(1)
27	28	29	30	31		
(2)	(3)	(4)	(5)	(6)		

April (Nisan 1)						
S	M	T	W	T	F	S
		1	2	3	4	5
		(9)	(10)	(11)	(12)	(13)
6	7	8	9	10	11	12
(14)	(15)	(16)	(17)	(18)	(19)	(20)
13	14	15	16	17	18	19
(21)	(22)	(23)	(24)	(25)	(26)	(27)
20	21	22	23	24	25	26
(28)	(29)	(30d)	(1)	(2)	(3)	(4)
27	28	29	30			
(5)	(6)	(7)	(8)			

February (Shebat 11)						
S	M	T	W	T	F	S
					1	2
					(7)	(8)
3	4	5	6	7	8	9
(9)	(10)	(11)	(12)	(13)	(14)	(15)
10	11	12	13	14	15	16
(16)	(17)	(18)	(19)	(20)	(21)	(22)
17	18	19	20	21	22	23
(23)	(24)	(25)	(26)	(27)	(28)	(29b)
24	25	26	27	28	29	
(1)	(2)	(3)	(4)	(5)	(6)	

May (Iyyar 2)						
S	M	T	W	T	F	S
				1	2	3
				(9)	(10)	(11)
4	5	6	7	8	9	10
(12)	(13)	(14)	(15)	(16)	(17)	(18)
11	12	13	14	15	16	17
(19)	(20)	(21)	(22)	(23)	(24)	(25)
18	19	20	21	22	23	24
(26)	(27)	(28)	(29e)	(1)	(2)	(3)
25	26	27	28	29	30	31
(4)	(5)	(6)	(7)	(8)	(9)	(10)

March (Adar 12)						
S	M	T	W	T	F	S
						1
						(7)
2	3	4	5	6	7	8
(8)	(9)	(10)	(11)	(12)	(13)	(14)
9	10	11	12	13	14	15
(15)	(16)	(17)	(18)	(19)	(20)	(21)
16	17	18	19	20	21	22
(22)	(23)	(24)	(25)	(26)	(27)	(28)
23	24	25	26	27	28	29
(29c)	(1)	(2)	(3)	(4)	(5)	(6)
30	31					

June (Sivan 3)						
S	M	T	W	T	F	S
1	2	3	4	5	6	7
(11)	(12)	(13)	(14)	(15)	(16)	(17)
8	9	10	11	12	13	14
(18)	(19)	(20)	(21)	(22)	(23)	(24)
15	16	17	18	19	20	21
(25)	(26)	(27)	(28)	(29f)	(1)	(2)
22	23	24	25	26	27	28
(3)	(4)	(5)	(6)	(7)	(8)	(9)
29	30					
(10)	(11)					

Passover Lamb Sacrificed — Nisan 14
Feast of First Fruits — 1st Sunday after Nisan 15

Feast of Unleavened Bread — Nisan 15-21
Pentecost — 8th Sunday after Nisan 15

Time of New Moon (Jerusalem) —   a1:33   b13:35   c22:59   d6:31   e13:15   f20:21

A.D. 8

July
(Tammuz 4)

S	M	T	W	T	F	S
		1	2	3	4	5
		(12)	(13)	(14)	(15)	(16)
6	7	8	9	10	11	12
(17)	(18)	(19)	(20)	(21)	(22)	(23)
13	14	15	16	17	18	19
(24)	(25)	(26)	(27)	(28)	(29)	(30g)
20	21	22	23	24	25	26
(1)	(2)	(3)	(4)	(5)	(6)	(7)
27	28	29	30	31		
(8)	(9)	(10)	(11)	(12)		

October
(Tishri 7)

S	M	T	W	T	F	S
		1	2	3	4	
		(15)	(16)	(17)	(18)	
5	6	7	8	9	10	11
(19)	(20)	(21)	(22)	(23)	(24)	(25)
12	13	14	15	16	17	18
(26)	(27)	(28)	(29j)	(1)	(2)	(3)
19	20	21	22	23	24	25
(4)	(5)	(6)	(7)	(8)	(9)	(10)
26	27	28	29	30	31	
(11)	(12)	(13)	(14)	(15)	(16)	

August
(Ab 5)

S	M	T	W	T	F	S
					1	2
					(13)	(14)
3	4	5	6	7	8	9
(15)	(16)	(17)	(18)	(19)	(20)	(21)
10	11	12	13	14	15	16
(22)	(23)	(24)	(25)	(26)	(27)	(28)
17	18	19	20	21	22	23
(29h)	(1)	(2)	(3)	(4)	(5)	(6)
24	25	26	27	28	29	30
(7)	(8)	(9)	(10)	(11)	(12)	(13)
31						

November
(Marheshvan 8)

S	M	T	W	T	F	S
						1
						(17)
2	3	4	5	6	7	8
(18)	(19)	(20)	(21)	(22)	(23)	(24)
9	10	11	12	13	14	15
(25)	(26)	(27)	(28)	(29)	(30k)	(1)
16	17	18	19	20	21	22
(2)	(3)	(4)	(5)	(6)	(7)	(8)
23	24	25	26	27	28	29
(9)	(10)	(11)	(12)	(13)	(14)	(15)
30						
(16)						

September
(Elul 6)

S	M	T	W	T	F	S
	1	2	3	4	5	6
	(15)	(16)	(17)	(18)	(19)	(20)
7	8	9	10	11	12	13
(21)	(22)	(23)	(24)	(25)	(26)	(27)
14	15	16	17	18	19	20
(28)	(29)	(30i)	(1)	(2)	(3)	(4)
21	22	23	24	25	26	27
(5)	(6)	(7)	(8)	(9)	(10)	(11)
28	29	30				
(12)	(13)	(14)				

December
(Kislev 9)

S	M	T	W	T	F	S
	1	2	3	4	5	6
	(17)	(18)	(19)	(20)	(21)	(22)
7	8	9	10	11	12	13
(23)	(24)	(25)	(26)	(27)	(28)	(29)
14	15	16	17	18	19	20
(30m)	(1)	(2)	(3)	(4)	(5)	(6)
21	22	23	24	25	26	27
(7)	(8)	(9)	(10)	(11)	(12)	(13)
28	29	30	31			
(14)	(15)	(16)	(17)			

ay of Trumpets — Tishri 1
east of Booths — Tishri 15-22

Day of Atonement — Tishri 10
Feast of Dedication — 8 days beginning Kislev 25

ime of the New Moon — g4:56 h15:50 i5:33 j22:07 k16:57 m12:46

A.D. 9

January
(Tebeth 10)

S	M	T	W	T	F	S
				1	2	3
				(18)	(19)	(20)
4	5	6	7	8	9	10
(21)	(22)	(23)	(24)	(25)	(26)	(27)
11	12	13	14	15	16	17
(28)	(29)	(30a)	(1)	(2)	(3)	(4)
18	19	20	21	22	23	24
(5)	(6)	(7)	(8)	(9)	(10)	(11)
25	26	27	28	29	30	31
(12)	(13)	(14)	(15)	(16)	(17)	(18)

April
(Nisan 1)

S	M	T	W	T	F	S
			1	2	3	4
			(19)	(20)	(21)	(22)
5	6	7	8	9	10	11
(23)	(24)	(25)	(26)	(27)	(28)	(29d)
12	13	14	15	16	17	18
(1)	(2)	(3)	(4)	(5)	(6)	(7)
19	20	21	22	23	24	25
(8)	(9)	(10)	(11)	(12)	(13)	(14)
26	27	28	29	30		
(15)	(16)	(17)	(18)	(19)		

February
(Shebat 11)

S	M	T	W	T	F	S
1	2	3	4	5	6	7
(19)	(20)	(21)	(22)	(23)	(24)	(25)
8	9	10	11	12	13	14
(26)	(27)	(28)	(29)	(30b)	(1)	(2)
15	16	17	18	19	20	21
(3)	(4)	(5)	(6)	(7)	(8)	(9)
22	23	24	25	26	27	28
(10)	(11)	(12)	(13)	(14)	(15)	(16)

May
(Iyyar 2)

S	M	T	W	T	F	S
					1	2
					(20)	(21)
3	4	5	6	7	8	9
(22)	(23)	(24)	(25)	(26)	(27)	(28)
10	11	12	13	14	15	16
(29)	(30e)	(1)	(2)	(3)	(4)	(5)
17	18	19	20	21	22	23
(6)	(7)	(8)	(9)	(10)	(11)	(12)
24	25	26	27	28	29	30
(13)	(14)	(15)	(16)	(17)	(18)	(19)
31						
(20)						

March
(Adar 12)

S	M	T	W	T	F	S
1	2	3	4	5	6	7
(17)	(18)	(19)	(20)	(21)	(22)	(23)
8	9	10	11	12	13	14
(24)	(25)	(26)	(27)	(28)	(29c)	(1)
15	16	17	18	19	20	21
(2)	(3)	(4)	(5)	(6)	(7)	(8)
22	23	24	25	26	27	28
(9)	(10)	(11)	(12)	(13)	(14)	(15)
29	30	31				
(16)	(17)	(18)				

June
(Sivan 3)

S	M	T	W	T	F	S
	1	2	3	4	5	6
	(21)	(22)	(23)	(24)	(25)	(26)
7	8	9	10	11	12	13
(27)	(28)	(29f)	(1)	(2)	(3)	(4)
14	15	16	17	18	19	20
(5)	(6)	(7)	(8)	(9)	(10)	(11)
21	22	23	24	25	26	27
(12)	(13)	(14)	(15)	(16)	(17)	(18)
28	29	30				
(19)	(20)	(21)				

Passover Lamb Sacrificed — Nisan 14
Feast of First Fruits — 1st Sunday after Nisan 15

Feast of Unleavened Bread — Nisan 15-21
Pentecost — 8th Sunday after Nisan 15

Time of New Moon (Jerusalem) —   a7:38   b23:52   c12:45   d22:37   e6:27   f13:24

A.D. 9

July
(Tammuz 4)

S	M	T	W	T	F	S
			1	2	3	4
			(22)	(23)	(24)	(25)
5	6	7	8	9	10	11
(26)	(27)	(28)	(29g)	(1)	(2)	(3)
12	13	14	15	16	17	18
(4)	(5)	(6)	(7)	(8)	(9)	(10)
19	20	21	22	23	24	25
(11)	(12)	(13)	(14)	(15)	(16)	(17)
26	27	28	29	30	31	
(18)	(19)	(20)	(21)	(22)	(23)	

October
(Tishri 7)

S	M	T	W	T	F	S
				1	2	3
				(26)	(27)	(28)
4	5	6	7	8	9	10
(29)	(30j)	(1)	(2)	(3)	(4)	(5)
11	12	13	14	15	16	17
(6)	(7)	(8)	(9)	(10)	(11)	(12)
18	19	20	21	22	23	24
(13)	(14)	(15)	(16)	(17)	(18)	(19)
25	26	27	28	29	30	31
(20)	(21)	(22)	(23)	(24)	(25)	(26)

August
(Ab 5)

S	M	T	W	T	F	S
						1
						(24)
2	3	4	5	6	7	8
(25)	(26)	(27)	(28)	(29)	(30h)	(1)
9	10	11	12	13	14	15
(2)	(3)	(4)	(5)	(6)	(7)	(8)
16	17	18	19	20	21	22
(9)	(10)	(11)	(12)	(13)	(14)	(15)
23	24	25	26	27	28	29
(16)	(17)	(18)	(19)	(20)	(21)	(22)
30	31					
(23)	(24)					

November
(Marheshvan 8)

S	M	T	W	T	F	S
1	2	3	4	5	6	7
(27)	(28)	(29k)	(1)	(2)	(3)	(4)
8	9	10	11	12	13	14
(5)	(6)	(7)	(8)	(9)	(10)	(11)
15	16	17	18	19	20	21
(12)	(13)	(14)	(15)	(16)	(17)	(18)
22	23	24	25	26	27	28
(19)	(20)	(21)	(22)	(23)	(24)	(25)
29	30					
(26)	(27)					

September
(Elul 6)

S	M	T	W	T	F	S
		1	2	3	4	5
		(25)	(26)	(27)	(28)	(29i)
6	7	8	9	10	11	12
(1)	(2)	(3)	(4)	(5)	(6)	(7)
13	14	15	16	17	18	19
(8)	(9)	(10)	(1)	(12)	(13)	(14)
20	21	22	23	24	25	26
(15)	(16)	(17)	(18)	(19)	(20)	(21)
27	28	29	30			
(22)	(23)	(24)	(25)			

December
(Kislev 9)

S	M	T	W	T	F	S
		1	2	3	4	5
		(28)	(29)	(30m)	(1)	(2)
6	7	8	9	10	11	12
(3)	(4)	(5)	(6)	(7)	(8)	(9)
13	14	15	16	17	18	19
(10)	(11)	(12)	(13)	(14)	(15)	(16)
20	21	22	23	24	25	26
(17)	(18)	(19)	(20)	(21)	(22)	(23)
27	28	29	30	31		
(24)	(25)	(26)	(27)	(28)		

Day of Trumpets — Tishri 1
Feast of Booths — Tishri 15-22

Day of Atonement — Tishri 10
Feast of Dedication — 8 days beginning Kislev 25

Time of the New Moon — g20:28 h4:31 i14:20 j2:37 k17:53 m11:58

A.D. 10

January (Tebeth 10)						
S	M	T	W	T	F	S
					1 (29)	2 (30a)
3 (1)	4 (2)	5 (3)	6 (4)	7 (5)	8 (6)	9 (7)
10 (8)	11 (9)	12 (10)	13 (11)	14 (12)	15 (13)	16 (14)
17 (15)	18 (16)	19 (17)	20 (18)	21 (19)	22 (20)	23 (21)
24 (22)	25 (23)	26 (24)	27 (25)	28 (26)	29 (27)	30 (28)
31 (29)						

April (Adar II 13)						
S	M	T	W	T	F	S
				1 (30d)	2 (1)	3 (2)
4 (3)	5 (4)	6 (5)	7 (6)	8 (7)	9 (8)	10 (9)
11 (10)	12 (11)	13 (12)	14 (13)	15 (14)	16 (15)	17 (16)
18 (17)	19 (18)	20 (19)	21 (20)	22 (21)	23 (22)	24 (23)
25 (24)	26 (25)	27 (26)	28 (27)	29 (28)	30 (29e)	

February (Shebat 11)						
S	M	T	W	T	F	S
	1 (30b)	2 (1)	3 (2)	4 (3)	5 (4)	6 (5)
7 (6)	8 (7)	9 (8)	10 (9)	11 (10)	12 (11)	13 (12)
14 (13)	15 (14)	16 (15)	17 (16)	18 (17)	19 (18)	20 (19)
21 (20)	22 (21)	23 (22)	24 (23)	25 (24)	26 (25)	27 (26)
28 (27)						

May (Iyyar 2)						
S	M	T	W	T	F	S
						1 (1)
2 (2)	3 (3)	4 (4)	5 (5)	6 (6)	7 (7)	8 (8)
9 (9)	10 (10)	11 (11)	12 (12)	13 (13)	14 (14)	15 (15)
16 (16)	17 (17)	18 (18)	19 (19)	20 (20)	21 (21)	22 (22)
23 (23)	24 (24)	25 (25)	26 (26)	27 (27)	28 (28)	29 (29)
30 (30f)	31 (1)					

March (Adar 12)						
S	M	T	W	T	F	S
	1 (28)	2 (29c)	3 (1)	4 (2)	5 (3)	6 (4)
7 (5)	8 (6)	9 (7)	10 (8)	11 (9)	12 (10)	13 (11)
14 (12)	15 (13)	16 (14)	17 (15)	18 (16)	19 (17)	20 (18)
21 (19)	22 (20)	23 (21)	24 (22)	25 (23)	26 (24)	27 (25)
28 (26)	29 (27)	30 (28)	31 (29)			

June (Sivan 3)						
S	M	T	W	T	F	S
		1 (2)	2 (3)	3 (4)	4 (5)	5 (6)
6 (7)	7 (8)	8 (9)	9 (10)	10 (11)	11 (12)	12 (13)
13 (14)	14 (15)	15 (16)	16 (17)	17 (18)	18 (19)	19 (20)
20 (21)	21 (22)	22 (23)	23 (24)	24 (25)	25 (26)	26 (27)
27 (28)	28 (29g)	29 (1)	30 (2)			

Passover Lamb Sacrificed — Nisan 14
Feast of First Fruits — 1st Sunday after Nisan 15

Feast of Unleavened Bread — Nisan 15-21
Pentecost — 8th Sunday after Nisan 15

Time of New Moon (Jerusalem) — a7:38   b2:48   c19:40   d9:31   e20:40   f5:46   g13:40

A.D. 10

July
(Tammuz 4)

S	M	T	W	T	F	S
				1	2	3
				(3)	(4)	(5)
4	5	6	7	8	9	10
(6)	(7)	(8)	(9)	(10)	(11)	(12)
11	12	13	14	15	16	17
(13)	(14)	(15)	(16)	(17)	(18)	(19)
18	19	20	21	22	23	24
(20)	(21)	(22)	(23)	(24)	(25)	(26)
25	26	27	28	29	30	31
(27)	(28)	(29h)	(1)	(2)	(3)	(4)

October
(Tishri 7)

S	M	T	W	T	F	S
					1	2
					(7)	(8)
3	4	5	6	7	8	9
(9)	(10)	(11)	(12)	(13)	(14)	(15)
10	11	12	13	14	15	16
(16)	(17)	(18)	(19)	(20)	(21)	(22)
17	18	19	20	21	22	23
(23)	(24)	(25)	(26)	(27)	(28)	(29)
24	25	26	27	28	29	30
(30k)	(1)	(2)	(3)	(4)	(5)	(6)
31						
(7)						

August
(Ab 5)

S	M	T	W	T	F	S
1	2	3	4	5	6	7
(5)	(6)	(7)	(8)	(9)	(10)	(11)
8	9	10	11	12	13	14
(12)	(13)	(14)	(15)	(16)	(17)	(18)
15	16	17	18	19	20	21
(19)	(20)	(21)	(22)	(23)	(24)	(25)
22	23	24	25	26	27	28
(26)	(27)	(28)	(29)	(30i)	(1)	(2)
29	30	31				
(3)	(4)	(5)				

November
(Marheshvan 8)

S	M	T	W	T	F	S
	1	2	3	4	5	6
	(8)	(9)	(10)	(11)	(12)	(13)
7	8	9	10	11	12	13
(14)	(15)	(16)	(17)	(18)	(19)	(20)
14	15	16	17	18	19	20
(21)	(22)	(23)	(24)	(25)	(26)	(27)
21	22	23	24	25	26	27
(28)	(29m)	(1)	(2)	(3)	(4)	(5)
28	29	30				
(6)	(7)	(8)				

September
(Elul 6)

S	M	T	W	T	F	S
			1	2	3	4
			(6)	(7)	(8)	(9)
5	6	7	8	9	10	11
(10)	(11)	(12)	(13)	(14)	(15)	(16)
12	13	14	15	16	17	18
(17)	(18)	(19)	(20)	(21)	(22)	(23)
19	20	21	22	23	24	25
(24)	(25)	(26)	(27)	(28)	(29j)	(1)
26	27	28	29	30		
(2)	(3)	(4)	(5)	(6)		

December
(Kislev 9)

S	M	T	W	T	F	S
			1	2	3	4
			(9)	(10)	(11)	(12)
5	6	7	8	9	10	11
(13)	(14)	(15)	(16)	(17)	(18)	(19)
12	13	14	15	16	17	18
(20)	(21)	(22)	(23)	(24)	(25)	(26)
19	20	21	22	23	24	25
(27)	(28)	(29)	(30n)	(1)	(2)	(3)
26	27	28	29	30	31	
(4)	(5)	(6)	(7)	(8)	(9)	

Day of Trumpets — Tishri 1
Feast of Booths — Tishri 15-22

Day of Atonement — Tishri 10
Feast of Dedication — 8 days beginning Kislev 25

Time of the New Moon — h21:10 i5:08 j14:24 k1:48 m15:51 n8:21

A.D. 11

January (Tebeth 10)						
S	M	T	W	T	F	S
						1 (10)
2 (11)	3 (12)	4 (13)	5 (14)	6 (15)	7 (16)	8 (17)
9 (18)	10 (19)	11 (20)	12 (21)	13 (22)	14 (23)	15 (24)
16 (25)	17 (26)	18 (27)	19 (28)	20 (29)	21 (30a)	22 (1)
23 (2)	24 (3)	25 (4)	26 (5)	27 (6)	28 (7)	29 (8)
30 (9)	31 (10)					

April (Nisan 1)						
S	M	T	W	T	F	S
					1 (11)	2 (12)
3 (13)	4 (14)	5 (15)	6 (16)	7 (17)	8 (18)	9 (19)
10 (20)	11 (21)	12 (22)	13 (23)	14 (24)	15 (25)	16 (26)
17 (27)	18 (28)	19 (29)	20 (30d)	21 (1)	22 (2)	23 (3)
24 (4)	25 (5)	26 (6)	27 (7)	28 (8)	29 (9)	30 (10)

February (Shebat 11)						
S	M	T	W	T	F	S
		1 (11)	2 (12)	3 (13)	4 (14)	5 (15)
6 (16)	7 (17)	8 (18)	9 (19)	10 (20)	11 (21)	12 (22)
13 (23)	14 (24)	15 (25)	16 (26)	17 (27)	18 (28)	19 (29b)
20 (1)	21 (2)	22 (3)	23 (4)	24 (5)	25 (6)	26 (7)
27 (8)	28 (9)					

May (Iyyar 2)						
S	M	T	W	T	F	S
1 (11)	2 (12)	3 (13)	4 (14)	5 (15)	6 (16)	7 (17)
8 (18)	9 (19)	10 (20)	11 (21)	12 (22)	13 (23)	14 (24)
15 (25)	16 (26)	17 (27)	18 (28)	19 (29e)	20 (1)	21 (2)
22 (3)	23 (4)	24 (5)	25 (6)	26 (7)	27 (8)	28 (9)
29 (10)	30 (11)	31 (12)				

March (Adar 12)						
S	M	T	W	T	F	S
		1 (10)	2 (11)	3 (12)	4 (13)	5 (14)
6 (15)	7 (16)	8 (17)	9 (18)	10 (19)	11 (20)	12 (21)
13 (22)	14 (23)	15 (24)	16 (25)	17 (26)	18 (27)	19 (28)
20 (29)	21 (30c)	22 (1)	23 (2)	24 (3)	25 (4)	26 (5)
27 (6)	28 (7)	29 (8)	30 (9)	31 (10)		

June (Sivan 3)						
S	M	T	W	T	F	S
			1 (13)	2 (14)	3 (15)	4 (16)
5 (17)	6 (18)	7 (19)	8 (20)	9 (21)	10 (22)	11 (23)
12 (24)	13 (25)	14 (26)	15 (27)	16 (28)	17 (29)	18 (30f)
19 (1)	20 (2)	21 (3)	22 (4)	23 (5)	24 (6)	25 (7)
26 (8)	27 (9)	28 (10)	29 (11)	30 (12)		

Passover Lamb Sacrificed — Nisan 14
Feast of First Fruits — 1st Sunday after Nisan 15

Feast of Unleavened Bread — Nisan 15-21
Pentecost — 8th Sunday after Nisan 15

Time of New Moon (Jerusalem) —   a2:18   b20:19   c13:10   d4:11   e17:05   f3:57

A.D. 11

July						
(Tammuz 4)						
S	M	T	W	T	F	S
					1	2
					(13)	(14)
3	4	5	6	7	8	9
(15)	(16)	(17)	(18)	(19)	(20)	(21)
10	11	12	13	14	15	16
(22)	(23)	(24)	(25)	(26)	(27)	(28)
17	18	19	20	21	22	23
(29g)	(1)	(2)	(3)	(4)	(5)	(6)
24	25	26	27	28	29	30
(7)	(8)	(9)	(10)	(11)	(12)	(13)
31						
(14)						

October						
(Tishri 7)						
S	M	T	W	T	F	S
						1
						(17)
2	3	4	5	6	7	8
(18)	(19)	(20)	(21)	(22)	(23)	(24)
9	10	11	12	13	14	15
(25)	(26)	(27)	(28)	(29j)	(1)	(2)
16	17	18	19	20	21	22
(3)	(4)	(5)	(6)	(7)	(8)	(9)
23	24	25	26	27	28	29
(10)	(11)	(12)	(13)	(14)	(15)	(16)
30	31					
(17)	(18)					

August						
(Ab 5)						
S	M	T	W	T	F	S
	1	2	3	4	5	6
	(15)	(16)	(17)	(18)	(19)	(20)
7	8	9	10	11	12	13
(21)	(22)	(23)	(24)	(25)	(26)	(27)
14	15	16	17	18	19	20
(28)	(29h)	(1)	(2)	(3)	(4)	(5)
21	22	23	24	25	26	27
(6)	(7)	(8)	(9)	(10)	(11)	(12)
28	29	30	31			
(13)	(14)	(15)	(16)			

November						
(Marheshvan 8)						
S	M	T	W	T	F	S
		1	2	3	4	5
		(19)	(20)	(21)	(22)	(23)
6	7	8	9	10	11	12
(24)	(25)	(26)	(27)	(28)	(29)	(30k)
13	14	15	16	17	18	19
(1)	(2)	(3)	(4)	(5)	(6)	(7)
20	21	22	23	24	25	26
(8)	(9)	(10)	(11)	(12)	(13)	(14)
27	28	29	30			
(15)	(16)	(17)	(18)			

September						
(Elul 6)						
S	M	T	W	T	F	S
				1	2	3
				(17)	(18)	(19)
4	5	6	7	8	9	10
(20)	(21)	(22)	(23)	(24)	(25)	(26)
11	12	13	14	15	16	17
(27)	(28)	(29)	(30i)	(1)	(2)	(3)
18	19	20	21	22	23	24
(4)	(5)	(6)	(7)	(8)	(9)	(10)
25	26	27	28	29	30	
(11)	(12)	(13)	(14)	(15)	(16)	

December						
(Kislev 9)						
S	M	T	W	T	F	S
				1	2	3
				(19)	(20)	(21)
4	5	6	7	8	9	10
(22)	(23)	(24)	(25)	(26)	(27)	(28)
11	12	13	14	15	16	17
(29m)	(1)	(2)	(3)	(4)	(5)	(6)
18	19	20	21	22	23	24
(7)	(8)	(9)	(10)	(11)	(12)	(13)
25	26	27	28	29	30	31
(14)	(15)	(16)	(17)	(18)	(19)	(20)

Day of Trumpets — Tishri 1
Feast of Booths — Tishri 15-22

Day of Atonement — Tishri 10
Feast of Dedication — 8 days beginning Kislev 25

Time of the New Moon — g13:13 h21:42 i6:18 j15:53 k2:51 m15:42

A.D. 12

January (Tebeth 10)						
S	M	T	W	T	F	S
1	2	3	4	5	6	7
(21)	(22)	(23)	(24)	(25)	(26)	(27)
8	9	10	11	12	13	14
(28)	(29)	(30a)	(1)	(2)	(3)	(4)
15	16	17	18	19	20	21
(5)	(6)	(7)	(8)	(9)	(10)	(11)
22	23	24	25	26	27	28
(12)	(13)	(14)	(15)	(16)	(17)	(18)
29	30	31				
(19)	(20)	(21)				

April (Nisan 1)						
S	M	T	W	T	F	S
1	2	3	4	5	6	7
(23)	(24)	(25)	(26)	(27)	(28)	(29)
8	9	10	11	12	13	14
(30d)	(1)	(2)	(3)	(4)	(5)	(6)
15	16	17	18	19	20	21
(7)	(8)	(9)	(10)	(11)	(12)	(13)
22	23	24	25	26	27	28
(14)	(15)	(16)	(17)	(18)	(19)	(20)
29	30					
(21)	(22)					

February (Shebat 11)						
S	M	T	W	T	F	S
			1	2	3	4
			(22)	(23)	(24)	(25)
5	6	7	8	9	10	11
(26)	(27)	(28)	(29b)	(1)	(2)	(3)
12	13	14	15	16	17	18
(4)	(5)	(6)	(7)	(8)	(9)	(10)
19	20	21	22	23	24	25
(11)	(12)	(13)	(14)	(15)	(16)	(17)
26	27	28	29			
(18)	(19)	(20)	(21)			

May (Iyyar 2)						
S	M	T	W	T	F	S
			1	2	3	4	5
			(23)	(24)	(25)	(26)	(27)
6	7	8	9	10	11	12
(28)	(29e)	(1)	(2)	(3)	(4)	(5)
13	14	15	16	17	18	19
(6)	(7)	(8)	(9)	(10)	(11)	(12)
20	21	22	23	24	25	26
(13)	(14)	(15)	(16)	(17)	(18)	(19)
27	28	29	30	31		
(20)	(21)	(22)	(23)	(24)		

March (Adar 12)						
S	M	T	W	T	F	S
				1	2	3
				(22)	(23)	(24)
4	5	6	7	8	9	10
(25)	(26)	(27)	(28)	(29)	(30c)	(1)
11	12	13	14	15	16	17
(2)	(3)	(4)	(5)	(6)	(7)	(8)
18	19	20	21	22	23	24
(9)	(10)	(11)	(12)	(13)	(14)	(15)
25	26	27	28	29	30	31
(16)	(17)	(18)	(19)	(20)	(21)	(22)

June (Sivan 3)						
S	M	T	W	T	F	S
					1	2
					(25)	(26)
3	4	5	6	7	8	9
(27)	(28)	(29)	(30f)	(1)	(2)	(3)
10	11	12	13	14	15	16
(4)	(5)	(6)	(7)	(8)	(9)	(10)
17	18	19	20	21	22	23
(11)	(12)	(13)	(14)	(15)	(16)	(17)
24	25	26	27	28	29	30
(18)	(19)	(20)	(21)	(22)	(23)	(24)

Passover Lamb Sacrificed — Nisan 14
Feast of First Fruits — 1st Sunday after Nisan 15

Feast of Unleavened Bread — Nisan 15-21
Pentecost — 8th Sunday after Nisan 15

Time of New Moon (Jerusalem) — a5:53　b21:12　c13:16　d5:32　e21:15　f11:38

A.D. 12

July						
(Tammuz 4)						
S	M	T	W	T	F	S
1	2	3	4	5	6	7
(25)	(26)	(27)	(28)	(29)	(30g)	(1)
8	9	10	11	12	13	14
(2)	(3)	(4)	(5)	(6)	(7)	(8)
15	16	17	18	19	20	21
(9)	(10)	(11)	(12)	(13)	(14)	(15)
22	23	24	25	26	27	28
(16)	(17)	(18)	(19)	(20)	(21)	(22)
29	30	31				
(23)	(24)	(25)				

October						
(Tishri 7)						
S	M	T	W	T	F	S
	1	2	3	4	5	6
	(29)	(30j)	(1)	(2)	(3)	(4)
7	8	9	10	11	12	13
(5)	(6)	(7)	(8)	(9)	(10)	(11)
14	15	16	17	18	19	20
(12)	(13)	(14)	(15)	(16)	(17)	(18)
21	22	23	24	25	26	27
(19)	(20)	(21)	(22)	(23)	(24)	(25)
28	29	30	31			
(26)	(27)	(28)	(29k)			

August						
(Ab 5)						
S	M	T	W	T	F	S
			1	2	3	4
			(26)	(27)	(28)	(29h)
5	6	7	8	9	10	11
(1)	(2)	(3)	(4)	(5)	(6)	(7)
12	13	14	15	16	17	18
(8)	(9)	(10)	(11)	(12)	(13)	(14)
19	20	21	22	23	24	25
(15)	(16)	(17)	(18)	(19)	(20)	(21)
26	27	28	29	30	31	
(22)	(23)	(24)	(25)	(26)	(27)	

November						
(Kislev 9)						
S	M	T	W	T	F	S
				1	2	3
				(1)	(2)	(3)
4	5	6	7	8	9	10
(4)	(5)	(6)	(7)	(8)	(9)	(10)
11	12	13	14	15	16	17
(11)	(12)	(13)	(14)	(15)	(16)	(17)
18	19	20	21	22	23	24
(18)	(19)	(20)	(21)	(22)	(23)	(24)
25	26	27	28	29	30	
(25)	(26)	(27)	(28)	(29)	(30m)	

September						
(Elul 6)						
S	M	T	W	T	F	S
						1
						(28)
2	3	4	5	6	7	8
(29i)	(1)	(2)	(3)	(4)	(5)	(6)
9	10	11	12	13	14	15
(7)	(8)	(9)	(10)	(11)	(12)	(13)
16	17	18	19	20	21	22
(14)	(15)	(16)	(17)	(18)	(19)	(20)
23	24	25	26	27	28	29
(21)	(22)	(23)	(24)	(25)	(26)	(27)
30						
(28)						

December						
(Tebeth 10)						
S	M	T	W	T	F	S
						1
						(1)
2	3	4	5	6	7	8
(2)	(3)	(4)	(5)	(6)	(7)	(8)
9	10	11	12	13	14	15
(9)	(10)	(11)	(12)	(13)	(14)	(15)
16	17	18	19	20	21	22
(16)	(17)	(18)	(19)	(20)	(21)	(22)
23	24	25	26	27	28	29
(23)	(24)	(25)	(26)	(27)	(28)	(29n)
30	31					
(1)	(2)					

Day of Trumpets — Tishri 1

Feast of Booths — Tishri 15-22

Day of Atonement — Tishri 10

Feast of Dedication — 8 days beginning Kislev 25

Time of the New Moon — g0:17   h11:25   i21:43   j7:53   k18:22   m5:16   n16:35

Gregorian

A.D. 13

January
(Shebat 11)

S	M	T	W	T	F	S
		1	2	3	4	5
		(3)	(4)	(5)	(6)	(7)
6	7	8	9	10	11	12
(8)	(9)	(10)	(11)	(12)	(13)	(14)
13	14	15	16	17	18	19
(15)	(16)	(17)	(18)	(19)	(20)	(21)
20	21	22	23	24	25	26
(22)	(23)	(24)	(25)	(26)	(27)	(28)
27	28	29	30	31		
(29)	(30a)	(1)	(2)	(3)		

April
(Nisan 1)

S	M	T	W	T	F	S
		1	2	3	4	5	6
	(4)	(5)	(6)	(7)	(8)	(9)
7	8	9	10	11	12	13
(10)	(11)	(12)	(13)	(14)	(15)	(16)
14	15	16	17	18	19	20
(17)	(18)	(19)	(20)	(21)	(22)	(23)
21	22	23	24	25	26	27
(24)	(25)	(26)	(27)	(28)	(29d)	(1)
28	29	30				
(2)	(3)	(4)				

February
(Adar 12)

S	M	T	W	T	F	S
					1	2
					(4)	(5)
3	4	5	6	7	8	9
(6)	(7)	(8)	(9)	(10)	(11)	(12)
10	11	12	13	14	15	16
(13)	(14)	(15)	(16)	(17)	(18)	(19)
17	18	19	20	21	22	23
(20)	(21)	(22)	(23)	(24)	(25)	(26)
24	25	26	27	28		
(27)	(28)	(29b)	(1)	(2)		

May
(Iyyar 2)

S	M	T	W	T	F	S
			1	2	3	4
			(5)	(6)	(7)	(8)
5	6	7	8	9	10	11
(9)	(10)	(11)	(12)	(13)	(14)	(15)
12	13	14	15	16	17	18
(16)	(17)	(18)	(19)	(20)	(21)	(22)
19	20	21	22	23	24	25
(23)	(24)	(25)	(26)	(27)	(28)	(29)
26	27	28	29	30	31	
(30e)	(1)	(2)	(3)	(4)	(5)	

March
(Adar II 13)

S	M	T	W	T	F	S
					1	2
					(3)	(4)
3	4	5	6	7	8	9
(5)	(6)	(7)	(8)	(9)	(10)	(11)
10	11	12	13	14	15	16
(12)	(13)	(14)	(15)	(16)	(17)	(18)
17	18	19	20	21	22	23
(19)	(20)	(21)	(22)	(23)	(24)	(25)
24	25	26	27	28	29	30
(26)	(27)	(28)	(29)	(30c)	(1)	(2)
31						
(3)						

June
(Sivan 3)

S	M	T	W	T	F	S
						1
						(6)
2	3	4	5	6	7	8
(7)	(8)	(9)	(10)	(11)	(12)	(13)
9	10	11	12	13	14	15
(14)	(15)	(16)	(17)	(18)	(19)	(20)
16	17	18	19	20	21	22
(21)	(22)	(23)	(24)	(25)	(26)	(27)
23	24	25	26	27	28	29
(28)	(29)	(30f)	(1)	(2)	(3)	(4)
30						
(5)						

Passover Lamb Sacrificed — Nisan 14
Feast of First Fruits — 1st Sunday after Nisan 15

Feast of Unleavened Bread — Nisan 15-21
Pentecost — 8th Sunday after Nisan 15

Time of New Moon (Jerusalem) — a4:28 b17:13 c7:06 d21:57 e13:14 f4:16

A.D. 13

July
(Tammuz 4)

S	M	T	W	T	F	S
	1	2	3	4	5	6
	(6)	(7)	(8)	(9)	(10)	(11)
7	8	9	10	11	12	13
(12)	(13)	(14)	(15)	(16)	(17)	(18)
14	15	16	17	18	19	20
(19)	(20)	(21)	(22)	(23)	(24)	(25)
21	22	23	24	25	26	27
(26)	(27)	(28)	(29g)	(1)	(2)	(3)
28	29	30	31			
(4)	(5)	(6)	(7)			

October
(Tishri 7)

S	M	T	W	T	F	S
		1	2	3	4	5
		(10)	(11)	(12)	(13)	(14)
6	7	8	9	10	11	12
(15)	(16)	(17)	(18)	(19)	(20)	(21)
13	14	15	16	17	18	19
(22)	(23)	(24)	(25)	(26)	(27)	(28)
20	21	22	23	24	25	26
(29)	(30j)	(1)	(2)	(3)	(4)	(5)
27	28	29	30	31		
(6)	(7)	(8)	(9)	(10)		

August
(Ab 5)

S	M	T	W	T	F	S
				1	2	3
				(8)	(9)	(10)
4	5	6	7	8	9	10
(11)	(12)	(13)	(14)	(15)	(16)	(17)
11	12	13	14	15	16	17
(18)	(19)	(20)	(21)	(22)	(23)	(24)
18	19	20	21	22	23	24
(25)	(26)	(27)	(28)	(29)	(30h)	(1)
25	26	27	28	29	30	31
(2)	(3)	(4)	(5)	(6)	(7)	(8)

November
(Marheshvan 8)

S	M	T	W	T	F	S
					1	2
					(11)	(12)
3	4	5	6	7	8	9
(13)	(14)	(15)	(16)	(17)	(18)	(19)
10	11	12	13	14	15	16
(20)	(21)	(22)	(23)	(24)	(25)	(26)
17	18	19	20	21	22	23
(27)	(28)	(29k)	(1)	(2)	(3)	(4)
24	25	26	27	28	29	30
(5)	(6)	(7)	(8)	(9)	(10)	(11)

September
(Elul 6)

S	M	T	W	T	F	S
1	2	3	4	5	6	7
(9)	(10)	(11)	(12)	(13)	(14)	(15)
8	9	10	11	12	13	14
(16)	(17)	(18)	(19)	(20)	(21)	(22)
15	16	17	18	19	20	21
(23)	(24)	(25)	(26)	(27)	(28)	(29i)
22	23	24	25	26	27	28
(1)	(2)	(3)	(4)	(5)	(6)	(7)
29	30					
(8)	(9)					

December
(Kislev 9)

S	M	T	W	T	F	S
1	2	3	4	5	6	7
(12)	(13)	(14)	(15)	(16)	(17)	(18)
8	9	10	11	12	13	14
(19)	(20)	(21)	(22)	(23)	(24)	(25)
15	16	17	18	19	20	21
(26)	(27)	(28)	(29)	(30m)	(1)	(2)
22	23	24	25	26	27	28
(3)	(4)	(5)	(6)	(7)	(8)	(9)
29	30	31				
(10)	(11)	(12)				

Day of Trumpets — Tishri 1
Feast of Booths — Tishri 15-22

Day of Atonement — Tishri 10
Feast of Dedication — 8 days beginning Kislev 25

Time of the New Moon — g18:37   h8:14   i21:11   j9:27   k20:58   m7:44

A.D. 14

January						
(Tebeth 10)						
S	M	T	W	T	F	S
			1	2	3	4
			(13)	(14)	(15)	(16)
5	6	7	8	9	10	11
(17)	(18)	(19)	(20)	(21)	(22)	(23)
12	13	14	15	16	17	18
(24)	(25)	(26)	(27)	(28)	(29a)	(1)
19	20	21	22	23	24	25
(2)	(3)	(4)	(5)	(6)	(7)	(8)
26	27	28	29	30	31	
(9)	(10)	(11)	(12)	(13)	(14)	

April						
(Nisan 1)						
S	M	T	W	T	F	S
		1	2	3	4	5
		(15)	(16)	(17)	(18)	(19)
6	7	8	9	10	11	12
(20)	(21)	(22)	(23)	(24)	(25)	(26)
13	14	15	16	17	18	19
(27)	(28)	(29)	(30d)	(1)	(2)	(3)
20	21	22	23	24	25	26
(4)	(5)	(6)	(7)	(8)	(9)	(10)
27	28	29	30			
(11)	(12)	(13)	(14)			

February						
(Shebat 11)						
S	M	T	W	T	F	S
						1
						(15)
2	3	4	5	6	7	8
(16)	(17)	(18)	(19)	(20)	(21)	(22)
9	10	11	12	13	14	15
(23)	(24)	(25)	(26)	(27)	(28)	(29)
16	17	18	19	20	21	22
(30b)	(1)	(2)	(3)	(4)	(5)	(6)
23	24	25	26	27	28	
(7)	(8)	(9)	(10)	(11)	(12)	

May						
(Iyyar 2)						
S	M	T	W	T	F	S
				1	2	3
				(15)	(16)	(17)
4	5	6	7	8	9	10
(18)	(19)	(20)	(21)	(22)	(23)	(24)
11	12	13	14	15	16	17
(25)	(26)	(27)	(28)	(29e)	(1)	(2)
18	19	20	21	22	23	24
(3)	(4)	(5)	(6)	(7)	(8)	(9)
25	26	27	28	29	30	31
(10)	(11)	(12)	(13)	(14)	(15)	(16)

March						
(Adar 12)						
S	M	T	W	T	F	S
						1
						(13)
2	3	4	5	6	7	8
(14)	(15)	(16)	(17)	(18)	(19)	(20)
9	10	11	12	13	14	15
(21)	(22)	(23)	(24)	(25)	(26)	(27)
16	17	18	19	20	21	22
(28)	(29c)	(1)	(2)	(3)	(4)	(5)
23	24	25	26	27	28	29
(6)	(7)	(8)	(9)	(10)	(11)	(12)
30	31					
(13)	(14)					

June						
(Sivan 3)						
S	M	T	W	T	F	S
1	2	3	4	5	6	7
(17)	(18)	(19)	(20)	(21)	(22)	(23)
8	9	10	11	12	13	14
(24)	(25)	(26)	(27)	(28)	(29)	(30f)
15	16	17	18	19	20	21
(1)	(2)	(3)	(4)	(5)	(6)	(7)
22	23	24	25	26	27	28
(8)	(9)	(10)	(11)	(12)	(13)	(14)
29	30					
(15)	(16)					

Passover Lamb Sacrificed — Nisan 14
Feast of First Fruits — 1st Sunday after Nisan 15

Feast of Unleavened Bread — Nisan 15-21
Pentecost — 8th Sunday after Nisan 15

Time of New Moon (Jerusalem) — a18:00   b4:13   c14:54   d2:28   e15:06   f4:54

A.D. 14

July
(Tammuz 4)

S	M	T	W	T	F	S
		1	2	3	4	5
		(17)	(18)	(19)	(20)	(21)
6	7	8	9	10	11	12
(22)	(23)	(24)	(25)	(26)	(27)	(28)
13	14	15	16	17	18	19
(29g)	(1)	(2)	(3)	(4)	(5)	(6)
20	21	22	23	24	25	26
(7)	(8)	(9)	(10)	(11)	(12)	(13)
27	28	29	30	31		
(14)	(15)	(16)	(17)	(18)		

October
(Tishri 7)

S	M	T	W	T	F	S
		1	2	3	4	
		(20)	(21)	(22)	(23)	
5	6	7	8	9	10	11
(24)	(25)	(26)	(27)	(28)	(29j)	(1)
12	13	14	15	16	17	18
(2)	(3)	(4)	(5)	(6)	(7)	(8)
19	20	21	22	23	24	25
(9)	(10)	(11)	(12)	(13)	(14)	(15)
26	27	28	29	30	31	
(16)	(17)	(18)	(19)	(20)	(21)	

August
(Ab 5)

S	M	T	W	T	F	S
					1	2
					(19)	(20)
3	4	5	6	7	8	9
(21)	(22)	(23)	(24)	(25)	(26)	(27)
10	11	12	13	14	15	16
(28)	(29)	(30h)	(1)	(2)	(3)	(4)
17	18	19	20	21	22	23
(5)	(6)	(7)	(8)	(9)	(10)	(11)
24	25	26	27	28	29	30
(12)	(13)	(14)	(15)	(16)	(17)	(18)
31						
(19)						

November
(Marheshvan 8)

S	M	T	W	T	F	S
						1
						(22)
2	3	4	5	6	7	8
(23)	(24)	(25)	(26)	(27)	(28)	(29)
9	10	11	12	13	14	15
(30k)	(1)	(2)	(3)	(4)	(5)	(6)
16	17	18	19	20	21	22
(7)	(8)	(9)	(10)	(11)	(12)	(13)
23	24	25	26	27	28	29
(14)	(15)	(16)	(17)	(18)	(19)	(20)
30						
(21)						

September
(Elul 6)

S	M	T	W	T	F	S
	1	2	3	4	5	6
	(20)	(21)	(22)	(23)	(24)	(25)
7	8	9	10	11	12	13
(26)	(27)	(28)	(29)	(30i)	(1)	(2)
14	15	16	17	18	19	20
(3)	(4)	(5)	(6)	(7)	(8)	(9)
21	22	23	24	25	25	27
(10)	(11)	(12)	(13)	(14)	(15)	(16)
28	29	30				
(17)	(18)	(19)				

December
(Kislev 9)

S	M	T	W	T	F	S
	1	2	3	4	5	6
	(22)	(23)	(24)	(25)	(26)	(27)
7	8	9	10	11	12	13
(28)	(29m)	(1)	(2)	(3)	(4)	(5)
14	15	16	17	18	19	20
(6)	(7)	(8)	(9)	(10)	(11)	(12)
21	22	23	24	25	26	27
(13)	(14)	(15)	(16)	(17)	(18)	(19)
28	29	30	31			
(20)	(21)	(22)	(23)			

Day of Trumpets — Tishri 1
Feast of Booths — Tishri 15-22

Day of Atonement — Tishri 10
Feast of Dedication — 8 days beginning Kislev 25

Time of the New Moon — g19:51 h11:45 i4:00 j19:45 k10:07 m22:46

A.D. 15

January
(Tebeth 10)

S	M	T	W	T	F	S
				1	2	3
				(24)	(25)	(26)
4	5	6	7	8	9	10
(27)	(28)	(29)	(30a)	(1)	(2)	(3)
11	12	13	14	15	16	17
(4)	(5)	(6)	(7)	(8)	(9)	(10)
18	19	20	21	22	23	24
(11)	(12)	(13)	(14)	(15)	(16)	(17)
25	26	27	28	28	30	31
(18)	(19)	(20)	(21)	(22)	(23)	(24)

February
(Shebat 11)

S	M	T	W	T	F	S
1	2	3	4	5	6	7
(25)	(26)	(27)	(28)	(29b)	(1)	(2)
8	9	10	11	12	13	14
(3)	(4)	(5)	(6)	(7)	(8)	(9)
15	16	17	18	19	20	21
(10)	(11)	(12)	(13)	(14)	(15)	(16)
22	23	24	25	26	27	28
(17)	(18)	(19)	(20)	(21)	(22)	(23)

March
(Adar 12)

S	M	T	W	T	F	S
1	2	3	4	5	6	7
(24)	(25)	(26)	(27)	(28)	(29)	(30c)
8	9	10	11	12	13	14
(1)	(2)	(3)	(4)	(5)	(6)	(7)
15	16	17	18	19	20	21
(8)	(9)	(10)	(11)	(12)	(13)	(14)
22	23	24	25	26	27	28
(15)	(16)	(17)	(18)	(19)	(20)	(21)
29	30	31				
(22)	(23)	(24)				

April
(Nisan 1)

S	M	T	W	T	F	S
			1	2	3	4
			(25)	(26)	(27)	(28)
5	6	7	8	9	10	11
(29d)	(1)	(2)	(3)	(4)	(5)	(6)
12	13	14	15	16	17	18
(7)	(8)	(9)	(10)	(11)	(12)	(13)
19	20	21	22	23	24	25
(14)	(15)	(16)	(17)	(18)	(19)	(20)
26	27	28	29	30		
(21)	(22)	(23)	(24)	(25)		

May
(Iyyar 2)

S	M	T	W	T	F	S
					1	2
					(26)	(27)
3	4	5	6	7	8	9
(28)	(29e)	(1)	(2)	(3)	(4)	(5)
10	11	12	13	14	15	16
(6)	(7)	(8)	(9)	(10)	(11)	(12)
17	18	19	20	21	22	23
(13)	(14)	(15)	(16)	(17)	(18)	(19)
24	25	26	27	28	29	30
(20)	(21)	(22)	(23)	(24)	(25)	(26)
31						
(27)						

June
(Sivan 3)

S	M	T	W	T	F	S
	1	2	3	4	5	6
	(28)	(29)	(30f)	(1)	(2)	(3)
7	8	9	10	11	12	13
(4)	(5)	(6)	(7)	(8)	(9)	(10)
14	15	16	17	18	19	20
(11)	(12)	(13)	(14)	(15)	(16)	(17)
21	22	23	24	25	26	27
(18)	(19)	(20)	(21)	(22)	(23)	(24)
28	29	30				
(25)	(26)	(27)				

Passover Lamb Sacrificed — Nisan 14

Feast of First Fruits — 1st Sunday after Nisan 15

Feast of Unleavened Bread — Nisan 15-21

Pentecost — 8th Sunday after Nisan 15

Time of New Moon (Jerusalem) — a9:51 b1948 c5:02 d13:59 e23:13 f4:28

A.D. 15

July
(Tammuz 4)

S	M	T	W	T	F	S
			1	2	3	4
			(28)	(29g)	(1)	(2)
5	6	7	8	9	10	11
(3)	(4)	(5)	(6)	(7)	(8)	(9)
12	13	14	15	16	17	18
(10)	(11)	(12)	(13)	(14)	(15)	(16)
19	20	21	22	23	24	25
(17)	(18)	(19)	(20)	(21)	(22)	(23)
26	27	28	29	30	31	
(24)	(25)	(26)	(27)	(28)	(29)	

October
(Marheshvan 8)

S	M	T	W	T	F	S
				1	2	3
				(2)	(3)	(4)
4	5	6	7	8	9	10
(5)	(6)	(7)	(8)	(9)	(10)	(11)
11	12	13	14	15	16	17
(12)	(13)	(14)	(15)	(16)	(17)	(18)
18	19	20	21	22	23	24
(19)	(20)	(21)	(22)	(23)	(24)	(25)
25	26	27	28	29	30	31
(26)	(27)	(28)	(29)	(30k)	(1)	(2)

August
(Ab 5)

S	M	T	W	T	F	S
						1
						(30h)
2	3	4	5	6	7	8
(1)	(2)	(3)	(4)	(5)	(6)	(7)
9	10	11	12	13	14	15
(8)	(9)	(10)	(11)	(12)	(13)	(14)
16	17	18	19	20	21	22
(15)	(16)	(17)	(18)	(19)	(20)	(21)
23	24	25	26	27	28	29
(22)	(23)	(24)	(25)	(26)	(27)	(28)
30	31					
(29)	(30i)					

November
(Kislev 9)

S	M	T	W	T	F	S
1	2	3	4	5	6	7
(3)	(4)	(5)	(6)	(7)	(8)	(9)
8	9	10	11	12	13	14
(10)	(11)	(12)	(13)	(14)	(15)	(16)
15	16	17	18	19	20	21
(17)	(18)	(19)	(20)	(21)	(22)	(23)
22	23	24	25	26	27	28
(24)	(25)	(26)	(27)	(28)	(29)	(30m)
29	30					
(1)	(2)					

September
(Tishri 7)

S	M	T	W	T	F	S
		1	2	3	4	5
		(1)	(2)	(3)	(4)	(5)
6	7	8	9	10	11	12
(6)	(7)	(8)	(9)	(10)	(11)	(12)
13	14	15	16	17	18	19
(13)	(14)	(15)	(16)	(17)	(18)	(19)
20	21	22	23	24	25	26
(20)	(21)	(22)	(23)	(24)	(25)	(26)
27	28	29	30			
(27)	(28)	(29j)	(1)			

December
(Tebeth 10)

S	M	T	W	T	F	S
		1	2	3	4	5
		(3)	(4)	(5)	(6)	(7)
6	7	8	9	10	11	12
(8)	(9)	(10)	(11)	(12)	(13)	(14)
13	14	15	16	17	18	19
(15)	(16)	(17)	(18)	(19)	(20)	(21)
20	21	22	23	24	25	26
(22)	(23)	(24)	(25)	(26)	(27)	(28)
27	28	29	30	31		
(29n)	(1)	(2)	(3)	(4)		

Day of Trumpets — Tishri 1
Feast of Booths — Tishri 15-22

Day of Atonement — Tishri 10
Feast of Dedication — 8 days beginning Kislev 25

Time of the New Moon — g21:33 h12:02 i4:49 j22:56 k16:48 m9:09 n23:22

A.D. 16

January (Shebat 11)

S	M	T	W	T	F	S
					1	2
					(5)	(6)
3	4	5	6	7	8	9
(7)	(8)	(9)	(10)	(11)	(12)	(13)
10	11	12	13	14	15	16
(14)	(15)	(16)	(17)	(18)	(19)	(20)
17	18	19	20	21	22	23
(21)	(22)	(23)	(24)	(25)	(26)	(27)
24	25	26	27	28	29	30
(28)	(29)	(30a)	(1)	(2)	(3)	(4)
31						
(5)						

February (Adar 12)

S	M	T	W	T	F	S
	1	2	3	4	5	6
	(6)	(7)	(8)	(9)	(10)	(11)
7	8	9	10	11	12	13
(12)	(13)	(14)	(15)	(16)	(17)	(18)
14	15	16	17	18	19	20
(19)	(20)	(21)	(22)	(23)	(24)	(25)
21	22	23	24	25	26	27
(26)	(27)	(28)	(29b)	(1)	(2)	(3)
28	29					
(4)	(5)					

March (Adar II 13)

S	M	T	W	T	F	S
	1	2	3	4	5	
	(6)	(7)	(8)	(9)	(10)	
6	7	8	9	10	11	12
(11)	(12)	(13)	(14)	(15)	(16)	(17)
13	14	15	16	17	18	19
(18)	(19)	(20)	(21)	(22)	(23)	(24)
20	21	22	23	24	25	26
(25)	(26)	(27)	(28)	(29)	(30c)	(1)
27	28	29	30	31		
(2)	(3)	(4)	(5)	(6)		

April (Nisan 1)

S	M	T	W	T	F	S
					1	2
					(7)	(8)
3	4	5	6	7	8	9
(9)	(10)	(11)	(12)	(13)	(14)	(15)
10	11	12	13	14	15	16
(16)	(17)	(18)	(19)	(20)	(21)	(22)
17	18	19	20	21	22	23
(23)	(24)	(25)	(26)	(27)	(28)	(29d)
24	25	26	27	28	29	30
(1)	(2)	(3)	(4)	(5)	(6)	(7)

May (Iyyar 2)

S	M	T	W	T	F	S
1	2	3	4	5	6	7
(8)	(9)	(10)	(11)	(12)	(13)	(14)
8	9	10	11	12	13	14
(15)	(16)	(17)	(18)	(19)	(20)	(21)
15	16	17	18	19	20	21
(22)	(23)	(24)	(25)	(26)	(27)	(28)
22	23	24	25	26	27	28
(29e)	(1)	(2)	(3)	(4)	(5)	(6)
29	30	31				
(7)	(8)	(9)				

June (Sivan 3)

S	M	T	W	T	F	S
			1	2	3	4
			(10)	(11)	(12)	(13)
5	6	7	8	9	10	11
(14)	(15)	(16)	(17)	(18)	(19)	(20)
12	13	14	15	16	17	18
(21)	(22)	(23)	(24)	(25)	(26)	(27)
19	20	21	22	23	24	25
(28)	(29)	(30f)	(1)	(2)	(3)	(4)
26	27	28	29	30		
(5)	(6)	(7)	(8)	(9)		

Passover Lamb Sacrificed — Nisan 14
Feast of First Fruits — 1st Sunday after Nisan 15

Feast of Unleavened Bread — Nisan 15-21
Pentecost — 8th Sunday after Nisan 15

Time of New Moon (Jerusalem) —   a11:27   b21:36   c6:10   d13:44   e21:12   f5:44

July
(Tammuz 4)

S	M	T	W	T	F	S
					1	2
					(10)	(11)
3	4	5	6	7	8	9
(12)	(13)	(14)	(15)	(16)	(17)	(18)
10	11	12	13	14	15	16
(19)	(20)	(21)	(22)	(23)	(24)	(25)
17	18	19	20	21	22	23
(26)	(27)	(28)	(29g)	(1)	(2)	(3)
24	25	26	27	28	29	30
(4)	(5)	(6)	(7)	(8)	(9)	(10)
31						
(11)						

August
(Ab 5)

S	M	T	W	T	F	S
	1	2	3	4	5	6
	(12)	(13)	(14)	(15)	(16)	(17)
7	8	9	10	11	12	13
(18)	(19)	(20)	(21)	(22)	(23)	(24)
14	15	16	17	18	19	20
(25)	(26)	(27)	(28)	(29)	(30h)	(1)
21	22	23	24	25	26	27
(2)	(3)	(4)	(5)	(6)	(7)	(8)
28	29	30	31			
(9)	(10)	(11)	(12)			

September
(Elul 6)

S	M	T	W	T	F	S
				1	2	3
				(13)	(14)	(15)
4	5	6	7	8	9	10
(16)	(17)	(18)	(19)	(20)	(21)	(22)
11	12	13	14	15	16	17
(23)	(24)	(25)	(26)	(27)	(28)	(29i)
18	19	20	21	22	23	24
(1)	(2)	(3)	(4)	(5)	(6)	(7)
25	26	27	28	29	30	
(8)	(9)	(10)	(11)	(12)	(13)	

October
(Tishri 7)

S	M	T	W	T	F	S
						1
						(14)
2	3	4	5	6	7	8
(15)	(16)	(17)	(18)	(19)	(20)	(21)
9	10	11	12	13	14	15
(22)	(23)	(24)	(25)	(26)	(27)	(28)
16	17	18	19	20	21	22
(29)	(30j)	(1)	(2)	(3)	(4)	(5)
23	24	25	26	27	28	29
(6)	(7)	(8)	(9)	(10)	(11)	(12)
30	31					
(13)	(14)					

November
(Marheshvan 8)

S	M	T	W	T	F	S
		1	2	3	4	5
		(15)	(16)	(17)	(18)	(19)
6	7	8	9	10	11	12
(20)	(21)	(22)	(23)	(24)	(25)	(26)
13	14	15	16	17	18	19
(27)	(28)	(29)	(30k)	(1)	(2)	(3)
20	21	22	23	24	25	26
(4)	(5)	(6)	(7)	(8)	(9)	(10)
27	28	29	30			
(11)	(12)	(13)	(14)			

December
(Kislev 9)

S	M	T	W	T	F	S
				1	2	3
				(15)	(16)	(17)
4	5	6	7	8	9	10
(18)	(19)	(20)	(21)	(22)	(23)	(24)
11	12	13	14	15	16	17
(25)	(26)	(27)	(28)	(29)	(30m)	(1)
18	19	20	21	22	23	24
(2)	(3)	(4)	(5)	(6)	(7)	(8)
25	26	27	28	29	30	31
(9)	(10)	(11)	(12)	(13)	(14)	(15)

Day of Trumpets — Tishri 1
Feast of Booths — Tishri 15-22

Day of Atonement — Tishri 10
Feast of Dedication — 8 days beginning Kislev 25

Time of the New Moon — g16:26 h6:04 i22:35 j17:08 k12:15 m6:28

A.D. 17

January
(Tebeth 10)

S	M	T	W	T	F	S
1	2	3	4	5	6	7
(16)	(17)	(18)	(19)	(20)	(21)	(22)
8	9	10	11	12	13	14
(23)	(24)	(25)	(26)	(27)	(28)	(29a)
15	16	17	18	19	20	21
(1)	(2)	(3)	(4)	(5)	(6)	(7)
22	23	24	25	26	27	28
(8)	(9)	(10)	(11)	(12)	(13)	(14)
29	30	31				
(15)	(16)	(17)				

April
(Nisan 1)

S	M	T	W	T	F	S
						1
						(18)
2	3	4	5	6	7	8
(19)	(20)	(21)	(22)	(23)	(24)	(25)
9	10	11	12	13	14	15
(26)	(27)	(28)	(29)	(30d)	(1)	(2)
16	17	18	19	20	21	22
(3)	(4)	(5)	(6)	(7)	(8)	(9)
23	24	25	26	27	28	29
(10)	(11)	(12)	(13)	(14)	(15)	(16)
30						
(17)						

February
(Shebat 11)

S	M	T	W	T	F	S
			1	2	3	4
			(18)	(19)	(20)	(21)
5	6	7	8	9	10	11
(22)	(23)	(24)	(25)	(26)	(27)	(28)
12	13	14	15	16	17	18
(29)	(30b)	(1)	(2)	(3)	(4)	(5)
19	20	21	22	23	24	25
(6)	(7)	(8)	(9)	(10)	(11)	(12)
26	27	28				
(13)	(14)	(15)				

May
(Iyyar 2)

S	M	T	W	T	F	S
	1	2	3	4	5	6
	(18)	(19)	(20)	(21)	(22)	(23)
7	8	9	10	11	12	13
(24)	(25)	(26)	(27)	(28)	(29e)	(1)
14	15	16	17	18	19	20
(2)	(3)	(4)	(5)	(6)	(7)	(8)
21	22	23	24	25	26	27
(9)	(10)	(11)	(12)	(13)	(14)	(15)
28	29	30	31			
(16)	(17)	(18)	(19)			

March
(Adar 12)

S	M	T	W	T	F	S
			1	2	3	4
			(16)	(17)	(18)	(19)
5	6	7	8	9	10	11
(20)	(21)	(22)	(23)	(24)	(25)	(26)
12	13	14	15	16	17	18
(27)	(28)	(29c)	(1)	(2)	(3)	(4)
19	20	21	22	23	24	25
(5)	(6)	(7)	(8)	(9)	(10)	(11)
26	27	28	29	30	31	
(12)	(13)	(14)	(15)	(16)	(17)	

June
(Sivan 3)

S	M	T	W	T	F	S
				1	2	3
				(20)	(21)	(22)
4	5	6	7	8	9	10
(23)	(24)	(25)	(26)	(27)	(28)	(29f)
11	12	13	14	15	16	17
(1)	(2)	(3)	(4)	(5)	(6)	(7)
18	19	20	21	22	23	24
(8)	(9)	(10)	(11)	(12)	(13)	(14)
25	26	27	28	29	30	
(15)	(16)	(17)	(18)	(19)	(20)	

Passover Lamb Sacrificed — Nisan 14
Feast of First Fruits — 1st Sunday after Nisan 15

Feast of Unleavened Bread — Nisan 15-21
Pentecost — 8th Sunday after Nisan 15

Time of New Moon (Jerusalem) —   a22:37   b12:00   c22:33   d6:48   e13:41   f20:25

A.D. 17

July
(Tammuz 4)

S	M	T	W	T	F	S
						1
						(21)
2	3	4	5	6	7	8
(22)	(23)	(24)	(25)	(26)	(27)	(28)
9	10	11	12	13	14	15
(29)	(30g)	(1)	(2)	(3)	(4)	(5)
16	17	18	19	20	21	22
(6)	(7)	(8)	(9)	(10)	(11)	(12)
23	24	25	26	27	28	29
(13)	(14)	(15)	(16)	(17)	(18)	(19)
30	31					
(20)	(21)					

October
(Tishri 7)

S	M	T	W	T	F	S
1	2	3	4	5	6	7
(24)	(25)	(26)	(27)	(28)	(29j)	(1)
8	9	10	11	12	13	14
(2)	(3)	(4)	(5)	(6)	(7)	(8)
15	16	17	18	19	20	21
(9)	(10)	(11)	(12)	(13)	(14)	(15)
22	23	24	25	26	27	28
(16)	(17)	(18)	(19)	(20)	(21)	(22)
29	30	31				
(23)	(24)	(25)				

August
(Ab 5)

S	M	T	W	T	F	S
		1	2	3	4	5
		(22)	(23)	(24)	(25)	(26)
6	7	8	9	10	11	12
(27)	(28)	(29h)	(1)	(2)	(3)	(4)
13	14	15	16	17	18	19
(5)	(6)	(7)	(8)	(9)	(10)	(11)
20	21	22	23	24	25	26
(12)	(13)	(14)	(15)	(16)	(17)	(18)
27	28	29	30	31		
(19)	(20)	(21)	(22)	(23)		

November
(Marheshvan 8)

S	M	T	W	T	F	S
			1	2	3	4
			(26)	(27)	(28)	(29)
5	6	7	8	9	10	11
(30k)	(1)	(2)	(3)	(4)	(5)	(6)
12	13	14	15	16	17	18
(7)	(8)	(9)	(10)	(11)	(12)	(13)
19	20	21	22	23	24	25
(14)	(15)	(16)	(17)	(18)	(19)	(20)
26	27	28	29	30		
(21)	(22)	(23)	(24)	(25)		

September
(Elul 6)

S	M	T	W	T	F	S
					1	2
					(24)	(25)
3	4	5	6	7	8	9
(26)	(27)	(28)	(29)	(30i)	(1)	(2)
10	11	12	13	14	15	16
(3)	(4)	(5)	(6)	(7)	(8)	(9)
17	18	19	20	21	22	23
(10)	(11)	(12)	(13)	(14)	(15)	(16)
24	25	26	27	28	29	30
(17)	(18)	(19)	(20)	(21)	(22)	(23)

December
(Kislev 9)

S	M	T	W	T	F	S
					1	2
					(26)	(27)
3	4	5	6	7	8	9
(28)	(29)	(30m)	(1)	(2)	(3)	(4)
10	11	12	13	14	15	16
(5)	(6)	(7)	(8)	(9)	(10)	(11)
17	18	19	20	21	22	23
(12)	(13)	(14)	(15)	(16)	(17)	(18)
24	25	26	27	28	29	30
(19)	(20)	(21)	(22)	(23)	(24)	(25)
31						
(26)						

Day of Trumpets — Tishri 1
Feast of Booths — Tishri 15-22

Day of Atonement — Tishri 10
Feast of Dedication — 8 days beginning Kislev 25

Time of the New Moon — g4:08 h13:50 i2:12 j17:27 k11:20 m6:54

A.D. 18

January
(Tebeth 10)

S	M	T	W	T	F	S
	1	2	3	4	5	6
	(27)	(28)	(29)	(30a)	(1)	(2)
7	8	9	10	11	12	13
(3)	(4)	(5)	(6)	(7)	(8)	(9)
14	15	16	17	18	19	20
(10)	(11)	(12)	(13)	(14)	(15)	(16)
21	22	23	24	25	26	27
(17)	(18)	(19)	(20)	(21)	(22)	(23)
28	29	30	31			
(24)	(25)	(26)	(27)			

April
(Adar II 13)

S	M	T	W	T	F	S
1	2	3	4	5	6	7
(28)	(29d)	(1)	(2)	(3)	(4)	(5)
8	9	10	11	12	13	14
(6)	(7)	(8)	(9)	(10)	(11)	(12)
15	16	17	18	19	20	21
(13)	(14)	(15)	(16)	(17)	(18)	(19)
22	23	24	25	26	27	28
(20)	(21)	(22)	(23)	(24)	(25)	(26)
29	30					
(27)	(28)					

February
(Shebat 11)

S	M	T	W	T	F	S
				1	2	3
				(28)	(29b)	(1)
4	5	6	7	8	9	10
(2)	(3)	(4)	(5)	(6)	(7)	(8)
11	12	13	14	15	16	17
(9)	(10)	(11)	(12)	(13)	(14)	(15)
18	19	20	21	22	23	24
(16)	(17)	(18)	(19)	(20)	(21)	(22)
25	26	27	28			
(23)	(24)	(25)	(26)			

May
(Nisan 1)

S	M	T	W	T	F	S
		1	2	3	4	5
		(29)	(30e)	(1)	(2)	(3)
6	7	8	9	10	11	12
(4)	(5)	(6)	(7)	(8)	(9)	(10)
13	14	15	16	17	18	19
(11)	(12)	(13)	(14)	(15)	(16)	(17)
20	21	22	23	24	25	26
(18)	(19)	(20)	(21)	(22)	(23)	(24)
27	28	29	30	31		
(25)	(26)	(27)	(28)	(29f)		

March
(Adar 12)

S	M	T	W	T	F	S
				1	2	3
				(27)	(28)	(29)
4	5	6	7	8	9	10
(30c)	(1)	(2)	(3)	(4)	(5)	(6)
11	12	13	14	15	16	17
(7)	(8)	(9)	(10)	(11)	(12)	(13)
18	19	20	21	22	23	24
(14)	(15)	(16)	(17)	(18)	(19)	(20)
25	26	27	28	29	30	31
(21)	(22)	(23)	(24)	(25)	(26)	(27)

June
(Sivan 3)

S	M	T	W	T	F	S
					1	2
					(1)	(2)
3	4	5	6	7	8	9
(3)	(4)	(5)	(6)	(7)	(8)	(9)
10	11	12	13	14	15	16
(10)	(11)	(12)	(13)	(14)	(15)	(16)
17	18	19	20	21	22	23
(17)	(18)	(19)	(20)	(21)	(22)	(23)
24	25	26	27	28	29	30
(24)	(25)	(26)	(27)	(28)	(29g)	(1)

Passover Lamb Sacrificed — Nisan 14
Feast of First Fruits — 1st Sunday after Nisan 15

Feast of Unleavened Bread — Nisan 15-21
Pentecost — 8th Sunday after Nisan 15

Time of New Moon (Jerusalem) — a2:28 b20:07 c10:36 d21:48 e6:28 f13:43 g20:38

A.D. 18

July (Tammuz 4)						
S	M	T	W	T	F	S
1	2	3	4	5	6	7
(2)	(3)	(4)	(5)	(6)	(7)	(8)
8	9	10	11	12	13	14
(9)	(10)	(11)	(12)	(13)	(14)	(15)
15	16	17	18	19	20	21
(16)	(17)	(18)	(19)	(20)	(21)	(22)
22	23	24	25	26	27	28
(23)	(24)	(25)	(26)	(27)	(28)	(29)
29	30	31				
(30h)	(1)	(2)				

October (Tishri 7)						
S	M	T	W	T	F	S
	1	2	3	4	5	6
	(5)	(6)	(7)	(8)	(9)	(10)
7	8	9	10	11	12	13
(11)	(12)	(13)	(14)	(15)	(16)	(17)
14	15	16	17	18	19	20
(18)	(19)	(20)	(21)	(22)	(23)	(24)
21	22	23	24	25	26	27
(25)	(26)	(27)	(28)	(29k)	(1)	(2)
28	29	30	31			
(3)	(4)	(5)	(6)			

August (Ab 5)						
S	M	T	W	T	F	S
			1	2	3	4
			(3)	(4)	(5)	(6)
5	6	7	8	9	10	11
(7)	(8)	(9)	(10)	(11)	(12)	(13)
12	13	14	15	16	17	18
(14)	(15)	(16)	(17)	(18)	(19)	(20)
19	20	21	22	23	24	25
(21)	(22)	(23)	(24)	(25)	(26)	(27)
26	27	28	29	30	31	
(28)	(29i)	(1)	(2)	(3)	(4)	

November (Marheshvan 8)						
S	M	T	W	T	F	S
				1	2	3
				(7)	(8)	(9)
4	5	6	7	8	9	10
(10)	(11)	(12)	(13)	(14)	(15)	(16)
11	12	13	14	15	16	17
(17)	(18)	(19)	(20)	(21)	(22)	(23)
18	19	20	21	22	23	24
(24)	(25)	(26)	(27)	(28)	(29)	(30m)
25	26	27	28	29	30	
(1)	(2)	(3)	(4)	(5)	(6)	

September (Elul 6)						
S	M	T	W	T	F	S
						1
						(5)
2	3	4	5	6	7	8
(6)	(7)	(8)	(9)	(10)	(11)	(12)
9	10	11	12	13	14	15
(13)	(14)	(15)	(16)	(17)	(18)	(19)
16	17	18	19	20	21	22
(20)	(21)	(22)	(23)	(24)	(25)	(26)
23	24	25	26	27	28	29
(27)	(28)	(29)	(30j)	(1)	(2)	(3)
30						
(4)						

December (Kislev 9)						
S	M	T	W	T	F	S
						1
						(7)
2	3	4	5	6	7	8
(8)	(9)	(10)	(11)	(12)	(13)	(14)
9	10	11	12	13	14	15
(15)	(16)	(17)	(18)	(19)	(20)	(21)
16	17	18	19	20	21	22
(22)	(23)	(24)	(25)	(26)	(27)	(28)
23	24	25	26	27	28	29
(29)	(30n)	(1)	(2)	(3)	(4)	(5)
30	31					
(6)	(7)					

Day of Trumpets — Tishri 1
Feast of Booths — Tishri 15-22

Day of Atonement — Tishri 10
Feast of Dedication — 8 days beginning Kislev 25

Time of the New Moon — h4:12 i13:09 j0:13 k14:01 m6:45 n1:46

A.D. 19

January
(Tebeth 10)

S	M	T	W	T	F	S
		1	2	3	4	5
		(8)	(9)	(10)	(11)	(12)
6	7	8	9	10	11	12
(13)	(14)	(15)	(16)	(17)	(18)	(19)
13	14	15	16	17	18	19
(20)	(21)	(22)	(23)	(24)	(25)	(26)
20	21	22	23	24	25	26
(27)	(28)	(29a)	(1)	(2)	(3)	(4)
27	28	29	30	31		
(5)	(6)	(7)	(8)	(9)		

April
(Nisan 1)

S	M	T	W	T	F	S
	1	2	3	4	5	6
	(9)	(10)	(11)	(12)	(13)	(14)
7	8	9	10	11	12	13
(15)	(16)	(17)	(18)	(19)	(20)	(21)
14	15	16	17	18	19	20
(22)	(23)	(24)	(25)	(26)	(27)	(28)
21	22	23	24	25	26	27
(29d)	(1)	(2)	(3)	(4)	(5)	(6)
28	29	30				
(7)	(8)	(9)				

February
(Shebat 11)

S	M	T	W	T	F	S
					1	2
					(10)	(11)
3	4	5	6	7	8	9
(12)	(13)	(14)	(15)	(16)	(17)	(18)
10	11	12	13	14	15	16
(19)	(20)	(21)	(22)	(23)	(24)	(25)
17	18	19	20	21	22	23
(26)	(27)	(28)	(29)	(30b)	(1)	(2)
24	25	26	27	28		
(3)	(4)	(5)	(6)	(7)		

May
(Iyyar 2)

S	M	T	W	T	F	S
			1	2	3	4
			(10)	(11)	(12)	(13)
5	6	7	8	9	10	11
(14)	(15)	(16)	(17)	(18)	(19)	(20)
12	13	14	15	16	17	18
(21)	(22)	(23)	(24)	(25)	(26)	(27)
19	20	21	22	23	24	25
(28)	(29)	(30e)	(1)	(2)	(3)	(4)
26	27	28	29	30	31	
(5)	(6)	(7)	(8)	(9)	(10)	

March
(Adar 12)

S	M	T	W	T	F	S
					1	2
					(8)	(9)
3	4	5	6	7	8	9
(10)	(11)	(12)	(13)	(14)	(15)	(16)
10	11	12	13	14	15	16
(17)	(18)	(19)	(20)	(21)	(22)	(23)
17	18	19	20	21	22	23
(24)	(25)	(26)	(27)	(28)	(29)	(30)
24	25	26	27	28	29	30
(1)	(2)	(3)	(4)	(5)	(6)	(7)
31						
(8)						

June
(Sivan 3)

S	M	T	W	T	F	S
						1
						(11)
2	3	4	5	6	7	8
(12)	(13)	(14)	(15)	(16)	(17)	(18)
9	10	11	12	13	14	15
(19)	(20)	(21)	(22)	(23)	(24)	(25)
16	17	18	19	20	21	22
(26)	(27)	(28)	(29f)	(1)	(2)	(3)
23	24	25	26	27	28	29
(4)	(5)	(6)	(7)	(8)	(9)	(10)
30						
(11)						

Passover Lamb Sacrificed — Nisan 14
Feast of First Fruits — 1st Sunday after Nisan 15

Feast of Unleavened Bread — Nisan 15-21
Pentecost — 8th Sunday after Nisan 15

Time of New Moon (Jerusalem) —   a21:18   b15:20   c6:37   d18:59   e5:02   f13:30

A.D. 19

July
(Tammuz 4)

S	M	T	W	T	F	S
	1	2	3	4	5	6
	(12)	(13)	(14)	(15)	(16)	(17)
7	8	9	10	11	12	13
(18)	(19)	(20)	(21)	(22)	(23)	(24)
14	15	16	17	18	19	20
(25)	(26)	(27)	(28)	(29g)	(1)	(2)
21	22	23	24	25	26	27
(3)	(4)	(5)	(6)	(7)	(8)	(9)
28	29	30	31			
(10)	(11)	(12)	(13)			

October
(Tishri 7)

S	M	T	W	T	F	S
		1	2	3	4	5
		(16)	(17)	(18)	(19)	(20)
6	7	8	9	10	11	12
(21)	(22)	(23)	(24)	(25)	(26)	(27)
13	14	15	16	17	18	19
(28)	(29)	(30j)	(1)	(2)	(3)	(4)
20	21	22	23	24	25	26
(5)	(6)	(7)	(8)	(9)	(10)	(11)
27	28	29	30	31		
(12)	(13)	(14)	(15)	(16)		

August
(Ab 5)

S	M	T	W	T	F	S
				1	2	3
				(14)	(15)	(16)
4	5	6	7	8	9	10
(17)	(18)	(19)	(20)	(21)	(22)	(23)
11	12	13	14	15	16	17
(24)	(25)	(26)	(27)	(28)	(29)	(30h)
18	19	20	21	22	23	24
(1)	(2)	(3)	(4)	(5)	(6)	(7)
25	26	27	28	29	30	31
(8)	(9)	(10)	(11)	(12)	(13)	(14)

November
(Marheshvan 8)

S	M	T	W	T	F	S
					1	2
					(17)	(18)
3	4	5	6	7	8	9
(19)	(20)	(21)	(22)	(23)	(24)	(25)
10	11	12	13	14	15	16
(26)	(27)	(28)	(29k)	(1)	(2)	(3)
17	18	19	20	21	22	23
(4)	(5)	(6)	(7)	(8)	(9)	(10)
24	25	26	27	28	29	30
(11)	(12)	(13)	(14)	(15)	(16)	(17)

September
(Elul 6)

S	M	T	W	T	F	S
1	2	3	4	5	6	7
(15)	(16)	(17)	(18)	(19)	(20)	(21)
8	9	10	11	12	13	14
(22)	(23)	(24)	(25)	(26)	(27)	(28)
15	16	17	18	19	20	21
(29i)	(1)	(2)	(3)	(4)	(5)	(6)
22	23	24	25	26	27	28
(7)	(8)	(9)	(10)	(11)	(12)	(13)
29	30					
(14)	(15)					

December
(Kislev 9)

S	M	T	W	T	F	S
1	2	3	4	5	6	7
(18)	(19)	(20)	(21)	(22)	(23)	(24)
8	9	10	11	12	13	14
(25)	(26)	(27)	(28)	(29)	(30m)	(1)
15	16	17	18	19	20	21
(2)	(3)	(4)	(5)	(6)	(7)	(8)
22	23	24	25	26	27	28
(9)	(10)	(11)	(12)	(13)	(14)	(15)
29	30	31				
(16)	(17)	(18)				

Day of Trumpets — Tishri 1
Feast of Booths — Tishri 15-22

Day of Atonement — Tishri 10
Feast of Dedication — 8 days beginning Kislev 25

Time of the New Moon — g21:15 h5:02 i13:42 j0:04 k12:47 m4:03

Gregorian

A.D. 20

January
(Tebeth 10)

S	M	T	W	T	F	S
			1	2	3	4
			(19)	(20)	(21)	(22)
5	6	7	8	9	10	11
(23)	(24)	(25)	(26)	(27)	(28)	(29a)
12	13	14	15	16	17	18
(1)	(2)	(3)	(4)	(5)	(6)	(7)
19	20	21	22	23	24	25
(8)	(9)	(10)	(11)	(12)	(13)	(14)
26	27	28	29	30	31	
(15)	(16)	(17)	(18)	(19)	(20)	

April
(Nisan 1)

S	M	T	W	T	F	S
			1	2	3	4
			(21)	(22)	(23)	(24)
5	6	7	8	9	10	11
(25)	(26)	(27)	(28)	(29)	(30d)	(1)
12	13	14	15	16	17	18
(2)	(3)	(4)	(5)	(6)	(7)	(8)
19	20	21	22	23	24	25
(9)	(10)	(11)	(12)	(13)	(14)	(15)
26	27	28	29	30		
(16)	(17)	(18)	(19)	(20)		

February
(Shebat 11)

S	M	T	W	T	F	S
						1
						(21)
2	3	4	5	6	7	8
(22)	(23)	(24)	(25)	(26)	(27)	(28)
9	10	11	12	13	14	15
(29)	(30b)	(1)	(2)	(3)	(4)	(5)
16	17	18	19	20	21	22
(6)	(7)	(8)	(9)	(10)	(11)	(12)
23	24	25	26	27	28	29
(13)	(14)	(15)	(16)	(17)	(18)	(19)

May
(Iyyar 2)

S	M	T	W	T	F	S
					1	2
					(21)	(22)
3	4	5	6	7	8	9
(23)	(24)	(25)	(26)	(27)	(28)	(29e)
10	11	12	13	14	15	16
(1)	(2)	(3)	(4)	(5)	(6)	(7)
17	18	19	20	21	22	23
(8)	(9)	(10)	(11)	(12)	(13)	(14)
24	25	26	27	28	29	30
(15)	(16)	(17)	(18)	(19)	(20)	(21)
31						
(22)						

March
(Adar 12)

S	M	T	W	T	F	S
1	2	3	4	5	6	7
(20)	(21)	(22)	(23)	(24)	(25)	(26)
8	9	10	11	12	13	14
(27)	(28)	(29)	(30c)	(1)	(2)	(3)
15	16	17	18	19	20	21
(4)	(5)	(6)	(7)	(8)	(9)	(10)
22	23	24	25	26	27	28
(11)	(12)	(13)	(14)	(15)	(16)	(17)
29	30	31				
(18)	(19)	(20)				

June
(Sivan 3)

S	M	T	W	T	F	S
	1	2	3	4	5	6
	(23)	(24)	(25)	(26)	(27)	(28)
7	8	9	10	11	12	13
(29)	(30f)	(1)	(2)	(3)	(4)	(5)
14	15	16	17	18	19	20
(6)	(7)	(8)	(9)	(10)	(11)	(12)
21	22	23	24	25	26	27
(13)	(14)	(15)	(16)	(17)	(18)	(19)
28	29	30				
(20)	(21)	(22)				

Passover Lamb Sacrificed — Nisan 14
Feast of First Fruits — 1st Sunday after Nisan 15

Feast of Unleavened Bread — Nisan 15-21
Pentecost — 8th Sunday after Nisan 15

Time of New Moon (Jerusalem) —   a21:15   b15:10   c8:24   d0:21   e14:17   f2:13

A.D. 20

July
(Tammuz 4)

S	M	T	W	T	F	S
			1	2	3	4
			(23)	(24)	(25)	(26)
5	6	7	8	9	10	11
(27)	(28)	(29g)	(1)	(2)	(3)	(4)
12	13	14	15	16	17	18
(5)	(6)	(7)	(8)	(9)	(10)	(11)
19	20	21	22	23	24	25
(12)	(13)	(14)	(15)	(16)	(17)	(18)
26	27	28	29	30	31	
(19)	(20)	(21)	(22)	(23)	(24)	

October
(Tishri 7)

S	M	T	W	T	F	S
				1	2	3
				(27)	(28)	(29j)
4	5	6	7	8	9	10
(1)	(2)	(3)	(4)	(5)	(6)	(7)
11	12	13	14	15	16	17
(8)	(9)	(10)	(11)	(12)	(13)	(14)
18	19	20	21	22	23	24
(15)	(16)	(17)	(18)	(19)	(20)	(21)
25	26	27	28	29	30	31
(22)	(23)	(24)	(25)	(26)	(27)	(28)

August
(Ab 5)

S	M	T	W	T	F	S
						1
						(25)
2	3	4	5	6	7	8
(26)	(27)	(28)	(29h)	(1)	(2)	(3)
9	10	11	12	13	14	15
(4)	(5)	(6)	(7)	(8)	(9)	(10)
16	17	18	19	20	21	22
(11)	(12)	(13)	(14)	(15)	(16)	(17)
23	24	25	26	27	28	29
(18)	(19)	(20)	(21)	(22)	(23)	(24)
30	31					
(25)	(26)					

November
(Marheshvan 8)

S	M	T	W	T	F	S
1	2	3	4	5	6	7
(29)	(30k)	(1)	(2)	(3)	(4)	(5)
8	9	10	11	12	13	14
(6)	(7)	(8)	(9)	(10)	(11)	(12)
15	16	17	18	19	20	21
(13)	(14)	(15)	(16)	(17)	(18)	(19)
22	23	24	25	26	27	28
(20)	(21)	(22)	(23)	(24)	(25)	(26)
29	30					
(27)	(28)					

September
(Elul 6)

S	M	T	W	T	F	S
		1	2	3	4	5
		(27)	(28)	(29)	(30i)	(1)
6	7	8	9	10	11	12
(2)	(3)	(4)	(5)	(6)	(7)	(8)
13	14	15	16	17	18	19
(9)	(10)	(11)	(12)	(13)	(14)	(15)
20	21	22	23	24	25	26
(16)	(17)	(18)	(19)	(20)	(21)	(22)
27	28	29	30			
(23)	(24)	(25)	(26)			

December
(Kislev 9)

S	M	T	W	T	F	S
		1	2	3	4	5
		(29m)	(1)	(2)	(3)	(4)
6	7	8	9	10	11	12
(5)	(6)	(7)	(8)	(9)	(10)	(11)
13	14	15	16	17	18	19
(12)	(13)	(14)	(15)	(16)	(17)	(18)
20	21	22	23	24	25	26
(19)	(20)	(21)	(22)	(23)	(24)	(25)
27	28	29	30	31		
(26)	(27)	(28)	(29)	(30n)		

Day of Trumpets — Tishri 1
Feast of Booths — Tishri 15-22

Day of Atonement — Tishri 10
Feast of Dedication — 8 days beginning Kislev 25

Time of the New Moon — g12:23 h21:22 i6:01 j15:13 k1:37 m13:31 n2:53

January
(Shebat 11)

S	M	T	W	T	F	S
					1	2
					(1)	(2)
3	4	5	6	7	8	9
(3)	(4)	(5)	(6)	(7)	(8)	(9)
10	11	12	13	14	15	16
(10)	(11)	(12)	(13)	(14)	(15)	(16)
17	18	19	20	21	22	23
(17)	(18)	(19)	(20)	(21)	(22)	(23)
24	25	26	27	28	29	30
(24)	(25)	(26)	(27)	(28)	(29a)	(1)
31						
(2)						

April
(Nisan 1)

S	M	T	W	T	F	S
				1	2	3
				(2)	(3)	(4)
4	5	6	7	8	9	10
(5)	(6)	(7)	(8)	(9)	(10)	(11)
11	12	13	14	15	16	17
(12)	(13)	(14)	(15)	(16)	(17)	(18)
18	19	20	21	22	23	24
(19)	(20)	(21)	(22)	(23)	(24)	(25)
25	26	27	28	29	30	
(26)	(27)	(28)	(29d)	(1)	(2)	

February
(Adar 12)

S	M	T	W	T	F	S
	1	2	3	4	5	6
	(3)	(4)	(5)	(6)	(7)	(8)
7	8	9	10	11	12	13
(9)	(10)	(11)	(12)	(13)	(14)	(15)
14	15	16	17	18	19	20
(16)	(17)	(18)	(19)	(20)	(21)	(22)
21	22	23	24	25	26	27
(23)	(24)	(25)	(26)	(27)	(28)	(29)
28						
(30b)						

May
(Iyyar 2)

S	M	T	W	T	F	S
						1
						(3)
2	3	4	5	6	7	8
(4)	(5)	(6)	(7)	(8)	(9)	(10)
9	10	11	12	13	14	15
(11)	(12)	(13)	(14)	(15)	(16)	(17)
16	17	18	19	20	21	22
(18)	(19)	(20)	(21)	(22)	(23)	(24)
23	24	25	26	27	28	29
(25)	(26)	(27)	(28)	(29)	(30e)	(1)
30	31					
(2)	(3)					

March
(Adar II 13)

S	M	T	W	T	F	S
	1	2	3	4	5	6
	(1)	(2)	(3)	(4)	(5)	(6)
7	8	9	10	11	12	13
(7)	(8)	(9)	(10)	(11)	(12)	(13)
14	15	16	17	18	19	20
(14)	(15)	(16)	(17)	(18)	(19)	(20)
21	22	23	24	25	26	27
(21)	(22)	(23)	(24)	(25)	(26)	(27)
28	29	30	31			
(28)	(29)	(30c)	(1)			

June
(Sivan 3)

S	M	T	W	T	F	S
		1	2	3	4	5
		(4)	(5)	(6)	(7)	(8)
6	7	8	9	10	11	12
(9)	(10)	(11)	(12)	(13)	(14)	(15)
13	14	15	16	17	18	19
(16)	(17)	(18)	(19)	(20)	(21)	(22)
20	21	22	23	24	25	26
(23)	(24)	(25)	(26)	(27)	(28)	(29f)
27	28	29	30			
(1)	(2)	(3)	(4)			

Passover Lamb Sacrificed — Nisan 14

Feast of First Fruits — 1st Sunday after Nisan 15

Feast of Unleavened Bread — Nisan 15-21

Pentecost — 8th Sunday after Nisan 15

Time of New Moon (Jerusalem) — a17:26 b8:52 c050 d16:46 e7:53 f21:33

A.D. 21

July
(Tammuz 4)

S	M	T	W	T	F	S
				1	2	3
				(5)	(6)	(7)
4	5	6	7	8	9	10
(8)	(9)	(10)	(11)	(12)	(13)	(14)
11	12	13	14	15	16	17
(15)	(16)	(17)	(18)	(19)	(20)	(21)
18	19	20	21	22	23	24
(22)	(23)	(24)	(25)	(26)	(27)	(28)
25	26	27	28	29	30	31
(29)	(30g)	(1)	(2)	(3)	(4)	(5)

October
(Tishri 7)

S	M	T	W	T	F	S
					1	2
					(8)	(9)
3	4	5	6	7	8	9
(10)	(11)	(12)	(13)	(14)	(15)	(16)
10	11	12	13	14	15	16
(17)	(18)	(19)	(20)	(21)	(22)	(23)
17	18	19	20	21	22	23
(24)	(25)	(26)	(27)	(28)	(29j)	(1)
24	25	26	27	28	29	30
(2)	(3)	(4)	(5)	(6)	(7)	(8)
31						
(9)						

August
(Ab 5)

S	M	T	W	T	F	S
1	2	3	4	5	6	7
(6)	(7)	(8)	(9)	(10)	(11)	(12)
8	9	10	11	12	13	14
(13)	(14)	(15)	(16)	(17)	(18)	(19)
15	16	17	18	19	20	21
(20)	(21)	(22)	(23)	(24)	(25)	(26)
22	23	24	25	26	27	28
(27)	(28)	(29h)	(1)	(2)	(3)	(4)
29	30	31				
(5)	(6)	(7)				

November
(Marheshvan 8)

S	M	T	W	T	F	S
	1	2	3	4	5	6
	(10)	(11)	(12)	(13)	(14)	(15)
7	8	9	10	11	12	13
(16)	(17)	(18)	(19)	(20)	(21)	(22)
14	15	16	17	18	19	20
(23)	(24)	(25)	(26)	(27)	(28)	(29)
21	22	23	24	25	26	27
(30k)	(1)	(2)	(3)	(4)	(5)	(6)
28	29	30				
(7)	(8)	(9)				

September
(Elul 6)

S	M	T	W	T	F	S
			1	2	3	4
			(8)	(9)	(10)	(11)
5	6	7	8	9	10	11
(12)	(13)	(14)	(15)	(16)	(17)	(18)
12	13	14	15	16	17	18
(19)	(20)	(21)	(22)	(23)	(24)	(25)
19	20	21	22	23	24	25
(26)	(27)	(28)	(29)	(30i)	(1)	(2)
26	27	28	29	30		
(3)	(4)	(5)	(6)	(7)		

December
(Kislev 9)

S	M	T	W	T	F	S
			1	2	3	4
			(10)	(11)	(12)	(13)
5	6	7	8	9	10	11
(14)	(15)	(16)	(17)	(18)	(19)	(20)
12	13	14	15	16	17	18
(21)	(22)	(23)	(24)	(25)	(26)	(27)
19	20	21	22	23	24	25
(28)	(29m)	(1)	(2)	(3)	(4)	(5)
26	27	28	29	30	31	
(6)	(7)	(8)	(9)	(10)	(11)	

Day of Trumpets — Tishri 1
Feast of Booths — Tishri 15-22

Day of Atonement — Tishri 10
Feast of Dedication — 8 days beginning Kislev 25

Time of the New Moon — g9:37   h20:32   i6:57   j17:26   k4:13   m15:17

A.D. 22

January
(Tebeth 10)

S	M	T	W	T	F	S
						1
						(12)
2	3	4	5	6	7	8
(13)	(14)	(15)	(16)	(17)	(18)	(19)
9	10	11	12	13	14	15
(20)	(21)	(22)	(23)	(24)	(25)	(26)
16	17	18	19	20	21	22
(27)	(28)	(29)	(30a)	(1)	(2)	(3)
23	24	25	26	27	28	29
(4)	(5)	(6)	(7)	(8)	(9)	(10)
30	31					
(11)	(12)					

April
(Nisan 1)

S	M	T	W	T	F	S
					1	2
					(13)	(14)
3	4	5	6	7	8	9
(15)	(16)	(17)	(18)	(19)	(20)	(21)
10	11	12	13	14	15	16
(22)	(23)	(24)	(25)	(26)	(27)	(28)
17	18	19	20	21	22	23
(29d)	(1)	(2)	(3)	(4)	(5)	(6)
24	25	26	27	28	29	30
(7)	(8)	(9)	(10)	(11)	(12)	(13)

February
(Shebat 11)

S	M	T	W	T	F	S
		1	2	3	4	5
		(13)	(14)	(15)	(16)	(17)
6	7	8	9	10	11	12
(18)	(19)	(20)	(21)	(22)	(23)	(24)
13	14	15	16	17	18	19
(25)	(26)	(27)	(28)	(29b)	(1)	(2)
20	21	22	23	24	25	26
(3)	(4)	(5)	(6)	(7)	(8)	(9)
27	28					
(10)	(11)					

May
(Iyyar 2)

S	M	T	W	T	F	S
1	2	3	4	5	6	7
(14)	(15)	(16)	(17)	(18)	(19)	(20)
8	9	10	11	12	13	14
(21)	(22)	(23)	(24)	(25)	(26)	(27)
15	16	17	18	19	20	21
(28)	(29)	(30e)	(1)	(2)	(3)	(4)
22	23	24	25	26	27	28
(5)	(6)	(7)	(8)	(9)	(10)	(11)
29	30	31				
(12)	(13)	(14)				

March
(Adar 12)

S	M	T	W	T	F	S
		1	2	3	4	5
		(12)	(13)	(14)	(15)	(16)
6	7	8	9	10	11	12
(17)	(18)	(19)	(20)	(21)	(22)	(23)
13	14	15	16	17	18	19
(24)	(25)	(26)	(27)	(28)	(29)	(30c)
20	21	22	23	24	25	26
(1)	(2)	(3)	(4)	(5)	(6)	(7)
27	28	29	30	31		
(8)	(9)	(10)	(11)	(12)		

June
(Sivan 3)

S	M	T	W	T	F	S
			1	2	3	4
			(15)	(16)	(17)	(18)
5	6	7	8	9	10	11
(19)	(20)	(21)	(22)	(23)	(24)	(25)
12	13	14	15	16	17	18
(26)	(27)	(28)	(29)	(30f)	(1)	(2)
19	20	21	22	23	24	25
(3)	(4)	(5)	(6)	(7)	(8)	(9)
26	27	28	29	30		
(10)	(11)	(12)	(13)	(14)		

Passover Lamb Sacrificed — Nisan 14
Feast of First Fruits — 1ˢᵗ Sunday after Nisan 15

Feast of Unleavened Bread — Nisan 15-21
Pentecost — 8ᵗʰ Sunday after Nisan 15

Time of New Moon (Jerusalem) — a2:41 b14:41 c3:41 d17:49 e8:47 f0:00

July
(Tammuz 4)

S	M	T	W	T	F	S
					1 (15)	2 (16)
3 (17)	4 (18)	5 (19)	6 (20)	7 (21)	8 (22)	9 (23)
10 (24)	11 (25)	12 (26)	13 (27)	14 (28)	15 (29g)	16 (1)
17 (2)	18 (3)	19 (4)	20 (5)	21 (6)	22 (7)	23 (8)
24 (9)	25 (10)	26 (11)	27 (12)	28 (13)	29 (14)	30 (15)
31 (16)						

October
(Tishri 7)

S	M	T	W	T	F	S
						1 (19)
2 (20)	3 (21)	4 (22)	5 (23)	6 (24)	7 (25)	8 (26)
9 (27)	10 (28)	11 (29)	12 (30j)	13 (1)	14 (2)	15 (3)
16 (4)	17 (5)	18 (6)	19 (7)	20 (8)	21 (9)	22 (10)
23 (11)	24 (12)	25 (13)	26 (14)	27 (15)	28 (16)	29 (17)
30 (18)	31 (19)					

August
(Ab 5)

S	M	T	W	T	F	S
	1 (17)	2 (18)	3 (19)	4 (20)	5 (21)	6 (22)
7 (23)	8 (24)	9 (25)	10 (26)	11 (27)	12 (28)	13 (29)
14 (30h)	15 (1)	16 (2)	17 (3)	18 (4)	19 (5)	20 (6)
21 (7)	22 (8)	23 (9)	24 (10)	25 (11)	26 (12)	27 (13)
28 (14)	29 (15)	30 (16)	31 (17)			

November
(Marheshvan 8)

S	M	T	W	T	F	S
		1 (20)	2 (21)	3 (22)	4 (23)	5 (24)
6 (25)	7 (26)	8 (27)	9 (28)	10 (29k)	11 (1)	12 (2)
13 (3)	14 (4)	15 (5)	16 (6)	17 (7)	18 (8)	19 (9)
20 (10)	21 (11)	22 (12)	23 (13)	24 (14)	25 (15)	26 (16)
27 (17)	28 (18)	29 (19)	30 (20)			

September
(Elul 6)

S	M	T	W	T	F	S
			1 (18)	2 (19)	3 (20)	
4 (21)	5 (22)	6 (23)	7 (24)	8 (25)	9 (26)	10 (27)
11 (28)	12 (29i)	13 (1)	14 (2)	15 (3)	16 (4)	17 (5)
18 (6)	19 (7)	20 (8)	21 (9)	22 (10)	23 (11)	24 (12)
25 (13)	26 (14)	27 (15)	28 (16)	29 (17)	30 (18)	

December
(Kislev 9)

S	M	T	W	T	F	S
				1 (21)	2 (22)	3 (23)
4 (24)	5 (25)	6 (26)	7 (27)	8 (28)	9 (29)	10 (30m)
11 (1)	12 (2)	13 (3)	14 (4)	15 (5)	16 (6)	17 (7)
18 (8)	19 (9)	20 (10)	21 (11)	22 (12)	23 (13)	24 (14)
25 (15)	26 (16)	27 (17)	28 (18)	29 (19)	30 (20)	31 (21)

Day of Trumpets — Tishri 1
Feast of Booths — Tishri 15-22

Day of Atonement — Tishri 10
Feast of Dedication — 8 days beginning Kislev 25

Time of the New Moon — g14:52 h5:07 i18:42 j7:37 k19:42 m6:53

Gregorian

A.D. 23

January
(Tebeth 10)

S	M	T	W	T	F	S
1	2	3	4	5	6	7
(22)	(23)	(24)	(25)	(26)	(27)	(28)
8	9	10	11	12	13	14
(29a)	(1)	(2)	(3)	(4)	(5)	(6)
15	16	17	18	19	20	21
(7)	(8)	(9)	(10)	(11)	(12)	(13)
22	23	24	25	26	27	28
(14)	(15)	(16)	(17)	(18)	(19)	(20)
29	30	31				
(21)	(22)	(23)				

April
(Nisan 1)

S	M	T	W	T	F	S
						1
						(24)
2	3	4	5	6	7	8
(25)	(26)	(27)	(28)	(29)	(30d)	(1)
9	10	11	12	13	14	15
(2)	(3)	(4)	(5)	(6)	(7)	(8)
16	17	18	19	20	21	22
(9)	(10)	(11)	(12)	(13)	(14)	(15)
23	24	25	26	27	28	29
(16)	(17)	(18)	(19)	(20)	(21)	(22)
30						
(23)						

February
(Shebat 11)

S	M	T	W	T	F	S
			1	2	3	4
			(24)	(25)	(26)	(27)
5	6	7	8	9	10	11
(28)	(29)	(30b)	(1)	(2)	(3)	(4)
12	13	14	15	16	17	18
(5)	(6)	(7)	(8)	(9)	(10)	(11)
19	20	21	22	23	24	25
(12)	(13)	(14)	(15)	(16)	(17)	(18)
26	27	28				
(19)	(20)	(21)				

May
(Iyyar 2)

S	M	T	W	T	F	S
	1	2	3	4	5	6
	(24)	(25)	(26)	(27)	(28)	(29e)
7	8	9	10	11	12	13
(1)	(2)	(3)	(4)	(5)	(6)	(7)
14	15	16	17	18	19	20
(8)	(9)	(10)	(11)	(12)	(13)	(14)
21	22	23	24	25	26	27
(15)	(16)	(17)	(18)	(19)	(20)	(21)
28	29	30	31			
(22)	(23)	(24)	(25)			

March
(Adar 12)

S	M	T	W	T	F	S
			1	2	3	4
			(22)	(23)	(24)	(25)
5	6	7	8	9	10	11
(26)	(27)	(28)	(29c)	(1)	(2)	(3)
12	13	14	15	16	17	18
(4)	(5)	(6)	(7)	(8)	(9)	(10)
19	20	21	22	23	24	25
(11)	(12)	(13)	(14)	(15)	(16)	(17)
26	27	28	29	30	31	
(18)	(19)	(20)	(21)	(22)	(23)	

June
(Sivan 3)

S	M	T	W	T	F	S
				1	2	3
				(26)	(27)	(28)
4	5	6	7	8	9	10
(29)	(30f)	(1)	(2)	(3)	(4)	(5)
11	12	13	14	15	16	17
(6)	(7)	(8)	(9)	(10)	(11)	(12)
18	19	20	21	22	23	24
(13)	(14)	(15)	(16)	(17)	(18)	(19)
25	26	27	28	29	30	
(20)	(21)	(22)	(23)	(24)	(25)	

Passover Lamb Sacrificed — Nisan 14

Feast of First Fruits — 1st Sunday after Nisan 15

Feast of Unleavened Bread — Nisan 15-21

Pentecost — 8th Sunday after Nisan 15

Time of New Moon (Jerusalem) —   a17:17   b3:17   c13:25   d0:13   e12:03   f1:07

A.D. 23

July
(Tammuz 4)

S	M	T	W	T	F	S
						1
						(26)
2	3	4	5	6	7	8
(27)	(28)	(29g)	(1)	(2)	(3)	(4)
9	10	11	12	13	14	15
(5)	(6)	(7)	(8)	(9)	(10)	(11)
16	17	18	19	20	21	22
(12)	(13)	(14)	(15)	(16)	(17)	(18)
23	24	25	26	27	28	29
(19)	(20)	(21)	(22)	(23)	(24)	(25)
30	31					
(26)	(27)					

October
(Tishri 7)

S	M	T	W	T	F	S
1	2	3	4	5	6	7
(29j)	(1)	(2)	(3)	(4)	(5)	(6)
8	9	10	11	12	13	14
(7)	(8)	(9)	(10)	(11)	(12)	(13)
15	16	17	18	19	20	21
(14)	(15)	(16)	(17)	(18)	(19)	(20)
22	23	24	25	26	27	28
(21)	(22)	(23)	(24)	(25)	(26)	(27)
29	30	31				
(28)	(29)	(30k)				

August
(Ab 5)

S	M	T	W	T	F	S
		1	2	3	4	5
		(28)	(29)	(30h)	(1)	(2)
6	7	8	9	10	11	12
(3)	(4)	(5)	(6)	(7)	(8)	(9)
13	14	15	16	17	18	19
(10)	(11)	(12)	(13)	(14)	(15)	(16)
20	21	22	23	24	25	26
(17)	(18)	(19)	(20)	(21)	(22)	(23)
27	28	29	30	31		
(24)	(25)	(26)	(27)	(28)		

November
(Kislev 9)

S	M	T	W	T	F	S
			1	2	3	4
			(1)	(2)	(3)	(4)
5	6	7	8	9	10	11
(5)	(6)	(7)	(8)	(9)	(10)	(11)
12	13	14	15	16	17	18
(12)	(13)	(14)	(15)	(16)	(17)	(18)
19	20	21	22	23	24	25
(19)	(20)	(21)	(22)	(23)	(24)	(25)
26	27	28	29	30		
(26)	(27)	(28)	(29m)	(1)		

September
(Elul 6)

S	M	T	W	T	F	S
					1	2
					(29)	(30i)
3	4	5	6	7	8	9
(1)	(2)	(3)	(4)	(5)	(6)	(7)
10	11	12	13	14	15	16
(8)	(9)	(`10)	(11)	(12)	(13)	(14)
17	18	19	20	21	22	23
(15)	(16)	(17)	(18)	(19)	(20)	(21)
24	25	26	27	28	29	30
(22)	(23)	(24)	(25)	(26)	(27)	(28)

December
(Tebeth 10)

S	M	T	W	T	F	S
					1	2
					(2)	(3)
3	4	5	6	7	8	9
(4)	(5)	(6)	(7)	(8)	(9)	(10)
10	11	12	13	14	15	16
(11)	(12)	(13)	(14)	(15)	(16)	(17)
17	18	19	20	21	22	23
(18)	(19)	(20)	(21)	(22)	(23)	(24)
24	25	26	27	28	29	30
(25)	(26)	(27)	(28)	(29)	(30n)	(1)
31						
(2)						

Day of Trumpets — Tishri 1
Feast of Booths — Tishri 15-22

Day of Atonement — Tishri 10
Feast of Dedication — 8 days beginning Kislev 25

Time of the New Moon — g15:24 h7:05 i23:31 j15:57 k7:21 m21:02 n8:53

A.D. 24

January (Shebat 11)						
S	M	T	W	T	F	S
	1	2	3	4	5	6
	(3)	(4)	(5)	(6)	(7)	(8)
7	8	9	10	11	12	13
(9)	(10)	(11)	(12)	(13)	(14)	(15)
14	15	16	17	18	19	20
(16)	(17)	(18)	(19)	(20)	(21)	(22)
21	22	23	24	25	26	27
(23)	(24)	(25)	(26)	(27)	(28)	(29a)
28	29	30	31			
(1)	(2)	(3)	(4)			

April (Nisan 1)						
S	M	T	W	T	F	S
	1	2	3	4	5	6
	(6)	(7)	(8)	(9)	(10)	(11)
7	8	9	10	11	12	13
(12)	(13)	(14)	(15)	(16)	(17)	(18)
14	15	16	17	18	19	20
(19)	(20)	(21)	(22)	(23)	(24)	(25)
21	22	23	24	25	26	27
(26)	(27)	(28)	(29d)	(1)	(2)	(3)
28	29	30				
(4)	(5)	(6)				

February (Adar 12)						
S	M	T	W	T	F	S
				1	2	3
				(5)	(6)	(7)
4	5	6	7	8	9	10
(8)	(9)	(10)	(11)	(12)	(13)	(14)
11	12	13	14	15	16	17
(15)	(16)	(17)	(18)	(19)	(20)	(21)
18	19	20	21	22	23	24
(22)	(23)	(24)	(25)	(26)	(27)	(28)
25	26	27	28	29		
(29)	(30b)	(1)	(2)	(3)		

(Iyyar 2) May						
S	M	T	W	T	F	S
			1	2	3	4
			(7)	(8)	(9)	(10)
5	6	7	8	9	10	11
(11)	(12)	(13)	(14)	(15)	(16)	(17)
12	13	14	15	16	17	18
(18)	(19)	(20)	(21)	(22)	(23)	(24)
19	20	21	22	23	24	25
(25)	(26)	(27)	(28)	(29)	(30e)	(1)
26	27	28	29	30	31	
(2)	(3)	(4)	(5)	(6)	(7)	

March (Adar II 13)						
S	M	T	W	T	F	S
					1	2
					(4)	(5)
3	4	5	6	7	8	9
(6)	(7)	(8)	(9)	(10)	(11)	(12)
10	11	12	13	14	15	16
(13)	(14)	(15)	(16)	(17)	(18)	(19)
17	18	19	20	21	22	23
(20)	(21)	(22)	(23)	(24)	(25)	(26)
24	25	26	27	28	29	30
(27)	(28)	(29c)	(1)	(2)	(3)	(4)
31						
(5)						

June (Sivan 3)						
S	M	T	W	T	F	S
						1
						(8)
2	3	4	5	6	7	8
(9)	(10)	(11)	(12)	(13)	(14)	(15)
9	10	11	12	13	14	15
(16)	(17)	(18)	(19)	(20)	(21)	(22)
16	17	18	19	20	21	22
(23)	(24)	(25)	(26)	(27)	(28)	(29f)
23	24	25	26	27	28	29
(1)	(2)	(3)	(4)	(5)	(6)	(7)
30						
(8)						

Passover Lamb Sacrificed — Nisan 14
Feast of First Fruits — 1ˢᵗ Sunday after Nisan 15

Feast of Unleavened Bread — Nisan 15-21
Pentecost — 8ᵗʰ Sunday after Nisan 15

Time of New Moon (Jerusalem) — a19:15 b4:36 c13:25 d22:13 e7:41 f18:39

July
(Tammuz 4)

S	M	T	W	T	F	S
	1	2	3	4	5	6
	(9)	(10)	(11)	(12)	(13)	(14)
7	8	9	10	11	12	13
(15)	(16)	(17)	(18)	(19)	(20)	(21)
14	15	16	17	18	19	20
(22)	(23)	(24)	(25)	(26)	(27)	(28)
21	22	23	24	25	26	27
(29)	(30g)	(1)	(2)	(3)	(4)	(5)
28	29	30	31			
(6)	(7)	(8)	(9)			

October
(Tishri 7)

S	M	T	W	T	F	S
		1	2	3	4	5
		(12)	(13)	(14)	(15)	(16)
6	7	8	9	10	11	12
(17)	(18)	(19)	(20)	(21)	(22)	(23)
13	14	15	16	17	18	19
(24)	(25)	(26)	(27)	(28)	(29)	(30j)
20	21	22	23	24	25	26
(1)	(2)	(3)	(4)	(5)	(6)	(7)
27	28	29	30	31		
(8)	(9)	(10)	(11)	(12)		

August
(Ab 5)

S	M	T	W	T	F	S
				1	2	3
				(10)	(11)	(12)
4	5	6	7	8	9	10
(13)	(14)	(15)	(16)	(17)	(18)	(19)
11	12	13	14	15	16	17
(20)	(21)	(22)	(23)	(24)	(25)	(26)
18	19	20	21	22	23	24
(27)	(28)	(29)	(30h)	(1)	(2)	(3)
25	26	27	28	29	30	31
(4)	(5)	(6)	(7)	(8)	(9)	(10)

October
(Tishri 7)

S	M	T	W	T	F	S
		1	2	3	4	5
		(12)	(13)	(14)	(15)	(16)
6	7	8	9	10	11	12
(17)	(18)	(19)	(20)	(21)	(22)	(23)
13	14	15	16	17	18	19
(24)	(25)	(26)	(27)	(28)	(29)	(30j)
20	21	22	23	24	25	26
(1)	(2)	(3)	(4)	(5)	(6)	(7)
27	28	29	30	31		
(8)	(9)	(10)	(11)	(12)		

September
(Elul 6)

S	M	T	W	T	F	S
1	2	3	4	5	6	7
(11)	(12)	(13)	(14)	(15)	(16)	(17)
8	9	10	11	12	13	14
(18)	(19)	(20)	(21)	(22)	(23)	(24)
15	16	17	18	19	20	21
(25)	(26)	(27)	(28)	(29i)	(1)	(2)
22	23	24	25	26	27	28
(3)	(4)	(5)	(6)	(7)	(8)	(9)
29	30					
(10)	(11)					

December
(Kislev 9)

S	M	T	W	T	F	S
1	2	3	4	5	6	7
(13)	(14)	(15)	(16)	(17)	(18)	(19)
8	9	10	11	12	13	14
(20)	(21)	(22)	(23)	(24)	(25)	(26)
15	16	17	18	19	20	21
(27)	(28)	(29m)	(1)	(2)	(3)	(4)
22	23	24	25	26	27	28
(5)	(6)	(7)	(8)	(9)	(10)	(11)
29	30	31				
(12)	(13)	(14)				

Day of Trumpets — Tishri 1
Feast of Booths — Tishri 15-22

Day of Atonement — Tishri 10
Feast of Dedication — 8 days beginning Kislev 25

Time of the New Moon —   g7:53   h22:42   i17:32   j11:58   k5:24   m20:49

A.D. 25

January
(Tebeth 10)

S	M	T	W	T	F	S
			1	2	3	4
			(15)	(16)	(17)	(18)
5	6	7	8	9	10	11
(19)	(20)	(21)	(22)	(23)	(24)	(25)
12	13	14	15	16	17	18
(26)	(27)	(28)	(29)	(30a)	(1)	(2)
19	20	21	22	23	24	25
(3)	(4)	(5)	(6)	(7)	(8)	(9)
26	27	28	29	30	31	
(10)	(11)	(12)	(13)	(14)	(15)	

February
(Shebat 11)

S	M	T	W	T	F	S
						1
						(16)
2	3	4	5	6	7	8
(17)	(18)	(19)	(20)	(21)	(22)	(23)
9	10	11	12	13	14	15
(24)	(25)	(26)	(27)	(28)	(29b)	(1)
16	17	18	19	20	21	22
(2)	(3)	(4)	(5)	(6)	(7)	(8)
23	24	25	26	27	28	
(9)	(10)	(11)	(12)	(13)	(14)	

March
(Adar 12)

S	M	T	W	T	F	S
						1
						(15)
2	3	4	5	6	7	8
(16)	(17)	(18)	(19)	(20)	(21)	(22)
9	10	11	12	13	14	15
(23)	(24)	(25)	(26)	(27)	(28)	(29)
16	17	18	19	20	21	22
(30c)	(1)	(2)	(3)	(4)	(5)	(6)
23	24	25	26	27	28	29
(7)	(8)	(9)	(10)	(11)	(12)	(13)
30	31					
(14)	(15)					

April
(Nisan 1)

S	M	T	W	T	F	S
		1	2	3	4	5
		(16)	(17)	(18)	(19)	(20)
6	7	8	9	10	11	12
(21)	(22)	(23)	(24)	(25)	(26)	(27)
13	14	15	16	17	18	19
(28)	(29d)	(1)	(2)	(3)	(4)	(5)
20	21	22	23	24	25	26
(6)	(7)	(8)	(9)	(10)	(11)	(12)
27	28	29	30			
(13)	(14)	(15)	(16)			

May
(Iyyar 2)

S	M	T	W	T	F	S
				1	2	3
				(17)	(18)	(19)
4	5	6	7	8	9	10
(20)	(21)	(22)	(23)	(24)	(25)	(26)
11	12	13	14	15	16	17
(27)	(28)	(29e)	(1)	(2)	(3)	(4)
18	19	20	21	22	23	24
(5)	(6)	(7)	(8)	(9)	(10)	(11)
25	26	27	28	29	30	31
(12)	(13)	(14)	(15)	(16)	(17)	(18)

June
(Sivan 3)

S	M	T	W	T	F	S
1	2	3	4	5	6	7
(19)	(20)	(21)	(22)	(23)	(24)	(25)
8	9	10	11	12	13	14
(26)	(27)	(28)	(29)	(30f)	(1)	(2)
15	16	17	18	19	20	21
(3)	(4)	(5)	(6)	(7)	(8)	(9)
22	23	24	25	26	27	28
(10)	(11)	(12)	(13)	(14)	(15)	(16)
29	30					
(17)	(18)					

Passover Lamb Sacrificed — Nisan 14
Feast of First Fruits — 1st Sunday after Nisan 15

Feast of Unleavened Bread — Nisan 15-21
Pentecost — 8th Sunday after Nisan 15

Time of New Moon (Jerusalem) —   a9:57   b20:55   c6:04   d13:53   e21:08   f4:53

July
(Tammuz 4)

S	M	T	W	T	F	S
		1	2	3	4	5
		(19)	(20)	(21)	(22)	(23)
6	7	8	9	10	11	12
(24)	(25)	(26)	(27)	(28)	(29g)	(1)
13	14	15	16	17	18	19
(2)	(3)	(4)	(5)	(6)	(7)	(8)
20	21	22	23	24	25	26
(9)	(10)	(11)	(12)	(13)	(14)	(15)
27	28	29	30	31		
(16)	(17)	(18)	(19)	(20)		

October
(Tishri 7)

S	M	T	W	T	F	S
			1	2	3	4
			(23)	(24)	(25)	(26)
5	6	7	8	9	10	11
(27)	(28)	(29)	(30j)	(1)	(2)	(3)
12	13	14	15	16	17	18
(4)	(5)	(6)	(7)	(8)	(9)	(10)
19	20	21	22	23	24	25
(11)	(12)	(13)	(14)	(15)	(16)	(17)
26	27	28	29	30	31	
(18)	(19)	(20)	(21)	(22)	(23)	

August
(Ab 5)

S	M	T	W	T	F	S
					1	2
					(21)	(22)
3	4	5	6	7	8	9
(23)	(24)	(25)	(26)	(27)	(28)	(29)
10	11	12	13	14	15	16
(30h)	(1)	(2)	(3)	(4)	(5)	(6)
17	18	19	20	21	22	23
(7)	(8)	(9)	(10)	(11)	(12)	(13)
24	25	26	27	28	29	30
(14)	(15)	(16)	(17)	(18)	(19)	(20)
31						
(21)						

November
(Marheshvan 8)

S	M	T	W	T	F	S
						1
						(24)
2	3	4	5	6	7	8
(25)	(26)	(27)	(28)	(29)	(30k)	(1)
9	10	11	12	13	14	15
(2)	(3)	(4)	(5)	(6)	(7)	(8)
16	17	18	19	20	21	22
(9)	(10)	(11)	(12)	(13)	(14)	(15)
23	24	25	26	27	28	29
(16)	(17)	(18)	(19)	(20)	(21)	(22)
30						
(23)						

September
(Elul 6)

S	M	T	W	T	F	S
	1	2	3	4	5	6
	(22)	(23)	(24)	(25)	(26)	(27)
7	8	9	10	11	12	13
(28)	(29i)	(1)	(2)	(3)	(4)	(5)
14	15	16	17	18	19	20
(6)	(7)	(8)	(9)	(10)	(11)	(12)
21	22	23	24	25	25	27
(13)	(14)	(15)	(16)	(17)	(18)	(19)
28	29	30				
(20)	(21)	(22)				

December
(Kislev 9)

S	M	T	W	T	F	S
	1	2	3	4	5	6
	(24)	(25)	(26)	(27)	(28)	(29)
7	8	9	10	11	12	13
(30m)	(1)	(2)	(3)	(4)	(5)	(6)
14	15	16	17	18	19	20
(7)	(8)	(9)	(10)	(11)	(12)	(13)
21	22	23	24	25	26	27
(14)	(15)	(16)	(17)	(18)	(19)	(20)
28	29	30	31			
(21)	(22)	(23)	(24)			

Day of Trumpets — Tishri 1
Feast of Booths — Tishri 15-22

Day of Atonement — Tishri 10
Feast of Dedication — 8 days beginning Kislev 25

Time of the New Moon — g14:20 h2:24 i17:43 j11:33 k6:44 m1:40

A.D. 26

January
(Tebeth 10)

S	M	T	W	T	F	S
				1	2	3
				(25)	(26)	(27)
4	5	6	7	8	9	10
(28)	(29a)	(1)	(2)	(3)	(4)	(5)
11	12	13	14	15	16	17
(6)	(7)	(8)	(9)	(10)	(11)	(12)
18	19	20	21	22	23	24
(13)	(14)	(15)	(16)	(17)	(18)	(19)
25	26	27	28	29	30	31
(20)	(21)	(22)	(23)	(24)	(25)	(26)

April
(Adar II 13)

S	M	T	W	T	F	S
			1	2	3	4
			(27)	(28)	(29)	(30d)
5	6	7	8	9	10	11
(1)	(2)	(3)	(4)	(5)	(6)	(7)
12	13	14	15	16	17	18
(8)	(9)	(10)	(11)	(12)	(13)	(14)
19	20	21	22	23	24	25
(15)	(16)	(17)	(18)	(19)	(20)	(21)
26	27	28	29	30		
(22)	(23)	(24)	(25)	(26)		

February
(Shebat 11)

S	M	T	W	T	F	S
1	2	3	4	5	6	7
(27)	(28)	(29)	(30a)	(1)	(2)	(3)
8	9	10	11	12	13	14
(4)	(5)	(6)	(7)	(8)	(9)	(10)
15	16	17	18	19	20	21
(11)	(12)	(13)	(14)	(15)	(16)	(17)
22	23	24	25	26	27	28
(18)	(19)	(20)	(21)	(22)	(23)	(24)

May
(Nisan 1)

S	M	T	W	T	F	S
					1	2
					(27)	(28)
3	4	5	6	7	8	9
(29e)	(1)	(2)	(3)	(4)	(5)	(6)
10	11	12	13	14	15	16
(7)	(8)	(9)	(10)	(11)	(12)	(13)
17	18	19	20	21	22	23
(14)	(15)	(16)	(17)	(18)	(19)	(20)
24	25	26	27	28	29	30
(21)	(22)	(23)	(24)	(25)	(26)	(27)
31						
(28)						

March
(Adar 12)

S	M	T	W	T	F	S
1	2	3	4	5	6	7
(25)	(26)	(27)	(28)	(29c)	(1)	(2)
8	9	10	11	12	13	14
(3)	(4)	(5)	(6)	(7)	(8)	(9)
15	16	17	18	19	20	21
(10)	(11)	(12)	(13)	(14)	(15)	(16)
22	23	24	25	26	27	28
(17)	(18)	(19)	(20)	(21)	(22)	(23)
29	30	31				
(24)	(25)	(26)				

June
(Iyyar 2)

S	M	T	W	T	F	S
	1	2	3	4	5	6
	(29f)	(1)	(2)	(3)	(4)	(5)
7	8	9	10	11	12	13
(6)	(7)	(8)	(9)	(10)	(11)	(12)
14	15	16	17	18	19	20
(13)	(14)	(15)	(16)	(17)	(18)	(19)
21	22	23	24	25	26	27
(20)	(21)	(22)	(23)	(24)	(25)	(26)
28	29	30				
(27)	(28)	(29)				

Passover Lamb Sacrificed — Nisan 14

Feast of First Fruits — 1st Sunday after Nisan 15

Feast of Unleavened Bread — Nisan 15-21

Pentecost — 8th Sunday after Nisan 15

Time of New Moon (Jerusalem) —   a19:00   b9:46   c21:37   d6:48   e14:08   f20:45

July
(Sivan 3)

S	M	T	W	T	F	S
			1	2	3	4
			(30g)	(1)	(2)	(3)
5	6	7	8	9	10	11
(4)	(5)	(6)	(7)	(8)	(9)	(10)
12	13	14	15	16	17	18
(11)	(12)	(13)	(14)	(15)	(16)	(17)
19	20	21	22	23	24	25
(18)	(19)	(20)	(21)	(22)	(23)	(24)
26	27	28	29	30	31	
(25)	(26)	(27)	(28)	(29h)	(1)	

October
(Tishri 7)

S	M	T	W	T	F	S
				1	2	3
				(4)	(5)	(6)
4	5	6	7	8	9	10
(7)	(8)	(9)	(10)	(11)	(12)	(13)
11	12	13	14	15	16	17
(14)	(15)	(16)	(17)	(18)	(19)	(20)
18	19	20	21	22	23	24
(21)	(22)	(23)	(24)	(25)	(26)	(27)
25	26	27	28	29	30	31
(28)	(29)	(30k)	(1)	(2)	(3)	(4)

August
(Ab 5)

S	M	T	W	T	F	S
						1
						(2)
2	3	4	5	6	7	8
(3)	(4)	(5)	(6)	(7)	(8)	(9)
9	10	11	12	13	14	15
(10)	(11)	(12)	(13)	(14)	(15)	(16)
16	17	18	19	20	21	22
(17)	(18)	(19)	(20)	(21)	(22)	(23)
23	24	25	26	27	28	29
(24)	(25)	(26)	(27)	(28)	(29)	(30i)
30	31					
(1)	(2)					

September
(Elul 6)

S	M	T	W	T	F	S
		1	2	3	4	5
		(3)	(4)	(5)	(6)	(7)
6	7	8	9	10	11	12
(8)	(9)	(10)	(11)	(12)	(13)	(14)
13	14	15	16	17	18	19
(15)	(16)	(17)	(18)	(19)	(20)	(21)
20	21	22	23	24	25	26
(22)	(23)	(24)	(25)	(26)	(27)	(28)
27	28	29	30			
(29j)	(1)	(2)	(3)			

September
(Elul 6)

S	M	T	W	T	F	S
		1	2	3	4	5
		(3)	(4)	(5)	(6)	(7)
6	7	8	9	10	11	12
(8)	(9)	(10)	(11)	(12)	(13)	(14)
13	14	15	16	17	18	19
(15)	(16)	(17)	(18)	(19)	(20)	(21)
20	21	22	23	24	25	26
(22)	(23)	(24)	(25)	(26)	(27)	(28)
27	28	29	30			
(29j)	(1)	(2)	(3)			

December
(Kislev 9)

S	M	T	W	T	F	S
		1	2	3	4	5
		(5)	(6)	(7)	(8)	(9)
6	7	8	9	10	11	12
(10)	(11)	(12)	(13)	(14)	(15)	(16)
13	14	15	16	17	18	19
(17)	(18)	(19)	(20)	(21)	(22)	(23)
20	21	22	23	24	25	26
(24)	(25)	(26)	(27)	(28)	(29n)	(1)
27	28	29	30	31		
(2)	(3)	(4)	(5)	(6)		

Day of Trumpets — Tishri 1
Feast of Booths — Tishri 15-22

Day of Atonement — Tishri 10
Feast of Dedication — 8 days beginning Kislev 25

Time of the New Moon — g3:49 h12:28 i23:31 j13:25 k6:06 m1:03 n20:50

A.D. 27

January
(Tebeth 10)

S	M	T	W	T	F	S
					1	2
					(7)	(8)
3	4	5	6	7	8	9
(9)	(10)	(11)	(12)	(13)	(14)	(15)
10	11	12	13	14	15	16
(16)	(17)	(18)	(19)	(20)	(21)	(22)
17	18	19	20	21	22	23
(23)	(24)	(25)	(26)	(27)	(28)	(29)
24	25	26	27	28	29	30
(30a)	(1)	(2)	(3)	(4)	(5)	(6)
31						
(7)						

February
(Shebat 11)

S	M	T	W	T	F	S
	1	2	3	4	5	6
	(8)	(9)	(10)	(11)	(12)	(13)
7	8	9	10	11	12	13
(14)	(15)	(16)	(17)	(18)	(19)	(20)
14	15	16	17	18	19	20
(21)	(22)	(23)	(24)	(25)	(26)	(27)
21	22	23	24	25	26	27
(28)	(29)	(30b)	(1)	(2)	(3)	(4)
28						
(5)						

March
(Adar 12)

S	M	T	W	T	F	S
	1	2	3	4	5	6
	(6)	(7)	(8)	(9)	(10)	(11)
7	8	9	10	11	12	13
(12)	(13)	(14)	(15)	(16)	(17)	(18)
14	15	16	17	18	19	20
(19)	(20)	(21)	(22)	(23)	(24)	(25)
21	22	23	24	25	26	27
(26)	(27)	(28)	(29c)	(1)	(2)	(3)
28	29	30	31			
(4)	(5)	(6)	(7)			

April
(Nisan 1)

S	M	T	W	T	F	S
				1	2	3
				(8)	(9)	(10)
4	5	6	7	8	9	10
(11)	(12)	(13)	(14)	(15)	(16)	(17)
11	12	13	14	15	16	17
(18)	(19)	(20)	(21)	(22)	(23)	(24)
18	19	20	21	22	23	24
(25)	(26)	(27)	(28)	(29)	(30d)	(1)
25	26	27	28	29	30	
(2)	(3)	(4)	(5)	(6)	(7)	

May
(Iyyar 2)

S	M	T	W	T	F	S
						1
						(8)
2	3	4	5	6	7	8
(9)	(10)	(11)	(12)	(13)	(14)	(15)
9	10	11	12	13	14	15
(16)	(17)	(18)	(19)	(20)	(21)	(22)
16	17	18	19	20	21	22
(23)	(24)	(25)	(26)	(27)	(28)	(29e)
23	24	25	26	27	28	29
(1)	(2)	(3)	(4)	(5)	(6)	(7)
30	31					
(8)	(9)					

June
(Sivan 3)

S	M	T	W	T	F	S
		1	2	3	4	5
		(10)	(11)	(12)	(13)	(14)
6	7	8	9	10	11	12
(15)	(16)	(17)	(18)	(19)	(20)	(21)
13	14	15	16	17	18	19
(22)	(23)	(24)	(25)	(26)	(27)	(28)
20	21	22	23	24	25	26
(29f)	(1)	(2)	(3)	(4)	(5)	(6)
27	28	29	30			
(7)	(8)	(9)	(10)			

Passover Lamb Sacrificed — Nisan 14
Feast of First Fruits — 1st Sunday after Nisan 15

Feast of Unleavened Bread — Nisan 15-21
Pentecost — 8th Sunday after Nisan 15

Time of New Moon (Jerusalem) —   a15:35   b7:39   c20:22   d6:08   e13:55   f20:55

A.D. 27

July
(Tammuz 4)

S	M	T	W	T	F	S
				1	2	3
				(11)	(12)	(13)
4	5	6	7	8	9	10
(14)	(15)	(16)	(17)	(18)	(19)	(20)
11	12	13	14	15	16	17
(21)	(22)	(23)	(24)	(25)	(26)	(27)
18	19	20	21	22	23	24
(28)	(29)	(30g)	(1)	(2)	(3)	(4)
25	26	27	28	29	30	31
(5)	(6)	(7)	(8)	(9)	(10)	(11)

October
(Tishri 7)

S	M	T	W	T	F	S
					1	2
					(15)	(16)
3	4	5	6	7	8	9
(17)	(18)	(19)	(20)	(21)	(22)	(23)
10	11	12	13	14	15	16
(24)	(25)	(26)	(27)	(28)	(29)	(30j)
17	18	19	20	21	22	23
(1)	(2)	(3)	(4)	(5)	(6)	(7)
24	25	26	27	28	29	30
(8)	(9)	(10)	(11)	(12)	(13)	(14)
31						
(15)						

August
(Ab 5)

S	M	T	W	T	F	S
1	2	3	4	5	6	7
(12)	(13)	(14)	(15)	(16)	(17)	(18)
8	9	10	11	12	13	14
(19)	(20)	(21)	(22)	(23)	(24)	(25)
15	16	17	18	19	20	21
(26)	(27)	(28)	(29h)	(1)	(2)	(3)
22	23	24	25	26	27	28
(4)	(5)	(6)	(7)	(8)	(9)	(10)
29	30	31				
(11)	(12)	(13)				

November
(Marheshvan 8)

S	M	T	W	T	F	S
	1	2	3	4	5	6
	(16)	(17)	(18)	(19)	(20)	(21)
7	8	9	10	11	12	13
(22)	(23)	(24)	(25)	(26)	(27)	(28)
14	15	16	17	18	19	20
(29)	(30k)	(1)	(2)	(3)	(4)	(5)
21	22	23	24	25	26	27
(6)	(7)	(8)	(9)	(10)	(11)	(12)
28	29	30				
(13)	(14)	(15)				

September
(Elul 6)

S	M	T	W	T	F	S
			1	2	3	4
			(14)	(15)	(16)	(17)
5	6	7	8	9	10	11
(18)	(19)	(20)	(21)	(22)	(23)	(24)
12	13	14	15	16	17	18
(25)	(26)	(27)	(28)	(29i)	(1)	(2)
19	20	21	22	23	24	25
(3)	(4)	(5)	(6)	(7)	(8)	(9)
26	27	28	29	30		
(10)	(11)	(12)	(13)	(14)		

December
(Kislev 9)

S	M	T	W	T	F	S
			1	2	3	4
			(16)	(17)	(18)	(19)
5	6	7	8	9	10	11
(20)	(21)	(22)	(23)	(24)	(25)	(26)
12	13	14	15	16	17	18
(27)	(28)	(29m)	(1)	(2)	(3)	(4)
19	20	21	22	23	24	25
(5)	(6)	(7)	(8)	(9)	(10)	(11)
26	27	28	29	30	31	
(12)	(13)	(14)	(15)	(16)	(17)	

Passover Lamb Sacrificed — Nisan 14
Feast of First Fruits — 1st Sunday after Nisan 15

Feast of Unleavened Bread — Nisan 15-21
Pentecost — 8th Sunday after Nisan 15

Time of the New Moon — g4:08   h12:25   i22:27   j10:54   k2:12   m20:09

A.D. 28

January
(Tebeth 10)

S	M	T	W	T	F	S
						1
						(18)
2	3	4	5	6	7	8
(19)	(20)	(21)	(22)	(23)	(24)	(25)
9	10	11	12	13	14	15
(26)	(27)	(28)	(29)	(30a)	(1)	(2)
16	17	18	19	20	21	22
(3)	(4)	(5)	(6)	(7)	(8)	(9)
23	24	25	26	27	28	29
(10)	(11)	(12)	(13)	(14)	(15)	(16)
30	31					
(17)	(18)					

April
(Nisan 1)

S	M	T	W	T	F	S
						1
						(19)
2	3	4	5	6	7	8
(20)	(21)	(22)	(23)	(24)	(25)	(26)
9	10	11	12	13	14	15
(27)	(28)	(29d)	(1)	(2)	(3)	(4)
16	17	18	19	20	21	22
(5)	(6)	(7)	(8)	(9)	(10)	(11)
23	24	25	26	27	28	29
(12)	(13)	(14)	(15)	(16)	(17)	(18)
30						
(19)						

February
(Shebat 11)

S	M	T	W	T	F	S
		1	2	3	4	5
		(19)	(20)	(21)	(22)	(23)
6	7	8	9	10	11	12
(24)	(25)	(26)	(27)	(28)	(29)	(30b)
13	14	15	16	17	18	19
(1)	(2)	(3)	(4)	(5)	(6)	(7)
20	21	22	23	24	25	26
(8)	(9)	(10)	(11)	(12)	(13)	(14)
27	28	29				
(15)	(16)	(17)				

May
(Iyyar 2)

S	M	T	W	T	F	S
	1	2	3	4	5	6
	(20)	(21)	(22)	(23)	(24)	(25)
7	8	9	10	11	12	13
(26)	(27)	(28)	(29)	(30e)	(1)	(2)
14	15	16	17	18	19	20
(3)	(4)	(5)	(6)	(7)	(8)	(9)
21	22	23	24	25	26	27
(10)	(11)	(12)	(13)	(14)	(15)	(16)
28	29	30	31			
(17)	(18)	(19)	(20)			

March
(Adar 12)

S	M	T	W	T	F	S
			1	2	3	4
			(18)	(19)	(20)	(21)
5	6	7	8	9	10	11
(22)	(23)	(24)	(25)	(26)	(27)	(28)
12	13	14	15	16	17	18
(29)	(30c)	(1)	(2)	(3)	(4)	(5)
19	20	21	22	23	24	25
(6)	(7)	(8)	(9)	(10)	(11)	(12)
26	27	28	29	30	31	
(13)	(14)	(15)	(16)	(17)	(18)	

June
(Sivan 3)

S	M	T	W	T	F	S
				1	2	3
				(21)	(22)	(23)
4	5	6	7	8	9	10
(24)	(25)	(26)	(27)	(28)	(29f)	(1)
11	12	13	14	15	16	17
(2)	(3)	(4)	(5)	(6)	(7)	(8)
18	19	20	21	22	23	24
(9)	(10)	(11)	(12)	(13)	(14)	(15)
25	26	27	28	29	30	
(16)	(17)	(18)	(19)	(20)	(21)	

Day of Trumpets — Tishri 1
Feast of Booths — Tishri 15-22

Day of Atonement — Tishri 10
Feast of Dedication — 8 days beginning Kislev 25

Time of New Moon (Jerusalem) —   a15:33   b10:23   c2:54   d16:42   e3:49   f13:03

A.D. 28

July
(Tammuz 4)

S	M	T	W	T	F	S
						1
						(22)
2	3	4	5	6	7	8
(23)	(24)	(25)	(26)	(27)	(28)	(29g)
9	10	11	12	13	14	15
(1)	(2)	(3)	(4)	(5)	(6)	(7)
16	17	18	19	20	21	22
(8)	(9)	(10)	(11)	(12)	(13)	(14)
23	24	25	26	27	28	29
(15)	(16)	(17)	(18)	(19)	(20)	(21)
30	31					
(22)	(23)					

October
(Tishri 7)

S	M	T	W	T	F	S
1	2	3	4	5	6	7
(26)	(27)	(28)	(29j)	(1)	(2)	(3)
8	9	10	11	12	13	14
(4)	(5)	(6)	(7)	(8)	(9)	(10)
15	16	17	18	19	20	21
(11)	(12)	(13)	(14)	(15)	(16)	(17)
22	23	24	25	26	27	28
(18)	(19)	(20)	(21)	(22)	(23)	(24)
29	30	31				
(25)	(26)	(27)				

August
(Ab 5)

S	M	T	W	T	F	S
		1	2	3	4	5
		(24)	(25)	(26)	(27)	(28)
6	7	8	9	10	11	12
(29)	(30h)	(1)	(2)	(3)	(4)	(5)
13	14	15	16	17	18	19
(6)	(7)	(8)	(9)	(10)	(11)	(12)
20	21	22	23	24	25	26
(13)	(14)	(15)	(16)	(17)	(18)	(19)
27	28	29	30	31		
(20)	(21)	(22)	(23)	(24)		

November
(Marheshvan 8)

S	M	T	W	T	F	S
			1	2	3	4
			(28)	(29)	(30k)	(1)
5	6	7	8	9	10	11
(2)	(3)	(4)	(5)	(6)	(7)	(8)
12	13	14	15	16	17	18
(9)	(10)	(11)	(12)	(13)	(14)	(15)
19	20	21	22	23	24	25
(16)	(17)	(18)	(19)	(20)	(21)	(22)
26	27	28	29	30		
(23)	(24)	(25)	(26)	(27)		

September
(Elul 6)

S	M	T	W	T	F	S
					1	2
					(25)	(26)
3	4	5	6	7	8	9
(27)	(28)	(29i)	(1)	(2)	(3)	(4)
10	11	12	13	14	15	16
(5)	(6)	(7)	(8)	(9)	(10)	(11)
17	18	19	20	21	22	23
(12)	(13)	(14)	(15)	(16)	(17)	(18)
24	25	26	27	28	29	30
(19)	(20)	(21)	(22)	(23)	(24)	(25)

December
(Kislev 9)

S	M	T	W	T	F	S
					1	2
					(28)	(29)
3	4	5	6	7	8	9
(30m)	(1)	(2)	(3)	(4)	(5)	(6)
10	11	12	13	14	15	16
(7)	(8)	(9)	(10)	(11)	(12)	(13)
17	18	19	20	21	22	23
(14)	(15)	(16)	(17)	(18)	(19)	(20)
24	25	26	27	28	29	30
(21)	(22)	(23)	(24)	(25)	(26)	(27)
31						
(28)						

Passover Lamb Sacrificed — Nisan 14
Feast of First Fruits — 1st Sunday after Nisan 15

Feast of Unleavened Bread — Nisan 15-21
Pentecost — 8th Sunday after Nisan 15

Time of the New Moon —   g21:11   h5:01   i13:14   j22:52   k10:25   m0:23

A.D. 29

January
(Tebeth 10)

S	M	T	W	T	F	S
	1	2	3	4	5	6
	(29a)	(1)	(2)	(3)	(4)	(5)
7	8	9	10	11	12	13
(6)	(7)	(8)	(9)	(10)	(11)	(12)
14	15	16	17	18	19	20
(13)	(14)	(15)	(16)	(17)	(18)	(19)
21	22	23	24	25	26	27
(20)	(21)	(22)	(23)	(24)	(25)	(26)
28	29	30	31			
(27)	(28)	(29)	(30b)			

April
(Nisan 1)

S	M	T	W	T	F	S
1	2	3	4	5	6	7
(1)	(2)	(3)	(4)	(5)	(6)	(7)
8	9	10	11	12	13	14
(8)	(9)	(10)	(11)	(12)	(13)	(14)
15	16	17	18	19	20	21
(15)	(16)	(17)	(18)	(19)	(20)	(21)
22	23	24	25	26	27	28
(22)	(23)	(24)	(25)	(26)	(27)	(28)
29	30					
(29)	(30e)					

February
(Adar 12)

S	M	T	W	T	F	S
				1	2	3
				(1)	(2)	(3)
4	5	6	7	8	9	10
(4)	(5)	(6)	(7)	(8)	(9)	(10)
11	12	13	14	15	16	17
(11)	(12)	(13)	(14)	(15)	(16)	(17)
18	19	20	21	22	23	24
(18)	(19)	(20)	(21)	(22)	(23)	(24)
25	26	27	28			
(25)	(26)	(27)	(28)			

May
(Iyyar 2)

S	M	T	W	T	F	S
		1	2	3	4	5
		(1)	(2)	(3)	(4)	(5)
6	7	8	9	10	11	12
(6)	(7)	(8)	(9)	(10)	(11)	(12)
13	14	15	16	17	18	19
(13)	(14)	(15)	(16)	(17)	(18)	(19)
20	21	22	23	24	25	26
(20)	(21)	(22)	(23)	(24)	(25)	(26)
27	28	29	30	31		
(27)	(28)	(29)	(30f)	(1)		

March
(Adar 12)

S	M	T	W	T	F	S
				1	2	3
				(29)	(30c)	(1)
4	5	6	7	8	9	10
(2)	(3)	(4)	(5)	(6)	(7)	(8)
11	12	13	14	15	16	17
(9)	(10)	(11)	(12)	(13)	(14)	(15)
18	19	20	21	22	23	24
(16)	(17)	(18)	(19)	(20)	(21)	(22)
25	26	27	28	29	30	31
(23)	(24)	(25)	(26)	(27)	(28)	(29d)

June
(Sivan 3)

S	M	T	W	T	F	S
					1	2
					(2)	(3)
3	4	5	6	7	8	9
(4)	(5)	(6)	(7)	(8)	(9)	(10)
10	11	12	13	14	15	16
(11)	(12)	(13)	(14)	(15)	(16)	(17)
17	18	19	20	21	22	23
(18)	(19)	(20)	(21)	(22)	(23)	(24)
24	25	26	27	28	29	30
(25)	(26)	(27)	(28)	(29g)	(1)	(2)

Day of Trumpets — Tishri 1
Feast of Booths — Tishri 15-22

Day of Atonement — Tishri 10
Feast of Dedication — 8 days beginning Kislev 25

Time of New Moon (Jerusalem) — a16:35   b10:04   c3:34   d20:04   e10:55   f23:54   g11:02

A.D. 29

July
(Tammuz 4)

S	M	T	W	T	F	S
1	2	3	4	5	6	7
(3)	(4)	(5)	(6)	(7)	(8)	(9)
8	9	10	11	12	13	14
(10)	(11)	(12)	(13)	(14)	(15)	(16)
15	16	17	18	19	20	21
(17)	(18)	(19)	(20)	(21)	(22)	(23)
22	23	24	25	26	27	28
(24)	(25)	(26)	(27)	(28)	(29h)	(1)
29	30	31				
(2)	(3)	(4)				

October
(Tishri 7)

S	M	T	W	T	F	S
	1	2	3	4	5	6
	(7)	(8)	(9)	(10)	(11)	(12)
7	8	9	10	11	12	13
(13)	(14)	(15)	(16)	(17)	(18)	(19)
14	15	16	17	18	19	20
(20)	(21)	(22)	(23)	(24)	(25)	(26)
21	22	23	24	25	26	27
(27)	(28)	(29)	(30k)	(1)	(2)	(3)
28	29	30	31			
(4)	(5)	(6)	(7)			

August
(Ab 5)

S	M	T	W	T	F	S
			1	2	3	4
			(5)	(6)	(7)	(8)
5	6	7	8	9	10	11
(9)	(10)	(11)	(12)	(13)	(14)	(15)
12	13	14	15	16	17	18
(16)	(17)	(18)	(19)	(20)	(21)	(22)
19	20	21	22	23	24	25
(23)	(24)	(25)	(26)	(27)	(28)	(29)
26	27	28	29	30	31	
(30i)	(1)	(2)	(3)	(4)	(5)	

November
(Marheshvan 8)

S	M	T	W	T	F	S
				1	2	3
				(8)	(9)	(10)
4	5	6	7	8	9	10
(11)	(12)	(13)	(14)	(15)	(16)	(17)
11	12	13	14	15	16	17
(18)	(19)	(20)	(21)	(22)	(23)	(24)
18	19	20	21	22	23	24
(25)	(26)	(27)	(28)	(29m)	(1)	(2)
25	26	27	28	29	30	
(3)	(4)	(5)	(6)	(7)	(8)	

September
(Elul 6)

S	M	T	W	T	F	S
						1
						(6)
2	3	4	5	6	7	8
(7)	(8)	(9)	(10)	(11)	(12)	(13)
9	10	11	12	13	14	15
(14)	(15)	(16)	(17)	(18)	(19)	(20)
16	17	18	19	20	21	22
(21)	(22)	(23)	(24)	(25)	(26)	(27)
23	24	25	26	27	28	29
(28)	(29j)	(1)	(2)	(3)	(4)	(5)
30						
(6)						

December
(Kislev 9)

S	M	T	W	T	F	S
						1
						(9)
2	3	4	5	6	7	8
(10)	(11)	(12)	(13)	(14)	(15)	(16)
9	10	11	12	13	14	15
(17)	(18)	(19)	(20)	(21)	(22)	(23)
16	17	18	19	20	21	22
(24)	(25)	(26)	(27)	(28)	(29)	(30n)
23	24	25	26	27	28	29
(1)	(2)	(3)	(4)	(5)	(6)	(7)
30	31					
(8)	(9)					

Passover Lamb Sacrificed — Nisan 14

Feast of First Fruits — 1st Sunday after Nisan 15

Feast of Unleavened Bread — Nisan 15-21

Pentecost — 8th Sunday after Nisan 15

Time of the New Moon — h20:45   i5:41   j14:43   k0:36   m11:47   n0:21

A.D. 30

January (Tebeth 10)						
S	M	T	W	T	F	S
		1	2	3	4	5
		(10)	(11)	(12)	(13)	(14)
6	7	8	9	10	11	12
(15)	(16)	(17)	(18)	(19)	(20)	(21)
13	14	15	16	17	18	19
(22)	(23)	(24)	(25)	(26)	(27)	(28)
20	21	22	23	24	25	26
(29a)	(1)	(2)	(3)	(4)	(5)	(6)
27	28	29	30	31		
(7)	(8)	(9)	(10)	(11)		

April (Nisan 1)						
S	M	T	W	T	F	S
	1	2	3	4	5	6
	(12)	(13)	(14)	(15)	(16)	(17)
7	8	9	10	11	12	13
(18)	(19)	(20)	(21)	(22)	(23)	(24)
14	15	16	17	18	19	20
(25)	(26)	(27)	(28)	(29)	(30d)	(1)
21	22	23	24	25	26	27
(2)	(3)	(4)	(5)	(6)	(7)	(8)
28	29	30				
(9)	(10)	(11)				

February (Shebat 11)						
S	M	T	W	T	F	S
					1	2
					(12)	(13)
3	4	5	6	7	8	9
(14)	(15)	(16)	(17)	(18)	(19)	(20)
10	11	12	13	14	15	16
(21)	(22)	(23)	(24)	(25)	(26)	(27)
17	18	19	20	21	22	23
(28)	(29)	(30b)	(1)	(2)	(3)	(4)
24	25	26	27	28		
(5)	(6)	(7)	(8)	(9)		

May (Iyyar 2)						
S	M	T	W	T	F	S
			1	2	3	4
			(12)	(13)	(14)	(15)
5	6	7	8	9	10	11
(16)	(17)	(18)	(19)	(20)	(21)	(22)
12	13	14	15	16	17	18
(23)	(24)	(25)	(26)	(27)	(28)	(29)
19	20	21	22	23	24	25
(30e)	(1)	(2)	(3)	(4)	(5)	(6)
26	27	28	29	30	31	
(7)	(8)	(9)	(10)	(11)	(12)	

March (Adar 12)						
S	M	T	W	T	F	S
					1	2
					(10)	(11)
3	4	5	6	7	8	9
(12)	(13)	(14)	(15)	(16)	(17)	(18)
10	11	12	13	14	15	16
(19)	(20)	(21)	(22)	(23)	(24)	(25)
17	18	19	20	21	22	23
(26)	(27)	(28)	(29c)	(1)	(2)	(3)
24	25	26	27	28	29	30
(4)	(5)	(6)	(7)	(8)	(9)	(10)
31						
(11)						

June (Sivan 3)						
S	M	T	W	T	F	S
						1
						(13)
2	3	4	5	6	7	8
(14)	(15)	(16)	(17)	(18)	(19)	(20)
9	10	11	12	13	14	15
(21)	(22)	(23)	(24)	(25)	(26)	(27)
16	17	18	19	20	21	22
(28)	(29f)	(1)	(2)	(3)	(4)	(5)
23	24	25	26	27	28	29
(6)	(7)	(8)	(9)	(10)	(11)	(12)
30						
(13)						

Day of Trumpets — Tishri 1
Feast of Booths — Tishri 15-22

Day of Atonement — Tishri 10
Feast of Dedication — 8 days beginning Kislev 25

Time of New Moon (Jerusalem) —   a14:08   b4:02   c20:20   d12:09   e3:42   f18:13

A.D. 30

July
(Tammuz 4)

S	M	T	W	T	F	S
	1	2	3	4	5	6
	(14)	(15)	(16)	(17)	(18)	(19)
7	8	9	10	11	12	13
(20)	(21)	(22)	(23)	(24)	(25)	(26)
14	15	16	17	18	19	20
(27)	(28)	(29)	(30g)	(1)	(2)	(3)
21	22	23	24	25	26	27
(4)	(5)	(6)	(7)	(8)	(9)	(10)
28	29	30	31			
(11)	(12)	(13)	(14)			

October
(Tishri 7)

S	M	T	W	T	F	S
		1	2	3	4	5
		(17)	(18)	(19)	(20)	(21)
6	7	8	9	10	11	12
(22)	(23)	(24)	(25)	(26)	(27)	(28)
13	14	15	16	17	18	19
(29j)	(1)	(2)	(3)	(4)	(5)	(6)
20	21	22	23	24	25	26
(7)	(8)	(9)	(10)	(11)	(12)	(13)
27	28	29	30	31		
(14)	(15)	(16)	(17)	(18)		

August
(Ab 5)

S	M	T	W	T	F	S
				1	2	3
				(15)	(16)	(17)
4	5	6	7	8	9	10
(18)	(19)	(20)	(21)	(22)	(23)	(24)
11	12	13	14	15	16	17
(25)	(26)	(27)	(28)	(29h)	(1)	(2)
18	19	20	21	22	23	24
(3)	(4)	(5)	(6)	(7)	(8)	(9)
25	26	27	28	29	30	31
(10)	(11)	(12)	(13)	(14)	(15)	(16)

November
(Marheshvan 8)

S	M	T	W	T	F	S
					1	2
					(19)	(20)
3	4	5	6	7	8	9
(21)	(22)	(23)	(24)	(25)	(26)	(27)
10	11	12	13	14	15	16
(28)	(29)	(30k)	(1)	(2)	(3)	(4)
17	18	19	20	21	22	23
(5)	(6)	(7)	(8)	(9)	(10)	(11)
24	25	26	27	28	29	30
(12)	(13)	(14)	(15)	(16)	(17)	(18)

September
(Elul 6)

S	M	T	W	T	F	S
1	2	3	4	5	6	7
(17)	(18)	(19)	(20)	(21)	(22)	(23)
8	9	10	11	12	13	14
(24)	(25)	(26)	(27)	(28)	(29)	(30i)
15	16	17	18	19	20	21
(1)	(2)	(3)	(4)	(5)	(6)	(7)
22	23	24	25	26	27	28
(8)	(9)	(10)	(11)	(12)	(13)	(14)
29	30					
(15)	(16)					

December
(Kislev 9)

S	M	T	W	T	F	S
1	2	3	4	5	6	7
(19)	(20)	(21)	(22)	(23)	(24)	(25)
8	9	10	11	12	13	14
(26)	(27)	(28)	(29m)	(1)	(2)	(3)
15	16	17	18	19	20	21
(4)	(5)	(6)	(7)	(8)	(9)	(10)
22	23	24	25	26	27	28
(11)	(12)	(13)	(14)	(15)	(16)	(17)
29	30	31				
(18)	(19)	(20)				

Passover Lamb Sacrificed — Nisan 14
Feast of First Fruits — 1st Sunday after Nisan 15

Feast of Unleavened Bread — Nisan 15-21
Pentecost — 8th Sunday after Nisan 15

Time of the New Moon —   g7:16   h18:57   i5:49   j16:37   k3:13   m14:10

A.D. 31

January
(Tebeth 10)

S	M	T	W	T	F	S
			1	2	3	4
			(21)	(22)	(23)	(24)
5	6	7	8	9	10	11
(25)	(26)	(27)	(28)	(29)	(30a)	(1)
12	13	14	15	16	17	18
(2)	(3)	(4)	(5)	(6)	(7)	(8)
19	20	21	22	23	24	25
(9)	(10)	(11)	(12)	(13)	(14)	(15)
26	27	28	29	30	31	
(16)	(17)	(18)	(19)	(20)	(21)	

February
(Shebat 11)

S	M	T	W	T	F	S
						1
						(22)
2	3	4	5	6	7	8
(23)	(24)	(25)	(26)	(27)	(28)	(29b)
9	10	11	12	13	14	15
(1)	(2)	(3)	(4)	(5)	(6)	(7)
16	17	18	19	20	21	22
(8)	(9)	(10)	(11)	(12)	(13)	(14)
23	24	25	26	27	28	
(15)	(16)	(17)	(18)	(19)	(20)	

March
(Adar 12)

S	M	T	W	T	F	S
						1
						(21)
2	3	4	5	6	7	8
(22)	(23)	(24)	(25)	(26)	(27)	(28)
9	10	11	12	13	14	15
(29)	(30c)	(1)	(2)	(3)	(4)	(5)
16	17	18	19	20	21	22
(6)	(7)	(8)	(9)	(10)	(11)	(12)
23	24	25	26	27	28	29
(13)	(14)	(15)	(16)	(17)	(18)	(19)
30	31					
(20)	(21)					

April
(Nisan 1)

S	M	T	W	T	F	S
		1	2	3	4	5
		(22)	(23)	(24)	(25)	(26)
6	7	8	9	10	11	12
(27)	(28)	(29d)	(1)	(2)	(3)	(4)
13	14	15	16	17	18	19
(5)	(6)	(7)	(8)	(9)	(10)	(11)
20	21	22	23	24	25	26
(12)	(13)	(14)	(15)	(16)	(17)	(18)
27	28	29	30			
(19)	(20)	(21)	(22)			

May
(Iyyar 2)

S	M	T	W	T	F	S
				1	2	3
				(23)	(24)	(25)
4	5	6	7	8	9	10
(26)	(27)	(28)	(29)	(30e)	(1)	(2)
11	12	13	14	15	16	17
(3)	(4)	(5)	(6)	(7)	(8)	(9)
18	19	20	21	22	23	24
(10)	(11)	(12)	(13)	(14)	(15)	(16)
25	26	27	28	29	30	31
(17)	(18)	(19)	(20)	(21)	(22)	(23)

June
(Sivan 3)

S	M	T	W	T	F	S
1	2	3	4	5	6	7
(24)	(25)	(26)	(27)	(28)	(29f)	(1)
8	9	10	11	12	13	14
(2)	(3)	(4)	(5)	(6)	(7)	(8)
15	16	17	18	19	20	21
(9)	(10)	(11)	(12)	(13)	(14)	(15)
22	23	24	25	26	27	28
(16)	(17)	(18)	(19)	(20)	(21)	(22)
29	30					
(23)	(24)					

Day of Trumpets — Tishri 1
Feast of Booths — Tishri 15-22

Day of Atonement — Tishri 10
Feast of Dedication — 8 days beginning Kislev 25

Time of New Moon (Jerusalem) — a1:15 b12:40 c0:50 d14:06 e4:29 f19:35

A.D. 31

July						
(Tammuz 4)						
S	M	T	W	T	F	S
		1	2	3	4	5
		(25)	(26)	(27)	(28)	(29)
6	7	8	9	10	11	12
(30g)	(1)	(2)	(3)	(4)	(5)	(6)
13	14	15	16	17	18	19
(7)	(8)	(9)	(10)	(11)	(12)	(13)
20	21	22	23	24	25	26
(14)	(15)	(16)	(17)	(18)	(19)	(20)
27	28	29	30	31		
(21)	(22)	(23)	(24)	(25)		

October						
(Tishri 7)						
S	M	T	W	T	F	S
			1	2	3	4
			(28)	(29)	(30j)	(1)
5	6	7	8	9	10	11
(2)	(3)	(4)	(5)	(6)	(7)	(88)
12	13	14	15	16	17	18
(9)	(10)	(11)	(12)	(13)	(14)	(15)
19	20	21	22	23	24	25
(16)	(17)	(18)	(19)	(20)	(21)	(22)
26	27	28	29	30	31	
(23)	(24)	(25)	(26)	(27)	(28)	

August						
(Ab 5)						
S	M	T	W	T	F	S
					1	2
					(26)	(27)
3	4	5	6	7	8	9
(28)	(29)	(30h)	(1)	(2)	(3)	(4)
10	11	12	13	14	15	16
(5)	(6)	(7)	(8)	(9)	(10)	(11)
17	18	19	20	21	22	23
(12)	(13)	(14)	(15)	(16)	(17)	(18)
24	25	26	27	28	29	30
(19)	(20)	(21)	(22)	(23)	(24)	(25)
31						
(26)						

November						
(Marheshvan 8)						
S	M	T	W	T	F	S
						1
						(29k)
2	3	4	5	6	7	8
(1)	(2)	(3)	(4)	(5)	(6)	(7)
9	10	11	12	13	14	15
(8)	(9)	(10)	(11)	(12)	(13)	(14)
16	17	18	19	20	21	22
(15)	(16)	(17)	(18)	(19)	(20)	(21)
23	24	25	26	27	28	29
(22)	(23)	(24)	(25)	(26)	(27)	(28)
30						
(29)						

September						
(Elul 6)						
S	M	T	W	T	F	S
	1	2	3	4	5	6
	(27)	(28)	(29i)	(1)	(2)	(3)
7	8	9	10	11	12	13
(4)	(5)	(6)	(7)	(8)	(9)	(10)
14	15	16	17	18	19	20
(11)	(12)	(13)	(14)	(15)	(16)	(17)
21	22	23	24	25	25	27
(18)	(19)	(20)	(21)	(22)	(23)	(24)
28	29	30				
(25)	(26)	(27)				

December						
(Kislev 9)						
S	M	T	W	T	F	S
	1	2	3	4	5	6
	(30m)	(1)	(2)	(3)	(4)	(5)
7	8	9	10	11	12	13
(6)	(7)	(8)	(9)	(10)	(11)	(12)
14	15	16	17	18	19	20
(13)	(14)	(15)	(16)	(17)	(18)	(19)
21	22	23	24	25	26	27
(20)	(21)	(22)	(23)	(24)	(25)	(26)
28	29	30	31			
(27)	(28)	(29n)	(1)			

Passover Lamb Sacrificed — Nisan 14
Feast of First Fruits — 1st Sunday after Nisan 15

Feast of Unleavened Bread — Nisan 15-21
Pentecost — 8th Sunday after Nisan 15

Time of the New Moon —   g10:46   h1:34   i15:47   j5:21   k18:06   m5:51   n16:35

A.D. 32

January
(Shebat 11)

S	M	T	W	T	F	S
				1	2	3
				(2)	(3)	(4)
4	5	6	7	8	9	10
(5)	(6)	(7)	(8)	(9)	(10)	(11)
11	12	13	14	15	16	17
(12)	(13)	(14)	(15)	(16)	(17)	(18)
18	19	20	21	22	23	24
(19)	(20)	(21)	(22)	(23)	(24)	(25)
25	26	27	28	29	30	31
(26)	(27)	(28)	(29)	(30a)	(1)	(2)

April
(Nisan 1)

S	M	T	W	T	F	S
				1	2	3
				(5)	(6)	(7)
4	5	6	7	8	9	10
(8)	(9)	(10)	(11)	(12)	(13)	(14)
11	12	13	14	15	16	17
(15)	(16)	(17)	(18)	(19)	(20)	(21)
18	19	20	21	22	23	24
(22)	(23)	(24)	(25)	(26)	(27)	(28)
25	26	27	28	29	30	
(29)	(30d)	(1)	(2)	(3)	(4)	

February
(Adar 12)

S	M	T	W	T	F	S
1	2	3	4	5	6	7
(3)	(4)	(5)	(6)	(7)	(8)	(9)
8	9	10	11	12	13	14
(10)	(11)	(12)	(13)	(14)	(15)	(16)
15	16	17	18	19	20	21
(17)	(18)	(19)	(20)	(21)	(22)	(23)
22	23	24	25	26	27	28
(24)	(25)	(26)	(27)	(28)	(29b)	(1)
29						
(2)						

May
(Iyyar 2)

S	M	T	W	T	F	S
						1
						(5)
2	3	4	5	6	7	8
(6)	(7)	(8)	(9)	(10)	(11)	(12)
9	10	11	12	13	14	15
(13)	(14)	(15)	(16)	(17)	(18)	(19)
16	17	18	19	20	21	22
(20)	(21)	(22)	(23)	(24)	(25)	(26)
23	24	25	26	27	28	29
(27)	(28)	(29e)	(1)	(2)	(3)	(4)
30	31					
(5)	(6)					

March
(Adar II 13)

S	M	T	W	T	F	S
	1	2	3	4	5	6
	(3)	(4)	(5)	(6)	(7)	(8)
7	8	9	10	11	12	13
(9)	(10)	(11)	(12)	(13)	(14)	(15)
14	15	16	17	18	19	20
(16)	(17)	(18)	(19)	(20)	(21)	(22)
21	22	23	24	25	26	27
(23)	(24)	(25)	(26)	(27)	(28)	(29c)
28	29	30	31			
(1)	(2)	(3)	(4)			

June
(Sivan 3)

S	M	T	W	T	F	S
		1	2	3	4	5
		(7)	(8)	(9)	(10)	(11)
6	7	8	9	10	11	12
(12)	(13)	(14)	(15)	(16)	(17)	(18)
13	14	15	16	17	18	19
(19)	(20)	(21)	(22)	(23)	(24)	(25)
20	21	22	23	24	25	26
(26)	(27)	(28)	(29)	(30f)	(1)	(2)
27	28	29	30			
(3)	(4)	(5)	(6)			

Day of Trumpets — Tishri 1
Feast of Booths — Tishri 15-22

Day of Atonement — Tishri 10
Feast of Dedication — 8 days beginning Kislev 25

Time of New Moon (Jerusalem) — a2:35 b12:21 c33:29 d9:30 e21:45 f11:23

July
(Tammuz 4)

S	M	T	W	T	F	S
				1	2	3
				(7)	(8)	(9)
4	5	6	7	8	9	10
(10)	(11)	(12)	(13)	(14)	(15)	(16)
11	12	13	14	15	16	17
(17)	(18)	(19)	(20)	(21)	(22)	(23)
18	19	20	21	22	23	24
(24)	(25)	(26)	(27)	(28)	(29)	(30g)
25	26	27	28	29	30	31
(1)	(2)	(3)	(4)	(5)	(6)	(7)

August
(Ab 5)

S	M	T	W	T	F	S
1	2	3	4	5	6	7
(8)	(9)	(10)	(11)	(12)	(13)	(14)
8	9	10	11	12	13	14
(15)	(16)	(17)	(18)	(19)	(20)	(21)
15	16	17	18	19	20	21
(22)	(23)	(24)	(25)	(26)	(27)	(28)
22	23	24	25	26	27	28
(29h)	(1)	(2)	(3)	(4)	(5)	(6)
29	30	31				
(7)	(8)	(9)				

September
(Elul 6)

S	M	T	W	T	F	S
			1	2	3	4
			(10)	(11)	(12)	(13)
5	6	7	8	9	10	11
(14)	(15)	(16)	(17)	(18)	(19)	(20)
12	13	14	15	16	17	18
(21)	(22)	(23)	(24)	(25)	(26)	(27)
19	20	21	22	23	24	25
(28)	(29)	(30i)	(1)	(2)	(3)	(4)
26	27	28	29	30		
(5)	(6)	(7)	(8)	(9)		

October
(Tishri 7)

S	M	T	W	T	F	S
					1	2
					(10)	(11)
3	4	5	6	7	8	9
(12)	(13)	(14)	(15)	(16)	(17)	(18)
10	11	12	13	14	15	16
(19)	(20)	(21)	(22)	(23)	(24)	(25)
17	18	19	20	21	22	23
(26)	(27)	(28)	(29)	(30j)	(1)	(2)
24	25	26	27	28	29	30
(3)	(4)	(5)	(6)	(7)	(8)	(9)
31						
(10)						

November
(Marheshvan 8)

S	M	T	W	T	F	S
	1	2	3	4	5	6
	(11)	(12)	(13)	(14)	(15)	(16)
7	8	9	10	11	12	13
(17)	(18)	(19)	(20)	(21)	(22)	(23)
14	15	16	17	18	19	20
(24)	(25)	(26)	(27)	(28)	(29k)	(1)
21	22	23	24	25	26	27
(2)	(3)	(4)	(5)	(6)	(7)	(8)
28	29	30				
(9)	(10)	(11)				

December
(Kislev 9)

S	M	T	W	T	F	S
			1	2	3	4
			(12)	(13)	(14)	(15)
5	6	7	8	9	10	11
(16)	(17)	(18)	(19)	(20)	(21)	(22)
12	13	14	15	16	17	18
(23)	(24)	(25)	(26)	(27)	(28)	(29)
19	20	21	22	23	24	25
(30m)	(1)	(2)	(3)	(4)	(5)	(6)
26	27	28	29	30	31	
(7)	(8)	(9)	(10)	(11)	(12)	

Passover Lamb Sacrificed — Nisan 14
Feast of First Fruits — 1st Sunday after Nisan 15

Feast of Unleavened Bread — Nisan 15-21
Pentecost — 8th Sunday after Nisan 15

Time of the New Moon — g2:28 h18:47 i11:37 j3:56 k18:44 m7:33

A.D. 33

January
(Tebeth 10)

S	M	T	W	T	F	S
						1
						(13)
2	3	4	5	6	7	8
(14)	(15)	(16)	(17)	(18)	(19)	(20)
9	10	11	12	13	14	15
(21)	(22)	(23)	(24)	(25)	(26)	(27)
16	17	18	19	20	21	22
(28)	(29a)	(1)	(2)	(3)	(4)	(5)
23	24	25	26	27	28	29
(6)	(7)	(8)	(9)	(10)	(11)	(12)
30	31					
(13)	(14)					

April
(Nisan 1)

S	M	T	W	T	F	S
					1	2
					(15)	(16)
3	4	5	6	7	8	9
(17)	(18)	(19)	(20)	(21)	(22)	(23)
10	11	12	13	14	15	16
(24)	(25)	(26)	(27)	(28)	(29d)	(1)
17	18	19	20	21	22	23
(2)	(3)	(4)	(5)	(6)	(7)	(8)
24	25	26	27	28	29	30
(9)	(10)	(11)	(12)	(13)	(14)	(15)

February
(Shebat 11)

S	M	T	W	T	F	S
		1	2	3	4	5
		(15)	(16)	(17)	(18)	(19)
6	7	8	9	10	11	12
(20)	(21)	(22)	(23)	(24)	(25)	(26)
13	14	15	16	17	18	19
(27)	(28)	(29)	(30b)	(1)	(2)	(3)
20	21	22	23	24	25	26
(4)	(5)	(6)	(7)	(8)	(9)	(10)
27	28					
(11)	(12)					

May
(Iyyar 2)

S	M	T	W	T	F	S
1	2	3	4	5	6	7
(16)	(17)	(18)	(19)	(20)	(21)	(22)
8	9	10	11	12	13	14
(23)	(24)	(25)	(26)	(27)	(28)	(29)
15	16	17	18	19	20	21
(30e)	(1)	(2)	(3)	(4)	(5)	(6)
22	23	24	25	26	27	28
(7)	(8)	(9)	(10)	(11)	(12)	(13)
29	30	31				
(14)	(15)	(16)				

March
(Adar 12)

S	M	T	W	T	F	S
		1	2	3	4	5
		(13)	(14)	(15)	(16)	(17)
6	7	8	9	10	11	12
(18)	(19)	(20)	(21)	(22)	(23)	(24)
13	14	15	16	17	18	19
(25)	(26)	(27)	(28)	(29c)	(1)	(2)
20	21	22	23	24	25	26
(3)	(4)	(5)	(6)	(7)	(8)	(9)
27	28	29	30	31		
(10)	(11)	(12)	(13)	(14)		

June
(Sivan 3)

S	M	T	W	T	F	S
			1	2	3	4
			(17)	(18)	(19)	(20)
5	6	7	8	9	10	11
(21)	(22)	(23)	(24)	(25)	(26)	(27)
12	13	14	15	16	17	18
(28)	(29f)	(1)	(2)	(3)	(4)	(5)
19	20	21	22	23	24	25
(6)	(7)	(8)	(9)	(10)	(11)	(12)
26	27	28	29	30		
(13)	(14)	(15)	(16)	(17)		

Day of Trumpets — Tishri 1
Feast of Booths — Tishri 15-22

Day of Atonement — Tishri 10
Feast of Dedication — 8 days beginning Kislev 25

Time of New Moon (Jerusalem) —   a18:33   b4:13   c13:02   d21:33   e6:24   f16:23

A.D. 33

July
(Tammuz 4)

S	M	T	W	T	F	S
					1	2
					(18)	(19)
3	4	5	6	7	8	9
(20)	(21)	(22)	(23)	(24)	(25)	(26)
10	11	12	13	14	15	16
(27)	(28)	(29)	(30g)	(1)	(2)	(3)
17	18	19	20	21	22	23
(4)	(5)	(6)	(7)	(8)	(9)	(10)
24	25	26	27	28	29	30
(11)	(12)	(13)	(14)	(15)	(16)	(17)
31						
(18)						

October
(Tishri 7)

S	M	T	W	T	F	S
						1
						(21)
2	3	4	5	6	7	8
(22	(23)	(24)	(25)	(26)	(27)	(28)
9	10	11	12	13	14	15
(29)	(30j)	(1)	(2)	(3)	(4)	(5)
16	17	18	19	20	21	22
(6)	(7)	(8)	(9)	(10)	(11)	(12)
23	24	25	26	27	28	29
(13)	(14)	(15)	(16)	(17)	(18)	(19)
30	31					
(20)	(21)					

August
(Ab 5)

S	M	T	W	T	F	S
	1	2	3	4	5	6
	(19)	(20)	(21)	(22)	(23)	(24)
7	8	9	10	11	12	13
(25)	(26)	(27)	(28)	(29h)	(1)	(2)
14	15	16	17	18	19	20
(3)	(4)	(5)	(6)	(7)	(8)	(9)
21	22	23	24	25	26	27
(10)	(11)	(12)	(13)	(14)	(15)	(16)
28	29	30	31			
(17)	(18)	(19)	(20)			

November
(Marheshvan 8)

S	M	T	W	T	F	S
		1	2	3	4	5
		(22)	(23)	(24)	(25)	(26)
6	7	8	9	10	11	12
(27)	(28)	(29)	(30k)	(1)	(2)	(3)
13	14	15	16	17	18	19
(4)	(5)	(6)	(7)	(8)	(9)	(10)
20	21	22	23	24	25	26
(11)	(12)	(13)	(14)	(15)	(16)	(17)
27	28	29	30			
(18)	(19)	(20)	(21)			

September
(Elul 6)

S	M	T	W	T	F	S
				1	2	3
				(21)	(22)	(23)
4	5	6	7	8	9	10
(24)	(25)	(26)	(27)	(28)	(29)	(30i)
11	12	13	14	15	16	17
(1)	(2)	(3)	(4)	(5)	(6)	(7)
18	19	20	21	22	23	24
(8)	(9)	(10)	(11)	(12)	(13)	(14)
25	26	27	28	29	30	
(15)	(16)	(17)	(18)	(19)	(20)	

December
(Kislev 9)

S	M	T	W	T	F	S
				1	2	3
				(22)	(23)	(24)
4	5	6	7	8	9	10
(25)	(26)	(27)	(28)	(29m)	(1)	(2)
11	12	13	14	15	16	17
(3)	(4)	(5)	(6)	(7)	(8)	(9)
18	19	20	21	22	23	24
(10)	(11)	(12)	(13)	(14)	(15)	(16)
25	26	27	28	29	30	31
(17)	(18)	(19)	(20)	(21)	(22)	(23)

Day of Trumpets — Tishri 1
Feast of Booths — Tishri 15-22

Day of Atonement — Tishri 10
Feast of Dedication — 8 days beginning Kislev 25

Time of the New Moon —   g4:22   h18:58   i12:05   j6:40   k1:00   m17:38

A.D. 34

January
(Tebeth 10)

S	M	T	W	T	F	S
1	2	3	4	5	6	7
(24)	(25)	(26)	(27)	(28)	(29)	(30a)
8	9	10	11	12	13	14
(1)	(2)	(3)	(4)	(5)	(6)	(7)
15	16	17	18	19	20	21
(8)	(9)	(10)	(11)	(12)	(13)	(14)
22	23	24	25	26	27	28
(15)	(16)	(17)	(18)	(19)	(20)	(21)
29	30	31				
(22)	(23)	(24)				

April
(Nisan 1)

S	M	T	W	T	F	S
						1
						(25)
2	3	4	5	6	7	8
(26)	(27)	(28)	(29d)	(1)	(2)	(3)
9	10	11	12	13	14	15
(4)	(5)	(6)	(7)	(8)	(9)	(10)
16	17	18	19	20	21	22
(11)	(12)	(13)	(14)	(15)	(16)	(17)
23	24	25	26	27	28	29
(18)	(19)	(20)	(21)	(22)	(23)	(24)
30						
(25)						

February
(Shebat 11)

S	M	T	W	T	F	S
			1	2	3	4
			(25)	(26)	(27)	(28)
5	6	7	8	9	10	11
(29b)	(1)	(2)	(3)	(4)	(5)	(6)
12	13	14	15	16	17	18
(7)	(8)	(9)	(10)	(11)	(12)	(13)
19	20	21	22	23	24	25
(14)	(15)	(16)	(17)	(18)	(19)	(20)
26	27	28				
(21)	(22)	(23)				

May
(Iyyar 2)

S	M	T	W	T	F	S
	1	2	3	4	5	6
	(26)	(27)	(28)	(29e)	(1)	(2)
7	8	9	10	11	12	13
(3)	(4)	(5)	(6)	(7)	(8)	(9)
14	15	16	17	18	19	20
(10)	(11)	(12)	(13)	(14)	(15)	(16)
21	22	23	24	25	26	27
(17)	(18)	(19)	(20)	(21)	(22)	(23)
28	29	30	31			
(24)	(25)	(26)	(27)			

March
(Adar 12)

S	M	T	W	T	F	S
			1	2	3	4
			(24)	(25)	(26)	(27)
5	6	7	8	9	10	11
(28)	(29)	(30c)	(1)	(2)	(3)	(4)
12	13	14	15	16	17	18
(5)	(6)	(7)	(8)	(9)	(10)	(11)
19	20	21	22	23	24	25
(12)	(13)	(14)	(15)	(16)	(17)	(18)
26	27	28	29	30	31	
(19)	(20)	(21)	(22)	(23)	(24)	

June
(Sivan 3)

S	M	T	W	T	F	S
				1	2	3
				(28)	(29)	(30f)
4	5	6	7	8	9	10
(1)	(2)	(3)	(4)	(5)	(6)	(7)
11	12	13	14	15	16	17
(8)	(9)	(10)	(11)	(12)	(13)	(14)
18	19	20	21	22	23	24
(15)	(16)	(17)	(18)	(19)	(20)	(21)
25	26	27	28	29	30	
(22)	(23)	(24)	(25)	(26)	(27)	

Passover Lamb Sacrificed — Nisan 14
Feast of First Fruits — 1st Sunday after Nisan 15

Feast of Unleavened Bread — Nisan 15-21
Pentecost — 8th Sunday after Nisan 15

Time of New Moon (Jerusalem) — a7:56 b19:53 c5:46 d14:01 e21:17 f4:38

A.D. 34

July
(Tammuz 4)

S	M	T	W	T	F	S
						1
						(28)
2	3	4	5	6	7	8
(29g)	(1)	(2)	(3)	(4)	(5)	(6)
9	10	11	12	13	14	15
(7)	(8)	(9)	(10)	(11)	(12)	(13)
16	17	18	19	20	21	22
(14)	(15)	(16)	(17)	(18)	(19)	(20)
23	24	25	26	27	28	29
(21)	(22)	(23)	(24)	(25)	(26)	(27)
30	31					
(28)	(29)					

August
(Ab 5)

S	M	T	W	T	F	S
		1	2	3	4	5
		(30h)	(1)	(2)	(3)	(4)
6	7	8	9	10	11	12
(5)	(6)	(7)	(8)	(9)	(10)	(11)
13	14	15	16	17	18	19
(12)	(13)	(14)	(15)	(16)	(17)	(18)
20	21	22	23	24	25	26
(19)	(20)	(21)	(22)	(23)	(24)	(25)
27	28	29	30	31		
(26)	(27)	(28)	(29i)	(1)		

September
(Tishri 7)

S	M	T	W	T	F	S
					1	2
					(2)	(3)
3	4	5	6	7	8	9
(4)	(5)	(6)	(7)	(8)	(9)	(10)
10	11	12	13	14	15	16
(11)	(12)	(13)	(14)	(15)	(16)	(17)
17	18	19	20	21	22	23
(18)	(19)	(20)	(21)	(22)	(23)	(24)
24	25	26	27	28	29	30
(25)	(26)	(27)	(28)	(29)	(30j)	(1)

October
(Marheshvan 8)

S	M	T	W	T	F	S
1	2	3	4	5	6	7
(2)	(3)	(4)	(5)	(6)	(7)	(8)
8	9	10	11	12	13	14
(9)	(10)	(11)	(12)	(13)	(14)	(15)
15	16	17	18	19	20	21
(16)	(17)	(18)	(19)	(20)	(21)	(22)
22	23	24	25	26	27	28
(23)	(24)	(25)	(26)	(27)	(28)	(29)
29	30	31				
(30k)	(1)	(2)				

November
(Kislev 9)

S	M	T	W	T	F	S
			1	2	3	4
			(3)	(4)	(5)	(6)
5	6	7	8	9	10	11
(7)	(8)	(9)	(10)	(11)	(12)	(13)
12	13	14	15	16	17	18
(14)	(15)	(16)	(17)	(18)	(19)	(20)
19	20	21	22	23	24	25
(21)	(22)	(23)	(24)	(25)	(26)	(27)
26	27	28	29	30		
(28)	(29m)	(1)	(2)	(3)		

December
(Tebeth 10)

S	M	T	W	T	F	S
					1	2
					(4)	(5)
3	4	5	6	7	8	9
(6)	(7)	(8)	(9)	(10)	(11)	(12)
10	11	12	13	14	15	16
(13)	(14)	(15)	(16)	(17)	(18)	(19)
17	18	19	20	21	22	23
(20)	(21)	(22)	(23)	(24)	(25)	(26)
24	25	26	27	28	29	30
(27)	(28)	(29)	(30n)	(1)	(2)	(3)
31						
(4)						

Day of Trumpets — Tishri 1
Feast of Booths — Tishri 15-22

Day of Atonement — Tishri 10
Feast of Dedication — 8 days beginning Kislev 25

Time of the New Moon — g12:57 h23:40 i13:26 j6:12 k1:02 m20:24 n14:44

A.D. 35

January
(Shebat 11)

S	M	T	W	T	F	S
	1	2	3	4	5	6
	(5)	(6)	(7)	(8)	(9)	(10)
7	8	9	10	11	12	13
(11)	(12)	(13)	(14)	(15)	(16)	(17)
14	15	16	17	18	19	20
(18)	(19)	(20)	(21)	(22)	(23)	(24)
21	22	23	24	25	26	27
(25)	(26)	(27)	(28)	(29)	(30a)	(1)
28	29	30	31			
(2)	(3)	(4)	(5)			

April
(Nisan 1)

S	M	T	W	T	F	S
1	2	3	4	5	6	7
(6)	(7)	(8)	(9)	(10)	(11)	(12)
8	9	10	11	12	13	14
(13)	(14)	(15)	(16)	(17)	(18)	(19)
15	16	17	18	19	20	21
(20)	(21)	(22)	(23)	(24)	(25)	(26)
22	23	24	25	26	27	28
(27)	(28)	(29d)	(1)	(2)	(3)	(4)
29	30					
(5)	(6)					

February
(Adar 12)

S	M	T	W	T	F	S
				1	2	3
				(6)	(7)	(8)
4	5	6	7	8	9	10
(9)	(10)	(11)	(12)	(13)	(14)	(15)
11	12	13	14	15	16	17
(16)	(17)	(18)	(19)	(20)	(21)	(22)
18	19	20	21	22	23	24
(23)	(24)	(25)	(26)	(27)	(28)	(29b)
25	26	27	28			
(1)	(2)	(3)	(4)			

May
(Iyyar 2)

S	M	T	W	T	F	S
		1	2	3	4	5
		(7)	(8)	(9)	(10)	(11)
6	7	8	9	10	11	12
(12)	(13)	(14)	(15)	(16)	(17)	(18)
13	14	15	16	17	18	19
(19)	(20)	(21)	(22)	(23)	(24)	(25)
20	21	22	23	24	25	26
(26)	(27)	(28)	(29e)	(1)	(2)	(3)
27	28	29	30	31		
(4)	(5)	(6)	(7)	(8)		

March
(Adar II 13)

S	M	T	W	T	F	S
				1	2	3
				(5)	(6)	(7)
4	5	6	7	8	9	10
(8)	(9)	(10)	(11)	(12)	(13)	(14)
11	12	13	14	15	16	17
(15)	(16)	(17)	(18)	(19)	(20)	(21)
18	19	20	21	22	23	24
(22)	(23)	(24)	(25)	(26)	(27)	(28)
25	26	27	28	29	30	31
(29)	(30c)	(1)	(2)	(3)	(4)	(5)

June
(Sivan 3)

S	M	T	W	T	F	S
					1	2
					(9)	(10)
3	4	5	6	7	8	9
(11)	(12)	(13)	(14)	(15)	(16)	(17)
10	11	12	13	14	15	16
(18)	(19)	(20)	(21)	(22)	(23)	(24)
17	18	19	20	21	22	23
(25)	(26)	(27)	(28)	(29)	(30f)	(1)
24	25	26	27	28	29	30
(2)	(3)	(4)	(5)	(6)	(7)	(8)

Passover Lamb Sacrificed — Nisan 14
Feast of First Fruits — 1st Sunday after Nisan 15

Feast of Unleavened Bread — Nisan 15-21
Pentecost — 8th Sunday after Nisan 15

Time of New Moon (Jerusalem) — a6:50   b20:04   c6:24   d14:27   e21:13   f3:54

July
(Tammuz 4)

S	M	T	W	T	F	S
1	2	3	4	5	6	7
(9)	(10)	(11)	(12)	(13)	(14)	(15)
8	9	10	11	12	13	14
(16)	(17)	(18)	(19)	(20)	(21)	(22)
15	16	17	18	19	20	21
(23)	(24)	(25)	(26)	(27)	(28)	(29g)
22	23	24	25	26	27	28
(1)	(2)	(3)	(4)	(5)	(6)	(7)
29	30	31				
(8)	(9)	(10)				

October
(Tishri 7)

S	M	T	W	T	F	S
	1	2	3	4	5	6
	(13)	(14)	(15)	(16)	(17)	(18)
7	8	9	10	11	12	13
(19)	(20)	(21)	(22)	(23)	(24)	(25)
14	15	16	17	18	19	20
(26)	(27)	(28)	(29)	(30j)	(1)	(2)
21	22	23	24	25	26	27
(3)	(4)	(5)	(6)	(7)	(8)	(9)
28	29	30	31			
(10)	(11)	(12)	(13)			

August
(Ab 5)

S	M	T	W	T	F	S
			1	2	3	4
			(11)	(12)	(13)	(14)
5	6	7	8	9	10	11
(15)	(16)	(17)	(18)	(19)	(20)	(21)
12	13	14	15	16	17	18
(22)	(23)	(24)	(25)	(26)	(27)	(28)
19	20	21	22	23	24	25
(29h)	(1)	(2)	(3)	(4)	(5)	(6)
26	27	28	29	30	31	
(7)	(8)	(9)	(10)	(11)	(12)	

November
(Marheshvan 8)

S	M	T	W	T	F	S
				1	2	3
				(14)	(15)	(16)
4	5	6	7	8	9	10
(17)	(18)	(19)	(20)	(21)	(22)	(23)
11	12	13	14	15	16	17
(24)	(25)	(26)	(27)	(28)	(29k)	(1)
18	19	20	21	22	23	24
(2)	(3)	(4)	(5)	(6)	(7)	(8)
25	26	27	28	29	30	
(9)	(10)	(11)	(12)	(13)	(14)	

September
(Elul 6)

S	M	T	W	T	F	S
						1
						(13)
2	3	4	5	6	7	8
(14)	(15)	(16)	(17)	(18)	(19)	(20)
9	10	11	12	13	14	15
(21)	(22)	(23)	(24)	(25)	(26)	(27)
16	17	18	19	20	21	22
(28)	(29)	(30i)	(1)	(2)	(3)	(4)
23	24	25	26	27	28	29
(5)	(6)	(7)	(8)	(9)	(10)	(11)
30						
(12)						

December
(Kislev 9)

S	M	T	W	T	F	S
						1
						(15)
2	3	4	5	6	7	8
(16)	(17)	(18)	(19)	(20)	(21)	(22)
9	10	11	12	13	14	15
(23)	(24)	(25)	(26)	(27)	(28)	(29)
16	17	18	19	20	21	22
(30m)	(1)	(2)	(3)	(4)	(5)	(6)
23	24	25	26	27	28	29
(7)	(8)	(9)	(10)	(11)	(12)	(13)
30	31					
(14)	(15)					

Day of Trumpets — Tishri 1
Feast of Booths — Tishri 15-22

Day of Atonement — Tishri 10
Feast of Dedication — 8 days beginning Kislev 25

Time of the New Moon — g11:40 h21:31 i10:03 j1:28 k19:26 m14:59

A.D. 36

January
(Tebeth 10)

S	M	T	W	T	F	S
		1	2	3	4	5
		(16)	(17)	(18)	(19)	(20)
6	7	8	9	10	11	12
(21)	(22)	(23)	(24)	(25)	(26)	(27)
13	14	15	16	17	18	19
(28)	(29)	(30a)	(1)	(2)	(3)	(4)
20	21	22	23	24	25	26
(5)	(6)	(7)	(8)	(9)	(10)	(11)
27	28	29	30	31		
(12)	(13)	(14)	(15)	(16)		

April
(Nisan 1)

S	M	T	W	T	F	S
		1	2	3	4	5
		(18)	(19)	(20)	(21)	(22)
6	7	8	9	10	11	12
(23)	(24)	(25)	(26)	(27)	(28)	(29)
13	14	15	16	17	18	19
(30d)	(1)	(2)	(3)	(4)	(5)	(6)
20	21	22	23	24	25	26
(7)	(8)	(9)	(10)	(11)	(12)	(13)
27	28	29	30			
(14)	(15)	(16)	(17)			

February
(Shebat 11)

S	M	T	W	T	F	S
					1	2
					(17)	(18)
3	4	5	6	7	8	9
(19)	(20)	(21)	(22)	(23)	(24)	(25)
10	11	12	13	14	15	16
(26)	(27)	(28)	(29)	(30b)	(1)	(2)
17	18	19	20	21	22	23
(3)	(4)	(5)	(6)	(7)	(8)	(9)
24	25	26	27	28	29	
(10)	(11)	(12)	(13)	(14)	(15)	

May
(Iyyar 2)

S	M	T	W	T	F	S
				1	2	3
				(18)	(19)	(20)
4	5	6	7	8	9	10
(21)	(22)	(23)	(24)	(25)	(26)	(27)
11	12	13	14	15	16	17
(28)	(29e)	(1)	(2)	(3)	(4)	(5)
18	19	20	21	22	23	24
(6)	(7)	(8)	(9)	(10)	(11)	(12)
25	26	27	28	29	30	31
(13)	(14)	(15)	(16)	(17)	(18)	(19)

March
(Adar 12)

S	M	T	W	T	F	S
						1
						(16)
2	3	4	5	6	7	8
(17)	(18)	(19)	(20)	(21)	(22)	(23)
9	10	11	12	13	14	15
(24)	(25)	(26)	(27)	(28)	(29c)	(1)
16	17	18	19	20	21	22
(2)	(3)	(4)	(5)	(6)	(7)	(8)
23	24	25	26	27	28	29
(9)	(10)	(11)	(12)	(13)	(14)	(15)
30	31					
(16)	(17)					

June
(Sivan 3)

S	M	T	W	T	F	S
1	2	3	4	5	6	7
(20)	(21)	(22)	(23)	(24)	(25)	(26)
8	9	10	11	12	13	14
(27)	(28)	(29f)	(1)	(2)	(3)	(4)
15	16	17	18	19	20	21
(5)	(6)	(7)	(8)	(9)	(10)	(11)
22	23	24	25	26	27	28
(12)	(13)	(14)	(15)	(16)	(17)	(18)
29	30					
(19)	(20)					

Passover Lamb Sacrificed — Nisan 14
Feast of First Fruits — 1ˢᵗ Sunday after Nisan 15

Feast of Unleavened Bread — Nisan 15-21
Pentecost — 8ᵗʰ Sunday after Nisan 15

Time of New Moon (Jerusalem) —　a10:26　b3:54　c18:13　d5:17　e13:53　f21:11

A.D. 36

July						
(Tammuz 4)						
S	M	T	W	T	F	S
		1	2	3	4	5
		(21)	(22)	(23)	(24)	(25)
6	7	8	9	10	11	12
(26)	(27)	(28)	(29)	(30g)	(1)	(2)
13	14	15	16	17	18	19
(3)	(4)	(5)	(6)	(7)	(8)	(9)
20	21	22	23	24	25	26
(10)	(11)	(12)	(13)	(14)	(15)	(16)
27	28	29	30	31		
(17)	(18)	(19)	(20)	(21)		

October						
(Tishri 7)						
S	M	T	W	T	F	S
			1	2	3	4
			(25)	(26)	(27)	(28)
5	6	7	8	9	10	11
(29)	(30j)	(1)	(2)	(3)	(4)	(5)
12	13	14	15	16	17	18
(6)	(7)	(8)	(9)	(10)	(11)	(12)
19	20	21	22	23	24	25
(13)	(14)	(15)	(16)	(17)	(18)	(19)
26	27	28	29	30	31	
(20)	(21)	(22)	(23)	(24)	(25)	

August						
(Ab 5)						
S	M	T	W	T	F	S
					1	2
					(22)	(23)
3	4	5	6	7	8	9
(24)	(25)	(26)	(27)	(28)	(29h)	(1)
10	11	12	13	14	15	16
(2)	(3)	(4)	(5)	(6)	(7)	(8)
17	18	19	20	21	22	23
(9)	(10)	(11)	(12)	(13)	(14)	(15)
24	25	26	27	28	29	30
(16)	(17)	(18)	(19)	(20)	(21)	(22)
31						
(23)						

November						
(Marheshvan 8)						
S	M	T	W	T	F	S
						1
						(26)
2	3	4	5	6	7	8
(27)	(28)	(29k)	(1)	(2)	(3)	(4)
9	10	11	12	13	14	15
(5)	(6)	(7)	(8)	(9)	(10)	(11)
16	17	18	19	20	21	22
(12)	(13)	(14)	(15)	(16)	(17)	(18)
23	24	25	26	27	28	29
(19)	(20)	(21)	(22)	(23)	(24)	(25)
30						
(26)						

September						
(Elul 6)						
S	M	T	W	T	F	S
	1	2	3	4	5	6
	(24)	(25)	(26)	(27)	(28)	(29i)
7	8	9	10	11	12	13
(1)	(2)	(3)	(4)	(5)	(6)	(7)
14	15	16	17	18	19	20
(8)	(9)	(10)	(11)	(12)	(13)	(14)
21	22	23	24	25	26	27
(15)	(16)	(17)	(18)	(19)	(20)	(21)
28	29	30				
(22)	(23)	(24)				

December						
(Kislev 9)						
S	M	T	W	T	F	S
	1	2	3	4	5	6
	(27)	(28)	(29)	(30m)	(1)	(2)
7	8	9	10	11	12	13
(3)	(4)	(5)	(6)	(7)	(8)	(9)
14	15	16	17	18	19	20
(10)	(11)	(12)	(13)	(14)	(15)	(16)
21	22	23	24	25	26	27
(17)	(18)	(19)	(20)	(21)	(22)	(23)
28	29	30	31			
(24)	(25)	(26)	(27)			

Day of Trumpets — Tishri 1

Feast of Booths — Tishri 15-22

Day of Atonement — Tishri 10

Feast of Dedication — 8 days beginning Kislev 25

Time of the New Moon —   g4:15   h12:81   i21:14   j8:30   k22:23   m15:02

A.D. 37

January (Tebeth 10)						
S	M	T	W	T	F	S
				1 (28)	2 (29)	3 (30a)
4 (1)	5 (2)	6 (3)	7 (4)	8 (5)	9 (6)	10 (7)
11 (8)	12 (9)	13 (10)	14 (11)	15 (12)	16 (13)	17 (14)
18 (15)	19 (16)	20 (17)	21 (18)	22 (19)	23 (20)	24 (21)
25 (22)	26 (23)	27 (24)	28 (25)	29 (26)	30 (27)	31 (28)

April (Adar II 13)						
S	M	T	W	T	F	S
			1 (29)	2 (30d)	3 (1)	4 (2)
5 (3)	6 (4)	7 (5)	8 (6)	9 (7)	10 (8)	11 (9)
12 (10)	13 (11)	14 (12)	15 (13)	16 (14)	17 (15)	18 (16)
19 (17)	20 (18)	21 (19)	22 (20)	23 (21)	24 (22)	25 (23)
26 (24)	27 (25)	28 (26)	29 (27)	30 (28)		

February (Shebat 11)						
S	M	T	W	T	F	S
1 (29)	2 (30b)	3 (1)	4 (2)	5 (3)	6 (4)	7 (5)
8 (6)	9 (7)	10 (8)	11 (9)	12 (10)	13 (11)	14 (12)
15 (13)	16 (14)	17 (15)	18 (16)	19 (17)	20 (18)	21 (19)
22 (20)	23 (21)	24 (22)	25 (23)	26 (24)	27 (25)	28 (26)

May (Nisan 1)						
S	M	T	W	T	F	S
					1 (29)	2 (30e)
3 (1)	4 (2)	5 (3)	6 (4)	7 (5)	8 (6)	9 (7)
10 (8)	11 (9)	12 (10)	13 (11)	14 (12)	15 (13)	16 (14)
17 (15)	18 (16)	19 (17)	20 (18)	21 (19)	22 (20)	23 (21)
24 (22)	25 (23)	26 (24)	27 (25)	28 (26)	29 (27)	30 (28)
31 (29f)						

March (Adar 12)						
S	M	T	W	T	F	S
1 (27)	2 (28)	3 (29c)	4 (1)	5 (2)	6 (3)	7 (4)
8 (5)	9 (6)	10 (7)	11 (8)	12 (9)	13 (10)	14 (11)
15 (12)	16 (13)	17 (14)	18 (15)	19 (16)	20 (17)	21 (18)
22 (19)	23 (20)	24 (21)	25 (22)	26 (23)	27 (24)	28 (25)
29 (26)	30 (27)	31 (28)				

June (Sivan 3)						
S	M	T	W	T	F	S
	1 (1)	2 (2)	3 (3)	4 (4)	5 (5)	6 (6)
7 (7)	8 (8)	9 (9)	10 (10)	11 (11)	12 (12)	13 (13)
14 (14)	15 (15)	16 (16)	17 (17)	18 (18)	19 (19)	20 (20)
21 (21)	22 (22)	23 (23)	24 (24)	25 (25)	26 (26)	27 (27)
28 (28)	29 (29g)	30 (1)				

Passover Lamb Sacrificed — Nisan 14

Feast of First Fruits — 1st Sunday after Nisan 15

Feast of Unleavened Bread — Nisan 15-21

Pentecost — 8th Sunday after Nisan 15

Time of New Moon (Jerusalem) — a9:48 b4:59 c22:41 d13:48 e2:04 f12:12 g20:54

		July (Tammuz 4)				
S	M	T	W	T	F	S
			1	2	3	4
			(2)	(3)	(4)	(5)
5	6	7	8	9	10	11
(6)	(7)	(8)	(9)	(10)	(11)	(12)
12	13	14	15	16	17	18
(13)	(14)	(15)	(16)	(17)	(18)	(19)
19	20	21	22	23	24	25
(20)	(21)	(22)	(23)	(24)	(25)	(26)
26	27	28	29	30	31	
(27)	(28)	(29)	(30h)	(1)	(2)	

		October (Tishri 7)				
S	M	T	W	T	F	S
				1	2	3
				(6)	(7)	(8)
4	5	6	7	8	9	10
(9)	(10)	(11)	(12)	(13)	(14)	(15)
11	12	13	14	15	16	17
(16)	(17)	(18)	(19)	(20)	(21)	(22)
18	19	20	21	22	23	24
(23)	(24)	(25)	(26)	(27)	(28)	(29)
25	26	27	28	29	30	31
(30k)	(1)	(2)	(3)	(4)	(5)	(6)

		August (Ab 5)				
S	M	T	W	T	F	S
						1
						(3)
2	3	4	5	6	7	8
(4)	(5)	(6)	(7)	(8)	(9)	(10)
9	10	11	12	13	14	15
(11)	(12)	(13)	(14)	(15)	(16)	(17)
16	17	18	19	20	21	22
(18)	(19)	(20)	(21)	(22)	(23)	(23)
23	24	25	26	27	28	29
(25)	(26)	(27)	(28)	(29i)	(1)	(2)
30	31					
(3)	(4)					

		November (Marheshvan 8)				
S	M	T	W	T	F	S
1	2	3	4	5	6	7
(7)	(8)	(9)	(10)	(11)	(12)	(13)
8	9	10	11	12	13	14
(14)	(15)	(16)	(17)	(18)	(19)	(20)
15	16	17	18	19	20	21
(21)	(22)	(23)	(24)	(25)	(26)	(27)
22	23	24	25	26	27	28
(28)	(29m)	(1)	(2)	(3)	(4)	(5)
29	30					
(6)	(7)					

		September (Elul 6)				
S	M	T	W	T	F	S
		1	2	3	4	5
		(5)	(6)	(7)	(8)	(9)
6	7	8	9	10	11	12
(10)	(11)	(12)	(13)	(14)	(15)	(16)
13	14	15	16	17	18	19
(17)	(18)	(19)	(20)	(21)	(22)	(23)
20	21	22	23	24	25	26
(24)	(25)	(26)	(27)	(28)	(29j)	(1)
27	28	29	30			
(2)	(3)	(4)	(5)			

		December (Kislev 9)				
S	M	T	W	T	F	S
		1	2	3	4	5
		(8)	(9)	(10)	(11)	(12)
6	7	8	9	10	11	12
(13)	(14)	(15)	(16)	(17)	(18)	(19)
13	14	15	16	17	18	19
(20)	(21)	(22)	(23)	(24)	(25)	(26)
20	21	22	23	24	25	26
(27)	(28)	(29)	(30n)	(1)	(2)	(3)
27	28	29	30	31		
(4)	(5)	(6)	(7)	(8)		

Day of Trumpets — Tishri 1
Feast of Booths — Tishri 15-22

Day of Atonement — Tishri 10
Feast of Dedication — 8 days beginning Kislev 25

Time of the New Moon —   h4:58   i13:07   j21:07   k8:41   m21:25   n12:47

A.D. 38

January
(Tebeth 10)

S	M	T	W	T	F	S
					1	2
					(9)	(10)
3	4	5	6	7	8	9
(11)	(12)	(13)	(14)	(15)	(16)	(17)
10	11	12	13	14	15	16
(18)	(19)	(20)	(21)	(22)	(23)	(24)
17	18	19	20	21	22	23
(25)	(26)	(27)	(28)	(29)	(30a)	(1)
24	25	26	27	28	29	30
(2)	(3)	(4)	(5)	(6)	(7)	(8)
31						
(9)						

April
(Nisan 1)

S	M	T	W	T	F	S
				1	2	3
				(10)	(11)	(12)
4	5	6	7	8	9	10
(13)	(14)	(15)	(16)	(17)	(18)	(19)
11	12	13	14	15	16	17
(20)	(21)	(22)	(23)	(24)	(25)	(26)
18	19	20	21	22	23	24
(27)	(28)	(29)	(30d)	(1)	(2)	(3)
25	26	27	28	29	30	
(4)	(5)	(6)	(7)	(8)	(9)	

February
(Shebat 11)

S	M	T	W	T	F	S
	1	2	3	4	5	6
	(10)	(11)	(12)	(13)	(14)	(15)
7	8	9	10	11	12	13
(17)	(17)	(18)	(19)	(20)	(21)	(22)
14	15	16	17	18	19	20
(23)	(24)	(25)	(26)	(27)	(28)	(29b)
21	22	23	24	25	26	27
(1)	(2)	(3)	(4)	(5)	(6)	(7)
28						
(8)						

May
(Iyyar 2)

S	M	T	W	T	F	S
						1
						(10)
2	3	4	5	6	7	8
(11)	(12)	(13)	(14)	(15)	(16)	(17)
9	10	11	12	13	14	15
(18)	(19)	(20)	(21)	(22)	(23)	(24)
16	17	18	19	20	21	22
(25)	(26)	(27)	(28)	(29e)	(1)	(2)
23	24	25	26	27	28	29
(3)	(4)	(5)	(6)	(7)	(8)	(9)
30	31					
(10)	(11)					

March
(Adar 12)

S	M	T	W	T	F	S
	1	2	3	4	5	6
	(9)	(10)	(11)	(12)	(13)	(14)
7	8	9	10	11	12	13
(15)	(16)	(17)	(18)	(19)	(20)	(21)
14	15	16	17	18	19	20
(22)	(23)	(24)	(25)	(26)	(27)	(28)
21	22	23	24	25	26	27
(29)	(30c)	(1)	(2)	(3)	(4)	(5)
28	29	30	31			
(6)	(7)	(8)	(9)			

June
(Sivan 3)

S	M	T	W	T	F	S
		1	2	3	4	5
		(12)	(13)	(14)	(15)	(16)
6	7	8	9	10	11	12
(17)	(18)	(19)	(20)	(21)	(22)	(23)
13	14	15	16	17	18	19
(24)	(25)	(26)	(27)	(28)	(29)	(30f)
20	21	22	23	24	25	26
(1)	(2)	(3)	(4)	(5)	(6)	(7)
27	28	29	30			
(8)	(9)	(10)	(11)			

Passover Lamb Sacrificed — Nisan 14

Feast of First Fruits — 1st Sunday after Nisan 15

Feast of Unleavened Bread — Nisan 15-21

Pentecost — 8th Sunday after Nisan 15

Time of New Moon (Jerusalem) —   a5:13   b22:35   c15:28   d7:04   e21:00   f9:10

A.D. 38

July
(Tammuz 4)

S	M	T	W	T	F	S
				1	2	3
				(12)	(13)	(14)
4	5	6	7	8	9	10
(15)	(16)	(17)	(18)	(19)	(20)	(21)
11	12	13	14	15	16	17
(22)	(23)	(24)	(25)	(26)	(27)	(28)
18	19	20	21	22	23	24
(29g)	(1)	(2)	(3)	(4)	(5)	(6)
25	26	27	28	29	30	31
(7)	(8)	(9)	(10)	(11)	(12)	(13)

October
(Tishri 7)

S	M	T	W	T	F	S
					1	2
					(16)	(17)
3	4	5	6	7	8	9
(18)	(19)	(20)	(21)	(22)	(23)	(24)
10	11	12	13	14	15	16
(25)	(26)	(27)	(28)	(29)	(30j)	(1)
17	18	19	20	21	22	23
(2)	(3)	(4)	(5)	(6)	(7)	(8)
24	25	26	27	28	29	30
(9)	(10)	(11)	(12)	(13)	(14)	(15)
31						
(16)						

August
(Ab 5)

S	M	T	W	T	F	S
1	2	3	4	5	6	7
(14)	(15)	(16)	(17)	(18)	(19)	(20)
8	9	10	11	12	13	14
(21)	(22)	(23)	(24)	(25)	(26)	(27)
15	16	17	18	19	20	21
(28)	(29)	(30h)	(1)	(2)	(3)	(4)
22	23	24	25	26	27	28
(5)	(6)	(7)	(8)	(9)	(10)	(11)
29	30	31				
(12)	(13)	(14)				

November
(Marheshvan 8)

S	M	T	W	T	F	S
	1	2	3	4	5	6
	(17)	(18)	(19)	(20)	(21)	(22)
7	8	9	10	11	12	13
(23)	(24)	(25)	(26)	(27)	(28)	(29k)
14	15	16	17	18	19	20
(1)	(2)	(3)	(4)	(5)	(6)	(7)
21	22	23	24	25	26	27
(8)	(9)	(10)	(11)	(12)	(13)	(14)
28	29	30				
(15)	(16)	(17)				

September
(Elul 6)

S	M	T	W	T	F	S
			1	2	3	4
			(15)	(16)	(17)	(18)
5	6	7	8	9	10	11
(19)	(20)	(21)	(22)	(23)	(24)	(25)
12	13	14	15	16	17	18
(26)	(27)	(28)	(29i)	(1)	(2)	(3)
19	20	21	22	23	24	25
(4)	(5)	(6)	(7)	(8)	(9)	(10)
26	27	28	29	30		
(11)	(12)	(13)	(14)	(15)		

December
(Kislev 9)

S	M	T	W	T	F	S
			1	2	3	4
			(18)	(19)	(20)	(21)
5	6	7	8	9	10	11
(22)	(23)	(24)	(25)	(26)	(27)	(28)
12	13	14	15	16	17	18
(29m)	(1)	(2)	(3)	(4)	(5)	(6)
19	20	21	22	23	24	25
(7)	(8)	(9)	(10)	(11)	(12)	(13)
26	27	28	29	30	31	
(14)	(15)	(16)	(17)	(18)	(19)	

Day of Trumpets — Tishri 1
Feast of Booths — Tishri 15-22

Day of Atonement — Tishri 10
Feast of Dedication — 8 days beginning Kislev 25

Time of the New Moon —   g19:43   h5:11   i14:18   j23:51   k10:26   m22:17

A.D. 39

January (Tebeth 10)						
S	M	T	W	T	F	S
						1 (20)
2 (21)	3 (22)	4 (23)	5 (24)	6 (25)	7 (26)	8 (27)
9 (28)	10 (29)	11 (30a)	12 (1)	13 (2)	14 (3)	15 (4)
16 (5)	17 (6)	18 (7)	19 (8)	20 (9)	21 (10)	22 (11)
23 (12)	24 (13)	25 (14)	26 (15)	27 (16)	28 (17)	29 (18)
30 (19)	31 (20)					

April (Nisan 1)						
S	M	T	W	T	F	S
					1 (21)	2 (22)
3 (23)	4 (24)	5 (25)	6 (26)	7 (27)	8 (28)	9 (29)
10 (30d)	11 (1)	12 (2)	13 (3)	14 (4)	15 (5)	16 (6)
17 (7)	18 (8)	19 (9)	20 (10)	21 (11)	22 (12)	23 (13)
24 (14)	25 (15)	26 (16)	27 (17)	28 (18)	29 (19)	30 (20)

February (Shebat 11)						
S	M	T	W	T	F	S
		1 (21)	2 (22)	3 (23)	4 (24)	5 (25)
6 (26)	7 (27)	8 (28)	9 (29)	10 (30b)	11 (1)	12 (2)
13 (3)	14 (4)	15 (5)	16 (6)	17 (7)	18 (8)	19 (9)
20 (10)	21 (11)	22 (12)	23 (13)	24 (14)	25 (15)	26 (16)
27 (17)	28 (18)					

May (Iyyar 2)						
S	M	T	W	T	F	S
1 (21)	2 (22)	3 (23)	4 (24)	5 (25)	6 (26)	7 (27)
8 (28)	9 (29e)	10 (1)	11 (2)	12 (3)	13 (4)	14 (5)
15 (6)	16 (7)	17 (8)	18 (9)	19 (10)	20 (11)	21 (12)
22 (13)	23 (14)	24 (15)	25 (16)	26 (17)	27 (18)	28 (19)
29 (20)	30 (21)	31 (22)				

March (Adar 12)						
S	M	T	W	T	F	S
		1 (19)	2 (20)	3 (21)	4 (22)	5 (23)
6 (24)	7 (25)	8 (26)	9 (27)	10 (28)	11 (29c)	12 (1)
13 (2)	14 (3)	15 (4)	16 (5)	17 (6)	18 (7)	19 (8)
20 (9)	21 (10)	22 (11)	23 (12)	24 (13)	25 (14)	26 (15)
27 (16)	28 (17)	29 (18)	30 (19)	31 (20)		

June (Sivan 3)						
S	M	T	W	T	F	S
			1 (23)	2 (24)	3 (25)	4 (26)
5 (27)	6 (28)	7 (29)	8 (30f)	9 (1)	10 (2)	11 (3)
12 (4)	13 (5)	14 (6)	15 (7)	16 (8)	17 (9)	18 (10)
19 (11)	20 (12)	21 (13)	22 (14)	23 (15)	24 (16)	25 (17)
26 (18)	27 (19)	28 (20)	29 (21)	30 (22)		

Passover Lamb Sacrificed — Nisan 14
Feast of First Fruits — 1ˢᵗ Sunday after Nisan 15

Feast of Unleavened Bread — Nisan 15-21
Pentecost — 8ᵗʰ Sunday after Nisan 15

Time of New Moon (Jerusalem) —   a11:19   b1"20   c15:09   d7:35   e23:13   f14:21

July
(Tammuz 4)

S	M	T	W	T	F	S
					1 (23)	2 (24)
3 (25)	4 (26)	5 (27)	6 (28)	7 (29)	8 (30g)	9 (1)
10 (2)	11 (3)	12 (4)	13 (5)	14 (6)	15 (7)	16 (8)
17 (9)	18 (10)	19 (11)	20 (12)	21 (13)	22 (14)	23 (15)
24 (16)	25 (17)	26 (18)	27 (19)	28 (20)	29 (21)	30 (22)
31 (23)						

August
(Ab 5)

S	M	T	W	T	F	S
	1 (24)	2 (25)	3 (26)	4 (27)	5 (28)	6 (29h)
7 (1)	8 (2)	9 (3)	10 (4)	11 (5)	12 (6)	13 (7)
14 (8)	15 (9)	16 (10)	17 (11)	18 (12)	19 (13)	20 (14)
21 (15)	22 (16)	23 (17)	24 (18)	25 (19)	26 (20)	27 (21)
28 (22)	29 (23)	30 (24)	31 (25)			

September
(Elul 6)

S	M	T	W	T	F	S
				1 (26)	2 (27)	3 (28)
4 (29)	5 (30i)	6 (1)	7 (2)	8 (3)	9 (4)	10 (5)
11 (6)	12 (7)	13 (8)	14 (9)	15 (10)	16 (11)	17 (12)
18 (13)	19 (14)	20 (15)	21 (16)	22 (17)	23 (18)	24 (19)
25 (20)	26 (21)	27 (22)	28 (23)	29 (24)	30 (25)	

October
(Tishri 7)

S	M	T	W	T	F	S
						1 (26)
2 (27)	3 (28)	4 (29j)	5 (1)	6 (2)	7 (3)	8 (4)
9 (5)	10 (6)	11 (7)	12 (8)	13 (9)	14 (10)	15 (11)
16 (12)	17 (13)	18 (14)	19 (15)	20 (16)	21 (17)	22 (18)
23 (19)	24 (20)	25 (21)	26 (22)	27 (23)	28 (24)	29 (25)
30 (26)	31 (27)					

November
(Marheshvan 8)

S	M	T	W	T	F	S
		1 (28)	2 (29)	3 (30k)	4 (1)	5 (2)
6 (3)	7 (4)	8 (5)	9 (6)	10 (7)	11 (8)	12 (9)
13 (10)	14 (11)	15 (12)	16 (13)	17 (14)	18 (15)	19 (16)
20 (17)	21 (18)	22 (19)	23 (20)	24 (21)	25 (22)	26 (23)
27 (24)	28 (25)	29 (26)	30 (27)			

December
(Kislev 9)

S	M	T	W	T	F	S
				1 (28)	2 (29m)	3 (1)
4 (2)	5 (3)	6 (4)	7 (5)	8 (6)	9 (7)	10 (8)
11 (9)	12 (10)	13 (11)	14 (12)	15 (13)	16 (14)	17 (15)
18 (16)	19 (17)	20 (18)	21 (19)	22 (20)	23 (21)	24 (22)
25 (23)	26 (24)	27 (25)	28 (26)	29 (27)	30 (28)	31 (29)

Day of Trumpets — Tishri 1
Feast of Booths — Tishri 15-22

Day of Atonement — Tishri 10
Feast of Dedication — 8 days beginning Kislev 25

Time of the New Moon — g4:14 h16:55 i4:24 j15:21 k2:13 m13:08

A.D. 40

January (Tebeth 10)						
S	M	T	W	T	F	S
1	2	3	4	5	6	7
(30a)	(1)	(2)	(3)	(4)	(5)	(6)
8	9	10	11	12	13	14
(7)	(8)	(9)	(10)	(11)	(12)	(13)
15	16	17	18	19	20	21
(14)	(15)	(16)	(17)	(18)	(19)	(20)
22	23	24	25	26	27	28
(21)	(22)	(23)	(24)	(25)	(26)	(27)
29	30	31				
(28)	(29b)	(1)				

April (Nisan 1)						
S	M	T	W	T	F	S
1	2	3	4	5	6	7
(3)	(4)	(5)	(6)	(7)	(8)	(9)
8	9	10	11	12	13	14
(10)	(11)	(12)	(13)	(14)	(15)	(16)
15	16	17	18	19	20	21
(17)	(18)	(19)	(20)	(21)	(22)	(23)
22	23	24	25	26	27	28
(24)	(25)	(26)	(27)	(28)	(29)	(30e)
29	30					
(1)	(2)					

February (Adar 12)						
S	M	T	W	T	F	S
			1	2	3	4
			(2)	(3)	(4)	(5)
5	6	7	8	9	10	11
(6)	(7)	(8)	(9)	(10)	(11)	(12)
12	13	14	15	16	17	18
(13)	(14)	(15)	(16)	(17)	(18)	(19)
19	20	21	22	23	24	25
(20)	(21)	(22)	(23)	(24)	(25)	(26)
26	27	28	29			
(27)	(28)	(29c)	(1)			

May (Iyyar 2)						
S	M	T	W	T	F	S
			1	2	3	4	5
			(3)	(4)	(5)	(6)	(7)
6	7	8	9	10	11	12
(8)	(9)	(10)	(11)	(12)	(13)	(14)
13	14	15	16	17	18	19
(15)	(16)	(17)	(18)	(19)	(20)	(21)
20	21	22	23	24	25	26
(22)	(23)	(24)	(25)	(26)	(27)	(28)
27	28	29	30	31		
(29f)	(1)	(2)	(3)	(4)		

March (Adar II 13)						
S	M	T	W	T	F	S
				1	2	3
				(2)	(3)	(4)
4	5	6	7	8	9	10
(5)	(6)	(7)	(8)	(9)	(10)	(11)
11	12	13	14	15	16	17
(12)	(13)	(14)	(15)	(16)	(17)	(18)
18	19	20	21	22	23	24
(19)	(20)	(21)	(22)	(23)	(24)	(25)
25	26	27	28	29	30	31
(26)	(27)	(28)	(29)	(30d)	(1)	(2)

June (Sivan 3)						
S	M	T	W	T	F	S
					1	2
					(5)	(6)
3	4	5	6	7	8	9
(7)	(8)	(9)	(10)	(11)	(12)	(13)
10	11	12	13	14	15	16
(14)	(15)	(16)	(17)	(18)	(19)	(20)
17	18	19	20	21	22	23
(21)	(22)	(23)	(24)	(25)	(26)	(27)
24	25	26	27	28	29	30
(28)	(29)	(30g)	(1)	(2)	(3)	(4)

Passover Lamb Sacrificed — Nisan 14

Feast of First Fruits — 1st Sunday after Nisan 15

Feast of Unleavened Bread — Nisan 15-21

Pentecost — 8th Sunday after Nisan 15

Time of New Moon (Jerusalem) — a0:04   b11:06   c22:33   d10:55   e0:30   f15:11   g6:25

A.D. 40

July
(Tammuz 4)

S	M	T	W	T	F	S
1	2	3	4	5	6	7
(5)	(6)	(7)	(8)	(9)	(10)	(11)
8	9	10	11	12	13	14
(12)	(13)	(14)	(15)	(16)	(17)	(18)
15	16	17	18	19	20	21
(19)	(20)	(21)	(22)	(23)	(24)	(25)
22	23	24	25	26	27	28
(26)	(27)	(28)	(29h)	(1)	(2)	(3)
29	30	31				
(4)	(5)	(6)				

October
(Tishri 7)

S	M	T	W	T	F	S
	1	2	3	4	5	6
	(8)	(9)	(10)	(11)	(12)	(13)
7	8	9	10	11	12	13
(14)	(15)	(16)	(17)	(18)	(19)	(20)
14	15	16	17	18	19	20
(21)	(22)	(23)	(24)	(25)	(26)	(27)
21	22	23	24	25	26	27
(28)	(29k)	(1)	(2)	(3)	(4)	(5)
28	29	30	31			
(6)	(7)	(8)	(9)			

August
(Ab 5)

S	M	T	W	T	F	S
			1	2	3	4
			(7)	(8)	(9)	(10)
5	6	7	8	9	10	11
(11)	(12)	(13)	(14)	(15)	(16)	(17)
12	13	14	15	16	17	18
(18)	(19)	(20)	(21)	(22)	(23)	(24)
19	20	21	22	23	24	25
(25)	(26)	(27)	(28)	(29)	(30i)	(1)
26	27	28	29	30	31	
(2)	(3)	(4)	(5)	(6)	(7)	

November
(Marheshvan 8)

S	M	T	W	T	F	S
				1	2	3
				(10)	(11)	(12)
4	5	6	7	8	9	10
(13)	(14)	(15)	(16)	(17)	(18)	(19)
11	12	13	14	15	16	17
(20)	(21)	(22)	(23)	(24)	(25)	(26)
18	19	20	21	22	23	24
(27)	(28)	(29)	(30m)	(1)	(2)	(3)
25	26	27	28	29	30	
(4)	(5)	(6)	(7)	(8)	(9)	

September
(Elul 6)

S	M	T	W	T	F	S
						1
						(8)
2	3	4	5	6	7	8
(9)	(10)	(11)	(12)	(13)	(14)	(15)
9	10	11	12	13	14	15
(16)	(17)	(18)	(19)	(20)	(21)	(22)
16	17	18	19	20	21	22
(23)	(24)	(25)	(26)	(27)	(28)	(29)
23	24	25	26	27	28	29
(30j)	(1)	(2)	(3)	(4)	(5)	(6)
30						
(7)						

December
(Kislev 9)

S	M	T	W	T	F	S
						1
						(10)
2	3	4	5	6	7	8
(11)	(12)	(13)	(14)	(15)	(16)	(17)
9	10	11	12	13	14	15
(18)	(19)	(20)	(21)	(22)	(23)	(24)
16	17	18	19	20	21	22
(25)	(26)	(27)	(28)	(29n)	(1)	(2)
23	24	25	26	27	28	29
(3)	(4)	(5)	(6)	(7)	(8)	(9)
30	31					
(10)	(11)					

Day of Trumpets — Tishri 1
Feast of Booths — Tishri 15-22

Day of Atonement — Tishri 10
Feast of Dedication — 8 days beginning Kislev 25

Time of the New Moon —   h21:37   i12:25   j2:38   k16:05   m4:30   n15:46

A.D. 41

	January					
	(Tebeth 10)					
S	M	T	W	T	F	S
		1	2	3	4	5
		(12)	(13)	(14)	(15)	(16)
6	7	8	9	10	11	12
(17)	(18)	(19)	(20)	(21)	(22)	(23)
13	14	15	16	17	18	19
(24)	(25)	(26)	(27)	(28)	(29)	(30a)
20	21	22	23	24	25	26
(1)	(2)	(3)	(4)	(5)	(6)	(7)
27	28	29	30	31		
(8)	(9)	(10)	(11)	(12)		

	April					
	(Nisan 1)					
S	M	T	W	T	F	S
	1	2	3	4	5	6
	(14)	(15)	(16)	(17)	(18)	(19)
7	8	9	10	11	12	13
(20)	(21)	(22)	(23)	(24)	(25)	(26)
14	15	16	17	18	19	20
(27)	(28)	(29)	(30d)	(1)	(2)	(3)
21	22	23	24	25	26	27
(4)	(5)	(6)	(7)	(8)	(9)	(10)
28	29	30				
(11)	(12)	(13)				

	February					
	(Shebat 11)					
S	M	T	W	T	F	S
					1	2
					(13)	(14)
3	4	5	6	7	8	9
(15)	(16)	(17)	(18)	(19)	(20)	(21)
10	11	12	13	14	15	16
(22)	(23)	(24)	(25)	(26)	(27)	(28)
17	18	19	20	21	22	23
(29b)	(1)	(2)	(3)	(4)	(5)	(6)
24	25	26	27	28		
(7)	(8)	(9)	(10)	(11)		

	May					
	(Iyyar 2)					
S	M	T	W	T	F	S
			1	2	3	4
			(14)	(15)	(16)	(17)
5	6	7	8	9	10	11
(18)	(19)	(20)	(21)	(22)	(23)	(24)
12	13	14	15	16	17	18
(25)	(26)	(27)	(28)	(29e)	(1)	(2)
19	20	21	22	23	24	25
(3)	(4)	(5)	(6)	(7)	(8)	(9)
26	27	28	29	30	31	
(10)	(11)	(12)	(13)	(14)	(15)	

	March					
	(Adar 12)					
S	M	T	W	T	F	S
					1	2
					(12)	(13)
3	4	5	6	7	8	9
(14)	(15)	(16)	(17)	(18)	(19)	(20)
10	11	12	13	14	15	16
(21)	(22)	(23)	(24)	(25)	(26)	(27)
17	18	19	20	21	22	23
(28)	(29c)	(1)	(2)	(3)	(4)	(5)
24	25	26	27	28	29	30
(6)	(7)	(8)	(9)	(10)	(11)	(12)
31						
(13)						

	June					
	(Sivan 3)					
S	M	T	W	T	F	S
						1
						(16)
2	3	4	5	6	7	8
(17)	(18)	(19)	(20)	(21)	(22)	(23)
9	10	11	12	13	14	15
(24)	(25)	(26)	(27)	(28)	(29)	(30f)
16	17	18	19	20	21	22
(1)	(2)	(3)	(4)	(5)	(6)	(7)
23	24	25	26	27	28	29
(8)	(9)	(10)	(11)	(12)	(13)	(14)
30						
(15)						

Passover Lamb Sacrificed — Nisan 14
Feast of First Fruits — 1st Sunday after Nisan 15

Feast of Unleavened Bread — Nisan 15-21
Pentecost — 8th Sunday after Nisan 15

Time of New Moon (Jerusalem) — a1:59 b11:36 c21:14 d7:29 e18:52 f7:40

A.D. 41

July
(Tammuz 4)

S	M	T	W	T	F	S
	1	2	3	4	5	6
	(16)	(17)	(18)	(19)	(20)	(21)
7	8	9	10	11	12	13
(22)	(23)	(24)	(25)	(26)	(27)	(28)
14	15	16	17	18	19	20
(29g)	(1)	(2)	(3)	(4)	(5)	(6)
21	22	23	24	25	26	27
(7)	(8)	(9)	(10)	(11)	(12)	(13)
28	29	30	31			
(14)	(15)	(16)	(17)			

October
(Tishri 7)

S	M	T	W	T	F	S
		1	2	3	4	5
		(19)	(20)	(21)	(22)	(23)
6	7	8	9	10	11	12
(24)	(25)	(26)	(27)	(28)	(29)	(30j)
13	14	15	16	17	18	19
(1)	(2)	(3)	(4)	(5)	(6)	(7)
20	21	22	23	24	25	26
(8)	(9)	(10)	(11)	(12)	(13)	(14)
27	28	29	30	31		
(15)	(16)	(17)	(18)	(19)		

August
(Ab 5)

S	M	T	W	T	F	S
				1	2	3
				(18)	(19)	(20)
4	5	6	7	8	9	10
(21)	(22)	(23)	(24)	(25)	(26)	(27)
11	12	13	14	15	16	17
(28)	(29)	(30h)	(1)	(2)	(3)	(4)
18	19	20	21	22	23	24
(5)	(6)	(7)	(8)	(9)	(10)	(11)
25	26	27	28	29	30	31
(12)	(13)	(14)	(15)	(16)	(17)	(18)

November
(Marheshvan 8)

S	M	T	W	T	F	S
					1	2
					(20)	(21)
3	4	5	6	7	8	9
(22)	(23)	(24)	(25)	(26)	(27)	(28)
10	11	12	13	14	15	16
(29k)	(1)	(2)	(3)	(4)	(5)	(6)
17	18	19	20	21	22	23
(7)	(8)	(9)	(10)	(11)	(12)	(13)
24	25	26	27	28	29	30
(14)	(15)	(16)	(17)	(18)	(19)	(20)

September
(Elul 6)

S	M	T	W	T	F	S
1	2	3	4	5	6	7
(19)	(20)	(21)	(22)	(23)	(24)	(25)
8	9	10	11	12	13	14
(26)	(27)	(28)	(29)	(30i)	(1)	(2)
15	16	17	18	19	20	21
(3)	(4)	(5)	(6)	(7)	(8)	(9)
22	23	24	25	26	27	28
(10)	(11)	(12)	(13)	(14)	(15)	(16)
29	30					
(17)	(18)					

December
(Kislev 9)

S	M	T	W	T	F	S
1	2	3	4	5	6	7
(21)	(22)	(23)	(24)	(25)	(26)	(27)
8	9	10	11	12	13	14
(28)	(29)	(30m)	(1)	(2)	(3)	(4)
15	16	17	18	19	20	21
(5)	(6)	(7)	(8)	(9)	(10)	(11)
22	23	24	25	26	27	28
(12)	(13)	(14)	(15)	(16)	(17)	(18)
29	30	31				
(19)	(20)	(21)				

Day of Trumpets — Tishri 1
Feast of Booths — Tishri 15-22

Day of Atonement — Tishri 10
Feast of Dedication — 8 days beginning Kislev 25

Time of the New Moon —   g22:03   h13:57   i6:54   j23:55   k15:49   m5:46

A.D. 42

January
(Tebeth 10)

S	M	T	W	T	F	S
			1	2	3	4
			(22)	(23)	(24)	(25)
5	6	7	8	9	10	11
(26)	(27)	(28)	(29a)	(1)	(2)	(3)
12	13	14	15	16	17	18
(4)	(5)	(6)	(7)	(8)	(9)	(10)
19	20	21	22	23	24	25
(11)	(12)	(13)	(14)	(15)	(16)	(17)
26	27	28	29	30	31	
(18)	(19)	(20)	(21)	(22)	(23)	

April
(Nisan 1)

S	M	T	W	T	F	S
		1	2	3	4	5
		(24)	(25)	(26)	(27)	(28)
6	7	8	9	10	11	12
(29d)	(1)	(2)	(3)	(4)	(5)	(6)
13	14	15	16	17	18	19
(7)	(8)	(9)	(10)	(11)	(12)	(13)
20	21	22	23	24	25	26
(14)	(15)	(16)	(17)	(18)	(19)	(20)
27	28	29	30			
(21)	(22)	(23)	(24)			

February
(Shebat 11)

S	M	T	W	T	F	S
						1
						(24)
2	3	4	5	6	7	8
(25)	(26)	(27)	(28)	(29)	(30b)	(1)
9	10	11	12	13	14	15
(2)	(3)	(4)	(5)	(6)	(7)	(8)
16	17	18	19	20	21	22
(9)	(10)	(11)	(12)	(13)	(14)	(15)
23	24	25	26	27	28	
(16)	(17)	(18)	(19)	(20)	(21)	

May
(Iyyar 2)

S	M	T	W	T	F	S
				1	2	3
				(25)	(26)	(27)
4	5	6	7	8	9	10
(28)	(29)	(30e)	(1)	(2)	(3)	(4)
11	12	13	14	15	16	17
(5)	(6)	(7)	(8)	(9)	(10)	(11)
18	19	20	21	22	23	24
(12)	(13)	(14)	(15)	(16)	(17)	(18)
25	26	27	28	29	30	31
(19)	(20)	(21)	(22)	(23)	(24)	(25)

March
(Adar 12)

S	M	T	W	T	F	S
						1
						(22)
2	3	4	5	6	7	8
(23)	(24)	(25)	(26)	(27)	(28)	(29c)
9	10	11	12	13	14	15
(1)	(2)	(3)	(4)	(5)	(6)	(7)
16	17	18	19	20	21	22
(8)	(9)	(10)	(11)	(12)	(13)	(14)
23	24	25	26	27	28	29
(15)	(16)	(17)	(18)	(19)	(20)	(21)
30	31					
(22)	(23)					

June
(Sivan 3)

S	M	T	W	T	F	S
1	2	3	4	5	6	7
(26)	(27)	(28)	(29f)	(1)	(2)	(3)
8	9	10	11	12	13	14
(4)	(5)	(6)	(7)	(8)	(9)	(10)
15	16	17	18	19	20	21
(11)	(12)	(13)	(14)	(15)	(16)	(17)
22	23	24	25	26	27	28
(18)	(19)	(20)	(21)	(22)	(23)	(24)
29	30					
(25)	(26)					

Passover Lamb Sacrificed — Nisan 14
Feast of First Fruits — 1st Sunday after Nisan 15

Feast of Unleavened Bread — Nisan 15-21
Pentecost — 8th Sunday after Nisan 15

Time of New Moon (Jerusalem) — a17:37 b3:46 c12:45 d21:04 e5:33 f16:43

A.D. 42

July
(Tammuz 4)

S	M	T	W	T	F	S
		1	2	3	4	5
		(27)	(28)	(29)	(30g)	(1)
6	7	8	9	10	11	12
(2)	(3)	(4)	(5)	(6)	(7)	(8)
13	14	15	16	17	18	19
(9)	(10)	(11)	(12)	(13)	(14)	(15)
20	21	22	23	24	25	26
(16)	(17)	(18)	(19)	(20)	(21)	(22)
27	28	29	30	31		
(23)	(24)	(25)	(26)	(27)		

October
(Tishri 7)

S	M	T	W	T	F	S
			1	2	3	4
			(30j)	(1)	(2)	(3)
5	6	7	8	9	10	11
(4)	(5)	(6)	(7)	(8)	(9)	(10)
12	13	14	15	16	17	18
(11)	(12)	(13)	(14)	(15)	(16)	(17)
19	20	21	22	23	24	25
(18)	(19)	(20)	(21)	(22)	(23)	(24)
26	27	28	29	30	31	
(25)	(26)	(27)	(28)	(29k)	(1)	

August
(Ab 5)

S	M	T	W	T	F	S
					1	2
					(28)	(29h)
3	4	5	6	7	8	9
(1)	(2)	(3)	(4)	(5)	(6)	(7)
10	11	12	13	14	15	16
(8)	(9)	(10)	(11)	(12)	(13)	(14)
17	18	19	20	21	22	23
(15)	(16)	(17)	(18)	(19)	(20)	(21)
24	25	26	27	28	29	30
(22)	(23)	(24)	(25)	(26)	(27)	(28)
31						
(29)						

November
(Kislev 9)

S	M	T	W	T	F	S
						1
						(2)
2	3	4	5	6	7	8
(3)	(4)	(5)	(6)	(7)	(8)	(9)
9	10	11	12	13	14	15
(10)	(11)	(12)	(13)	(14)	(15)	(16)
16	17	18	19	20	21	22
(17)	(18)	(19)	(20)	(21)	(22)	(23)
23	24	25	26	27	28	29
(24)	(25)	(26)	(27)	(28)	(29)	(30m)
30						
(1)						

September
(Elul 6)

S	M	T	W	T	F	S
	1	2	3	4	5	6
	(30i)	(1)	(2)	(3)	(4)	(5)
7	8	9	10	11	12	13
(6)	(7)	(8)	(9)	(10)	(11)	(12)
14	15	16	17	18	19	20
(13)	(14)	(15)	(16)	(17)	(18)	(19)
21	22	23	24	25	25	27
(20)	(21)	(22)	(23)	(24)	(25)	(26)
28	29	30				
(27)	(28)	(29)				

December
(Tebeth 10)

S	M	T	W	T	F	S
	1	2	3	4	5	6
	(2)	(3)	(4)	(5)	(6)	(7)
7	8	9	10	11	12	13
(8)	(9)	(10)	(11)	(12)	(13)	(14)
14	15	16	17	18	19	20
(15)	(16)	(17)	(18)	(19)	(20)	(21)
21	22	23	24	25	26	27
(22)	(23)	(24)	(25)	(26)	(27)	(28)
28	29	30	31			
(29)	(30n)	(1)	(2)			

Day of Trumpets — Tishri 1
Feast of Booths — Tishri 15-22

Day of Atonement — Tishri 10
Feast of Dedication — 8 days beginning Kislev 25

Time of the New Moon — g1:32 h14:48 i6:31 j1:06 k19:54 m13:46 n5:20

A.D. 43

January
(Shebat 11)

S	M	T	W	T	F	S
				1	2	3
				(3)	(4)	(5)
4	5	6	7	8	9	10
(6)	(7)	(8)	(9)	(10)	(11)	(12)
11	12	13	14	15	16	17
(13)	(14)	(15)	(16)	(17)	(18)	(19)
18	19	20	21	22	23	24
(20)	(21)	(22)	(23)	(24)	(25)	(26)
25	26	27	28	29	30	31
(27)	(28)	(29a)	(1)	(2)	(3)	(4)

April
(Nisan 1)

S	M	T	W	T	F	S
			1	2	3	4
			(5)	(6)	(7)	(8)
5	6	7	8	9	10	11
(9)	(10)	(11)	(12)	(13)	(14)	(15)
12	13	14	15	16	17	18
(16)	(17)	(18)	(19)	(20)	(21)	(22)
19	20	21	22	23	24	25
(23)	(24)	(25)	(26)	(27)	(28)	(29d)
26	27	28	29	30		
(1)	(2)	(3)	(4)	(5)		

February
(Adar 12)

S	M	T	W	T	F	S
1	2	3	4	5	6	7
(5)	(6)	(7)	(8)	(9)	(10)	(11)
8	9	10	11	12	13	14
(12)	(13)	(14)	(15)	(16)	(17)	(18)
15	16	17	18	19	20	21
(19)	(20)	(21)	(22)	(23)	(24)	(25)
22	23	24	25	26	27	28
(26)	(27)	(28)	(29)	(30b)	(1)	(2)

May
(Iyyar 2)

S	M	T	W	T	F	S
					1	2
					(6)	(7)
3	4	5	6	7	8	9
(8)	(9)	(10)	(11)	(12)	(13)	(14)
10	11	12	13	14	15	16
(15)	(16)	(17)	(18)	(19)	(20)	(21)
17	18	19	20	21	22	23
(22)	(23)	(24)	(25)	(26)	(27)	(28)
24	25	26	27	28	29	30
(29)	(30e)	(1)	(2)	(3)	(4)	(5)
31						
(6)						

March
(Adar II 13)

S	M	T	W	T	F	S
1	2	3	4	5	6	7
(3)	(4)	(5)	(6)	(7)	(8)	(9)
8	9	10	11	12	13	14
(10)	(11)	(12)	(13)	(14)	(15)	(16)
15	16	17	18	19	20	21
(17)	(18)	(19)	(20)	(21)	(22)	(23)
22	23	24	25	26	27	28
(24)	(25)	(26)	(27)	(28)	(29c)	(1)
29	30	31				
(2)	(3)	(4)				

June
(Sivan 3)

S	M	T	W	T	F	S
	1	2	3	4	5	6
	(7)	(8)	(9)	(10)	(11)	(12)
7	8	9	10	11	12	13
(13)	(14)	(15)	(16)	(17)	(18)	(19)
14	15	16	17	18	19	20
(20)	(21)	(22)	(23)	(24)	(25)	(26)
21	22	23	24	25	26	27
(27)	(28)	(29f)	(1)	(2)	(3)	(4)
28	29	30				
(5)	(6)	(7)				

Passover Lamb Sacrificed — Nisan 14

Feast of First Fruits — 1st Sunday after Nisan 15

Feast of Unleavened Bread — Nisan 15-21

Pentecost — 8th Sunday after Nisan 15

Time of New Moon (Jerusalem) — a18:24   b5:04   c14:01   d21:32   e4:34   f12:11

A.D. 43

July (Tammuz 4)

S	M	T	W	T	F	S
			1 (8)	2 (9)	3 (10)	4 (11)
5 (12)	6 (13)	7 (14)	8 (15)	9 (16)	10 (17)	11 (18)
12 (19)	13 (20)	14 (21)	15 (22)	16 (23)	17 (24)	18 (25)
19 (26)	20 (27)	21 (28)	22 (29g)	23 (1)	24 (2)	25 (3)
26 (4)	27 (5)	28 (6)	29 (7)	30 (8)	31 (9)	

October (Tishri 7)

S	M	T	W	T	F	S
				1 (11)	2 (12)	3 (13)
4 (14)	5 (15)	6 (16)	7 (17)	8 (18)	9 (19)	10 (20)
11 (21)	12 (22)	13 (23)	14 (24)	15 (25)	16 (26)	17 (27)
18 (28)	19 (29j)	20 (1)	21 (2)	22 (3)	23 (4)	24 (5)
25 (6)	26 (7)	27 (8)	28 (9)	29 (10)	30 (11)	31 (12)

August (Ab 5)

S	M	T	W	T	F	S
						1 (10)
2 (11)	3 (12)	4 (13)	5 (14)	6 (15)	7 (16)	8 (17)
9 (18)	10 (19)	11 (20)	12 (21)	13 (22)	14 (23)	15 (24)
16 (25)	17 (26)	18 (27)	19 (28)	20 (29)	21 (30h)	22 (1)
23 (2)	24 (3)	25 (4)	26 (5)	27 (6)	28 (7)	29 (8)
30 (9)	31 (10)					

November (Marheshvan 8)

S	M	T	W	T	F	S
1 (13)	2 (14)	3 (15)	4 (16)	5 (17)	6 (18)	7 (19)
8 (20)	9 (21)	10 (22)	11 (23)	12 (24)	13 (25)	14 (26)
15 (27)	16 (28)	17 (29)	18 (30k)	19 (1)	20 (2)	21 (3)
22 (4)	23 (5)	24 (6)	25 (7)	26 (8)	27 (9)	28 (10)
29 (11)	30 (12)					

September (Elul 6)

S	M	T	W	T	F	S
		1 (11)	2 (12)	3 (13)	4 (14)	5 (15)
6 (16)	7 (17)	8 (18)	9 (19)	10 (20)	11 (21)	12 (22)
13 (23)	14 (24)	15 (25)	16 (26)	17 (27)	18 (28)	19 (29)
20 (30i)	21 (1)	22 (2)	23 (3)	24 (4)	25 (5)	26 (6)
27 (7)	28 (8)	29 (9)	30 (10)			

December (Kislev 9)

S	M	T	W	T	F	S
		1 (13)	2 (14)	3 (15)	4 (16)	5 (17)
6 (18)	7 (19)	8 (20)	9 (21)	10 (22)	11 (23)	12 (24)
13 (25)	14 (26)	15 (27)	16 (28)	17 (29)	18 (30m)	19 (1)
20 (2)	21 (3)	22 (4)	23 (5)	24 (6)	25 (7)	26 (8)
27 (9)	28 (10)	29 (11)	30 (12)	31 (13)		

Day of Trumpets — Tishri 1
Feast of Booths — Tishri 15-22

Day of Atonement — Tishri 10
Feast of Dedication — 8 days beginning Kislev 25

Time of the New Moon — g21:37   h9:51   i1:17   j19:23   k14:48   m9:53

A.D. 44

January
(Tebeth 10)

S	M	T	W	T	F	S
					1	2
					(14)	(15)
3	4	5	6	7	8	9
(16)	(17)	(18)	(19)	(20)	(21)	(22)
10	11	12	13	14	15	16
(23)	(24)	(25)	(26)	(27)	(28)	(29)
17	18	19	20	21	22	23
(30a)	(1)	(2)	(3)	(4)	(5)	(6)
24	25	26	27	28	29	30
(7)	(8)	(9)	(10)	(11)	(12)	(13)
31						
(14)						

April
(Nisan 1)

S	M	T	W	T	F	S
					1	2
					(16)	(17)
3	4	5	6	7	8	9
(18)	(19)	(20)	(21)	(22)	(23)	(24)
10	11	12	13	14	15	16
(25)	(26)	(27)	(28)	(29d)	(1)	(2)
17	18	19	20	21	22	23
(3)	(4)	(5)	(6)	(7)	(8)	(9)
24	25	26	27	28	29	30
(10)	(11)	(12)	(13)	(14)	(15)	(16)

February
(Shebat 11)

S	M	T	W	T	F	S
	1	2	3	4	5	6
	(15)	(16)	(17)	(18)	(19)	(20)
7	8	9	10	11	12	13
(21)	(22)	(23)	(24)	(25)	(26)	(27)
14	15	16	17	18	19	20
(28)	(29b)	(1)	(2)	(3)	(4)	(5)
21	22	23	24	25	26	27
(6)	(7)	(8)	(9)	(10)	(11)	(12)
28	29					
(13)	(14)					

May
(Iyyar 2)

S	M	T	W	T	F	S
1	2	3	4	5	6	7
(17)	(18)	(19)	(20)	(21)	(22)	(23)
8	9	10	11	12	13	14
(24)	(25)	(26)	(27)	(28)	(29e)	(1)
15	16	17	18	19	20	21
(2)	(3)	(4)	(5)	(6)	(7)	(8)
22	23	24	25	26	27	28
(9)	(10)	(11)	(12)	(13)	(14)	(15)
29	30	31				
(16)	(17)	(18)				

March
(Adar 12)

S	M	T	W	T	F	S
		1	2	3	4	5
		(15)	(16)	(17)	(18)	(19)
6	7	8	9	10	11	12
(20)	(21)	(22)	(23)	(24)	(25)	(26)
13	14	15	16	17	18	19
(27)	(28)	(29)	(30c)	(1)	(2)	(3)
20	21	22	23	24	25	26
(4)	(5)	(6)	(7)	(8)	(9)	(10)
27	28	29	30	31		
(11)	(12)	(13)	(14)	(15)		

June
(Sivan 3)

S	M	T	W	T	F	S
			1	2	3	4
			(19)	(20)	(21)	(22)
5	6	7	8	9	10	11
(23)	(24)	(25)	(26)	(27)	(28)	(29)
12	13	14	15	16	17	18
(30f)	(1)	(2)	(3)	(4)	(5)	(6)
19	20	21	22	23	24	25
(7)	(8)	(9)	(10)	(11)	(12)	(13)
26	27	28	29	30		
(14)	(15)	(16)	(17)	(18)		

Passover Lamb Sacrificed — Nisan 14

Feast of First Fruits — 1st Sunday after Nisan 15

Feast of Unleavened Bread — Nisan 15-21

Pentecost — 8th Sunday after Nisan 15

Time of New Moon (Jerusalem) — a3:12 b17:50 c5:29 d14:29 e21:42 f4:15

A.D. 44

July
(Tammuz 4)

S	M	T	W	T	F	S
					1	2
					(19)	(20)
3	4	5	6	7	8	9
(21)	(22)	(23)	(24)	(25)	(26)	(27)
10	11	12	13	14	15	16
(28)	(29g)	(1)	(2)	(3)	(4)	(5)
17	18	19	20	21	22	23
(6)	(7)	(8)	(9)	(10)	(11)	(12)
24	25	26	27	28	29	30
(13)	(14)	(15)	(16)	(17)	(18)	(19)
31						
(20)						

October
(Tishri 7)

S	M	T	W	T	F	S
						1
						(23)
2	3	4	5	6	7	8
(24)	(25)	(26)	(27)	(28)	(29j)	(1)
9	10	11	12	13	14	15
(2)	(3)	(4)	(5)	(6)	(7)	(8)
16	17	18	19	20	21	22
(9)	(10)	(11)	(12)	(13)	(14)	(15)
23	24	25	26	27	28	29
(16)	(17)	(18)	(19)	(20)	(21)	(22)
30	31					
(23)	(24)					

August
(Ab 5)

S	M	T	W	T	F	S
	1	2	3	4	5	6
	(21)	(22)	(23)	(24)	(25)	(26)
7	8	9	10	11	12	13
(27)	(28)	(29h)	(1)	(2)	(3)	(4)
14	15	16	17	18	19	20
(5)	(6)	(7)	(8)	(9)	(10)	(11)
21	22	23	24	25	26	27
(12)	(13)	(14)	(15)	(16)	(17)	(18)
28	29	30	31			
(19)	(20)	(21)	(22)			

November
(Marheshvan 8)

S	M	T	W	T	F	S
		1	2	3	4	5
		(25)	(26)	(27)	(28)	(29)
6	7	8	9	10	11	12
(30k)	(1)	(2)	(3)	(4)	(5)	(6)
13	14	15	16	17	18	19
(7)	(8)	(9)	(10)	(11)	(12)	(13)
20	21	22	23	24	25	26
(14)	(15)	(16)	(17)	(18)	(19)	(20)
27	28	29	30			
(21)	(22)	(23)	(24)			

September
(Elul 6)

S	M	T	W	T	F	S
				1	2	3
				(23)	(24)	(25)
4	5	6	7	8	9	10
(26)	(27)	(28)	(29)	(30i)	(1)	(2)
11	12	13	14	15	16	17
(3)	(4)	(5)	(6)	(7)	(8)	(9)
18	19	20	21	22	23	24
(10)	(11)	(12)	(13)	(14)	(15)	(16)
25	26	27	28	29	30	
(17)	(18)	(19)	(20)	(21)	(22)	

December
(Kislev 9)

S	M	T	W	T	F	S
				1	2	3
				(25)	(26)	(27)
4	5	6	7	8	9	10
(28)	(29)	(30m)	(1)	(2)	(3)	(4)
11	12	13	14	15	16	17
(5)	(6)	(7)	(8)	(9)	(10)	(11)
18	19	20	21	22	23	24
(12)	(13)	(14)	(15)	(16)	(17)	(18)
25	26	27	28	29	30	31
(19)	(20)	(21)	(22)	(23)	(24)	(25)

Day of Trumpets — Tishri 1
Feast of Booths — Tishri 15-22

Day of Atonement — Tishri 10
Feast of Dedication — 8 days beginning Kislev 25

Time of the New Moon — g11:22   h20:08   i7:22   j21:25   k14:15   m9:10

Gregorian
A.D. 45

January
(Tebeth 10)

S	M	T	W	T	F	S
1	2	3	4	5	6	7
(26)	(27)	(28)	(29)	(30a)	(1)	(2)
8	9	10	11	12	13	14
(3)	(4)	(5)	(6)	(7)	(8)	(9)
15	16	17	18	19	20	21
(10)	(11)	(12)	(13)	(14)	(15)	(16)
22	23	24	25	26	27	28
(17)	(18)	(19)	(20)	(21)	(22)	(23)
29	30	31				
(24)	(25)	(26)				

April
(Adar 13)

S	M	T	W	T	F	S
						1
						(27)
2	3	4	5	6	7	8
(28)	(29)	(30d)	(1)	(2)	(3)	(4)
9	10	11	12	13	14	15
(5)	(6)	(7)	(8)	(9)	(10)	(11)
16	17	18	19	20	21	22
(12)	(13)	(14)	(15)	(16)	(17)	(18)
23	24	25	26	27	28	29
(19)	(20)	(21)	(22)	(23)	(24)	(25)
30						
(26)						

February
(Shebat 11)

S	M	T	W	T	F	S
			1	2	3	4
			(27)	(28)	(29)	(30b)
5	6	7	8	9	10	11
(1)	(2)	(3)	(4)	(5)	(6)	(7)
12	13	14	15	16	17	18
(8)	(9)	(10)	(11)	(12)	(13)	(14)
19	20	21	22	23	24	25
(15)	(16)	(17)	(18)	(19)	(20)	(21)
26	27	28				
(22)	(23)	(24)				

May
(Nisan 1)

S	M	T	W	T	F	S
	1	2	3	4	5	6
	(27)	(28)	(29e)	(1)	(2)	(3)
7	8	9	10	11	12	13
(4)	(5)	(6)	(7)	(8)	(9)	(10)
14	15	16	17	18	19	20
(11)	(12)	(13)	(14)	(15)	(16)	(17)
21	22	23	24	25	26	27
(18)	(19)	(20)	(21)	(22)	(23)	(24)
28	29	30	31			
(25)	(26)	(27)	(28)			

March
(Adar 12)

S	M	T	W	T	F	S
			1	2	3	4
			(25)	(26)	(27)	(28)
5	6	7	8	9	10	11
(29c)	(1)	(2)	(3)	(4)	(5)	(6)
12	13	14	15	16	17	18
(7)	(8)	(9)	(10)	(11)	(12)	(13)
19	20	21	22	23	24	25
(14)	(15)	(16)	(17)	(18)	(19)	(20)
26	27	28	29	30	31	
(21)	(22)	(23)	(24)	(25)	(26)	

June
(Iyyar 2)

S	M	T	W	T	F	S
				1	2	3
				(29f)	(1)	(2)
4	5	6	7	8	9	10
(3)	(4)	(5)	(6)	(7)	(8)	(9)
11	12	13	14	15	16	17
(10)	(11)	(12)	(13)	(14)	(15)	(16)
18	19	20	21	22	23	24
(17)	(18)	(19)	(20)	(21)	(22)	(23)
25	26	27	28	29	30	
(24)	(25)	(26)	(27)	(28)	(29)	

Passover Lamb Sacrificed — Nisan 14
Feast of First Fruits — 1st Sunday after Nisan 15

Feast of Unleavened Bread — Nisan 15-21
Pentecost — 8th Sunday after Nisan 15

Time of New Moon (Jerusalem) —   a4:50   b23:24   c15:16   d3:50   e13:31   f21:20

A.D. 45

			July (Sivan 3)			
S	M	T	W	T	F	S
						1
						(30g)
2	3	4	5	6	7	8
(1)	(2)	(3)	(4)	(5)	(6)	(7)
9	10	11	12	13	14	15
(8)	(9)	(10)	(11)	(12)	(13)	(14)
16	17	18	19	20	21	22
(15)	(16)	(17)	(18)	(19)	(20)	(21)
23	24	25	26	27	28	29
(22)	(23)	(24)	(25)	(26)	(27)	(28)
30	31					
(29h)	(1)					

			October (Tishri 7)			
S	M	T	W	T	F	S
1	2	3	4	5	6	7
(4)	(5)	(6)	(7)	(8)	(9)	(10)
8	9	10	11	12	13	14
(11)	(12)	(13)	(14)	(15)	(16)	(17)
15	16	17	18	19	20	21
(18)	(19)	(20)	(21)	(22)	(23)	(24)
22	23	24	25	26	27	28
(25)	(26)	(27)	(28)	(29k)	(1)	(2)
29	30	31				
(3)	(4)	(5)				

			August (Ab 5)			
S	M	T	W	T	F	S
		1	2	3	4	5
		(2)	(3)	(4)	(5)	(6)
6	7	8	9	10	11	12
(7)	(8)	(9)	(10)	(11)	(12)	(13)
13	14	15	16	17	18	19
(14)	(15)	(16)	(17)	(18)	(19)	(20)
20	21	22	23	24	25	26
(21)	(22)	(23)	(24)	(25)	(26)	(27)
27	28	29	30	31		
(28)	(29i)	(1)	(2)	(3)		

			November (Marheshvan 8)			
S	M	T	W	T	F	S
			1	2	3	4
			(6)	(7)	(8)	(9)
5	6	7	8	9	10	11
(10)	(11)	(12)	(13)	(14)	(15)	(16)
12	13	14	15	16	17	18
(17)	(18)	(19)	(20)	(21)	(22)	(23)
19	20	21	22	23	24	25
(24)	(25)	(26)	(27)	(28)	(29)	(30m)
26	27	28	29	30		
(1)	(2)	(3)	(4)	(5)		

			September (Elul 6)			
S	M	T	W	T	F	S
					1	2
					(4)	(5)
3	4	5	6	7	8	9
(6)	(7)	(8)	(9)	(10)	(11)	(12)
10	11	12	13	14	15	16
(13)	(14)	(15)	(16)	(17)	(18)	(19)
17	18	19	20	21	22	23
(20)	(21)	(22)	(23)	(24)	(25)	(26)
24	25	26	27	28	29	30
(27)	(28)	(29)	(30j)	(1)	(2)	(3)

			December (Kislev 9)			
S	M	T	W	T	F	S
					1	2
					(6)	(7)
3	4	5	6	7	8	9
(8)	(9)	(10)	(11)	(12)	(13)	(14)
10	11	12	13	14	15	16
(15)	(16)	(17)	(18)	(19)	(20)	(21)
17	18	19	20	21	22	23
(22)	(23)	(24)	(25)	(26)	(27)	(28)
24	25	26	27	28	29	30
(29)	(30n)	(1)	(2)	(3)	(4)	(5)
31						
(6)						

Day of Trumpets — Tishri 1
Feast of Booths — Tishri 15-22

Day of Atonement — Tishri 10
Feast of Dedication — 8 days beginning Kislev 25

Time of the New Moon — g4:27   h11:34   i21:26   j6:43   k19:18   m10:34   n4:19

A.D. 46

January (Tebeth 10)

S	M	T	W	T	F	S
	1	2	3	4	5	6
	(7)	(8)	(9)	(10)	(11)	(12)
7	8	9	10	11	12	13
(13)	(14)	(15)	(16)	(17)	(18)	(19)
14	15	16	17	18	19	20
(20)	(21)	(22)	(23)	(24)	(25)	(26)
21	22	23	24	25	26	27
(27)	(28)	(29a)	(1)	(2)	(3)	(4)
28	29	30	31			
(5)	(6)	(7)	(8)			

April (Nisan 1)

S	M	T	W	T	F	S
1	2	3	4	5	6	7
(8)	(9)	(10)	(11)	(12)	(13)	(14)
8	9	10	11	12	13	14
(15)	(16)	(17)	(18)	(19)	(20)	(21)
15	16	17	18	19	20	21
(22)	(23)	(24)	(25)	(26)	(27)	(28)
22	23	24	25	26	27	28
(29)	(30d)	(1)	(2)	(3)	(4)	(5)
29	30					
(6)	(7)					

February (Shebat 11)

S	M	T	W	T	F	S
				1	2	3
				(9)	(10)	(11)
4	5	6	7	8	9	10
(12)	(13)	(14)	(15)	(16)	(17)	(18)
11	12	13	14	15	16	17
(19)	(20)	(21)	(22)	(23)	(24)	(25)
18	19	20	21	22	23	24
(26)	(27)	(28)	(29)	(30b)	(1)	(2)
25	26	27	28			
(3)	(4)	(5)	(6)			

May (Iyyar 2)

S	M	T	W	T	F	S
		1	2	3	4	5
		(8)	(9)	(10)	(11)	(12)
6	7	8	9	10	11	12
(13)	(14)	(15)	(16)	(17)	(18)	(19)
13	14	15	16	17	18	19
(20)	(21)	(22)	(23)	(24)	(25)	(26)
20	21	22	23	24	25	26
(27)	(28)	(29e)	(1)	(2)	(3)	(4)
27	28	29	30	31		
(5)	(6)	(7)	(8)	(9)		

March (Adar 12)

S	M	T	W	T	F	S
				1	2	3
				(7)	(8)	(9)
4	5	6	7	8	9	10
(10)	(11)	(12)	(13)	(14)	(15)	(16)
11	12	13	14	15	16	17
(17)	(18)	(19)	(20)	(21)	(22)	(23)
18	19	20	21	22	23	24
(24)	(25)	(26)	(27)	(28)	(29)	(30c)
25	26	27	28	29	30	31
(1)	(2)	(3)	(4)	(5)	(6)	(7)

June (Sivan 3)

S	M	T	W	T	F	S
					1	2
					(10)	(11)
3	4	5	6	7	8	9
(12)	(13)	(14)	(15)	(16)	(17)	(18)
10	11	12	13	14	15	16
(19)	(20)	(21)	(22)	(23)	(24)	(25)
17	18	19	20	21	22	23
(26)	(27)	(28)	(29f)	(1)	(2)	(3)
24	25	26	27	28	29	30
(4)	(5)	(6)	(7)	(8)	(9)	(10)

Passover Lamb Sacrificed — Nisan 14
Feast of First Fruits — 1st Sunday after Nisan 15

Feast of Unleavened Bread — Nisan 15-21
Pentecost — 8th Sunday after Nisan 15

Time of New Moon (Jerusalem) —   a23:20   b17:48   c10:07   d23:43   e10:54   f20:14

A.D. 46

July
(Tammuz 4)

S	M	T	W	T	F	S
1	2	3	4	5	6	7
(11)	(12)	(13)	(14)	(15)	(16)	(17)
8	9	10	11	12	13	14
(18)	(19)	(20)	(21)	(22)	(23)	(24)
15	16	17	18	19	20	21
(25)	(26)	(27)	(28)	(29)	(30g)	(1)
22	23	24	25	26	27	28
(2)	(3)	(4)	(5)	(6)	(7)	(8)
29	30	31				
(9)	(10)	(11)				

October
(Tishri 7)

S	M	T	W	T	F	S
	1	2	3	4	5	6
	(15)	(16)	(17)	(18)	(19)	(20)
7	8	9	10	11	12	13
(21)	(22)	(23)	(24)	(25)	(26)	(27)
14	15	16	17	18	19	20
(28)	(29)	(30j)	(1)	(2)	(3)	(4)
21	22	23	24	25	26	27
(5)	(6)	(7)	(8)	(9)	(10)	(11)
28	29	30	31			
(12)	(13)	(14)	(15)			

August
(Ab 5)

S	M	T	W	T	F	S
			1	2	3	4
			(12)	(13)	(14)	(15)
5	6	7	8	9	10	11
(16)	(17)	(18)	(19)	(20)	(21)	(22)
12	13	14	15	16	17	18
(23)	(24)	(25)	(26)	(27)	(28)	(29h)
19	20	21	22	23	24	25
(1)	(2)	(3)	(4)	(5)	(6)	(7)
26	27	28	29	30	31	
(8)	(9)	(10)	(11)	(12)	(13)	

November
(Marheshvan 8)

S	M	T	W	T	F	S
				1	2	3
				(16)	(17)	(18)
4	5	6	7	8	9	10
(19)	(20)	(21)	(22)	(23)	(24)	(25)
11	12	13	14	15	16	17
(26)	(27)	(28)	(29k)	(1)	(2)	(3)
18	19	20	21	22	23	24
(4)	(5)	(6)	(7)	(8)	(9)	(10)
25	26	27	28	29	30	
(11)	(12)	(13)	(14)	(15)	(16)	

September
(Elul 6)

S	M	T	W	T	F	S
						1
						(14)
2	3	4	5	6	7	8
(15)	(16)	(17)	(18)	(19)	(20)	(21)
9	10	11	12	13	14	15
(22)	(23)	(24)	(25)	(26)	(27)	(28)
16	17	18	19	20	21	22
(29j)	(1)	(2)	(3)	(4)	(5)	(6)
23	24	25	26	27	28	29
(7)	(8)	(9)	(10)	(11)	(12)	(13)
30						
(14)						

December
(Kislev 9)

S	M	T	W	T	F	S
						1
						(17)
2	3	4	5	6	7	8
(18)	(19)	(20)	(21)	(22)	(23)	(24)
9	10	11	12	13	14	15
(25)	(26)	(27)	(28)	(29)	(30m)	(1)
16	17	18	19	20	21	22
(2)	(3)	(4)	(5)	(6)	(7)	(8)
23	24	25	26	27	28	29
(9)	(10)	(11)	(12)	(13)	(14)	(15)
30	31					
(16)	(17)					

Day of Trumpets — Tishri 1
Feast of Booths — Tishri 15-22

Day of Atonement — Tishri 10
Feast of Dedication — 8 days beginning Kislev 25

Time of the New Moon — g4:46   h12:58   i21:38   j7:28   k19:06   m8:56

A.D. 47

January
(Tebeth 10)

S	M	T	W	T	F	S
		1	2	3	4	5
		(18)	(19)	(20)	(21)	(22)
6	7	8	9	10	11	12
(23)	(24)	(25)	(26)	(27)	(28)	(29)
13	14	15	16	17	18	19
(30a)	(1)	(2)	(3)	(4)	(5)	(6)
20	21	22	23	24	25	26
(7)	(8)	(9)	(10)	(11)	(12)	(13)
27	28	29	30	31		
(14)	(15)	(16)	(17)	(18)		

February
(Shebat 11)

S	M	T	W	T	F	S
					1	2
					(19)	(20)
3	4	5	6	7	8	9
(21)	(22)	(23)	(24)	(25)	(26)	(27)
10	11	12	13	14	15	16
(28)	(29b)	(1)	(2)	(3)	(4)	(5)
17	18	19	20	21	22	23
(6)	(7)	(8)	(9)	(10)	(11)	(12)
24	25	26	27	28		
(13)	(14)	(15)	(16)	(17)		

March
(Adar 12)

S	M	T	W	T	F	S
					1	2
					(18)	(19)
3	4	5	6	7	8	9
(20)	(21)	(22)	(23)	(24)	(25)	(26)
10	11	12	13	14	15	16
(27)	(28)	(29)	(30c)	(1)	(2)	(3)
17	18	19	20	21	22	23
(4)	(5)	(6)	(7)	(8)	(9)	(10)
24	25	26	27	28	29	30
(11)	(12)	(13)	(14)	(15)	(16)	(17)
31						
(18)						

April
(Nisan 1)

S	M	T	W	T	F	S
	1	2	3	4	5	6
	(19)	(20)	(21)	(22)	(23)	(24)
7	8	9	10	11	12	13
(25)	(26)	(27)	(28)	(29)	(30d)	(1)
14	15	16	17	18	19	20
(2)	(3)	(4)	(5)	(6)	(7)	(8)
21	22	23	24	25	26	27
(9)	(10)	(11)	(12)	(13)	(14)	(15)
28	29	30				
(16)	(17)	(18)				

May
(Iyyar 2)

S	M	T	W	T	F	S
			1	2	3	4
			(19)	(20)	(21)	(22)
5	6	7	8	9	10	11
(23)	(24)	(25)	(26)	(27)	(28)	(29e)
12	13	14	15	16	17	18
(1)	(2)	(3)	(4)	(5)	(6)	(7)
19	20	21	22	23	24	25
(8)	(9)	(10)	(11)	(12)	(13)	(14)
26	27	28	29	30	31	
(15)	(16)	(17)	(18)	(19)	(20)	

June
(Sivan 3)

S	M	T	W	T	F	S
						1
						(21)
2	3	4	5	6	7	8
(22)	(23)	(24)	(25)	(26)	(27)	(28)
9	10	11	12	13	14	15
(29)	(30f)	(1)	(2)	(3)	(4)	(5)
16	17	18	19	20	21	22
(6)	(7)	(8)	(9)	(10)	(11)	(12)
23	24	25	26	27	28	29
(13)	(14)	(15)	(16)	(17)	(18)	(19)
30						
(20)						

Passover Lamb Sacrificed — Nisan 14
Feast of First Fruits — 1st Sunday after Nisan 15

Feast of Unleavened Bread — Nisan 15-21
Pentecost — 8th Sunday after Nisan 15

Time of New Moon (Jerusalem) — a0:45　b17:42　c10:41　d2:48　e17:33　f6:41

A.D. 47

July
(Tammuz 4)

S	M	T	W	T	F	S
	1	2	3	4	5	6
	(21)	(22)	(23)	(24)	(25)	(26)
7	8	9	10	11	12	13
(27)	(28)	(29g)	(1)	(2)	(3)	(4)
14	15	16	17	18	19	20
(5)	(6)	(7)	(8)	(9)	(10)	(11)
21	22	23	24	25	26	27
(12)	(13)	(14)	(15)	(16)	(17)	(18)
28	29	30	31			
(19)	(20)	(21)	(22)			

August
(Ab 5)

S	M	T	W	T	F	S
				1	2	3
				(23)	(24)	(25)
4	5	6	7	8	9	10
(26)	(27)	(28)	(29)	(30h)	(1)	(2)
11	12	13	14	15	16	17
(3)	(4)	(5)	(6)	(7)	(8)	(9)
18	19	20	21	22	23	24
(10)	(11)	(12)	(13)	(14)	(15)	(16)
25	26	27	28	29	30	31
(17)	(18)	(19)	(20)	(21)	(22)	(23)

September
(Elul 6)

S	M	T	W	T	F	S
1	2	3	4	5	6	7
(24)	(25)	(26)	(27)	(28)	(29i)	(1)
8	9	10	11	12	13	14
(2)	(3)	(4)	(5)	(6)	(7)	(8)
15	16	17	18	19	20	21
(9)	(10)	(11)	(12)	(13)	(14)	(15)
22	23	24	25	26	27	28
(16)	(17)	(18)	(19)	(20)	(21)	(22)
29	30					
(23)	(24)					

October
(Tishri 7)

S	M	T	W	T	F	S
		1	2	3	4	5
		(25)	(26)	(27)	(28)	(29j)
6	7	8	9	10	11	12
(1)	(2)	(3)	(4)	(5)	(6)	(7)
13	14	15	16	17	18	19
(8)	(9)	(10)	(11)	(12)	(13)	(14)
20	21	22	23	24	25	26
(15)	(16)	(17)	(18)	(19)	(20)	(21)
27	28	29	30	31		
(22)	(23)	(24)	(25)	(26)		

November
(Marheshvan 8)

S	M	T	W	T	F	S
					1	2
					(27)	(28)
3	4	5	6	7	8	9
(29)	(30k)	(1)	(2)	(3)	(4)	(5)
10	11	12	13	14	15	16
(6)	(7)	(8)	(9)	(10)	(11)	(12)
17	18	19	20	21	22	23
(13)	(14)	(15)	(16)	(17)	(18)	(19)
24	25	26	27	28	29	30
(20)	(21)	(22)	(23)	(24)	(25)	(26)

December
(Kislev 9)

S	M	T	W	T	F	S
1	2	3	4	5	6	7
(27)	(28)	(29m)	(1)	(2)	(3)	(4)
8	9	10	11	12	13	14
(5)	(6)	(7)	(8)	(9)	(10)	(11)
15	16	17	18	19	20	21
(12)	(13)	(14)	(15)	(16)	(17)	(18)
22	23	24	25	26	27	28
(19)	(20)	(21)	(22)	(23)	(24)	(25)
29	30	31				
(26)	(27)	(28)				

Day of Trumpets — Tishri 1
Feast of Booths — Tishri 15-22

Day of Atonement — Tishri 10
Feast of Dedication — 8 days beginning Kislev 25

Time of the New Moon — g18:12   h4:22   i13:48   j23:15   k9:24   m20:37

A.D. 48

January
(Tebeth 10)

S	M	T	W	T	F	S
			1	2	3	4
			(29)	(30a)	(1)	(2)
5	6	7	8	9	10	11
(3)	(4)	(5)	(6)	(7)	(8)	(9)
12	13	14	15	16	17	18
(10)	(11)	(12)	(13)	(14)	(15)	(16)
19	20	21	22	23	24	25
(17)	(18)	(19)	(20)	(21)	(22)	(23)
26	27	28	29	30	31	
(24)	(25)	(26)	(27)	(28)	(29b)	

April
(Nisan 1)

S	M	T	W	T	F	S
			1	2	3	4
			(1)	(2)	(3)	(4)
5	6	7	8	9	10	11
(5)	(6)	(7)	(8)	(9)	(10)	(11)
12	13	14	15	16	17	18
(12)	(13)	(14)	(15)	(16)	(17)	(18)
19	20	21	22	23	24	25
(19)	(20)	(21)	(22)	(23)	(24)	(25)
26	27	28	29	30		
(26)	(27)	(28)	(29e)	(1)		

February
(Adar 12)

S	M	T	W	T	F	S
						1
						(1)
2	3	4	5	6	7	8
(2)	(3)	(4)	(5)	(6)	(7)	(8)
9	10	11	12	13	14	15
(9)	(10)	(11)	(12)	(13)	(14)	(15)
16	17	18	19	20	21	22
(16)	(17)	(18)	(19)	(20)	(21)	(22)
23	24	25	26	27	28	29
(23)	(24)	(25)	(26)	(27)	(28)	(29)

May
(Iyyar 2)

S	M	T	W	T	F	S
					1	2
					(2)	(3)
3	4	5	6	7	8	9
(4)	(5)	(6)	(7)	(8)	(9)	(10)
10	11	12	13	14	15	16
(11)	(12)	(13)	(14)	(15)	(16)	(17)
17	18	19	20	21	22	23
(18)	(19)	(20)	(21)	(22)	(23)	(24)
24	25	26	27	28	29	30
(25)	(26)	(27)	(28)	(29)	(30f)	(1)
31						
(2)						

March
(Adar 12)

S	M	T	W	T	F	S
1	2	3	4	5	6	7
(30c)	(1)	(2)	(3)	(4)	(5)	(6)
8	9	10	11	12	13	14
(7)	(8)	(9)	(10)	(11)	(12)	(13)
15	16	17	18	19	20	21
(14)	(15)	(16)	(17)	(18)	(19)	(20)
22	23	24	25	26	27	28
(21)	(22)	(23)	(24)	(25)	(26)	(27)
29	30	31				
(28)	(29)	(30d)				

June
(Sivan 3)

S	M	T	W	T	F	S
	1	2	3	4	5	6
	(3)	(4)	(5)	(6)	(7)	(8)
7	8	9	10	11	12	13
(9)	(10)	(11)	(12)	(13)	(14)	(15)
14	15	16	17	18	19	20
(16)	(17)	(18)	(19)	(20)	(21)	(22)
21	22	23	24	25	26	27
(23)	(24)	(25)	(26)	(27)	(28)	(29)
28	29	30				
(30g)	(1)	(2)				

Passover Lamb Sacrificed — Nisan 14
Feast of First Fruits — 1st Sunday after Nisan 15

Feast of Unleavened Bread — Nisan 15-21
Pentecost — 8th Sunday after Nisan 15

Time of New Moon (Jerusalem) — a8:58   b23:17   c12:24   d3:16   e18:40   f10:05   go:48

A.D. 48

July
(Tammuz 4)

S	M	T	W	T	F	S
			1	2	3	4
			(3)	(4)	(5)	(6)
5	6	7	8	9	10	11
(7)	(8)	(9)	(10)	(11)	(12)	(13)
12	13	14	15	16	17	18
(14)	(15)	(16)	(17)	(18)	(19)	(20)
19	20	21	22	23	24	25
(21)	(22)	(23)	(24)	(25)	(26)	(27)
26	27	28	29	30	31	
(28)	(29h)	(1)	(2)	(3)	(4)	

October
(Tishri 7)

S	M	T	W	T	F	S
				1	2	3
				(7)	(8)	(9)
4	5	6	7	8	9	10
(10)	(11)	(12)	(13)	(14)	(15)	(16)
11	12	13	14	15	16	17
(17)	(18)	(19)	(20)	(21)	(22)	(23)
18	19	20	21	22	23	24
(24)	(25)	(26)	(27)	(28)	(29)	(30k)
25	26	27	28	29	30	31
(1)	(2)	(3)	(4)	(5)	(6)	(7)

August
(Ab 5)

S	M	T	W	T	F	S
						1
						(5)
2	3	4	5	6	7	8
(6)	(7)	(8)	(9)	(10)	(11)	(12)
9	10	11	12	13	14	15
(13)	(14)	(15)	(16)	(17)	(18)	(19)
16	17	18	19	20	21	22
(20)	(21)	(22)	(23)	(24)	(25)	(26)
23	24	25	26	27	28	29
(27)	(28)	(29)	(30i)	(1)	(2)	(3)
30	31					
(4)	(5)					

November
(Marheshvan 8)

S	M	T	W	T	F	S
1	2	3	4	5	6	7
(8)	(9)	(10)	(11)	(12)	(13)	(14)
8	9	10	11	12	13	14
(15)	(16)	(17)	(18)	(19)	(20)	(21)
15	16	17	18	19	20	21
(22)	(23)	(24)	(25)	(26)	(27)	(28)
22	23	24	25	26	27	28
(29m)	(1)	(2)	(3)	(4)	(5)	(6)
29	30					
(7)	(8)					

September
(Elul 6)

S	M	T	W	T	F	S
		1	2	3	4	5
		(6)	(7)	(8)	(9)	(10)
6	7	8	9	10	11	12
(11)	(12)	(13)	(14)	(15)	(16)	(17)
13	14	15	16	17	18	19
(18)	(19)	(20)	(21)	(22)	(23)	(24)
20	21	22	23	24	25	26
(25)	(26)	(27)	(28)	(29j)	(1)	(2)
27	28	29	30			
(3)	(4)	(5)	(6)			

December
(Kislev 9)

S	M	T	W	T	F	S
		1	2	3	4	5
		(9)	(10)	(11)	(12)	(13)
6	7	8	9	10	11	12
(14)	(15)	(16)	(17)	(18)	(19)	(20)
13	14	15	16	17	18	19
(21)	(22)	(23)	(24)	(25)	(26)	(27)
20	21	22	23	24	25	26
(28)	(29n)	(1)	(2)	(3)	(4)	(5)
27	28	29	30	31		
(6)	(7)	(8)	(9)	(10)		

Day of Trumpets — Tishri 1
Feast of Booths — Tishri 15-22

Day of Atonement — Tishri 10
Feast of Dedication — 8 days beginning Kislev 25

Time of the New Moon — h14:19   i2:35   j14:02   k1:07   m12:07   n23:02

Gregorian
A.D. 49

January (Tebeth 10)						
S	M	T	W	T	F	S
					1 (11)	2 (12)
3 (13)	4 (14)	5 (15)	6 (16)	7 (17)	8 (18)	9 (19)
10 (20)	11 (21)	12 (22)	13 (23)	14 (24)	15 (25)	16 (26)
17 (27)	18 (28)	19 (29)	20 (30a)	21 (1)	22 (2)	23 (3)
24 (4)	25 (5)	26 (6)	27 (7)	28 (8)	29 (9)	30 (10)
31 (11)						

April (Nisan 1)						
S	M	T	W	T	F	S
				1 (12)	2 (13)	3 (14)
4 (15)	5 (16)	6 (17)	7 (18)	8 (19)	9 (20)	10 (21)
11 (22)	12 (23)	13 (24)	14 (25)	15 (26)	16 (27)	17 (28)
18 (29d)	19 (1)	20 (2)	21 (3)	22 (4)	23 (5)	24 (6)
25 (7)	26 (8)	27 (9)	28 (10)	29 (11)	30 (12)	

February (Shebat 11)						
S	M	T	W	T	F	S
	1 (12)	2 (13)	3 (14)	4 (15)	5 (16)	6 (17)
7 (18)	8 (19)	9 (20)	10 (21)	11 (22)	12 (23)	13 (24)
14 (25)	15 (26)	16 (27)	17 (28)	18 (29b)	19 (1)	20 (2)
21 (3)	22 (4)	23 (5)	24 (6)	25 (7)	26 (8)	27 (9)
28 (10)						

May (Iyyar 2)						
S	M	T	W	T	F	S
						1 (13)
2 (14)	3 (15)	4 (16)	5 (17)	6 (18)	7 (19)	8 (20)
9 (21)	10 (22)	11 (23)	12 (24)	13 (25)	14 (26)	15 (27)
16 (28)	17 (29)	18 (30e)	19 (1)	20 (2)	21 (3)	22 (4)
23 (5)	24 (6)	25 (7)	26 (8)	27 (9)	28 (10)	29 (11)
30 (12)	31 (13)					

March (Adar 12)						
S	M	T	W	T	F	S
	1 (11)	2 (12)	3 (13)	4 (14)	5 (15)	6 (16)
7 (17)	8 (18)	9 (19)	10 (20)	11 (21)	12 (22)	13 (23)
14 (24)	15 (25)	16 (26)	17 (27)	18 (28)	19 (29)	20 (30c)
21 (1)	22 (2)	23 (3)	24 (4)	25 (5)	26 (6)	27 (7)
28 (8)	29 (9)	30 (10)	31 (11)			

June (Sivan 3)						
S	M	T	W	T	F	S
		1 (14)	2 (15)	3 (16)	4 (17)	5 (18)
6 (19)	7 (20)	8 (21)	9 (22)	10 (23)	11 (24)	12 (25)
13 (26)	14 (27)	15 (28)	16 (29)	17 (30f)	18 (1)	19 (2)
20 (3)	21 (4)	22 (5)	23 (6)	24 (7)	25 (8)	26 (9)
27 (10)	28 (11)	29 (12)	30 (13)			

Passover Lamb Sacrificed — Nisan 14
Feast of First Fruits — 1st Sunday after Nisan 15

Feast of Unleavened Bread — Nisan 15-21
Pentecost — 8th Sunday after Nisan 15

Time of New Moon (Jerusalem) —   a9:50   b20:46   c0:19   d21:00   e10:59   f1:57

A.D. 49

July
(Tammuz 4)

S	M	T	W	T	F	S
				1	2	3
				(14)	(15)	(16)
4	5	6	7	8	9	10
(17)	(18)	(19)	(20)	(21)	(22)	(23)
11	12	13	14	15	16	17
(24)	(25)	(26)	(27)	(28)	(29g)	(1)
18	19	20	21	22	23	24
(2)	(3)	(4)	(5)	(6)	(7)	(8)
25	26	27	28	29	30	31
(9)	(10)	(11)	(12)	(13)	(14)	(15)

October
(Tishri 7)

S	M	T	W	T	F	S
					1	2
					(17)	(18)
3	4	5	6	7	8	9
(19)	(20)	(21)	(22)	(23)	(24)	(25)
10	11	12	13	14	15	16
(26)	(27)	(28)	(29j)	(1)	(2)	(3)
17	18	19	20	21	22	23
(4)	(5)	(6)	(7)	(8)	(9)	(10)
24	25	26	27	28	29	30
(11)	(12)	(13)	(14)	(15)	(16)	(17)
31						
(18)						

August
(Ab 5)

S	M	T	W	T	F	S
1	2	3	4	5	6	7
(16)	(17)	(18)	(19)	(20)	(21)	(22)
8	9	10	11	12	13	14
(23)	(24)	(25)	(26)	(27)	(28)	(29)
15	16	17	18	19	20	21
(30h)	(1)	(2)	(3)	(4)	(5)	(6)
22	23	24	25	26	27	28
(7)	(8)	(9)	(10)	(11)	(12)	(13)
29	30	31				
(14)	(15)	(16)				

November
(Marheshvan 8)

S	M	T	W	T	F	S
	1	2	3	4	5	6
	(19)	(20)	(21)	(22)	(23)	(24)
7	8	9	10	11	12	13
(25)	(26)	(27)	(28)	(29)	(30k)	(1)
14	15	16	17	18	19	20
(2)	(3)	(4)	(5)	(6)	(7)	(8)
21	22	23	24	25	26	27
(9)	(10)	(11)	(12)	(13)	(14)	(15)
28	29	30				
(16)	(17)	(18)				

September
(Elul 6)

S	M	T	W	T	F	S
			1	2	3	4
			(17)	(18)	(19)	(20)
5	6	7	8	9	10	11
(21)	(22)	(23)	(24)	(25)	(26)	(27)
12	13	14	15	16	17	18
(28)	(29)	(30i)	(1)	(2)	(3)	(4)
19	20	21	22	23	24	25
(5)	(6)	(7)	(8)	(9)	(10)	(11)
26	27	28	29	30		
(12)	(13)	(14)	(15)	(16)		

December
(Kislev 9)

S	M	T	W	T	F	S
			1	2	3	4
			(19)	(20)	(21)	(22)
5	6	7	8	9	10	11
(23)	(24)	(25)	(26)	(27)	(28)	(29m)
12	13	14	15	16	17	18
(1)	(2)	(3)	(4)	(5)	(6)	(7)
19	20	21	22	23	24	25
(8)	(9)	(10)	(11)	(12)	(13)	(14)
26	27	28	29	30	31	
(15)	(16)	(17)	(18)	(19)	(20)	

Day of Trumpets — Tishri 1
Feast of Booths — Tishri 15-22

Day of Atonement — Tishri 10
Feast of Dedication — 8 days beginning Kislev 25

Time of the New Moon — g17:20   h8:37   i23:27   j13:37   k2:47   m14:43

Gregorian

A.D. 50

January
(Tebeth 10)

S	M	T	W	T	F	S
						1
						(21)
2	3	4	5	6	7	8
(22)	(23)	(24)	(25)	(26)	(27)	(28)
9	10	11	12	13	14	15
(29)	(30a)	(1)	(2)	(3)	(4)	(5)
16	17	18	19	20	21	22
(6)	(7)	(8)	(9)	(10)	(11)	(12)
23	24	25	26	27	28	29
(13)	(14)	(15)	(16)	(17)	(18)	(19)
30	31					
(20)	(21)					

April
(Nisan 1)

S	M	T	W	T	F	S
					1	2
					(23)	(24)
3	4	5	6	7	8	9
(25)	(26)	(27)	(28)	(29)	(30d)	(1)
10	11	12	13	14	15	16
(2)	(3)	(4)	(5)	(6)	(7)	(8)
17	18	19	20	21	22	23
(9)	(10)	(11)	(12)	(13)	(14)	(15)
24	25	26	27	28	29	30
(16)	(17)	(18)	(19)	(20)	(21)	(22)

February
(Shebat 11)

S	M	T	W	T	F	S
		1	2	3	4	5
		(22)	(23)	(24)	(25)	(26)
6	7	8	9	10	11	12
(27)	(28)	(29b)	(1)	(2)	(3)	(4)
13	14	15	16	17	18	19
(5)	(6)	(7)	(8)	(9)	(10)	(11)
20	21	22	23	24	25	26
(12)	(13)	(14)	(15)	(16)	(17)	(18)
27	28					
(19)	(20)					

May
(Iyyar 2)

S	M	T	W	T	F	S
1	2	3	4	5	6	7
(23)	(24)	(25)	(26)	(27)	(28)	(29e)
8	9	10	11	12	13	14
(1)	(2)	(3)	(4)	(5)	(6)	(7)
15	16	17	18	19	20	21
(8)	(9)	(10)	(11)	(12)	(13)	(14)
22	23	24	25	26	27	28
(15)	(16)	(17)	(18)	(19)	(20)	(21)
29	30	31				
(22)	(23)	(24)				

March
(Adar 12)

S	M	T	W	T	F	S
		1	2	3	4	5
		(21)	(22)	(23)	(24)	(25)
6	7	8	9	10	11	12
(26)	(27)	(28)	(29c)	(1)	(2)	(3)
13	14	15	16	17	18	19
(4)	(5)	(6)	(7)	(8)	(9)	(10)
20	21	22	23	24	25	26
(11)	(12)	(13)	(14)	(15)	(16)	(17)
27	28	29	30	31		
(18)	(19)	(20)	(21)	(22)		

June
(Sivan 3)

S	M	T	W	T	F	S
			1	2	3	4
			(25)	(26)	(27)	(28)
5	6	7	8	9	10	11
(29)	(30f)	(1)	(2)	(3)	(4)	(5)
12	13	14	15	16	17	18
(6)	(7)	(8)	(9)	(10)	(11)	(12)
19	20	21	22	23	24	25
(13)	(14)	(15)	(16)	(17)	(18)	(19)
26	27	28	29	30		
(20)	(21)	(22)	(23)	(24)		

Passover Lamb Sacrificed — Nisan 14
Feast of First Fruits — 1st Sunday after Nisan 15

Feast of Unleavened Bread — Nisan 15-21
Pentecost — 8th Sunday after Nisan 15

Time of New Moon (Jerusalem) —   a1:22   b11:04   c20:22   d5:58   e16:30   f4:25

A.D. 50

July
(Tammuz 4)

S	M	T	W	T	F	S
					1	2
					(25)	(26)
3	4	5	6	7	8	9
(27)	(28)	(29g)	(1)	(2)	(3)	(4)
10	11	12	13	14	15	16
(5)	(6)	(7)	(8)	(9)	(10)	(11)
17	18	19	20	21	22	23
(12)	(13)	(14)	(15)	(16)	(17)	(18)
24	25	26	27	28	29	30
(19)	(20)	(21)	(22)	(23)	(24)	(25)
31						
(26)						

October
(Tishri 7)

S	M	T	W	T	F	S
						1
						(28)
2	3	4	5	6	7	8
(29j)	(1)	(2)	(3)	(4)	(5)	(6)
9	10	11	12	13	14	15
(7)	(8)	(9)	(10)	(11)	(12)	(13)
16	17	18	19	20	21	22
(14)	(15)	(16)	(17)	(18)	(19)	(20)
23	24	25	26	27	28	29
(21)	(22)	(23)	(24)	(25)	(26)	(27)
30	31					
(28)	(29)					

August
(Ab 5)

S	M	T	W	T	F	S
	1	2	3	4	5	6
	(27)	(28)	(29)	(30h)	(1)	(2)
7	8	9	10	11	12	13
(3)	(4)	(5)	(6)	(7)	(8)	(9)
14	15	16	17	18	19	20
(10)	(11)	(12)	(13)	(14)	(15)	(16)
21	22	23	24	25	26	27
(17)	(18)	(19)	(20)	(21)	(22)	(23)
28	29	30	31			
(24)	(25)	(26)	(27)			

November
(Marheshvan 8)

S	M	T	W	T	F	S
		1	2	3	4	5
		(30k)	(1)	(2)	(3)	(4)
6	7	8	9	10	11	12
(5)	(6)	(7)	(8)	(9)	(10)	(11)
13	14	15	16	17	18	19
(12)	(13)	(14)	(15)	(16)	(17)	(18)
20	21	22	23	24	25	26
(19)	(20)	(21)	(22)	(23)	(24)	(25)
27	28	29	30			
(26)	(27)	(28)	(29)			

September
(Elul 6)

S	M	T	W	T	F	S
				1	2	3
				(28)	(29)	(30i)
4	5	6	7	8	9	10
(1)	(2)	(3)	(4)	(5)	(6)	(7)
11	12	13	14	15	16	17
(8)	(9)	(10)	(11)	(12)	(13)	(14)
18	19	20	21	22	23	24
(15)	(16)	(17)	(18)	(19)	(20)	(21)
25	26	27	28	29	30	
(22)	(23)	(24)	(25)	(26)	(27)	

December
(Kislev 9)

S	M	T	W	T	F	S
				1	2	3
				(30m)	(1)	(2)
4	5	6	7	8	9	10
(3)	(4)	(5)	(6)	(7)	(8)	(9)
11	12	13	14	15	16	17
(10)	(11)	(12)	(13)	(14)	(15)	(16)
18	19	20	21	22	23	24
(17)	(18)	(19)	(20)	(21)	(22)	(23)
25	26	27	28	29	30	31
(24)	(25)	(26)	(27)	(28)	(29n)	(1)

Day of Trumpets — Tishri 1
Feast of Booths — Tishri 15-22

Day of Atonement — Tishri 10
Feast of Dedication — 8 days beginning Kislev 25

Time of the New Moon — g17:58 h9:13 i1:57 j19:21 k12:13 m3:32 n16:17

A.D. 51

January
(Shebat 11)

S	M	T	W	T	F	S
1	2	3	4	5	6	7
(2)	(3)	(4)	(5)	(6)	(7)	(8)
8	9	10	11	12	13	14
(9)	(10)	(11)	(12)	(13)	(14)	(15)
15	16	17	18	19	20	21
(16)	(17)	(18)	(19)	(20)	(21)	(22)
22	23	24	25	26	27	28
(23)	(24)	(25)	(26)	(27)	(28)	(29)
29	30	31				
(30a)	(1)	(2)				

April
(Nisan 1)

S	M	T	W	T	F	S
						1
						(4)
2	3	4	5	6	7	8
(5)	(6)	(7)	(8)	(9)	(10)	(11)
9	10	11	12	13	14	15
(12)	(13)	(14)	(15)	(16)	(17)	(18)
16	17	18	19	20	21	22
(19)	(20)	(21)	(22)	(23)	(24)	(25)
23	24	25	26	27	28	29
(26)	(27)	(28)	(29)	(30d)	(1)	(2)
30						
(3)						

February
(Adar 12)

S	M	T	W	T	F	S
			1	2	3	4
			(3)	(4)	(5)	(6)
5	6	7	8	9	10	11
(7)	(8)	(9)	(10)	(11)	(12)	(13)
12	13	14	15	16	17	18
(14)	(15)	(16)	(17)	(18)	(19)	(20)
19	20	21	22	23	24	25
(21)	(22)	(23)	(24)	(25)	(26)	(27)
26	27	28				
(28)	(29b)	(1)				

May
(Iyyar 2)

S	M	T	W	T	F	S
	1	2	3	4	5	6
	(4)	(5)	(6)	(7)	(8)	(9)
7	8	9	10	11	12	13
(10)	(11)	(12)	(13)	(14)	(15)	(16)
14	15	16	17	18	19	20
(17)	(18)	(19)	(20)	(21)	(22)	(23)
21	22	23	24	25	26	27
(24)	(25)	(26)	(27)	(28)	(29e)	(1)
28	29	30	31			
(2)	(3)	(4)	(5)			

March
(Adar II 13)

S	M	T	W	T	F	S
			1	2	3	4
			(2)	(3)	(4)	(5)
5	6	7	8	9	10	11
(6)	(7)	(8)	(9)	(10)	(11)	(12)
12	13	14	15	16	17	18
(13)	(14)	(15)	(16)	(17)	(18)	(19)
19	20	21	22	23	24	25
(20)	(21)	(22)	(23)	(24)	(25)	(26)
26	27	28	29	30	31	
(27)	(28)	(29c)	(1)	(2)	(3)	

June
(Sivan 3)

S	M	T	W	T	F	S
				1	2	3
				(6)	(7)	(8)
4	5	6	7	8	9	10
(9)	(10)	(11)	(12)	(13)	(14)	(15)
11	12	13	14	15	16	17
(16)	(17)	(18)	(19)	(20)	(21)	(22)
18	19	20	21	22	23	24
(23)	(24)	(25)	(26)	(27)	(28)	(29)
25	26	27	28	29	30	
(30f)	(1)	(2)	(3)	(4)	(5)	

Passover Lamb Sacrificed — Nisan 14

Feast of First Fruits — 1st Sunday after Nisan 15

Feast of Unleavened Bread — Nisan 15-21

Pentecost — 8th Sunday after Nisan 15

Time of New Moon (Jerusalem) — a3:09   b12:30   c20:55   d5:03   e13:35   f23:22

A.D. 51

July
(Tammuz 4)

S	M	T	W	T	F	S
						1
						(6)
2	3	4	5	6	7	8
(7)	(8)	(9)	(10)	(11)	(12)	(13)
9	10	11	12	13	14	15
(14)	(15)	(16)	(17)	(18)	(19)	(20)
16	17	18	19	20	21	22
(21)	(22)	(23)	(24)	(25)	(26)	(27)
23	24	25	26	27	28	29
(28)	(29g)	(1)	(2)	(3)	(4)	(5)
30	31					
(6)	(7)					

October
(Tishri 7)

S	M	T	W	T	F	S
1	2	3	4	5	6	7
(10)	(11)	(12)	(13)	(14)	(15)	(16)
8	9	10	11	12	13	14
(17)	(18)	(19)	(20)	(21)	(22)	(23)
15	16	17	18	19	20	21
(24)	(25)	(26)	(27)	(28)	(29)	(30j)
22	23	24	25	26	27	28
(1)	(2)	(3)	(4)	(5)	(6)	(7)
29	30	31				
(8)	(9)	(10)				

August
(Ab 5)

S	M	T	W	T	F	S
		1	2	3	4	5
		(8)	(9)	(10)	(11)	(12)
6	7	8	9	10	11	12
(13)	(14)	(15)	(16)	(17)	(18)	(19)
13	14	15	16	17	18	19
(20)	(21)	(22)	(23)	(24)	(25)	(26)
20	21	22	23	24	25	26
(27)	(28)	(29)	(30h)	(1)	(2)	(3)
27	28	29	30	31		
(4)	(5)	(6)	(7)	(8)		

November
(Marheshvan 8)

S	M	T	W	T	F	S
			1	2	3	4
			(11)	(12)	(13)	(14)
5	6	7	8	9	10	11
(15)	(16)	(17)	(18)	(19)	(20)	(21)
12	13	14	15	16	17	18
(22)	(23)	(24)	(25)	(26)	(27)	(28)
19	20	21	22	23	24	25
(29)	(30k)	(1)	(2)	(3)	(4)	(5)
26	27	28	29	30		
(6)	(7)	(8)	(9)	(10)		

September
(Elul 6)

S	M	T	W	T	F	S
					1	2
					(9)	(10)
3	4	5	6	7	8	9
(11)	(12)	(13)	(14)	(15)	(16)	(17)
10	11	12	13	14	15	16
(18)	(19)	(20)	(21)	(22)	(23)	(24)
17	18	19	20	21	22	23
(25)	(26)	(27)	(28)	(29i)	(1)	(2)
24	25	26	27	28	29	30
(3)	(4)	(5)	(6)	(7)	(8)	(9)

December
(Kislev 9)

S	M	T	W	T	F	S
					1	2
					(11)	(12)
3	4	5	6	7	8	9
(13)	(14)	(15)	(16)	(17)	(18)	(19)
10	11	12	13	14	15	16
(20)	(21)	(22)	(23)	(24)	(25)	(26)
17	18	19	20	21	22	23
(27)	(28)	(29)	(30m)	(1)	(2)	(3)
24	25	26	27	28	29	30
(4)	(5)	(6)	(7)	(8)	(9)	(10)
31						
(11)						

Day of Trumpets — Tishri 1
Feast of Booths — Tishri 15-22

Day of Atonement — Tishri 10
Feast of Dedication — 8 days beginning Kislev 25

Time of the New Moon —   g11:18   h2:03   i19:31   j14:31   k9:14   m2:05

A.D. 52

January (Tebeth 10)						
S	M	T	W	T	F	S
	1	2	3	4	5	6
	(12)	(13)	(14)	(15)	(16)	(17)
7	8	9	10	11	12	13
(18)	(19)	(20)	(21)	(22)	(23)	(24)
14	15	16	17	18	19	20
(25)	(26)	(27)	(28)	(29a)	(1)	(2)
21	22	23	24	25	26	27
(3)	(4)	(5)	(6)	(7)	(8)	(9)
28	29	30	31			
(10)	(11)	(12)	(13)			

April (Nisan 1)						
S	M	T	W	T	F	S
	1	2	3	4	5	6
	(15)	(16)	(17)	(18)	(19)	(20)
7	8	9	10	11	12	13
(21)	(22)	(23)	(24)	(25)	(26)	(27)
14	15	16	17	18	19	20
(28)	(29d)	(1)	(2)	(3)	(4)	(5)
21	22	23	24	25	26	27
(6)	(7)	(8)	(9)	(10)	(11)	(12)
28	29	30				
(13)	(14)	(15)				

February (Shebat 11)						
S	M	T	W	T	F	S
				1	2	3
				(14)	(15)	(16)
4	5	6	7	8	9	10
(17)	(18)	(19)	(20)	(21)	(22)	(23)
11	12	13	14	15	16	17
(24)	(25)	(26)	(27)	(28)	(29)	(30b)
18	19	20	21	22	23	24
(1)	(2)	(3)	(4)	(5)	(6)	(7)
25	26	27	28	29		
(8)	(9)	(10)	(11)	(12)		

May (Iyyar 2)						
S	M	T	W	T	F	S
			1	2	3	4
			(16)	(17)	(18)	(19)
5	6	7	8	9	10	11
(20)	(21)	(22)	(23)	(24)	(25)	(26)
12	13	14	15	16	17	18
(27)	(28)	(29)	(30e)	(1)	(2)	(3)
19	20	21	22	23	24	25
(4)	(5)	(6)	(7)	(8)	(9)	(10)
26	27	28	29	30	31	
(11)	(12)	(13)	(14)	(15)	(16)	

March (Adar 12)						
S	M	T	W	T	F	S
					1	2
					(13)	(14)
3	4	5	6	7	8	9
(15)	(16)	(17)	(18)	(19)	(20)	(21)
10	11	12	13	14	15	16
(22)	(23)	(24)	(25)	(26)	(27)	(28)
17	18	19	20	21	22	23
(29c)	(1)	(2)	(3)	(4)	(5)	(6)
24	25	26	27	28	29	30
(7)	(8)	(9)	(10)	(11)	(12)	(13)
31						
(14)						

June (Sivan 3)						
S	M	T	W	T	F	S
						1
						(17)
2	3	4	5	6	7	8
(18)	(19)	(20)	(21)	(22)	(23)	(24)
9	10	11	12	13	14	15
(25)	(26)	(27)	(28)	(29f)	(1)	(2)
16	17	18	19	20	21	22
(3)	(4)	(5)	(6)	(7)	(8)	(9)
23	24	25	26	27	28	29
(10)	(11)	(12)	(13)	(14)	(15)	(16)
30						
(17)						

Passover Lamb Sacrificed — Nisan 14
Feast of First Fruits — 1st Sunday after Nisan 15

Feast of Unleavened Bread — Nisan 15-21
Pentecost — 8th Sunday after Nisan 15

Time of New Moon (Jerusalem) —   a16:23   b4:10   c13:47   d23:45   e4:47   f11:55

A.D. 52

July
(Tammuz 4)

S	M	T	W	T	F	S
	1	2	3	4	5	6
	(18)	(19)	(20)	(21)	(22)	(23)
7	8	9	10	11	12	13
(24)	(25)	(26)	(27)	(28)	(29g)	(1)
14	15	16	17	18	19	20
(2)	(3)	(4)	(5)	(6)	(7)	(8)
21	22	23	24	25	26	27
(9)	(10)	(11)	(12)	(13)	(14)	(15)
28	29	30	31			
(16)	(17)	(18)	(19)			

August
(Ab 5)

S	M	T	W	T	F	S
				1	2	3
				(20)	(21)	(22)
4	5	6	7	8	9	10
(23)	(24)	(25)	(26)	(27)	(28)	(29)
11	12	13	14	15	16	17
(30h)	(1)	(2)	(3)	(4)	(5)	(6)
18	19	20	21	22	23	24
(7)	(8)	(9)	(10)	(11)	(12)	(13)
25	26	27	28	29	30	31
(14)	(15)	(16)	(17)	(18)	(19)	(20)

September
(Elul 6)

S	M	T	W	T	F	S
1	2	3	4	5	6	7
(21)	(22)	(23)	(24)	(25)	(26)	(27)
8	9	10	11	12	13	14
(28)	(29i)	(1)	(2)	(3)	(4)	(5)
15	16	17	18	19	20	21
(6)	(7)	(8)	(9)	(10)	(11)	(12)
22	23	24	25	26	27	28
(13)	(14)	(15)	(16)	(17)	(18)	(19)
29	30					
(20)	(21)					

October
(Tishri 7)

S	M	T	W	T	F	S
		1	2	3	4	5
		(22)	(23)	(24)	(25)	(26)
6	7	8	9	10	11	12
(27)	(28)	(29)	(30j)	(1)	(2)	(3)
13	14	15	16	17	18	19
(4)	(5)	(6)	(7)	(8)	(9)	(10)
20	21	22	23	24	25	26
(11)	(12)	(13)	(14)	(15)	(16)	(17)
27	28	29	30	31		
(18)	(19)	(20)	(21)	(22)		

November
(Marheshvan 8)

S	M	T	W	T	F	S
					1	2
					(23)	(24)
3	4	5	6	7	8	9
(25)	(26)	(27)	(28)	(29)	(30k)	(1)
10	11	12	13	14	15	16
(2)	(3)	(4)	(5)	(6)	(7)	(8)
17	18	19	20	21	22	23
(9)	(10)	(11)	(12)	(13)	(14)	(15)
24	25	26	27	28	29	30
(16)	(17)	(18)	(19)	(20)	(21)	(22)

December
(Kislev 9)

S	M	T	W	T	F	S
1	2	3	4	5	6	7
(23)	(24)	(25)	(26)	(27)	(28)	(29)
8	9	10	11	12	13	14
(30m)	(1)	(2)	(3)	(4)	(5)	(6)
15	16	17	18	19	20	21
(7)	(8)	(9)	(10)	(11)	(12)	(13)
22	23	24	25	26	27	28
(14)	(15)	(16)	(17)	(18)	(19)	(20)
29	30	31				
(21)	(22)	(23)				

Day of Trumpets — Tishri 1
Feast of Booths — Tishri 15-22

Day of Atonement — Tishri 10
Feast of Dedication — 8 days beginning Kislev 25

Time of the New Moon — g20:17 h7:03 i20:58 j13:59 k9:02 m4:33

Gregorian

A.D. 53

January
(Tebeth 10)

S	M	T	W	T	F	S
			1	2	3	4
			(24)	(25)	(26)	(27)
5	6	7	8	9	10	11
(28)	(29a)	(1)	(2)	(3)	(4)	(5)
12	13	14	15	16	17	18
(6)	(7)	(8)	(9)	(10)	(11)	(12)
19	20	21	22	23	24	25
(13)	(14)	(15)	(16)	(17)	(18)	(19)
26	27	28	29	30	31	
(20)	(21)	(22)	(23)	(24)	(25)	

April
(Nisan 1)

S	M	T	W	T	F	S
		1	2	3	4	5
		(25)	(26)	(27)	(28)	(29d)
6	7	8	9	10	11	12
(1)	(2)	(3)	(4)	(5)	(6)	(7)
13	14	15	16	17	18	19
(8)	(9)	(10)	(11)	(12)	(13)	(14)
20	21	22	23	24	25	26
(15)	(16)	(17)	(18)	(19)	(20)	(21)
27	28	29	30			
(22)	(23)	(24)	(25)			

February
(Shebat 11)

S	M	T	W	T	F	S
						1
						(26)
2	3	4	5	6	7	8
(27)	(28)	(29)	(30b)	(1)	(2)	(3)
9	10	11	12	13	14	15
(4)	(5)	(6)	(7)	(8)	(9)	(10)
16	17	18	19	20	21	22
(11)	(12)	(13)	(14)	(15)	(16)	(17)
23	24	25	26	27	28	
(18)	(19)	(20)	(21)	(22)	(23)	

May
(Iyyar 2)

S	M	T	W	T	F	S
				1	2	3
				(26)	(27)	(28)
4	5	6	7	8	9	10
(29e)	(1)	(2)	(3)	(4)	(5)	(6)
11	12	13	14	15	16	17
(7)	(8)	(9)	(10)	(11)	(12)	(13)
18	19	20	21	22	23	24
(14)	(15)	(16)	(17)	(18)	(19)	(20)
25	26	27	28	29	30	31
(21)	(22)	(23)	(24)	(25)	(26)	(27)

March
(Adar 12)

S	M	T	W	T	F	S
						1
						(24)
2	3	4	5	6	7	8
(25)	(26)	(27)	(28)	(29)	(30c)	(1)
9	10	11	12	13	14	15
(2)	(3)	(4)	(5)	(6)	(7)	(8)
16	17	18	19	20	21	22
(9)	(10)	(11)	(12)	(13)	(14)	(15)
23	24	25	26	27	28	29
(16)	(17)	(18)	(19)	(20)	(21)	(22)
30	31					
(23)	(24)					

June
(Sivan 3)

S	M	T	W	T	F	S
1	2	3	4	5	6	7
(28)	(29)	(30f)	(1)	(2)	(3)	(4)
8	9	10	11	12	13	14
(5)	(6)	(7)	(8)	(9)	(10)	(11)
15	16	17	18	19	20	21
(12)	(13)	(14)	(15)	(16)	(17)	(18)
22	23	24	25	26	27	28
(19)	(20)	(21)	(22)	(23)	(24)	(25)
29	30					
(26)	(27)					

Passover Lamb Sacrificed — Nisan 14
Feast of First Fruits — 1st Sunday after Nisan 15

Feast of Unleavened Bread — Nisan 15-21
Pentecost — 8th Sunday after Nisan 15

Time of New Moon (Jerusalem) — a22;54   b14:54   c3:57   d14:07   e22:01   f4:44

A.D. 53

July						
(Tammuz 4)						
S	M	T	W	T	F	S
		1	2	3	4	5
		(28)	(29g)	(1)	(2)	(3)
6	7	8	9	10	11	12
(4)	(5)	(6)	(7)	(8)	(9)	(10)
13	14	15	16	17	18	19
(11)	(12)	(13)	(14)	(15)	(16)	(17)
20	21	22	23	24	25	26
(18)	(19)	(20)	(21)	(22)	(23)	(24)
27	28	29	30	31		
(25)	(26)	(27)	(28)	(29h)		

October						
(Marheshvan 8)						
S	M	T	W	T	F	S
			1	2	3	4
			(3)	(4)	(5)	(6)
5	6	7	8	9	10	11
(7)	(8)	(9)	(10)	(11)	(12)	(13)
12	13	14	15	16	17	18
(14)	(15)	(16)	(17)	(18)	(19)	(20)
19	20	21	22	23	24	25
(21)	(22)	(23)	(24)	(25)	(26)	(27)
26	27	28	29	30	31	
(28)	(29)	(30k)	(1)	(2)	(3)	

August						
(Elul 6)						
S	M	T	W	T	F	S
					1	2
					(1)	(2)
3	4	5	6	7	8	9
(3)	(4)	(5)	(6)	(7)	(8)	(9)
10	11	12	13	14	15	16
(10)	(11)	(12)	(13)	(14)	(15)	(16)
17	18	19	20	21	22	23
(17)	(18)	(19)	(20)	(21)	(22)	(23)
24	25	26	27	28	29	30
(24)	(25)	(26)	(27)	(28)	(29)	(30i)
31						
(1)						

November						
(Kislev 9)						
S	M	T	W	T	F	S
						1
						(4)
2	3	4	5	6	7	8
(5)	(6)	(7)	(8)	(9)	(10)	(11)
9	10	11	12	13	14	15
(12)	(13)	(14)	(15)	(16)	(17)	(18)
16	17	18	19	20	21	22
(19)	(20)	(21)	(22)	(23)	(24)	(25)
23	24	25	26	27	28	29
(26)	(27)	(28)	(29)	(30m)	(1)	(2)
30						
(3)						

September						
(Tishri 7)						
S	M	T	W	T	F	S
	1	2	3	4	5	6
	(2)	(3)	(4)	(5)	(6)	(7)
7	8	9	10	11	12	13
(8)	(9)	(10)	(11)	(12)	(13)	(14)
14	15	16	17	18	19	20
(15)	(16)	(17)	(18)	(19)	(20)	(21)
21	22	23	24	25	25	27
(22)	(23)	(24)	(25)	(26)	(27)	(28)
28	29	30				
(29j)	(1)	(2)				

December						
(Tebeth 10)						
S	M	T	W	T	F	S
	1	2	3	4	5	6
	(4)	(5)	(6)	(7)	(8)	(9)
7	8	9	10	11	12	13
(10)	(11)	(12)	(13)	(14)	(15)	(16)
14	15	16	17	18	19	20
(17)	(18)	(19)	(20)	(21)	(22)	(23)
21	22	23	24	25	26	27
(24)	(25)	(26)	(27)	(28)	(29n)	(1)
28	29	30	31			
(2)	(3)	(4)	(5)			

Day of Trumpets — Tishri 1
Feast of Booths — Tishri 15-22

Day of Atonement — Tishri 10
Feast of Dedication — 8 days beginning Kislev 25

Time of the New Moon — g11:26 h19:20 i5:21 j18:03 k9:36 m3:36 n22:02

A.D. 54

January
(Shebat 11)

S	M	T	W	T	F	S
				1	2	3
				(6)	(7)	(8)
4	5	6	7	8	9	10
(9)	(10)	(11)	(12)	(13)	(14)	(15)
11	12	13	14	15	16	17
(16)	(17)	(18)	(19)	(20)	(21)	(22)
18	19	20	21	22	23	24
(23)	(24)	(25)	(26)	(27)	(28)	(29)
25	26	27	28	29	30	31
(30a)	(1)	(2)	(3)	(4)	(5)	(6)

April
(Nisan 1)

S	M	T	W	T	F	S
			1	2	3	4
			(6)	(7)	(8)	(9)
5	6	7	8	9	10	11
(10)	(11)	(12)	(13)	(14)	(15)	(16)
12	13	14	15	16	17	18
(17)	(18)	(19)	(20)	(21)	(22)	(23)
19	20	21	22	23	24	25
(24)	(25)	(26)	(27)	(28)	(29d)	(1)
26	27	28	29	30		
(2)	(3)	(4)	(5)	(6)		

February
(Adar 12)

S	M	T	W	T	F	S
1	2	3	4	5	6	7
(7)	(8)	(9)	(10)	(11)	(12)	(13)
8	9	10	11	12	13	14
(14)	(15)	(16)	(17)	(18)	(19)	(20)
15	16	17	18	19	20	21
(21)	(22)	(23)	(24)	(25)	(26)	(27)
22	23	24	25	26	27	28
(28)	(29)	(30b)	(1)	(2)	(3)	(4)

May
(Iyyar 2)

S	M	T	W	T	F	S
					1	2
					(7)	(8)
3	4	5	6	7	8	9
(9)	(10)	(11)	(12)	(13)	(14)	(15)
10	11	12	13	14	15	16
(16)	(17)	(18)	(19)	(20)	(21)	(22)
17	18	19	20	21	22	23
(23)	(24)	(25)	(26)	(27)	(28)	(29e)
24	25	26	27	28	29	30
(1)	(2)	(3)	(4)	(5)	(6)	(7)
31						
(8)						

March
(Adar II 13)

S	M	T	W	T	F	S
1	2	3	4	5	6	7
(5)	(6)	(7)	(8)	(9)	(10)	(11)
8	9	10	11	12	13	14
(12)	(13)	(14)	(15)	(16)	(17)	(18)
15	16	17	18	19	20	21
(19)	(20)	(21)	(22)	(23)	(24)	(25)
22	23	24	25	26	27	28
(26)	(27)	(28)	(29)	(30c)	(1)	(2)
29	30	31				
(3)	(4)	(5)				

June
(Sivan 3)

S	M	T	W	T	F	S
	1	2	3	4	5	6
	(9)	(10)	(11)	(12)	(13)	(14)
7	8	9	10	11	12	13
(15)	(16)	(17)	(18)	(19)	(20)	(21)
14	15	16	17	18	19	20
(22)	(23)	(24)	(25)	(26)	(27)	(28)
21	22	23	24	25	26	27
(29)	(30f)	(1)	(2)	(3)	(4)	(5)
28	29	30				
(6)	(7)	(8)				

Passover Lamb Sacrificed — Nisan 14
Feast of First Fruits — 1ˢᵗ Sunday after Nisan 15

Feast of Unleavened Bread — Nisan 15-21
Pentecost — 8ᵗʰ Sunday after Nisan 15

Time of New Moon (Jerusalem) —   a18:16   b11:31   c1:39   d12:38   e21:15   f4:39

A.D. 54

July
(Tammuz 4)

S	M	T	W	T	F	S
			1	2	3	4
			(9)	(10)	(11)	(12)
5	6	7	8	9	10	11
(13)	(14)	(15)	(16)	(17)	(18)	(19)
12	13	14	15	16	17	18
(20)	(21)	(22)	(23)	(24)	(25)	(26)
19	20	21	22	23	24	25
(27)	(28)	(29g)	(1)	(2)	(3)	(4)
26	27	28	29	30	31	
(5)	(6)	(7)	(8)	(9)	(10)	

October
(Tishri 7)

S	M	T	W	T	F	S
			1	2	3	
			(13)	(14)	(15)	
4	5	6	7	8	9	10
(16)	(17)	(18)	(19)	(20)	(21)	(22)
11	12	13	14	15	16	17
(23)	(24)	(25)	(26)	(27)	(28)	(29j)
18	19	20	21	22	23	24
(1)	(2)	(3)	(4)	(5)	(6)	(7)
25	26	27	28	29	30	31
(8)	(9)	(10)	(11)	(12)	(13)	(14)

August
(Ab 5)

S	M	T	W	T	F	S
						1
						(11)
2	3	4	5	6	7	8
(12)	(13)	(14)	(15)	(16)	(17)	(18)
9	10	11	12	13	14	15
(19)	(20)	(21)	(22)	(23)	(24)	(25)
16	17	18	19	20	21	22
(26)	(27)	(28)	(29h)	(1)	(2)	(3)
23	24	25	26	27	28	29
(4)	(5)	(6)	(7)	(8)	(9)	(10)
30	31					
(11)	(12)					

November
(Marheshvan 8)

S	M	T	W	T	F	S
1	2	3	4	5	6	7
(15)	(16)	(17)	(18)	(19)	(20)	(21)
8	9	10	11	12	13	14
(22)	(23)	(24)	(25)	(26)	(27)	(28)
15	16	17	18	19	20	21
(29)	(30k)	(1)	(2)	(3)	(4)	(5)
22	23	24	25	26	27	28
(6)	(7)	(8)	(9)	(10)	(11)	(12)
29	30					
(13)	(14)					

September
(Elul 6)

S	M	T	W	T	F	S
		1	2	3	4	5
		(13)	(14)	(15)	(16)	(17)
6	7	8	9	10	11	12
(18)	(19)	(20)	(21)	(22)	(23)	(24)
13	14	15	16	17	18	19
(25)	(26)	(27)	(28)	(29)	(30i)	(1)
20	21	22	23	24	25	26
(2)	(3)	(4)	(5)	(6)	(7)	(8)
27	28	29	30			
(9)	(10)	(11)	(12)			

December
(Kislev 9)

S	M	T	W	T	F	S
		1	2	3	4	5
		(15)	(16)	(17)	(18)	(19)
6	7	8	9	10	11	12
(20)	(21)	(22)	(23)	(24)	(25)	(26)
13	14	15	16	17	18	19
(27)	(28)	(29m)	(1)	(2)	(3)	(4)
20	21	22	23	24	25	26
(5)	(6)	(7)	(8)	(9)	(10)	(11)
27	28	29	30	31		
(12)	(13)	(14)	(15)	(16)		

Day of Trumpets — Tishri 1
Feast of Booths — Tishri 15-22

Day of Atonement — Tishri 10
Feast of Dedication — 8 days beginning Kislev 25

Time of the New Moon — g11:56 h19:59 i5:27 j16:55 k6:50 m23:19

A.D. 55

January
(Tebeth 10)

S	M	T	W	T	F	S
					1	2
					(17)	(18)
3	4	5	6	7	8	9
(19)	(20)	(21)	(22)	(23)	(24)	(25)
10	11	12	13	14	15	16
(26)	(27)	(28)	(29)	(30a)	(1)	(2)
17	18	19	20	21	22	23
(3)	(4)	(5)	(6)	(7)	(8)	(9)
24	25	26	27	28	29	30
(10)	(11)	(12)	(13)	(14)	(15)	(15)
31						
(17)						

April
(Nisan 1)

S	M	T	W	T	F	S
				1	2	3
				(17)	(18)	(19)
4	5	6	7	8	9	10
(20)	(21)	(22)	(23)	(24)	(25)	(26)
11	12	13	14	15	16	17
(27)	(28)	(29d)	(1)	(2)	(3)	(4)
18	19	20	21	22	23	24
(5)	(6)	(7)	(8)	(9)	(10)	(11)
25	26	27	28	29	30	
(12)	(13)	(14)	(15)	(16)	(17)	

February
(Shebat 11)

S	M	T	W	T	F	S
	1	2	3	4	5	6
	(18)	(19)	(20)	(21)	(22)	(23)
7	8	9	10	11	12	13
(24)	(25)	(26)	(27)	(28)	(29)	(30b)
14	15	16	17	18	19	20
(1)	(2)	(3)	(4)	(5)	(6)	(7)
21	22	23	24	25	26	27
(8)	(9)	(10)	(11)	(12)	(13)	(14)
28						
(15)						

May
(Iyyar 2)

S	M	T	W	T	F	S
						1
						(18)
2	3	4	5	6	7	8
(19)	(20)	(21)	(22)	(23)	(24)	(25)
9	10	11	12	13	14	15
(26)	(27)	(28)	(29)	(30e)	(1)	(2)
16	17	18	19	20	21	22
(3)	(4)	(5)	(6)	(7)	(8)	(9)
23	24	25	26	27	28	29
(10)	(11)	(12)	(13)	(14)	(15)	(16)
30	31					
(17)	(18)					

March
(Adar 12)

S	M	T	W	T	F	S
	1	2	3	4	5	6
	(16)	(17)	(18)	(19)	(20)	(21)
7	8	9	10	11	12	13
(22)	(23)	(24)	(25)	(26)	(27)	(28)
14	15	16	17	18	19	20
(29)	(30c)	(1)	(2)	(3)	(4)	(5)
21	22	23	24	25	26	27
(6)	(7)	(8)	(9)	(10)	(11)	(12)
28	29	30	31			
(13)	(14)	(15)	(16)			

June
(Sivan 3)

S	M	T	W	T	F	S
		1	2	3	4	5
		(19)	(20)	(21)	(22)	(23)
6	7	8	9	10	11	12
(24)	(25)	(26)	(27)	(28)	(29f)	(1)
13	14	15	16	17	18	19
(2)	(3)	(4)	(5)	(6)	(7)	(8)
20	21	22	23	24	25	26
(9)	(10)	(11)	(12)	(13)	(14)	(15)
27	28	29	30			
(16)	(17)	(18)	(19)			

Passover Lamb Sacrificed — Nisan 14
Feast of First Fruits — 1st Sunday after Nisan 15

Feast of Unleavened Bread — Nisan 15-21
Pentecost — 8th Sunday after Nisan 15

Time of New Moon (Jerusalem) —   a17:44   b12:30   c5:51   d20:44   e9:03   f19:21

A.D. 55

July (Tammuz 4)						
S	M	T	W	T	F	S
				1 (20)	2 (21)	3 (22)
4 (23)	5 (24)	6 (25)	7 (26)	8 (27)	9 (28)	10 (29)
11 (30g)	12 (1)	13 (2)	14 (3)	15 (4)	16 (5)	17 (6)
18 (7)	19 (8)	20 (9)	21 (10)	22 (11)	23 (12)	24 (13)
25 (14)	26 (15)	27 (16)	28 (17)	29 (18)	30 (19)	31 (20)

October (Tishri 7)						
S	M	T	W	T	F	S
					1 (24)	2 (25)
3 (26)	4 (27)	5 (28)	6 (29)	7 (30j)	8 (1)	9 (2)
10 (3)	11 (4)	12 (5)	13 (6)	14 (7)	15 (8)	16 (9)
17 (10)	18 (11)	19 (12)	20 (13)	21 (14)	22 (15)	23 (16)
24 (17)	25 (18)	26 (19)	27 (20)	28 (21)	29 (22)	30 (23)
31 (24)						

August (Ab 5)						
S	M	T	W	T	F	S
1 (21)	2 (22)	3 (23)	4 (24)	5 (25)	6 (26)	7 (27)
8 (28)	9 (29h)	10 (1)	11 (2)	12 (3)	13 (4)	14 (5)
15 (6)	16 (7)	17 (8)	18 (9)	19 (10)	20 (11)	21 (12)
22 (13)	23 (14)	24 (15)	25 (16)	26 (17)	27 (18)	28 (19)
29 (20)	30 (21)	31 (22)				

November (Marheshvan 8)						
S	M	T	W	T	F	S
	1 (25)	2 (26)	3 (27)	4 (28)	5 (29k)	6 (1)
7 (2)	8 (3)	9 (4)	10 (5)	11 (6)	12 (7)	13 (8)
14 (9)	15 (10)	16 (11)	17 (12)	18 (13)	19 (14)	20 (15)
21 (16)	22 (17)	23 (18)	24 (19)	25 (20)	26 (21)	27 (22)
28 (23)	29 (24)	30 (25)				

September (Elul 6)						
S	M	T	W	T	F	S
			1 (23)	2 (24)	3 (25)	4 (26)
5 (27)	6 (28)	7 (29i)	8 (1)	9 (2)	10 (3)	11 (4)
12 (5)	13 (6)	14 (7)	15 (8)	16 (9)	17 (10)	18 (11)
19 (12)	20 (13)	21 (14)	22 (15)	23 (16)	24 (17)	25 (18)
26 (19)	27 (20)	28 (21)	29 (22)	30 (23)		

December (Kislev 9)						
S	M	T	W	T	F	S
			1 (26)	2 (27)	3 (28)	4 (29)
5 (30f)	6 (1)	7 (2)	8 (3)	9 (4)	10 (5)	11 (6)
12 (7)	13 (8)	14 (9)	15 (10)	16 (11)	17 (12)	18 (13)
19 (14)	20 (15)	21 (16)	22 (17)	23 (18)	24 (19)	25 (20)
26 (21)	27 (22)	28 (23)	29 (24)	30 (25)	31 (26)	

Day of Trumpets — Tishri 1
Feast of Booths — Tishri 15-22

Day of Atonement — Tishri 10
Feast of Dedication — 8 days beginning Kislev 25

Time of the New Moon — g4:31 h12:47 i21:19 j6:39 k17:23 m6:04

A.D. 56

January
(Tebeth 10)

S	M	T	W	T	F	S
						1
						(27)
2	3	4	5	6	7	8
(28)	(29a)	(1)	(2)	(3)	(4)	(5)
9	10	11	12	13	14	15
(6)	(7)	(8)	(9)	(10)	(11)	(12)
16	17	18	19	20	21	22
(13)	(14)	(15)	(16)	(17)	(18)	(19)
23	24	25	26	27	28	29
(20)	(21)	(22)	(23)	(24)	(25)	(26)
30	31					
(27)	(28)					

April
(Adar II 13)

S	M	T	W	T	F	S
						1
						(29d)
2	3	4	5	6	7	8
(1)	(2)	(3)	(4)	(5)	(6)	(7)
9	10	11	12	13	14	15
(8)	(9)	(10)	(11)	(12)	(13)	(14)
16	17	18	19	20	21	22
(15)	(16)	(17)	(18)	(19)	(20)	(21)
23	24	25	26	27	28	29
(22)	(23)	(24)	(25)	(26)	(27)	(28)
30						
(29)						

February
(Shebat 11)

S	M	T	W	T	F	S
		1	2	3	4	5
		(29)	(30b)	(1)	(2)	(3)
6	7	8	9	10	11	12
(4)	(5)	(6)	(7)	(8)	(9)	(10)
13	14	15	16	17	18	19
(11)	(12)	(13)	(14)	(15)	(16)	(17)
20	21	22	23	24	25	26
(18)	(19)	(20)	(21)	(22)	(23)	(24)
27	28	29				
(25)	(26)	(27)				

February
(Shebat 11)

S	M	T	W	T	F	S
		1	2	3	4	5
		(29)	(30b)	(1)	(2)	(3)
6	7	8	9	10	11	12
(4)	(5)	(6)	(7)	(8)	(9)	(10)
13	14	15	16	17	18	19
(11)	(12)	(13)	(14)	(15)	(16)	(17)
20	21	22	23	24	25	26
(18)	(19)	(20)	(21)	(22)	(23)	(24)
27	28	29				
(25)	(26)	(27)				

March
(Adar 12)

S	M	T	W	T	F	S
			1	2	3	4
			(28)	(29)	(30c)	(1)
5	6	7	8	9	10	11
(2)	(3)	(4)	(5)	(6)	(7)	(8)
12	13	14	15	16	17	18
(9)	(10)	(11)	(12)	(13)	(14)	(15)
19	20	21	22	23	24	25
(16)	(17)	(18)	(19)	(20)	(21)	(22)
26	27	28	29	30	31	
(23)	(24)	(25)	(26)	(27)	(28)	

June
(Sivan 3)

S	M	T	W	T	F	S
				1	2	3
				(1)	(2)	(3)
4	5	6	7	8	9	10
(4)	(5)	(6)	(7)	(8)	(9)	(10)
11	12	13	14	15	16	17
(11)	(12)	(13)	(14)	(15)	(16)	(17)
18	19	20	21	22	23	24
(18)	(19)	(20)	(21)	(22)	(23)	(24)
25	26	27	28	29	30	
(25)	(26)	(27)	(28)	(29g)	(1)	

Passover Lamb Sacrificed — Nisan 14
Feast of First Fruits — 1st Sunday after Nisan 15

Feast of Unleavened Bread — Nisan 15-21
Pentecost — 8th Sunday after Nisan 15

Time of New Moon (Jerusalem) — a20:48 b13:04 c5:52 d22:17 e13:40 f3:39 g16:06

July
(Tammuz 4)

S	M	T	W	T	F	S
						1
						(2)
2	3	4	5	6	7	8
(3)	(4)	(5)	(6)	(7)	(8)	(9)
9	10	11	12	13	14	15
(10)	(11)	(12)	(13)	(14)	(15)	(16)
16	17	18	19	20	21	22
(17)	(18)	(19)	(20)	(21)	(22)	(23)
23	24	25	26	27	28	29
(24)	(25)	(26)	(27)	(28)	(29)	(30h)
30	31					
(1)	.(2)					

October
(Tishri 7)

S	M	T	W	T	F	S
1	2	3	4	5	6	7
(6)	(7)	(8)	(9)	(10)	(11)	(12)
8	9	10	11	12	13	14
(13)	(14)	(15)	(16)	(17)	(18)	(19)
15	16	17	18	19	20	21
(20)	(21)	(22)	(23)	(24)	(25)	(26)
22	23	24	25	26	27	28
(27)	(28)	(29)	(30k)	(1)	(2)	(3)
29	30	31				
(4)	(5)	(6)				

August
(Ab 5)

S	M	T	W	T	F	S
		1	2	3	4	5
		(3)	(4)	(5)	(6)	(7)
6	7	8	9	10	11	12
(8)	(9)	(10)	(11)	(12)	(13)	(14)
13	14	15	16	17	18	19
(15)	(16)	(17)	(18)	(19)	(20)	(21)
20	21	22	23	24	25	26
(22)	(23)	(24)	(25)	(26)	(27)	(28)
27	28	29	30	31		
(29i)	(1)	(2)	(3)	(4)		

November
(Marheshvan 8)

S	M	T	W	T	F	S
			1	2	3	4
			(7)	(8)	(9)	(10)
5	6	7	8	9	10	11
(11)	(12)	(13)	(14)	(15)	(16)	(17)
12	13	14	15	16	17	18
(18)	(19)	(20)	(21)	(22)	(23)	(24)
19	20	21	22	23	24	25
(25)	(26)	(27)	(28)	(29m)	(1)	(2)
26	27	28	29	30		
(3)	(4)	(5)	(6)	(7)		

September
(Elul 6)

S	M	T	W	T	F	S
					1	2
					(5)	(6)
3	4	5	6	7	8	9
(7)	(8)	(9)	(10)	(11)	(12)	(13)
10	11	12	13	14	15	16
(14)	(15)	(16)	(17)	(18)	(19)	(20)
17	18	19	20	21	22	23
(21)	(22)	(23)	(24)	(25)	(26)	(27)
24	25	26	27	28	29	30
(28)	(29j)	(1)	(2)	(3)	(4)	(5)

December
(Kislev 9)

S	M	T	W	T	F	S
					1	2
					(8)	(9)
3	4	5	6	7	8	9
(10)	(11)	(12)	(13)	(14)	(15)	(16)
10	11	12	13	14	15	16
(17)	(18)	(19)	(20)	(21)	(22)	(23)
17	18	19	20	21	22	23
(24)	(25)	(26)	(27)	(28)	(29)	(30n)
24	25	26	27	28	29	30
(1)	(2)	(3)	(4)	(5)	(6)	(7)
31						
(8)						

Day of Trumpets — Tishri 1
Feast of Booths — Tishri 15-22

Day of Atonement — Tishri 10
Feast of Dedication — 8 days beginning Kislev 25

Time of the New Moon —   h3:07   i13:06   j22:41   k8:34   m19:18   n7:02

A.D. 57

January
(Tebeth 10)

S	M	T	W	T	F	S
	1	2	3	4	5	6
	(9)	(10)	(11)	(12)	(13)	(14)
7	8	9	10	11	12	13
(15)	(16)	(17)	(18)	(19)	(20)	(21)
14	15	16	17	18	19	20
(22)	(23)	(24)	(25)	(26)	(27)	(28)
21	22	23	24	25	26	27
(29a)	(1)	(2)	(3)	(4)	(5)	(6)
28	29	30	31			
(7)	(8)	(9)	(10)			

April
(Nisan 1)

S	M	T	W	T	F	S
1	2	3	4	5	6	7
(11)	(12)	(13)	(14)	(15)	(16)	(17)
8	9	10	11	12	13	14
(18)	(19)	(20)	(21)	(22)	(23)	(24)
15	16	17	18	19	20	21
(25)	(26)	(27)	(28)	(29)	(30d)	(1)
22	23	24	25	26	27	28
(2)	(3)	(4)	(5)	(6)	(7)	(8)
29	30					
(9)	(10)					

February
(Shebat 11)

S	M	T	W	T	F	S
				1	2	3
				(11)	(12)	(13)
4	5	6	7	8	9	10
(14)	(15)	(16)	(17)	(18)	(19)	(20)
11	12	13	14	15	16	17
(21)	(22)	(23)	(24)	(25)	(26)	(27)
18	19	20	21	22	23	24
(28)	(29)	(30b)	(1)	(2)	(3)	(4)
25	26	27	28			
(5)	(6)	(7)	(8)			

May
(Iyyar 2)

S	M	T	W	T	F	S
		1	2	3	4	5
		(11)	(12)	(13)	(14)	(15)
6	7	8	9	10	11	12
(16)	(17)	(18)	(19)	(20)	(21)	(22)
13	14	15	16	17	18	19
(23)	(24)	(25)	(26)	(27)	(28)	(29)
20	21	22	23	24	25	26
(30e)	(1)	(2)	(3)	(4)	(5)	(6)
27	28	29	30	31		
(7)	(8)	(9)	(10)	(11)		

March
(Adar 12)

S	M	T	W	T	F	S
				1	2	3
				(9)	(10)	(11)
4	5	6	7	8	9	10
(12)	(13)	(14)	(15)	(16)	(17)	(18)
11	12	13	14	15	16	17
(19)	(20)	(21)	(22)	(23)	(24)	(25)
18	19	20	21	22	23	24
(26)	(27)	(28)	(29c)	(1)	(2)	(3)
25	26	27	28	29	30	31
(4)	(5)	(6)	(7)	(8)	(9)	(10)

June
(Sivan 3)

S	M	T	W	T	F	S
					1	2
					(12)	(13)
3	4	5	6	7	8	9
(14)	(15)	(16)	(17)	(18)	(19)	(20)
10	11	12	13	14	15	16
(21)	(22)	(23)	(24)	(25)	(26)	(27)
17	18	19	20	21	22	23
(28)	(29f)	(1)	(2)	(3)	(4)	(5)
24	25	26	27	28	29	30
(6)	(7)	(8)	(9)	(10)	(11)	(12)

Passover Lamb Sacrificed — Nisan 14

Feast of First Fruits — 1st Sunday after Nisan 15

Feast of Unleavened Bread — Nisan 15-21

Pentecost — 8th Sunday after Nisan 15

Time of New Moon (Jerusalem) — a19:41   b9:07   c23:19   d14:14   e5:36   f20:48

A.D. 57

July (Tammuz 4)						
S	M	T	W	T	F	S
1	2	3	4	5	6	7
(13)	(14)	(15)	(16)	(17)	(18)	(19)
8	9	10	11	12	13	14
(20)	(21)	(22)	(23)	(24)	(25)	(26)
15	16	17	18	19	20	21
(27)	(28)	(29)	(30g)	(1)	(2)	(3)
22	23	24	25	26	27	28
(4)	(5)	(6)	(7)	(8)	(9)	(10)
29	30	31				
(11)	(12)	(13)				

October (Tishri 7)						
S	M	T	W	T	F	S
	1	2	3	4	5	6
	(16)	(17)	(18)	(19)	(20)	(21)
7	8	9	10	11	12	13
(22)	(23)	(24)	(25)	(26)	(27)	(28)
14	15	16	17	18	19	20
(29)	(30j)	(1)	(2)	(3)	(4)	(5)
21	22	23	24	25	26	27
(6)	(7)	(8)	(9)	(10)	(11)	(12)
28	29	30	31			
(13)	(14)	(15)	(16)			

August (Ab 5)						
S	M	T	W	T	F	S
			1	2	3	4
			(14)	(15)	(16)	(17)
5	6	7	8	9	10	11
(18)	(19)	(20)	(21)	(22)	(23)	(24)
12	13	14	15	16	17	18
(25)	(26)	(27)	(28)	(29)	(30h)	(1)
19	20	21	22	23	24	25
(2)	(3)	(4)	(5)	(6)	(7)	(8)
26	27	28	29	30	31	
(9)	(10)	(11)	(12)	(13)	(14)	

November (Marheshvan 8)						
S	M	T	W	T	F	S
				1	2	3
				(17)	(18)	(19)
4	5	6	7	8	9	10
(20)	(21)	(22)	(23)	(24)	(25)	(26)
11	12	13	14	15	16	17
(27)	(28)	(29k)	(1)	(2)	(3)	(4)
18	19	20	21	22	23	24
(5)	(6)	(7)	(8)	(9)	(10)	(11)
25	26	27	28	29	30	
(12)	(13)	(14)	(15)	(16)	(17)	

September (Elul 6)						
S	M	T	W	T	F	S
						1
						(15)
2	3	4	5	6	7	8
(16)	(17)	(18)	(19)	(20)	(21)	(22)
9	10	11	12	13	14	15
(23)	(24)	(25)	(26)	(27)	(28)	(29i)
16	17	18	19	20	21	22
(1)	(2)	(3)	(4)	(5)	(6)	(7)
23	24	25	26	27	28	29
(8)	(9)	(10)	(11)	(12)	(13)	(14)
30						
(15)						

December (Kislev 9)						
S	M	T	W	T	F	S
						1
						(18)
2	3	4	5	6	7	8
(19)	(20)	(21)	(22)	(23)	(24)	(25)
9	10	11	12	13	14	15
(26)	(27)	(28)	(29m)	(1)	(2)	(3)
16	17	18	19	20	21	22
(4)	(5)	(6)	(7)	(8)	(9)	(10)
23	24	25	26	27	28	29
(11)	(12)	(13)	(14)	(15)	(16)	(17)
30	31					
(18)	(19)					

Day of Trumpets — Tishri 1
Feast of Booths — Tishri 15-22

Day of Atonement — Tishri 10
Feast of Dedication — 8 days beginning Kislev 25

Time of the New Moon — g11:09 h0:18 i12:24 j23:51 k11:03 m22:02

A.D. 58

January
(Tebeth 10)

S	M	T	W	T	F	S
		1	2	3	4	5
		(20)	(21)	(22)	(23)	(24)
6	7	8	9	10	11	12
(25)	(26)	(27)	(28)	(29)	(30a)	(1)
13	14	15	16	17	18	19
(2)	(3)	(4)	(5)	(6)	(7)	(8)
20	21	22	23	24	25	26
(9)	(10)	(11)	(12)	(13)	(14)	(15)
27	28	29	30	31		
(16)	(17)	(18)	(19)	(20)		

April
(Nisan 1)

S	M	T	W	T	F	S
		1	2	3	4	5	6
		(21)	(22)	(23)	(24)	(25)	(26)
7	8	9	10	11	12	13
(27)	(28)	(29d)	(1)	(2)	(3)	(4)
14	15	16	17	18	19	20
(5)	(6)	(7)	(8)	(9)	(10)	(11)
21	22	23	24	25	26	27
(12)	(13)	(14)	(15)	(16)	(17)	(18)
28	29	30				
(19)	(20)	(21)				

February
(Shebat 11)

S	M	T	W	T	F	S
					1	2
					(21)	(22)
3	4	5	6	7	8	9
(23)	(24)	(25)	(26)	(27)	(28)	(29b)
10	11	12	13	14	15	16
(1)	(2)	(3)	(4)	(5)	(6)	(7)
17	18	19	20	21	22	23
(8)	(9)	(10)	(11)	(12)	(13)	(14)
24	25	26	27	28		
(15)	(16)	(17)	(18)	(19)		

May
(Iyyar 2)

S	M	T	W	T	F	S
			1	2	3	4
			(22)	(23)	(24)	(25)
5	6	7	8	9	10	11
(26)	(27)	(28)	(29)	(30e)	(1)	(2)
12	13	14	15	16	17	18
(3)	(4)	(5)	(6)	(7)	(8)	(9)
19	20	21	22	23	24	25
(10)	(11)	(12)	(13)	(14)	(15)	(16)
26	27	28	29	30	31	
(17)	(18)	(19)	(20)	(21)	(22)	

March
(Adar 12)

S	M	T	W	T	F	S
					1	2
					(20)	(21)
3	4	5	6	7	8	9
(22)	(23)	(24)	(25)	(26)	(27)	(28)
10	11	12	13	14	15	16
(29)	(30c)	(1)	(2)	(3)	(4)	(5)
17	18	19	20	21	22	23
(6)	(7)	(8)	(9)	(10)	(11)	(12)
24	25	26	27	28	29	30
(13)	(14)	(15)	(16)	(17)	(18)	(19)
31						
(20)						

June
(Sivan 3)

S	M	T	W	T	F	S
						1
						(23)
2	3	4	5	6	7	8
(24)	(25)	(26)	(27)	(28)	(29f)	(1)
9	10	11	12	13	14	15
(2)	(3)	(4)	(5)	(6)	(7)	(8)
16	17	18	19	20	21	22
(9)	(10)	(11)	(12)	(13)	(14)	(15)
23	24	25	26	27	28	29
(16)	(17)	(18)	(19)	(20)	(21)	(22)
30						
(23)						

Passover Lamb Sacrificed — Nisan 14

Feast of First Fruits — 1st Sunday after Nisan 15

Feast of Unleavened Bread — Nisan 15-21

Pentecost — 8th Sunday after Nisan 15

Time of New Moon (Jerusalem) —   a8:48   b19:24   c6:17   d18:04   e7:09   f21:34

July
(Tammuz 4)

S	M	T	W	T	F	S
	1	2	3	4	5	6
	(24)	(25)	(26)	(27)	(28)	(29)
7	8	9	10	11	12	13
(30g)	(1)	(2)	(3)	(4)	(5)	(6)
14	15	16	17	18	19	20
(7)	(8)	(9)	(10)	(11)	(12)	(13)
21	22	23	24	25	26	27
(14)	(15)	(16)	(17)	(18)	(19)	(20)
28	29	30	31			
(21)	(22)	(23)	(24)			

October
(Tishri 7)

S	M	T	W	T	F	S
		1	2	3	4	5
		(27)	(28)	(29)	(30j)	(1)
6	7	8	9	10	11	12
(2)	(3)	(4)	(5)	(6)	(7)	(8)
13	14	15	16	17	18	19
(9)	(10)	(11)	(12)	(13)	(14)	(15)
20	21	22	23	24	25	26
(16)	(17)	(18)	(19)	(20)	(21)	(22)
27	28	29	30	31		
(23)	(24)	(25)	(26)	(27)		

August
(Ab 5)

S	M	T	W	T	F	S
				1	2	3
				(25)	(26)	(27)
4	5	6	7	8	9	10
(28)	(29)	(30h)	(1)	(2)	(3)	(4)
11	12	13	14	15	16	17
(5)	(6)	(7)	(8)	(9)	(10)	(11)
18	19	20	21	22	23	24
(12)	(13)	(14)	(15)	(16)	(17)	(18)
25	26	27	28	29	30	31
(19)	(20)	(21)	(22)	(23)	(24)	(25)

November
(Marheshvan 8)

S	M	T	W	T	F	S
					1	2
					(28)	(29)
3	4	5	6	7	8	9
(30k)	(1)	(2)	(3)	(4)	(5)	(6)
10	11	12	13	14	15	16
(7)	(8)	(9)	(10)	(11)	(12)	(13)
17	18	19	20	21	22	23
(14)	(15)	(16)	(17)	(18)	(19)	(20)
24	25	26	27	28	29	30
(21)	(22)	(23)	(24)	(25)	(26)	(27)

September
(Elul 6)

S	M	T	W	T	F	S
1	2	3	4	5	6	7
(26)	(27)	(28)	(29i)	(1)	(2)	(3)
8	9	10	11	12	13	14
(4)	(5)	(6)	(7)	(8)	(9)	(10)
15	16	17	18	19	20	21
(11)	(12)	(13)	(14)	(15)	(16)	(17)
22	23	24	25	26	27	28
(18)	(19)	(20)	(21)	(22)	(23)	(24)
29	30					
(25)	(26)					

December
(Kislev 9)

S	M	T	W	T	F	S
1	2	3	4	5	6	7
(28)	(29m)	(1)	(2)	(3)	(4)	(5)
8	9	10	11	12	13	14
(6)	(7)	(8)	(9)	(10)	(11)	(12)
15	16	17	18	19	20	21
(13)	(14)	(15)	(16)	(17)	(18)	(19)
22	23	24	25	26	27	28
(20)	(21)	(22)	(23)	(24)	(25)	(26)
29	30	31				
(27)	(28)	(29)				

Day of Trumpets — Tishri 1
Feast of Booths — Tishri 15-22

Day of Atonement — Tishri 10
Feast of Dedication — 8 days beginning Kislev 25

Time of the New Moon —   g12:52   h4:27   i19:50   j10:40   k0:38   m13:20

Gregorian

A.D. 59

January (Tebeth 10)						
S	M	T	W	T	F	S
			1	2	3	4
			(30a)	(1)	(2)	(3)
5	6	7	8	9	10	11
(4)	(5)	(6)	(7)	(8)	(9)	(10)
12	13	14	15	16	17	18
(11)	(12)	(13)	(14)	(15)	(16)	(17)
19	20	21	22	23	24	25
(18)	(19)	(20)	(21)	(22)	(23)	(24)
26	27	28	29	30	31	
(25)	(26)	(27)	(28)	(29b)	(1)	

April (Nisan 1)						
S	M	T	W	T	F	S
		1	2	3	4	5
		(2)	(3)	(4)	(5)	(6)
6	7	8	9	10	11	12
(7)	(8)	(9)	(10)	(11)	(12)	(13)
13	14	15	16	17	18	19
(14)	(15)	(16)	(17)	(18)	(19)	(20)
20	21	22	23	24	25	26
(21)	(22)	(23)	(24)	(25)	(26)	(27)
27	28	29	30			
(28)	(29e)	(1)	(2)			

February (Adar 12)						
S	M	T	W	T	F	S
						1
						(2)
2	3	4	5	6	7	8
(3)	(4)	(5)	(6)	(7)	(8)	(9)
9	10	11	12	13	14	15
(10)	(11)	(12)	(13)	(14)	(15)	(16)
16	17	18	19	20	21	22
(17)	(18)	(19)	(20)	(21)	(22)	(23)
23	24	25	26	27	28	
(24)	(25)	(26)	(27)	(28)	(29c)	

May (Iyyar 2)						
S	M	T	W	T	F	S
				1	2	3
				(3)	(4)	(5)
4	5	6	7	8	9	10
(6)	(7)	(8)	(9)	(10)	(11)	(12)
11	12	13	14	15	16	17
(13)	(14)	(15)	(16)	(17)	(18)	(19)
18	19	20	21	22	23	24
(20)	(21)	(22)	(23)	(24)	(25)	(26)
25	26	27	28	29	30	31
(27)	(28)	(29)	(30f)	(1)	(2)	(3)

March (Adar II 13)						
S	M	T	W	T	F	S
						1
						(1)
2	3	4	5	6	7	8
(2)	(3)	(4)	(5)	(6)	(7)	(8)
9	10	11	12	13	14	15
(9)	(10)	(11)	(12)	(13)	(14)	(15)
16	17	18	19	20	21	22
(16)	(17)	(18)	(19)	(20)	(21)	(22)
23	24	25	26	27	28	29
(23)	(24)	(25)	(26)	(27)	(28)	(29)
30	31					
(30d)	(1)					

June (Sivan 3)						
S	M	T	W	T	F	S
1	2	3	4	5	6	7
(4)	(5)	(6)	(7)	(8)	(9)	(10)
8	9	10	11	12	13	14
(11)	(12)	(13)	(14)	(15)	(16)	(17)
15	16	17	18	19	20	21
(18)	(19)	(20)	(21)	(22)	(23)	(24)
22	23	24	25	26	27	28
(25)	(26)	(27)	(28)	(29g)	(1)	(2)
29	30					
(3)	(4)					

Passover Lamb Sacrificed — Nisan 14
Feast of First Fruits — 1st Sunday after Nisan 15

Feast of Unleavened Bread — Nisan 15-21
Pentecost — 8th Sunday after Nisan 15

Time of New Moon (Jerusalem) — a0:36 b10:35 c19:48 d4:56 e14:41 f1:41 g14:18

A.D. 59

July
(Tammuz 4)

S	M	T	W	T	F	S
		1	2	3	4	5
		(5)	(6)	(7)	(8)	(9)
6	7	8	9	10	11	12
(10)	(11)	(12)	(13)	(14)	(15)	(16)
13	14	15	16	17	18	19
(17)	(18)	(19)	(20)	(21)	(22)	(23)
20	21	22	23	24	25	26
(24)	(25)	(26)	(27)	(28)	(29)	(30h)
27	28	29	30	31		
(1)	(2)	(3)	(4)	(5)		

October
(Tishri 7)

S	M	T	W	T	F	S
			1	2	3	4
			(8)	(9)	(10)	(11)
5	6	7	8	9	10	11
(12)	(13)	(14)	(15)	(16)	(17)	(18)
12	13	14	15	16	17	18
(19)	(20)	(21)	(22)	(23)	(24)	(25)
19	20	21	22	23	24	25
(26)	(27)	(28)	(29)	(30k)	(1)	(2)
26	27	28	29	30	31	
(3)	(4)	(5)	(6)	(7)	(8)	

August
(Ab 5)

S	M	T	W	T	F	S
					1	2
					(6)	(7)
3	4	5	6	7	8	9
(8)	(9)	(10)	(11)	(12)	(13)	(14)
10	11	12	13	14	15	16
(15)	(16)	(17)	(18)	(19)	(20)	(21)
17	18	19	20	21	22	23
(22)	(23)	(24)	(25)	(26)	(27)	(28)
24	25	26	27	28	29	30
(29i)	(1)	(2)	(3)	(4)	(5)	(6)
31						
(7)						

November
(Marheshvan 8)

S	M	T	W	T	F	S
						1
						(9)
2	3	4	5	6	7	8
(10)	(11)	(12)	(13)	(14)	(15)	(16)
9	10	11	12	13	14	15
(17)	(18)	(19)	(20)	(21)	(22)	(23)
16	17	18	19	20	21	22
(24)	(25)	(26)	(27)	(28)	(29)	(30m)
23	24	25	26	27	28	29
(1)	(2)	(3)	(4)	(5)	(6)	(7)
30						
(8)						

September
(Elul 6)

S	M	T	W	T	F	S
	1	2	3	4	5	6
	(8)	(9)	(10)	(11)	(12)	(13)
7	8	9	10	11	12	13
(14)	(15)	(16)	(17)	(18)	(19)	(20)
14	15	16	17	18	19	20
(21)	(22)	(23)	(24)	(25)	(26)	(27)
21	22	23	24	25	25	27
(28)	(29)	(30i)	(1)	(2)	(3)	(4)
28	29	30				
(5)	(6)	(7)				

December
(Kislev 9)

S	M	T	W	T	F	S
	1	2	3	4	5	6
	(9)	(10)	(11)	(12)	(13)	(14)
7	8	9	10	11	12	13
(15)	(16)	(17)	(18)	(19)	(20)	(21)
14	15	16	17	18	19	20
(22)	(23)	(24)	(25)	(26)	(27)	(28)
21	22	23	24	25	26	27
(29n)	(1)	(2)	(3)	(4)	(5)	(6)
28	29	30	31			
(7)	(8)	(9)	(10)			

Day of Trumpets — Tishri 1
Feast of Booths — Tishri 15-22

Day of Atonement — Tishri 10
Feast of Dedication — 8 days beginning Kislev 25

Time of the New Moon —   h4:45   i20:58   j14:25   k7:59   m0:19   n14:27

A.D. 60

January
(Tebeth 10)

S	M	T	W	T	F	S
				1	2	3
				(11)	(12)	(13)
4	5	6	7	8	9	10
(14)	(15)	(16)	(17)	(18)	(19)	(20)
11	12	13	14	15	16	17
(21)	(22)	(23)	(24)	(25)	(26)	(27)
18	19	20	21	22	23	24
(28)	(29)	(30a)	(1)	(2)	(3)	(4)
25	26	27	28	29	30	31
(5)	(6)	(7)	(8)	(9)	(10)	(11)

April
(Nisan 1)

S	M	T	W	T	F	S
				1	2	3
				(14)	(15)	(16)
4	5	6	7	8	9	10
(17)	(18)	(19)	(20)	(21)	(22)	(23)
11	12	13	14	15	16	17
(24)	(25)	(26)	(27)	(28)	(29)	(30d)
18	19	20	21	22	23	24
(1)	(2)	(3)	(4)	(5)	(6)	(7)
25	26	27	28	29	30	
(8)	(9)	(10)	(11)	(12)	(13)	

February
(Shebat 11)

S	M	T	W	T	F	S
1	2	3	4	5	6	7
(12)	(13)	(14)	(15)	(16)	(17)	(18)
8	9	10	11	12	13	14
(19)	(20)	(21)	(22)	(23)	(24)	(25)
15	16	17	18	19	20	21
(26)	(27)	(28)	(29b)	(1)	(2)	(3)
22	23	24	25	26	27	28
(4)	(5)	(6)	(7)	(8)	(9)	(10)
29						
(11)						

May
(Iyyar 2)

S	M	T	W	T	F	S
						1
						(14)
2	3	4	5	6	7	8
(15)	(16)	(17)	(18)	(19)	(20)	(21)
9	10	11	12	13	14	15
(22)	(23)	(24)	(25)	(26)	(27)	(28)
16	17	18	19	20	21	22
(29e)	(1)	(2)	(3)	(4)	(5)	(6)
23	24	25	26	27	28	29
(7)	(8)	(9)	(10)	(11)	(12)	(13)
30	31					
(14)	(15)					

March
(Adar 12)

S	M	T	W	T	F	S
	1	2	3	4	5	6
	(12)	(13)	(14)	(15)	(16)	(17)
7	8	9	10	11	12	13
(18)	(19)	(20)	(21)	(22)	(23)	(24)
14	15	16	17	18	19	20
(25)	(26)	(27)	(28)	(29c)	(1)	(2)
21	22	23	24	25	26	27
(3)	(4)	(5)	(6)	(7)	(8)	(9)
28	29	30	31			
(10)	(11)	(12)	(13)			

June
(Sivan 3)

S	M	T	W	T	F	S
		1	2	3	4	5
		(16)	(17)	(18)	(19)	(20)
6	7	8	9	10	11	12
(21)	(22)	(23)	(24)	(25)	(26)	(27)
13	14	15	16	17	18	19
(28)	(29f)	(1)	(2)	(3)	(4)	(5)
20	21	22	23	24	25	26
(6)	(7)	(8)	(9)	(10)	(11)	(12)
27	28	29	30			
(13)	(14)	(15)	(16)			

Passover Lamb Sacrificed — Nisan 14　　　　　Feast of Unleavened Bread — Nisan 15-21
Feast of First Fruits — 1st Sunday after Nisan 15　　　Pentecost — 8th Sunday after Nisan 15

Time of New Moon (Jerusalem) —　a2:15　b12:09　c20:47　d4:48　e12:52　f21:48

July (Tammuz 4)						
S	M	T	W	T	F	S
				1	2	3
				(17)	(18)	(19)
4	5	6	7	8	9	10
(20)	(21)	(22)	(23)	(24)	(25)	(26)
11	12	13	14	15	16	17
(27)	(28)	(29)	(30g)	(1)	(2)	(3)
18	19	20	21	22	23	24
(4)	(5)	(6)	(7)	(8)	(9)	(10)
25	26	27	28	29	30	31
(11)	(12)	(13)	(14)	(15)	(16)	(17)

October (Tishri 7)						
S	M	T	W	T	F	S
					1	2
					(20)	(21)
3	4	5	6	7	8	9
(22)	(23)	(24)	(25)	(26)	(27)	(28)
10	11	12	13	14	15	16
(29)	(30j)	(1)	(2)	(3)	(4)	(5)
17	18	19	20	21	22	23
(6)	(7)	(8)	(9)	(10)	(11)	(12)
24	25	26	27	28	29	30
(13)	(14)	(15)	(16)	(17)	(18)	(19)
31						
(20)						

August (Ab 5)						
S	M	T	W	T	F	S
1	2	3	4	5	6	7
(18)	(19)	(20)	(21)	(22)	(23)	(24)
8	9	10	11	12	13	14
(25)	(26)	(27)	(28)	(29h)	(1)	(2)
15	16	17	18	19	20	21
(3)	(4)	(5)	(6)	(7)	(8)	(9)
22	23	24	25	26	27	28
(10)	(11)	(12)	(13)	(14)	(15)	(16)
29	30	31				
(17)	(18)	(19)				

November (Marheshvan 8)						
S	M	T	W	T	F	S
	1	2	3	4	5	6
	(21)	(22)	(23)	(24)	(25)	(26)
7	8	9	10	11	12	13
(27)	(28)	(29)	(30k)	(1)	(2)	(3)
14	15	16	17	18	19	20
(4)	(5)	(6)	(7)	(8)	(9)	(10)
21	22	23	24	25	26	27
(11)	(12)	(13)	(14)	(15)	(16)	(17)
28	29	30				
(18)	(19)	(20)				

September (Elul 6)						
S	M	T	W	T	F	S
			1	2	3	4
			(20)	(21)	(22)	(23)
5	6	7	8	9	10	11
(24)	(25)	(26)	(27)	(28)	(29)	(30i)
12	13	14	15	16	17	18
(1)	(2)	(3)	(4)	(5)	(6)	(7)
19	20	21	22	23	24	25
(8)	(9)	(10)	(11)	(12)	(13)	(14)
26	27	28	29	30		
(15)	(16)	(17)	(18)	(19)		

December (Kislev 9)						
S	M	T	W	T	F	S
			1	2	3	4
			(21)	(22)	(23)	(24)
5	6	7	8	9	10	11
(25)	(26)	(27)	(28)	(29m)	(1)	(2)
12	13	14	15	16	17	18
(3)	(4)	(5)	(6)	(7)	(8)	(9)
19	20	21	22	23	24	25
(10)	(11)	(12)	(13)	(14)	(15)	(16)
26	27	28	29	30	31	
(17)	(18)	(19)	(20)	(21)	(22)	

Day of Trumpets — Tishri 1
Feast of Booths — Tishri 15-22

Day of Atonement — Tishri 10
Feast of Dedication — 8 days beginning Kislev 25

Time of the New Moon —   g8:32   h21:52   i14:11   j2:48   k4:05   m22:08

A.D. 61

			January (Tebeth 10)			
S	M	T	W	T	F	S
						1 (23)
2 (24)	3 (25)	4 (26)	5 (27)	6 (28)	7 (29)	8 (30a)
9 (1)	10 (2)	11 (3)	12 (4)	13 (5)	14 (6)	15 (7)
16 (8)	17 (9)	18 (10)	19 (11)	20 (12)	21 (13)	22 (14)
23 (15)	24 (16)	25 (17)	26 (18)	27 (19)	28 (20)	29 (21)
30 (22)	31 (23)					

			April (Nisan 1)			
S	M	T	W	T	F	S
					1 (24)	2 (25)
3 (26)	4 (27)	5 (28)	6 (29d)	7 (1)	8 (2)	9 (3)
10 (4)	11 (5)	12 (6)	13 (7)	14 (8)	15 (9)	16 (10)
17 (11)	18 (12)	19 (13)	20 (14)	21 (15)	22 (16)	23 (17)
24 (18)	25 (19)	26 (20)	27 (21)	28 (22)	29 (23)	30 (24)

			February (Shebat 11)			
S	M	T	W	T	F	S
		1 (24)	2 (25)	3 (26)	4 (27)	5 (28)
6 (29)	7 (30b)	8 (1)	9 (2)	10 (3)	11 (4)	12 (5)
13 (6)	14 (7)	15 (8)	16 (9)	17 (10)	18 (11)	19 (12)
20 (13)	21 (14)	22 (15)	23 (16)	24 (17)	25 (18)	26 (19)
27 (20)	28 (21)					

			May (Iyyar 2)			
S	M	T	W	T	F	S
1 (25)	2 (26)	3 (27)	4 (28)	5 (29)	6 (30e)	7 (1)
8 (2)	9 (3)	10 (4)	11 (5)	12 (6)	13 (7)	14 (8)
15 (9)	16 (10)	17 (11)	18 (12)	19 (13)	20 (14)	21 (15)
22 (16)	23 (17)	24 (18)	25 (19)	26 (20)	27 (21)	28 (22)
29 (23)	30 (24)	31 (25)				

			March (Adar 12)			
S	M	T	W	T	F	S
		1 (22)	2 (23)	3 (24)	4 (25)	5 (26)
6 (27)	7 (28)	8 (29c)	9 (1)	10 (2)	11 (3)	12 (4)
13 (5)	14 (6)	15 (7)	16 (8)	17 (9)	18 (10)	19 (11)
20 (12)	21 (13)	22 (14)	23 (15)	24 (16)	25 (17)	26 (18)
27 (19)	28 (20)	29 (21)	30 (22)	31 (23)		

			June (Sivan 3)			
S	M	T	W	T	F	S
			1 (26)	2 (27)	3 (28)	4 (29f)
5 (1)	6 (2)	7 (3)	8 (4)	9 (5)	10 (6)	11 (7)
12 (8)	13 (9)	14 (10)	15 (11)	16 (12)	17 (13)	18 (14)
19 (15)	20 (16)	21 (17)	22 (18)	23 (19)	24 (20)	25 (21)
26 (22)	27 (23)	28 (24)	29 (25)	30 (26)		

Passover Lamb Sacrificed — Nisan 14
Feast of First Fruits — 1st Sunday after Nisan 15

Feast of Unleavened Bread — Nisan 15-21
Pentecost — 8th Sunday after Nisan 15

Time of New Moon (Jerusalem) — a13:46   b2:43   c13:15   d21:50   e5:08   f12:00

July
(Tammuz 4)

S	M	T	W	T	F	S
					1	2
					(27)	(28)
3	4	5	6	7	8	9
(29g)	(1)	(2)	(3)	(4)	(5)	(6)
10	11	12	13	14	15	16
(7)	(8)	(9)	(10)	(11)	(12)	(13)
17	18	19	20	21	22	23
(14)	(15)	(16)	(17)	(18)	(19)	(20)
24	25	26	27	28	29	30
(21)	(22)	(23)	(24)	(25)	(26)	(27)
31						
(28)						

October
(Marheshvan 8)

S	M	T	W	T	F	S
						1
						(1)
2	3	4	5	6	7	8
(2)	(3)	(4)	(5)	(6)	(7)	(8)
9	10	11	12	13	14	15
(9)	(10)	(11)	(12)	(13)	(14)	(15)
16	17	18	19	20	21	22
(16)	(17)	(18)	(19)	(20)	(21)	(22)
23	24	25	26	27	28	29
(23)	(24)	(25)	(26)	(27)	(28)	(29)
30	31					
(30k)	(1)					

August
(Ab 5)

S	M	T	W	T	F	S
	1	2	3	4	5	6
	(29)	(30h)	(1)	(2)	(3)	(4)
7	8	9	10	11	12	13
(5)	(6)	(7)	(8)	(9)	(10)	(11)
14	15	16	17	18	19	20
(12)	(13)	(14)	(15)	(16)	(17)	(18)
21	22	23	24	25	26	27
(19)	(20)	(21)	(22)	(23)	(24)	(25)
28	29	30	31			
(26)	(27)	(28)	(29i)			

November
(Kislev 9)

S	M	T	W	T	F	S
		1	2	3	4	5
		(2)	(3)	(4)	(5)	(6)
6	7	8	9	10	11	12
(7)	(8)	(9)	(10)	(11)	(12)	(13)
13	14	15	16	17	18	19
(14)	(15)	(16)	(17)	(18)	(19)	(20)
20	21	22	23	24	25	26
(21)	(22)	(23)	(24)	(25)	(26)	(27)
27	28	29	30			
(28)	(29m)	(1)	(2)			

September
(Tishri 7)

S	M	T	W	T	F	S
				1	2	3
				(1)	(2)	(3)
4	5	6	7	8	9	10
(4)	(5)	(6)	(7)	(8)	(9)	(10)
11	12	13	14	15	16	17
(11)	(12)	(13)	(14)	(15)	(16)	(17)
18	19	20	21	22	23	24
(18)	(19)	(20)	(21)	(22)	(23)	(24)
25	26	27	28	29	30	
(25)	(26)	(27)	(28)	(29)	(30j)	

December
(Tebeth 10)

S	M	T	W	T	F	S
				1	2	3
				(3)	(4)	(5)
4	5	6	7	8	9	10
(6)	(7)	(8)	(9)	(10)	(11)	(12)
11	12	13	14	15	16	17
(13)	(14)	(15)	(16)	(17)	(18)	(19)
18	19	20	21	22	23	24
(20)	(21)	(22)	(23)	(24)	(25)	(26)
25	26	27	28	29	30	31
(27)	(28)	(29)	(30n)	(1)	(2)	(3)

Day of Trumpets — Tishri 1
Feast of Booths — Tishri 15-22

Day of Atonement — Tishri 10
Feast of Dedication — 8 days beginning Kislev 25

Time of the New Moon —   g19:34   h5:02   i17:24   j9:01   k3:20   m22:54   n18:01

A.D. 62

January (Shebat 11)

S	M	T	W	T	F	S
1	2	3	4	5	6	7
(4)	(5)	(6)	(7)	(8)	(9)	(10)
8	9	10	11	12	13	14
(11)	(12)	(13)	(14)	(15)	(16)	(17)
15	16	17	18	19	20	21
(18)	(19)	(20)	(21)	(22)	(23)	(24)
22	23	24	25	26	27	28
(25)	(26)	(27)	(28)	(29)	(30a)	(1)
29	30	31				
(2)	(3)	(4)				

April (Nisan 1)

S	M	T	W	T	F	S
						1
						(5)
2	3	4	5	6	7	8
(6)	(7)	(8)	(9)	(10)	(11)	(12)
9	10	11	12	13	14	15
(13)	(14)	(15)	(16)	(17)	(18)	(19)
16	17	18	19	20	21	22
(20)	(21)	(22)	(23)	(24)	(25)	(26)
23	24	25	26	27	28	29
(27)	(28)	(29d)	(1)	(2)	(3)	(4)
30						
(5)						

February (Adar 12)

S	M	T	W	T	F	S
			1	2	3	4
			(5)	(6)	(7)	(8)
5	6	7	8	9	10	11
(9)	(10)	(11)	(12)	(13)	(14)	(15)
12	13	14	15	16	17	18
(16)	(17)	(18)	(19)	(20)	(21)	(22)
19	20	21	22	23	24	25
(23)	(24)	(25)	(26)	(27)	(28)	(29)
26	27	28				
(30b)	(1)	(2)				

May (Iyyar 2)

S	M	T	W	T	F	S
		1	2	3	4	5	6
	(6)	(7)	(8)	(9)	(10)	(11)
7	8	9	10	11	12	13
(12)	(13)	(14)	(15)	(16)	(17)	(18)
14	15	16	17	18	19	20
(19)	(20)	(21)	(22)	(23)	(24)	(25)
21	22	23	24	25	26	27
(26)	(27)	(28)	(29)	(30e)	(1)	(2)
28	29	30	31			
(3)	(4)	(5)	(6)			

March (Adar II 13)

S	M	T	W	T	F	S
			1	2	3	4
			(3)	(4)	(5)	(6)
5	6	7	8	9	10	11
(7)	(8)	(9)	(10)	(11)	(12)	(13)
12	13	14	15	16	17	18
(14)	(15)	(16)	(17)	(18)	(19)	(20)
19	20	21	22	23	24	25
(21)	(22)	(23)	(24)	(25)	(26)	(27)
26	27	28	29	30	31	
(28)	(29c)	(1)	(2)	(3)	(4)	

June (Sivan 3)

S	M	T	W	T	F	S
				1	2	3
				(7)	(8)	(9)
4	5	6	7	8	9	10
(10)	(11)	(12)	(13)	(14)	(15)	(16)
11	12	13	14	15	16	17
(17)	(18)	(19)	(20)	(21)	(22)	(23)
18	19	20	21	22	23	24
(24)	(25)	(26)	(27)	(28)	(29f)	(1)
25	26	27	28	29	30	
(2)	(3)	(4)	(5)	(6)	(7)	

Passover Lamb Sacrificed — Nisan 14

Feast of First Fruits — 1st Sunday after Nisan 15

Feast of Unleavened Bread — Nisan 15-21

Pentecost — 8th Sunday after Nisan 15

Time of New Moon (Jerusalem) —   a11:15   b1:44   c13:13   d22:04   e5:12   f11:46

A.D. 62

July
(Tammuz 4)

S	M	T	W	T	F	S
						1
						(8)
2	3	4	5	6	7	8
(9)	(10)	(11)	(12)	(13)	(14)	(15)
9	10	11	12	13	14	15
(16)	(17)	(18)	(19)	(20)	(21)	(22)
16	17	18	19	20	21	22
(23)	(24)	(25)	(26)	(27)	(28)	(29g)
23	24	25	26	27	28	29
(1)	(2)	(3)	(4)	(5)	(6)	(7)
30	31					
(8)	(9)					

October
(Tishri 7)

S	M	T	W	T	F	S
1	2	3	4	5	6	7
(12)	(13)	(14)	(15)	(16)	(17)	(18)
8	9	10	11	12	13	14
(19)	(20)	(21)	(22)	(23)	(24)	(25)
15	16	17	18	19	20	21
(26)	(27)	(28)	(29)	(30j)	(1)	(2)
22	23	24	25	26	27	28
(3)	(4)	(5)	(6)	(7)	(8)	(9)
29	30	31				
(10)	(11)	(12)				

August
(Ab 5)

S	M	T	W	T	F	S
		1	2	3	4	5
		(10)	(11)	(12)	(13)	(14)
6	7	8	9	10	11	12
(15)	(16)	(17)	(18)	(19)	(20)	(21)
13	14	15	16	17	18	19
(22)	(23)	(24)	(25)	(26)	(27)	(28)
20	21	22	23	24	25	26
(29)	(30h)	(1)	(2)	(3)	(4)	(5)
27	28	29	30	31		
(6)	(7)	(8)	(9)	(10)		

November
(Marheshvan 8)

S	M	T	W	T	F	S
			1	2	3	4
			(13)	(14)	(15)	(16)
5	6	7	8	9	10	11
(17)	(18)	(19)	(20)	(21)	(22)	(23)
12	13	14	15	16	17	18
(24)	(25)	(26)	(27)	(28)	(29k)	(1)
19	20	21	22	23	24	25
(2)	(3)	(4)	(5)	(6)	(7)	(8)
26	27	28	29	30		
(9)	(10)	(11)	(12)	(13)		

September
(Elul 6)

S	M	T	W	T	F	S
					1	2
					(11)	(12)
3	4	5	6	7	8	9
(13)	(14)	(15)	(16)	(17)	(18)	(19)
10	11	12	13	14	15	16
(20)	(21)	(22)	(23)	(24)	(25)	(26)
17	18	19	20	21	22	23
(27)	(28)	(29i)	(1)	(2)	(3)	(4)
24	25	26	27	28	29	30
(5)	(6)	(7)	(8)	(9)	(10)	(11)

December
(Kislev 9)

S	M	T	W	T	F	S
					1	2
					(14)	(15)
3	4	5	6	7	8	9
(16)	(17)	(18)	(19)	(20)	(21)	(22)
10	11	12	13	14	15	16
(23)	(24)	(25)	(26)	(27)	(28)	(29)
17	18	19	20	21	22	23
(30m)	(1)	(2)	(3)	(4)	(5)	(6)
24	25	26	27	28	29	30
(7)	(8)	(9)	(10)	(11)	(12)	(13)
31						
(14)						

Day of Trumpets — Tishri 1
Feast of Booths — Tishri 15-22

Day of Atonement — Tishri 10
Feast of Dedication — 8 days beginning Kislev 25

Time of the New Moon —   g19:00   h3:57   i15:22   j5:35   k22:27   m17:16

A.D. 63

January
(Tebeth 10)

S	M	T	W	T	F	S
	1	2	3	4	5	6
	(15)	(16)	(17)	(18)	(19)	(20)
7	8	9	10	11	12	13
(21)	(22)	(23)	(24)	(25)	(26)	(27)
14	15	16	17	18	19	20
(28)	(29)	(30a)	(1)	(2)	(3)	(4)
21	22	23	24	25	26	27
(5)	(6)	(7)	(8)	(9)	(10)	(11)
28	29	30	31			
(12)	(13)	(14)	(15)			

February

S	M	T	W	T	F	S
				1	2	3
				(16)	(17)	(18)
4	5	6	7	8	9	10
(19)	(20)	(21)	(22)	(23)	(24)	(25)
11	12	13	14	15	16	17
(26)	(27)	(28)	(29)	(30b)	(1)	(2)
18	19	20	21	22	23	24
(3)	(4)	(5)	(6)	(7)	(8)	(9)
25	26	27	28			
(10)	(11)	(12)	(13)			

March
(Adar 12)

S	M	T	W	T	F	S
				1	2	3
				(14)	(15)	(16)
4	5	6	7	8	9	10
(17)	(18)	(19)	(20)	(21)	(22)	(23)
11	12	13	14	15	16	17
(24)	(25)	(26)	(27)	(28)	(29c)	(1)
18	19	20	21	22	23	24
(2)	(3)	(4)	(5)	(6)	(7)	(8)
25	26	27	28	29	30	31
(9)	(10)	(11)	(12)	(13)	(14)	(15)

April
(Nisan 1)

S	M	T	W	T	F	S
1	2	3	4	5	6	7
(16)	(17)	(18)	(19)	(20)	(21)	(22)
8	9	10	11	12	13	14
(23)	(24)	(25)	(26)	(27)	(28)	(29)
15	16	17	18	19	20	21
(30d)	(1)	(2)	(3)	(4)	(5)	(6)
22	23	24	25	26	27	28
(7)	(8)	(9)	(10)	(11)	(12)	(13)
29	30					
(14)	(15)					

May
(Iyyar 2)

S	M	T	W	T	F	S
			1	2	3	4	5
			(16)	(17)	(18)	(19)	(20)
6	7	8	9	10	11	12
(21)	(22)	(23)	(24)	(25)	(26)	(27)
13	14	15	16	17	18	19
(28)	(29e)	(1)	(2)	(3)	(4)	(5)
20	21	22	23	24	25	26
(6)	(7)	(8)	(9)	(10)	(11)	(12)
27	28	29	30	31		
(13)	(14)	(15)	(16)	(17)		

June
(Sivan 3)

S	M	T	W	T	F	S
					1	2
					(18)	(19)
3	4	5	6	7	8	9
(20)	(21)	(22)	(23)	(24)	(25)	(26)
10	11	12	13	14	15	16
(27)	(28)	(29)	(30f)	(1)	(2)	(3)
17	18	19	20	21	22	23
(4)	(5)	(6)	(7)	(8)	(9)	(10)
24	25	26	27	28	29	30
(11)	(12)	(13)	(14)	(15)	(16)	(17)

Passover Lamb Sacrificed — Nisan 14
Feast of First Fruits — 1st Sunday after Nisan 15

Feast of Unleavened Bread — Nisan 15-21
Pentecost — 8th Sunday after Nisan 15

Time of New Moon (Jerusalem) — a12:44 b7:02 c22:42 d11:08 e20:49 f4:44

A.D. 63

July (Tammuz 4)						
S	M	T	W	T	F	S
1	2	3	4	5	6	7
(18)	(19)	(20)	(21)	(22)	(23)	(24)
8	9	10	11	12	13	14
(25)	(26)	(27)	(28)	(29g)	(1)	(2)
15	16	17	18	19	20	21
(3)	(4)	(5)	(6)	(7)	(8)	(9)
22	23	24	25	26	27	28
(10)	(11)	(12)	(13)	(14)	(15)	(16)
29	30	31				
(17)	(18)	(19)				

October (Tishri 7)						
S	M	T	W	T	F	S
	1	2	3	4	5	6
	(22)	(23)	(24)	(25)	(26)	(27)
7	8	9	10	11	12	13
(28)	(29j)	(1)	(2)	(3)	(4)	(5)
14	15	16	17	18	19	20
(6)	(7)	(8)	(9)	(10)	(11)	(12)
21	22	23	24	25	26	27
(13)	(14)	(15)	(16)	(17)	(18)	(19)
28	29	30	31			
(20)	(21)	(22)	(23)			

August (Ab 5)						
S	M	T	W	T	F	S
			1	2	3	4
			(20)	(21)	(22)	(23)
5	6	7	8	9	10	11
(24)	(25)	(26)	(27)	(28)	(29h)	(1)
12	13	14	15	16	17	18
(2)	(3)	(4)	(5)	(6)	(7)	(8)
19	20	21	22	23	24	25
(9)	(10)	(11)	(12)	(13)	(14)	(15)
26	27	28	29	30	31	
(16)	(17)	(18)	(19)	(20)	(21)	

November (Marheshvan 8)						
S	M	T	W	T	F	S
				1	2	3
				(24)	(25)	(26)
4	5	6	7	8	9	10
(27)	(28)	(29)	(30k)	(1)	(2)	(3)
11	12	13	14	15	16	17
(4)	(5)	(6)	(7)	(8)	(9)	(10)
18	19	20	21	22	23	24
(11)	(12)	(13)	(14)	(15)	(16)	(17)
25	26	27	28	29	30	
(18)	(19)	(20)	(21)	(22)	(23)	

September (Elul 6)						
S	M	T	W	T	F	S
						1
						(22)
2	3	4	5	6	7	8
(23)	(24)	(25)	(26)	(27)	(28)	(29)
9	10	11	12	13	14	15
(30i)	(1)	(2)	(3)	(4)	(5)	(6)
16	17	18	19	20	21	22
(7)	(8)	(9)	(10)	(11)	(12)	(13)
23	24	25	26	27	28	29
(14)	(15)	(16)	(17)	(18)	(19)	(20)
30						
(21)						

December (Kislev 9)						
S	M	T	W	T	F	S
						1
						(24)
2	3	4	5	6	7	8
(25)	(26)	(27)	(28)	(29m)	(1)	(2)
9	10	11	12	13	14	15
(3)	(4)	(5)	(6)	(7)	(8)	(9)
16	17	18	19	20	21	22
(10)	(11)	(12)	(13)	(14)	(15)	(16)
23	24	25	26	27	28	29
(17)	(18)	(19)	(20)	(21)	(22)	(23)
30	31					
(24)	(25)					

Day of Trumpets — Tishri 1
Feast of Booths — Tishri 15-22

Day of Atonement — Tishri 10
Feast of Dedication — 8 days beginning Kislev 25

Time of the New Moon — g12:04 h14:46 i4:36 j15:07 k3:48 m18:58

Gregorian

A.D. 64

January
(Tebeth 10)

S	M	T	W	T	F	S
		1	2	3	4	5
		(26)	(27)	(28)	(29)	(30a)
6	7	8	9	10	11	12
(1)	(2)	(3)	(4)	(5)	(6)	(7)
13	14	15	16	17	18	19
(8)	(9)	(10)	(11)	(12)	(13)	(14)
20	21	22	23	24	25	26
(15)	(16)	(17)	(18)	(19)	(20)	(21)
27	28	29	30	31		
(22)	(23)	(24)	(25)	(26)		

April
(Adar II 13)

S	M	T	W	T	F	S
		1	2	3	4	5
		(27)	(28)	(29d)	(1)	(2)
6	7	8	9	10	11	12
(3)	(4)	(5)	(6)	(7)	(8)	(9)
13	14	15	16	17	18	19
(10)	(11)	(12)	(13)	(14)	(15)	(16)
20	21	22	23	24	25	26
(17)	(18)	(19)	(20)	(21)	(22)	(23)
27	28	29	30			
(24)	(25)	(26)	(27)			

February
(Shebat 11)

S	M	T	W	T	F	S
					1	2
					(27)	(28)
3	4	5	6	7	8	9
(29)	(30b)	(1)	(2)	(3)	(4)	(5)
10	11	12	13	14	15	16
(6)	(7)	(8)	(9)	(10)	(11)	(12)
17	18	19	20	21	22	23
(13)	(14)	(15)	(16)	(17)	(18)	(19)
24	25	26	27	28	29	
(20)	(21)	(22)	(23)	(24)	(25)	

May
(Nisan 1)

S	M	T	W	T	F	S
				1	2	3
				(28)	(29)	(30e)
4	5	6	7	8	9	10
(1)	(2)	(3)	(4)	(5)	(6)	(7)
11	12	13	14	15	16	17
(8)	(9)	(10)	(11)	(12)	(13)	(14)
18	19	20	21	22	23	24
(15)	(16)	(17)	(18)	(19)	(20)	(21)
25	26	27	28	29	30	31
(22)	(23)	(24)	(25)	(26)	(27)	(28)

March
(Adar 12)

S	M	T	W	T	F	S
						1
						(26)
2	3	4	5	6	7	8
(27)	(28)	(29)	(30c)	(1)	(2)	(3)
9	10	11	12	13	14	15
(4)	(5)	(6)	(7)	(8)	(9)	(10)
16	17	18	19	20	21	22
(11)	(12)	(13)	(14)	(15)	(16)	(17)
23	24	25	26	27	28	29
(18)	(19)	(20)	(21)	(22)	(23)	(24)
30	31					
(25)	(26)					

June
(Iyyar 2)

S	M	T	W	T	F	S
1	2	3	4	5	6	7
(29f)	(1)	(2)	(3)	(4)	(5)	(6)
8	9	10	11	12	13	14
(7)	(8)	(9)	(10)	(11)	(12)	(13)
15	16	17	18	19	20	21
(14)	(15)	(16)	(17)	(18)	(19)	(20)
22	23	24	25	26	27	28
(21)	(22)	(23)	(24)	(25)	(26)	(27)
29	30					
(28)	(29)					

Passover Lamb Sacrificed — Nisan 14

Feast of First Fruits — 1st Sunday after Nisan 15

Feast of Unleavened Bread — Nisan 15-21

Pentecost — 8th Sunday after Nisan 15

Time of New Moon (Jerusalem) — a12:24 b7:00 c1:02 d17:06 e6:37 f17:55

July
(Sivan 3)

S	M	T	W	T	F	S
		1	2	3	4	5
		(30g)	(1)	(2)	(3)	(4)
6	7	8	9	10	11	12
(5)	(6)	(7)	(8)	(9)	(10)	(11)
13	14	15	16	17	18	19
(12)	(13)	(14)	(15)	(16)	(17)	(18)
20	21	22	23	24	25	26
(19)	(20)	(21)	(22)	(23)	(24)	(25)
27	28	29	30	31		
(26)	(27)	(28)	(29h)	(1)		

October
(Tishri 7)

S	M	T	W	T	F	S
			1	2	3	4
			(4)	(5)	(6)	(7)
5	6	7	8	9	10	11
(8)	(9)	(10)	(11)	(12)	(13)	(14)
12	13	14	15	16	17	18
(15)	(16)	(17)	(18)	(19)	(20)	(21)
19	20	21	22	23	24	25
(22)	(23)	(24)	(25)	(26)	(27)	(28)
26	27	28	29	30	31	
(29k)	(1)	(2)	(3)	(4)	(5)	

August
(Ab 5)

S	M	T	W	T	F	S
					1	2
					(2)	(3)
3	4	5	6	7	8	9
(4)	(5)	(6)	(7)	(8)	(9)	(10)
10	11	12	13	14	15	16
(11)	(12)	(13)	(14)	(15)	(16)	(17)
17	18	19	20	21	22	23
(18)	(19)	(20)	(21)	(22)	(23)	(24)
24	25	26	27	28	29	30
(25)	(26)	(27)	(28)	(29i)	(1)	(2)
31						
(3)						

November
(Marheshvan 8)

S	M	T	W	T	F	S
						1
						(6)
2	3	4	5	6	7	8
(7)	(8)	(9)	(10)	(11)	(12)	(13)
9	10	11	12	13	14	15
(14)	(15)	(16)	(17)	(18)	(19)	(20)
16	17	18	19	20	21	22
(21)	(22)	(23)	(24)	(25)	(26)	(27)
23	24	25	26	27	28	29
(28)	(29)	(30m)	(1)	(2)	(3)	(4)
30						
(5)						

September
(Elul 6)

S	M	T	W	T	F	S
	1	2	3	4	5	6
	(4)	(5)	(6)	(7)	(8)	(9)
7	8	9	10	11	12	13
(10)	(11)	(12)	(13)	(14)	(15)	(16)
14	15	16	17	18	19	20
(17)	(18)	(19)	(20)	(21)	(22)	(23)
21	22	23	24	25	26	27
(24)	(25)	(26)	(27)	(28)	(29)	(30i)
28	29	30				
(1)	(2)	(3)				

December
(Kislev 9)

S	M	T	W	T	F	S
	1	2	3	4	5	6
	(6)	(7)	(8)	(9)	(10)	(11)
7	8	9	10	11	12	13
(12)	(13)	(14)	(15)	(16)	(17)	(18)
14	15	16	17	18	19	20
(19)	(20)	(21)	(22)	(23)	(24)	(25)
21	22	23	24	25	26	27
(26)	(27)	(28)	(29n)	(1)	(2)	(3)
28	29	30	31			
(4)	(5)	(6)	(7)			

Day of Trumpets — Tishri 1
Feast of Booths — Tishri 15-22

Day of Atonement — Tishri 10
Feast of Dedication — 8 days beginning Kislev 25

Time of the New Moon — g3:36 h12:26 i21:03 j6:05 k16:09 m3:50 n17:27

A.D. 65

January
(Tebeth 10)

S	M	T	W	T	F	S
				1	2	3
				(8)	(9)	(10)
4	5	6	7	8	9	10
(11)	(12)	(13)	(14)	(15)	(16)	(17)
11	12	13	14	15	16	17
(18)	(19)	(20)	(21)	(22)	(23)	(24)
18	19	20	21	22	23	24
(25)	(26)	(27)	(28)	(29)	(30a)	(1)
25	26	27	28	29	30	31
(2)	(3)	(4)	(5)	(6)	(7)	(8)

April
(Nisan 1)

S	M	T	W	T	F	S
			1	2	3	4
			(9)	(10)	(11)	(12)
5	6	7	8	9	10	11
(13)	(14)	(15)	(16)	(17)	(18)	(19)
12	13	14	15	16	17	18
(20)	(21)	(22)	(23)	(24)	(25)	(26)
19	20	21	22	23	24	25
(27)	(28)	(29)	(30d)	(1)	(2)	(3)
26	27	28	29	30		
(4)	(5)	(6)	(7)	(8)		

February
(Shebat 11)

S	M	T	W	T	F	S
1	2	3	4	5	6	7
(9)	(10)	(11)	(12)	(13)	(14)	(15)
8	9	10	11	12	13	14
(16)	(17)	(18)	(19)	(20)	(21)	(22)
15	16	17	18	19	20	21
(23)	(24)	(25)	(26)	(27)	(28)	(29)
22	23	24	25	26	27	28
(30b)	(1)	(2)	(3)	(4)	(5)	(6)

May
(Iyyar 2)

S	M	T	W	T	F	S
					1	2
					(9)	(10)
3	4	5	6	7	8	9
(11)	(12)	(13)	(14)	(15)	(16)	(17)
10	11	12	13	14	15	16
(18)	(19)	(20)	(21)	(22)	(23)	(24)
17	18	19	20	21	22	23
(25)	(26)	(27)	(28)	(29)	(30e)	(1)
24	25	26	27	28	29	30
(2)	(3)	(4)	(5)	(6)	(7)	(8)
31						
(9)						

March
(Adar 12)

S	M	T	W	T	F	S
1	2	3	4	5	6	7
(7)	(8)	(9)	(10)	(11)	(12)	(13)
8	9	10	11	12	13	14
(14)	(15)	(16)	(17)	(18)	(19)	(20)
15	16	17	18	19	20	21
(21)	(22)	(23)	(24)	(25)	(26)	(27)
22	23	24	25	26	27	28
(28)	(29c)	(1)	(2)	(3)	(4)	(5)
29	30	31				
(6)	(7)	(8)				

June
(Sivan 3)

S	M	T	W	T	F	S
	1	2	3	4	5	6
	(10)	(11)	(12)	(13)	(14)	(15)
7	8	9	10	11	12	13
(16)	(17)	(18)	(19)	(20)	(21)	(22)
14	15	16	17	18	19	20
(23)	(24)	(25)	(26)	(27)	(28)	(29f)
21	22	23	24	25	26	27
(1)	(2)	(3)	(4)	(5)	(6)	(7)
28	29	30				
(8)	(9)	(10)				

Passover Lamb Sacrificed — Nisan 14
Feast of First Fruits — 1st Sunday after Nisan 15

Feast of Unleavened Bread — Nisan 15-21
Pentecost — 8th Sunday after Nisan 15

Time of New Moon (Jerusalem) —   a8:49   b1:12   c17:38   d9:26   e0:07   f13:27

A.D. 65

July
(Tammuz 4)

S	M	T	W	T	F	S
			1	2	3	4
			(11)	(12)	(13)	(14)
5	6	7	8	9	10	11
(15)	(16)	(17)	(18)	(19)	(20)	(21)
12	13	14	15	16	17	18
(22)	(23)	(24)	(25)	(26)	(27)	(28)
19	20	21	22	23	24	25
(29)	(30g)	(1)	(2)	(3)	(4)	(5)
26	27	28	29	30	31	
(6)	(7)	(8)	(9)	(10)	(11)	

October 17
(Tishri 7)

S	M	T	W	T	F	S
				1	2	3
				(15)	(16)	(17)
4	5	6	7	8	9	10
(18)	(19)	(20)	(21)	(22)	(23)	(24)
11	12	13	14	15	16	17
(25)	(26)	(27)	(28)	(29)	(30j)	(1)
18	19	20	21	22	23	24
(2)	(3)	(4)	(5)	(6)	(7)	(8)
25	26	27	28	29	30	31
(9)	(10)	(11)	(12)	(13)	(14)	(15)

August
(Ab 5)

S	M	T	W	T	F	S
						1
						(12)
2	3	4	5	6	7	8
(13)	(14)	(15)	(16)	(17)	(18)	(19)
9	10	11	12	13	14	15
(20)	(21)	(22)	(23)	(24)	(25)	(26)
16	17	18	19	20	21	22
(27)	(28)	(29h)	(1)	(2)	(3)	(4)
23	24	25	26	27	28	29
(5)	(6)	(7)	(8)	(9)	(10)	(11)
30	31					
(12)	(13)					

November
(Marheshvan 8)

S	M	T	W	T	F	S
1	2	3	4	5	6	7
(16)	(17)	(18)	(19)	(20)	(21)	(22)
8	9	10	11	12	13	14
(23)	(24)	(25)	(26)	(27)	(28)	(29k)
15	16	17	18	19	20	21
(1)	(2)	(3)	(4)	(5)	(6)	(7)
22	23	24	25	26	27	28
(8)	(9)	(10)	(11)	(12)	(13)	(14)
29	30					
(15)	(16)					

September
(Elul 6)

S	M	T	W	T	F	S
		1	2	3	4	5
		(14)	(15)	(16)	(17)	(18)
6	7	8	9	10	11	12
(19)	(20)	(21)	(22)	(23)	(24)	(25)
13	14	15	16	17	18	19
(26)	(27)	(28)	(29i)	(1)	(2)	(3)
20	21	22	23	24	25	26
(4)	(5)	(6)	(7)	(8)	(9)	(10)
27	28	29	30			
(11)	(12)	(13)	(14)			

December
(Kislev 9)

S	M	T	W	T	F	S
		1	2	3	4	5
		(17)	(18)	(19)	(20)	(21)
6	7	8	9	10	11	12
(22)	(23)	(24)	(25)	(26)	(27)	(28)
13	14	15	16	17	18	19
(29)	(30m)	(1)	(2)	(3)	(4)	(5)
20	21	22	23	24	25	26
(6)	(7)	(8)	(9)	(10)	(11)	(12)
27	28	29	30	31		
(13)	(14)	(15)	(16)	(17)		

Day of Trumpets — Tishri 1
Feast of Booths — Tishri 15-22

Day of Atonement — Tishri 10
Feast of Dedication — 8 days beginning Kislev 25

Time of the New Moon — g1:23 h12:04 i22:01 j7:53 k18:16 m5:28

A.D. 66

January (Tebeth 10)						
S	M	T	W	T	F	S
					1 (18)	2 (19)
3 (20)	4 (21)	5 (22)	6 (23)	7 (24)	8 (25)	9 (26)
10 (27)	11 (28)	12 (29a)	13 (1)	14 (2)	15 (3)	16 (4)
17 (5)	18 (6)	19 (7)	20 (8)	21 (9)	22 (10)	23 (11)
24 (12)	25 (13)	26 (14)	27 (15)	28 (16)	29 (17)	30 (18)
31 (19)						

April (Nisan 1)						
S	M	T	W	T	F	S
				1 (20)	2 (21)	3 (22)
4 (23)	5 (24)	6 (25)	7 (26)	8 (27)	9 (28)	10 (29)
11 (30d)	12 (1)	13 (2)	14 (3)	15 (4)	16 (5)	17 (6)
18 (7)	19 (8)	20 (9)	21 (10)	22 (11)	23 (12)	24 (13)
25 (14)	26 (15)	27 (16)	28 (17)	29 (18)	30 (19)	

February (Shebat 11)						
S	M	T	W	T	F	S
	1 (20)	2 (21)	3 (22)	4 (23)	5 (24)	6 (25)
7 (26)	8 (27)	9 (28)	10 (29)	11 (30b)	12 (1)	13 (2)
14 (3)	15 (4)	16 (5)	17 (6)	18 (7)	19 (8)	20 (9)
21 (10)	22 (11)	23 (12)	24 (13)	25 (14)	26 (15)	27 (16)
28 (17)						

May (Iyyar 2)						
S	M	T	W	T	F	S
						1 (20)
2 (21)	3 (22)	4 (23)	5 (24)	6 (25)	7 (26)	8 (27)
9 (28)	10 (29)	11 (30e)	12 (1)	13 (2)	14 (3)	15 (4)
16 (5)	17 (6)	18 (7)	19 (8)	20 (9)	21 (10)	22 (11)
23 (12)	24 (13)	25 (14)	26 (15)	27 (16)	28 (17)	29 (18)
30 (19)	31 (20)					

March (Adar 12)						
S	M	T	W	T	F	S
	1 (18)	2 (19)	3 (20)	4 (21)	5 (22)	6 (23)
7 (24)	8 (25)	9 (26)	10 (27)	11 (28)	12 (29c)	13 (1)
14 (2)	15 (3)	16 (4)	17 (5)	18 (6)	19 (7)	20 (8)
21 (9)	22 (10)	23 (11)	24 (12)	25 (13)	26 (14)	27 (15)
28 (16)	29 (17)	30 (18)	31 (19)			

June (Sivan 3)						
S	M	T	W	T	F	S
		1 (21)	2 (22)	3 (23)	4 (24)	5 (25)
6 (26)	7 (27)	8 (28)	9 (29f)	10 (1)	11 (2)	12 (3)
13 (4)	14 (5)	15 (6)	16 (7)	17 (8)	18 (9)	19 (10)
20 (11)	21 (12)	22 (13)	23 (14)	24 (15)	25 (16)	26 (17)
27 (18)	28 (19)	29 (20)	30 (21)			

Passover Lamb Sacrificed — Nisan 14
Feast of First Fruits — 1st Sunday after Nisan 15

Feast of Unleavened Bread — Nisan 15-21
Pentecost — 8th Sunday after Nisan 15

Time of New Moon (Jerusalem) — a17:31 b6:19 c19:49 d10:06 e1:06 f16:27

A.D. 66

July
(Tammuz 4)

S	M	T	W	T	F	S
				1	2	3
				(22)	(23)	(24)
4	5	6	7	8	9	10
(25)	(26)	(27)	(28)	(29)	(30g)	(1)
11	12	13	14	15	16	17
(2)	(3)	(4)	(5)	(6)	(7)	(8)
18	19	20	21	22	23	24
(9)	(10)	(11)	(12)	(13)	(14)	(15)
25	26	27	28	29	30	31
(16)	(17)	(18)	(19)	(20)	(21)	(22)

October
(Tishri 7)

S	M	T	W	T	F	S
					1	2
					(25)	(26)
3	4	5	6	7	8	9
(27)	(28)	(29j)	(1)	(2)	(3)	(4)
10	11	12	13	14	15	16
(5)	(6)	(7)	(8)	(9)	(10)	(11)
17	18	19	20	21	22	23
(12)	(13)	(14)	(15)	(16)	(17)	(18)
24	25	26	27	28	29	30
(19)	(20)	(21)	(22)	(23)	(24)	(25)
31						
(26)						

August
(Ab 5)

S	M	T	W	T	F	S
1	2	3	4	5	6	7
(23)	(24)	(25)	(26)	(27)	(28)	(29h)
8	9	10	11	12	13	14
(1)	(2)	(3)	(4)	(5)	(6)	(7)
15	16	17	18	19	20	21
(8)	(9)	(10)	(11)	(12)	(13)	(14)
22	23	24	25	26	27	28
(15)	(16)	(17)	(18)	(19)	(20)	(21)
29	30	31				
(22)	(23)	(24)				

November
(Marheshvan 8)

S	M	T	W	T	F	S
	1	2	3	4	5	6
	(27)	(28)	(29)	(30k)	(1)	(2)
7	8	9	10	11	12	13
(3)	(4)	(5)	(6)	(7)	(8)	(9)
14	15	16	17	18	19	20
(10)	(11)	(12)	(13)	(14)	(15)	(16)
21	22	23	24	25	26	27
(17)	(18)	(19)	(20)	(21)	(22)	(23)
28	29	30				
(24)	(25)	(26)				

September
(Elul 6)

S	M	T	W	T	F	S
			1	2	3	4
			(25)	(26)	(27)	(28)
5	6	7	8	9	10	11
(29)	(30i)	(1)	(2)	(3)	(4)	(5)
12	13	14	15	16	17	18
(6)	(7)	(8)	(9)	(10)	(11)	(12)
19	20	21	22	23	24	25
(13)	(14)	(15)	(16)	(17)	(18)	(19)
26	27	28	29	30		
(20)	(21)	(22)	(23)	(24)		

December
(Kislev 9)

S	M	T	W	T	F	S
			1	2	3	4
			(27)	(28)	(29m)	(1)
5	6	7	8	9	10	11
(2)	(3)	(4)	(5)	(6)	(7)	(8)
12	13	14	15	16	17	18
(9)	(10)	(11)	(12)	(13)	(14)	(15)
19	20	21	22	23	24	25
(16)	(17)	(18)	(19)	(20)	(21)	(22)
26	27	28	29	30	31	
(23)	(24)	(25)	(26)	(27)	(28)	

Day of Trumpets — Tishri 1
Feast of Booths — Tishri 15-22

Day of Atonement — Tishri 10
Feast of Dedication — 8 days beginning Kislev 25

Time of the New Moon — g7:26   h21:27   i10:27   j22:2   k19:51   m21:02

A.D. 67

January (Tebeth 10)						
S	M	T	W	T	F	S
						1
						(29)
2	3	4	5	6	7	8
(30a)	(1)	(2)	(3)	(4)	(5)	(6)
9	10	11	12	13	14	15
(7)	(8)	(9)	(10)	(11)	(12)	(13)
16	17	18	19	20	21	22
(14)	(15)	(16)	(17)	(18)	(19)	(20)
23	24	25	26	27	28	29
(21)	(22)	(23)	(24)	(25)	(26)	(27)
30	31					
(28)	(29b)					

April (Nisan 1)						
S	M	T	W	T	F	S
					1	2
					(1)	(2)
3	4	5	6	7	8	9
(3)	(4)	(5)	(6)	(7)	(8)	(9)
10	11	12	13	14	15	16
(10)	(11)	(12)	(13)	(14)	(15)	(16)
17	18	19	20	21	22	23
(17)	(18)	(19)	(20)	(21)	(22)	(23)
24	25	26	27	28	29	30
(24)	(25)	(26)	(27)	(28)	(29)	(30e)

February (Adar 12)						
S	M	T	W	T	F	S
		1	2	3	4	5
		(1)	(2)	(3)	(4)	(5)
6	7	8	9	10	11	12
(6)	(7)	(8)	(9)	(10)	(11)	(12)
13	14	15	16	17	18	19
(13)	(14)	(15)	(16)	(17)	(18)	(19)
20	21	22	23	24	25	26
(20)	(21)	(22)	(23)	(24)	(25)	(26)
27	28					
(27)	(28)					

May (Iyyar 2)						
S	M	T	W	T	F	S
1	2	3	4	5	6	7
(1)	(2)	(3)	(4)	(5)	(6)	(7)
8	9	10	11	12	13	14
(8)	(9)	(10)	(11)	(12)	(13)	(14)
15	16	17	18	19	20	21
(15)	(16)	(17)	(18)	(19)	(20)	(21)
22	23	24	25	26	27	28
(22)	(23)	(24)	(25)	(26)	(27)	(28)
29	30	31				
(29f)	(1)	(2)				

March (Adar 12)						
S	M	T	W	T	F	S
		1	2	3	4	5
		(29)	(30c)	(1)	(2)	(3)
6	7	8	9	10	11	12
(4)	(5)	(6)	(7)	(8)	(9)	(10)
13	14	15	16	17	18	19
(11)	(12)	(13)	(14)	(15)	(16)	(17)
20	21	22	23	24	25	26
(18)	(19)	(20)	(21)	(22)	(23)	(24)
27	28	29	30	31		
(25)	(26)	(27)	(28)	(29d)		

June (Sivan 3)						
S	M	T	W	T	F	S
			1	2	3	4
			(3)	(4)	(5)	(6)
5	6	7	8	9	10	11
(7)	(8)	(9)	(10)	(11)	(12)	(13)
12	13	14	15	16	17	18
(14)	(15)	(16)	(17)	(18)	(19)	(20)
19	20	21	22	23	24	25
(21)	(22)	(23)	(24)	(25)	(26)	(27)
26	27	28	29	30		
(28)	(29)	(30g)	(1)	(2)		

Passover Lamb Sacrificed — Nisan 14
Feast of First Fruits — 1st Sunday after Nisan 15

Feast of Unleavened Bread — Nisan 15-21
Pentecost — 8th Sunday after Nisan 15

Time of New Moon (Jerusalem) — a7:51 b18:20 c4:45 d15:43 e3:51 f17:28 g8:22

A.D. 67

July
(Tammuz 4)

S	M	T	W	T	F	S
					1	2
					(3)	(4)
3	4	5	6	7	8	9
(5)	(6)	(7)	(8)	(9)	(10)	(11)
10	11	12	13	14	15	16
(12)	(13)	(14)	(15)	(16)	(17)	(18)
17	18	19	20	21	22	23
(19)	(20)	(21)	(22)	(23)	(24)	(25)
24	25	26	27	28	29	30
(26)	(27)	(28)	(29)	(30h)	(1)	(2)
31						
(3)						

October
(Tishri 7)

S	M	T	W	T	F	S
						1
						(6)
2	3	4	5	6	7	8
(7)	(8)	(9)	(10)	(11)	(12)	(13)
9	10	11	12	13	14	15
(14)	(15)	(16)	(17)	(18)	(19)	(20)
16	17	18	19	20	21	22
(21)	(22)	(23)	(24)	(25)	(26)	(27)
23	24	25	26	27	28	29
(28)	(29k)	(1)	(2)	(3)	(4)	(5)
30	31					
(6)	(7)					

August
(Ab 5)

S	M	T	W	T	F	S
	1	2	3	4	5	6
	(4)	(5)	(6)	(7)	(8)	(9)
7	8	9	10	11	12	13
(10)	(11)	(12)	(13)	(14)	(15)	(16)
14	15	16	17	18	19	20
(17)	(18)	(19)	(20)	(21)	(22)	(23)
21	22	23	24	25	26	27
(24)	(25)	(26)	(27)	(28)	(29i)	(1)
28	29	30	31			
(2)	(3)	(4)	(5)			

November
(Marheshvan 8)

S	M	T	W	T	F	S
		1	2	3	4	5
		(8)	(9)	(10)	(11)	(12)
6	7	8	9	10	11	12
(13)	(14)	(15)	(16)	(17)	(18)	(19)
13	14	15	16	17	18	19
(20)	(21)	(22)	(23)	(24)	(25)	(26)
20	21	22	23	24	25	26
(27)	(28)	(29)	(30m)	(1)	(2)	(3)
27	28	29	30			
(4)	(5)	(6)	(7)			

September
(Elul 6)

S	M	T	W	T	F	S
				1	2	3
				(6)	(7)	(8)
4	5	6	7	8	9	10
(9)	(10)	(11)	(12)	(13)	(14)	(15)
11	12	13	14	15	16	17
(16)	(17)	(18)	(19)	(20)	(21)	(22)
18	19	20	21	22	23	24
(23)	(24)	(25)	(26)	(27)	(28)	(29)
25	26	27	28	29	30	
(30j)	(1)	(2)	(3)	(4)	(5)	

December
(Kislev 9)

S	M	T	W	T	F	S
				1	2	3
				(8)	(9)	(10)
4	5	6	7	8	9	10
(11)	(12)	(13)	(14)	(15)	(16)	(17)
11	12	13	14	15	16	17
(18)	(19)	(20)	(21)	(22)	(23)	(24)
18	19	20	21	22	23	24
(25)	(26)	(27)	(28)	(29)	(30n)	(1)
25	26	27	28	29	30	31
(2)	(3)	(4)	(5)	(6)	(7)	(8)

Day of Trumpets — Tishri 1
Feast of Booths — Tishri 15-22

Day of Atonement — Tishri 10
Feast of Dedication — 8 days beginning Kislev 25

Time of the New Moon —   h0:01   i15:48   j7:15   k21:55   m11:31   n23:34

Gregorian

A.D. 68

January
(Tebeth 10)

S	M	T	W	T	F	S
1	2	3	4	5	6	7
(9)	(10)	(11)	(12)	(13)	(14)	(15)
8	9	10	11	12	13	14
(16)	(17)	(18)	(19)	(20)	(21)	(22)
15	16	17	18	19	20	21
(23)	(24)	(25)	(26)	(27)	(28)	(29a)
22	23	24	25	26	27	28
(1)	(2)	(3)	(4)	(5)	(6)	(7)
29	30	31				
(8)	(9)	(10)				

April
(Nisan)

S	M	T	W	T	F	S
1	2	3	4	5	6	7
(12)	(13)	(14)	(15)	(16)	(17)	(18)
8	9	10	11	12	13	14
(19)	(20)	(21)	(22)	(23)	(24)	(25)
15	16	17	18	19	20	21
(26)	(27)	(28)	(29d)	(1)	(2)	(3)
22	23	24	25	26	27	28
(4)	(5)	(6)	(7)	(8)	(9)	(10)
29	30					
(11)	(12)					

February
(Shebat 11)

S	M	T	W	T	F	S
			1	2	3	4
			(11)	(12)	(13)	(14)
5	6	7	8	9	10	11
(15)	(16)	(17)	(18)	(19)	(20)	(21)
12	13	14	15	16	17	18
(22)	(23)	(24)	(25)	(26)	(27)	(28)
19	20	21	22	23	24	25
(29b)	(1)	(2)	(3)	(4)	(5)	(6)
26	27	28	29			
(7)	(8)	(9)	(10)			

May
(Iyyar 2)

S	M	T	W	T	F	S
			1	2	3	4	5
			(13)	(14)	(15)	(16)	(17)
6	7	8	9	10	11	12
(18)	(19)	(20)	(21)	(22)	(23)	(24)
13	14	15	16	17	18	19
(25)	(26)	(27)	(28)	(29)	(30e)	(1)
20	21	22	23	24	25	26
(2)	(3)	(4)	(5)	(6)	(7)	(8)
27	28	29	30	31		
(9)	(10)	(11)	(12)	(13)		

March
(Adar 12)

S	M	T	W	T	F	S
				1	2	3
				(11)	(12)	(13)
4	5	6	7	8	9	10
(14)	(15)	(16)	(17)	(18)	(19)	(20)
11	12	13	14	15	16	17
(21)	(22)	(23)	(24)	(25)	(26)	(27)
18	19	20	21	22	23	24
(28)	(29)	(30c)	(1)	(2)	(3)	(4)
25	26	27	28	29	30	31
(5)	(6)	(7)	(8)	(9)	(10)	(11)

June
(Sivan 3)

S	M	T	W	T	F	S
					1	2
					(14)	(15)
3	4	5	6	7	8	9
(16)	(17)	(18)	(19)	(20)	(21)	(22)
10	11	12	13	14	15	16
(23)	(24)	(25)	(26)	(27)	(28)	(29f)
17	18	19	20	21	22	23
(1)	(2)	(3)	(4)	(5)	(6)	(7)
24	25	26	27	28	29	30
(8)	(9)	(10)	(11)	(12)	(13)	(14)

Passover Lamb Sacrificed — Nisan 14
Feast of First Fruits — 1st Sunday after Nisan 15

Feast of Unleavened Bread — Nisan 15-21
Pentecost — 8th Sunday after Nisan 15

Time of New Moon (Jerusalem) — a10:04 b19:25 c4:16 d13:23 e23:30 f11:08

A.D. 68

July
(Tammuz 4)

S	M	T	W	T	F	S
1	2	3	4	5	6	7
(15)	(16)	(17)	(18)	(19)	(20)	(21)
8	9	10	11	12	13	14
(22)	(23)	(24)	(25)	(26)	(27)	(28)
15	16	17	18	19	20	21
(29)	(30g)	(1)	(2)	(3)	(4)	(5)
22	23	24	25	26	27	28
(6)	(7)	(8)	(9)	(10)	(11)	(12)
29	30	31				
(13)	(14)	(15)				

October
(Tishri 7)

S	M	T	W	T	F	S
	1	2	3	4	5	6
	(18)	(19)	(20)	(21)	(22)	(23)
7	8	9	10	11	12	13
(24)	(25)	(26)	(27)	(28)	(29)	(30j)
14	15	16	17	18	19	20
(1)	(2)	(3)	(4)	(5)	(6)	(7)
21	22	23	24	25	26	27
(8)	(9)	(10)	(11)	(12)	(13)	(14)
28	29	30	31			
(15)	(16)	(17)	(18)			

August
(Ab 5)

S	M	T	W	T	F	S
			1	2	3	4
			(16)	(17)	(18)	(19)
5	6	7	8	9	10	11
(20)	(21)	(22)	(23)	(24)	(25)	(26)
12	13	14	15	16	17	18
(27)	(28)	(29h)	(1)	(2)	(3)	(4)
19	20	21	22	23	24	25
(5)	(6)	(7)	(8)	(9)	(10)	(11)
26	27	28	29	30	31	
(12)	(13)	(14)	(15)	(16)	(17)	

November
(Marheshvan 8)

S	M	T	W	T	F	S
				1	2	3
				(19)	(20)	(21)
4	5	6	7	8	9	10
(22)	(23)	(24)	(25)	(26)	(27)	(28)
11	12	13	14	15	16	17
(29k)	(1)	(2)	(3)	(4)	(5)	(6)
18	19	20	21	22	23	24
(7)	(8)	(9)	(10)	(11)	(12)	(13)
25	26	27	28	29	30	
(14)	(15)	(16)	(17)	(18)	(19)	

September
(Elul 6)

S	M	T	W	T	F	S
						1
						(18)
2	3	4	5	6	7	8
(19)	(20)	(21)	(22)	(23)	(24)	(25)
9	10	11	12	13	14	15
(26)	(27)	(28)	(29)	(30i)	(1)	(2)
16	17	18	19	20	21	22
(3)	(4)	(5)	(6)	(7)	(8)	(9)
23	24	25	26	27	28	29
(10)	(11)	(12)	(13)	(14)	(15)	(16)
30						
(17)						

December
(Kislev 9)

S	M	T	W	T	F	S
						1
						(20)
2	3	4	5	6	7	8
(21)	(22)	(23)	(24)	(25)	(26)	(27)
9	10	11	12	13	14	15
(28)	(29)	(30m)	(1)	(2)	(3)	(4)
16	17	18	19	20	21	22
(5)	(6)	(7)	(8)	(9)	(10)	(11)
23	24	25	26	27	28	29
(12)	(13)	(14)	(15)	(16)	(17)	(18)
30	31					
(19)	(20)					

Day of Trumpets — Tishri 1
Feast of Booths — Tishri 15-22

Day of Atonement — Tishri 10
Feast of Dedication — 8 days beginning Kislev 25

Time of the New Moon —   g0:38   h16:07   i9:17   j3:13   k20:34   m11:59

Gregorian

A.D. 69

January
(Tebeth 10)

S	M	T	W	T	F	S
		1	2	3	4	5
		(21)	(22)	(23)	(24)	(25)
6	7	8	9	10	11	12
(26)	(27)	(28)	(29)	(30a)	(1)	(2)
13	14	15	16	17	18	19
(3)	(4)	(5)	(6)	(7)	(8)	(9)
20	21	22	23	24	25	26
(10)	(11)	(12)	(13)	(14)	(15)	(16)
27	28	29	30	31		
(17)	(18)	(19)	(20)	(21)		

April
(Nisan 1)

S	M	T	W	T	F	S
		1	2	3	4	5	6
		(23)	(24)	(25)	(26)	(27)	(28)
7	8	9	10	11	12	13
(29)	(30d)	(1)	(2)	(3)	(4)	(5)
14	15	16	17	18	19	20
(6)	(7)	(8)	(9)	(10)	(11)	(12)
21	22	23	24	25	26	27
(13)	(14)	(15)	(16)	(17)	(18)	(19)
28	29	30				
(20)	(21)	(22)				

February
(Shebat 11)

S	M	T	W	T	F	S
					1	2
					(22)	(23)
3	4	5	6	7	8	9
(24)	(25)	(26)	(27)	(28)	(29b)	(1)
10	11	12	13	14	15	16
(2)	(3)	(4)	(5)	(6)	(7)	(8)
17	18	19	20	21	22	23
(9)	(10)	(11)	(12)	(13)	(14)	(15)
24	25	26	27	28		
(16)	(17)	(18)	(19)	(20)		

May
(Iyyar 2)

S	M	T	W	T	F	S
			1	2	3	4
			(23)	(24)	(25)	(26)
5	6	7	8	9	10	11
(27)	(28)	(29e)	(1)	(2)	(3)	(4)
12	13	14	15	16	17	18
(5)	(6)	(7)	(8)	(9)	(10)	(11)
19	20	21	22	23	24	25
(12)	(13)	(14)	(15)	(16)	(17)	(18)
26	27	28	29	30	31	
(19)	(20)	(21)	(22)	(23)	(24)	

March
(Adar 12)

S	M	T	W	T	F	S
					1	2
					(21)	(22)
3	4	5	6	7	8	9
(23)	(24)	(25)	(26)	(27)	(28)	(29c)
10	11	12	13	14	15	16
(1)	(2)	(3)	(4)	(5)	(6)	(7)
17	18	19	20	21	22	23
(8)	(9)	(10)	(11)	(12)	(13)	(14)
24	25	26	27	28	29	30
(15)	(16)	(17)	(18)	(18)	(20)	(21)
31						
(22)						

June
(Sivan 3)

S	M	T	W	T	F	S
						1
						(25)
2	3	4	5	6	7	8
(26)	(27)	(28)	(29f)	(1)	(2)	(3)
9	10	11	12	13	14	15
(4)	(5)	(6)	(7)	(8)	(9)	(10)
16	17	18	19	20	21	22
(11)	(12)	(13)	(14)	(15)	(16)	(17)
23	24	25	26	27	28	29
(18)	(19)	(20)	(21)	(22)	(23)	(24)
30						
(25)						

Passover Lamb Sacrificed — Nisan 14
Feast of First Fruits — 1st Sunday after Nisan 15

Feast of Unleavened Bread — Nisan 15-21
Pentecost — 8th Sunday after Nisan 15

Time of New Moon (Jerusalem) — a0:56 b11:37 c20:39 d5:43 e12:30 f20:47

A.D. 59

July
(Tammuz 4)

S	M	T	W	T	F	S
	1	2	3	4	5	6
	(26)	(27)	(28)	(29)	(30g)	(1)
7	8	9	10	11	12	13
(2)	(3)	(4)	(5)	(6)	(7)	(8)
14	15	16	17	18	19	20
(9)	(10)	(11)	(12)	(13)	(14)	(15)
21	22	23	24	25	26	27
(16)	(17)	(18)	(19)	(20)	(21)	(22)
28	29	30	31			
(23)	(24)	(25)	(26)			

August
(Ab 5)

S	M	T	W	T	F	S
				1	2	3
				(27)	(28)	(29h)
4	5	6	7	8	9	10
(1)	(2)	(3)	(4)	(5)	(6)	(7)
11	12	13	14	15	16	17
(8)	(9)	(10)	(11)	(12)	(13)	(14)
18	19	20	21	22	23	24
(15)	(16)	(17)	(18)	(19)	(20)	(21)
25	26	27	28	29	30	31
(22)	(23)	(24)	(25)	(26)	(27)	(28)

September
(Elul 6)

S	M	T	W	T	F	S
1	2	3	4	5	6	7
(29)	(30i)	(1)	(2)	(3)	(4)	(5)
8	9	10	11	12	13	14
(6)	(7)	(8)	(9)	(10)	(11)	(12)
15	16	17	18	19	20	21
(13)	(14)	(15)	(16)	(17)	(18)	(19)
22	23	24	25	26	27	28
(20)	(21)	(22)	(23)	(24)	(25)	(26)
29	30					
(27)	(28)					

October
(Tishri 7)

S	M	T	W	T	F	S
		1	2	3	4	5
		(29)	(30j)	(1)	(2)	(3)
6	7	8	9	10	11	12
(4)	(5)	(6)	(7)	(8)	(9)	(10)
13	14	15	16	17	18	19
(11)	(12)	(13)	(14)	(15)	(16)	(17)
20	21	22	23	24	25	26
(18)	(19)	(20)	(21)	(22)	(23)	(24)
27	28	29	30	31		
(25)	(26)	(27)	(28)	(29k)		

November
(Kislev 9)

S	M	T	W	T	F	S
					1	2
					(1)	(2)
3	4	5	6	7	8	9
(3)	(4)	(5)	(6)	(7)	(8)	(9)
10	11	12	13	14	15	16
(10)	(11)	(12)	(13)	(14)	(15)	(16)
17	18	19	20	21	22	23
(17)	(18)	(19)	(20)	(21)	(22)	(23)
24	25	26	27	28	29	30
(24)	(25)	(26)	(27)	(28)	(29)	(30m)

December
(Tebeth 10)

S	M	T	W	T	F	S
1	2	3	4	5	6	7
(1)	(2)	(3)	(4)	(5)	(6)	(7)
8	9	10	11	12	13	14
(8)	(9)	(10)	(11)	(12)	(13)	(14)
15	16	17	18	19	20	21
(15)	(16)	(17)	(18)	(19)	(20)	(21)
22	23	24	25	26	27	28
(22)	(23)	(24)	(25)	(26)	(27)	(28)
29	30	31				
(29)	(30n)	(1)				

Day of Trumpets — Tishri 1
Feast of Booths — Tishri 15-22

Day of Atonement — Tishri 10
Feast of Dedication — 8 days beginning Kislev 25

Time of the New Moon — g6:26 h18:24 i9:19 j3:06 k22:29 m17:29 n10:28

Gregorian

A.D. 70

January
(Shebat 11)

S	M	T	W	T	F	S
			1	2	3	4
			(2)	(3)	(4)	(5)
5	6	7	8	9	10	11
(6)	(7)	(8)	(9)	(10)	(11)	(12)
12	13	14	15	16	17	18
(13)	(14)	(15)	(16)	(17)	(18)	(19)
19	20	21	22	23	24	25
(20)	(21)	(22)	(23)	(24)	(25)	(26)
26	27	28	29	30	31	
(27)	(28)	(29)	(30a)	(1)	(2)	

April
(Nisan 1)

S	M	T	W	T	F	S
			1	2	3	4	5
			(4)	(5)	(6)	(7)	(8)
6	7	8	9	10	11	12
(9)	(10)	(11)	(12)	(13)	(14)	(15)
13	14	15	16	17	18	19
(16)	(17)	(18)	(19)	(20)	(21)	(22)
20	21	22	23	24	25	26
(23)	(24)	(25)	(26)	(27)	(28)	(29)
27	28	29	30			
(30d)	(1)	(2)	(3)			

February
(Adar 12)

S	M	T	W	T	F	S
						1
						(3)
2	3	4	5	6	7	8
(4)	(5)	(6)	(7)	(8)	(9)	(10)
9	10	11	12	13	14	15
(11)	(12)	(13)	(14)	(15)	(16)	(17)
16	17	18	19	20	21	22
(18)	(19)	(20)	(21)	(22)	(23)	(24)
23	24	25	26	27	28	
(25)	(26)	(27)	(28)	(29b)	(1)	

May
(Iyyar 2)

S	M	T	W	T	F	S
				1	2	3
				(4)	(5)	(6)
4	5	6	7	8	9	10
(7)	(8)	(9)	(10)	(11)	(12)	(13)
11	12	13	14	15	16	17
(14)	(15)	(16)	(17)	(18)	(19)	(20)
18	19	20	21	22	23	24
(21)	(22)	(23)	(24)	(25)	(26)	(27)
25	26	27	28	29	30	31
(28)	(29e)	(1)	(2)	(3)	(4)	(5)

March
(Adar II 13)

S	M	T	W	T	F	S
						1
						(2)
2	3	4	5	6	7	8
(3)	(4)	(5)	(6)	(7)	(8)	(9)
9	10	11	12	13	14	15
(10)	(11)	(12)	(13)	(14)	(15)	(16)
16	17	18	19	20	21	22
(17)	(18)	(19)	(20)	(21)	(22)	(23)
23	24	25	26	27	28	29
(24)	(25)	(26)	(27)	(28)	(29c)	(1)
30	31					
(2)	(3)					

June
(Sivan 3)

S	M	T	W	T	F	S
1	2	3	4	5	6	7
(6)	(7)	(8)	(9)	(10)	(11)	(12)
8	9	10	11	12	13	14
(13)	(14)	(15)	(16)	(17)	(18)	(19)
15	16	17	18	19	20	21
(20)	(21)	(22)	(23)	(24)	(25)	(26)
22	23	24	25	26	27	28
(27)	(28)	(29f)	(1)	(2)	(3)	(4)
29	30					
(5)	(6)					

Passover Lamb Sacrificed — Nisan 14
Feast of First Fruits — 1st Sunday after Nisan 15

Feast of Unleavened Bread — Nisan 15-21
Pentecost — 8th Sunday after Nisan 15

Time of New Moon (Jerusalem) — a0:43 b12:19 c21:41 d5:25 e12:18 f19:20

A.D. 70

July
(Tammuz 4)

S	M	T	W	T	F	S
		1	2	3	4	5
		(7)	(8)	(9)	(10)	(11)
6	7	8	9	10	11	12
(12)	(13)	(14)	(15)	(16)	(17)	(18)
13	14	15	16	17	18	19
(19)	(21)	(22)	(23)	(23)	(24)	(25)
20	21	22	23	24	25	26
(26)	(27)	(28)	(29)	(30g)	(1)	(2)
27	28	29	30	31		
(3)	(4)	(5)	(6)	(7)		

October
(Tishri 7)

S	M	T	W	T	F	S
			1	2	3	4
			(10)	(11)	(12)	(13)
5	6	7	8	9	10	11
(14)	(15)	(16)	(17)	(18)	(19)	(20)
12	13	14	15	16	17	18
(21)	(22)	(23)	(24)	(25)	(26)	(27)
19	20	21	22	23	24	25
(28)	(29j)	(1)	(2)	(3)	(4)	(5)
26	27	28	29	30	31	
(6)	(7)	(8)	(9)	(10)	(11)	

August
(Ab 5)

S	M	T	W	T	F	S
					1	2
					(8)	(9)
3	4	5	6	7	8	9
(10)	(11)	(12)	(13)	(14)	(15)	(16)
10	11	12	13	14	15	16
(17)	(18)	(19)	(20)	(21)	(22)	(23)
17	18	19	20	21	22	23
(24)	(25)	(26)	(27)	(28)	(29h)	(1)
24	25	26	27	28	29	30
(2)	(3)	(4)	(5)	(6)	(7)	(8)
31						
(9)						

November
(Marheshvan 8)

S	M	T	W	T	F	S
						1
						(12)
2	3	4	5	6	7	8
(13)	(14)	(15)	(16)	(17)	(18)	(19)
9	10	11	12	13	14	15
(20)	(21)	(22)	(23)	(24)	(25)	(26)
16	17	18	19	20	21	22
(27)	(28)	(29)	(30k)	(1)	(2)	(3)
23	24	25	26	27	28	29
(4)	(5)	(6)	(7)	(8)	(9)	(10)
30						
(11)						

September
(Elul 6)

S	M	T	W	T	F	S
	1	2	3	4	5	6
	(10)	(11)	(12)	(13)	(14)	(15)
7	8	9	10	11	12	13
(16)	(17)	(18)	(19)	(20)	(21)	(22)
14	15	16	17	18	19	20
(23)	(24)	(25)	(26)	(27)	(28)	(29)
21	22	23	24	25	25	27
(30i)	(1)	(2)	(3)	(4)	(5)	(6)
28	29	30				
(7)	(8)	(9)				

December
(Kislev 9)

S	M	T	W	T	F	S
	1	2	3	4	5	6
	(12)	(13)	(14)	(15)	(16)	(17)
7	8	9	10	11	12	13
(18)	(19)	(20)	(21)	(22)	(23)	(24)
14	15	16	17	18	19	20
(25)	(26)	(27)	(28)	(29)	(30m)	(1)
21	22	23	24	25	26	27
(2)	(3)	(4)	(5)	(6)	(7)	(8)
28	29	30	31			
(9)	(10)	(11)	(12)			

Day of Trumpets — Tishri 1
Feast of Booths — Tishri 15-22

Day of Atonement — Tishri 10
Feast of Dedication — 8 days beginning Kislev 25

Time of the New Moon —   g3:44 h14:36 i4:42 j21:54 k17:07 m12:40

Appendix E

Daniel's Seventy "Sevens" Prophecy

"Seventy 'sevens' are decreed for your people and your holy city to finish transgression, to put an end to sin, to atone for wickedness, to bring in everlasting righteousness, to seal up vision and prophecy and to anoint the most holy. Know and understand this: From the issuing of the decree to restore and rebuild Jerusalem until the Anointed One, the ruler, comes, there will be seven 'sevens,' and sixty-two 'sevens.' It will be rebuilt with streets and a trench, but in times of trouble. After the sixty-two 'sevens,' the Anointed One will be cut off and will have nothing. The people of the ruler who will come will destroy the city and the sanctuary. The end will come like a flood: War will continue until the end, and desolations have been decreed. He will confirm a covenant with many for one 'seven.' In the middle of the 'seven' he will put an end to sacrifice and offering. And on a wing of the temple he will set up an abomination that causes desolation, until the end that is decreed is poured out on him." (Daniel 9:24-27)

The unit of time for the sevens in this prophecy is not stated; however, the seven probably means seven years. Thus seventy "sevens" would probably be 70 × 7 = 490 years. The starting point for the prophecy is "from the issuing of the decree to restore and rebuild Jerusalem." There are actually three decrees concerning the rebuilding of Jerusalem after the Babylonian captivity: one under Cyrus (Ezra 1:1-4), one under Darius (Ezra 6:1-12) and one under Artaxerxes (Ezra 7:7-26); however, only the degree by Artaxerxes fits the coming of the Anointed One (Jesus). Artaxerxes' decree was sent out on the first day of the first month of the seventh year of his reign. Artaxerxes was the king of Persia from 464 until 425 B.C. (Chambers Biographical Dictionary page 67). Thus, 464 B.C. would probably be his ascension year and 463 B.C. would be his first year of reign. Therefore, his seventh year would be 457 B.C. The actual date of the letter in terms of our calendar would probably have been March 21, 457 B.C. (Gregorian) since their calendar was essentially the same as the Jewish solar-lunar calendar.

Amazingly 490 years after 457 B.C. (counting inclusively) brings us to A.D. 33 the year that Christ was crucified and rose from the tomb. Daniel 9:24 says: "Seventy 'sevens' are decreed for your people and your holy city to finish transgression, to put an end to sin, to atone for wickedness, to bring in everlasting righteousness, to seal up vision and prophecy and to anoint the most holy." This prophecy was fulfilled with the death, burial and resurrection of Jesus! Jesus of course began his ministry after seven sevens and sixty-two sevens or after 69 × 7 = 483 years or after A.D. 26. This is consistent with the date Jesus began His ministry, A.D. 30. However, the primary focus of the prophecy is Jesus' death, burial and resurrection. Similarly the destruction of the Temple occurred in A.D. 70, after the Anointed One was cut off, in accordance with the prophecy.

This prophecy illustrates the purpose of prophecy which doesn't seem to be to tell us the date of future events before they occur. This is shown by the fact that there were three decrees and it was only after the event occurred that we knew which one was correct. The purpose of the unfulfilled prophecy was to give the people knowledge of what would take place in the future, but not exactly when.   After the prophecy was fulfilled, we have a demonstration of the sovereignty of God since we can see that the events took place exactly in accordance with God's plan.

The 490th year of this prophecy began at sunset on March 18, A.D. 33, according to the Jewish calendar of the Bible. Just 15 days later, on April 3, A.D. 33 this prophecy was fulfilled with Jesus' resurrection. As 2 Peter 3:9 says, "The Lord is not slow in keeping his promise, as some understand slowness. He is patient with you, not wanting anyone to perish, but everyone to come to repentance."

Glossary

A.D. The abbreviation for *Anno Domini* (in the Year of our Lord).

Agrippa (Herod Agrippa II). Herod Agrippa II was the King Agrippa before whom Paul made his defense in Acts 25:23. He was the son of Herod Agrippa I and received the title of king from the Roman Emperor Claudius.

Antigonus. The king and high priest of Judea from 40-37 B.C. and its last Jewish king. He was succeeded by Herod I.

Antioch (Pisidian). A city that was located in what today is central Turkey where Paul preached a sermon recorded in Acts 13:14-43 on his first missionary journey. Paul established a Christian Church in this city.

Antioch (Syria). The capital of the Roman province of Syria and the site of the first Gentile Christian Church. The disciples were first called Christians in Antioch and it was from Antioch that Paul and Barnabas began their first missionary journey.

Antiochus Epiphanes. Ruler of the Seleukid Kingdom from 175 to 164 B.C. who defiled the Temple in Jerusalem in 168 B.C.

Archelaus. A son of Herod I who was made ethnarch of Judea and Samaria after the death of King Herod I (Matthew 2:22).

Aretus IV. Nabataean king from c.9 BC - AD 40 whose ethnarch of Damascus attempted to arrest Paul (2 Cor.11:32).

Astronomical Year. For A.D. years the astronomical year is the same as the A.D. year, but for B.C. years the astronomical year is one minus the B.C. year. Thus 1 B.C. becomes 1 - 1 B.C. = astronomical year 0.

Autumn (Autumnal) Equinox. The apparent position of the sun when its path through the sky crosses the celestial equator going south. At this position the sun has a celestial longitude of 180 degrees. The sun reaches this position in the sky on approximately December 23 (Gregorian) with some variation due to leap year (see Figure 1.5, page 39).

B.C. The abbreviation for Before Christ (in calendar usage).

Benedictus. The prophecy of Zechariah, father of John the Baptist, recorded in Luke 1:68-79. The name Benedictus comes from the first word of the first verse of the Latin version of this Scripture.

Bernice. The daughter of King Herod Agrippa I. She is mention in Acts 25:13 as accompanying King Agrippa (Herod Agrippa II) when he visited Festus and heard Paul's defense while Paul was imprisoned in Caesarea.

Bishop. In the New Testament, a term used interchangeably with the term elder for one of the overseers of a single Christian congregation.

Celestial Equator. The projection of the earth's equator on the celestial sphere.

Celestial Longitude. The angular distance of a celestial object from the spring equinox measured eastward along the ecliptic to the great circle that passes through the object at right angels to the ecliptic.

Celestial Sphere. A representation of the sky as a spherical shell on which the celestial bodies appear to be projected.

Church Fathers. The church leaders and writers, beginning with the apostles, who preserved and transmitted the teachings and history of Christ's Church.

Conjunction. Two celestial bodies are said to be in conjunction when their apparent position in the sky is close together.

Consul. Either of the two chief magistrates appointed annually in the Roman republic and later in the Roman empire. These consuls served from January 1 to December 31 (Julian) unless replaced prior to the expiration of their term. The consuls at the beginning of the year were used by some historians, such as Josephus, to identify the year of occurrence of ancient events.

Duchan. The platform in the Temple of Jerusalem on which the Levites stood when they chanted the Psalms.

Ecliptic. The apparent annual path of the sun on the celestial sphere.

Egeria. A fourth century nun who traveled in the Holy Land from A.D. 381 to 384 and whose observation were preserved in a diary in the form of letters to the sisters of her community.

Elder. In the New Testament, a term used interchangeably with the term bishop for one of the overseers of a single Christian congregation.

Epiphany. A term from a Geek word which means appearance or manifestation which was applied to Jesus as the appearance or manifestation of God. A festival call Epiphany was celebrated on January 6 (Julian) to commemorate Jesus' baptism and also His birth by the Eastern Christian Churches.

Ethnarch. A title, superior to tetrarch but inferior to king, given by the Romans to some provincial rulers. Archelaus was made ethnarch of Judea and Samaria.

Gregorian Calendar. The calendar that we currently use which was introduced under Pope Gregory XIII (1572-1585). The Gregorian Calendar was just like its predecessor, the Julian Calendar, except years ending in 00 were not leap years unless they were evenly divisible by 400 (see Appendix A).

Helena. A queen of Adiabene who converted to Judaism and bought grain for the relief of a famine in Jerusalem which was probably the same famine predicted by Agabus in Acts 11:28 (see Josephus, *Antiquities*, 20.2.6).

Herod I. The king of Judea at the birth of Jesus (Matthew 2:1). King Herod's father was the Idumean Antipater.

Herod Agrippa I. A grandson of King Herod I who was given the title of king by the Emperor Gaius (Caligula). Herod Agrippa I killed the Apostle James, the brother of the Apostles John, and had Peter imprisoned (Acts 12:1-3).

Herod Antipas. A son of King Herod I who was given the title of tetrarch of Galilee (Luke 3:1) following the death of Herod I. Herod Antipas examined Jesus prior to His crucifixion (Luke 23:8-11).

Intercalation. A system used to keep the Jewish Calendar in step with the seasons by periodically introducing a thirteenth month into the Jewish year (see Chapter 1, page 41).

Judas Maccabaeus. The leader of a Jewish revolt against Antiochus Epiphanes. This revolt freed Jerusalem and Judas Maccabaeus rededicated the Temple in 165 B.C. on Kislev 25, the anniversary of its defilement by Antiochus Epiphanes.

Julian Calendar. The calendar introduced under Julius Caesar in 46 B.C. which had a year of 365 days with every fourth year a leap year with 366 days. This calendar year proved to be slightly too long and was modified by the Gregorian calendar introduced in 1582 (see Appendix A).

Julian Day Number. A number associated with each date on the Julian calendar equal to the number of days separating a given date from January 1,4713 B.C.(Julian).

Level of Confidence I. Level of Confidence I dates are dates that the author believes have a high probability of being exactly correct since they are supported by clear chronological information given in Scripture.

Level of Confidence II. Level of Confidence II dates represents the author's best estimate of the date of the given event; however, these dates have a lower probability of being of being exactly correct because they depend on interpolation between Level of Confidence I dates and may involve the interpretation of less clear Bible passages. Confidence Level II dates may also depend more heavily on extra-Biblical ancient sources.

Lord's Supper. The Holy Communion (Eucharist), instituted by Jesus on Thursday, March 31, A.D. 33. Acts 20:7 indicates that the Apostolic Church celebrated the Lord's Supper on the first day (Sunday) of every week. The Lord's Supper together with Christian Baptism were the primary ordinances of the Apostolic Church.

Magnificat.   The song of praise spoken by Mary at her meeting with Elizabeth of Luke 1:46-55. The term Magnificat comes from the first word of the first verse of the Latin version of this Scripture.

Mishmir.   The priestly order serving in the Temple (see Chapter 3).

Mishnah.   A compilation and commentary of the Jewish Oral law. Rabbi Akiba (c A.D. 110-135) or possibly an earlier scholar made a comprehensive collection of the traditional oral law and Judah Prince of Galilee (c A.D. 200) produced the Mishnah in written form.

Nabatean Kingdom.   A kingdom in north-Arabia, with its capital in Petra, that continued in existence into the 2nd Century A.D. , when the emperor Trajan created the Roman province of Arabia.

New American Standard Bible (NASB).   The English translation of the Bible used for most of the Scripture quotations in this book. The NASB version used in this book was copyrighted in 1995 by the Lockman Foundation which has sponsored the NASB translation. This translation of the Bible is probably the most literal of any of the available English translations.

Passion.   A term referring to Jesus' suffering immediately before and during His death on the cross.

Philip the Apostle.   One of Jesus' original twelve Apostles (Matthew 10:3).

Philip the Evangelist.   One of the original seven deacons (Acts 6:5) who later became an evangelist (Acts 8:5-40).

Philip the Tetrarch.   The son of Herod I and Cleopatra of Jerusalem who was made tetrarch of the region of Iturea and Trachonitis on the death of Herod I (Luke 3:1).

Philip.   A son of Herod I and Manamne II. His wife, Herodias, left him and married Herod Antipas the tetrarch of Galilee (Matthew 14:3).

Pisidian Antioch.   See Antioch (Pisidian)

Shekinah Light. The light indicating the presence of God that shown during the Exodus (Exodus 40:38).

Spring (Vernal) Equinox. The position of the sun when its apparent path through the sky (Ecliptic) crosses the Celestial Equator on its way north. At this point the sun has a Celestial Longitude of 0 degrees and the sun reaches this position on approximately March 21 (Gregorian) with some variation due to leap year (see Figure 1.5 page 39).

Summer Solstice. The northern most position of the sun on the ecliptic (see Figure 1.5 page 39). The sun reaches this position on approximately June 22 (Gregorian).

Talmud. A combination of the Mishnah (the Jewish oral law) and the Gemara (comments of Jewish rabbis on the Mishnah). There are two Talmuds, the Palestinian and Babylonian Talmuds, named for the area in which they were written. The Babylonian Talmud is more complete and is generally considered to be more authoritative. Reference to the Talmud in this book are to the Babylonian Talmud.

Tekufah. A season of the Jewish calendar. The Jewish calendar had four tekufoth just as we have four seasons.

Tetrarch. In Greek usage, the ruler of a fourth part of a region; however in Roman usage the title could be giver to the ruler of any part of an Oriental province.

Watches. In New Testament Judea the night was divided into four watches: evening, midnight, cockcrowing and morning (Mark 13:35).

Winter Solstice. The southern most position of the sun on the ecliptic (see Figure 1.5 page 39). The sun reaches this position on approximately December 22 (Gregorian).

Zodiac. An imaginary belt around the apparent annual path of the sun through the sky (ecliptic) which is divided into twelve equal parts and each part is named for the major constellation of stars it contains.

References

Aharoni, Yohanan and Avi-yonah, Michael, *The Macmillan Bible Atlas,* The Macmillan Company, Collier-Macmillan Limited, London 1969.

Ante-Nicene Fathers, Translations of *The Writings of the Fathers down to A.D. 325,* Edited by The Rev. A.R. Roberts, D.D., and J. Donaldson, LL. D.,Wm. B. Eerdmans Publishing Co., Grand Rapids, Michigan, 1977.

Boorstin, Daniel J., *The Discoverers,* Random House, New York,1983.

Bruce, F.F., *Commentary On The Book Of Acts,* Wm. B. Eerdmans Publishing Co., 1979.

Chadwick, Henry, *The Early Church,* Dorset Press, New York, 1967.

Chambers Dictionary of World History, Edited by B.P. Lenman and K. Boyd, Chambers Harrap Publishers Ltd., Edinburgh, 1993.

Doggett, LeRoy E., and Schaefer, Bradley E., *Moonwatch - July 14, 1988,* Sky & Telescope, July 1988.

Doggett, LeRoy E., and Schaefer, Bradley E., *Results of the July Moonwatch,* Sky & Telescope, April 1989.

Early Christian Writings-The Apostolic Fathers, Translated by Maxwell Staniforth, Dorset Press, New York, 1986.

Encylopedia of the Early Church, Produced by the Institutum Patristicum Augustinaum and Edited by Angelo Di Berardino, Translated from the Italian by Adrian Walford, Oxford University Press, 1992.

Eusebius, *The History of the Church from Christ to Constantine,* Translated with an Introduction by G.A. Williamson, Dorset Press, New York, 1965.

Faulstich, F. W., *History, Harmony & The Hebrew Kings,* Chronology Books, Spencer, Iowa, 1986.

Finegan, J., *Handbook of Biblical Chronology*, Princeton Univ. Press, 1986.

Goldstine, Herman H., *New and Full Moons 1001 B.C. to A.D. 1651*, American Philosophical Society, Philadelphia, 1973.

Havey, O., *Calendar Conversion by way of the Julian Day Number*, American Philosophical Society, Philadelphia, 1983.

Hendin, David, *Guide to Biblical Coins,* Amphora Books, New York, 1987.

Hendriksen, William, *New Testament Commentary-Exposition of the Gospel of Luke,* Baker Book House, Grand Rapids, Michigan, 1978.

Humpheys, C.J. and W.G. Waddington, *Dating the Crucifixion,* Nature, 306: 743-746, December 1983.

Hydrographic Department, Ministry of Defence, *Ocean Passages for the World,* Crown, Great Britain, 1973.

Josephus, *The Works of Josephus,* Translated by William Whiston, A.M., Hendrickson Publishers, Peabody, Massachusetts, 1987.

Josephus, *The Jewish War,* General Editor Gaalya Cornfeld, Zondervan Publishing House, Grand Rapids, Michigan, 1982.

Martin, Ernest L., *The Birth of Christ Recalculated,* Foundation for Biblical Research, Pasadena, California, 1980.

Meeus, Jean, *Astronomical Tables of the Sun, Moon, and Planets,* Williman-Bell, Inc., Richmond, Virginia 1983.

Meshorer, Ya'akov, *Ancient Jewish Coinage,* Amphora Books, Dix Hills, New York, 1982.

Metzger, Bruce M., *Manuscripts of the Greek Bible An Introduction to Greek Palaeography,* Oxford University Press, 1981.

Meyers, Eric M., *Early Judaism and Christianity in the Light of Archaeology,* Biblical Archaeologist, Volume 51, Number 2, June 1988.

Mishnah, Edited by Herbert Danby, Oxford University Press, England, 1933.

Mosley, John, *The Christmas Star,* Griffith Observatory, Los Angeles, California, 1987.

Parise, Frank, Editor, *The Book of Calendars*, Facts On File, Inc., New York, 1982.

Philo, *The Works of Philo,* Translated by C.D. Yonge, Hendrickson Publishers, Peabody, Massachusetts, 1993.

QuickYerse Deluxe Bible Collection for CD-ROM, Parsons Technology, Hiawatha, Iowa, 1995.

Robinson, John A.T., *Redating The New Testament,* The Westminster Press, Philadelphia, 1976.

Schaff, Philip, *History of the Christian Church,* Wm. B. Eerdman Publishing Company, Grand Rapids, Michigan, 1977.

Schürer, Emil, *The History of the Jewish People in the Age of Jesus Christ,* a New English Version Revised and Edited by Geza Vermes, Fergus Miller and Martin Goodman, T. & T. Clark LTD, Edinburgh, 1987.

Sear, David R., *Greek Coins and Their Value,* Seaby, London, 1979.

Sear, David R., *Greek Imperial Coins and Their Value- The Local Coinage of the Roman Empire*, Seaby Publishing Ltd., London, 1982.

Sear, David R., *Roman Coins and Their Value,*Seaby, London, 1981.

Sinnott, Roger W., *Computing the Star of Bethlehem*, Sky & Telescope, December 1986.

Stevenson, Seth W., *A Dictionary of Roman Coins-Republic and Imperial,* B.A. Seaby LTD., London, 1982.

Student Map Manual-Historical Geography of the Bible Lands, Pictorial Archive (Near East History) Est., Zondervan Publishing House, Grand Rapids, Michigan, 1983.

Suetonius, *The Twelve Caesars,* Translated by Robert Graves, Penguin Books, Middlesex, England, 1986.

Tacitus, *The Annals of Imperial Rome,* Translated by Michael Grant, Dorset Press, New York, 1971.

Talmud, *The Babylonian Talmud,* Translated under the editorship of Rabbi Dr. I. Epstein, The Soncino Press, London, 1935.

The Cambridge Encyclopedia, D. Crystal editor, Cambridge Press, 1990

The Illustrated Bible Dictionary, Tyndale House Publishers, Wheaton, Illinois, 1980.

The International Atlas, Rand McNally & Company, Chicago, 1969.

The New Encyclopedia of Archaeological Excavations in the Holy Land, Ephraim Stern, Editor, The Israel Exploration Society & Carta, Jerusalem, Simon & Schuster, New York, 1993.

The Sky - Astronomy Software Version 4, Software Bisque, Golden, Colorado, 1996.

Tuckerman, B., *Planetary, Lunar, and Solar Positions 501 B.C. to A.D. 1,* The American Philosophical Society, Philadelphia, 1962

Webster's Third New International Dictionary, G. & C. Merriam Company, Springfield, Massachusetts, 1961.

The World Almanac and Book of Facts 1994, World Almanac, Mahwah, New Jersey, 1993.

World Christian Encyclopedia-A Comparative Survey of Churches and Religions in the Modern World A.D. 1900-2000, Edited by David B. Barrett, Oxford University Press, 1982.

Index of New Testament Passages
(Page Numbers are for Summary Tables at the End of Chapters)

Index of Names and Subjects